THE COMPLETE
GATHERED GOLD

THE COMPLETE GATHERED GOLD

A treasury of quotations for Christians

John Blanchard

 EVANGELICAL PRESS

EVANGELICAL PRESS
Faverdale North, Darlington, DL3 0PH, England
e-mail: sales@evangelicalpress.org

Evangelical Press USA
P. O. Box 825, Webster, New York 14580, USA
e-mail: usa.sales@evangelicalpress.org

web: http://www.evangelicalpress.org

Complete Gathered Gold — first published 2006
ISBN 0 85234 644 1

Complete Gathered Gold — reprint 2007

Gathered Gold — first published 1984
ISBN 0 85234 186 5 (paperback)
ISBN 0 85234 197 0 (hardback)

More Gathered Gold — first published 1986
ISBN 0 85234 218 7 (hardback)
ISBN 0 85234 219 5 (paperback)

Sifted Silver — first published 1995
ISBN 0 85234 334 5

British Library Cataloguing in Publication Data available

Printed and bound by Gutenberg Press, Malta.

Gratefully dedicated to
HG and the mighty M

Introduction

Ever since I became a Christian I have had a trawling eye and an insatiable appetite to hoard pithy statements that summarized important truths or expressed valuable insights in memorable ways. I soon began to arrange my growing collection into an indexed system, where they were joined by hundreds of other statements I read or heard as the years went by.

Some time later I toyed with the idea that at some point I might gather all of them into a published anthology in order to share my treasures with others. In 1978 I came across *The Golden Treasury of Puritan Quotations*, compiled by my good friend Dr I. D. E. Thomas, a Welsh preacher living in California, and he graciously invited me to make as much use as I wished of his material. Shortly afterwards I was given a time-worn copy of *The Puritan Remembrancer*, edited by The Rev. H. J. Horn and by then out of print for over half a century. I was already hugely indebted to the Puritans and fascinated by the works of people like Thomas Brooks, John Flavel, William Secker, John Trapp and Thomas Watson, with their agile army of aphorisms. These men were spiritual giants and we can still benefit from their wit and wisdom today. Browsing through its tiny, packed pages was like discovering a private gold-mine and this was the final spur I needed to press ahead with the publication of my now greatly augmented collection.

In 1984 this resulted in Evangelical Press publishing a selection of 5,000 quotations under the title *Gathered Gold* and this was so enthusiastically received that it was joined two years later by another 5,000 items (inventively entitled *More Gathered Gold*)! This was meant to mark the end of the story, but two things changed the plot. Firstly, both volumes continued to be widely used in many countries around the world; and secondly, hundreds of further quotations were finding their way into my filing system every year. As a result, a third volume of 5,000 entries, entitled *Sifted Silver*, was published in 1995.

Ten years on, another tide of material was clamouring for inclusion and my publisher and I felt it best to pull the entire available collection together: the present volume is the result.

It will soon be seen that the entries are drawn from a very wide circle. Some are from people with whom I would have substantial doctrinal differences, but their inclusion does not imply my endorsement of the authors' stance on other matters. To go even further, not all of those whose names appear in these pages are even Christians, but this in no way devalues the quotations being used. Readers with raised eyebrows at this are referred to Acts 17:28 for an apostolic precedent!

Not all of the quotations have the same depth or tone. Some are technical explanations and others have a devotional or practical slant, while mingled with the deeply serious are those in which wit or humour is the vehicle used to convey the point being made.

In assembling the material for publication I have avoided cluttering up the pages with titles, ranks, positions and dates, so leaving the quotations to stand on their own, but a subject index has been provided, including cross-references where it was thought that these would be helpful.

I have deliberately excluded from the mountains of material at my disposal any quotations that are of a negative nature, such as those reflecting anti-Christian attitudes about God, life, man, death and eternity. These have their place as counter-points in otherwise positive presentations, but I wanted this collection to be wholly positive and more widely useful than as a technical reference book. It will obviously be a comprehensive resource for preachers, teachers and other Christian communicators, but I trust that it will also be a means of direction, inspiration, insight and encouragement to countless 'ordinary' Christians in the rough and tumble of their daily lives.

At my publisher's request a limited number of items from my own written and spoken ministry have been included where it was felt that this be helpful — though I obviously make no personal claim that they qualify as 'gold'!

I am grateful to members of the Evangelical Press team who have contributed so much to this project. David Clark and Anthony Gosling have encouraged me from the very beginning and Pete Cooper has once again come up with a superb and original cover design. I am especially indebted to the editor, Patricia Rubens who has worked tirelessly and efficiently in collating the three previous volumes with all the additional material. The entire anthology is now sent out with the prayer that the wit and wisdom of mere mortals gathered over the passing years might help to illuminate the unchanging truth of 'the living and enduring word of God' (1 Peter 1:23).

John Blanchard
Banstead
Surrey

October 2006

ABANDONMENT

(See also: Consecration, Submission, Zeal)

The greatness of a man's power is the measure of his surrender. *William Booth*

Oh, how greatly has the man advanced who has learned not to be his own, not to be governed by his own reason, but to surrender his mind to God! *John Calvin*

To be another than I am, I must abandon that I am. *Chrysostom*

God doesn't want our success; he wants us. He doesn't demand our achievements; he demands our obedience.

Charles Colson

A life abandoned to Christ cannot be cut short. *Sherwood Day*

My Saviour, I am thine,
By everlasting bands;
My name, my heart, I would resign;
My soul is in thy hands.

Philip Doddridge

I have this day been before God and have given myself — all that I have and am — to God; so that I am in no respect my own. I have given myself clean away.

Jonathan Edwards

It is when God appears to have abandoned us that we must abandon ourselves most wholly to God. *François Fenelon*

Self, service, substance is the divine order, and nothing counts until we give ourselves. *Vance Havner*

(God) cannot bless us until he has us. When we try to keep within us an area that is our own, we try to keep an area of death. Therefore, in love, he claims all. There's no bargaining with him.

C. S Lewis

It is not so much of our time and so much of our attention that God demands; it is not even all of our time and all of our attention: it is ourselves. *C. S. Lewis*

I will place no value on anything I have or may possess, except in relation to the kingdom of Christ. *David Livingstone*

Before we can pray, 'Thy kingdom come', we must be willing to pray, 'My kingdom go'. *Alan Redpath*

Christianity is the total commitment of all I know of me to all I know of Jesus Christ. *William Temple*

Were the whole realm of nature mine,
That were an offering far too small;
Love so amazing, so divine,
Demands my soul, my life, my all.

Isaac Watts

If so poor a worm as I
May to thy great glory live;
All my actions sanctify,
All my words and thoughts receive.
Claim me for thy service, claim
All I have and all I am.

Charles Wesley

ABORTION

Abortion must be looked upon as an eventuation that runs counter to the biological stream of life. *L Galdston*

To eliminate the scourge of illegitimate children more self-discipline to prevent their conception is required, not more freedom to destroy them in the womb.

Immanuel Jakobovits

Abortion

If human life can be taken before birth, there is no logical reason why it cannot be taken after birth. _Francis Schaeffer_

Since the Bible teaches that life in the womb is human life, one cannot accept abortion without denying the authority and truth of Scripture in practice.
Francis Schaeffer

Every induced abortion, whether legal or criminal, is an expression of failure — failed contraceptive technique, irresponsibility by one or both partners, ignorance, betrayal of trust or denial of human dignity. _John Stallworthy_

It is only a short step from disposable babies to disposable people.
Margaret White

ACTIONS
(See also: Duty; Good Deeds; Service)

Practice is the soul of knowledge.
Thomas Adams

Words are leaves — deeds are fruit. _Anon._

Do every act in thy life as if it were the last. _Marcus Antoninus_

Think like a man of action and act like a man of thought. _Henri Bergson_

All our activity is sowing; and so is our inactivity. _John Blanchard_

The gospel is not a doctrine of the tongue, but of life. _John Calvin_

Every action of our lives touches on some chord that will vibrate in eternity.
E. H. Chapin

Man's practices are the best indexes of his principles. _Stephen Charnock_

Unless a man has to do more than he can do, he will not do all that he can do.
Gordon Cooper

It is not enough that our actions be good and praise worthy, if our intentions are not pure and upright. It is to profane the good to do it with a bad end in view.
Jean Daillé

Action is the proper fruit of knowledge.
Thomas Fuller

An acre of performance is worth a whole world of promise. _James Howell_

No conduct of any man may be neutral.
John Hus

Great ideas need landing gears as well as wings. _C. D. Jackson_

There are no non-religious activities; only religious and irreligious. _C. S. Lewis_

Sympathy is no substitute for action.
David Livingstone

The actions of men are the best interpreters of their thoughts. _John Locke_

What or whom we worship determines our behaviour. _John Murray_

Practice is the very life of piety.
William S. Plumer

Make no distinction in your conduct between small things and great.
William Taylor

Affection without action is like Rachel, beautiful but barren. _John Trapp_

Behaviour is a mirror in which everyone displays his own image.
Johann Wolfgang von Goethe

Knowing is not enough; we must apply. Willing is not enough; we must do.
Johann Wolfgang von Goethe

The actions of men form an infallible index of their own character.
Geoffrey B. Wilson

The conduct of our lives is the only proof of the sincerity of our hearts.
Robert Wilson

ACTIVISM
(See also: Service)

Beware of the urgent crowding out the important. *Anon.*

Busyness in the King's business is no excuse for neglecting the King. *Anon.*

God's service is sometimes hindered by a feverish attempt to do it. *Anon.*

What is the use of running when we are not on the right road? *Anon.*

No man has a right to lead such a life of contemplation as to forget in his own ease the service due to his neighbour; nor has any man a right to be so immersed in active life as to neglect the contemplation of God. *Augustine*

Activity and theology are no substitutes for God. *John Blanchard*

Activity can be a hiding place from reality. *John Blanchard*

In too many churches today we have the motion but not the unction.
John Blanchard

It is dangerously possible for activity to be no more than a dizzy whirl around a central emptiness. *John Blanchard*

Let us beware of feeling that unless we personally are up and doing the Lord is not at work. *John Blanchard*

There is a world of difference between activity and progress. *John Blanchard*

Velocity is no substitute for direction or purpose. *John Blanchard*

I think the devil has made it his business to monopolize on three elements: noise, hurry, crowds . . . Satan is quite aware of the power of silence. *Jim Elliot*

It is possible to be so active in the service of Christ as to forget to love him.
R. T. Forsyth

I am convinced that if the devil cannot make us lazy he will make us so busy here and there that the best is sacrificed for the good. *Vance Havner*

Idleness is the devil's workshop, but so is busyness if, while we are busy here and there we fail in our main responsibility.
Vance Havner

The work of God cannot be done in the energy of the flesh. Too much religious activity is just old Adam in his Sunday clothes. *Vance Havner*

Those dear souls who argue that the devil never takes a vacation should remember that we are not supposed to imitate the devil. *Vance Havner*

We have been too busy chopping wood to take time out to sharpen the axe.
Vance Havner

When we are too busy to sharpen the axe we are too busy. *Vance Havner*

Activism

To concentrate on service and activity for God may often actively thwart our attaining of the true, God himself. *Roy Hession*

It is difficult to see Jesus when you are in a hurry. *Joel Horne*

We are not always doing the most business for God when we are the busiest. *John Henry Jowett*

Many Christians are so busy they can only hear the click and clatter of church machinery. *Walter B. Knight*

What is the use of travelling at a fast speed when you are going in the wrong direction? *Bernhard Langer*

As long as we continue to trust to our own abilities and activities we shall avail nothing. *D. Martyn Lloyd-Jones*

One of the greatest dangers in the spiritual life is to live on your own activities. In other words, the activity is not in its right place as something which you do, but has become something that keeps you going. *D. Martyn Lloyd-Jones*

The child is generally much more active than the adult person; so that if we estimate our growth merely in terms of activity we are setting up a characteristic of childhood and the childish state as the measure of growth. *D. Martyn Lloyd-Jones*

The flesh loves excitement. It is always ready to jump and run somewhere. It hurries us into action. The Holy Spirit does not. Satan rushes men. God leads them. *F. B. Meyer*

One of Satan's methods today is to start so many organizations in a church that the members have no time for communion with God. *G. Campbell Morgan*

Activity which lacks thought is blind. *John Murray*

It is more important to know where you are going than to get there quickly. Do not mistake activity for achievement. *Mabel Newcomer*

Beware the barrenness of a busy life. *Len North*

Satan is far more anxious to keep us off our knees than he is to keep us off our feet! *Ivor Powell*

We have many irons in the fire, but none ever get hot. *Ivor Powell*

There is too much working before men and too little waiting before God. There is more and more motion and less and less unction. *Alan Redpath*

We won't get rid of the malady of sin by increasing our activity. *Alan Redpath*

Of what use is it to have many irons in the fire if the fire is going out? *Eric Roberts*

To be always preaching, teaching, speaking, writing and working public works is unquestionably a sign of zeal. But it is not a sign of zeal according to knowledge. *J. C. Ryle*

In an effort to get the work of the Lord done, we often lose contact with the Lord of the work. *A. W. Tozer*

Our religious activities should be ordered in such a way as to have plenty of time for the cultivation of the fruits of solitude and silence. *A. W. Tozer*

Sometimes I think the church would be better off if we would call a moratorium on activity for about six weeks and just waited on God to see what he is waiting to do for us.   *A. W. Tozer*

We of the nervous West are victims of the philosophy of activism tragically misunderstood. If we are not making plans or working to carry out plans already made we feel we are failures. *A. W. Tozer*

Many a Christian worker's activity is the grave of his spiritual life. *C. J. Vaughan*

Apart from God every activity is merely a passing whiff of insignificance.
Alfred Whitehead

The conduct of our lives is the only proof of the sincerity of our hearts.
Robert Wilson

The actions of men form an infallible index of their character. *Geoffrey R Wilson*

ADDICTION — See Habit

ADOPTION

The Christian is far more than a guest with God.   *Donald Grey Barnhouse*

Only if we walk in the beauty of God's law do we become sure of our adoption as children of the Father.   *John Calvin*

We can only begin an upright course of life when God, of his good pleasure, adopts us into his family.   *John Calvin*

Adoption gives us the *privilege* of sons, regeneration the *nature* of sons.
Stephen Charnock

Understanding adoption should mean that our own sense of the great goodness and love of God is immeasurably enriched.
Sinclair Ferguson

I am a pilgrim and a stranger on the earth, but I am not an orphan.   *Vance Havner*

Adoption, as the term clearly implies, is an act of transfer from an alien family into the family of God himself. This is surely the apex of grace and privilege.
John Murray

The spirit of prayer is the fruit and token of the Spirit of adoption.   *John Newton*

Adoption … is the highest privilege that the gospel offers: higher even than justification.   *J. I. Packer*

Adoption is a greater mercy than Adam had in paradise.   *Thomas Watson*

God has made his children, by adoption, nearer to himself than the angels. The angels are the friends of Christ; believers are his members.   *Thomas Watson*

Since God has a Son of his own, and such a Son, how wonderful God's love in adopting us! We needed a Father, but he did not need sons.   *Thomas Watson*

ADORATION — See Awe; Worship

ADVERSITY — See Pain; Sickness; Suffering; Trials

ADVICE

We give advice by the bucket, but take it by the grain.   *W. R. Alger*

Four eyes see more than two.   *Anon.*

Most of us would get along well if we used the advice we give to others.   *Anon.*

Two quick ways to disaster are to take nobody's advice and to take everybody's advice.   *Anon.*

To profit from good advice requires more wisdom than to give it. *Churton Collins*

It takes a great man to give sound advice tactfully, but a greater to accept it graciously.   *J. C. MacAulay*

Men give advice; God gives guidance.
Leonard Ravenhill

I not only use all the brains I'd have but all I can borrow.   *Woodrow Wilson*

AFFECTIONS

The fundamental distinction between the godly and ungodly men consists in the object to which their affections are directed.   *Anon.*

The true worth of a man is to be measured by the objects he pursues.
Marcus Aurelius

Grace comes not to take away a man's affections, but to take them up.
William Fenner

The nearer to heaven in hopes, the farther from earth in desires.
William Gurnall

The tree will not only lie as it falls, but it will fall as it leans. What is the inclination of my soul?   *J. J. Gurney*

Affection is the answer to apathy.
Vance Havner

The real test of the genuineness of any inward affection is not so much the character of the feeling as it reveals itself in our consciousness, as the course of action to which it leads.   *Charles Hodge*

There is a close connection between the affections and the understanding: if we love evil, we cannot understand that which is good.   *C. H. Spurgeon*

Whatever is your greatest joy and treasure, that is your god.   *C. H. Spurgeon*

Likeness comes from liking. We grow to be like that which we like.
Augustus H. Strong

Affection without action is like Rachel, beautiful but barren.   *John Trapp*

AFFLICTION — See Pain; Sickness; Suffering; Trials

AGE — See Old Age

AGNOSTICISM
(See also: Atheism; Unbelief)

Agnosticism is the philosophical, ethical and religious dry rot of the modern world.
F. E. Abbot

Is it wise to leave massive questions about life, death and eternity hanging in the air?
John Blanchard

The hard-core agnostic says that on the question of God's existence the only knowable truth is that there no such thing as knowable truth — in other words that there can be no agnosticism about agnosticism. Does this make sense?
John Blanchard

Since we cannot suspend judgement about life itself, in the end we cannot be neutral about religious faith.
C. Stephen Evans

I remain an agnostic, and the practical outcome of agnosticism is that you act as though God did not exist.
W. Somerset Maugham

Agnosticism leads inevitably to moral indifference. *Thomas Merton*

Agnosticism is not grounds for rejecting Christianity; rather it is grounds for examining Christianity. *Josh McDowell*

When agnosticism has done its withering work in the mind of man, the mysteries remain as before; all that has been added to them is a settled despair.
Vincent McNabb

Atheism and agnosticism are not merely defective theories that need to be corrected by further study and more information. They are sin for which men are called to repent because God has made himself known to them.
R. C. Sproul

I could not bear to be an 'ignoramus' or an 'agnostic' about God! I must have a God! I cannot do without him.
C. H. Spurgeon

We should all be incurably agnostic if God had not revealed himself.
David Watson

There are no agnostics in hell.
Geoffrey B. Wilson

AIM — See Purpose

ALCOHOL
(See also: Drunkenness)

Alcohol does not make people able to do things better. It makes them less ashamed of doing them badly. *Anon.*

Alcohol never drowns sorrows; it irrigates them. *Anon.*

Drink like a fish only if you drink what a fish drinks. *Anon.*

The youth who stands with a glass of liquor in his hand would do well to consider which he had best throw away, the liquor or himself. *Anon.*

Wine is a turncoat: first a friend, then a deceiver, then an enemy. *Anon.*

Is it any merit to abstain from wine if one is intoxicated with anger? *Augustine*

Drink has drained more blood, hung more crepe, sold more homes, armed more villains, slain more children, snapped more wedding rings, defiled more innocents, blinded more eyes, twisted more limbs, dethroned more reasons, wrecked more manhood, dishonoured more womanhood, broken more hearts, driven more to suicide than any other scourge that ever swept across the world.
Evangeline Cory Booth

If we could sweep intemperance out of the country, there would be hardly poverty enough left to give healthy exercise to the charitable impulses. *Phillips Brooks*

Strong drink is not only the devil's way into a man, but man's way to the devil.
Adam Clarke

I have better use for my brain than to poison it with alcohol. To put alcohol in the human brain is like putting sand in the bearings of an engine. *Thomas Edison*

Alcohol does not drown care, but waters it and makes it grow faster.
Benjamin Franklin

Every moderate drinker could abandon the intoxicating cup, if he would; every inebriate would if he could. *J. B. Gough*

I have four good reasons for being an abstainer — my head is clearer, my health is better, my heart is lighter and my purse is heavier. *Thomas Guthrie*

Whisky is a good thing in its place. There is nothing like it for preserving a man when he is dead. If you want to keep a dead man, put him in whisky; if you want to kill a live man, put whisky in him.
Thomas Guthrie

I am more afraid of King Alcohol than of all the bullets of the enemy. *Robert E. Lee*

I never see a sign 'Licensed to sell spirits' without thinking that it is a licence to ruin souls.   *Robert Murray M'Cheyne*

No drug known to man is more widely used nor more frequently responsible for deaths, injuries or crimes than is ethyl alcohol.   *S. L. McMillen*

Wine has drowned more than the sea.
Publitius Syrus

AMBITION

Ambition, like the grave, is never full.
Thomas Adams

It's dangerous to try to be number one, because it's next to nothing.   *Anon.*

Honour ought to seek thee, not thou seek it.   *Augustine*

Ambition is like hunger; it obeys no law but its appetite.   *Josh Billings*

If there is anything worse than social climbing in the world it is ecclesiastical climbing in the church. *John Blanchard*

The man who desires honour does not deserve it.   *John Blanchard*

Seek not great things for yourself in this world, for if your garments be long they will make you stumble. *William Bridge*

Ambition is a gilded misery, a secret poison, a hidden plague, the engineer of deceit, the mother of hypocrisy, the parent of envy, the original of vices, the moth of holiness and blinder of hearts, turning medicines into maladies and remedies into diseases. High seats are never but uneasy and crowns are always stuffed with thorns.   *Thomas Brooks*

Ambition can creep as well as soar.
Edmund Burke

Ambition deludes men so much that by its sweetness it not only intoxicates but drives them mad.   *John Calvin*

Ambition is blind — man's favour is blind — the world's applause is blind.
John Calvin

There is nothing less tolerable in the servants of Christ than ambition and vanity.
John Calvin

To live happily the evils of ambition and self-love must be plucked from our hearts by the roots.   *John Calvin*

Ambition is greed for power. *C. C. Colton*

Ambition is the mind's immodesty.
William Davenant

Ambition is like love, impatient both of delays and rivals. *John Denham*

Most of the trouble in the world is caused by people wanting to be important.
T. S. Eliot

The fruit of the Spirit is not push, drive, climb, grasp and trample ... Life is more than a climb to the top of the heap.
Richard J. Foster

Nothing arouses ambition so much in the heart as the trumpet-clang of another's fame. *Baltasar Gracian*

When we seek honours we depart from Jesus. *Hugh of St Victor*

Where ambition can cover its enterprises, even to the person himself, under the appearance of principle, it is the most incurable and inflexible of passions.
David Hume

Ambition is pitiless; any merit that it cannot use it finds despicable.
Joseph Joubert

Ambition is but avarice on stilts.
W. S. Landor

Seek not greatness, but seek truth, and you will find both. *Horace Mann*

Ambition is a lust that is never quenched, but grows more inflamed and madder by enjoyment. *Thomas Otway*

It is doubtless an easy enough matter to drop certain forms of outer worldliness

... but quite another to lay carnal ambition in the dust. *James Philip*

When we have yearnings and cravings that never seem to be satisfied, we should ask ourselves whether in fact there is something wrong with the desire itself.
James Philip

Ambition is the grand enemy of all peace.
John C. Powys

You may get to the very top of the ladder, and then find it has not been leaning against the right wall. *A. Raine*

There are people who want to be everywhere at once and they seem to get nowhere. *Carl Sandburg*

I charge thee, fling away ambition: by that sin fell the angels. *William Shakespeare*

I know of nothing which I would choose to have as the subject of my ambition for life than to be kept faithful to my God till death. *C. H. Spurgeon*

Some climb so high that they break their necks. *George Swinnock*

There is no greater unreasonableness in the world than in the designs of ambition. *Jeremy Taylor*

The itch to have the pre-eminence is one disease for which no natural cure has ever been found. *A. W. Tozer*

Ambition rides without reins. *John Trapp*

If we are taken up with our own personal needs, or if we are looking for position and status in the church, we shall be of little use to God. *David Watson*

17

Your ambition, not your worded prayer, is your real creed.   *Ella Wheeler Wilcox*

AMUSEMENTS
(See also: Recreation)

Many so-called innocent amusements are but contrivances of the devil to make us forget God.   *Anon.*

Amusements are to virtue like breezes to the flame; gentle ones will fan it, but strong ones will put it out.
David Thomas

Is it not a strange thing and a wonder that, with the shadow of atomic destruction hanging over the world and with the coming of Christ drawing near, the professed followers of the Lord should be giving themselves up to religious amusements?
A. W. Tozer

ANGELS
(See also: Demons)

Jacob saw angels ascending and descending, but none standing still.   *Anon.*

Angels mean messengers and ministers. Their function is to execute the plan of divine providence, even in earthly things.
Thomas Aquinas

Angels will never be kings. They will always be servants.   *Andrew Bonar*

Angels are the dispensers and administrators of the divine beneficence towards us.   *John Calvin*

Angels are the ministers of God's wrath, as well as of his grace.   *John Calvin*

They who think that each of us is defended by one angel only wickedly depreciate the kindness of God.
John Calvin

Under Christ, as the Head, angels are the guardians of the church.   *John Calvin*

The Bible assumes, rather than asserts, the existence of angels, as it does the fact of God himself.   *C. T. Cook*

According to Scripture, the angels praise God chiefly for two things: God's creation of the world and God's redemption of the world through Jesus Christ. Let us follow the angels' example.
William Dembski

Angels have a much more important place in the Bible than the devil and his demons.   *Billy Graham*

We must not get so busy counting demons that we forget the holy angels.
Billy Graham

Angels are clothed with God's powers to accomplish his will in the realm of nature.   *T. Hewitt*

I meditate on the blessed obedience and order of angels, without which no peace could be in heaven, and oh that it might be so on earth!   *Richard Hooker*

An angel is a spiritual creature created by God without a body, for the services of Christendom and of the church.
Martin Luther

Angels both good and bad have a greater influence on this world than men are generally aware of.   *Increase Mather*

Millions of spiritual creatures walk the earth unseen, both when we sleep and when we awake.   *John Milton*

If two angels were sent from heaven to execute a divine command, one to conduct an empire and the other to sweep a street in it, they would feel no inclination to change employments.   *John Newton*

We rob ourselves of much joy if we forget the loving and caring presence all round about us of the angels of God.
Maurice Roberts

Activity is the mark of holy spirits and should be the mark of holy men.
C. H. Spurgeon

Take away purity from an angel and he is no more an angel but a devil.
Thomas Watson

ANGELS — Fallen — See Demons

ANGER
(See also: Hatred; Revenge; Passion)

He that is inebriated with a passion is unfit for an action.   *Thomas Adams*

When anger enters the mind wisdom departs.   *Thomas à Kempis*

Anger is a wind which blows out the lamp of the mind.   *Anon.*

Anger is an acid that can do more harm to the vessel in which it is stored than to anything on which it is poured.   *Anon.*

Anger is as a stone cast into a wasp's nest.
Anon.

Anger is just one letter short of danger.
Anon.

Anger is often more hurtful than the injury that caused it.   *Anon.*

Don't fly into a rage unless you are prepared for a rough landing.   *Anon.*

He who can suppress a moment's anger may prevent a day of sorrow.   *Anon.*

Nothing can cook your goose quicker than boiling anger.   *Anon.*

One thing that improves the longer it is kept is your temper.   *Anon.*

Sharp words make more wounds than surgeons can heal.   *Anon.*

The anger of today is the remorse of tomorrow.   *Anon.*

Two things a man should never be angry at: what he can help, and what he cannot help.   *Anon.*

Angry men are blind and foolish.
Pietro Aretino

It is easy to fly into a passion — anybody can do that — but to be angry with the right person at the right time and with the right object and in the right way — that is not easy, and it is not everyone who can do it.   *Aristotle*

Our anger and impatience often proves much more mischievous than the things about which we are angry or impatient.
Marcus Aurelius

A man that does not know how to be angry does not know how to be good. Now and then a man should be shaken to the core with indignation over things evil.
Henry Ward Beecher

It is better to swallow angry words than to have to eat them afterwards.
John Blanchard

Anger

The worst of slaves is he whom passion rules. *Phillips Brooks*

Anger is usually inexhaustible. *John Calvin*

Intemperate anger deprives men of their senses. *John Calvin*

The sun should not set upon our anger, neither should it rise upon our confidence. *C. C. Colton*

Anger and jealously can no more bear to lose sight of their objects than love. *George Eliot*

Anger is seldom without a reason, but seldom a good one. *Benjamin Franklin*

A man in a passion rides a horse that runs away with him. *Thomas Fuller*

Act nothing in a furious passion. It is putting to sea in a storm. *Thomas Fuller*

Anger is a sin that is its own punishment. *Matthew Henry*

Angry men have good memories. *Matthew Henry*

It is the great duty of all Christians to put off anger. It unfits for duty … a man cannot wrestle with God and wrangle with his neighbour at the same time. *Philip Henry*

The worst thing we can bring to a religious controversy is anger. *Matthew Henry*

When anger was in Cain's heart, murder was not far off. *Matthew Henry*

When passion is on the throne reason is out of doors. *Matthew Henry*

Human anger never practises the things that God can approve. *D. Edmond Hiebert*

Anger at God is a symptom. The basic problem is unbelief. *Gladys Hunt*

Do not do to others what angers you if done to you by others. *Isocrates*

When angry, count ten before you speak; if very angry, count a hundred. *Thomas Jefferson*

Anger should not be destroyed but sanctified. *William Jenkyn*

Anger's the anaesthetic of the mind. *C. S. Lewis*

When passion enters a situation, human reasoning (unassisted by grace) has as much chance of retaining its hold on truth as a snowflake in the mouth of a blast furnace. *C. S. Lewis*

When you are in the right, you can afford to keep your temper; and when you are in the wrong you cannot afford to lose it. *G. C. Lorimer*

Nothing makes room for Satan more than wrath. *Thomas Manton*

No man can think clearly when his fists are clenched. *George J. Nathan*

Anger begins in folly and ends in repentance. *Pythagoras*

People who fly into a rage always make a bad landing. *Will Rogers*

The greatest remedy for anger is delay. *Seneca*

Unrestrained anger is often more hurtful to us than the injury that provoked it.
Seneca

There is no old age for a man's anger.
Sophocles

Passion is the drunkenness of the mind.
Robert South

When anger is present, look for the pain.
R. C. Sproul

Anger is temporary insanity.
C. H. Spurgeon

I have no more right as a Christian to allow a bad temper to dwell in me than I have to allow the devil himself to dwell there. *C. H. Spurgeon*

To be angry against sin is a high and holy thing. *C. H. Spurgeon*

Wrath in man is a tormenting fiend.
David Thomas

The fury of man never furthered the glory of God. *A. W. Tozer*

Anger and malice differ but in age.
John Trapp

Anger may rush into a wise man's bosom, but should not rest there. *John Trapp*

Ask permission from God before you dare do anything in an angry way.
John Trapp

ANGER — Righteous

Anger is one of the holy feet of the soul when it goes in the right direction.
C. H. Spurgeon

It is not a sin to be angry, but hard not to sin when we are angry. *John Trapp*

That anger is without sin that is against sin. *Thomas Watson*

ANNIHILATION
(See also: Death; Eternity; Judgement)

God does not annihilate his work, however much he may change its form. The biblical idea of death has nothing in common with annihilation. *Louis Berkhof*

The Bible annihilates annihilationism.
John Blanchard

The concept of annihilationism is a doctrine of despair. *John Blanchard*

In every culture, and apparently throughout history, it has been normal for man to assume that he has some continuance beyond the grave. *Arthur C. Custance*

The philosophy that man will fall into oblivion, snuffed out like a candle, makes no sense of the inequalities of life.
Brian Edwards

What men fear is not that death is annihilation but that it is not. *Epicurus*

That man is a spiritual being, who survives the death of his physical body, is a basic human instinct which is denied only with the greatest effort. *Dave Hunt*

The wicked will not be annihilated by the second death as judgement for their sins any more than Christ was annihilated when he paid the penalty for our sins.
R. A. Killen

No man, regardless of his theoretical system, is content to look at himself as a

finally meaningless machine which can and will be discarded totally and for ever.
Francis Schaeffer

ANTICHRIST
(See also: Satan — Existence and Nature)

The name Antichrist does not designate a single individual, but a single kingdom, which extends throughout many generations.
John Calvin

When Scripture speaks of Antichrist it includes the whole duration of his reign.
John Calvin

ANTINOMIANISM

The person who claims he can live carelessly because he is not under law but under grace needs to be sure that he is not under wrath.
John Blanchard

We are not cleansed by Christ so that we can immerse ourselves continually in fresh dirt, but in order that our purity may serve the glory of God.
John Calvin

Antinomianism sets up the grace of God in opposition to his government.
Richard Cecil

Nothing could be further from the truth than the suggestion that God's choice destroys moral effort on our part.
Sinclair Ferguson

The greatest curse that ever entered the church of God is dirty antinomianism.
Rowland Hill

To argue from mercy to sin is the devil's logic.
James Janeway

If the 'grace' you have received does not help you to keep the law, you have not received grace.
D. Martyn Lloyd-Jones

The gospel no more excuses sin than the law does. What is repugnant to the moral law of God is also contrary to the gospel of Christ.
Henry T. Mahan

In the denial of the permanent authority and sanctity of the moral law there is a direct thrust at the very centre of our holy faith, for it is a thrust at the veracity and authority of our Lord himself.
John Murray

Such as will not have Christ to be their King to rule over them shall never have his blood to save them.
Thomas Watson

ANXIETY
(See also Fear; Worry)

Anxiety and prayer are more opposed to each other than fire and water.
J. A. Bengel

Anxiety is the poison of human life.
Hugh Blair

Anxiety never strengthens you for tomorrow; it only weakens you for today.
John Blanchard

Anxiety is a word of unbelief or unreasoning dread. We have no right to allow it. Full faith in God puts it to rest.
Horace Bushnell

Anxiety is the rust of life, destroying its brightness and weakening its power. A childlike and abiding trust in providence is its best preventative and remedy.
Tryon Edwards

Anxiety is the fundamental phenomenon and the central problem of neurosis.
Sigmund Freud

Anxiety is the natural result when our hopes are centered in anything short of God and his will for us.   *Billy Graham*

To carry care to bed is to sleep with a pack on your back.   *Thomas Haliburton*

Anxiety is the interest paid on trouble before it is due.   *William R. Inge*

Anxiety is not only a pain which we must ask God to assuage but also a weakness we must ask him to pardon — for he's told us to take no care for the morrow.
    C. S. Lewis

Anxious care rests upon a basis of heathen worldly-mindedness and of heathen misunderstanding of the character of God.   *Alexander Maclaren*

Two things come between our souls and unshadowed fellowship — sin and care. We must be as resolute to cast our care upon the Lord as to confess our sins to him.   *F. B. Meyer*

The beginning of anxiety is the end of faith, and the beginning of true faith is the end of anxiety.   *George Muller*

All the care in the world will not make us continue a minute beyond the time God has appointed.   *J. C. Ryle*

Can we gain anything by fearing and fuming? Do we not unfit ourselves for action, and unhinge our minds for wise decision? We are sinking by our struggles when we might float by faith.
    C. H. Spurgeon

Unquiet minds and hearts will be uncertain in decision and unsettled in grace.
    J. Charles Stern

Anxiety is a self-contradiction to true humility.   *Kenneth Wuest*

Anxious care is out of place in a heavenly Father's presence.   *Kenneth Wuest*

APATHY
(See also: Complacency; Indifference)

One does evil enough when one does nothing good.   *Anon.*

Still water and still religion freeze the quickest.   *Anon.*

When apathy is the master, all men are slaves.   *Anon.*

When God has spoken, apathy is evidence of practical atheism. *Joyce Baldwin*

Nothing is so fatal to religion as indifference.   *Edmund Burke*

The only thing necessary for the triumph of evil is for good men to do nothing.
    Edmund Burke

Some Christians are not only like salt that has lost its savour, but like pepper that has lost its pep.   *Albert George Butzer*

If we once become listless to duty, we shall quickly become lifeless in it.
    Stephen Charnock

An appeaser is one who feeds a crocodile — hoping it will eat him last.
    Winston Churchill

No man need stay the way he is.
    Harry Emerson Fosdick

If the doctrine of sinless perfection is a heresy, the doctrine of contentment with sinful imperfection is a greater heresy.
    A. J. Gordon

Many Christians have enough religion to make them decent, but not enough to make them dynamic. *Kenneth Grider*

None will have such a sad parting from Christ as those who went halfway with him and then left him. *William Gurnall*

Affection is the answer to apathy.
Vance Havner

Never before have we had so many degrees in the church and yet so little temperature. *Vance Havner*

Nothing is more dangerous to our spiritual well-being than a mild amiability that smiles at sin. *Vance Havner*

Some of us simmer all our lives and never come to the boil. *Vance Havner*

The same church members who yell like Comanche Indians at a ball game on Saturday sit like wooden Indians in church on Sunday. *Vance Havner*

We've got too many comfortable saints expanding their physical waistline instead of extending their spiritual coastline.
Vance Havner

He who passively accepts evil is as much involved in it as he who helps to perpetrate it. *Martin Luther King*

Spiritual indifference is always the result of losing God as the centre and source of spiritual vitality. *Festo Kivengere*

At the final bar of judgement the gravest charge that will be made against us Christians will be that we were so unconcerned.
D. Martyn Lloyd-Jones

Christians are the more cold and careless in the spiritual life because they do not oftener think of heaven. *Thomas Manton*

He who aims at nothing never achieves anything else. *J. I. Packer*

Nothing is so offensive to Christ as luke-warmness in religion. *J. C. Ryle*

Apathy is the acceptance of the unacceptable. *John R. W. Stott*

Our problems of spiritual coldness and apathy in the churches would quickly disappear if Christian believers generally would confess their great need for redis-covering the loveliness of Jesus Christ, their Saviour. *A. W. Tozer*

The low level of moral enthusiasm among us may have a significance far deeper than we are willing to believe. *A. W. Tozer*

No man can sit down and withhold his hands from the warfare against wrong and get peace from his acquiescence.
Woodrow Wilson

APOSTASY

It is the creed of every sound evangelical church that those who do go back to perdition were persons who never really believed in Jesus. *A. A. Bonar*

The apostate must perish, not because the sacrifice of Christ is not of efficacy enough to expiate even his guilt, but because, continuing in his apostasy, he will have nothing to do with that sacri-fice which is the only available sacrifice for sin. *John Brown*

Apostasy is a perversion to evil after a seemingly conversion from it.
Timothy Cruso

None sink so far into hell as those that come nearest heaven, because they fall from the greatest height. *William Gurnall*

None will have such a sad parting from Christ as those who went halfway with him and then left him. *William Gurnall*

The evil consequences of apostasy from God are not confined to the original apostates. *Charles Hodge*

To forsake Christ for the world is to leave a treasure for a trifle … eternity for a moment, reality for a shadow, all things for nothing. *William Jenkyn*

It is better not to have known the way of truth than not to persist in it. *John King*

Scripture does not need to be denied for apostasy to begin: all that is needed is that Scripture takes second place in our calculations. *Iain H. Murray*

How can they be true who have departed from the truth? *James Philip*

None prove so hopelessly wicked as those who, after experiencing strong religious convictions, have gone back again to sin and the world. *J. C. Ryle*

Apostasy must be called what it is — a spiritual adultery. *Francis Schaeffer*

To see a ship sink in the harbour of profession is more grievous than if it had perished in the open sea of profaneness. *William Secker*

Judas betrayed his Master with a kiss. That is how apostates do it; it is always with a kiss. *C. H. Spurgeon*

The essence of apostasy is changing sides from that of the crucified to that of the crucifier. *John R. W. Stott*

He falls deepest into hell who falls backwards. *Thomas Watson*

The apostate drops as a windfall into the devil's mouth. *Thomas Watson*

The root of all apostasy is the primal sin of unbelief. *Geoffrey B. Wilson*

APPRECIATION

Lord, help us to glow in the other man's gift. *Tom Butler*

The deepest principle in human nature is the craving to be appreciated. *William Jones*

Next to excellence is the appreciation of it. *William Makepeace Thackery*

ARROGANCE — See Boasting; Conceit; Egotism; Pride; Vanity

ART

All arts proceed from God and ought to be held as divine inventions. *John Calvin*

True art is reverent imitation of God. *Tryon Edwards*

Every artist writes his own autobiography. *Havelock Ellis*

Art is a collaboration between God and the artist, and the less the artist does the better. *Andre Gide*

Art leads to a more profound concept of life, because art itself is a profound expression of feeling. *Hans Hofmann*

Art is the gift of God, and must be used unto his glory.
Henry Wordsworth Longfellow

Since I have known God in a saving manner, painting, poetry and music have had charms unknown to me before.
Henry Martyn

Art is the gift of God and must be used for his glory. That in art is the highest which aims at this.
Buonarroti Michelangelo

The true work of art is but a shadow of the divine perfection.
Buonarroti Michelangelo

Genuine art was never created for its own sake, it was always a means of worship, an affirmation of belief, an aspiration pointing beyond itself. The beauty of art is reflected beauty.   *Thomas Molnar*

Art ultimately exists for God's glory.
Robert A. Morey

We shall have no art until we remember that it is a reward, given us only when we reach beyond ourselves to the Author of beauty.   *George Roche*

Art is here because God meant it to be here.   *Hans Rookmaaker*

All great art is the expression of man's delight in God's work, not his own.
John Ruskin

ASCENSION — See Jesus Christ — Ascension

ASSURANCE

That faith which is never assaulted with doubting is but a fancy. Assuredly that assurance which is ever secure is but a dream.   *Robert Bolton*

A soul under assurance is unwilling to go to heaven without company.
Thomas Brooks

A well-grounded assurance is always attended by three fair handmaids: love, humility and holy joy.   *Thomas Brooks*

Assurance is glory in the bud, it is the suburbs of paradise.   *Thomas Brooks*

Assurance is optimum maximum, the best and greatest mercy; and therefore God will only give it to his best and dearest friends.   *Thomas Brooks*

Assurance makes heavy afflictions light, long afflictions short, bitter afflictions sweet.   *Thomas Brooks*

Assurance makes most for your comfort but holiness makes most for God's honour.   *Thomas Brooks*

Faith cannot be lost, but assurance may; therefore assurance is not faith.
Thomas Brooks

Many a Christian has his pardon sealed in the court of heaven before it is sealed in the court of his own conscience.
Thomas Brooks

Perfect signs of grace can never spring from imperfect grace.   *Thomas Brooks*

Reason's arm is too short to reach the jewel of assurance.   *Thomas Brooks*

The more the soul is conformed to Christ, the more confident it will be of its interest in Christ.   *Thomas Brooks*

Though no man merits assurance by his obedience, yet God usually crowns obedience with assurance.   *Thomas Brooks*

Without the diligent use of means a lazy Christian has no right to expect to receive assurance.   *Thomas Brooks*

Let us not seek any other ground of assurance than God's own testimony.
John Calvin

The inward testimony of conscience, the sealing of the conscience, the sealing of the Spirit ... far exceeds all the evidence of the senses.   *John Calvin*

There is no better assurance of salvation to he found anywhere than can he gained from the decree of God.   *John Calvin*

Assurance is the fruit that grows out of the root of faith.   *Stephen Charnock*

Assurance is from God every bit as much as faith is.   *J. C. P. Cockerton*

Assurance does not grow like a hothouse plant, pampered in an even temperature and sheltered from every puff of wind! It is an outdoor species, meant to flourish in the ever-changing weather conditions of the world.   *J. C. P. Cockerton*

The gospel is the ground of the believer's assurance, while the Holy Spirit is its cause.   *J. C. P. Cockerton*

Assurance does not lie in what we are, be we great or small. It lies in what God has done in his plan of salvation to secure us to himself. *Sinclair Ferguson*

Assurance is our reaction to the gift of salvation and our reflection on our trust in Christ.   *Sinclair Ferguson*

Faith alone justifies, through Christ alone. Assurance is the enjoyment of that justification.   *Sinclair Ferguson*

Assurance hath a narrow throat, and may be choked with a small sin.
Thomas Fuller

Fear to fall and assurance to stand are two sisters.   *Thomas Fuller*

Assurance is, as it were, the cream of faith.   *William Gurnall*

A well-grounded assurance of heaven and happiness, instead of puffing a man up with pride, will make and keep him very humble.   *Matthew Henry*

I think the first essential mark of the difference between true and false assurance is to be found in the fact that the true works humility.   *A. A. Hodge*

None have assurance at all times. As in a walk that is shaded with trees and chequered with light and shadow, some tracks and paths in it are dark and others are sunshine. Such is usually the life of the most assured Christian. *Ezekiel Hopkins*

Faith rests on the naked Word of God; that Word believed gives full assurance.
H. A. Ironside

Sin can never quite bereave a saint of his jewel, his grace; but it may steal away the key of the cabinet, his assurance.
William Jenkyn

The Holy Spirit is no sceptic, and the things he has written in our hearts are not doubts or opinions, but assertions – surer and more certain than sense or life itself.
Martin Luther

None walk so evenly with God as they who are assured of the love of God.
Thomas Manton

Our assurance must be founded, built up and established on the mercy of God alone. *Will Metzger*

The doctrine of assurance, biblically understood, keeps the saint on his toes.
J. A. Motyer

Faith is our seal; assurance of faith is God's seal. *Christopher Nesse*

Feelings of confidence about our salvation need to be tested before they are trusted. *J. I. Packer*

The assurance that we are called of God, chosen in Christ before the foundation of the world, affords a safe and secure anchorage from which no tempest can ever dislodge us. *James Philip*

Where the eternal interests of the soul are concerned only a fool will give himself the benefit of the doubt. *A. W Pink*

Your Rock is Christ, and it is not the Rock which ebbs and flows, but your sea.
Samuel Rutherford

Assurance … enables a child of God to feel that the great business of life is a settled business, the great debt a paid debt, the great disease a healed disease and the great work a finished work. *J. C. Ryle*

Assurance is a most delicate plant. It needs daily, hourly, watering, tending, cherishing. So watch and pray the more when you have got it. *J. C. Ryle*

Assurance of hope is more than life. It is health, strength, power, vigour, activity, energy, manliness, and beauty. *J. C. Ryle*

No less a person than God is needed to assure us of God's love. *Richard Sibbes*

Christians should never rest until the soul evidences that it is the Lord's … While our interest in his favour is doubtful, what happiness can we enjoy? *Charles Simeon*

Our assurance is only as strong as our faith. *R. C. Sproul*

Assurance is a jewel for worth but not for rarity. *C. H. Spurgeon*

Assurance of faith can never come by the works of the law. It is an evangelical virtue, and can only reach us in a gospel way. *C. H. Spurgeon*

Faith saves us, but assurance satisfies us.
C. H. Spurgeon

Full assurance is not essential to salvation, but it is essential to satisfaction.
C. H. Spurgeon

No believer should be content with hoping and trusting, he should ask the Lord to lead him on to full assurance, so that matters of hope may become matters of certainty. *C. H. Spurgeon*

We count it no presumption to say that we are saved, for the Word of God has told us so in those places where salvation is promised to faith in Christ. The presumption would lie in doubting the Word of God. *C. H. Spurgeon*

If the priesthood of all believers is the first fruit of justification, 'assurance' is the second. *John R. W. Stott*

A letter may be written, when it is not sealed; so grace may be written in the heart, and the Spirit may not set the seal of assurance to it. *Thomas Watson*

Faith will make us walk, but assurance will make us run.   *Thomas Watson*

Sanctification is the seed; assurance is the flower which grows out of it.
Thomas Watson

The jewel of assurance is best kept in the cabinet of the heart.   *Thomas Watson*

The inward witness, son, the inward witness; that is proof, the strongest proof of Christianity.   *Samuel Wesley*

ATHEISM
(See also: Agnosticism; Unbelief)

Atheism is the main disease of the soul.
Thomas Adams

To be an atheist requires an infinitely greater measure of faith than to receive all the great truths which atheism would deny.   *Joseph Addison*

An atheist is someone who believes that what you see is all you get.   *Anon.*

Atheism has no moral power to change lives.   *Anon.*

Atheism is not an institution; it is a destitution.   *Anon.*

Atheism is the death of hope, the suicide of the soul.   *Anon.*

For an atheist to find God is as difficult as for a thief to find a policeman and for the same reason.   *Anon.*

One trouble with being an atheist is that you have nobody to talk to when you are alone.   *Anon.*

Philosophically speaking, atheism is much closer to superstition and wishful thinking than to science.   *Anon.*

No man says, 'There is no God' but he whose interest it is there should be none.
Augustine

Atheism is rather in the lip than in the heart of man.   *Francis Bacon*

God never wrought miracles to convince atheism because his ordinary works convince it.   *Francis Bacon*

There are more atheists than believe themselves to be such.   *Albert Barnes*

An atheist is a man who looks through a telescope and tries to explain what he can't see.   *O. A. Battista*

Where there is no God there is no man.
Nicolai Berdyaev

Those who deny the existence of God are hard put to explain the existence of man.
Harold Berry

An atheist is not lacking in faith — he is lacking in evidence.   *John Blanchard*

Atheism is the ultimate ignorance.
John Blanchard

Atheism knows of no foundation for logical thinking.   *John Blanchard*

It takes greater faith to be an atheist than to be a Christian.   *John Blanchard*

One of the bleakest things about atheism is that it provides no basis for virtue.
John Blanchard

Strictly speaking, the atheist has no questions to ask about suffering; neither does he have any answers.   *John Blanchard*

The world is still waiting for the first wise atheist. *John Blanchard*

I have yet to meet a person whose life was in a terrible mess who claimed that atheism suddenly revealed a truth that changed his or her life for lasting good. *Joe Boot*

Atheism is the most cruel hypothesis of all. For it says that in the end, injustice cannot be righted, suffering cannot be redeemed, evil triumphs after all. *Francis Bridger*

He that doth not believe that there is a God is more vile than a devil. To deny there is a God is a sort of atheism that is not to be found in hell. *Thomas Brooks*

An atheist is a man without any visible means of support. *John Buchan*

This is, indeed, the proper business of the whole life, in which men should daily exercise themselves, to consider the infinite goodness, justice, power and wisdom of God, in this magnificent theatre of God. *John Calvin*

Every atheist is a grand fool. *Stephen Charnock*

People think that when they do not believe in God they believe in nothing, but the fact is they will believe in anything. *G. K. Chesterton*

How did the atheist get his idea of that God whom he denies? *Samuel Taylor Coleridge*

It is hard to see how a great man can be an atheist. Doubters do not achieve. Sceptics do not contribute. Cynics do not create. *Calvin Coolidge.*

A denial of God is practically always the result of shutting one eye. It may be for this reason that God gave us two. *C. A. Coulson*

If there is no God, everything is permitted. *Fydor Dostoyevski*

It takes no brains to be an atheist. *Dwight D. Eisenhower*

The question of God cannot be finally avoided because it is a question about the kind of universe we live in. This is a real question and it must have a real answer. We need to know the truth about God if we are to live our lives rightly. *C. Stephen Evans*

Atheism stabs the soul to death at one stroke. *John Flavel*

Atheists are worse than devils, for they believe, and tremble; these banish God out of their thoughts. *John Flavel*

Men may deny God with their voices, but cannot escape his presence or judgement with fanciful theories and exculpatory formulas. *P. G. Fothergill*

Atheism is a universal negative, and therefore impossible to prove. It is little wonder, therefore, that many claim that it takes more faith to be an atheist than to believe in God. *Rob Frost*

Some are atheists only in fair weather. *Thomas Fuller*

It amazes me to find an intelligent person who fights against something which he does not at all believe exists. *Mohandas Gandhi*

It has always seemed to me utterly absurd for the atheist to profess such deep regard for the random products of a universe where chance is king.

Michael Green

It isn't very rational to argue that the world which is based on cause and effect is itself uncaused.   *Michael Green*

If 'God is dead' all sorts of other things die too, including truth, selfhood, character, the power of words to describe reality and for some people even reality itself.   *Os Guinness*

Atheism is folly, and atheists are the greatest fools in nature, for they see there is a world that could not make itself, and yet they will not own there is a God that made it.   *Matthew Henry*

No man will say, 'There is no God' till he is so hardened in sin that it has become his interest that there should be none to call him to account.   *Matthew Henry*

The devil divides the world between atheism and superstition.   *George Herbert*

Atheistic morality is not impossible, but it will never answer our purpose.

Roswell D. Hitchcock

Unless the being of God be presupposed, no tolerable account can be given of the being of any thing.   *Ezekiel Hopkins*

No man is a consistent atheist.

R. B. Kuiper

Atheism turns out to be too simple. If the whole universe has no meaning, we should never have found out that it has no meaning: just as, if there were no light in the universe and therefore no creatures with eyes, we should never know it was dark.   *C. S. Lewis*

I was … living, like so many atheists or antitheists, in a whirl of contradictions. I maintained that God did not exist. I was also very angry with God for not existing. I was equally angry with him for creating a world.   *C. S. Lewis*

I can see how it might be possible to look down upon the earth and be an atheist, but I cannot conceive how he could look into the heavens and say there is no God.

Abraham Lincoln

Every effort to prove there is no God is in itself an effort to reach for God.

Charles Edward Locke.

If there is no God, what else is there to celebrate and believe in as a source of significance?   *Pete Lowman*

Atheism, like all other worldviews, is a matter of faith.   *Alister McGrath*

When people tell me they are atheists, they are not just telling me about the way they think. They also tell me something about the way they live.   *Will Metzer*

The footprint of the savage in the sand is sufficient to attest the presence of man to the atheist, yet he will not recognize God, whose hand is impressed upon the entire universe.   *Hugh Miller*

It is philosophically and logically absurd to state such a universal negative as 'There is no God.'   *Robert A. Morey*

To say with assurance that there was, is and never shall be any deity of any kind in the entire universe would require the atheist to travel throughout time, be everywhere at the same moment in time, and know all things. To do all this, he would have to be omnipotent, omnipresent and omniscient. In short, he would have to become the very God that he wishes so much to deny. *Robert A. Morey*

The best reply to an atheist is to give him a good dinner and ask him if he believes there is a cook. *Louis Nizer*

God's world is never friendly to those who forget its Maker. *J. I. Packer*

There is no greater blasphemy than to will God out of existence. *J. I. Packer*

There are more atheists in lip than in life. *Clark H. Pinnock*

Atheists put on a false courage and alacrity in the midst of their darkness and apprehensions, like children who, when they fear to go in the dark, will sing for fear. *Alexander Pope*

To be absolutely sure of anything, an atheist must know everything. *Edgar Powell*

It is non-believers who are most vociferous in demanding some explanation from God. *Frank Retief*

No one is so much alone in the universe as a denier of God. *Johann P. F. Richter*

The worst moment for the atheist is when he is really thankful and has nobody to thank. *Dante Gabriel Rossetti*

Atheism is a cruel, long-term business. *Jean-Paul Sartre*

That God does not exist, I cannot deny. That my whole being cries out for God, I cannot forget. *Jean-Paul Sartre*

The adoption of atheism is a sin without necessity. It is the voluntary action of man. *W. G. T. Shedd*

The atheist is always alone. *Ignazio Silone*

Naturalists who deny the existence of any transcendent, personal God cannot successfully solve the problem of good. They cannot explain why there is a difference between right and wrong. *James W. Sire*

Atheism and agnosticism are not merely defective theories that need to be corrected by further study and more information. They are sin for which men are called to repent because God has made himself known to them.
R. C. Sproul

The problem is not that there is insufficient evidence to convince rational beings that there is a God, but that rational beings have a natural hostility to the being of God. *R. C. Sproul*

If ever man appears as a consummate ass, it's when he denies the existence of God.
Billy Sunday

The atheist has got one point beyond the devil. *Jonathan Swift*

An atheist is a man who believes himself an accident. *Francis Thompson*

Was every man on earth to become an atheist, it could not affect God in any way.
A. W. Tozer

All atheists are wilful atheists.
John Urquhart

Those who hope for no other life are dead even for this.
Johann Wolfgang von Goethe

Atheism springs not from a clear head but from a disordered heart.
W. L. Watkinson

The religion of the atheist has a God-shaped blank at its heart. *H. G. Wells*

There are no atheists in foxholes and rubber rafts. *James Whitaker*

To see and hear an atheist die will more demonstrate that there is a God than all the learned can do by their arguments.
Zeno

ATONEMENT
(See also: Cross; Forgiveness by God; Jesus Christ — Death; Redemption)

The Lord Jesus took our place that we might have his peace; he took our sin that we might have his salvation. *Anon.*

When you can add brightness to the sun, beauty to the rainbow and strength to the everlasting hills, then you may try to improve the finished work of Christ. *Anon.*

The cross of Jesus Christ is a two-way street; we have been brought to God and God has been brought to us.
Donald Grey Barnhouse

Just as surely as there was an actual cross, an actual body, actual blood, an actual death, an actual tomb, an actual resurrection so there was an actual atonement, not merely the possibility of one.
John Blanchard

The death of Christ was an atonement which totally succeeded, not an attempt which partially failed. *John Blanchard*

The death of Jesus was not a proposition for sinners but the purchase of salvation.
John Blanchard

Bearing shame and scoffing rude,
In my place condemned he stood;
Sealed my pardon with his blood:
Hallelujah! what a Saviour!
Philipp Paul Bliss

The nature of the atonement settles its extent. If it merely made salvation possible, it applied to all men. If it effectively secured salvation, it had reference only to the elect. *Loraine Boettner*

The atonement is the real reason for the Incarnation. *James Montgomery Boice*

I hear the words of love,
I gaze upon the blood,
I see the mighty sacrifice,
And I have peace with God.
Horatius Bonar

When the Lord Jesus Christ had our sins laid upon him, he did give more perfect satisfaction unto divine justice for our sins than if . . . all of us had been damned in hell unto all eternity. *William Bridge*

Christ hath crossed out the black lines of our sin with the red lines of his own blood.
Thomas Brooks

Christ rose again, but our sins did not: they are buried for ever in his grave.
John Brown

Blest cross! Blest sepulchre!
  Blest rather be
The man that there was put to
  shame for me.
John Bunyan

Because the sinless Saviour died,
My sinful soul is counted free;
For God the Just is satisfied
To look on him, and pardon me.
Charitie Lees de Chenez

Atonement is not something contrived, as it were, behind the Father's back; it is the Father's way of making it possible for the sinful to have fellowship with him.
James Denney

'Reconciliation' in the New Testament sense is not something which we accomplish when we lay aside our enmity to God; it is something which God accomplished when in the death of Christ he put away everything that on his side meant estrangement.   *James Denney*

The simplest word of faith is the deepest word of theology: Christ died for our sins.
James Denney

Grace first inscribed my name
In God's eternal book;
'Twas grace that gave me to the Lamb,
Who all my sorrows took.
Philip Doddridge

The work of atonement took place in the presence of the God of heaven. Indeed, it involved a transaction within the fellowship of the eternal Trinity in their love for us: the Son was willing, with the aid of the Spirit, to experience the hiding of the face of the Father. *Sinclair Ferguson*

Sin's debt, that fearful burden,
Let not your soul distress;
Your guilt the Lord will pardon,
And cover by his grace.
He comes for men procuring
The peace of sins forgiven;
For all God's sons securing
Their heritage in heaven.
Paul Gerhardt

God in his love pitcheth upon persons … Christ died not for propositions only, but for persons. He loved *us,* not ours.
Thomas Goodwin

It was to save sinners that Christ Jesus came into the world. He did not come to help them save themselves, nor to induce them to save themselves, nor even to enable them to save themselves. He came to save them!   *William Hendriksen*

There is room enough in Christ for all comers.   *Matthew Henry*

Great is the gospel of our glorious God,
Where mercy met the anger of God's rod;
A penalty was paid and pardon bought,
And sinners lost at last to him were
   brought.
William Vernon Higham

The evidence that the death of Christ has been accepted as an expiation for sin, of infinite value and efficiency, is the fact that God has commissioned his ministers to announce to all men that God is reconciled and ready to forgive, so that whosoever will may turn to him and live.
Charles Hodge

The wrong that man hath done to the divine majesty *should* be expiated by none but man and *could* be by none but God.   *John Howe*

Our answer to the devil's charge is not an alibi, but a plea of guilty and a claim that the demands of justice have been satisfied in the blood of the Lord Jesus Christ.   *Russell Howden*

If our Saviour had committed all the sins of the world … his agony that he suffered should have been no greater nor grievouser than it was.   *Hugh Latimer*

It was not for societies or states that Christ died, but for me.   *C. S. Lewis*

To deny the necessity of atonement is to deny the existence of a real moral order.
J. Gresham Machen.

There is no clearer note in the Christian gospel than this: that God has put us right with himself entirely of his own free grace and at an inward cost to himself of which, in human history, Calvary is the index.
Leslie S. McCaw

There is not a ray of hope for man outside of substitution.   *D. L. Moody*

The atonement is the crucial doctrine of the faith. Unless we are right here, it matters not, it seems to me, what we are like elsewhere.   *Leon Morris*

Out of the wealth of his resources, God has paid debts which were no concern of his.   *J. A. Motyer*

Christ discharged the debt of sin. He bore our sins and purged them. He did not make a token payment which God accepts in place of the whole. Our debts are not cancelled; they are liquidated.
John Murray

Those for whom Christ died are those for whom he rose again and his heavenly saving activity is of equal extent with his once-for-all redemptive accomplishments.   *John Murray*

Unless we believe in the final restoration of all men we cannot have an unlimited atonement. If we universalize the extent we limit the efficacy.   *John Murray*

What is offered to men in the gospel? It is not the possibility of salvation, not simply the opportunity of salvation. What is offered is salvation.   *John Murray*

All peace with God is resolved into a purging atonement made for sin.
John Owen

Christ did not die for any upon condition, if they do believe; but he died for all God's elect, that they should believe.
John Owen

If Christ had not died, sin had never died in any sinner unto eternity.   *John Owen*

Nothing can give perfect peace of conscience with God but what can make atonement for sin. And whoever attempt it any other way but by virtue of that atonement will never attain it, in this world or hereafter.   *John Owen*

There is no death of sin without the death of Christ.   *John Owen*

It cannot be over-emphasized that we have not seen the full meaning of the cross till we have seen it as the centre of the gospel, flanked on the one hand by total inability and unconditional election and on the other by irresistible grace and final preservation.   *J. I. Packer*

The question of the extent of the atonement does not arise in evangelistic preaching; the message to be delivered is simply this — that Christ Jesus, the sovereign Lord, who died for sinners, now invites sinners freely to himself. God commands all to repent and believe; Christ promises joy and peace to all who do so.   *J. I. Packer*

The Redeemer's death actually saves his people, as it was meant to do. *J. I. Packer*

The atonement was not the cause but the effect of God's love.   *A. W. Pink*

Do not believe the devil's gospel, which is a *chance* of salvation; a chance of salvation is a chance of damnation.
Adolph Saphir

Nothing needs to be added to Christ's finished work, and nothing *can* be added to Christ's finished work. *Francis Schaeffer*

The atonement is not offered to an individual either as an elect man, or as a non-elect man; but as a man, and a sinner, simply. *W. G. T. Shedd*

Christ assumed both body and soul; and he offered both in our room, as was necessary to expiate guilt incurred in body and by both. *G. Smeaton*

All are not saved by Christ's death, but all which are saved are saved by Christ's death; his death is sufficient to save all, as the sun is sufficient to lighten all.
Henry Smith

Atonement by the blood of Jesus is not an arm of Christian truth; it is the heart of it. *C. H. Spurgeon*

Atonement is the brain and spinal cord of Christianity *C. H. Spurgeon*

If our Lord's bearing our sin for us is not the gospel, I have no gospel to preach.
C. H. Spurgeon

One thing I know substitution. And one thing I do preach it. *C. H. Spurgeon*

Sin mingles even with our holy things, and our best repentance, faith, prayer and thanksgiving could not be received of God were it not for the merit of the atoning sacrifice. *C. H. Spurgeon*

Until God can be unjust, and demand two payments for one debt, he cannot destroy the soul for whom Jesus died.
C. H. Spurgeon

Dear Lord, what heavenly wonders dwell
In thy atoning blood!
By this are sinners snatched from hell,
And rebels brought to God.
Anne Steele

What God was satisfying on the cross was his very own self. It was not the law conceived as something above him, but the law of his own infinite being.
John R. W. Stott

Because Christ is man, he can make atonement for man and sympathize with man. Because Christ is God his atonement has infinite value and the union which he effects with God is complete.
Augustus H. Strong

Christ's atonement is no passion-play. Hell cannot be cured by homoeopathy.
Augustus H. Strong

God requires satisfaction because he is holiness, but he makes satisfaction because he is love *Augustus H. Strong*

Payment God cannot twice demand;
First at my bleeding Saviour's hand,
And then again at mine.
Augustus M. Toplady

The things we have to choose between are an atonement of high value, or an atonement of wide extension. The two cannot go together. *Benjamin B. Warfield*

Christ's blood has value enough to redeem the whole world, but the virtue of it is applied only to such as believe.
Thomas Watson

Well might the sun in darkness hide,
And shut his glories in,
When God, the mighty Maker, died
For man, the creature's sin.
Isaac Watts

The resurrection is the proof of our reconciliation. *Geoffrey B. Wilson*

AUTHORITY

A leading authority is anyone who has guessed right more than once. *Anon.*

There is nothing holier, or better, or safer, than to content ourselves with the authority of Christ alone. *John Calvin*

The authority of the saints rests upon the authority of the Scriptures, the Saviour and the Spirit. *Vance Havner*

When authority goes out anarchy comes in. *Vance Havner*

The overriding issue of the twentieth century is the crisis in authority.
Carl F. H. Henry

Obedience to legitimate authority is one of the fruits and evidences of Christian sincerity. *Charles Hodge*

The source of all authority is not Scripture, but Christ … Nowhere are we told that the Scripture of itself is able to convince a sinner or bring him to God.
Augustus H. Strong

We are finite and sinful, and we need authority. *Augustus H. Strong*

AVARICE — See Greed

AWE
(See also: Adoration; Fear of God; Worship)

Awe is the primary religious emotion.
Anon.

We should give God the same place in our hearts that he holds in the universe.
Anon.

Christ never permitted anybody to be commonly familiar with him, and if you knew him you would never be familiar with him — you would be reverent.
Rolfe Barnard

We are encouraged to come freely to God but not flippantly. *John Blanchard*

The man who cannot wonder is but a pair of spectacles behind which there is no eye. *Thomas Carlyle*

The world will never starve for want of wonders; but only for want of wonder.
G. K. Chesterton

Where there is no awe the highest love is surely lacking. *Peter Green*

Nothing else under the sun can be as dry, flat, tedious and exhausting as religious work without the wonder. *Vance Havner*

We must rejoice in God, but still with a holy trembling. *Matthew Henry*

When we cannot, by searching, find the bottom, we must sit down at the brink and adore the depth. *Matthew Henry*

When we have found God good, we must not forget to pronounce him great; and his kind thoughts of us must not abate our high thoughts of him. *Matthew Henry*

Reverence excludes speculation about things that God has not mentioned in his Word. *J. I. Packer*

The more we lose sight of the otherness of God, the more shallow our worship will be. *Alwyn Pritchard*

The true scientist never loses the faculty of amazement. It is the essence of his being. *Hans Seyle*

The larger the island of knowledge, the longer the shoreline of wonder. *Ralph W. Sockman*

Christ can never be known without a sense of awe and fear accompanying the knowledge . . . No one who knows him intimately can ever be flippant in his presence. *A. W. Tozer*

The greatest need of the moment is that light-hearted, superficial religionists be struck down with a vision of God high and lifted up, with his train filling the temple. *A. W. Tozer*

BACKSLIDING

Whoever strives to withdraw from obedience withdraws from grace. *Thomas à Kempis*

If thou wilt fly from God, the devil will lend thee both spurs and a horse. *Thomas Adams*

However deep you fall, you are never out of God's reach. *Anon.*

If you are not as close to God as you used to be, you do not have to guess who moved. *Anon.*

Life's greatest tragedy is to lose God and not miss him. *Anon.*

Never look back unless you want to go that way. *Anon.*

It is better to help our friends to recover lost grace than lost money. *Augustine*

Withering is a slow process, barely perceptible at first either to one who is being withered or to those who look on. *Donald Grey Barnhouse*

Backsliding never begins with a loud bang ... it begins quietly, slowly, subtly, insidiously. *John Blanchard*

It is possible to be back-slapping and backsliding at the same time. *John Blanchard*

It is possible to be diligent in our religion, yet distant in our relationship. *John Blanchard*

No Christian is ever going in the right direction when he has his back to God. *John Blanchard*

There's no slipping uphill again, and no standing still when once you've begun to slip down. *George Eliot*

A declining Christian must needs be a doubting Christian. *William Gurnall*

Grace in a decay is like a man pulled off his legs by sickness. *William Gurnall*

The Christian in a declining condition ... is as unfit to die as he is to live. *William Gurnall*

To backslide in heart is more than to backslide. *William Gurnall*

If you find yourself loving any pleasure more than your prayers, any book better

than the Bible, any house better than the house of the Lord, any table better than the Lord's table, any persons better than Christ, or any indulgence better than the hope of heaven — be alarmed.
Thomas Guthrie

Taking it easy is often the prelude to backsliding. Comfort precedes collapse.
Vance Havner

We are so subnormal that if we ever became normal people would think we were abnormal.   *Vance Havner*

God will preserve you in your ways, not in your wanderings.   *William Jenkyn*

For some of us, our greatest ability seems to be the ability for getting away from the Shepherd.   *Geoffrey King*

Collapse in the Christian life is seldom a blowout. It is usually a slow leak.
Paul E. Little

The backslider is a man who, because of relationship to God, never really enjoy anything else.   *D. Martyn Lloyd-Jones*

We are all constantly backsliding but for the grace of God.   *Dick Lucas*

The man who has lost contact with God lives on the same dead-end street as the man who denies him.   *Milton Marcy*

Backsliding is caused by slack abiding.
Ernest Plant

If we know anything of true, saving religion, let us ever beware of the beginnings of backsliding.   *J. C. Ryle*

It is a miserable thing to be a backslider. Of all unhappy things that can befall a

man, I suppose it is the worst. A stranded ship, an eagle with a broken wing, a garden covered with weeds, a harp without strings, a church in ruins — all these are sad sights, but a backslider is a sadder sight still.   *J. C. Ryle*

Men fall in private long before they fall in public.   *J. C. Ryle*

Of all decays, the decay of goodness is the most lamentable.   *Richard Sibbes*

Backsliders begin with dusty Bibles and end with filthy garments. *C. H. Spurgeon*

It is dangerous to backslide in any degree, for we know not to what it may lead.   *C. H. Spurgeon*

It may be hard going forward, but it is worse going back.   *C. H. Spurgeon*

Unsaintly saints are the tragedy of Christianity.   *A. W. Tozer*

BEAUTY

Beauty without virtue is a flower without perfume.   *Anon.*

Beauty is a gift of God.   *Aristotle*

Beauty is God's handwriting.
Ralph Waldo Emerson

Never lose an opportunity to see anything beautiful. Beauty is God's handwriting.
Charles Kingsley

Our being cannot be satisfied unless the thirst for beauty is quenched.
H. R. Rookmaaker

The beautiful can have but only one source — God.   *Arthur Schopenhauer*

There is a beauty in holiness as well as a beauty of holiness.   *George Swinnock*

BEHAVIOUR — See Actions

BELIEF — See Faith

BIBLE — Authority
(See also: Bible — Divine Authority and Authorship)

The faith will totter if the authority of the Holy Scriptures loses its hold on men. We must surrender ourselves to the authority of Holy Scripture, for it can neither mislead nor be misled.   *Augustine*

The authority of the Bible comes not from the calibre of its human authors but from the character of its divine Author.
John Blanchard

The Bible is the sceptre by which the heavenly King rules his church.
John Calvin

Whether we happen to like it or not, we are closed up to the teaching of the Bible for our information about all doctrines in the Christian faith, and this includes the doctrine of the Bible's view of itself.
Edward John Carnell

The Word of God is more credible than a visitor from the dead.   *B. H. Carroll*

The authority of Scripture is not one that binds, but one that sets free.
William Newton Clarke

The Word of God is above the church.
Thomas Cranmer

God's Word is its own best argument.
Vance Havner

The Word of God is either absolute or obsolete.   *Vance Havner*

There is only one real inevitability: it is necessary that the Scripture be fulfilled.
Carl F. Henry

The best evidence the Bible's being the Word of God is found between its covers.   *Charles Hodge*

The Bible is the statute-book of God's kingdom.   *Ezekiel Hopkins*

All experience must be subservient to the discipline of Scripture.   *Erroll Hulse*

Never mind the scribes — what saith the Scripture?   *Martin Luther*

We glory most in the fact that Scripture so commends itself to the conscience, and experience so bears out the Bible, that the gospel can go round the world and carry with it, in all its travel, its own mighty credentials.   *Henry Melvill*

The Bible was the only book Jesus ever quoted, and then never as a basis for discussion but to decide the point at issue.   *Leon Morris*

What does not agree with Scripture does not come from God.   *Leon Morris*

Our vision of God must be controlled not by what we see in the world but by what Scripture authorizes us to believe.
Iain H. Murray

It is for the Bible to form and reform the church . . . it is for the church to keep and keep to the Bible.   *J. I. Packer*

The church no more created the canon than Newton created the law of gravity; recognition is not creation.   *J. I. Packer*

God demands complete loyalty to his Word. *Richard L. Pratt*

A partially inspired Bible is little better than no Bible at all. *J. C. Ryle*

If the difficulties of plenary inspiration are to be numbered by thousands, the difficulties of any other view of inspiration are to be numbered by tens of thousands. *J. C. Ryle*

The ordinary Christian with the Bible in his hand can say that the majority is wrong. *Francis Schaeffer*

The truth of Scripture demolishes speculation. *R. C. Sproul*

The Bible, the whole Bible, and nothing but the Bible is the religion of Christ's church. *C. H. Spurgeon*

This we believe, when we first begin to believe, that we ought not to believe anything beyond Scripture. *Tertullian*

The truly wise man is he who always believes the Bible against the opinion of any man. *R. A. Torrey*

The only authoritative word ever published is that which comes from the Holy Scriptures. *A. W. Tozer*

Inspiration, in the full apostolic meaning of the word, ceased when the canon of Scripture was brought to completion. Without such apostolic inspiration there can be no infallible revelation. *Geoffrey B. Wilson*

BIBLE — and Christ

A man who can read the New Testament and not see that Christ claims to be more than mere man can look all over the sky at high noon on a cloudless day and not see the sun. *W. E. Biederwolf*

We do not find Christ in the Old Testament by spotting accidental references or similarities here and there; he is the centre, the structure of the whole history of the Old Testament. *Edmund P. Clowney*

We cannot have a reliable Saviour without a reliable Scripture. *Brian H. Edwards*

The entire Bible carries the certification of the Son of God, which brings with it infallible authority. Thus the written Word of God has the seal of the living Word of God. *John H. Gerstner*

The Old Testament Scriptures are intelligible only when understood as predicting and prefiguring Christ.
Charles Hodge

Ignorance of the Scripture is ignorance of Christ. *Jerome*

It is Christ himself, not the Bible, that is the true Word of God. The Bible, read in the right spirit and with the guidance of good teachers, will bring us to him.
C. S. Lewis

As we go to the cradle only in order to find the baby, so we go to the Scriptures only to find Christ. *Martin Luther*

Believing and reading Scripture means that we hear the word from Christ's mouth. *Martin Luther*

Every word in the Bible points to Christ.
Martin Luther

Here you will find the swaddling clothes and manger in which Christ lies.
Martin Luther

If you want to interpret well and confidently, set Christ before you, for he is the man to whom it all applies, every bit of it.
Martin Luther

I see nothing in Scripture except Christ and him crucified. *Martin Luther*

Take Christ out of the Scriptures and what will you find remaining in them?
Martin Luther

There is not a word in the Bible which is *extra crucem*, which can be understood without reference to the cross.
Martin Luther

The Jesus of the New Testament has at least one advantage over the Jesus of modern reconstruction — he is real.
J. Gresham Machen

When you are reading a book in a dark room, and find it difficult, you take it to a window to get more light. So take your Bible to Christ.
Robert Murray M'Cheyne

Jesus saw himself as the key to Scripture and it as the key to himself. *J. I. Packer*

The deity of Christ is the key doctrine of the Scriptures. Reject it, and the Bible becomes a jumble of words without any unifying theme. Accept it, and the Bible becomes an intelligible and ordered revelation of God in the person of Jesus Christ. *J. Oswald Sanders*

Christ is the scope of the Scripture.
Richard Sibbes

Christ is figured in the law, foretold in the prophets and fulfilled in the gospel.
Henry Smith

Scripture is the royal chariot in which Jesus rides. *C. H. Spurgeon*

The Scriptures are in print what Christ is in person. The inspired Word is like a faithful portrait of Christ. *A. W. Tozer*

You can be perfectly free to go to your Bible with assurance that you will find Jesus Christ everywhere in its pages.
A. W. Tozer

BIBLE — Divine Authority and Authorship
(See also: Revelation)

As in paradise, God walks in the Holy Scriptures, seeking man. *Ambrose*

In God's work we see his hand, but in his Word we see his face. *Anon.*

When you drink from the stream, remember the spring. *Anon.*

The Bible is a volume of letters from the heavenly country. *Augustine*

The shortest road to an understanding of the Bible is the acceptance of the fact that God is speaking in every line.
Donald Grey Barnhouse

The fact that for fifteen centuries no attempt was made to formulate a definition of the doctrine of inspiration of the Bible testifies to the universal belief of the church that the Scriptures were the handiwork of the Holy Ghost.
George Duncan Barry

A man can only deny the divine integrity of Scripture by trampling Scripture itself under his feet. *John Blanchard*

The Bible does not say that its words were inspired by God but that they were expired by him.   *John Blanchard*

The Bible is none other than the voice of him that sitteth upon the throne. Every book of it, every chapter of it, every syllable of it, every letter of it, is the direct utterance of the Most High.
John William Burgon

God cannot endure the contempt of his Word.   *John Calvin*

God is not to be separated from his Word.
John Calvin

Observe . . . that the same reverence that we have for God is due also to the Scripture, because it has proceeded from him alone, and has nothing of man mixed with it.
John Calvin

The first thing that is essential when anyone begins to read the Bible is to know what it claims for itself. *Brian H. Edwards*

Throughout its pages the Bible never expresses one sentence or word of doubt about either its divine origin or its absolute trustworthiness; on the contrary, it constantly asserts both. *Brian H. Edwards*

There is abundant evidence that the Bible, though written by man, is not the product of the human mind.
Ambrose Fleming

If God's speech has an obvious location, that location must be the Holy Scriptures. There simply is no other candidate.
John M. Frame

Scripture does not merely claim to be the Word of God. It also presents us with reasons for believing its claims. It

presents its claims in a credible way.
John M. Frame

The entire Bible carries the certification of the Son of God, which brings with it infallible authority. Thus the written Word of God has the seal of the living Word of God.   *John H. Gerstner*

God can be described as a heavenly Father, a caring parent who brings human persons into existence and continues to watch over them. Part of that caring is shown in God's desire to communicate with us.   *Walter R. Hearn*

The Bible is a letter God has sent to us; prayer is a letter we send to him.
Matthew Henry

The very words of Scripture are to be accounted the words of the Holy Ghost.
Matthew Henry

God has favoured us with his autobiography so that we might know and think his thoughts in every department of our lives.   *Robert M. Horn*

Inspiration is the name of that all-comprehensive operation of the Holy Spirit whereby he has bestowed on the church a complete and infallible Scripture.
Abraham Kuyper

A belief in strictly verbal inspiration will indeed make all Scripture a book by a single Author.   *C. S. Lewis*

We have a speaking God ... the clear speech of a God who reveals himself in words which we can grasp, that are meaningful.   *Peter Lewis*

All the words of God are weighed, counted and measured.   *Martin Luther*

Divinity is nothing but a grammar of the language of the Holy Ghost.
Martin Luther

The Holy Scriptures did not grow on earth.
Martin Luther

You are so to deal with the Scriptures that you bear in mind that God himself is saying this.
Martin Luther

The Bible is God's book, not man's book.
J. Gresham Machen

The sacred Scriptures come from the fullness of the Spirit; so that there is nothing in the Prophets, or the Law, or the Gospel, or the Epistles, which descends not from divine majesty.
Origen

The biblical vented not writers in their words themselves, suited to the things that they learned, but only expressed the words they received.
John Owen

Scripture is not only human witness to God, it is also divine self-testimony.
J. I. Packer

The Bible appears like a symphony orchestra, with the Holy Ghost as its Toscanini; each instrument has been brought willingly, spontaneously, creatively, to play his notes just as the great conductor desired, though none of them could ever hear the music as a whole.
J. I. Packer

The divine Author of Scripture is not dead.
J. I. Packer

One proof of the inspiration of the Bible is that it has withstood so much poor preaching.
A.T. Robertson

The view which I maintain is that every book, and chapter, and verse and syllable of the Bible was given by inspiration of God.
J. C. Ryle

Because we believe the Scriptures to be God's Word and we believe God does not lie, we begin by accepting all its statements, including those which are historical, as true, rather than suspending judgement about them until they are proved to be true.
David Samuel

The Scriptures do not breathe out God. God breathes out Scripture.
Robert Sheehan

If the Bible is trustworthy then we must take seriously the claim that it is more than trustworthy.
R. C. Sproul

Inerrancy affirms that the Bible is nothing less than revelation, revelation that comes to us from a transcendent personal God.
R. C. Sproul

The Bible speaks to you in the very tones of God's voice.
C. H. Spurgeon

There is a living God. He has spoken in the Bible. He means what he says and will do all he has promised.
J. Hudson Taylor

The Scriptures sprang out of God.
William Tyndale

The Scriptures owe their origin to an activity of God the Holy Ghost and in the highest and truest sense are his creation.
Benjamin B. Warfield

What the Bible says, God says.
Benjamin B. Warfield

Scripture is the library of the Holy Ghost.
Thomas Watson

Think in every line you read that God is speaking to you.   *Thomas Watson*

The heavens declare thy glory, Lord,
In every star thy wisdom shines;
But when our eyes behold thy Word,
We read thy name in fairer lines.
                              Isaac Watts

God means what he says and says what he means.   *John Wilmot*

BIBLE — Fulness

The completeness of the Bible is as full as any other gift of God.   *Anon.*

Old truths are always new to us if they come with the smell of heaven upon them.   *John Bunyan*

I have worked over the Bible, prayed over the Bible for more than sixty years, and I tell you there is no book like the Bible. It is a miracle of literature, a perennial spring of wisdom, a wonderful book of surprises, a revelation of mystery, an infallible guide of conduct, an unspeakable source of comfort. *Samuel Chadwick*

The Bible presents us with a doctrine of the Bible.   *John M. Frame*

The difference between John's Gospel and the book of Chronicles is like the difference between man's brain and the hair of his head; nevertheless the life of the body is as truly in the hair as in the brain.   *A. A. Hodge*

The Bible is an inexhaustible fountain of all truths. The existence of the Bible is the greatest blessing which humanity ever experienced.   *Immanuel Kant*

The Bible … transcends all our categories and increasingly supplies our finite minds from its inexhaustible store of treasures.
                    D. Martyn Lloyd-Jones

There is no justification for any new interpretation of the faith.   *R. C. Lucas*

I have made a covenant with God that he sends me neither visions, dreams, nor even angels. I am well satisfied with the gift of the Holy Scriptures, which give me abundant instruction and all that I need to know both for this life and for that which is to come.   *Martin Luther*

In Scripture, every little daisy is a meadow.   *Martin Luther*

The Word is an ocean, without bottom or banks.   *Thomas Manton*

We can never exhaust all the treasure and worth that is in the Word. *Thomas Manton*

One gem from that ocean is worth all the pebbles from earthly streams.
                    Robert Murray M'Cheyne

In the divine Scriptures, there are shallows and there are deeps; shallows where the lamb may wade, and deeps where the elephant may swim.   *John Owen*

There is a fulness in all Scripture far beyond our conception.   *J. C. Ryle*

There is an inexhaustible fulness in Scripture.   *J. C. Ryle*

The great argument of Scripture is the glory of God's own name.
                              Charles Simeon

If when I get to heaven the Lord shall say to me, 'Spurgeon, I want you to preach for all eternity,' I would reply,

'Lord, give me a Bible, that is all I need.'
C. H. Spurgeon

Nobody ever outgrows Scripture; the book widens and deepens with our years.
C. H. Spurgeon

Father of mercies, in thy Word
What endless glory shines!
For ever be thy name adored
For these celestial lines.
Anne Steele

We do not expect any new worlds in our astronomy, nor do we expect any new Scriptures in our theology.
Augustus H. Strong

I adore the fulness of the Scriptures.
Tertullian

The Bible is a rock of diamonds, a chain of pearls, the sword of the Spirit; a chart by which the Christian sails to eternity; the map by which he daily walks; the sundial by which he sets his life; the balance in which he weighs his actions.
Thomas Watson

All the knowledge you want in one book, the Bible.
John Wesley

BIBLE — and the Holy Spirit

God does not bestow the Spirit on his people in order to set aside the use of his Word, but rather to render it fruitful.
John Calvin

The Word is the chariot of the Spirit, the Spirit the guider of the Word.
Stephen Charnock

Unless God imparts the spiritual ability to hear his voice, one hears nothing but meaningless words.
Ronald Dunn

Revelation is the act of communicating divine knowledge by the Spirit to the mind. Inspiration is the act of the same Spirit, controlling those who make the truth known.
Charles Hodge

If God does not open and explain Holy Writ, no one can understand it; it will remain a closed book, enveloped in darkness.
Martin Luther

Proper understanding of the Scriptures comes only through the Holy Spirit.
Martin Luther

The Holy Ghost must be the only master to teach us, and let youth and scholar not be ashamed to learn of this tutor.
Martin Luther

He who has the Holy Spirit in his heart and the Scriptures in his hands has all he needs.
Alexander MacLaren

God's mind is revealed in Scripture, but we can see nothing without the spectacles of the Holy Ghost.
Thomas Manton

If the Holy Spirit guides us at all, he will do it according to the Scriptures, and never contrary to them.
George Muller

(The Holy Spirit) has not promised to reveal new truths, but to enable us to understand what we read in the Bible; and if we venture beyond the pale of Scripture we are upon enchanted ground and exposed to all the illusions of imagination and enthusiasm.
John Newton

We are directed to expect the teaching and assistance of the Holy Spirit only within the limitations and by the medium of the written word.
John Newton

If you want to understand the Bible, get

on your knees … You will learn more in one hour of prayerful communion with the Spirit than in a thousand years in all the schools of human culture.
A. T. Pierson

The Holy Spirit is always in, with and by the Word. *Philipp Spener*

There is a real nutriment for the soul in Scripture brought home to the heart by the Holy Spirit. *C. H. Spurgeon*

The Bible is a supernatural book and can be understood only by supernatural aid.
A. W. Tozer

The Holy Spirit who inspired the Scriptures will expect obedience to the Scriptures, and if we do not give that obedience we will quench him. *A. W. Tozer*

BIBLE — Inerrancy and Infallibility

There can be no falsehood anywhere in the literal sense of Holy Scripture.
Thomas Aquinas

I believe most firmly that no one of those authors has erred in any respect in writing. *Augustine*

This I have learned to do: to hold only those books which are called the Holy Scriptures in such honour that I finally believe that not one of the holy writers ever erred. *Augustine*

Men do not reject the Bible because they find faults in it, but because it finds fault in them. *John Blanchard*

If the Bible contains errors, it is not God's Word itself, however reliable it may be.
James Montgomery Boice

Scripture bears upon the face of it as clear evidence of its truth as black and white do of their colour, sweet and bitter of their taste. *John Calvin*

We believe that the most scientific view, the most up-to-date and rationalistic conception, will find its fullest satisfaction in taking the Bible story literally.
Winston Churchill

It may be stated categorically that no archaeological discovery has ever controverted a biblical reference. Scores of archaeological finds have been made which confirm in clear outline or in exact detail historical statements in the Bible. *Nelson Glueck*

Well knowing that the Scriptures are perfect as dictated (or spoken) by the Word of God, and his Spirit, a heavy punishment awaits those who add to, or take from, the Scriptures. *Irenaeus*

God's Word is such perfect truth and righteousness that it needs no patching or repair; in its course it makes a perfectly straight line, without any bends in any direction. *Martin Luther*

I have learned to ascribe infallibility only to the books which are termed canonical, so that I confidently believe that not one of their authors erred. *Martin Luther*

It is impossible that Scripture should contradict itself, only that it so appears to the senseless and obstinate hypocrites.
Martin Luther

The Scriptures have never erred.
Martin Luther

The Word of God is perfect; it is precious and pure; it is truth itself. *Martin Luther*

The gospel is not speculation but fact. It is truth, because it is the record of a person who is the Truth. *Alexander Maclaren*

Our belief in the infallibility of Scripture arises not from an ability to prove that Scripture is perfect from start to finish. Rather it rests on Jesus' own witness to Scripture. He believed and taught that it was the Word of God and therefore inherently trustworthy. Our belief in Scripture is dependent on our belief in Jesus. *Peter C. Moore*

No sciences are better attested than the religion of the Bible. *Isaac Newton*

There are more sure marks of authenticity in the Bible than in any profane history. *Isaac Newton*

I will put down all apparent inconsistencies in the Bible to my own ignorance. *John Newton*

The veracity of God guarantees the trustworthiness of Scripture. *J. I. Packer*

Here is rock; all else is sand. *J. C. Ryle*

Nothing is written by chance in the Word of God. There is a special reason for the selection of every single expression. *J. C. Ryle*

We have the truth and we need not be afraid to say so. *J. C. Ryle*

The Bible is objective, absolute truth in all areas it touches upon. *Francis Schaeffer*

Unless the Bible is without error, not only when it speaks of salvation matters, but also when it speaks of history and the cosmos, we have no foundation for answering questions concerning the existence of the universe and its form and the uniqueness of man. *Francis Schaeffer*

If the Bible is trustworthy then we must take seriously the claim that it is more than trust-worthy. *R. C. Sproul*

God writes with a pen that never blots, speaks with a tongue that never slips, acts with a hand that never fails. *C H. Spurgeon*

I am prepared to believe whatever it says, and to take it believing it to be the Word of God. For if it is not all true, it is not worth one solitary penny to me. *C. H. Spurgeon*

If I did not believe in the infallibility of this book I would rather be without it. If I am to judge the book, it is no judge of me. *C. H. Spurgeon*

My brethren, when you hear that a learned man has made a new discovery which contradicts the Scriptures, do not feel alarmed. Do not imagine that he is really a great man, but believe that he is just an educated idiot or a self-conceited fool. *C H. Spurgeon*

Opinions alter, but truth certified by God can no more change than the God who uttered it. *C H. Spurgeon*

We must never edit God. *A. W. Tozer*

If there be any mistakes in the Bible, there may as well be a thousand. If there be one falsehood in that book, it did not come from the God of truth. *John Wesley*

We affirm that the Bible is the Word of God, and that it is not marred with human infirmities. *Christopher Wordsworth*

BIBLE — Influence and Power

The Word generates faith and regenerates us. *Joseph Alleine*

God brings about reformation when his people return to the Word of God as their sole source of doctrine and practice. *John H. Armstrong*

It is not the man who brings the Word that saves the soul, but the Word which the man brings. *Thomas Arthur*

Our faith is fed by what is plain in Scripture and tried by what is obscure. *Augustine*

The Word of the Lord is a light to guide you, a counsellor to counsel you, a comforter to comfort you, a staff to support you, a sword to defend you, and a physician to cure you. The Word is a mine to enrich you, a robe to clothe you, and a crown to crown you. *Thomas Brooks*

The Lord does not shine upon us, except when we take his Word as our light. *John Calvin*

Unless God's Word illumine the way, the whole life of men is wrapped in darkness and mist, so that they cannot but miserably stray. *John Calvin*

I know the Bible is inspired because it finds me at a greater depth of my being than any other book. *Samuel Taylor Coleridge*

Nothing has affected the rise and fall of civilization, the character of cultures, the structure of governments, and the lives of the inhabitants of this planet as profoundly as the words of the Bible. *Charles Colson*

What though no answering voice is heard?
Thine oracles, the written Word,
Counsel and guidance still impart,
Responsive to the upright heart. *Josiah Conder*

The foundation of every reformation of the Holy Spirit is the Word of God made plain to the people. *Frank Cooke*

The only true reformation is that which emanates from the Word of God. *J. H. Merle d'Aubigné*

Philosophy and religion may reform, but only the Bible can transform. *Brian H. Edwards*

The Scriptures teach us the best way of living, the noblest way of suffering and the most comfortable way of dying. *John Flavel*

We must not … view the Bible merely as a record of what God has done but actually as a part of the saving process. *Don Garlington*

Hold fast to the Bible as the sheet-anchor of our liberties; write its precepts on your hearts and practise them in your lives. To the influence of this book we are indebted for the progress made in true civilization, and to this we must look for our guide in the future. *Ulysees S. Grant*

The mightier any is in the Word, the more mighty he will be in prayer. *William Gurnall*

It is not the Word hidden in the head but in the heart that keeps us from sin. *Vance Havner*

The Bible is a disturbing book, a hammer, a fire and a sword. *Vance Havner*

The old book has been 'buried' many times, even as now men would bury God. However, the 'corpse' has a habit of coming to life in the midst of interment to outlive all the pallbearers. *Vance Havner*

There is no devil in the first two chapters of the Bible and no devil in the last two chapters. Thank God for a book that disposes of the devil! *Vance Havner*

God's Word is the instrument by which God's Spirit transforms the Christian.
Robert M. Horn

If half the strength spent in attacking or defending the Bible were spent in releasing it, how the level of ordinary life would be raised! *Will H. Houghton*

The divine law, as seen by the Christian, exhibits liberty, gives liberty, is liberty.
Robert Johnstone

The Bible redirects my will, cleanses my emotions, enlightens my mind, and quickens my total being. *E. Stanley Jones*

A single line in the Bible has consoled me more than all the books I have ever read. *Immanuel Kant*

The first thing the Bible does is to make man take a serious view of life.
D. Martin Lloyd-Jones

I have done nothing: the Word has done and accomplished everything.
Martin Luther

The Bible is alive, it speaks to me; it has feet, it runs after me; it has hands, it lays hold on me. *Martin Luther*

The Bible is not antique, or modern. It is eternal. *Martin Luther*

The true Christian church is the work of the Word communicated by every available means. *Martin Luther*

The world is conquered by the Word, and by the Word the church is served and rebuilt. *Martin Luther*

The Christians who have turned the world upside down have been men and women with a vision in their hearts and the Bible in their hands. *T. B. Maston*

God's chosen instrument in conversion is his Word, not our reasoning ability.
Will Metzger

All of God's work is done by God's Word.
Stuart Olyott

While other books inform, and some few reform, this one book transforms.
A. T. Pierson

Scripture is not only pure but purifying.
William S. Plumer

There is no other upon which we can rest in a dying moment, but the Bible.
John Selden

The man of one book is always formidable; but when that book is the Bible he is irresistible. *William M. Taylor*

Scripture is the spiritual glass to dress our souls by. *Thomas Watson*

The Word is both a glass to show us the spots of our soul and a laver to wash them away. *Thomas Watson*

The sum of all the counsel I can give you, necessary for the regulating of your behaviour towards God and man, in every station, place and condition of your lives,

is contained in that blessed Word of God.
Isaac Watts, Snr.

When you have read the Bible, you will know it is the Word of God, because you will have found it the key to your own heart, your own happiness and your own duty. *Woodrow Wilson*

BIBLE — Preservation

There are two dominant themes in the Bible: the one is the story of man's seduction by sin; the other, man's salvation by Christ. *S. Barton Babbage*

The Bible, as a revelation from God, was not designed to give us all the information we might desire, nor to solve all the questions about which the human soul is perplexed, but to impart enough to be a safe guide to the haven of eternal rest.
Albert Barnes

The same God who amazingly provided the Bible has amazingly preserved it.
John Blanchard

The Christian can take the whole Bible in his hand and say without fear or hesitation that he holds in it the true Word of God, handed down without essential loss from generation to generation.
Frederick Kenyon

It is a miracle how God has so long preserved his book! How great and glorious it is to have the Word of God!
Martin Luther

The Jews would die 10,000 times rather than to permit one single word to be altered of their Scriptures. *Philo*

A thousand times over the death-knell of the Bible has been sounded, the funeral procession formed, the inscription cut on the tombstone, and committal read. But somehow the corpse never stays put.
Bernard Ramm

The Christian feels that the tooth of time gnaws all books but the Bible … Nineteen centuries of experience have tested it. It has passed through critical fires no other volume has suffered, and its spiritual truth has endured the flames and come out without so much as a *smell* of burning. *W. E. Sangster*

When the dust of battle dies down we shall hear all sixty-six books declare with the apostle Paul, 'Do thyself no harm, for we are all here.' *W. H. Griffith Thomas*

In his mysterious providence, God has preserved his Word. We do not have a Bible which is unreliable and glutted with error, but one that in most wondrous fashion presents the Word of God and the text of the original. *Edward J. Young*

BIBLE — Purpose

Salvation, the salvation of man, is the final purpose of the whole Bible.
J. H. Bernard

Only one means and one way of cure has been given us and that is the teaching of the Word. Without it nothing else will avail. *Chrysostom*

The Bible is a window in this prison world through which we may look into eternity. *Timothy Dwight*

How precious is the Book divine,
By inspiration given!
Bright as a lamp its doctrines shine,
To guide our souls to heaven.
John Fawcett

The intention of the Holy Ghost is to teach us how one goes to heaven, not how heaven goes.   *Galileo Galilei*

As seed is made for soil and soil for seed, so the heart is made for God's truth and God's truth for the heart. *Richard Glover*

The storehouse of God's Word was never meant for mere scrutiny, even primarily for study but for sustenance.
                    Vance Havner

The Bible calls itself food. The value of food is not in the discussion it arouses but in the nourishment it imparts.
                    Will H. Houghton

The entire content of Scripture may be summarized under these heads: man's creation, man's fall and man's salvation.
                    R. B. Kuiper

At the heart of everything that the Bible says are two great truths, which belong inseparably together the majesty of the law of God, and sin as an offence against that law.   *J. Gresham Machen*

The Scriptures were not given to increase our knowledge but to change our lives.
                    D. L. Moody

Apart from the first two chapters of Genesis, which set the stage, the real subject of every character of the Bible is what God does about our sins. *J. I. Packer*

The Bible is not an entertainment. It was never designed to amuse.   *J. I. Packer*

The Bible is not primarily about man at all. Its subject is God… Its main theme is not human salvation, but the work of God vindicating his purposes and glorifying himself in a sinful and disordered cosmos.   *J. I. Packer*

Everything in Scripture has in view the promotion of holiness.   *A. W. Pink*

God's design in all that he has revealed to us is to the purifying of our affections and the transforming of our characters.
                    A. W. Pink

If you wish to know God you must know his Word.   *C. H. Spurgeon*

When we go to the doctor and are given a prescription, his purpose is that we should eat the medicine, not the prescription!   *John R. W. Stott*

The Scripture is both the breeder and feeder of grace.   *Thomas Watson*

I want to know one thing, the way to heaven ... God himself has condescended to teach the way . . . He hath written it down in a book. Oh, give me that book! At any price give me the book of God!
                    John Wesley

BIBLE — Relevance

The Bible is meant to be bread for our daily use, not just cake for special occasions.   *Anon.*

No other literature can match its standards of truth, love, honesty or humility, its opposition to injustices, racism, oppression and greed, or its concern for the sick, the weak, the homeless, the poor and the dying.   *John Blanchard*

There is nothing on which the Bible has nothing to say.   *John Blanchard*

Where Scripture leads we may safely follow.   *Loraine Boettner*

Do not try to make the Bible relevant; its relevance is axiomatic.
Dietrich Bonhoeffer

All Scripture is profitable for us, even passages that seem so difficult to understand.
Jerry Bridges

The entire Bible is a book on godliness.
Jerry Bridges

The doctrines of the Bible are all practical and its laws all reasonable. Every doctrine has its practical *therefore* and every law its doctrinal *because.* *John Brown*

Our inklings of the realities of God will be vague and smudged until we learn from Scripture to think correctly about the realities of which we are already aware.
John Calvin

There can be no courage in men unless God supports them by his Word.
John Calvin

There is no faith without God's Word.
John Calvin

Unless God's Word illumine the way, the whole life of men is wrapped in darkness and mist, so that they cannot but miserably stray.
John Calvin

All in the Bible that is vital is clear, and all that is not clear is not vital.
Guthrie Clark

The Bible never grows old.
Edith Deen

It is not commentaries, councils or creeds that should mould our Christian beliefs, however valuable some of them may be, but the Word of God.
Brian Edwards

All that needs to be spoken or written about prayer is in the Bible. *E. F. Hallock*

Any spiritual experience that is not Bible-based is not of God but of the devil. It may be spiritual, but it is the wrong spirit.
Vance Havner

The Holy Scripture, as it is a rule both of our duty to God and of our expectation from him, is of much greater use and benefit to us than day or night, than the air we breathe in, or the light of the sun.
Matthew Henry

The Bible clearly presents a unified view of reality, consistent and coherent, that accurately describes the human situation.
W. Andrew Hoffecker

He who hath heard the Word of God can bear his silences. *Ignatius of Loyola*

According to Christianity, the acid test of truth and goodness is scripturalness.
R. B. Kuiper

He who rejects the Bible has nothing to live by. Neither does he have anything to die by.
R. B. Kuiper

All things desirable to men are contained in the Bible.
Abraham Lincoln

God has provided very wonderfully for the plain man who is not a scholar.
J. Gresham Machen

The Bible is not a ladder but a foundation.
J. Gresham Machen

He who has the Holy Spirit in his heart and the Scriptures in his hands has all he needs.
Alexander MacLaren

The biblical worldview is relevant because it gives a coherent, consistent view of the world into which we can put 'truths' learned from all the disciplines: science, psychology, art, literature, economics.
Peter C. Moore

There's far more truth in the book of Genesis than in the quantum theory.
Malcolm Muggeridge

There is no situation in which we are placed, no demand that arises, for which Scripture as the deposit of the manifold wisdom of God is not adequate and sufficient. *John Murray*

Holy Writ is to be kept not under a bushel, but under men's noses. Its message is to be held forth as diligently as it is held fast. *J. I. Packer*

Scripture is the most up-to-date and relevant reading that ever comes my way.
J. I. Packer

The fundamental mode whereby our rational Creator guides his rational creatures is by rational understanding and application of his written Word.
J. I. Packer

Scripture is relevant to a disenchanted era, for it holds the only hope of its deliverance. *Clark H. Pinnock*

God's Word interprets nature, providence and grace. *William S. Plumer*

If we want to know where our pathway is to lead and where our feet are to walk, the best place to look is into that Book which God has called the Light and the Lamp. *Robert G. Rayburn*

The Lord has more truth yet to break forth out of his holy Word. *John Robinson*

I know no rule by which to judge of a man's estate but the Bible. *J. C. Ryle*

Take away the cross of Christ from the Bible and it is a dark book. *J. C. Ryle*

Compromising the full authority of Scripture eventually affects what it means to be a Christian theologically and how we live in the full spectrum of human life.
Francis Schaeffer

The Bible gives not just moral limits but absolutes and truth in regard to the whole spectrum of life. *Francis Schaeffer*

I hold one single sentence out of God's Word to be of more certainty and of more power than all the discoveries of all the learned men of all the ages.
C. H. Spurgeon

It is impossible to rightly govern the world without God and the Bible.
George Washington

We need every word that God speaks.
David Watson

Scratch the surface of Scripture wherever you wish and you will uncover a slice of life. *Arthur Skevington Wood*

There is no ancient history in the Bible.
Dinsdale T. Young

BIBLE — Submission to

On the Day of Judgement you will not be asked, 'What did you read?' but 'What did you do?' *Thomas à Kempis*

We are not to make our experience the rule of Scripture, but Scripture the rule of our experience.   *Anon.*

The primary qualification demanded in the reader of the Bible is not scholarship but surrender, not expert knowledge but willingness to be led by the Spirit of God.
Martin Anstey

If you believe what you like in the Bible, and reject what you like, it is not the Bible you believe but yourself.*Augustine*

To the canonical Scriptures alone I owe agreement without dissent.   *Augustine*

We must surrender ourselves to the authority of Holy Scripture, for it can neither mislead nor be misled. *Augustine*

Let us beware of being wiser than God. What he has written he has written not for our opinion but for our obedience.
John Blanchard

The man who is not prepared to heed the Word of God obediently will not even be able to hear it correctly. This is why the parables become windows to some people and walls to others. *John Blanchard*

There are parts of the Bible which cause me difficulty, but none which cause me doubt.   *John Blanchard*

We are to submit without reservation to every word of Scripture without exception.   *John Blanchard*

We have no more right to tamper with Scripture than a postman has to edit our mail.   *John Blanchard*

As we search the Scriptures, we must allow them to search us, to sit in judge-

ment upon our character and conduct.
Jerry Bridges

All who forsake the Word fall into idolatry.   *John Calvin*

I do not venture to make any assertion where Scripture is silent.   *John Calvin*

Let us so adhere to the Word of God that no novelty may captivate us and lead us astray.   *John Calvin*

Men are fools till they submit to the Word of God.   *John Calvin*

Our wisdom ought to consist in embracing with gentle docility, and without any exception, all that is delivered in the sacred Scriptures.   *John Calvin*

We should yield this honour to the Word, to believe what is otherwise incredible.
John Calvin

We have hungered to be masters of the Word much more than we have hungered to be mastered by it.   *Don Carson*

Beware of reasoning about God's Word — obey it!   *Oswald Chambers*

The sum and substance of the preparation needed for a coming eternity is that you believe what the Bible tells you and do what the Bible bids you.
Thomas Chalmers

There was never anything of false doctrine brought into the church, or anything of false worship imposed upon the church, but either it was by neglecting the Scripture, or by introducing something above the Scripture. *John Collins*

Of all commentaries upon the Scriptures,

good examples are the best and the liveliest. *John Donne*

Knowledge of the Scriptures does not help if it is not accompanied by a believing submission to the word of the cross, the wisdom of God. *F. W. Grosheide*

If you stand on the Word you do not stand in with the world. *Vance Havner*

The more reverence we have for the Word of God the more joy we shall find in it.
Matthew Henry

Those who would have the blessings of God's testimonies must come under the bonds of his statutes. *Matthew Henry*

Men do not reject the Bible because it contradicts itself, but because it contradicts them. *E. Paul Hovey*

I rest with the conviction that every word of Christ is true; and what I do not understand I commit to his grace in the hope that I shall understand it after my death.
John Hus

Before the Word everyone must give way.
Martin Luther

My conscience is captive to the Word of God. *Martin Luther*

Some people are critical of everything; some embrace anything. The wise weigh all things by the Word. *Henry T. Mahan*

Few *tremble* at the Word of God. Few, in reading it, hear the voice of Jehovah, which is full of majesty.
Robert Murray M'Cheyne

We are to live under the dominion of the Word of God. *J. A. Motyer*

The law of God is the royal law of liberty and liberty consists in being captive to the word and law of God. All other liberty is not liberty but the thraldom of servitude to sin. *John Murray*

I'm tired of hearing people say, 'I'm standing on the Word of God.' We should be standing under it. *Stephen Olford*

It is for the Bible to form and reform the church ... it is for the church to keep and keep to the Bible. *J. I. Packer*

To defer to God's Word is an act of faith; any querying and editing of it on our own initiative is an exhibition of unbelief.
J. I. Packer

When we reach the outer limits of what Scripture says it is time to stop arguing and start worshipping. *J. I. Packer*

I believe that even now, when we cannot explain alleged difficulties in Holy Scripture, the wisest course is to blame the interpreter and not the text, to suspect our own ignorance to be in fault, and not any defect in God's Word. *J. C. Ryle*

The Bible would not be the book of God if it had not deep places here and there which man has no line to fathom.
J. C. Ryle

What makes the difference is not how many times you have been through the Bible, but how many times and how thoroughly the Bible has been through you.
Rodney ('Gipsy') Smith

Be walking Bibles. *C. H. Spurgeon*

Never be afraid of your Bibles. If there is a text of Scripture you dare not meet, humble yourself till you can.
C. H. Spurgeon

The place for God's Word is not an outside place, but an inside place.
C. H. Spurgeon

Where the Scripture hath no tongue we must have no ears. *John Trapp*

Doers of the Word are the best hearers.
Thomas Watson

Till we are above sin, we are not above Scripture. *Thomas Watson*

I am a Bible bigot. I follow it in all things, both great and small. *John Wesley*

The Bible is a book which from beginning to end insists that God is not there primarily to be explored but to be listened to. *David Wilkinson*

BIBLE — Supremacy

The Bible among books is what Christ is among men. *Anon.*

No man is uneducated who knows the Bible, and no one is wise who is ignorant of its teachings. *Samuel Chadwick*

A glory gilds the sacred page,
Majestic like the sun;
It gives a light to every age,
It gives, but borrows none.
William Cowper

The New Testament is the best book the world has ever known or will know.
Charles Dickens

The Bible never claims to be one holy book among many, but the holy book above all. *William H. Edwards*

As God is the only holy person, so Scripture is the only holy book. *William Gurnall*

In regard to this great book I have but to say it is the best gift God has given to men. All that the good Saviour gave to the world was communicated through this book. *Abraham Lincoln*

I put the Scriptures above all the sayings of the fathers, angels, men and devils. Here I take my stand. *Martin Luther*

I account the Scriptures of God the most sublime philosophy. *Isaac Newton*

The Bible … the most majestic thing in our literature and … the most spiritually living thing we inherit.
Arthur Quiller-Couch

The Bible is not only the book of God but also the god of books. *John Ruskin*

Many books in my library are now behind and beneath me. They were good in their way once, and so were the clothes I wore when I was ten years old; but I have outgrown them. Nobody ever outgrows Scripture; the book widens and deepens with our years. *C. H. Spurgeon*

Had I the tongue of angels, I could not sufficiently set forth the excellency of Scripture. *Thomas Watson*

BIBLE — Unity

All Scripture is the context in which any Scripture is to be considered and applied.
Anon.

Any part of the human body can only be properly explained in reference to the whole body. And any part of the Bible can only be properly explained in reference to the whole Bible. *F. F. Bruce*

The Bible is not simply an anthology;

there is a unity which binds the whole together. An anthology is compiled by an anthologist, but no anthologist compiled the Bible.   *F. F. Bruce*

The new covenant does not destroy the old in substance, but only in form.
John Calvin

The Bible has a story-line. It traces an unfolding drama.   *Edmund P. Clowney*

The Bible is a unity, and this unity is such that the New Testament functions as an infallible interpreter of the Old.
Richard B. Gaffin

Thy Word is like a glorious choir,
And loud its anthems ring;
Though many parts and tongues unite,
It is one song they sing.
Edwin Hodder

The doctrines of the Bible are not isolated but interlaced; and the view of one doctrine must necessarily affect the view taken of another.   *A. A. Hodge*

Scriptural paradoxes are seeming, not actual, contradictions. Scripture is its own infallible interpreter and every part of it must be interpreted in the light of the whole of it.   *R. B. Kuiper*

The Bible is a self-consistent unit. What it teaches in one place it does not contradict elsewhere.   *R. B. Kuiper*

I take it as a first principle that we must not interpret any one part of Scripture so that it contradicts other parts. *C. S. Lewis*

It is impossible that Scripture should contradict itself; it only appears so to senseless and obstinate hypocrites.
Martin Luther

Truly, the inner unity of the Bible is miraculous; a sign and wonder, challenging the unbelief of our sceptical age.
J. I. Packer

The Scriptures explain themselves.
A. W Pink

God's truth always agrees with itself.
Richard Sibbes

The same Testator made both Testaments.
Thomas Taylor

The Old Testament is the Bible from the waist down and the New Testament is the Bible from the waist up.   *A. W. Tozer.*

BIBLE STUDY

The study of God's Word for the purpose of discovering God's will is the secret discipline which has formed the greatest characters.   *James W. Alexander*

It is possible to be full of Scripture and full of carnality.   *Anon.*

Scripture knowledge is the candle without which faith cannot see to do its work.
Anon.

Study the Bible to be wise; believe it to be safe; practise it to be holy.   *Anon.*

The devil is not afraid of the Bible that has got dust on it.   *Anon.*

The study of God's Word for the purpose of discovering God's will is the greatest discipline which has formed the greatest character.   *Anon.*

There is no substitute for reading the Bible; it throws a great deal of light on the commentaries!   *Anon.*

When the Bible is put on the shelf the church will surely follow it.   *Anon.*

Let no man think or maintain that a man can search too far or be too well studied in the book of God's word or in the book of God's works.   *Francis Bacon*

To reject study on pretence of the sufficiency of the Spirit is to reject the Scripture itself.   *Richard Baxter*

Apply yourself to the whole text, and apply the whole text to yourself.
        J. A. Bengel

Hit-and-run Bible reading can often become hit and miss.   *John Blanchard*

The man who reads on the surface will live on the surface — and a superficial Christian is a pathetic parody of the truth.
        John Blanchard

There is more to Christian growth than knowing what the Bible says; nobody is ever nourished by memorizing menus.
        John Blanchard

We must study the Bible more. We must not only lay it up within us, but transfuse it through the whole texture of the soul.
        Horatius Bonar

As we search the Scriptures, we must allow them to search us, to sit in judgement upon our character and conduct.
        Jerry Bridges

It is impossible to practise godliness without a constant, consistent and balanced intake of the Word of God in our lives.
        Jerry Bridges

Memorization is the first step to meditation.   *Jerry Bridges*

Reading gives us breadth, but study gives us depth.   *Jerry Bridges*

A man can't always be defending the truth; there must be a time to feed on it.
        John Brown

I have sometimes seen more in a line of the Bible than I could well tell how to stand under, and yet at another time the whole Bible hath been to me as dry as a stick.   *John Bunyan*

I was never out of my Bible. *John Bunyan*

Sin will keep you from this book, or this book will keep you from sin.
        John Bunyan

Continual meditation on the Word is not ineffectual … God, by one and another promise, establishes our faith.
        John Calvin.

Those only are worthy students of the law who come to it with a cheerful mind, and are so delighted with its instruction as to account nothing more desirable or delicious than to make progress therein.
        John Calvin

The source of all our troubles is in not knowing the Scriptures.   *Chrysostom*

Explain the Scriptures by the Scriptures.
        Clement of Alexandria

The longer I'm a Christian, the more I'm in fear of misinterpreting the Bible. It's an awesome responsibility.
        Charles Colson

Never leave a passage of Scripture until it has said something to you. *Robert Cook*

Bible reading is not an exceptional thing

for the literate Christian. It is part of his response to God. *Oscar Feucht*

The difference between reading and study is like the difference between drifting in a boat and rowing toward a destination. *Oscar Feucht*

Compare Scripture with Scripture. False doctrines, like false witnesses, agree not among themselves. *William Gurnall*

The Christian is bred by the Word and he must be fed by it. *William Gurnall*

A well-understood Bible is the only basis of a sound theology, an enlightened piety, practical godliness, solid comfort and extensive usefulness. *E. F. Hallock*

If I had to choose between reading the Bible and prayer, I would choose to read the Bible. It is more important for me to hear what God is saying than for God to hear what I am saying. *E. F. Hallock*

No one ever graduates from Bible study until he meets its Author face to face. *Everett Harris*

The Bible that is falling apart usually belongs to someone who isn't. *Vance Havner*

They who would grow in grace must be inquisitive. *Matthew Henry*

If the Bible is to get into us we must get into the Bible. *Robert M. Horn*

Lay hold on the Bible until the Bible lays hold on you. *Will H. Houghton*

The jewel of the Word should not hang in our ears, but be locked up in a believing heart. *William Jenkyn*

Every time we consider or study the Bible we are, of necessity, worshipping. *D. Martyn Lloyd-Jones*

It is a good thing to be a student of the Word, but only in order to be a practiser and experiencer of the Word. *D. Martyn Lloyd-Jones*

Let us never forget that the message of the Bible is addressed primarily to the mind, to the understanding. *D. Martyn Lloyd-Jones*

Faith is not an achievement, it is a gift. Yet it comes only through the hearing and study of the Word. *Martin Luther*

I study my Bible as I gather apples. First, I shake the whole tree that the ripest may fall. Then I shake each limb, and when I have shaken each limb I shake each branch and every twig. Then I look under every leaf. *Martin Luther*

Nothing but faith can comprehend the truth. *Martin Luther*

Our first concern will be for the grammatical meaning, for this is the truly theological meaning. *Martin Luther*

Pause at every verse of Scripture and shake, as it were, every bough of it, that if possible some fruit at least may drop down. *Martin Luther*

The Bible was written for a man with a head upon his shoulders. *Martin Luther*

To read without faith is to walk in darkness. *Martin Luther*

I am tempted to say that one of the most obvious effects of the new birth should be the restoration of plain common sense in the understanding of the perfectly plain utterances of Holy Scripture.

J. Gresham Machen

I hold that the Bible is essentially a plain book. Common sense is a wonderful help in reading it.   *J. Gresham Machen*

We should always be chewing and sucking out the sweetness of this cud.

Thomas Manton

What we take in by the Word we digest by meditation and let out by prayer.

Thomas Manton

Devout meditation on the Word is more important to soul-health even than prayer. It is more needful for you to hear God's words than that God should hear yours, though the one will always lead to the other.   *F. B. Meyer*

Our natural eyesight is so defective that to read the Bible aright we must put on the spectacles of faith.   *Graham Miller*

I never saw a useful Christian who was not a student of the Bible.   *D. L. Moody*

If all the neglected Bibles were dusted simultaneously, we would have a record dust storm and the sun would go into eclipse for a whole week.

David A. Nygren

Meditate on the Word in the Word.

John Owen

If I were the devil, one of my first aims would be to stop folk from digging into the Bible.   *J. I. Packer*

The reading of Scripture is intended to awaken our minds, not to send them to sleep.   *J. I. Packer*

The Spirit is not given to make Bible study needless, but to make it effective

J. I. Packer

The Scriptures make prayer a reality and not a reverie.   *Austin Phelps*

Partial examination will result in partial views of truth, which are necessarily imperfect; only careful comparison will show the complete mind of God.

A. T. Pierson

No verse of Scripture yields its meaning to lazy people.   *A. W. Pink*

Nowhere in Scripture is there any promise to the dilatory.   *A. W. Pink*

Those who know most of God's testimonies desire to know more.

William S. Plumer

Without the knowledge of Scripture a biblical defence is practically impossible

Richard L. Pratt

What is needed, in times when crisis assaults faith and difficulty spawns doubt, is a fresh examination of the New Testament, that utterly amazing book of realism and hope.   *Paul S. Rees*

The Christian who is careless in Bible reading is careless in Christian living.

Max Reich

The longer you read the Bible, the more you will like it; it will grow sweeter and sweeter; and the more you get into the spirit of it, the more you will get into the spirit of Christ.   *William Romaine*

A thorough knowledge of the Bible is worth more than a college education.

Theodore D. Roosevelt

Make it the first morning business of your life to understand some part of the Bible clearly, and make it your daily business to obey it in all that you do understand.
John Ruskin

The Bible is the one book to which any thoughtful man may go with any honest question of life or destiny and find the answer of God by honest searching.
John Ruskin

A humble and prayerful spirit will find a thousand things in the Bible which the proud, self-conceited student will utterly fail to discern.   *J. C. Ryle*

Ignorance of the Scriptures is the root of all error.   *J. C. Ryle*

Knowledge of the Bible never comes by intuition.   *J. C. Ryle*

We must read our Bibles like men digging for hidden treasure.   *J. C. Ryle*

Neglect the Word and you neglect the Lord.   *Leith Samuel*

If such a diligent study of Scripture should interfere with our reading of religious literature, we may rest satisfied that we shall not be the losers, to say the least of it.   *Adolph Saphir*

Salvation comes by faith, but knowledge of the Bible by works.   *Charles Simeon*

Blame none but yourself if all the Bible you get is that little bit from under the calendar hurriedly snatched as a sop to conscience.   *David Shepherd*

Read it to get the facts, study it to get the meaning, meditate on it to get the benefit.   *David Shepherd*

Inerrancy is never a licence for superficiality. It is not a ticket to skate lightly over the surface of the text. *R. C. Sproul*

The main reason why we should study the Bible is because it is our duty. God is our Sovereign, it is his Word, and he commands that we study it.   *R. C. Sproul*

The Word of God is deeper than a flannelgraph. It demands the closest possible scrutiny. It calls for the most excellent scholarship. It makes the finest point of technical analysis worth the effort. The yield of such effort is truth. *R. C. Sproul*

Backsliders begin with dusty Bibles and end with filthy garments. *C. H. Spurgeon*

Bible study is the metal that makes a Christian.   *C. H. Spurgeon*

I have always found that the meaning of a text can be better learned by prayer than in any other way.   *C. H. Spurgeon*

The deeper you dig into Scripture, the more you find that it is a great abyss of truth.   *C. H. Spurgeon*

The sight of the promises themselves is good for the eye of faith; the more we study the words of grace, the more grace shall we derive from the words.
C. H. Spurgeon

One of the highest and noblest functions of a man's mind is to listen to God's Word, and so to read his mind and think his thoughts after him.   *John R. W. Stott*

The Bible only comforts those who think.
Geoff Thomas

Ninety-nine Christians in every hundred are merely playing at Bible study; and therefore ninety-nine Christians in every hundred are merely weaklings when they might be giants. *R. A. Torrey*

An honest man with an open Bible and a pad and pencil is sure to find out what is wrong with him very quickly. *A. W. Tozer*

It is not mere words that nourish the soul, but God himself. *A. W. Tozer*

Nothing less than a whole Bible can make a whole Christian. *A. W. Tozer*

The Bible was written in tears and to tears it will yield its best treasure. God has nothing to say to the frivolous man. *A. W. Tozer*

Whatever keeps me from my Bible is my enemy, however harmless it may appear to me. *A. W. Tozer*

Leave not off reading the Bible till you find your hearts warmed. Let it not only inform you but inflame you. *Thomas Watson*

Nothing can cut the diamond but the diamond; nothing can interpret Scripture but Scripture. *Thomas Watson*

You can only understand Scripture on your knees. *Maurice Zundel*

BIGOTRY

No physician can cure the blind in mind. *Anon.*

A bigot is either narrow-minded in the best sense or small-minded in the worst. *John Blanchard*

Bigotry is like the pupil of the eye — the more light you pour into it, the more it contracts. *Oliver Wendell Holmes*

It is with narrow minded as with narrow-necked bottles; the less they have in them, the more noise they make in pouring out. *Alexander Pope*

BLASPHEMY

There is nothing worse than blasphemy. *Chrysostom*

God himself is out of the sinner's reach, and not capable of receiving any real injury; and therefore enmity to God spits at his name, and shows its ill-will. *Matthew Henry*

To pray to saints is idolatry advanced to blasphemy. *Thomas Watson*

BLESSINGS — See Spiritual Gifts

BOASTING
(See also: Conceit; Egotism; Pride; Vanity)

He who sings his own praise is usually off key. *Anon.*

People who sing their own praises usually do so without accompaniment. *Anon.*

Self-praise is no recommendation. *Anon.*

Men arrogate too much to themselves when they think that they excel in anything. *John Calvin*

Nobody's so apt to be a soloist as the fellow who blows his own horn. *Franklin P. Jones*

Anyone who thinks he can live the Christian life himself is just proclaiming that he is not a Christian. *D. Martyn Lloyd-Jones*

Do you wish people to think well of you? Don't speak well of yourself.
Blaise Pascal

Boasting is an evidence that we are pleased with self; belittling, that we are disappointed in it. Either way, we reveal that we have a high opinion of ourselves.
A. W. Tozer

There is not a more dangerous precipice than self-righteousness. *Thomas Watson*

BRAVERY — See Courage

BROKENNESS — See Humility; Repentance; Self-Crucifixion; Submission

---

CHANCE

The doctrine of chances is the bible of the fool.
Anon.

If anything in this world is the result of chance then God is not sovereign over all.
Wilson Benton

If life is an accident, it cannot conceivably have any purpose, for accident and purpose are mutually exclusive.
John Blanchard

If your Christianity is comfortable, it is compromised.
John Blanchard

There is no such thing as an easy Christianity. If it is easy, it is not Christianity; if it is Christianity, it is not easy.
John Blanchard

There is no such thing as chance or accident; the words merely signify our ignorance of some real and immediate cause.
Adam Clarke

No evolutionary biologist has ever produced any quantitive proof that the designs of nature are in fact within the reach of chance.   *Michael Denton*

I cannot believe that God plays dice with the world.
Albert Einstein

Why should I assume that chance has equipped me with eyes and a brain so that I can actually see what I am doing? Isn't it equally possible that when I think I'm a seminary professor typing at my desk in California, I am really a cockroach running around the New York City subway?
John M. Frame

For the materialist, chance is the magic wand to make not only rabbits but entire universes appear out of nothing.
R. C. Sproul

What are the chances that the universe was created by the power of chance? Not a chance.
R. C. Sproul

CHARACTER

What thou art in the sight of God, that thou truly art.
Thomas à Kempis

A man's character is accurately measured by his reaction to life's inequities. *Anon.*

A man shows his character by what he laughs at.
Anon.

Being a character and having a character are poles apart.
Anon.

Character is always lost when a high ideal is sacrificed on the altar of conformity and compromise.
Anon.

Character is best revealed by a person's dislikes.
Anon.

Character, like embroidery, is made stitch by stitch. *Anon.*

It's what you do when you have nothing to do that reveals what you are. *Anon.*

No amount of riches can atone for poverty of character. *Anon.*

Reputation is precious, but character is priceless. *Anon.*

Reputation is what men think you are; character is what God knows you are. *Anon.*

The mark of a man is how he treats a person who can be of no possible use to him. *Anon.*

The pinnacle of a man's greatness is the height of his own character. *Anon.*

The two great tests of character are wealth and poverty. *Anon.*

The true worth of a man is to be measured by the objects he pursues. *Marcus Antoninus*

Character is better than ancestry. *Thomas Barnado*

One of the surest marks of good character is a man's ability to accept personal criticism without malice to the one who gives it. *O. A. Battista*

Happiness is not the end of life; character is. *Henry Ward Beecher*

Reputation is sometimes as wide as the horizon when character is the point of a needle. *Henry Ward Beecher*

Character is more important than lifestyle. *John Blanchard*

Character is what we are when nobody sees us except God. *John Blanchard*

Circumstances never create character; they merely reveal it. *John Blanchard*

Everything in life is a test of character. *John Blanchard*

There is no such thing as salvation by character; what men need is salvation from character. *John Blanchard*

God-like character is both the fruit of the Spirit as he works within us and the result of our personal efforts. We are both totally dependent upon his working within us and totally responsible for our own character development. *Jerry Bridges*

Though the power for godly character comes from Christ, the responsibility for developing and displaying that character is ours. *Jerry Bridges*

If we would judge rightly of any man we must see how he bears good and bad fortune. *John Calvin*

Lighter is the loss of money than of character. *John Calvin*

The character wherewith we sink into the grave at death is the very character wherewith we shall reappear at the resurrection. *Thomas Chalmers*

The conduct of our lives is the true mirror of our doctrine. *Michel de Montaigne*

The fruit of the Spirit is not excitement or orthodoxy: it is character. *G. B. Duncan*

Character is that which can do without success. *Ralph Waldo Emerson*

Character

Character is not made in a crisis — it is only exhibited. *Robert Freeman*

A character, no more than a fence, can be strengthened by whitewash. *Paul Frost*

You cannot dream yourself into a character; you must hammer and forge yourself one. *James Froude*

Men and brethren, a simple trust in God is the most essential ingredient in moral sublimity of character. *Richard Fuller*

The finest test of character is seen in the amount and the power of gratitude we have. *Milo H. Gates*

A man is what he is, not what men say he is. His character no man can touch. His character is what he is before his God and his Judge; and only himself can damage that. *John B. Gough*

Character tends to congeal, to solidify as time goes on. *Vance Havner*

The Lord knows them that are his by name, but we must know them by their character. *Matthew Henry*

Character is destiny. *Heraclitus*

I have learned by experience that no man's character can be eventually injured but by his own acts. *Rowland Hill*

Many a man's reputation would not know his character if they met on the street. *Elbert Hubbard*

Material abundance without character is the surest way to destruction. *Thomas Jefferson*

Character and reputation are not synonymous. *George Johnstone Jeffrey*

The test of your character is what you would do if you knew no one would ever know. *Bob Jones*

A man's heart is what he is. *R. B. Kuiper*

Character is like a tree and reputation its shadow. The shadow is what we think of it; the tree is the real thing. *Abraham Lincoln*

Nearly all men can stand adversity, but if you want to test a man's character, give him power. *Abraham Lincoln*

Our behaviour in times of need and crisis proclaims what we really are. *D. Martyn Lloyd-Jones*

Reputation is what folks think you are. Personality is what you seem to be. Character is what you really are. *Alfred Montapert*

Character is what a man is in the dark. *D. L. Moody*

Character tells upon others. *G. Campbell Morgan*

No man can climb out beyond the limitations of his own character. *John Morley*

Strive to be like a well-regulated watch, of pure gold, with open face, busy hands, and full of good works. *David C. Newquist*

Orthodoxy of words is blasphemy unless it is backed up by superiority of character. *Blaise Pascal*

Thoughts, even more than overt acts, reveal character. *William S. Plumer*

There is no stronger test of a man's character than power and authority. *Plutarch*

God is more concerned about character than our comfort.   *Paul W. Powell*

Man makes holy what he believes as he makes beautiful what he loves.
Ernest Renan

All men are good company in fair weather; but the storms of life prove spiritual character.   *Maurice Roberts*

Character on earth will prove an everlasting possession in the world to come.
J. C. Ryle

Men best show their character in trifles, where they are not on their guard.
Arthur Schopenhauer

The grace of God will do very little for us if we resolve to do nothing for ourselves. God calls us to co-operate with him in the perfecting of character.
W. Graham Scroggie

Human character is worthless in proportion as abhorrence of sin is lacking in it.
W. G. T. Shedd

Daylight can be seen through very small holes, so little things will illustrate a person's character.   *Samuel Smiles*

Not on the stage alone, in the world also, a man's real character comes out best in his asides.   *Alexander Smith*

It is in little things not in great that weakness of character is to be found.
Charles Simeon

Characters that are really great are always simple.   *C. H. Spurgeon*

I am quite certain that the safest way to defend your character is never to say a word about it.   *C. H. Spurgeon*

The actions of men form an infallible index of their character. *Geoffrey Wilson*

Character is a plant that grows more sturdily for some cutting back. *Verna Wright*

CHARITY
(See also: Generosity; Giving; Kindness)

The river of charity springs from the fountain of piety.   *Thomas Adams*

Charity gives itself rich; covetousness hoards itself poor.   *Anon.*

He that has no charity deserves no mercy.
Anon.

The word 'alms' has no singular, as if to teach us that a solitary act of charity scarcely deserves the name.   *Anon.*

In necessary things, unity; in doubtful things, liberty; in all things, charity.
Richard Baxter

Piety is the root of charity. *John Calvin*

Charity to the soul is the soul of charity.
Elizabeth Fry

Charity is the very livery of Christ.
Hugh Latimer

We have made the slogan 'Charity begins at home' a part of our religion — although it was invented by a Roman pagan and is directly contrary to the story of the Good Samaritan. Charity begins where the need is greatest and the crisis is most dangerous.   *Frank C. Laubach*

Christian life consists in faith and charity.   *Martin Luther*

The greatest charity in the world is the communication of divine truth to the ignorant. *Alexander Maclaren*

The brightest blaze of intelligence is of incalculably less value than the smallest spark of charity. *William Nevins*

Proportion thy charity to the strength of thy estate, lest God proportion thy estate to the weakness of thy charity.
Francis Quarles

The place of charity, like that of God, is everywhere. *Francis Quarles*

There is nothing that the world understands and values more than true charity.
J. C. Ryle

Charity is money put to interest in another world. *Robert Southey*

Charity is the best way to plenty; he gets most that gives most. *George Swinnock*

Charity offers honey to a bee without wings. *John Trapp*

The lamp of faith must be filled with the oil of charity. *Thomas Watson*

CHASTENING
(See also: Trials)

When God takes away correction, damnation enters the doors. *Thomas Adams*

By chastening, the Lord separates the sin that he hates from the sinner whom he loves. *Anon.*

Not till the loom is silent,
And the shuffles cease to fly,
Shall God unfold the pattern
And explain the reason why

The dark threads were as needful
(In the Master's skilful hand)
As the threads of gold and silver
In the pattern which he planned.
Anon.

Heaven often smites in mercy, even when the blow is severest. *Joanna Baillie*

Any chastisement that ever reaches us comes for our profit, that we might be partakers of God's holiness.
Donald Grey Barnhouse

God punishes his enemies but chastises his children. *Alistair Begg*

Our sovereign God never lets so much as a shadow fall across our lives without intending it to be for his glory and our good. *John Blanchard*

God's corrections are our instructions, his lashes our lessons, his scourges our schoolmasters. *Thomas Brooks*

God would not rub so hard, were it not to fetch out the dirt and spots that be in his people. *Thomas Brooks*

Mercy and punishment, they flow from God, as the honey and the sting from the bee. *Thomas Brooks*

Where God loves, he afflicts in love, and wherever God afflicts in love there he will, first or last, teach such souls such lessons as shall do them good to all eternity. *Thomas Brooks*

Let us learn like Christians to kiss the rod, and love it. *John Bunyan*

Adversity does not fall out to us by chance, but is the method by which God arouses us to repentance. *John Calvin*

The Lord blesses us more by punishing us than he would have done by sparing us. *John Calvin*

The scourges by which God chastises his children are testimonies of his love. *John Calvin*

There is nothing more to be dreaded than that the Lord should allow us loose reins. *John Calvin*

God teaches us, by affliction, to prize and long for heaven. *Thomas Case*

God denies a Christian nothing but with a design to give him something better. *Richard Cecil*

All the judgements of God upon his own are for correction. *Lewis Sperry Chafer*

God gives gifts that we may love him, and stripes that we may fear him. Yea, oftentimes he mixes frowns with his favours. *George Downame*

The Lord does not measure out our afflictions according to our faults, but according to our strength, and looks not what we have deserved, but what we are able to bear. *George Downame*

God will go to any lengths to bring us to an acknowledgement of who he is. *Elisabeth Elliot*

Fear not the knife that God wields, for his hand is sure. *François Fenelon*

God never strikes except for motives of love, and never takes away but in order to give. *François Fenelon*

The very proof that God loves you is that he does not spare you, but lays upon you the cross of Jesus Christ. *François Fenelon*

There is comfort to be found even in God's condemnations. *François Fenelon*

God kills thy comforts from no other design but to kill thy corruptions; wants are ordained to kill wantonness; poverty is appointed to kill pride; reproaches are permitted to destroy ambition. *John Flavel*

God's wounds cure; sin's kisses kill. *William Gurnall*

God dries up the channels, that you may be compelled to plunge into an infinite ocean of happiness. *Robert Hall*

God's chastening originates in his love. *Vance Havner*

God delights not in the death of sinners, or the disquiet of the saints, but punishes with a kind of reluctance. *Matthew Henry*

God never afflicts us but when we give him cause to do it. He does not dispense his frowns as he does his favours, from his mere good pleasure. *Matthew Henry*

God warns before he wounds. *Matthew Henry*

Good men, even when God frowns upon them, think well of him. *Matthew Henry*

When we are chastened we must pray to be taught, and look into the law as the best expositor of providence. It is not the chastening itself that does good, but the teaching that goes along with it and is the exposition of it. *Matthew Henry*

He who hath heard the Word of God can bear his silences. *Ignatius*

Chastening

Such is the condition of grace, that it shines the brighter for scouring, and is most glorious when it is most clouded.

William Jenkyn

Chastening is simultaneous wrath and mercy. *R. T. Kendall*

Believer, think not of undisturbed repose until the flesh be dropped. There is a ceaseless cycle of sorrow and temptation here. But despise not the scourge. It has a teaching voice. It is held by a loving Father's hand. *Henry Law*

The bitterest cup with Christ is better than the sweetest cup without him.

Ian Macpherson

If nothing else will do to sever me from my sins, Lord, send me such sore and trying calamities as shall awake me from earthly slumbers.

Robert Murray M'Cheyne

The heavenly Father has no spoiled children. He loves them too much to allow that. *Fred Mitchell*

The rough hewing of reproof is only to square us for the heavenly build.

D. L. Moody

God often makes his people pass through the furnace, not that they may perish, but that they may be purified, and thus reach a better salvation. *Thomas V. Moore*

Our heavenly father never takes anything from his children unless he means to give them something better. *George Muller*

There is no chastisement in heaven, nor in hell. Not in heaven, because there is no sin; not in hell, because there is no amendment. Chastisement is a companion of them that are in the way, and of them only. *John Owen*

I thank thee more that all our joy is
    touched with pain;
That shadows fall on brightest hours, that
    thorns remain;
So that earth's bliss may be our guide,
    and not our chain.
For thou, who knowest, Lord, how soon
    our weak heart clings,
Hast given us joys, tender and true, yet
    all with wings;
So that we see, gleaming on high, diviner
    things.

Adelaide Anne Proctor

It is God's way commonly to deepen his people by placing them under periodic providential strains and pressures.

Maurice Roberts

Whatever is good for God's children, they shall have it, for all is theirs to further them to heaven. If crosses be good, they shall have them, if disgrace be good, they shall have it, for all is ours, to serve our main good. *Richard Sibbes*

The anvil, the fire and the hammer are the making of us; we do not get fashioned much by anything else. That heavy hammer falling on us helps to shape us; therefore, let affliction and trouble and trial come. *C. H. Spurgeon*

The sword of justice no longer threatens us, but the rod of parental correction is still in use. *C. H. Spurgeon*

The painful pruning knife is in safe hands.
John R. W. Stott

God will wean us from the earth some way — the easy way if possible, the hard way if necessary. *A. W. Tozer*

It is doubtful if God can bless a man greatly without hurting him deeply.
A. W. Tozer

It is in mercy and in measure that God chastiseth his children. *John Trapp*

We must lay our hands upon our mouths when God's hand is upon our backs.
John Trapp

God parts that and us which would part us and him. *Ralph Venning*

God punishes most when he does not punish. *Thomas Watson*

The vessels of mercy are first seasoned with affliction, and then the wine of glory is poured in. *Thomas Watson*

CHILDREN — See Family Life

CHRIST — See Jesus Christ

CHRISTIAN
(See also: Christianity)

A Christian is a man possessed. *Anon.*

A true Christian is both a beggar and an heir. *Anon.*

Christ's sheep are marked in the ear and the foot; they hear his voice and they follow him. *Anon.*

It doesn't take much of a man to be a Christian, but it takes all of him. *Anon.*

It is natural to be religious; it is supernatural to be Christian. *Anon.*

The best Christians we have among us are only Christians in the making. They are by no means finished products. *Anon.*

Every believer is God's miracle.
Philip Bailey

The Christian is called upon to live a supernatural life, and he has been given the power to live that life.
Donald Grey Barnhouse

We believers ... are the library of Christ's doings ... At present we are a poor edition, but the great Bookbinder has promised to bring out a new edition on indestructible paper and clear type with no errata, imprints of the Son of God, bound in his likeness for ever.
Donald Grey Barnhouse

A Christian is not a person who has made a new start in life, but a person who has received a new life to start with.
John Blanchard

A Christian no longer has a secular life.
John Blanchard

Holiness is to be the driving ambition of the Christian. *John Blanchard*

Jesus has always had more fans than followers. *John Blanchard*

Believers are not hired servants, supporting themselves by their own work, but children maintained at their Father's expense. *Horatius Bonar*

There is no higher compliment that can be paid to a Christian than to call him godly. *Jerry Bridges*

There is nothing that can stand the touchstone of God's justice. Christ is my all, and I am nothing. *John Bunyan*

No true Christian is his own man.
John Calvin

Christian

The goal of the new life is that God's children exhibit melody and harmony in their conduct. What melody? The song of God's justice. What harmony? The harmony between God's righteousness and our obedience. *John Calvin*

Holiness is the everyday business of every Christian. *Charles Colson*

If we really understand what being a Christian means — that this Christ, the living God, actually comes in to rule one's life — then everything change: values, goals, priorities, desires and habits.
Charles Colson

The Christian family is entered by calling and evidenced by character.
Herbert W. Cragg

Knowing God is your single greatest privilege as a Christian. *Sinclair Ferguson*

A Christian in this world is but gold in the ore; at death, the pure gold is smelted out and separated and the dross cast away and consumed. *John Flavel*

The Scripture gives four names to Christians — saints, for their holiness; believers, for their faith; brethren, for their love; disciples, for their knowledge.
Andrew Fuller

If you were arrested for being a Christian, would there be enough evidence to convict you? *David Otis Fuller*

The Christian should stand out like a sparkling diamond. *Billy Graham*

The Christian life is the only true adventure. *Wilfred Grenfell*

Christians are not just nice people. They are new creatures. If you are what you have always been you are not a Christian. *Vance Havner*

If you are a Christian, you are not a citizen of this world trying to get to heaven; you are a citizen of heaven making your way through this world. *Vance Havner*

I reckon him a Christian indeed that is neither ashamed of the gospel nor a shame to it. *Matthew Henry*

The saints are God's jewels, highly esteemed by and dear to him; they are a royal diadem in his hand. *Matthew Henry*

A Christian is one who seeks and enjoys the grace of the Lord Jesus, the love of God and the communion of the Holy Ghost. *Charles Hodge*

He is only a Christian who lives for Christ. *Charles Hodge*

Faith makes a Christian; life proves a Christian; trials confirm a Christian; and death crowns a Christian.
Johann G. C. Hopfner

Holiness is the distinguishing mark of the Christian. *Michael Howell*

A Christian's life is a state of holy desire.
Jerome

Christians are made, not born. *Jerome*

A Christ not in us is a Christ not ours.
William Law

The Christian is a part of Christ, a member of his body. *J. B. Lightfoot*

A Christian is something before he does anything; and we have to be Christian before we can live the Christian life.
D. Martyn Lloyd-Jones

A man finally proclaims whether he is a Christian or not by the view he takes of this world.   *D. Martyn Lloyd-Jones*

By definition a Christian should be a problem and an enigma to every person who is not a Christian.
D. Martyn Lloyd-Jones

The Christian faith is ultimately not only a matter of understanding or of intellect, it is a condition of the heart.
D. Martyn Lloyd-Jones

The Christian is a man who expects nothing from this world. He does not pin his hopes on it, because he knows that it is doomed.   *D. Martyn Lloyd-Jones*

The Christian is not a good man. He is a vile wretch who has been saved by the grace of God.   *D. Martyn Lloyd-Jones*

The Christian is sorrowful, but not morose; serious, but not solemn; sober-minded, but not solemn; grave, but never cold or prohibitive; his joy is a holy joy; his happiness a serious happiness.
D. Martyn Lloyd-Jones

The more Christian a person is, the simpler will that person's life be.
D. Martyn Lloyd-Jones

The ordinary Christian knows more about life than the greatest philosopher who is not a Christian.   *D. Martyn Lloyd-Jones*

A Christian is never in a state of completion but always in a process of becoming.   *Martin Luther*

A Christian man is a perfectly free lord of all, subject to none. A Christian man is a perfectly dutiful servant, subject to all.
Martin Luther

Christian life consists in faith and charity.   *Martin Luther*

All Christians are saints and he who is not a saint is not a Christian.
Alexander Maclaren

A Christian's life is full of mysteries: poor, and yet rich; base, and yet exalted; shut out of the world, and yet admitted into the company of saints and angels; slighted, yet dear to God; the world's dirt, and God's jewels.   *Thomas Manton*

Every Christian is born great because he is born for heaven. *Jean Baptiste Massillon*

The true reason for becoming a Christian is not that we may have a wonderful life but that we may be in a right relationship to God.   *Will Metzger*

A Christian is the world's Bible — and some of them need revising. *D. L. Moody*

There is one single fact that one may oppose to all the wit and argument of infidelity; namely, that no man ever repented of being a Christian on his death bed.   *Hannah More*

A saint is not merely a professing follower of Christ, but a professing follower presumed to be what he professes.
Handley C. G. Moule

What is a Christian? The question can be answered in many ways, but the richest answer I know is that a Christian is one who has God as his Father.   *J. I. Packer*

The Christian who has the smile of Christ needs no status symbols.
Leonard Ravenhill

What God did in Christ's crucifixion and resurrection holds true of every believer. He is crucified, dead, buried, risen and ascended with Christ, and his life is hidden with Christ in God. *Klaas Runia*

They lose nothing who gain Christ.
Samuel Rutherford

In themselves, believers have no life, or strength, or spiritual power. All that they have of vital religion comes from Christ. They are what they are, and feel what they feel, and do what they do, because they draw out of Jesus a continual supply of grace, help and ability. *J. C. Ryle*

Saints on earth are not perfect angels, but only converted sinners. *J. C. Ryle*

The true Christian is in all countries a pilgrim and a stranger. *George Santayana*

The meaning of the word 'Christian' has been reduced to practically nothing. Surely, there is no word that has been so devalued unless it is the word 'God' itself. *Francis Schaeffer*

There will be no possibility of standing before Christ but by standing in Christ.
William Secker

A Christian is a strange person. He is both dead and alive, he is miserable and glorious. He grows downwards and upwards at the same time; for as he dies in sin and misery and natural death approaching, so he lives the life of grace, and grows more and more till he end in glory.
Richard Sibbes

A Christian is not his own man.
Richard Sibbes

Christians are in the world to be witnesses, and they must concentrate on their calling. *Paul B. Smith*

For the Christian, all of life is sacred.
Paul B. Smith

The distinguishing mark of a Christian is his confidence in the love of Christ, and the yielding of his affections to Christ in return. *C. H. Spurgeon*

To a man who lives unto God nothing is secular, everything is sacred.
C. H. Spurgeon

The Christian has been transplanted into a new soil and a new climate, and both soil and climate are Christ.
James S. Stewart

A Christian is, in essence, somebody personally related to Jesus Christ.
John R. W. Stott

Nobody can call himself a Christian who does not worship Jesus. *John R. W. Stott*

The Christian should resemble a fruit tree, not a Christmas tree! For the gaudy decorations of a Christmas tree are only tied on, whereas fruit grows on a fruit tree.
John R. W. Stott

A genuine Christian should be a walking mystery because he is surely a walking miracle. Through the leading and the power of the Holy Spirit, the Christian is involved in a daily life and habit that cannot be explained. *A. W. Tozer*

The Christian is strong or weak depending upon how closely he has cultivated the knowledge of God. *A. W. Tozer*

There is a sense in which the people of the Lord are a people apart, belonging to each other in a sense in which they don't belong to anyone else.   *A. W. Tozer*

All Christ's subjects are kings.
Thomas Watson

The saints are the walking pictures of God.   *Thomas Watson*

Whatever makes men good Christians makes them good citizens.
Daniel Webster

What distinguishes the Christian is not that he practises religion but that he is in Christ.   *Douglas Webster*

The Christian is a God explorer.
Tom Wells

CHRISTIANITY — Characteristics

If Christianity is true it is true for everybody, everywhere, and at all times.
John Blanchard

If your Christianity is comfortable, it is compromised.   *John Blanchard*

In true Christianity, there are no short-term commitments and no escape clauses.
John Blanchard

Our conduct should be modelled on that of Christ dying on the cross. *John Cassian*

The Christian ideal has not been tried and found wanting. It has been found difficult and left untried.   *G. K Chesterton*

There is no Christianity without the practice of it.   *John R. De Witt*

The proper temperature of Christianity is red-hot.   *Alexander Duff*

Christianity is not about how to escape from the difficulties of life, but about how to face them.   *Brian Edwards*

It is unnatural for Christianity to be popular.   *Billy Graham*

The supernatural is the native air of Christianity.   *Dora Greenwell*

A Christianity that does not lead to a transformation of the whole person is not Christianity.   *Edward N. Gross*

Christianity is not true because it works. It works because it is true. *Os Guinness*

Salt seasons, purifies, preserves. But somebody ought to remind us that salt also irritates. Real living Christianity rubs this world the wrong way. *Vance Havner*

The fresh air of normal New Testament Christianity would be a shock to the average professing Christian.
Vance Havner

Whatever else may be in question, a Christian's view of the world begins with allegiance to the God who created us and gave his son Jesus to draw us to himself. If others have a different 'bottom line', so be it. Nobody said the Christian life would be easy or popular.
Walter R. Hearn

Christianity promises to make men free; it never promises to make them independent.   *William R. Inge*

The Holy Spirit is the only authenticator of Christianity.   *Arthur P. Johnson*

Authentic Christianity is not sophisticated but simple.   *R. T. Kendall*

Christianity begins with the doctrine of sin.   *Soren Kierkegaard*

Christian living is not fighting for a position but from a position.   *Paul O. Kroon*

According to the Bible, Christianity is a matter of history, a matter of doctrine and a matter of conduct.   *R. B. Kuiper*

To strip Christianity of the supernatural is to destroy Christianity.   *R. B. Kuiper*

Christianity, if false, is of no importance, and, if true, of infinite importance. The one thing it cannot be is moderately important.   *C. S. Lewis*

If you want a religion to make you feel comfortable, I certainly don't recommend Christianity.   *C. S. Lewis*

One of the reasons why it needs no special education to be a Christian is that Christianity is an education in itself.
                                    C. S. Lewis

The mind which asks for a non-miraculous Christianity is a mind in process of relapsing from Christianity into mere 'religion'.   *C. S. Lewis*

Christianity starts with repentance.
                                    D. Martyn Lloyd-Jones

Nothing in the Scripture indicates the church should lure people to Christ by presenting Christianity as an attractive option.   *John MacArthur*

Christianity is not engrossed by this transitory world, but measures all things by the thought of eternity.
                                    J. Gresham Machen

Christianity is essentially and fundamentally a sinner's religion.   *Al Martin*

In Christianity, creed has always to do with Christ.   *G. Campbell Morgan*

Doctrinal Christianity is not a pastime for intellectuals. It is a matter of life and death.   *Iain H. Murray*

Real doctrinal Christianity has an obstinacy about it which no amount of modern opinion or religious excitement can change.   *Iain H. Murray*

Supernatural living through supernatural empowering is at the very heart of New Testament Christianity.   *J. I. Packer*

Christianity is a battle — not a dream.
                                    Wendell Phillips

Christianity is nothing without its history.
                                    Clark H. Pinnock

Christianity is a demanding and serious religion. When it is delivered as easy and amusing, it is another kind of religion altogether.   *Neil Postman*

Christianity did not originate in a lie, and we can and ought to demonstrate this, as well as to believe it.   *William Ramsay*

The pessimist is not a representative of Christianity.   *A. T. Robertson*

Christianity is no more a bondage to men than wings are to birds.
                                    O. Palmer Robertson

Christianity without dogma is a powerless thing.   *J. C. Ryle*

We must aim to have a Christianity which, like the sap of a tree, runs through twig and leaf of our character and sanctifies all. *J. C. Ryle*

We may call the doctrine of the Christian faith exhilarating or we may call it devastating. We may call it revelation or we may call it rubbish. But if we call it dull, words simply have no meaning.
Dorothy L. Sayers

It is quite possible that some day there might evolve a world religion, but the Christianity of the Bible will never be a part of it. *Paul B. Smith*

Christianity is summed up in the two facts: Christ for us and Christ in us.
Augustus H. Strong

Christ is the centre of Christianity; all else is circumference. *John R. W. Stott*

Nobody has understood Christianity who does not understand ... the word 'justified'. *John R. W. Stott*

There is no authentic biblical Christianity without the cross at its centre.
John R. W. Stott

If Christianity has never disturbed us, we have not yet learned what it is.
William Temple

Christianity can do without the favour of the world. *David Thomas*

Christianity promises us no escape from the opposition of wicked men; indeed it teaches us to expect it. *David Thomas*

Justification is the very hinge and pillar of Christianity. *Thomas Watson*

Christianity is not merely a programme of conduct; it is the power of a new life.
Benjamin B. Warfield

A godly life is always the best advertisement for Christianity. *Geoffrey B. Wilson*

CHRISTIANITY — Definition

Christianity can be expressed in three sentences. I deserve hell. Jesus Christ took my hell. There is nothing left for me but his heaven. *Anon.*

Christianity is life under sealed orders.
Anon.

Christianity is obedience. *Anon.*

Religion is man's search for God. Christianity is God's search for man. *Anon.*

Christianity is not the religion of Jesus ... but Christ religion. Christianity is now as dependent on him, moment by moment, as when he trod this earth.
Herman Bavinck

Christianity is the land of beginning again. *W. A. Criswell*

Christianity is the way of the cross ... and your blood and sweat may mingle with Christ's before your life is finished.
Lionel Fletcher

'Crucified' is the only definitive adjective by which to describe the Christian life. *J. Furman Miller*

Christianity is a rescue religion.
Michael Green

Christianity is either relevant all the time or useless any time. It is not just a phase of life; it is life itself. *Richard Halverson*

Christ plus Christians equals Christianity. *Geoffrey King*

Christianity is a universal holiness in every part of life. *William Law*

Christianity is the story of how the rightful King has landed, you might say landed in disguise, and is calling us all to take part in a great campaign of sabotage. *C. S. Lewis*

In science we have been reading only the notes to a poem; in Christianity we find the poem itself. *C. S. Lewis*

Some tend to think that Christianity is a matter of being nice. But niceness is purely biological. One dog is nicer than another dog! *D. Martyn Lloyd-Jones*

Christianity is not a way of life as distinguished from a doctrine, nor a way of life expressing itself in a doctrine, but a way of life founded upon a doctrine. *J. Gresham Machen*

Christianity is a religion about a cross. *Leon Morris*

Christianity is the power of God in the soul of man. *Robert B. Munger*

Christianity is primarily about truth and the doctrine of salvation. *Iain H. Murray*

There must be many serious minded believers who, as they look at what is often portrayed as Christianity today, wonder if it pertains to the same God in whom we ourselves profess to believe. *John J. Murray*

Christianity is not the acceptance of certain ideas. It is a personal attitude of trust and devotion to a person. *Stephen Neill*

Christianity is not a system of doctrine but a new creature. *John Newton*

Christian doctrine is grace, and Christian conduct is gratitude. *J. I. Packer*

Christianity is more than a storm cellar; it is a way of life. *Gilbert Peters*

Christianity is very much greater than Christian doctrine ... Theology can never take the place of faith. *Theodore Robinson*

Christianity is neither a creed nor a ceremonial, but life vitally connected with a loving Christ. *Josiah Strong*

Christianity is the total commitment of all I know of me to all I know of Jesus Christ. *William Temple*

Christianity is all about relationships with God and with others. *David Watson*

Christianity can be condensed into four words: admit, submit, commit and transmit. *Samuel Wilberforce*

Christianity is not merely an assurance policy to take us to heaven; it is a bowing of the knee to the lordship of Christ. *Frederick R. Wood*

CHRISTIANITY — Uniqueness

Only for Christianity is God both transcendent and immanent — at once the eternal Creator of the cosmos and the earthly redeemer of mankind, as well as its indwelling spirit, omnipresent as well as omnipotent. *Mortimer J. Adler*

The distinction between Christianity and all other Systems of religion consists largely in this, that in these others men are found seeking after God, while Christianity is God seeking after men. *Thomas Arnold*

The glory of Christianity is to conquer by forgiveness.   *William Blake*

Christianity can no more be compared with other religions than Jesus Christ can be compared with other people.
John Blanchard

Christianity is based upon historical acts and facts. All other faiths centre on the subjective ethical teaching of their founders.   *Joe Boot*

Christianity is not a mere development of the ancient world, but a new and supernatural beginning.   *Jonathan Edwards*

All religions other than Christianity have a kind of points system for obtaining eternal life.   *Stephen Gaukroger*

As you look into other faiths you will find an enormous amount that is true and worthy, that is moral and good, as well as much that is not. But you will not find anything that is good and true which cannot be found in Christ. *Michael Green*

It is quite plain that, if treated fairly on its own premises, Christianity excludes the full truth and final validity of other religions.   *Os Guinness*

The Christian faith is not true because it works; it works because it is true.
Os Guinness

You won't get rid of your difficulties by putting away Christianity, because they will come up under philosophy.
A. A. Hodge

Where idolatry ends, there Christianity begins; and where idolatry begins, there Christianity ends.   *Friedrich H. Jacobi*

All other religions are oblique: the founder stands aside and introduces another speaker … Christianity alone is direct speech.   *Soren Kierkegaard*

We must never talk about the failure of Christianity. It is impossible for Christianity to fail. What fails is the shabby counterfeit of the real thing that we are willing to put up with.   *Geoffrey King*

Christianity has the only true God; all other gods are idols. Christianity has the only true Saviour; every other saviour so called leaves and leads men to destruction.   *R. B. Kuiper*

Christianity has the only true morality; no other religion conduces to true holiness.   *R. B. Kuiper*

Do not attempt to water Christianity down. There must be no pretence that you can have it with the supernatural left out. So far as I can see Christianity is precisely the one religion from which the miraculous cannot be separated.   *C. S. Lewis*

I believe in Christianity as I believe in the sun — not only because I see it, because by it I see everything else.
C. S. Lewis

There is no Christianity apart from revelation.   *D. Martyn Lloyd-Jones*

The life of Christianity consists in possessive pronouns.   *Martin Luther*

Christianity knows nothing of hopeless cases. It professes its ability to take the most crooked stick and bring it straight, to flash a new power into the blackest carbon, which will turn it into a diamond.
Alexander Maclaren

In the Christian religion all moral duties are advanced and heightened to their greatest perfection.   *Thomas Manton*

The uniqueness of Christianity is in Jesus Christ.   *John Mbiti*

The difficulties of Christianity no doubt are great; but depend on it, they are nothing compared to the difficulties of infidelity.   *J. C. Ryle*

The primary emphasis of biblical Christianity is the teaching that the infinite-personal God is the ultimate reality, the Creator of all else, and that an individual can come openly to the holy God upon the basis of the finished work of Christ and that alone.   *Francis Schaeffer*

Christianity is beyond religion.
      Robert Scott

No religion except Christianity has an atonement.   *R. C. Sproul*

Christianity is essentially a religion of resurrection.   *James S. Stewart*

Christianity … is the revelation of God, not the research of man. *James S. Stewart*

Christianity is in its very essence a resurrection religion. The concept of resurrection lies at its heart. If you remove it, Christianity is destroyed. *John R. W. Stott*

Christianity without Christ is a chest without a treasure, a frame without a portrait, a corpse without breath. *John R. W. Stott*

So Christianity is old, and is getting older every year. Yet it is also new, new every morning.   *John R. W. Stott*

Union with Christ is a unique emphasis

among the world's religion.
      John R. W. Stott

Christianity is the one revealed religion.
      Benjamin B. Warfield

Christianity did not begin in a school of Philosophy or a mystical conception or an ideological panacea, but with a group of very ordinary men who came into vital contact with the person of Jesus Christ.   *Fredrick P. Wood*

CHRISTLIKENESS
(See also: Godliness; Holiness)

If you are in Christ, and Christ is in you, then the world should see nothing else.
      Anon.

To be much like Christ, be much with Christ.   *Anon.*

The most deeply felt obligation on earth is that which the Christian feels to imitate the Redeemer   *Albert Barnes*

The universal command of the gospel, that comprises all our duties, is to walk as Christ walked.   *William Bates*

A Christian's life should be nothing but a visible representation of Christ.
      Thomas Brooks

The more the soul is conformed to Christ, the more confident it will be of its interest in Christ.   *Thomas Brooks*

We are not merely to serve Christ, we are to be like him.   *Derek Copley*

To become like Christ is the only thing in the world worth caring for, the thing before which every ambition of man is folly and all lower achievement vain.
      John Drummond

The fear of the Lord was a lovely grace in the perfect humanity of Jesus. Let it be the test of our 'predestination to be conformed to his image'. *Sinclair Ferguson*

The gospel does not make us like Adam in his innocence — it makes us like Christ, in all the perfection of his reflection of God. *Sinclair Ferguson*

Even when we can cite chapter and verse for creation, corruption, predestination, election, vocation, regeneration, justification, adoption, sanctification and glorification, the test of discipleship remains incomplete; we must still deal with the crucial question of our likeness to the Master who is gentle and humble in heart. *Mariano Di Gangi*

The duty as well as the destiny of believers is to be conformed to the image of God's Son. *William Hendriksen*

None can know their election but by their conformity to Christ; for all that are chosen are chosen to sanctification. *Matthew Henry*

The Christian's task is to make the Lord Jesus visible, intelligible and desirable. *Len Jones*

All our salvation consists in the manifestation of the nature, life and Spirit of Jesus in our inward new man. *William Law*

From morning to night keep Jesus in your heart, long for nothing, desire nothing, hope for nothing, but to have all that is within you changed into the sprit and temper of the holy Jesus. *William Law*

'Putting on Christ' is not one among many jobs a Christian has to do; and it is not a sort of special exercise for the top class. It is the whole of Christianity. Christianity offers nothing else at all. *C. S. Lewis*

If you try to imitate Christ, the world will praise you; if you become like Christ, the world will hate you!
D. Martyn Lloyd-Jones

The goal of sanctification is to be conformed to Christ's image, not to be self-satisfied. *John MacArthur*

God never gave man a thing to do concerning which it were irreverent to ponder how the Son of God would have done it. *George MacDonald*

To gain entire likeness to Christ, I ought to get a high esteem of the happiness of it. *Robert Murray M'Cheyne*

Conformity to the world can be overcome by nothing but conformity to Jesus.
Andrew Murray

It is not great talents that God blesses, so much as great likeness to Jesus.
Robert Murray M'Cheyne

We are never more like Christ than in prayers of intercession. *Austin Phelps*

To be like Christ in any measure is grace; to be like him in perfection is glory.
William S. Plumer

However holy or Christlike a Christian may become, he is still in the condition of 'being changed'. *John R. W. Stott*

If we had to sum up in a single brief sentence what life is all about, why Jesus Christ came into this world to live and die and rise, and what God is up to in the long-drawn-out historical process both

BC and AD, it would be difficult to find a more succinct explanation than this: God is making human beings more human by making them more like Christ.
John R. W. Stott

You and I were created to tell the truth about God by reflecting his likeness. That is normality. How many lies have you told about God today? *Ian Thomas*

No Christian is where he ought to be spiritually until the beauty of the Lord Jesus Christ is being reproduced in daily Christian life. *A. W. Tozer*

Our lives should be as many sermons upon Christ's life. *John Trapp*

Holiness is not the laborious acquisition of virtue from without, but the expression of the Christ-life from within.
J. W. C. Wand

When no mark of the cross appears in our discipleship, we may doubt the ownership. We should be branded for Christ. *Mary S. Wood*

CHURCH — Attendance and Membership

Don't stay away from church because there are so many hypocrites. There's always room for one more. *A. R. Adams*

He cannot have God for his Father who refuses to have the church for his mother.
Augustine

No local church is perfect — but there is no way in which it can be improved by the absence of spiritually-minded Christians. *John Blanchard*

A person who says he believes in God but never goes to church is like one who says he believes in education but never goes to school. *Franklin Clark Fry*

There is no place for any loose stone in God's edifice. *Joseph Hall*

Any man in a church should be one whose character qualifies him for any office the church offers. *E. F. Hallock*

An avoidable absence from church is an infallible evidence of spiritual decay.
Frances Ridley Havergal

Don't ever come to church without coming as though it were the first time, as though it could be the best time and as though it might be the last time.
Vance Havner

I believe in loyalty to the local church. I don't believe in that view of the invisible church that makes you invisible at church! *Vance Havner*

How lovely is the sanctuary in the eyes of those who are truly sanctified!
Matthew Henry

Those that would enjoy the dignities and privileges of Christ's family must submit to the discipline of it. *Matthew Henry*

Those whom God leads, he leads to his holy hill, and to his tabernacles; those therefore who pretend to be led by the Spirit and yet turn their backs upon instituted ordinances, certainly deceive themselves. *Matthew Henry*

The New Testament knows nothing of freelance Christianity. It is the corporate witness of the redeemed fellowship that is used by the Spirit of God.
Geoffrey King

The church is the only institution in the world that has lower entrance requirements than those for getting on a bus.
William Laroe

The New Testament does not envisage solitary religion. *C. S. Lewis*

The question whether or not to join the church or belong to the church is not one that is open for the Christian believer.
Donald MacLeod

A church membership does not make a Christian any more than owning a piano makes a musician. *Douglas Meador*

The Christian church is the only society in the world in which membership is based upon the qualification that the candidate shall be unworthy of membership.
Charles Clayton Morrison

You don't see the church on Sunday morning any more than you see the army when it's on dress parade. *Bill Popejoy*

The church of Christ needs servants of all kinds, and instruments of every sort; penknives as well as swords, axes as well as hammers, chisels as well as saws, Marthas as well as Marys, Peters as well as Johns. *J. C. Ryle*

We don't go to church; we are the church.
Ernest Southcott

To stay away from church is to spit in God's face and despise his gift of the kingdom. *R. C. Sproul*

Going to church doesn't make you a Christian any more than going to a garage makes you an automobile.
Billy Sunday

Stating it in just about the most simple terms we know, the Christian church is the assembly of redeemed saints.
A. W. Tozer

We must meet with the Church Militant if ever we hope to meet with the Church Triumphant. Together in grace, God's people make ready for glory.
Malcolm Watts

There is nothing more unchristian than a solitary Christian. *John Wesley*

No new Christian is born in a vacuum. He is delivered into the fellowship of the church. He is baptized by the one Spirit into the body of Christ. He joins the society of the saints.
Arthur Skevington Wood

CHURCH — Blemishes

It is a poor worship to move our hats, not our hearts. *Thomas Adams*

A church without the truth is not a true church, and a church without the Spirit is not a true church. *Anon.*

A cold church, like cold butter, never spreads well. *Anon.*

The pastor cannot lead unless the people get behind him. *Anon.*

Our whole problem is that we meet, and go through the motions, and the Lord is not there. *Rolfe Barnard*

The levity in our services shows the blindness of our hearts. *Rolfe Barnard*

The idea of a church in politics can come only from that false postulate that the purpose of the church is to save the world.
Donald Grey Barnhouse

Some churches' programmes are so full their members have no time left to be Christians.   *John Blanchard*

Whenever doctrine is devalued the church's worship is diminished, and no amount of enthusiasm, excitement or energy can replace what is lost.
John Blanchard

Before the church can make an impact on the culture it must break with the idolatries and misconceptions that dominate the culture.   *Donald Bloesch*

I looked for the church and I found it in the world; I looked for the world and I found it in the church.   *Horatius Bonar*

The church has halted somewhere between Calvary and Pentecost. *J. L Brice*

The greatest sin of the church is that she withholds the gospel from herself and the world.   *Emil Brumner*

People are driven from the church not so much by stern truth that makes them uneasy as by weak nothings that make them contemptuous.   *George Buttrick*

God's sacred barn-floor will not be perfectly cleansed before the last day.
John Calvin

The church cannot be rightly reformed except it be trained to obedience by the frequent scourges of God.   *John Calvin*

Those who wish to build the church by rejecting the doctrine of the Word build a hog's sty, and not the church of God.
John Calvin

A church with a little creed is a church with a little life.   *B. H. Carroll*

We do not want, as the newspapers say, a church that will move with the world. We want a church that will move the world.
G. K. Chesterton

Nothing will so avail to divide the church as love of power.   *Chrysostom*

A church without authority is like a crocodile without teeth; it can open its mouth as wide and as often as it likes, but who cares?   *Brian H. Edwards*

It is one of Satan's deep devices to call off the attention of the church from her own state to the condition of the world without and around her.   *H. C. Fish*

The average church is often like a congested lung with only a few cells doing the breathing.   *A. J. Gordon*

It is a stark tragedy to love the church and its work and not to love Jesus.
E. F. Hallock

Nothing will destroy a church and its power in a community and the world any quicker than to lose its first love.
E. F. Hallock

From the days of Constantine to this hour Christianity fares badly when the world takes the church under its patronizing wing. I am not impressed by the smiling sponsorship of this age.   *Vance Hanver*

If even half of our church membership ever took Jesus Christ seriously we would start a major revolution!   *Vance Havner*

It would be frightening to know how little of our church activity is the spontaneous expression of our love for Christ.
Vance Havner

Many a Christian, many a church, has everything on the showcase and nothing on the shelves. *Vance Havner*

Many church people do not give Satan enough trouble to arouse his opposition. *Vance Havner*

Never before have we had so many degrees in the church and yet so little temperature. *Vance Havner*

One serious malady of the church is infantile paralysis — too many babies who never grow. *Vance Havner*

The besetting sin of our Christianity today, in private and public, is insipidity. *Vance Havner*

The church can do many things after she repents, but she can do nothing else until she repents. *Vance Havner*

The church has no greater need today than to fall in love with Jesus all over again. *Vance Havner*

The devil's main business today is getting people to join a church without being saved. *Vance Havner*

Too many church members are starched and ironed but not washed. *Vance Havner*

Too many church services begin at eleven o'clock sharp and end at twelve o'clock dull. *Vance Havner*

We are long on membership but short on discipleship. We are more anxious to gather statistics than to grow saints. *Vance Havner*

When recreation gets ahead of re-creation, then God's house has become a den of thieves. *Vance Havner*

When the nightclub invades the sanctuary it ought not to be difficult for any Bible Christian to discern the time of day. *Vance Havner*

Worldliness is rampant in the church. The devil is not fighting churches, he is joining them! He isn't persecuting Christianity, he is professing it. *Vance Havner*

The chief trouble with the church is that you and I are in it. *Charles H. Heimsath*

It is not only a mistake but a sin to trust attractions for the ear and the eyes, and to draw people to the church by the same methods by which they are drawn to a place of entertainment. *William G. Hughes*

The more exalted pomp there be of men's devising, there will be the less spiritual truth. *George Hutcheson*

I can think of some churches that would be even emptier if the gospel were preached in them. *William R. Inge*

I know that the church has its stupidities and inanities and irrelevancies; but I love my mother in spite of her weaknesses and wrinkles. *E. Stanley Jones*

Many Christians are so busy they can only hear the click and clatter of church machinery. *Walter B. Knight*

A self-satisfied church is either dead or dying. *R. B. Kuiper*

By and large people do not go to church to learn about God from his infallible Word, but rather to be tranquillized. *R. B. Kuiper*

If the church were strong and active, as it

ought to be, the world would oppose much more vigorously.   *R. B. Kuiper*

Middle-of-the-road pacifism in significant doctrinal controversy has ruined many a church.   *R. B. Kuiper*

The problem of the church today is not that the gospel has lost its power but that the church has lost its audience.
Paul Little

I have no hesitation again in asserting that the failure of the church to have a greater impact upon the life of men and women in the world today is due entirely to the fact that her own life is not in order.
D. Martyn Lloyd-Jones

It is the lack of solid biblical conviction in the pulpit which has begotten the almost total absence of decisiveness in the pews.   *Conrad Mbewe*

To play little religious games in church with those of one's own kind may well be a prime index of man's fallenness.
Samuel J. Mlikolaski

Depend upon it, as long as the church is living so much like the world, we cannot expect our children to be brought into the fold.   *D. L. Moody*

One of Satan's methods today is to start so many organizations in a church that the members have no time for communion with God.   *G. Campbell Morgan*

We are producing Christian activities faster than we are producing Christian experience and Christian faith. *J. R. Mott*

The church is most evangelistic when she is least concerned about impressing the world or with adding to her numbers.
Iain H. Murray

The church must never beg for money as if this were the secret of her strength.
Andrew Murray

The early church was not wrecked on the rocks of mere activism; nor did it sink in the quicksands of blasphemous idleness.
Stuart Olyott

The real need of the church is not for new methods of evangelism or increased activity, but for a deep moral cleansing and a readjustment of heart and life that will clear away barriers to fruitful communication of the gospel.   *James Philip*

The average church knows more about promotion than prayer.
Leonard Ravenhill

Going through any physical motions apart from the lifting of one's spirit to God or the humbling of one's spirit before God is without significance.
Robert G. Rayburn

One of the main causes of present troubles in the church is the neglect of discipline.   *Klaas Runia*

Neither a church conformed to the world, nor a church ignorant of the world can fulfil her mission in the world.
Ernst Schrupp

It would take a theologian with a fine-toothed comb to find the Holy Spirit recognizably present with power in much of our ecclesiastical routine.
Samuel M. Shoemaker

I believe that in public worship we should do well to be bound by no human rules, and constrained by no stereotyped order.
C. H. Spurgeon

I believe that one reason why the church of God at this present moment has so little influence over the world is because the world has so much influence over the church. *C. H. Spurgeon*

That in some parts of the world the church as the new community is more a dream than a reality is a disgrace with which sensitive Christians must never come to terms. *John R. W. Stott*

Some may say, 'If the minister preached better, we should be better hearers'; but the minister might say, 'If I had better hearers, I should preach better.' *William Tiptaft*

Are we just holding on to the painted mane of the painted horse, repeating a trip of very insignificant circles to a pleasing musical accompaniment? *A. W. Tozer*

I can safely say, on the authority of all that is revealed in the Word of God, that any man or woman on this earth who is bored and turned off by worship is not ready for heaven. *A. W. Tozer*

I do not believe it is necessarily true that we are worshipping God when we are making a lot of racket. *A. W. Tozer*

In the average church we hear the same prayers repeated each Sunday year in and year out with, one would suspect, not the remotest expectation that they will be answered. *A. W. Tozer*

Much church work and activity is thrown back upon a shaky foundation of psychology and natural talents. *A. W. Tozer*

Much that passes for New Testament Christianity is little more than objective truth sweetened with song and made palatable by religious entertainment. *A. W. Tozer*

My observations have led me to the belief that many, perhaps most, of the activities engaged in by the average church do not contribute in any way to the accomplishing of the true work of Christ on earth. I hope I am wrong, but I am afraid I am right. *A. W. Tozer*

There are churches so completely out of the hands of God that if the Holy Spirit withdrew from them they wouldn't find it out for many months. *A. W. Tozer*

God preserve our churches from becoming mere bless-me-clubs! *George Verwer*

The Christian church today suffers because so many of its members feel that they have made a decision for Christ, or that they have chosen to join a church. Such man-centred notions spell spiritual weakness and imbalance. *David Watson*

When social action is mistaken for evangelism, the church has ceased to manufacture its own blood cells and is dying of leukaemia. *Sherwood Wirt*

CHURCH — and Christ

The church is heir to the cross. *Thomas Adams*

The church is Christ's body and the body of a man goes by the same name as the head. *Anon.*

The church is a community of the works and words of Jesus. *Donald English*

As the church endures hardness and humiliation as united to him who was on the cross, so she should exhibit something

Church — and Christ

of supernatural energy as united with him who is on the throne.   *A. J. Gordon*

The church is nothing but Christ displayed.   *William Gurnall*

The church is taken out of dying Jesus' side, as Eve out of sleeping Adam's.
          William Gurnall

What the world needs is neither a Christless churchianity nor a churchless Christianity, but Christ the Head living afresh in his body, the church.
          Vance Havner

The church comes out of Christ's side in the sleep of his death.   *William Jenkyn*

The church is the fruit of the gospel.
          Hywel R. Jones

No aspect of Christ's relationship to the church looms larger in Holy Writ than the fact that he is its Head.   *R. B. Kuiper*

The church was originated not only by Christ, but also from him, and cannot continue to exist for even a moment apart from him.   *R. B. Kuiper*

If we accept the divine entry of God into human history through the man Jesus Christ, we cannot help accepting the unique nature of the fellowship which he founded. For in a true sense it is an extension of the actual visit, sustained by the living God.   *J. B. Phillips*

Christ is the essence of worship, and our understanding of the church's worship must take its starting-point from him.
          Robert G. Rayburn

Christ is the King of his church, and the church is the greatest queen in the world.
          Richard Sibbes

The church's one foundation
Is Jesus Christ her Lord;
She is his new creation
By water and the Word;
From heaven he came and sought her
To be his holy bride;
With his own blood he bought her,
And for her life he died.
          Samuel John Stone

If the church goes wrong on Christ it goes wrong on everything.   *John R. W. Stott*

CHURCH — Divisions

Better a holy discord than a profane concord.   *Thomas Adams*

You can't build a church with stumbling blocks.   *Fred Beck*

It is better to have divisions than an evil uniformity.   *Walter Cradock*

In the great things of religion, be of a mind: but when there is not a unity of sentiment, let there be a union of affections.   *Matthew Henry*

Division is better than agreement in evil.
          George Hutcheson

Divisions between Christians are a sin and a scandal, and Christians ought at all times to be making contributions towards reunion, if it is only by their prayers.
          C. S. Lewis

Let's have no barriers against saints, only sins.   *R. C. Lucas*

The division of Christians is the sin of fratricide.   *J. A. Motyer*

It is a fearful sin to make a rent and a hole in Christ's mystical body because there is a spot in it.   *Samuel Rutherford*

The existence of over 9,000 Christian denominations throughout the world is an insult to Christ and a hindrance to the spread of the kingdom of God.
David Watson

CHURCH — Duties

A church is a hospital for sinners, not a museum for saints. *Anon.*

The church is not a yachting club but a fleet of fishing boats. *Anon.*

No church is obedient that is not evangelistic. *John Blanchard*

The church exists by mission as a fire exists by burning. *Emil Brunner*

As the saving doctrine of Christ is the life of the church, so discipline is, as it were, its sinews. *John Calvin*

The highest honour in the church is not government but service. *John Calvin*

Wherever we see the Word of God purely preached and heard, there a church of God exists, even if it swarms with many faults. *John Calvin*

The church that ceases to be evangelistic will soon cease to be evangelical.
Alexander Duff

The aim of the church is to reach the rest of the world. *Donald English*

The church is meant to be a working model of what God wants to do with the rest of society. *Donald English*

Only a virtuoso in exegetical evasion would dare to deny that the mission of the church is to make disciples.
Mariano di Gangi

The business of the church is to demonstrate God. *Vance Havner*

The Christian church is not just a 'doctrine club'. *Paul Helm*

How blessed a constitution were the Christian church if all the members did their duty! *Matthew Henry*

The Lord God hath given us three principal signs and marks by which we may know this his church, that is to say, the Word, the sacraments and discipline
John Hooper

It is the church's task to turn adherents to the church into possessors of Christ.
Kenneth Kirk

Today's church ... has no more solemn duty than to maintain purity of doctrine.
R. B. Kuiper

The only valid consideration for the church to realize at all times must be what serves the gospel, its credibility, its deepening, its propagation. What forms, customs and ordinances must be removed, changed or avoided, lest the church itself be a burden to faith in the gospel?
Walter Kunneth

God never intended his church to be a refrigerator in which to preserve perishable piety. He intended it to be an incubator in which to hatch out converts.
F. Lincicome

The Scriptures know no clericalism. To all the people of God belongs the work of the ministry. *R. C. Lucas*

The church is a workshop, not a dormitory. *Alexander MacLaren*

If a church does not evangelize it will fossilize. *A. W. Pink*

Anything which makes it easier for us to worship spiritually should be encouraged while anything that draws attention to itself rather than to God should be eliminated from our corporate worship services. *Robert G. Rayburn*

Church greatness consists in being greatly serviceable. *J. C. Ryle*

Prayer meetings are the throbbing machinery of the church. *C. H. Spurgeon*

We shall never see much change for the better in our churches in general till the prayer meeting occupies a higher place in the esteem of Christians.
C. H. Spurgeon

If we ever forget our basic charter – 'My house is a house of prayer' – we might as well shut the church doors.
James S. Stewart

Every church should be engaged in continuous self-reformation. *John R. W. Stott*

Congregations never honour God more than when they reverently listen to his Word, intending not just to hear but to obey in response to what he has done, is doing and will do for them.
Geoff Thomas

I believe a local church exists to do corporately what each Christian believer should be doing individually – and that is to worship God. It is to show forth the excellencies of him who has called us out of darkness into his marvellous light. It is to reflect the glories of Christ ever shining upon us through the ministries of the Holy Spirit. *A. W. Tozer*

The church has nothing to do but to save souls; therefore spend and be spent in this work. It is not your business to speak so many times, but to save souls as you can; to bring as many sinners as you possibly can to repentance. *John Wesley*

CHURCH — Fellowship

Christians may not see eye to eye, but they should walk arm in arm. *Anon.*

The church of Jesus Christ is not a building where people come together for a religious service, but it is a gathering of people who come together in order to worship God and to build each other by mutual faith and strength.
Donald Grey Barnhouse

The Christian church is a truly classless society. *John Blanchard*

There are no insignificant members in the church. *Herbert M. Carson*

The church should be a community of encouragement. *Fred Catherwood*

It is best to be with those in time we hope to be with in eternity. *Thomas Fuller*

In public worship all should join. The little strings go to make up a concert, as well as the great. *Thomas Goodwin*

There is no place for any loose stone in God's edifice. *Joseph Hall*

Local churches are to be thought of not as churches of individuals but, primarily, churches of families. *Paul Helm*

As those who are grown Christians must be willing to hear the plainest truths preached for the sake of the weak, so the

weak must be willing to hear the more difficult and mysterious truths preached for the sake of those who are strong.
Matthew Henry

When we take God for our God, we take his people for our people. *Matthew Henry*

We are neither made nor redeemed for self-sufficient aloneness.   *J. I. Packer*

We are not entitled to infer from the fact that a group of people are drawing nearer to each other that any of them is drawing nearer to the truth.   *J. I. Packer*

Our Lord has many weak children in his family, many dull pupils in his school, many raw soldiers in his army, many lame sheep in his flock. Yet he bears with them all, and casts none away. Happy is that Christian who has learned to do likewise with his brethren.   *J. C. Ryle*

We should always regard communion with other believers as an eminent means of grace.   *J. C. Ryle*

The secret of good relationships in the Christian community is the recognition that Jesus Christ is Lord and that Christians live 'unto him'.   *John R. W. Stott*

Christians in concert are an abridgement of heaven, shining like a firmament of bright stars.   *George Swinnock*

Be united with other Christians. A wall with loose bricks is not good. The bricks must be cemented together.
Corrie ten Boom

There is no room in the church for any intellectual, spiritual or social elite which separates itself from fellow-believers whom Christ has accepted.
Geoffrey R. Wilson

CHURCH — Glory

The church has many critics but no rivals.   *Anon.*

Although God is concerned about the sin of the nation, he is more concerned about the spirituality of the church. *John Benton*

Purity of doctrine is the soul of the church.
John Calvin

The excellence of the church does not consist in multitude but in purity.
John Calvin

The source and origin of the church is the free love of God.   *John Calvin*

The most wonderful things that are now done on earth are wrought in the public ordinances.   *David Clarkson*

Is not the church the very cork on which the world remains afloat?
William Hendriksen

As the beauty of the human body is brought out by the variety of its parts, so the glory of the body of Christ appears in the diversity of its members. *R. B. Kuiper*

In the counsel of God the church existed even before the creation of man.
R. B. Kuiper

The Christian church is glorious in its very nature.   *R. B. Kuiper*

The glory of the greatest, wealthiest, most powerful and most resplendent empire of all history was as nothing, yes less than nothing, in comparison with the glory of the church of Christ.   *R. B. Kuiper*

The glory of the gospel is that when the church is absolutely different from the world she invariably attracts it.
D. Martyn Lloyd-Jones

The true Christian church is the work of the Word communicated by every available means. *Martin Luther*

Sound doctrine always has been, is today, and ever will be the foremost mark of the true church. *Geoff Thomas*

The highest expression of the will of God in this age is the church which he purchased with his own blood. *A. W. Tozer*

There are no little churches; all churches are the same size in God's sight.
A. W. Tozer

CHURCH — Oneness

The church and the churches are not the same. *Donald Grey Barnhouse*

There is not doubt but that if there be one God, there is but one church; if there be but one Christ, there is but one church; if there be but one cross, there is but one church; if there be but one Holy Ghost, there is but one church. *A. A. Hodge*

The real unity of the church must not be organized but exercised. *Johannes Lilje*

The church is not a great community made up of an accumulation of small communities, but is truly present in its wholeness in every company of believers, however small. *K. L. Schmidt*

The church is one body – you cannot touch a toe without affecting the whole body. *Friedrich Tholuck*

CHURCH — Power

The church has many critics but no rivals. *Anon.*

If it were not for the church, Satan would already have turned this world into hell.
Paul E. Billheier

The one reaction the Christian church ought never to produce in the community is indifference. *John Blanchard*

The church upon its knees would bring heaven upon the earth. *E .M Bounds*

The past has not exhausted the possibilities nor the demands for doing great things for God. The church that is dependent on its past history for its miracles of power and grace is a fallen church.
E. M. Bounds

The church that does not work miracles is dead and ought to be buried.
Samuel Chadwick

There ought to be enough electricity in every church service to give everybody in the congregation either a charge or a shock! *Vance Havner*

The Christian church has the resurrection written all over it. *F. G. Robinson*

A holy church is an awful weapon in the hand of God. *C. H. Spurgeon*

The church is still to be reckoned with.
A. W. Tozer

CHURCH — Security in God's purposes

The church is not a democracy in which we have chosen God, but a theocracy in which he has chosen us. *John Blanchard*

The church is the only society in the world that never loses any of its members, even by death.   *John Blanchard*

The preservation of the church depends on the mere favour of God. *John Calvin*

The salvation of the church is so precious in the sight of God that he regards the wrong done to the faithful as done to himself.   *John Calvin*

The welfare of the church is inseparably connected with the righteousness of God.
John Calvin

Never futile is the work of the church, for it is a product not of the mind of man but of the sovereign grace of God.
William Hendriksen

The church shall survive the world, and be in bliss when that is in ruins.
Matthew Henry

We may with the greatest assurance depend upon God for the safety of his church.   *Matthew Henry*

When men are projecting the church's ruin God is preparing for its salvation.
Matthew Henry

While the world stands God will have a church in it.   *Matthew Henry*

The church will outlive the universe; in it the individual person will outlive the universe. Everything that is joined to the immortal Head will share his immortality.   *C. S. Lewis*

The church of God is a nation without any capital on earth. *G. Campbell Morgan*

Ever since God had a church of redeemed sinners on earth the future of her destiny has been brighter than her past history.
William S. Plumer

The household of Abraham is the prototype of the church of God. The promise which accrued to him is the secret of the maintenance of the church.
Herman N. Ridderbos

No history ought to receive so much of our attention as the past and present history of the church of Christ. The rise and fall of worldly empires are events of comparatively small importance in the sight of God.   *J. C. Ryle*

I believe in the final perseverance of every saint as an individual. Furthermore, I believe in the final perseverance of the saints as a body: the church of God shall live, and continue her work till she has accomplished it. But far diviner is the thought to me of the final perseverance of the Christ of God.   *C. H. Spurgeon*

God has twisted together his glory and our good.   *Thomas Watson*

CHURCH UNITY

Peace is not purchased by the sacrifice of truth.   *Anon.*

When the Bible speaks about church unity, it speaks of unity not at the expense of truth but on the basis of it.
John Blanchard

Unity must not he sought at the expense of the gospel.   *Walter J. Chantry*

Division is better than agreement in evil.
George Hutcheson

To strive without sacrifice of truth for the visible unity of the body of Christ is to enhance its glory.   *R. B. Kuiper*

Unity is of the essence of the body of Christ.   *R. B. Kuiper*

Unity must be ordered according to God's holy Word, or else it were better war than peace.   *Hugh Latimer*

If all the churches in the world became amalgamated, it would not make the slightest difference to the man in the street. He is not outside the churches because the churches are disunited, he is outside because he likes his sin, because he is a sinner, because he is ignorant of spiritual realities. He is no more interested in unity than the man in the moon!
D. Martyn Lloyd-Jones

Putting all the ecclesiastical corpses into one graveyard will not bring about a resurrection.   *D. Martyn Lloyd-Jones*

Cursed be that unity for which the Word of God is put at stake.   *Martin Luther*

We cannot expect the world to believe that the Father sent the Son, that Jesus' claims are true and that Christianity is true, unless the world sees some reality of the oneness of true Christians.
Francis Schaeffer

I am quite sure that the best way to promote union is to promote truth.
C. H. Spurgeon

That union which is not based on the truth of God is rather a conspiracy than a communion.   *C. H. Spurgeon*

The way to the union of Christendom does not lie through committee-rooms ...

It lies through personal union with the Lord so deep and real as to be comparable with his union with the Father.
William Temple

Unity in Christ is not something to be achieved: it is something to be recognized.   *A. W. Tozer*

Unity without verity is not better than conspiracy.   *John Trapp*

CIRCUMSTANCES

No Christian should feel 'under' the circumstances, because the circumstances are under God.   *John Blanchard*

God doesn't want to keep changing your circumstances; he wants to change you.
J. Sidlow Baxter

Worship God in the difficult circumstances and, when he chooses, he will alter them in two seconds.
Oswald Chambers

The answer to decision-making is not putting the Lord to the test by ascribing arbitrary significance to events in his providence ... God has not authorized us to make oracles of events.
Edmund P. Clowney

Events of all sorts creep and fly exactly as God pleases.   *William Cowper*

Things do not happen in this world — they are brought about.   *Will Hays*

My whole outlook upon everything that happens to me should be governed by these three things: my realization of who I am, my consciousness of where I am going, and my knowledge of what awaits me when I get there.
D. Martyn Lloyd-Jones

All things harden the wicked for hell and ripen the godly for heaven.
Daniel Rowland

CLEANSING — See Forgiveness by God

CLOTHING

Clothes are the ensigns of our sin and covers of our shame. To be proud of them is as great a folly as for a beggar to be proud of his rags or a thief of his halter.
John Trapp

As to matters of dress, I would recommend one never to be first in the fashion not last out of it.
John Wesley

COMMITMENT — See Abandonment; Consecration; Submission; Zeal

COMMON GRACE — See Grace — Common Grace

COMMUNION WITH CHRIST
(See also: Communion with God; Love for Christ; Meditation; Prayer)

Let us use the world but enjoy the Lord.
Thomas Adams

Attachment to Christ is the secret of detachment from the world.
Anon.

To be much like Christ, be much with Christ.
Anon.

My soul's cry is still for more acquaintance with the Lord Jesus, and the Father in him.
Andrew Bonar

The more any man loves Christ, the more he delights to be with Christ alone. Lovers love to be alone.
Thomas Brooks

Holiness is not a merit by which we can attain communion with God, but a gift of Christ, which enables us to cling to him and to follow him.
John Calvin

No one has any communion with Christ but he who has received the true knowledge of him from the word of the gospel.
John Calvin

The power to live a new life depends upon daily communion with the living Lord.
John Eadie

Concentration on Christ is not primarily a matter of the intellect, but rather a matter of the condition of the heart.
Sinclair Ferguson

Union with Christ is the foundation of all our spiritual experience and all our spiritual blessings.
Sinclair Ferguson

A test of Christian devotion is the extent to which, in happiness as well as in sorrow, we think of Jesus.
Frank Gabelein

It is tragic to go through our days making Christ the subject of our study but not the sustenance of our souls.
Vance Havner

Jesus showed to his disciples his hands and his side; he cannot send us into the world unless we are identified with him in his crucifixion.
Vance Havner

The supreme experience is to get past all lesser experiences to Christ himself.
Vance Havner

Unless you live in Christ, you are dead to God.
Rowland Hill

A dungeon with Christ is a throne, and a throne without Christ a hell. *Martin Luther*

Communion with Christ

I thirst for the knowledge of the Word, but most of all for Jesus himself, the true Word.   *Robert Murray M'Cheyne*

It is good to be among the twelve, but it is far better to be among the three.
      Robert Murray M'Cheyne

The more a person is satisfied with Christ, the more he will find his satisfaction in satisfying him.   *J. A. Motyer*

By union with Christ the whole complexion of time and eternity is changed and the people of God may rejoice with joy unspeakable and full of glory.
      John Murray

To please Christ is to live a life in such deep fellowship with him that our walk is characterized by an eagerness to explore his every wish.
      W. Graham Scroggie

Have your heart right with Christ, and he will visit you often, and so turn weekdays into Sundays, meals into sacraments, homes into temples, and earth into heaven.   *C. H. Spurgeon*

In forty years I have not spent fifteen waking minutes without thinking of Jesus.   *C. H. Spurgeon*

Living is sustained by feeding. We must support the spiritual life by spiritual food, and that spiritual food is the Lord Jesus.
      C. H. Spurgeon

There is no cure for lukewarmness like a good supper with Christ. *C. H. Spurgeon*

True communion with Christ is not a mere spasm, not just an excitement of ecstasy.
      C. H. Spurgeon

Union with Christ is a unique emphasis among the world's religions.
      John R. W. Stott

Our task is to live our personal communion with Christ with such intensity as to make it contagious.   *Paul Toumier*

To accept Christ is to know the meaning of the words 'as he is, so are we in this world'. We accept his friends as our friends, his enemies as our enemies, his ways as our ways, his rejection as our rejection, his cross as our cross, his life as our life, and his future as our future.
      A. W. Tozer

COMMUNION WITH GOD
(See also: Communion with Christ; Love for God; Meditation; Prayer)

Everybody who belongs to Jesus belongs to everybody who belongs to Jesus. *Anon.*

God is closest to those whose hearts are broken.   *Anon.*

The life rooted in God cannot be uprooted.   *Anon.*

To walk with God you must walk in the direction in which God goes.   *Anon.*

God finds pleasure in us when we find pleasure in him.   *Augustine*

God is the country of the soul. *Augustine*

The Christian has to live in the world, but he must draw all his resources from outside of the world.
      Donald Grey Barnhouse

The Christian must fight to be alone with God and to keep time for knowing God.
      Donald Grey Barnhouse

Communion with God is the beginning of heaven. *William Bates*

I have more to do with God than with all the world; yea, more and greater business with him in one day than with all the world in all my life. *Richard Baxter*

Our sense of sin is in proportion to our nearness to God. *Thomas D. Bernard*

If you are a failure in your devotional life, you are a phoney in every other part.
John Blanchard

It is impossible to be too preoccupied with God, and it is only as we fill our hearts and minds with him that we become melted out of our likeness and moulded into his. *John Blanchard*

Nothing promotes the activity of the devil more than the Christian's proximity to God. *John Blanchard*

You will never get far for God unless you get far with him. *John Blanchard*

Look into the Fountain, and the very looking will make you thirsty. *Andrew Bonar*

No man who lives near to God lives in vain. *Horatius Bonar*

Our ability to stay with God in our closet measures our ability to stay with God out of the closet. *E. M. Bounds*

To be little with God is to be little for God. *E. M. Bounds*

I would rather walk with God in the dark than go alone in the light.
Mary Gardiner Brainard

A Christian may have as choice communion with God when his eyes are full of tears as he can have when his heart is full of joy. *Thomas Brooks*

Access to God lies open to none but his pure worshippers. *John Calvin*

Man never achieves a clear knowledge of himself until he has *first* looked upon God's face, and then descends from contemplating him to scrutinize himself.
John Calvin

I can afford to lose everything except the touch of God on my life. *Willard Cantelon*

God does not give us power to imitate him; he gives us his very self.
Oswald Chambers

We must learn to spend quality time with God. *Derek Copley*

None reverence the Lord more than they who know him best. *William Cowper*

I count all that part of my life lost which I spent not in communion with God or in doing good. *John Donne*

True grace delights in secret converse with God. *Jonathan Edwards*

Seeking the face of God turns us in a definite direction which cannot be confused with entertainment or superficiality.
Jim Elliff

Only to sit and think of God,
Oh what a joy it is!
To think the thought, to breathe the name
Earth has no higher bliss.
Frederick W. Faber

It is misguided to think that God will revive a people who find no time to commune with him from the heart.
Jim Faucett

How rare it is to find a soul quiet enough to hear God speak!   *François Fenelon*

Fellowship with God means warfare with the world.   *Charles F. Fuller*

Count not that thou hast lived that day in which thou hast not lived with God.
Richard Fuller

We need to sit before God long enough for the sacredness and holiness of his person to overshadow the spirit and mind.
E. F. Hallock

God has no favourites, but he does have intimates.   *Vance Havner*

If our lives and ministry are to count for anything today we must solemnly resolve to make time for God.   *Vance Havner*

One man with a glowing experience of God is worth a library full of arguments.
Vance Havner

The man who lives in God is never out of season.   *Vance Havner*

Though the gracious soul still desires more of God, it never desires more than God.   *Matthew Henry*

To wait on God is to live a life of desire toward him, delight in him, dependence on him, and devotedness to him.
Matthew Henry

We must live a life of communion with God, even while our conversation is with the world.   *Matthew Henry*

Whenever we enter into communion with God it becomes us to have a due sense of the vast distance and disproportion that there are between us and the holy angels, and of the infinite distance, and no proportion at all, between us and the holy God.   *Matthew Henry*

Adequate time for daily waiting on God … is the only way I can escape the tyranny of the urgent.   *Charles Hummel*

If we spend sixteen hours a day dealing with tangible things and only five minutes a day dealing with God, is it any wonder that tangible things are 200 times more real to us than God? *William R. Inge*

Man is at his greatest and highest when, upon his knees, he comes face to face with God.   *D. Martyn Lloyd-Jones*

I am so busy at this present time I cannot do with less than four hours each day in the presence of God.   *Martin Luther*

Most Christians learned at an early age how to talk to God, but they did not learn to listen as well.   *Gordon MacDonald*

Did you ever lose by communion with God? … How quietly we enjoy ourselves when we have enjoyed our God!
Thomas Manton

How can we expect to live with God in heaven if we love not to live with him on earth?   *John Mason*

I ought to spend the best hours of the day in communion with God. It is my noblest and most fruitful employment, and is not to be thrust into any corner.
Robert Murray M'Cheyne

Live near to God and all things will appear little to you in comparison with eternal realities.

Robert Murray M'Cheyne

Oh for closest communion with God, till soul and body – hand, face and heart – shine with divine brilliancy! But oh for a holy ignorance of our shining!

Robert Murray M'Cheyne

Perhaps there are no truths about the Spirit that Christian people more urgently need to learn today than those which relate to the inner life of fellowship with God.

J. I. Packer

We may lay it down as an elemental principle of religion that no large growth in holiness was ever gained by one who did not take time to be often long alone with God.

Austin Phelps

A man in touch with God has access to unimagined divine energies and is able to bend them to earth in blessing to men.

James Philip

In the light of God, human vision clears.

James Philip

Trees which stand on top of a cliff need to send their roots deep.

Ivor Powell

Great eagles fly alone; great lions hunt alone; great souls walk alone — alone with God.

Leonard Ravenhill

No man ever said, at the end of his days, 'I have read my Bible too much, I have thought of God too much, I have prayed too much, I have been too careful with my soul.'

J. C. Ryle

It is not sufficient to commune with the truth, for truth is impersonal. We must commune with the God of truth.

W. G. T. Shedd

My God and I are good company.

Richard Sibbes

Water is not lost when it emptieth itself into the sea, for there it is in its proper element. A Christian is not lost when he loseth himself in his God, in his Saviour.

Richard Sibbes

It is scarcely ever that we can intercede with fervour unless we enjoy habitual nearness to God.

Charles Simeon

Dwell deep in the hidden life of God. The cedar grows more beneath the ground than above it.

A. B. Simpson

There is a pattern to human responses to the presence of God. The more righteous the person, the more he trembles when he enters the immediate presence of God.

R. C. Sproul

If we are weak in communion with God we are weak everywhere.

C. H. Spurgeon

The nearer we come to God, the more graciously will he reveal himself to us.

C. H. Spurgeon

Take away everything I have, but do not take away the sweetness of walking and talking with the King of glory!

John Stam

Communion with God is one thing; familiarity with God is quite another thing.

A. W. Tozer

God being who he is must always be sought for himself, never as a means towards something else.

A. W. Tozer

God has not bowed to our nervous haste nor embraced the methods of our machine age. *The man who would know God must give time to him.*   *A. W. Tozer*

I know that people do not want to be alone with God, but if your longing heart ever finds the living water, it will be alone.
                                A. W. Tozer

In God's presence the Christian feels overwhelmed and undone, yet there is nowhere he would rather be than in that presence.   *A. W. Tozer*

Only engrossment with God can maintain perpetual spiritual enthusiasm, because only God can supply everlasting novelty.   *A. W. Tozer*

The Christian is strong or weak depending upon how closely he has cultivated the knowledge of God.   *A. W. Tozer*

The fellowship of God is delightful beyond all telling.   *A. W. Tozer*

We are called to an everlasting preoccupation with God.   *A. W. Tozer*

We know the intercourse between God and the soul in conscious personal awareness.   *A. W. Tozer*

At the profoundest depths in life, men talk not about God, but with him.
                                D. Elton Trueblood

The more familiar a man becomes with the meeting of God face to face the less likely he is to be deceived as to the gulf which parts him, limited, finite, defective, from the Infinite and Perfect.
                                Newport J. D. White

How much better I might serve God if I had cultivated a closer communion with him!   *William Wilberforce*

Talk with us, Lord, thyself reveal,
While here on earth we rove;
Speak to our hearts, and let us feel
The kindling of thy love.
                                Charles Wesley

COMMUNISM

The only difference between capitalism and Communism is that with capitalism man exploits man, but with Communism the reverse is the case!   *Anon.*

The Communists offer one precious, fatal boon: they take away the sense of sin.   *Murray Kempton*

What does it matter if 90% of the Russian people perish provided the surviving 10% be converted to the Communist faith?   *Lenin*

Everyone must be an atheist. We will never attain our goal until the myth of God has been removed from the thoughts of man.   *Lenin*

Communism is an enemy of God. It attacks and denies him who created heaven and earth.   *Andrew Ben Loo*

The greatest obstacle to evangelism today is the international conspiracy of Communism.   *Andrew Ben Loo*

We oppose Communism not because of politics but primarily because of faith in God, in Christ, in his Word the Bible and in his church.   *Andrew Ben Loo*

Communism is the devil's latest substitute for the Christian concept of the kingdom of God.   *Frederick H. Olert*

Communism levels men down; Christ levels men up.   *Leonard Ravenhill*

Communism is the corruption of a dream of justice.   *Adlai Stevenson*

Communism is the devil's enemy of Christianity.   *A. W. Tozer*

Who ever heard of a Marxist on his death-bed asking for Das Kapital to be read to him …?   *Stephen Travis*

COMPANIONSHIP — See Fellowship; Friendship

COMPASSION
(See also Kindness; Love for Others; Mercy to Others)

Compassion is what makes a person feel pain when somebody else hurts.   *Anon.*

People will not care what you know until they know that you care.   *Anon.*

The Christian should show the same concern for compassion as for creeds.
          John Blanchard

There is no exercise better for the heart than reaching down and lifting people up.
          John Andrew Holmer

As soon as we cease to bleed we cease to bless.   *John Henry Jowett*

Biblical orthodoxy without compassion is surely the ugliest thing in the world.
          Francis Schaeffer

God cares, God is concerned. And since God is concerned his people have an obligation to be concerned too.
          Foy Valentine

COMPLACENCY
(See also: Apathy)

Show me a thoroughly satisfied man and I will show you a failure.   *Anon.*

The fatal blow to progress is self-satis-faction.   *Anon.*

A Christian never falls asleep in the fire or in the water, but grows in the sunshine.
          John Berridge

No Christian should be complacent about his spiritual condition.   *John Blanchard*

He that is too secure is not safe.
          Thomas Fuller

The quickest and shortest way to crush whatever laurels you have won is for you to rest on them.   *Donald P. Jones*

He who accepts evil without protesting against it is really co-operating with it.
          Martin Luther King

When we are best at ease, when all things go with us according to our will and pleas-ure, then we are commonly furthest from God.   *Hugh Latimer*

God's greatest curse out of hell is to allow an unsaved soul to be at peace.
          Brownlow North

The calm which puts us to sleep may be more fatal than a storm which keeps us wide awake.   *William S. Plumer*

A man who is always satisfied with him-self is seldom satisfied with others.
          Francois Rochefoucauld

Complacency is the deadly enemy of spir-itual progress.   *A. W. Tozer*

Complacency

Keep me, Lord, from ever hardening down into the state of being just another average Christian. *A. W. Tozer*

Spiritual complacency is more deadly than anything the devil can bring against us in our upward struggle. *A. W. Tozer*

When I find someone who is settled down too snugly into this world and its system, I am forced to doubt whether he has ever truly been born again. *A. W. Tozer*

COMPLAINING — See Murmuring

COMPROMISE

Please all and you will please none. *Aesop*

People who always bend backwards to please everybody soon weaken their spine. *Anon.*

The middle of the road is where most accidents happen. *Anon.*

Those who follow the crowd are quickly lost in it. *Anon.*

Every lesser good has an essential element of sin. *Augustine*

If you are holding something back from God, then God is holding something back from you. *John Blanchard*

It is impossible to compromise with sin and conquer it at the same time. *John Blanchard*

It is perhaps the greatest sin of the greatest number of Christians that in so many details of life they put God second. *John Blanchard*

We must never settle for harmony at the expense of holiness, nor for peace at the expense of principle. *John Blanchard*

It is not lawful for you to make a compromise with God: to try to fulfil part of your duties, and to omit others at your own pleasure. *John Calvin*

Some people want to be vaccinated with a mild dose of Christianity so as to be protected from the real thing. *William Culbertson*

Lines of least resistance make crooked rivers and crooked men. *William H. Danforth*

Compromise is but the sacrifice of one right or good in the hope of retaining another too often ending in the loss of both. *Tryon Edwards*

Conformity is the ape of harmony. *Ralph Waldo Emerson*

It is madness for sheep to talk peace with a wolf. *Thomas Fuller*

A dog that follows everybody is of no good to anybody. *Vance Havner*

A soft and sheltered Christianity, afraid to be lean and lone, unwilling to face the storms and brave the heights, will end up fat and foul in the cages of conformity. *Vance Havner*

If you try to be everything to everybody, you will end up being nothing to anybody. *Vance Havner*

It is better to die for a conviction than to live with a compromise. *Vance Havner*

The middle of the road is a poor place to walk. It is a poor place to drive. It is a poor place to live. *Vance Havner*

To withhold one thing from God is theft, for everything is his.   *Vance Havner*

We have been accustomed to the sacrifice of the ideal on the altar of the convenient and immediately profitable.
                                          Stuart Holden

Compromise makes a good umbrella but a poor roof; it is a temporary expedient.
                              James Russell Lowell

You cannot play with sin and overcome it at the same time.   *J. C. MacAulay*

We must eternally bid defiance to that peace with men which is inconsistent with peace with God.   *John Owen*

To do what others do when, deep down, one knows it is wrong is moral cowardice, which does not lessen guilt but increases it.   *J. I. Packer*

It is impossible at one and the same time to make earthly and heavenly things the principal subject of your thoughts.
                                             A. W. Pink

He who offers to God a second place offers him no place.   *John Ruskin*

Accommodation leads to accommodation — which leads to accommodation.
                                        Francis Schaeffer

To accommodate to the world spirit about us in our age is nothing less than the most gross form of worldliness in the proper definition of that word. *Francis Schaeffer*

Compromise must always be impossible where the truth is essential and fundamental.   *C. H. Spurgeon*

May God save us from intermittent religion!   *C. H. Spurgeon*

You cannot compromise a proposition with God.   *Billy Sunday*

There is no such cruelty to men's souls as clemency to their sins.
                                        George Swinnock

Anything that takes God's place is out of place.   *Abe Van der Puy*

We can tell when we have been influenced by the world. It is when we find ourselves neither hot nor cold, just compromised.   *Malcolm Watts*

Compromise is like dry rot in the fabric of the Christian church; sooner or later the structure will give way. *Mary S. Wood*

CONCEIT
(See also: Boasting; Egotism; Pride; Vanity)

The smaller the mind the greater the conceit.   *Aesop*

Every man is his own greatest dupe.
                                           W. R. Alger

Conceit makes a little squirt think that he is a fountain of knowledge.   *Anon.*

Confidence is keeping your chin up; over-confidence is sticking your neck out.
                                              Anon.

If you will but totally disregard a conceited man, he will, after a while, be out of breath in blowing his own trumpet.
                                              Anon.

Most self-made men worship their creator.   *Anon.*

Self-conceit is a magnifying glass through which we look at ourselves; we seem much bigger than we are. Plain window glass is better. *Anon.*

The best remedy for conceit is to sit down and make a list of all the things you don't know. *Anon.*

Conceit is the most incurable disease that is known to the human soul.
Henry Ward Beecher

Conceited men are a harmless kind of creature, who, by their overweening self-respect, relieve others from the duty of respecting them at all.
Henry Ward Beecher

Don't think yourself so big that other people look small. *Confucius*

Of all fools the conceited fool is the worst.
William Gurnall

Conceit is vanity driven from all other shifts, and forced to appeal to itself for admiration. *William Hazlitt*

It is wonderful how near conceit is to insanity! *Douglas Jerrold*

He who gives himself airs of importance, exhibits the credentials of impotence.
John C. Lavater

Self-opinion is the bane of all virtue.
Edward Marbury

Ignorance and confidence are often twins.
George Swinnock

He is two fools that is wise in his own eyes. *John Trapp*

CONFESSION
(See also Contrition; Conviction of Sin; Penitence; Repentance

Confessing your sins is no substitute for forsaking them. *Anon.*

Confession of sin puts the soul under the blessing of God. *Anon.*

Confession must be salted with contrition. *Anon.*

Before God can deliver us we must undeceive ourselves. *Augustine*

The confession of evil works is the first beginning of good works. *Augustine*

When man uncovers his sin, God covers it. When man cloaks, God strips bare. When man confesses, God pardons.
Augustine

Acknowledging that one is a sinner is no more conviction of sin than believing the truth about Jesus is saving faith.
John Blanchard

Sins concealed by man are never cancelled by God. *John Blanchard*

Confessing sin is not informing God, it is agreeing with him. *Derek Cleave*

Confession is the first step to repentance.
Edmund Gayton

How easily sin gets into the heart; how hardly it gets out of the mouth.
Joseph Hall

A great part of our worthiness lies in an acknowledgement of our own unworthiness. *Matthew Henry*

Little credit is to be given to confessions upon the rack. *Matthew Henry*

For him who confesses, shams are over and realities have begun. *William James*

The recognition of sin is the beginning of salvation. *Martin Luther*

Wounds cannot be healed until they are revealed and sins cannot be forgiven until they are confessed. *Martin Luther*

Confession is, as it were, the vomit of the soul. *Thomas Manton*

Never suffer sin to remain upon you; let it not grow old in you; wipe it off while it is fresh, else it will stain; let it not eat its way in and rust in you.
John Henry Newman

The time lag between the moment of sinning and the moment of forsaking and confessing is a sure indication of the true nature of a man's walk with God.
Alan Redpath

We confess small faults in order to insure that we have no great ones.
Francis Rochefoucauld

Many blush to confess their faults who never blush to commit them.
William Secker

Confession is verbal humiliation.
Richard Sibbes

The way to cover our sin is to uncover it by confession. *Richard Sibbes*

You can pray till doomsday for revival, but you will never get it without repentance and confession of sin in the Christian life. *Erlo Stegan*

Do not give fair names to foul sins. Call them what you will, they will smell no sweeter. *C. H. Spurgeon*

It does not spoil your happiness to confess your sin. The unhappiness is in not making the confession. *C. H. Spurgeon*

Confessing of our faults is the next thing to innocence. *Publilius Syrus*

CONFIDENCE — See Assurance

CONFLICT — See Spiritual Warfare

CONFORMITY — See Compromise

CONSCIENCE — and the Bible

My conscience is captive to the Word of God. *Martin Luther*

Order my footsteps by thy Word.
And make my heart sincere;
Let sin have no dominion, Lord,
But keep my conscience clear.
Isaac Watts

If conscience is to be directed by the Spirit of God it must be governed by the Word of God. *Mary S. Wood*

CONSCIENCE — and God

Conscience is God's deputy, God's spy, God's notary, God's viceroy.
Thomas Brooks

Conscience is God's preacher in the bosom. *Thomas Brooks*

Man's conscience is the oracle of God.
George G. N. Byron

Distinction between virtuous and vicious actions has been engraven by the Lord on the heart of every man. *John Calvin*

If there were no God, consciences were useless. *John Calvin*

I have been a man of great sins, but he has been a God of great mercies, and now, through his mercies, I have a conscience as sound and quiet as if I had never sinned. *Donald Cargill*

Conscience is God's deputy, and must in the exercise of this office confine itself to the orders and instructions of the sovereign Lord. *D. Clarkson*

Conscience, which is the voice of God, is higher than all the voices of men. *J. H. Merle d'Aubigne*

When men turn their back on God's revelation in Scripture he still sets the truth of it in their hearts. *Michael Green*

Conscience is God's sergeant. He employs it to arrest the sinner. *William Gurnall*

Nothing can take off conscience from accusing but that which takes off God from threatening. *William Gurnall*

A Christian's enlightened conscience is his sense of obligation to God. *William Hendriksen*

Conscience is that candle of the Lord which was not quite put out. *Matthew Henry*

There is a conscience in man, therefore there is a God in heaven. *Ezekiel Hopkins*

Two things strike me with awe: the starry heavens above and the moral law within. *Immanuel Kant*

Conscience holds us accountable to God. Drop the idea of God and the vitality of conscience is destroyed. Mere abstract ideas of 'right' and 'wrong' do not bind the conscience; the idea of God and judgement does. *R. C. H. Lenski*

Every conscience is primed by God. He embosses upon our human nature an awareness of his standards. *Peter Masters*

Whether trained in moral or religious values or not, all people have God's moral code written within them, and no technique on earth can totally delete or change it. *Peter Masters*

Conscience hath somewhat divine in it. *Richard Sibbes*

Conscience is God's vicar. *Richard Sibbes*

Conscience is a mirror of God's holiness. *Augustus H. Strong*

Conscience is not an original authority. It points to something higher than itself. *Augustus H. Strong*

Conscience is the deputy-deity in the little world man. *George Swinnock*

Conscience is God's spy and man's overseer. *John Trapp*

Conscience, the domestic chaplain. *John Trapp*

If there were no Bible to tell us there is a God, yet conscience might. *Thomas Watson*

We never do anything so secretly but that it is in the presence of two witnesses: God and our own conscience. *Benjamin Whichcote*

CONSCIENCE — Importance

Conscience is to the soul as the stomach is to the body. *Thomas Adams*

Knowledge directs conscience; conscience perfects knowledge.
Thomas Adams

The glory of good men is in their conscience, and not in the mouths of men.
Thomas à Kempis

The testimony of a good conscience is the glory of a good man.
Thomas à Kempis

A good conscience is a soft pillow. *Anon.*

A quiet conscience sleeps in thunder.
Anon.

Conscience warns us as a friend before it punishes us as a judge. *Anon.*

The best tranquillizer is a clear conscience. *Anon.*

When a man says he has a clear conscience it often means he has a bad memory. *Anon.*

When a man won't listen to his conscience, it may be because he doesn't want advice from a total stranger. *Anon.*

When you have only one thing on your conscience, it is probably a silencer.
Anon.

Conscience is a man's judgement of himself, according to the judgement of God of him. *Thomas Aquinas*

A good conscience is the palace of Christ, the temple of the Holy Ghost, the paradise of delight, the standing Sabbath of the saints. *Augustine*

A good conscience is the inseparable attendant of faith. *John Calvin*

A happy life depends on a good conscience. *John Calvin*

Conscience is the root of all true courage; if a man would be brave let him obey his conscience. *J. F Clarke*

Religion's home is in the conscience.
T L. Cuyler

Of all human experiences, the most universal is a bad conscience. *James Denney*

A quiet conscience never produced an unquiet conversation. *John Flavel*

A good conscience is the best divinity.
Thomas Fuller

Conscience is the moral consciousness that an action is or is not in accord with moral judgement. *John H. Gerstner*

Most of us follow our conscience as we follow a wheelbarrow; we push it in front of us in the direction we want to go.
Billy Graham

Better to have a dog that will, by his barking, tell us a thief is in our yard, than one that will sit still and let us be robbed before we have any notice of our danger.
William Gurnall

If faith be a jewel, a good conscience is the cabinet in which it is kept.
William Gurnall

Peace of conscience is but a discharge under God's hand that the debt due to

divine justice is fully paid.
William Gurnall

Peace of conscience is nothing but the echo of pardoning mercy.
William Gurnall

The pen with which conscience writes down our sins hath a sharp nib.
William Gurnall

Happy is that man who can be acquitted by himself in private, by others in public and by God in both. *Joseph Hall*

A dull conscience leads only to halfway reconciliations with God. *Ole Hallesby*

Conscience is a living thing, subject to growth and development. *Ole Hallesby*

If we take care to keep a good conscience, we may leave it to God to take care of our good name. *Matthew Henry*

Never was the voice of conscience silenced without retribution.
Anna Jameson

Cleanse your conscience and your faith will be out of danger. *William Jenkyn*

That man can never have good days that keeps an evil conscience.
Benjamin Keach

All men stand condemned, not by alien codes of ethics, but by their own, and all men therefore are conscious of guilt.
C. S. Lewis

Disobedience to conscience makes conscience ...The moral blindness consequent on being a bad man must therefore fall on everyone who is not a good man.
C. S. Lewis

Money dishonestly acquired is never worth its cost, while a good conscience never costs as much as it is worth.
S. P. Senn

My prison shall be my grave before I will budge a jot, for I owe my conscience to no mortal man. Right is right, even if everyone is against it; and wrong is wrong, even if everyone is for it. *William Penn*

Conscience is the rudder of the ship of faith. *James Philip*

Faith is strong only when the conscience is clear and the heart is pure. *James Philip*

A good conscience is the best treasure ever held, the best pleasure ever tasted, the best honour ever conferred.
William S. Plumer

Cowardice asks, 'Is it safe?' Expediency asks, 'Is it politic?' Vanity asks, 'Is it popular?' Conscience asks, 'Is it *right?*'
William Morley Punshon

We can do nothing well without joy, and a good conscience, which is the ground of joy. *Richard Sibbes*

No man's conscience is to be a judge for another. *C. H. Spurgeon*

Before our conscience punishes us as a judge, it warns us as a friend. *Stanislus*

Trust that man in nothing who has not a conscience in everything.
Lawrence Sterne

A scar on the conscience is the same as a wound. *Publilius Syrus*

Even when there is no law, there is conscience. *Publilius Syrus*

Conscience is that inner voice that keeps speaking within our beings — and it deserves something better from us than wisecracks and humour.   *A. W. Tozer*

A good conscience and a good name is like a gold ring set with a rich diamond.
Thomas Watson

A good conscience can sleep in the mouth of a cannon.   *Thomas Watson*

No flattery can heal a bad conscience, so no slander can hurt a good one.
Thomas Watson

Preserve your conscience always soft and sensitive. If but one sin force its way into that tender part of the soul and is suffered to dwell there, the road is paved for a thousand iniquities.   *Isaac Watts*

A conscience void of offence before God and man is an inheritance for eternity.
Daniel Webster

A pure conscience is the home of faith.
A. Paget Wilkes

Even if different people's consciences tell them to do or avoid doing different things, everyone accepts the moral absolute, 'Never disobey your conscience.'
Peter S. Williams

CONSCIENCE — Power

A good conscience is to the soul what health is to the body; it preserves a constant ease and serenity within us.
Joseph Addison

A guilty conscience is like a whirlpool, drawing in all to itself which would otherwise pass by.   *Thomas Fuller*

A wounded conscience is able to un paradise paradise itself.   *Thomas Fuller*

The only tyrant I accept in this world is the still voice within. *Mahatma Gandhi*

Faith and good conscience are hope's two wings.   *William Gurnall*

A evil conscience is like a raging sea, which can only be calmed by the sign of the cross of Christ. It is a gnawing worm in the bones, for the removal of which nothing less is required than the blood of the Son of God. *Friedrich Krummacher*

Conscience is the still small voice that makes you feel still smaller.
James A. Sanaker

A gnawing conscience keeps the memory terribly alert.   *W. E. Sangster*

Our consciences tell us that we might have done a great deal better than we have.   *Richard Sibbes*

I would bear any affliction rather than be burdened with a guilty conscience.
C. H. Spurgeon

An uneasy conscience is a hair on the mouth.   *Mark Twain*

CONSCIENCE — and Sin

A guilty conscience is a hell on earth, and points to one beyond.   *Anon.*

A guilty conscience needs no accuser.
Anon.

Quite often when a man thinks his mind is getting broader it is only his conscience stretching.   *Anon.*

Conscience — and Sin

A seared conscience is the sinner's heritage.   *Horatius Bonar*

What we call conscience is, in many instances, only a wholesome fear of the constable.   *Christian Bovee*

Neglect of duty will never get guilt off the conscience.   *Thomas Brooks*

The torture of a bad conscience is the hell of a living soul.   *John Calvin*

There is no greater torment than an evil conscience.   *John Calvin*

Conscience alone has witnessed sufficiently to the moral law, so that every man is 'without excuse'.   *Walter J. Chantry*

An evil conscience is the devil's anvil, on which he fabricates all those swords and spears on which the guilty sinner pierces and wounds himself. *John Flavel*

The greatest violation of conscience is the greatest of sins.   *John Flavel*

No torment in the world is comparable to an accusing conscience.
William Gurnall

We must never be overawed either by majesty or multitude to do a sinful thing and go against our consciences.
Matthew Henry

The most painful wound in the world is a stab of conscience.   *John Ellis Large*

All the floods of sin can never distinguish God's love to his people; but one single drop of sin upon the believer's conscience will distinguish his peace.
William Mason

Our consciences take no account of the Fall.   *Donald MacLeod*

Nothing can give perfect peace of conscience with God but what can make atonement for sin. And whoever attempt it in any other way but by virtue of that atonement will never attain it, in this world or hereafter.   *John Owen*

Many a man has enough conscience to scare him in sin, but not enough to save him from sin.   *C. H. Spurgeon*

Never, on any account whatever, let us do that which our conscience cannot justify.   *C. H. Spurgeon*

This side of hell, what can be worse than the tortures of an awakened conscience?
C. H. Spurgeon

Though consciences have to be educated, they are never to be violated, even when they are wrong.   *John R. W. Stott*

Some serve their consciences as David did Uriah; make it drunk that they may be rid of it.   *George Swinnock*

An evil conscience is often quiet, but never secure.   *Publilius Syrus*

Conscience never lets you lean on someone else.   *A. W. Tozer*

One small drop of an evil conscience troubles a whole sea of outward comforts.
John Trapp

Sin makes sad convulsions in the conscience.   *Thomas Watson*

CONSECRATION

(See also: Abandonment; Submission; Zeal)

Consecration is resolution that is not afraid of sacrifice. *Anon.*

To my God, a heart of flame; to my fellow men, a heart of love; to myself, a heart of steel. *Augustine*

Henceforth may no profane delight
Divide this consecrated soul;
Possess it thou, who hast the right,
As Lord and Master of the whole.
Antoinette Bourignon

The child of God has only one dread — to offend his Father; only one desire — to please and delight in him.
Charles Bridges

It does not take great men to do great things; it only takes consecrated men.
Phillips Brooks

Rid me, good Lord, of every diverting thing. *Amy Carmichael*

Consecration is not so much a step as a course, not so much an act as a position to which a course of action inseparably belongs. *Frances Ridley Havergal*

God wants self before substance and service. *Vance Havner*

If religion be worth anything it is worth everything. *Matthew Henry*

Consecration isn't our giving anything to God. It is our taking our hands off what already belongs to God. *Walter B. Knight*

Consecration is handing God a blank sheet to fill in with your name signed at the bottom. *M. H. Miller*

The body has two eyes, but the soul must have but one. *William Secker*

Whatever the cost in rearrangement, including bravely coming to terms with loved ones, friends, not to say pursuits, pleasures and indulgences, you must turn to the Lord and give yourself afresh to him. *William Still*

CONSISTENCY — See Faithfulness

CONTEMPT

Contempt leaves a deeper scar than anger. *Anon.*

Christ saw much in this world to weep over, and much to pray over, but he saw nothing in it to look upon with contempt.
E. H. Chaplin

CONTENTMENT

A contented mind is a continual feast.
Anon.

Contentment is an inexhaustible treasure.
Anon.

Let your riches consist, not in the largeness of your possessions, but in the fewness of your wants. *Anon.*

A contented spirit is a fruit of divine grace.
George Barlow

The Christian is called upon to make his material possessions immaterial.
John Blanchard

Contentment with what we have is absolutely vital to our spiritual health.
Jerry Bridges

To be content with one's possessions is

one of the most strongly worded exhortations in Scripture.   *Jerry Bridges*

It is the best riches not to desire riches.
Thomas Brooks

If we have not quiet in our minds, outward comfort will do no more for us than a golden slipper on a gouty foot.
John Bunyan

The contented man is never poor, the discontented never rich.   *George Eliot*

I am always content with what happens, for what God chooses is better than what I choose.   *Epictetus*

Content makes poor men rich; discontent makes rich men poor. *Benjamin Franklin*

Better a little fire to warm us than a great one to burn us.   *Thomas Fuller*

Contentment consisteth not in adding more fuel, but in taking away some fire; not in multiplying of wealth, but in subtracting men's desires. *Thomas Fuller*

The holy person is the only contented man in the world.   *William Gurnall*

A mind at leisure from itself beats all rest cures.   *Vance Havner*

He is much happier that is always content, though he has ever so little, than he that is always coveting, though he has ever so much.   *Matthew Henry*

That condition of life is best for every man which is best for his soul, and keeps him most clear of the cares and snares of the world.   *Matthew Henry*

He who desires nothing will always be free.   *Edouard Laboulaye*

Be content with what you have, but never with what you are.   *W. B. Millard*

The only person in this world who enjoys complete contentment is the person who knows that the only worthwhile and satisfying life is to be a means, however humble, to God's chief end his own glory and praise.   *J. I. Packer*

Contentment is an embracing of the providence of God.   *George Seevers*

Contentment is natural wealth; luxury is artificial poverty.   *Socrates*

The wealthiest man is he who is contented with least.   *Socrates*

If you are not content with what you have, you would not be satisfied if it were doubled.   *C. H. Spurgeon*

No chance is evil to him that is content.
Jeremy Taylor

The more we count the blessings we have, the less we crave the luxuries we haven't.
William A. Ward

There is no better antidote against coveting that which is another's than being content with that which is our own.
Thomas Watson

The fewer desires, the more peace.
Joseph Wilson

CONTRITION
(See also: Confession; Conviction of Sin; Penitence; Repentance)

God can do wonders with a broken heart if you give him all the pieces.
Victor Alfsen

The only things that are improved by breaking are the hearts of sinners. *Anon.*

Sorrow for sin as long as you have sin to sorrow for. *Anon.*

There is no progress possible to the man who does not see and mourn over his defects. *George Barlow*

Godly sorrow is a gift from God. No hand but a divine hand can make the heart soft and tender under the sight and sense of sin. *Thomas Brooks*

Remorse is the pain of sin. *Theodore Parker*

Sorrow for sin should be the keenest sorrow; joy in the Lord should be the loftiest joy. *C. H. Spurgeon*

The best rubics of worship are those which are written on broken hearts. *C. H. Spurgeon*

We can stand before the cross only with a bowed head and a broken spirit. *John R. W. Stott*

He grieves truly that mourns without a witness. *George Swinnock*

The broken heart is the only sound heart. *John Trapp*

CONTROVERSY

The devil falls in when saints fall out. *Anon.*

Some arguments are sound — and nothing more. *Richard Armour*

There are some controversies prickly like brambles, and apt to scratch those that handle them, but yielding no savoury or wholesome fruit. *Isaac Barrow*

Never encourage any degrees of heat without light. *David Brainerd*

Dissolution is the daughter of dissension. *Thomas Brooks*

Christianity cannot flourish in a time of strife and contention among its professors. *Jonathan Edwards*

Religious contention is the devil's harvest. *Charles Fontaine*

Hot heads and cold hearts never solved anything. *Billy Graham*

The worst thing we can bring to a religious controversy is anger. *Matthew Henry*

Our divisions should never be discussed except in the presence of those who have already come to believe that there is one God and that Jesus Christ is his only Son. *C. S. Lewis*

Division has done more to hide Christ from the view of men than all the infidelity that has ever been spoken. *George Macdonald*

The itch of disputing and zeal for an opinion, rather than religion in the main, are bad characters. *Thomas Manton*

I have never yet known the Spirit of God to work where the Lord's people were divided. *D. L. Moody*

The devil's master stroke is that of dividing forces that ought to stand together. *G. Campbell Morgan*

Controversy

Controversy is a serious thing. All those who enter upon it are in great need of more grace. *Iain H. Murray*

Truth often suffers more by the heat of its defenders than by the arguments of its opposers. *William Penn*

I have other things to do than to be a contentious man. *John Penry*

Five minutes before I die it will not matter one whit to me who won the last argument. I will have other things of far greater importance on my mind. *Frank Retief*

One of the marks of a mature person is the ability to dissent without creating dissension. *Don Robinson*

Nothing does so much harm to the cause of religion as the quarrels of Christians. *J. C. Ryle*

Beware of the habits we learn in controversy. *Francis Schaeffer*

Fractions always breed factions. *Richard Sibbes*

Contention is sooner stirred than stinted. *John Trapp*

The devil loves to fish in troubled waters. *John Trapp*

It is not controversy we have to dread so much as the spirit of controversy. *Richard Treffry*

Divisions are Satan's powder-plot, to blow up religion. *Thomas Watson*

That religion is suspicious which is full of faction and discord. *Thomas Watson*

The gospel seldom thrives where the apple of strife grows. *Thomas Watson*

CONVERSION
(See also: Faith — Saving; Regeneration; Repentance)

It is a sign of true conversion when a man's heart is melted to love God's eternal law and when his will is bent to obey it. *Richard Alderson*

Conversion is a deep work — a heart-work. It goes throughout the man, throughout the mind, throughout the members, throughout the entire life. *Joseph Alleine*

Conversion is no repairing of the old building; but it takes all down and erects a new structure. *Joseph Alleine*

Nature forms us; sin deforms us; school informs us; Christ transforms us. *Anon.*

Man is not converted because he wills to be, but he wills to be because he is ordained to election. *Augustine*

God does not convert men without design; and his designs are not new, but are eternal. *Albert Barnes*

If a person claims to be converted, we are entitled to ask two questions: 'From what?' and 'Into what?' *John Blanchard*

I remember this, that everything looked new to me... the fields, the cattle, the trees. I was like a new man in a new world. *Billy Bray*

Conversion is not the smooth, easy-going process some men seem to think it otherwise man's heart would never have been compared to fallow ground and God's Word to a plough. *John Bunyan*

Conversion cannot be separated from prayer.   *John Calvin*

In the conversion of man, the properties of our original nature remain entire.
                     John Calvin

Men by their own free will cannot turn to God until he first change their stony hearts into hearts of flesh. *John Calvin*

True conversion is proved by the constant tenor of the life.   *John Calvin*

Regeneration is a spiritual change; conversion is a spiritual motion.
                     Stephen Charnock

If Christ's lordship does not disrupt our own lordship, then the reality of our conversion must be questioned.
                     Charles Colson

Conversion is but the first step in the divine life. As long as we live we should more and more be turning from all that is evil and to all that is good. *Tryon Edwards*

Conversion is an empty-handed turning from sin to the Saviour.   *Vance Havner*

It takes a radical break to turn from earth's trash to heaven's treasure. *Vance Havner*

Consideration is the first step towards conversion.   *Matthew Henry*

If no conversion, no salvation.
                     Matthew Henry

Regeneration is a single act, complete in itself, and never repeated; conversion, as the beginning of holy living, is the commencement of a series, constant, endless and progressive.   *A. A. Hodge*

The almighty power of God in the conversion of a sinner is the most mysterious of all the works of God.
                     Thomas Hooker

If a man is as passionate, malicious, resentful, sullen, moody or morose after his conversion as before it, what is he converted from or to? *John Angell James*

Conversion requires an alteration of the will, and an alteration which, in the last resort, does not occur without the intervention of the supernatural. *C. S. Lewis*

Every conversion is the story of a blessed defeat.   *C. S. Lewis*

Unless God changes a person's heart, nothing lasting will be achieved.
                     Will Metzger

We must not make the mistake of thinking that people are converted because they follow our line of reasoning as we explain the gospel.   *Will Metzger*

Whenever a profession of conversion is not accompanied by holiness of life it must be understood that the person concerned is not yet a Christian.
                     Iain H. Murray

Conversions need to be weighed as well as counted.   *Joseph Parker*

True conversion is the heart turning from Satan's control to God's, from sin to holiness, from the world to Christ. *A. W. Pink*

I found that I was not only converted, but I was invaded.   *Eugenia Price*

The surest mark of true conversion is humility.   *J. C. Ryle*

Conversion

Conversion is the standing miracle of the church.   *C. H. Spurgeon*

True conversion gives a man security, but it does not allow him to leave off being watchful.   *C. H. Spurgeon*

True conversion gives a man strength and holiness, but it never lets him boast.
C. H. Spurgeon

When the Word of God converts a man, it takes away from him his despair, but it does not take from him his repentance.
C. H. Spurgeon

When Christ came into my life I came about like a well-handled ship.
Robert Louis Stevenson

We are not truly converted if we are not intellectually and morally converted, and we are not intellectually and morally converted if we have not subjected our minds and our wills to the yoke of Jesus Christ.
John R. W. Stott

Conversion for the early New Testament Christians was not a destination; it was the beginning of a journey.   *A. W. Tozer*

The change of a sinner's heart is as great a miracle as any Jesus Christ wrought on earth.   *Joseph Wilson*

Before Christ, a man loves things and uses people; after Christ he loves people and uses things.   *Horace Wood*

CONVICTION — See Assurance

CONVICTION OF SIN
(See also: Confession; Contrition; Penitence; Repentance)

Conviction is not repentance. It is one thing to be awakened at five o'clock in the morning, but it is another thing to get up.   *Anon.*

It is a universal law of the higher life that the better a man becomes, the more sensitive he is to sin.   *Anon.*

The worst sinners are sometimes those who feel the least sinful.   *Anon.*

Nobody has ever been convicted of his sinfulness until he has been confronted with the living Lord in his holiness.
Rolfe Barnard

As the heart is more washed, we grow more sensible of its remaining defilement; just as we are more displeased with a single spot on a new coat than with a hundred stains on an old one.
John Berridge

The greater our view of Christ, the greater our view of sin.   *John Blanchard*

No man begins to be good till he sees himself to be bad.   *Thomas Brooks*

The flesh cannot endure the doctrine of the gospel; none can endure to have their vices reproved.   *John Calvin*

There is precious instruction to be got by finding we were wrong. *Thomas Carlyle*

Measure your growth in grace by your sensitiveness to sin. *Oswald Chambers*

Our salvation begins when we condemn ourselves.   *Didymus*

The greater the saint, the greater the sense of sinfulness.   *G. B. Duncan*

116

The conviction that causes men to think it worth the while to seek salvation is hardly ever a conviction of the worth of the reward, but of the dreadfulness of the punishment.   *Jonathan Edwards*

No man can ever enter heaven until he is first convinced he deserves hell.
                              John W. Everett

Grace often grows strongest where conviction of sin has pierced deepest.
                              Sinclair Ferguson

The deepest levels of conviction may be experienced after rather than before conversion.   *Sinclair Ferguson*

Those who are most conscious of forgiveness are invariably those who have been most acutely convicted of their sin.
                              Sinclair Ferguson

Christ is not sweet till sin is made bitter to us.   *John Flavel*

Conviction of sin is conviction of sinnership ... it is a conviction of a wrong relationship with God, of falling completely short of what man is meant to be.
                              Bryan Green

Men must see sin to be sin and themselves to be sinners before they will want a Saviour.   *Vance Havner*

Who was the guilty? Who brought this
   upon thee?
Alas, my treason, Lord Jesus, hath
   undone thee.
'Twas I, Lord Jesus, I it was denied thee;
I crucified thee!
                              Johann Heermann

Christ will be sweet to us if sin be bitter.
                              Matthew Henry

When men begin to complain more of their sins than of their afflictions then there begins to be some hope of them.
                              Matthew Henry

If faith without works is dead, then conviction without action is worthless.
                              Jay Hudson

The sorest injury we can do to any man is to lighten his conception of the enormity of sin.   *John Henry Jowett*

Conviction of sin is an indispensable pre-requisite of faith in Christ.
                              R. B. Kuiper

When one is born of the Spirit one does not suddenly become perfect or even nearly so. Rather, one becomes exceedingly sinful in one's own estimation. That is to say, one comes under conviction of sin.   *R. B. Kuiper*

A man only comes to Christ when he is desperate.   *D. Martyn Lloyd-Jones*

The first sign of spiritual life is to feel that you are dead! *D. Martyn Lloyd-Jones*

A man must completely despair of himself in order to become fit to obtain the grace of Christ.   *Martin Luther*

I have no other name than sinner; sinner is my name, sinner is my surname.
                              Martin Luther

Rightly to feel sin is the torture of all tortures.   *Martin Luther*

The recognition of sin is the beginning of salvation.   *Martin Luther*

The consciousness of sin alone leads men to turn to the Saviour from sin, and the consciousness of sin comes only when men are brought face to face with the law of God. *J. Gresham Machen*

The real prelude to a conviction of sin is the conviction of God's holiness.
Douglas Macmillan

You cannot command convictions of sin to come when you like.
Robert Murray M'Cheyne

A full conviction of sin is a great and shaking surprisal unto a guilty soul.
John Owen

Until men know themselves better, they will care very little to know Christ at all.
John Owen

A sense of defilement before God is not morbid, neurotic or unhealthy in any way. It is natural, realistic, healthy, and a true perception of our condition. *J. I. Packer*

Conviction of sin is essentially an awareness of a wrong relationship with God.
J. I. Packer

A right knowledge of the way to heaven is to feel that we are on the way to hell.
J. C. Ryle

The beginning of the way to heaven is to feel that we are on the way to hell.
J. C. Ryle

To be sensible of our corruption and abhor our own transgressions is the first symptom of spiritual health. *J. C. Ryle*

We must know the depth and malignancy of our disease in order to appreciate the Great Physician. *J. C. Ryle*

The very first and indispensable sign of

regeneration is self-loathing and abhorrence. *Charles Simeon*

If you can look on sin without sorrow then you have never looked on Christ.
C. H. Spurgeon

Only let a man once feel sin for half an hour, really feel its tortures, and I warrant you he would prefer to dwell in a pit of snakes than to live with his sins.
C. H. Spurgeon

Whenever you think about your own conversion, regard it as a miracle.
C. H. Spurgeon

The only way to arrive at faith in the Holy Spirit is along the road of self-despair.
John R. W. Stott

They tell me I rub the fur the wrong way. I don't. Let the cat turn around!
Billy Sunday

In review of God's manifold blessings, the thing I most seem to thank him for is the conviction of sin. *Friedrich Tholuck*

Until a man has got into trouble with his heart he is not likely to get out of trouble with God. *A. W. Tozer*

No man shall be in heaven but he that sees himself fully qualified for hell, as a faggot that is bound up for eternal burnings unless mercy plucks the brand out of the fire. *Robert Traill*

It is part of our worthiness to see our unworthiness. *Thomas Watson*

No man can feel sin, but by grace.
Thomas Watson

Sin must have tears. *Thomas Watson*

To mourn only for fear of hell is like a thief that weeps for the penalty rather than the offence. *Thomas Watson*

A sense of spiritual poverty is a blessing when it leads the humble soul to God. *Edwin T. Winkler*

CONVICTIONS

A belief is what you hold; a conviction is what holds you. *Anon.*

A conviction is not truly a conviction unless it includes a commitment to live by what we claim to believe. *Jerry Bridges*

You can have such an open mind that it is too porous to hold a conviction. *George Crane*

Beware lest we mistake our prejudices for our convictions. *Harry A. Ironside*

A dogmatic belief in objective value is necessary to the very idea of a rule which is not tyranny or an obedience which is not slavery. *C. S. Lewis*

You never know how much you really believe anything until its truth or falsehood becomes a matter of life and death to you. *C. S. Lewis*

Great saints have always been dogmatic. We need a return to a gentle dogmatism that smiles while it stands stubborn and firm on the Word of God. *A. W. Tozer*

Convictions are the root on which the tree of vital Christianity grows. *Benjamin B. Warfield*

COURAGE

Bravery is not the absence of fear, but the mastery of it. *Anon.*

Courage is fear that has said its prayers. *Anon.*

The scars you acquire by exercising courage will never make you feel inferior. *O. A. Battista*

Show when you are tempted to hide, and hide when you are tempted to show. *A. R. Bruce*

There can be no courage in men unless God supports them by his Word. *John Calvin*

A man without courage is a knife without an edge. *Benjamin Franklin*

Courage is absolutely necessary for goodness. *Richard Glover*

One man with courage makes a majority. *Andrew Jackson*

I fear not the tyranny of man, neither yet what the devil can invent against me. *John Knox*

Only he who can say, 'The Lord is the strength of my life' can say, 'Of whom shall I be afraid?' *Alexander MacLaren*

Take courage. We walk in the wilderness today and in the Promised Land tomorrow. *D. L Moody*

Courage consists not in hazarding without fear, but being resolutely minded in a just cause. *Plutarch*

Perfect courage consists in doing without a witness all that we should be capable of doing before the whole world.
Francois Rochefoucauld

Courage is the mastery of fear, not the absence of fear. *Mark Twain*

COURTESY

Courtesy is a Christian duty, fully consistent with the exercise of Christian faithfulness. *Charles Bridges*

Life is short, but there is always time for courtesy. *Ralph Waldo Emerson*

All doors open to courtesy. *Thomas Fuller*

Politeness is like an air cushion; there may be nothing in it, but it eases our jolts wonderfully. *Samuel Johnson*

If you will be cherished when you are old, be courteous while you are young.
John Lyly

Sanctity is no enemy to courtesy.
John Trapp

Nothing is ever lost by courtesy. It is the cheapest of the pleasures; costs nothing and conveys much. *Erastus Wiman*

COVENANT

Every breach of peace with God is not a breach of covenant with God.
Thomas Brooks

The covenant of grace is the saint's original title to heaven. *Thomas Brooks*

The whole covenant is a bundle of promises. *Thomas Brooks*

The covenant is an expression of God's will, not man's, and man must listen to its terms, trust God that they are holy and just and good, and order his life accordingly. *J. Gresham Machen*

As we are under the covenant of grace, we are secured against departing from the living God by the sure declaration of the covenant. *C. H. Spurgeon*

Faith always sees the bow of covenant promise whenever sense sees the cloud of affliction. *C. H. Spurgeon*

The covenant is a rocky foundation to build on for life or for death.
C. H. Spurgeon

The bond of the covenant is able to bear the weight of the believer's heaviest burden. *William S. Plummer*

COVETOUSNESS
(See also: Gluttony; Greed)

Wealth is the devil's stirrup whereby he gets up and rides the covetous.
Thomas Adams

He who covets is poor, notwithstanding all he may have acquired. *Ambrose*

Charity gives itself rich; covetousness hoards itself poor. *Anon.*

Gold is the heaviest of all metals, but it is made more heavy by covetousness. *Anon.*

Much trouble is caused by our yearnings getting ahead of our earnings. *Anon.*

Seeking empties a life; giving fills it.
Anon.

Covetousness is a sin that comes earliest into the human heart, and is the last and most difficult to be driven out.
George Barlow

Covetousness makes us the slaves of the devil. *John Calvin*

Faith is the sovereign antidote to covetousness. *John Calvin*

Covetousness is the blight that is withering our church life in all directions.
Samuel Chadwick

When all sins are old in us and go upon crutches, covetousness does but then lie in her cradle. *Thomas Decker*

Riches have made more covetous men than covetousness has made rich men.
Thomas Fuller

Covetousness is commonly a master-sin and has the command of other lusts.
Matthew Henry

Covetousness is spiritual idolatry; it is the giving of that love and regard to worldly wealth which are due to God only.
Matthew Henry

He is much happier that is always content, though he has ever so little, than he that is always coveting, though he has ever so much. *Matthew Henry*

Poor people are as much in danger from an inordinate desire towards the wealth of the world as rich people from an inordinate delight in it. *Matthew Henry*

The covetous man sits hatching upon his wealth and brooding over it, till it is fledged, as the young ones under the hen, and then it is gone. *Matthew Henry*

Covetousness swallows down any lie.
William Jenkyn

The soul of man is infinite in what it covets. *Ben Jonson*

Beware ... of the beginnings of covetousness, for you know not where it will end.
Thomas Manton

There are two sins which were Christ's sorest enemies, covetousness and envy. Covetousness sold Christ and envy delivered him. *Thomas Manton*

Coveting is something we do with our hearts, not our hands or feet. *Will Metzger*

We may love money without having it, just as we may have money without loving it. *J. C. Ryle*

One can be covetous when he has little, much, or anything between, for covetousness comes from the heart, not from the circumstances of life.
Charles Caldwell Ryrie

Covetousness is both the beginning and the end of the devil's alphabet — the first vice in corrupt nature that moves, and the last which dies. *Robert South*

We need not covet money, for we shall always have our God, and God is better than gold, his favour is better than fortune. *C. H. Spurgeon*

Covetous men, though they have enough to sink them yet have they never enough to satisfy them. *John Trapp*

A man may be said to be given to covetousness when he takes more pains for getting earth than for getting heaven.
Thomas Watson

Covetousness is dry drunkenness.
Thomas Watson

Covetousness is not only in getting riches unjustly, but in loving them inordinately, which is a key that opens the door to all sin. *Thomas Watson*

The itch of covetousness makes a man scratch what he can from another.
Thomas Watson

The sin of covetousness is the most hard to root out. *Thomas Watson*

There is no better antidote against coveting that which is another's than being content with that which is our own.
Thomas Watson

I have heard thousands of confessions, but never one of covetousness.
Francis Xavier

COWARDICE

Cowards run the greatest danger of any men in a battle. *Anon.*

A coward is one who in perilous emergency thinks with his legs.
Ambrose Bierce

There are times when silence is golden, but there are also times when it is just plain yellow. *John Blanchard*

A dog barks when his master is attacked. I would be a coward if I saw that God's truth is attacked and yet would remain silent, without giving any sound.
John Calvin

A man without courage cannot long remain virtuous, for he is unable to resist vice. *Chrysostom*

Many would be cowards if they had enough courage. *Thomas Fuller*

Many that are swift-footed enough when there is no danger are cow-hearted when there is. *Matthew Henry*

To sin by silence when they should protest makes cowards out of men.
Abraham Lincoln

Some people deliberately avoid anything that may lead them to the divine encounter. *J. B. Phillips*

I can't abide cowardice. I refuse to make my God and Saviour a nonentity.
C. T. Studd

He is a base servant that is ashamed of his lord's livery. *George Swinnock*

It is a significant fact that the Bible gives no record of a coward ever being cured of his malady. *A. W. Tozer*

CREATION
(See also: Evolution; Nature)

The Eternal Word stood in the same relation to the created universe as the incarnate Christ to the church. *T. K. Abbott*

God has left his fingerprints all over creation. *Anon.*

In God's works we see his hand, but in his Word we see his face. *Anon.*

The glory of creation is its infinite diversity. *Anon.*

Because he is all-powerful and good, he made everything exceedingly good.
Augustine

The Himalayas are the raised letters upon which we blind children put our fingers to spell out the name of God.

J. H. Barrows

The solitary, sublime, simple reason the Bible gives for the existence of everything in all creation is that it came into being by God's will, because he chose that it should. For the unbeliever, no further explanation is possible; for the believer none is necessary.

John Blanchard

Whether special creation is endorsed by every scientist in the world or rejected by all of them is of monumental irrelevance. The Christian says God created the world because the Bible says so.

John Blanchard

What are the heavens, the earth, the sea, but a sheet of riyal paper, written all over with the wisdom and the power of God?

Thomas Brooks

God is not a copyist — the devil is that because he can be no other: but everything God makes is original. *John Caiger*

The work of God was completed, not in one moment but in six days, that it might not be tedious to us to occupy the whole of life in the consideration of it.

John Calvin

The probability of life originating by accident is comparable to the probability of the complete dictionary resulting from an explosion in a printing factory.

Edwin Conklin

If a universe could create itself, it would embody the powers of a creator, and we should be forced to conclude that the universe itself is a god. *George Davis*

All I have seen teaches me to trust the Creator for all I have not seen.

Ralph Waldo Emerson

God is the true origin of species.

Don Garlington

Every work of God serves to display his glory, and set off the greatness of his majesty. *John Gill*

We cannot discover by scientific investigations anything about the creative processes used by God. *Duane Gish*

We do not know how God created, what processes he used, for God used processes which are not now operating anywhere in the natural universe. *Duane Gish*

If the universe was created we can view ourselves as purposeful creatures bearing the stamp of God's intentions. Human life takes on a sacred dimension. We become obligated to treat each other with dignity and respect. *John Halver*

The Bible does not set forth a detailed description of the created world, as scientists seek to do, but repeatedly refers to that world as evidence of God's purposeful activity. The biblical answer to the question, 'Why does anything exist at all?' has not been superseded by scientific discoveries or surpassed by philosophical reasoning. *Walter R. Hearn*

The universe seems to have been designed by a pure mathematician.

James Jeans

The question is: How must creation have occurred if we assume that God had nothing to do with it? *Phillip E. Johnson*

What the science educators propose to teach us as 'evolution', and label as fact, is based not only upon any incontrovertible empirical evidence, but upon a highly controversial philosophical presupposition. *Phillip E. Johnson*

Two things strike me with awe: the starry heavens above and the moral law within. *Immanuel Kant*

Either one begins with faith in an eternal God or with faith in eternal matter. There is nothing in between. *Douglas F. Kelly*

God in his Word has given us information concerning creation that we could have received in no other way than by divine revelation, for no one was there to observe it, and it cannot be repeated as an experiment in a laboratory. *Douglas F. Kelly*

Nothing could be more logical or more intelligent than to accept the information from the One who made it, from the One who was the eye-witness, from the One who is truth itself. *Douglas F. Kelly*

No philosophical theory which I have yet come across is a radical improvement on the words of Genesis, that 'in the beginning God made heaven and earth'. *C. S. Lewis*

There never was a theory of the universe that did not need a god to make it go. *James Clerk Maxwell*

The argument from design is irresistible. Nature does testify to its Creator. *John Stuart Mill*

The serious scientist's comment on Genesis 1 is 'I have nothing to say. I was not there.' *Graham Miller*

No account of the universe can be true unless that account leaves it possible for our thinking to be a real insight. *Robert A. Morey*

Without all doubt this world... could arise from nothing but the perfectly free will of God. *Isaac Newton*

Nobody can plead that he is ignorant of the existence of God. It can clearly be seen that there is an Unseen. *Stuart Olyott*

Posterity will some day laugh at the foolishness of modern materialistic philosophy. The more I study nature, the more I am amazed at the Creator. *Louis Pasteur*

Every one of God's works is in its way great. All angels and all men united could not make one grasshopper. *William S. Plumer*

Everything above us speaks of the greatness of God, not of man. *William S. Plumer*

No human can claim to have seen the origin of the universe — let alone be able to repeat it, and therefore no one has any right to say they have disproved the Bible. *Edgar Powell*

If the universe reveals its order to us through rational science, it is because the universe is so ordered by the Author of reason. *George Roche*

The supreme justification for all creation is that God has willed it to be. *Hans Rookmaaker*

The idea of creation confounds me and surpasses my conception, though I believe as much of it as I am able to conceive. But I know that God has formed

the universe and all that exists in the most consummate order.
Jean Jacques Rousseau

Man is the captain of creation, and thus his job is to work with the world, organizing it and transforming it for God's glory. *R. C. Sproul*

Our ecological responsibility rests in our prior responsibility to obey our Creator.
R. C. Sproul

What are the chances that the universe was created by the power of chance? Not a chance. *R. C. Sproul*

That the universe was formed by a fortuitous concourse of atoms, I will no more believe than that the accidental jumbling of the alphabet would fall into a most ingenious treatise of philosophy.
Jonathan Swift

What can be more foolish than to think that all this rare fabric of heaven and earth could come by chance, when all the skill of art is not able to make an oyster?
Jeremy Taylor

Creation is the setting forth of Jesus Christ as Lord and Sovereign. *A. W. Tozer*

The problems of origin and destiny have escaped the philosopher and the scientist, but the humblest follower of Christ knows the answer to both. *A. W. Tozer*

The creation is both a monument of God's power and a looking glass in which we may see his wisdom. *Thomas Watson*

To create requires infinite power. All the world cannot make a fly. *Thomas Watson*

We may see God's glory blazing in the sun and twinkling in the stars.
Thomas Watson

Creation itself is distinct from God. He is related to it as he sustains it, but he is different to it. *David Wilkinson*

If something already existed out of which God made the universe then God would not be absolute. *David Wilkinson*

Without God the world would be a maze without a clue. *Woodrow Wilson*

CRITICISM BY OTHERS
(See also: Criticism of Others)

If men speak ill of you, live so that no one will believe them. *Anon.*

If you are not big enough to stand criticism, you are too small to be praised.
Anon.

It is just as much a Christian's duty to avoid taking offence as it is to avoid giving offence. *Anon.*

Many can bear adversity, but few contempt. *Anon.*

Prophets of God have usually been on the receiving end of more mud than medals. *Anon.*

To reply to a nasty remark with another nasty remark is like trying to remove dirt with mud. *Anon.*

We would rather be ruined by praise than saved by criticism. *Anon.*

Never be afraid to test yourself by your critic's words. *John Blanchard*

If you are slandered, never mind; it will

all come off when it is dry
Charles G. Finney

The most unspotted innocence and the most unparalleled excellency will not always be a fence against the reproach of tongues. *Matthew Henry*

Wisdom teaches us to wink at many of the injuries that are done to us, and act as if we did not see them. *Matthew Henry*

I had rather that true and faithful teachers should rebuke and condemn me, and reprove my ways, than that hypocrites should flatter me and applaud me as a saint. *Martin Luther*

I have seldom ever heard a criticism about myself that didn't indeed contain a kernel of useful truth.
Gordon MacDonald

Slander has a marvellous way of driving us into the arms of our heavenly Father.
Stuart Olyott

When people kick us, it is sometimes a sign that we are in front of them.
Percy Ray

If you were not strangers here the dogs of the world would not bark at you.
Samuel Rutherford

To be irritated by criticism is to acknowledge it was deserved. *Tacitus*

Don't defend your church or your organization against criticism. If the criticism is false it can do no harm. If it is true you need to hear it and do something about it. *A. W. Tozer*

Many people believe that admitting a fault means they no longer have to correct it. *Marie von Ebner-Eschenbach*

CRITICISM OF OTHERS
(See also: Criticism by Others)

Many are like barbers, that trim all men but themselves. *Thomas Adams*

Blowing out the other fellow's candle doesn't make yours shine any brighter.
Anon.

Criticism is often a form of self-boasting. *Anon.*

Do not condemn the judgement of another because it differs from yours. You may both be wrong. *Anon.*

Do not remove a fly from your friend's forehead with a hatchet. *Anon.*

Fault-finders seldom find anything else.
Anon.

It is a vital moment of truth when a man discovers that what he condemns most vehemently in others is that to which he is himself prone. *Anon.*

It is but a short step from the critical to the hypocritical. *Anon.*

Never put your finger on someone's faults unless it is part of a helping hand. *Anon.*

Rare is the person who can weigh the faults of others without putting his thumb on the scales. *Anon.*

The best place to criticize your neighbour is in front of your own mirror. *Anon.*

The critic who starts with himself will have no time to take on outside contracts.
Anon.

We do not get forward ourselves by keeping others back. *Anon.*

When looking for faults, use a mirror, not a telescope. *Anon.*

You have to be little to belittle. *Anon.*

The accuser should be better than the accused. *Aristotle*

Christians would never dream of intentionally running down other people with their cars; then why do we do it with our tongues? *Doug Barnett*

Finding fault is not difficult to those who are determined to find it. *John Blanchard*

Remember, that wherever you throw mud at somebody you lose ground. *John Blanchard*

The man who seems unusually concerned with the demotion of others is usually concerned with the promotion of himself. *John Blanchard*

We must not be busy bishops in other men's dioceses. *John Boys*

It is not what we gain by detracting from others, but what we have without any comparison, that is truly praiseworthy. *John Calvin*

Any fool can criticize, condemn and complain — and usually does. *Dale Carnegie*

No one so thoroughly appreciates the value of constructive criticism as the one who is giving it. *Hal Chadwick*

It is the peculiar quality of a fool to perceive the faults of others and forget his own. *Cicero*

Criticism, like rain, should be gentle enough to nourish a man's growth without destroying his roots. *Frank A. Clark*

A blurred finger is unfit to wipe away a blot. *Jean Daille*

It is not necessary to blow out your neighbour's light to let your own shine. *M. R. de Haan*

It is much easier to be critical than to be correct. *Benjamin Disraeli*

To speak ill of others is a dishonest way of praising ourselves. *Will Durant*

Taking to pieces is the trade of those who cannot construct. *Ralph Waldo Emerson*

The unspiritual are out of court as religious critics; they are deaf men judging music. *C. G. Findlay*

Clean your fingers before you point at my spots. *Benjamin Franklin*

None are such critics of small faults as those guilty of grave ones. *Richard Glover*

We have a bat's eye for our own faults, and an eagle's for the faults of others. *James L. Gordon*

It is a barren kind of criticism which tells you what a thing is not. *Rufus Wilmot Griswold*

Unless we are willing to help a person overcome his faults, there is little value in pointing them out. *Robert J. Hastings*

Giving away pieces of our mind is poor business. We can't afford it, for one thing, because we do not have that much mind to spare! *Vance Havner*

In judging and censuring our brethren we meddle with that which does not belong to us. *Matthew Henry*

Pass no sentence which cannot ask God in faith to confirm.   *Matthew Henry*

No man can be severe in his judgement who feels that the mild eyes of Christ are fixed upon him.   *Charles Hodge*

Two things are very bad for the heart — running up stairs and running down people.   *C. A. Joyce*

God has a habit of saving people in ways I especially dislike, therefore I have to be careful what I say.   *C. S. Lewis*

He has the right to criticize who has the heart to help.   *Abraham Lincoln*

The man that is most busy in censuring others is always least employed in examining himself.   *Thomas Lye*

Criticism is asserted superiority.
     Henry E. Manning

Censuring is a pleasing sin, extremely compliant with nature.   *Thomas Manton*

They only have a right to censure that have a heart to help; the rest is cruelty and injustice.   *Samuel Medley*

Defamation begins and lives in the mind.
     J. A. Motyer

Nowhere does the self-centred heart of man more quickly take control than when it comes to the machinery of criticism and the promptings of self-interest.
     J. A. Motyer

The nature and end of judgement ... must be corrective, not vindictive; for healing, not destruction.   *John Owen*

Never throw mud. You may miss your mark; but you must have dirty hands.
     Joseph Parker

Criticism often takes from the tree caterpillars and blossoms together.
     Jean Paul Richter

They are fittest to find fault in whom there is no fault to be found.   *William Secker*

Forebear to judge, for we are sinners all.
     William Shakespeare

I would rather play with the forked lightning, or take in my hands living wires with their fiery current, than speak a reckless word against any servant of Christ.
     A. B. Simpson

Stoning prophets is poor work.
     Harold St. John

A smile in giving honest criticism can make the difference between resentment and reform.   *Phillip Steinmetz*

A desire to disgrace others never sprang from grace.   *George Swinnock*

Reproofs should be as oils or ointments, gently rubbed in by the warm fire of love.
     George Swinnock

Some men would receive blows with more patience if they were given them with more prudence.   *George Swinnock*

There is no readier way for a man to bring his own worth into question, than by endeavouring to detract from the worth of other men.   *John Tillotson*

Some warmth must be in a reproof, but it must not be scalding hot.   *John Trapp*

One of the easiest habits for any human being to acquire is the habit of criticizing others. *Spiros Zodhiates*

CROSS
(See also: Atonement; Jesus Christ — Death)

The cross is the cost of my forgiveness.
Anon.

The cross of Christ is the key of paradise. *Anon.*

The cross of Christ will always be an offence to the natural man. *John Blanchard*

The cross is the only ladder high enough to touch the threshold of heaven.
George Boardman

The cross of Christ destroyed the equation religion equals happiness.
Dietrich Bonhoeffer

Our salvation consists in the doctrine of the cross. *John Calvin*

The righteous One upon the cross is the sinner's only point of contact with the saving power of God.
Lewis Sperry Chafer

Every doctrine that is not embedded in the cross of Jesus will lead astray.
Oswald Chambers

The cross means nothing apart from the law. *Walter J. Chantry*

Freed to draw by its own power, the cross remains the magnet of the souls of men.
Kenneth Cragg

The wonder of the cross is not the blood, but whose blood, and to what purpose.
Donald English

You do not understand Christ until you understand his cross. *P. T. Forsyth*

A crossless Christ would mean no more than a Christless cross. *Vance Havner*

The sufferings of our Saviour were designed to display the glory of God as the moral ruler of the universe. *William Jay*

The cross of Christ runs through the whole of Scripture. *Martin Luther*

There is not a word in the Bible, which is *extra crucem*, which can be understood without reference to the cross.
Martin Luther

What brought Jesus to the cross was ultimately not the authorities of the Jews and the Romans but God's love and purpose.
Alex Luc

The cross is the centre of the world's history. The incarnation of Christ and the crucifixion of our Lord are the pivot round which all the events of the ages revolve. *Alexander MacLaren*

The meaning of the cross is to be found not in the physical suffering, the scorning, the forsaking by the disciples. No. In the crucifixion the vertical, not the horizontal dimension, is central.
Will Metzger

Among the categorical imperatives of the faith, the saving power of the cross is central and inescapable.
C. Campbell Morgan

In the cross, sin is cursed and cancelled. In the cross, grace is victorious and available. *G. Campbell Morgan*

Nobody who has truly seen the cross of Christ can ever again speak of hopeless cases. *C. Campbell Morgan*

Christianity is a religion about a cross. *Leon Morris*

The cross dominates the New Testament. *Leon Morris*

The glory of the cross of Christ is bound up with the effectiveness of its accomplishment. *John Murray*

The saving power of the cross does not depend on faith being added to it; its saving power is such that faith flows from it. *J. I. Packer*

God was the master of ceremonies at the cross. *Ernest Reisinger*

The cross was not a tragic failure; it was a triumphant rescue. *Vaughan Roberts*

As long as the world stands the cross will seem foolishness to natural man. *J. C. Ryle*

Take away the cross of Christ from the Bible and it is a dark book. *J. C. Ryle*

It is the cross … that reveals the most violent and mysterious outpouring of the wrath of God that we find anywhere in Scripture. *R. C. Sproul*

I wish that our ministry — and mine especially — might be tied and tethered to the cross. *C. H. Spurgeon*

Nothing provokes the devil like the cross. *C. H. Spurgeon*

The world's one and only remedy is the cross. *C. H. Spurgeon*

There are some sciences that may be learned by the head, but the science of Christ crucified can only be learned by the heart. *C. H. Spurgeon*

This one event of the cross of Christ is a final revelation both of the character and consequence of human sin and of the wonder and sacrifice of divine love. *Alan Stibbs*

The cross is the resting place for sin, the tomb for self and the throne for our fears. *Harold St. John*

All God's justice and all God's love are focused in the cross, so that it teaches more of God and his truth than all space and time beside. *Augustus H. Strong*

The cross of Christ is the most revolutionary thing ever to appear among men. *A. W. Tozer*

The cross stands high above the opinions of men and to that cross all opinions must come at last for judgement. *A. W. Tozer*

The cross stands in bold opposition to the natural man. Its philosophy runs contrary to the processes of the unregenerate mind. *A. W. Tozer*

To try to find a common ground between the message of the cross and man's fallen reason is to try the impossible, and if persisted in must result in an impaired reason, a meaningless cross and a powerless Christianity. *A. W. Tozer*

We must do something about the cross and one of two things only we can do — flee it or die upon it. *A. W. Tozer*

Calvary shows how far men will go in sin, and how far God will go for man's salvation. *H. C. Trumbull*

CURIOSITY

Almost all men are affected with the disease of desiring to obtain useless knowledge. *John Calvin*

It is easy to mistake curiosity for spiritual hunger. *François Fenelon*

Curiosity is looking over other people's affairs and overlooking our own.
H. L. Wayland

CYNICISM

Never, never, never be a cynic, even a gentle one. Never help out a sneer, even at the devil. *Vachel Lindsay*

Sour godliness is the devil's religion.
John Wesley

What is a cynic? A man who knows the price of everything and the value of nothing. *Oscar Wilde*

DARKNESS — See Spiritual Darkness

DEATH — Anticipation

Those who have welcomed Christ may welcome death. *Anon.*

Nothing has contributed more powerfully to wean me from all that held me down to earth than the thought, constantly dwelt upon, of death and of the last judgement.
Augustine

But this is the privilege of saints, that they shall not die until the best time, not until when, if they were but rightly informed, they would desire to die. *Samuel Bolton*

Lord, give me Simeon's dismissal: Christ in my arms. *Andrew Bonar*

Although we must still meet death, let us nevertheless be calm and serene in living and dying, when we have Christ going before us. If anyone cannot set his mind at rest by disregarding death, that man should know that he has not yet gone far enough in the faith of Christ.
John Calvin

If we remember that by death we are called back from exile to home, to our heavenly fatherland, shall we then not be filled with comfort? *John Calvin*

We may positively state that nobody has made any progress in the school of Christ, unless he cheerfully looks forward towards the day of his death, and towards the day of the final resurrection.
John Calvin

My dying shows me to be mortal, but I shall be immortal after that.
Donald Cargill

He who always waits upon God is ready whensoever he calls. He is a happy man who so lives that death at all times may find him at leisure to die. *Owen Feltham*

A good life fears not life nor death.
Thomas Fuller

Ah! Is this dying? How have I dreaded as an enemy this smiling friend!
Thomas Goodwin

Let thy hope of heaven master thy fear of death. Why shouldest thou be afraid to die, who hopest to live by dying?
William Gurnall

He whose head is in heaven need not fear to put his feet into the grave.
Matthew Henry

How pleasantly does the good man speak of dying; as if it were but undressing and going to bed! *Matthew Henry*

When Christ calls me home I shall go with the gladness of a boy bounding away from school. *Adoniram Judson*

To me there is nothing more fatuous about mankind than the statement that to think about death is morbid. The man who refuses to face facts is a fool.
D. Martyn Lloyd-Jones

This is my coronation day. I have been looking forward to it for years.
D. L. Moody

I am packed, sealed and waiting for the post. *John Newton*

Who would live always in such a world as this? *John Newton*

Through Christ death is become friendly to me. *Richard Sibbes*

If I may die as I have seen some die, I court the grand occasion. I would not wish to escape death by some by-road if I may sing as they sang. *C. H. Spurgeon*

It is the very joy of this earthly life to think that it will come to an end.
C. H. Spurgeon

Be sure to celebrate my funeral scripturally and send Hallelujahs all round. It is a better day than one's wedding day.
C. T. Studd

Death is never sudden to a saint; no guest comes unawares to him who keeps a constant table. *George Swinnock*

I lie down in comfort at night, not being anxious whether I awake in this world or another. *Isaac Watts*

Lord, keep me from a sinful and too eager desire after death. I desire not to be impatient. I wish quietly to wait till my blessed change comes. *George Whitefield*

My gems are falling away; but it is because God is making up his jewels.
Charles Wolfe

My happiest moment will be when God puts his hand on my heart and stops it beating. *Arthur S. Wood*

DEATH — Blessings
(See also: Death — and Heaven)

What is death but the burial of vices?
Ambrose

Death cancels everything but truth. *Anon.*

Death for the Christian is an honourable discharge from the battles of life. *Anon.*

Death is but a physical incident in an immortal career. *Anon.*

Death is not extinguishing the light; it is putting out the lamp because dawn has come. *Anon.*

Those who live in the Lord never see each other for the last time. *Anon.*

When death becomes the property of the believer it receives a new name and is called sleep. *William Arnot*

A believer's last day is his best day.
Thomas Brooks

Christ has made of death a narrow starlit strip between the companionships of

yesterday and the reunions of tomorrow.
William Jennings Bryan

Death is God's delightful way of giving us life. *Oswald Chambers*

Death is a blessing insomuch as it puts an end to all temptation.
François Fenelon

All life is surrounded by a great circumference of death; but to the believer in Jesus, beyond this surrounding death is a boundless sphere of life. He only has to die once to be done with death for ever.
James Hamilton

Dying saints may be justly envied, while living sinners are justly pitied.
Matthew Henry

Death is not death if it rids us of doubt and fear, of chance and change, of space and time, and all which space and time bring forth and then destroy.
Charles Kingsley

Death is the foreshadowing of life. We die that we may die no more.
Thomas Hooker

What message from heaven speaks louder to us than the daily dying and departure of our fellow creature? *William Law*

Has this world been so kind to you that you would leave it with regret? There are better things ahead than any we leave behind. *C. S. Lewis*

If we really believe that home is elsewhere and that this life is a 'wandering to find home', why should we not look forward to the arrival? *C. S. Lewis*

By death I shall escape from death.
James Montgomery

Death is not so much something which happens to the Christian as something God works for him. *J. A. Motyer*

Death mingles sceptres with spades.
William S. Plumer

Satan may chase him to the gates of death, but he cannot pursue the Christian through the gates. *David C. Potter*

Death will cut us down, but he shall not eternally keep us down. *William Secker*

A dying man is a balloon throwing down its ballast. *Petit Senn*

Death is not now the death of me, but death will be the death of my misery, the death of my sins; it will be the death of my corruptions. But death will be my birthday in regard of happiness.
Richard Sibbes

Death is only a grim porter to let us into a stately palace. *Richard Sibbes*

Death is the waiting room where we robe ourselves for immortality. *C. H. Spurgeon*

I have heard of people being afraid of the pains of death. There are no pains of death: the pain is in life. Death is the end of pain. It is all over. Put the saddle on the right horse. Do not blame death for what he does not do. It is life that brings pain. *C. H. Spurgeon*

Jesus has transformed death from a dreary cavern into a passage leading to glory.
C. H. Spurgeon

The best moment of a Christian's life is his last one, because it is the one that is nearest heaven. *C. H. Spurgeon*

To the Christian, death is an exodus, an unmooring, a home-coming. Here, we are as ships on the stocks; at death, we are launched into our true element.
Augustus H. Strong

The worst of a saint is past when he dies.
George Swinnock

If you have one grain of grace, you must die to know how rich you are.
William Tiptaft

Death is only putting out the lamp at the rise of a new dawn. *David Watson*

Death is the funeral of all our sorrows.
Thomas Watson

Death will set a true saint out of gunshot and free him from sin and trouble.
Thomas Watson

The wheels of death's chariot may rattle and make a noise, but they are to carry a believer to Christ. *Thomas Watson*

At a funeral we bury something not someone; it is the house not the tenant that is lowered into the grave. *Verna Wright*

Faith builds a bridge across the gulf of death. *Edward Young*

DEATH — Certainty

All the world is a hospital and every person in it a terminal patient. *Anon.*

Men may live in crowds, but they die one by one. *Anon.*

The power of mortality thrusts every generation into the graveyard.
Donald Grey Barnhouse

Death is the greatest fact of life.
John Blanchard

Man can defy gravity, but not the grave.
John Blanchard

Nobody has to ask the question: 'Is there death after life?' *John Blanchard*

The two greatest facts in life are sin and death. *John Blanchard*

We are not here to stay; we are here to go. *John Blanchard*

As many pores as there are in the skin, so many windows there are for death to enter at. *Thomas Brooks*

The time of every man's death has been fixed by God … We are safe from all risk until God is pleased to call us away.
John Calvin

In light of the fact that we must all die, the exact timing, surely, is of relatively little consequence. *D. A. Carson*

Death is oftentimes as near to the young man's back as it is to the old man's face.
Bernard of Clairvaux

All human things are subject to decay,
And when fate summons, monarchs must obey. *John Dryden*

You know death is strong; it is the king of terrors and the terror of kings.
William Dyer

Death takes no denial. *Euripides*

Death takes no bribes. *Benjamin Franklin*

Death keeps no calendar. *Thomas Fuller*

Our death was bred when our life was first conceived.   *William Gurnall*

We can as soon run from ourselves as run from death.   *William Gurnall*

Death borders on our birth, and our cradle stands in the grave.   *Joseph Hall*

Dying my death is the one thing no one else can do for me.   *Martin Heidegger*

Righteousness delivers from the sting of death, but not from the stroke of it.
Matthew Henry

We are but tenants, and … shortly the great Landlord will give us notice that our lease has expired.   *Joseph Jefferson*

It is hard to have patience with people who say 'There is no death' or 'Death doesn't matter.' There is death. And whatever is matters. And whatever happens has consequences, and it and they are irrevocable and irreversible. You might as well say that birth doesn't matter.
C. S. Lewis

The moment you come into this world you are beginning to go out of it.
D. Martyn Lloyd-Jones

Every man must do two things alone: he must do his own believing, and his own dying.   *Martin Luther*

The longest life is a lingering death.
John Mason

Even Rome cannot grant us a dispensation from death.   *Moliere*

The death rate is still one per person.
Robert A. Morey

To reckon with death is no more than sober realism, since death is life's one and only certainty.   *J. I. Packer*

All that is here is condemned to die — to pass away like a snowball before a summer sun.   *Samuel Rutherford*

All the care in the world will not make us continue a minute beyond the time God has appointed.   *J. C. Ryle*

One out of one dies.
George Bernard Shaw

We were earth, we are flesh, we shall be worm's meat.   *Henry Smith*

Against this arrest there is no bail.
George Swinnock

Death waits upon sin as the wages on the work.   *Thomas Taylor*

Death is not a spectator sport.
Samuel E. Waldron

DEATH — and Heaven
(See also: Death — Blessings)

Death *shortens* our way to heaven, but grace *sweetens* our way to heaven. *Anon.*

Death for the Christian is not a miserable cul-de-sac, but a glorious open road into the presence of God.   *Doug Barnett*

Death does not put our relationship with God into the past tense. *John Blanchard*

When death strikes the Christian down, he falls into heaven.   *John Blanchard*

That to which we react with natural sorrow is something to which God reacts with supernatural joy.   *John Blanchard*

Death to a saint is nothing but the taking of a sweet flower out of this wilderness, and planting of it in the garden of paradise. *Thomas Brooks*

It is no credit to your heavenly Father for you to be loath to go home. *Thomas Brooks*

Death is but a passage out of a prison into a palace. *John Bunyan*

Death is not a descent, but a never-ending ascent into the larger spaces and the fuller delights. *J. Ossian Davies*

This world is the land of the dying; the next is the land of the living. *Tryon Edwards*

I have talked to doctors and nurses who have held the hands of dying people, and they say that there is as much difference between the death of a Christian and a non-Christian as there is between heaven and hell. *Billy Graham*

To the Christian death has redemptive significance. It is the portal through which we enter the presence of our Lord. *Hilys Jasper*

The grave has a door on its inner side. *Alexander Maclaren*

Death to a Christian is a putting off of rags for robes. *John Mason*

First infancy dies, then childhood, then youth, then manhood, then old age; and then we make an end of dying. *John Mason*

Some day you will read in the papers that D. L. Moody, of East Northfield, is dead. Don't you believe a word of it! At that moment I shall be more alive than I am now. *D. L. Moody*

Death is that delightful moment when the friendly flood heaves beneath the freed keel, and the prow is set straight and finally towards the shore of home, and the Pilot stands on board, at length seen 'face to face'. *Handley C. G. Moule*

Shall I be afraid to die, when in death I commend my soul to such a sweet Lord, and go to my Husband and to my King? *Richard Sibbes*

The belief that we shall never die is the foundation of our dying well. *Francois Turretin*

The dust of a believer is part of Christ's mystic body. *Thomas Watson*

DEATH — Indiscriminate

Death takes away the difference between king and beggar, and tumbles both the knight and the pawn into one bag. *Thomas Adams*

There are no pockets in a shroud. *Anon.*

There's no dying by proxy. *Anon.*

Death surprises us in the midst of our hopes. *Thomas Fuller*

All ages are threatened with death. *Thomas Manton*

Death is a mighty leveller. *J. C. Ryle*

As men, we are all equal in the presence of death. *Publitius Syrus*

Death, which levels all men, is the most effective sermon for earthly rulers. *Friedrich Tholuck*

DEATH — and Judgement

At death we leave behind all we have and take with us all we are. *Anon.*

Where death finds you, eternity binds you. *Anon.*

Death puts us all in our place.
John Blanchard

As death leaves us, so judgement will find us. *Thomas Brooks*

The character wherewith we sink into the grave at death is the very character wherewith we shall reappear at the resurrection. *Thomas Chalmers*

It is no miracle if he that lives like a beast dies like a beast. *Francis Cheynell*

If the second birth hath no place in you, the second death shall have power over you. *William Dyer*

Death stamps the characters and conditions of men for eternity. As death finds them in this world, so will they be in the next. *Nathaniel Emmons*

Damned sinners in hell shall not be allowed their light, being cast into utter darkness; and glorified saints in heaven shall not need their light, for God himself will be their everlasting light.
Matthew Henry

Death ... strips the soul of all the disguises wherein it appeared before men, that it may appear naked and open before God. Our grave-clothes are night-clothes. *Matthew Henry*

Death to a godly man is like a fair gale of wind to convey him to the heavenly country; but to a wicked man it is an east wind, a storm, a tempest, that hurries him away in confusion and amazement, to destruction. *Matthew Henry*

Let us make a friend of death and our Judge; and then we shall die out of choice as well as necessity. *John Mason*

If you die wrong the first time you cannot come back to die better a second time. *Robert Murray M'Cheyne*

He who never thirsts for God here will thirst for him before he has been dead a minute. *Brownlow North*

Death and what is beyond it will show who is wise and who is a fool.
William S. Plumer

With the same heart that men die, with that heart they will rise again. *J. C. Ryle*

Death brings with it the exposure of our entire life. *Basilea Schlink*

Just as the tree cut down, that falls
To north or southward, there it lies;
So man departs to heav'n or hell,
Fix'd in the state wherein he dies.
Isaac Watts

One may live as a conqueror, a king or a magistrate; but he must die as a man.
Daniel Webster

The bed of death brings every human being to his pure individuality, to the intense contemplation of that deepest and most solemn of all relations the relation between the creature and his Creator.
Daniel Webster

DEATH — Meaning

The very existence of the fear of death, which is the root of practically all human fears, is a clear indication that death is unnatural even though its incidence is universal. *Akbar Abdul-Haqq*

Death is that damp that puts out all the dim lights of vanity. *Thomas Adams*

The human body is formed for immortality ... By sinking into death it does not utterly perish. *John Calvin*

Death is fundamentally God's imposed limitation on human arrogance. *D. A. Carson*

We are not gods; and by death we learn that we are only human. *D. A. Carson*

If God exists, then it is possible for me confidently to affirm that my existence does not end with my death. *Stephen T. Davies*

Were it not for sin, death had never had a beginning, and were it not for death sin would never have had an ending. *William Dyer*

What men fear is not that death is annihilation but that it is not. *Epicurus*

When death speaks, there is an instant hush in the whole house; everything else is stilled that we may listen. *Arthur John Gossip*

Death is an incident, not an end. *Billy Graham*

We have a date with Deity, an appointment with the Almighty. *Vance Havner*

Death is as due to a sinner as wages are to a servant. *Matthew Henry*

Death by definition is something which is completely unfruitful. *D. Martyn Lloyd-Jones*

The intellectual critic is soon answered. We have but to ask him to explain the meaning of life and death. *D. Martyn Lloyd-Jones*

Life, according to the Bible, is not just existence, but it is existence in the presence and with the favour of God; and death is not just the death of the body but it is separation from God and a doom that should fill the heart of man with a nameless dread. *J. Gresham Machen*

Any worldview that cannot cope with death is fatally deficient. *Alister McGrath*

Death is not part of the natural process, but is the judgement of God on sin. *Peter Misselbrook*

Man is not naturally mortal; death is not the debt of nature but the wages of sin. *John Murray*

All death is unnatural. *J. I. Packer*

Death is only a horizon; and a horizon is nothing save the limit of our sight. *R. W. Raymond*

Death is not extinction in any uses of the word. It is always separation. *Charles Caldwell Ryrie*

Death is not a terminus but only a junction. *J. Charles Stern*

DEATH — Preparation for

If men are prepared to die they are ready for anything. *Joseph Addison Alexander*

The readiness which Christ requires of us is a personal readiness to leave the world and meet our God.
Joseph Addison Alexander

It is never too soon to begin to make friends with death. *Anon.*

There is nothing more certain than death, nothing more uncertain than the time of dying. I will therefore be prepared at all times for that which may come at any time. *Anon.*

Until you are free to die, you are not free to live. *Anon.*

Do every act in thy life as if it were the last. *Marcus Antoninus*

It is not too soon to go to hell at a hundred years old, and not too soon to go to heaven at twenty. *Richard Baxter*

All living is preparation for dying.
John Blanchard

Happy is that Christian who falls asleep with his Lord's work in his hand.
Francis Burkitt

The mind of a Christian ought not to be filled with thoughts of earthly things, or find satisfaction in them, for we ought to be living as if we might have to leave this world at any moment. *John Calvin*

You cannot pass a day devoutly unless you think of it as your last. *John Climacus*

Look upon death as a thing you must meet with; look upon yourselves as a thing you must part with. *William Dyer*

He has lived ill who knows not how to die well. *Thomas Fuller*

It is difficult for me to understand how an intelligent person can spend all of his time building for this world and have no time for the future world. *Billy Graham*

There is nothing morbid about getting ready to die. For a Christian, it is preparation for life's greatest adventure.
Vance Havner

It ought to be the business of every day to prepare for our last day.
Matthew Henry

We should be alarmed if we were not sure to live a month and yet we are careless though we are not sure to live a day.
Matthew Henry

Where you die, when you die, or by what means, is scarcely worth a thought, if you do but die in Christ. *Rowland Hill*

When death comes, having nothing to do, but just to die. *Henry Law*

There are, aren't there, only three things we can do about death: to desire it, to fear it, or to ignore it. *C. S. Lewis*

If a philosophy of life cannot help me to die, then in a sense it cannot help me to live. *D. Martyn Lloyd-Jones*

If life be short, then moderate your worldly cares and projects; do not cumber yourselves with too much provision for a short voyage. *Thomas Manton*

We should think of death, not as though we were thinking, but as though we were dying. *John Mason*

Live mindful of death — it will have a mighty tendency to make you serious, discreet and industrious. *Cotton Mather*

Live so as to be missed.
Robert Murray M'Cheyne

Plan your life, budgeting for seventy years ... and understand that if your time proves shorter that will not be unfair deprivation but rapid promotion. *J. I. Packer*

How many Christians live their lives packed up and ready to go? *J. I. Packer*

Above all things, let us every day think of our last day. *Pachomius*

He who lives to live forever never fears dying. *William Penn*

Live so that when death comes you may embrace like friends, not encounter like enemies. *Francis Quarles*

All deaths are solemn events. Nothing in the whole history of a man is so important as his end. *J. C. Ryle*

Death is a great fact that all acknowledge, but very few seem to realize. *J. C. Ryle*

It is an easy matter for one to die that hath died in heart and affection before.
Richard Sibbes

Is it not dangerous living one hour at a time in a state that we would not die in.
Richard Sibbes

He who does not prepare for death is more than an ordinary fool. He is a madman.
C. H. Spurgeon

No man would find it difficult to die who died every day. He would have practised it so often, that he would only have to die but once more; like the singer who has been through his rehearsals, and is perfect in his part, and has but to pour forth the notes once for all, and have done.
C. H. Spurgeon

To be familiar with the grave is prudence.
C. H. Spurgeon

Let us live as people who are prepared to die, and die as people who are prepared to live. *James S. Stewart*

If thou would'st die comfortably, live conscientiously. *George Swinnock*

If rich men only knew when they died, how their relatives would scramble for their money, the worms for their bodies, and the devil for their souls, they would not be so anxious to save money.
William Tiptaft

No one can live well until they can die well. *David Watson*

He may look on death with joy who can look on forgiveness with faith.
Thomas Watson

Take care of your life and the Lord will take care of your death.
George Whitefield

DEATH — Triumph over

Death may be the king of terrors but Jesus is the King of kings. *Anon.*

The fear of death is worse than death.
Robert Burton

Christians out-die pagans and the resurrection of Christ is the reason. *T. R. Glover*

No man ever repented of being a Christian on his deathbed. *Hannah More*

No philosophy that will not teach us how

to master death is worth twopence to us.
J. I. Packer

Since Christ has made full atonement for the believer's sins and obtained remission for him, death can no more harm him than could a wasp whose venomous sting had been removed — though it might still buzz and hiss and attempt to disturb him.
A. W. Pink

The only real answer to death is life.
Derek Prime

Death stung itself to death when he stung Christ. *William Romaine*

What greater encouragement can a man have to fight against his enemy than when he is sure of the victory before he fights — of final victory? *Richard Sibbes*

No Christian has ever been known to recant on his deathbed. *C. M. Ward*

Our people die well. *John Wesley*

There is nothing in the fact of death, nothing in the consequences of death, which Christ has not endured for us.
Brooke Foss Westcott

DECEIT — See Dishonesty; Lying

DEMOCRACY

Democracy is not an infallible way for getting things right. The democratic vote among the Israelites in the wilderness was to go back to Egypt. *John Blanchard*

Democracy assumes that there are extraordinary possibilities in ordinary people. *Harry Emerson Fosdick*

Numbers can never turn evil into good or error into truth. *F. J. Harris*

A society which becomes democratic in ethos as well as in constitution is doomed. And not much loss either. *C. S. Lewis*

Democracy is all very well as a political device. It must not be allowed to intrude into the spiritual, or even the aesthetic, world. *C. S. Lewis*

Public opinion does not decide whether things are good or bad. *Cornelius Tacitus*

DEMONS
(See also: Angels)

There are two equal and opposite errors into which our race can fall about the devils. One is to disbelieve in their existence. The other is to believe, and to feel an excessive and unhealthy interest in them. *C. S. Lewis*

It is no more difficult to believe in demons than to believe in God, Christ, the Holy Spirit, angels or the devil.
J. W. Roberts

DEPRAVITY
(See also: Guilt; Man — a Sinner;

Since man is depraved, he will not ask ultimate questions until he is dislodged from his temporal illusion. *Anon.*

We all come from the same mould — and some of us are mouldier than others!
Anon.

At the Fall, man's natural gifts were corrupted through sin, while his supernatural gifts were entirely lost. *Augustine*

The Bible does not teach that there is no good in man; the doctrine of total depravity does not mean that. The Bible teaches, rather, that there is no good in man that can satisfy God. *Donald Grey Barnhouse*

Fallen human nature has neither grace nor truth in it, but the human nature of Christ was full of grace and truth.   *W. E. Best*

Original sin is more than negative absence of original righteousness; it is positive corruption.   *W. E. Best*

An unconverted person is deliberately off course.   *John Blanchard*

Man sins not because he is deprived, but because he is depraved. *John Blanchard*

One of the clearest proofs of the depravity of man is his implacable hatred of the only solution to his greatest problem.
John Blanchard

The natural man is capable of natural good, but he is incapable of any spiritual good.   *John Blanchard*

We are born in sin and spend our lives coping with the consequences.
John Blanchard

There is the seed of all sins — of the vilest and worst of sins — in the best of men.   *Thomas Brooks*

Man naturally is apt to crown anything but Christ.   *Thomas Brooks*

Our corrupted hearts are the factories of the devil.   *Thomas Browne*

According to the constitution of our nature, oil might be extracted from a stone sooner than we could perform a good work.   *John Calvin*

Every sin should convince us of the general truth of the corruption of our nature.
John Calvin

Original sin is sufficient for the condemnation of all men.   *John Calvin*

The general character of men's lives is nothing else but a continual departure from the law of God.   *John Calvin*

The Holy Spirit teaches us in Scripture that our mind is smitten with so much blindness, that the affections of our heart are so depraved and perverted, that our whole nature is vitiated, that we can do nothing but sin until he forms a new will within us.   *John Calvin*

There is not a man who knows the hundredth part of his own sin. *John Calvin*

We ... are born lions, tigers, wolves and bears, until the Spirit of Christ tames us, and from wild and savage beasts forms us to be mild sheep.   *John Calvin*

Man, by his fall, wounded his head and his heart; the wound in the head made him unstable in the truth, and that in his heart unsteadfast in his affections.
Stephen Charnock

We owe our creation to God, our corruption to ourselves.   *Stephen Charnock*

Unconverted men would kill God if they could get to him.   *Jonathan Edwards*

When I look into my heart, and take a view of my wickedness, it looks like an abyss infinitely deeper than hell.
Jonathan Edwards

Men sometimes affect to deny the depravity of our race; but it is as clearly taught in the lawyer's office and in courts of justice, as in the Bible itself. Every prison and fetter and scaffold and bolt and bar and chain is evidence that man believes in the depravity of man.   *Tyron Edwards*

The true problem lies in the hearts and thoughts of men... What terrifies us is not the explosive force of the atomic bomb, but the power of the wickedness of the human heart.   *Albert Einstein*

As we get to know ourselves better we always find ourselves to be more depraved than we thought.
François Fenelon

The magnitude of man's sin is also the measure of his need of salvation.
Sinclair Ferguson

The ultimate tragedy of man's self-understanding is that he believes himself to be free, has all the feelings of a free agent, but does not realize that he is a slave to sin and serves the will of Satan.
Sinclair Ferguson

Whoever has a proper knowledge of himself will be convinced that naturally there is nothing good in him. *Robert Haldane*

I never say that civilization is going to the dogs. I still have some respect for dogs! Mankind without the grace of God is doing things beneath the dignity of the beasts of the field.   *Vance Havner*

Man is not evolving upwards towards a knowledge of God. He was created with a knowledge of God and has been going the other way ever since. *Vance Havner*

Grace does not run in the blood, but corruption does. A sinner begets a sinner, but a saint does not beget a saint.
Matthew Henry

Temptation has its source not in the outer lure but in the inner lust.
D. Edmund Hiebert

The rejection of the gospel is as clear proof of moral depravity as inability to see the sun at noon is proof of blindness.
Charles Hodge

Crime is inherent in human nature; the germ is in every man.   *H. B. Irving*

In the last analysis, we sin not because we have to but because we want to.
Henry Jacobsen

The wickedness of the ordinary man can be explained only by recognizing a radical defect that runs from top to bottom in his moral nature.   *C. E. Joad*

The decisive seat of evil ... is not in social and political institutions ... but simply in the weakness and imperfection of the human soul.   *George Kennan*

Depravity spells moral inability. Sin has so crippled man's moral powers that he cannot perform anything that is truly spiritual and acceptable to God.
Ernest F. Kevan

Man is totally destitute of that love to God which constitutes the very essence of holiness, and in its place he is possessed of an aversion to God which, though sometimes latent, becomes active enmity so soon as God's will comes into conflict with his own.   *Ernest F. Kevin*

Man was born and lives in sin. He cannot do anything for himself but can only do harm to himself. *Soren Kierkeggard*

If it were left to sinners, totally depraved as they are, to respond of their own volition to the gospel in faith, not one would respond.   *R. B. Kuiper*

So great is the depravity of unregenerate man that although there is nothing that he needs more than the gospel, there is nothing that he desires less. *R. B. Kuiper*

The Fall is simply and solely disobedience — doing what you have been told not to do; and it results from pride — from being too big for your boots, forgetting your place, thinking you are God.
C. S. Lewis

We are all fallen creatures and all very hard to live with. *C. S. Lewis*

We have all come to realize that a man can be educated and cultured and still be a beast! *D. Martyn Lloyd-Jones*

When a man truly sees himself, he knows that nobody can say anything about him that is too bad. *D. Martyn Lloyd-Jones*

As no man can give himself faith, neither can he take away his unbelief.
Martin Luther

Original sin is in us, like the beard. We are shaved today and look clean, and have a smooth chin; tomorrow our beard has grown again, nor does it cease growing while we remain on earth. In like manner original sin cannot be extirpated from us; it springs up in us as long as we live.
Martin Luther

The real state of human nature after the fall of man is not that one part of it has been cut off or can attain only a stunted growth, but that all of it is corrupt.
J. Gresham Machen

Man has more grandeur than the Milky Way, but how easy evil is for him, how inevitable! *Jacques Maritain*

Total depravity means … that conversion is beyond the capacity of the natural man.
Donald MacLeod

The history of man is his attempt to escape his own corruption. *Daniel Mullis*

Nothing in man is as good as it should be. *J. I. Packer*

We are born unrighteous; for each one tends to himself, and the bent toward self is the beginning of all disorder.
Blaise Pascal

The sinner is free to do as he pleases … but his pleasure is to sin. *A. W. Pink*

Man's deepest problems lie within himself. *Clark Pinnock*

If God were not omniscient (the human heart) would deceive *him*.
William S. Plumer

It is in our hearts that the evil lies, and it is from our hearts that it must be plucked out. *Bertrand Russell*

Wrong views about holiness are generally traceable to wrong views about human corruption. *J. C. Ryle*

Since the tree of knowledge has been tasted, the key of knowledge has been rusted. *William Secker*

There never yet was a mother who taught her child to be an infidel. *Henry W. Shaw*

The sinner in his sinful nature could never have a will according to God.
J. Denham Smith

Man's will is free to follow his inclinations, but fallen man's inclinations are

always and invariably away from God.
R. C. Sproul

Alas! Our heart is our greatest enemy.
C. H. Spurgeon

As the salt flavours every drop in the Atlantic, so does sin affect every atom of our nature. *C. H. Spurgeon*

I would never have been saved if I could have helped it. *C. H. Spurgeon*

Man is a double-dyed villain. He is corrupted by nature and afterwards by practice. *Augustus H. Strong*

Sinners, like water, if simply let alone, will run downhill to ruin.
Augustus H. Strong

The root of all evil in human nature is the corruption of the will. *A. W. Tozer*

One of the products of the Fall is that we remember the things we ought to forget — and forget the things we ought to remember. *Paul Tucker*

'Know thyself? If I knew myself I would run away. *Johann Wolfgang von Goethe*

Sin not only makes us unlike God but contrary to God. *Thomas Watson*

How sad our state by nature is!
Our sin how deep it stains!
And Satan binds our captive minds
Fast in his slavish chains. *Isaac Watts*

Depravity is the great hindrance to faith, but grace is God's way of overcoming the hindrance. *Malcolm Watts*

If depravity is not preached, grace will be ignored. *Malcolm Watts*

The answer to the wickedness of human nature is not found in human eloquence or attractiveness. It is not even found in the miraculous. The answer is found in God! *Tom Wells*

DEPRESSION
(See also: Despair)

Our feelings of depression and despair tell more about ourselves than about the way things really are. *Anon.*

The Christian's chief occupational hazards are depression and discouragement. *John R. W. Stott*

DESIRES
(See also: Lust)

A wise man will desire no more than he may get justly, use soberly, distribute cheerfully and leave contentedly. *Anon.*

Desire without discipline breeds disappointment, but discipline without desire breeds drudgery. *Anon.*

We often desire most what we ought not to have. *Anon.*

If your desires be endless, your cares and fears will be so too. *Thomas Fuller*

Our desires must not only be offered up to God, but they must all terminate in him, desiring nothing more than God, but still more and more of him. *Matthew Henry*

A Christian's life is a state of holy desire.
Jerome

Carnal desire is a gulf that is never filled up.
Thomas Manton

The habitual inclination of the heart in

145

believers is unto good, unto God, unto holiness, unto obedience.   *John Owen*

If all our wishes were gratified, most of our pleasures would be destroyed.
Richard Whateley

DESPAIR
(See also: Depression)

Despair is hope stark dead, as presumption is hope stark mad.   *Thomas Adams*

The logical outcome of genuine despair would seem to be suicide. If a man is not prepared for that, he does not really despair, but only fancies so.   *Anon.*

Despair is Satan's masterpiece; it carries men headlong to hell as the devils did the herd of swine into the deep.
Thomas Brooks

Despair is the damp of hell, as joy is the serenity of heaven.   *John Donne*

He that despairs degrades the Deity.
Owen Feltham

I will never despair, because I have a God; I will never presume, because I am but a man.   *Owen Feltham*

You may despair of yourself as much as you like, but never of God.
François Fenelon

In a really dark night of the soul it is always three in the morning, day after day.
F. Scott Fitzgerald

God does not despair of you, therefore you ought not to despair of yourself.
C. C. Grafton

Hopeless and lifeless go together.
William Gurnall

We do not usually learn that Christ is all we need until we reach that point where he is all we have!   *Vance Havner*

When there is no hope there can be no endeavour.   *Samuel Johnson*

Despair is a greater sin than any of the sins which provoke it.   *C. S. Lewis*

To this truth give all the Scriptures witness: that while in hell there is no place for hope, on earth there is no place for despair.   *Brownlow North*

The pessimist is not a representative of Christianity.   *A. T. Robertson*

The Christian's chief occupational hazards are depression and discouragement.   *John R. W. Stott*

It is impossible for that man to despair who remembers that his Helper is omnipotent.   *Jeremy Taylor*

Despair is Satan's master piece.
John Trapp

Despair cuts the sinews of endeavour.
Thomas Watson

The devil would make us wade so far in the waters of repentance that we should get beyond our depth and be drowned in the gulf of despair.   *Thomas Watson*

Let us never despair while we have Christ as our leader!   *George Whitefield*

DESTINY
(See also: Eternal Life; Eternity; Heaven; Hell; Judgement)

Let it be considered that if our lives be not a journey to heaven they will be a journey to hell.   *Jonathan Edwards*

Destiny waits in the hands of God, not in the hands of statesmen. *T. S. Eliot*

God, in his glory and presence, forms the destiny of the Christian.
Sinclair Ferguson

DETERMINATION
(See also: Perseverance)

Great souls have wills, feeble ones have only wishes. *Anon.*

I can plod. *William Carey*

It is not theology that makes a man of valour what he is, but 'plodology'!
Leslie Carter

All excellence involves discipline and tenacity of purpose. *John W. Gardner*

Christ wants not nibblers at the possible, but grabbers of the impossible. *C. T. Studd*

DEVIL — See Satan

DIFFICULTIES

An obstacle is often an unrecognized opportunity. *Anon.*

Difficulties either make us better or bitter. *Anon.*

In the presence of trouble some people grow wings; others buy crutches. *Anon.*

Difficulties are God's errands; and when we are sent upon them we should esteem it a proof of God's confidence — as a compliment from God.
Henry Ward Beecher

No crisis is greater than Christ.
John Blanchard

When problems get Christians praying they do more good than harm.
John Blanchard

There are no difficulties with God. Difficulties wholly exist in our own unbelieving minds. *Thomas Charles*

It is difficulties which show what men are. *Epictetus*

Shall light troubles make you forget weighty mercies? *John Flavel*

The reason some people know the solution is because they created the problem.
Kelly Fordyce

You must live with people to see their problems, and live with God in order to solve them. *P. T. Forsyth*

Nothing is more offensive to God than disbelief of his promise and despair of the performance of it because of some difficulties that seem to lie in the way.
Matthew Henry

Problems are opportunities in work clothes. *Henry J. Kaiser*

Difficulties in the way to heaven serve to bring us to a despair of ourselves, not of God. *Thomas Manton*

The more terrible the storm, the more necessary the anchor. *William S. Plumer*

If a man in his heart is right with God, God will deal with the problem.
Alan Redpath

If God be God, then no insoluble problems exist. And if God be *my* God, then no problem of mine is without its appropriate solution. *Maurice Roberts*

Many men owe the grandeur of their lives to their tremendous difficulties.
C. H. Spurgeon

Let God's promises shine on your problems.
Corrie ten Boom

Our greatest problem in suffering is unbelief.
Geoff Thomas

Difficulties prove men.
Johann Wolfgang von Goethe

DIGNITY

If your dignity cannot take care of itself, but requires nursing, it is worth but little.
Anon.

The easiest way to dignity is humility.
Anon.

Dignity does not consist in possessing honours, but in deserving them. *Aristotle*

I know of no case when a man added to his dignity by standing on it.
Winston Churchill

Where is there dignity unless there is honesty.
Cicero

Man's dignity rests in God, who assigns an inestimable worth to every person. Man's origin is not an accident, but a profoundly intelligent act by One who has eternal value; by One who stamps his image on each person.   *R. C. Sproul*

DISAPPOINTMENTS

We mount to heaven mostly on the ruins of our cherished schemes, finding our failures were successes.   *A. B. Alcott*

Disappointments are his appointments.
Anon.

There are no disappointments to those whose wills are buried in the will of God.
Frederick W. Faber

In the light of eternity we shall see that what we desired would have been fatal to us, and that what we would have avoided was essential to our wellbeing.
François Fenelon

There is many a thing which the world calls disappointment, but there is no such a word in the dictionary of faith. What to others are disappointments are to believers intimations of the way of God.
John Newton

Disappointment is often the salt of life.
Theodore Parker

DISCIPLESHIP

It costs to follow Jesus Christ, but it costs more not to.   *Anon.*

Jesus didn't commit the gospel to an advertising agency; he commissioned disciples.   *Joseph Bayly*

Salvation without discipleship is 'cheap grace'.   *Dietrich Bonhoeffer*

No man is qualified to be a disciple of Christ until he has been divested of self.
John Calvin

Our Lord had only one desire, and that was to do the will of his Father, and to have this desire is characteristic of a disciple.   *Oswald Chambers*

The walk of a disciple is gloriously different, but gloriously certain.
Oswald Chambers

When we learn to hold the world with a

loose grip we are learning to take hold of the world to come with a firm grip.
Sinclair Ferguson

To leave all and follow Christ is the biggest thing that a living soul on this earth can do. *A. Lindsay Glegg*

Salvation is free, but discipleship costs everything we have. *Billy Graham*

Our Lord made discipleship hard and lost many prospective followers because he called them to a pilgrimage, not to a parade — to a *fight,* not to a frolic.
Vance Havner

As long as we live we must be scholars in Christ's school and sit at his feet; but we should aim to be headscholars and to get into the highest form. *Matthew Henry*

Jesus promised his disciples three things — that they would be completely fearless, absurdly happy and in constant trouble. *F. R. Maitby*

A disciple is a person who learns to live the life his teacher lives.
Juan Carlos Ortiz

Discipleship is more than getting to know what the teacher knows. It is getting to be what he is. *Juan Carlos Ortiz*

The making of a disciple means the creating of a duplicate. *Juan Carlos Ortiz*

Does it not fill our hearts with a thrilling excitement to think that the costly disciplines and lonely agonies that make up our earthly discipleship may at any moment, and without any warning, be transformed into everlasting splendours the like of which we can scarcely conceive, let alone understand?
James Philip

As the soldier follows his general, as the servant follows his master, as the scholar follows his teacher, as the sheep follows its shepherd, just so ought the professing Christian to follow Christ. *J. C. Ryle*

The new Christian is like a man who has learned to drive in a country where the traffic moves on the left side of the highway and suddenly finds himself in another country and forced to drive on the right. He must unlearn his old habit and learn a new one and, more serious than all, he must learn in heavy traffic.
A. W. Tozer

DISCIPLINE

Desire without discipline breeds disappointment, but discipline without desire breeds drudgery. *Anon.*

Discipline is a privilege because it is an evidence of our sonship. *Alistair Begg*

Discipline is proof of sonship.
John Blanchard

Guarding our hearts begins with guarding our eyes and ears. *Jerry Bridges*

There is a certain kind of maturity that can be attained only through the discipline of suffering. *D. A. Carson*

The alternative to discipline is disaster.
Vance Havner

You cannot sharpen an axe on a cake of butter. *Vance Havner*

Discipline, while the word is unfallen, exists for the sake of what seems its very opposite — for freedom, almost for extravagance. *C. S. Lewis*

149

The great need in the Christian life is for self-discipline. This is not something that happens to you in a meeting; you have got to do it!   *D. Martyn Lloyd-Jones*

There is no point in praying for spiritual growth unless we do our best to live disciplined Christian lives.
Nigel McCullough

Discipline is the basic set of tools we require to solve life's problems.
M. Scott Peck

Better be pruned to grow than cut up to burn.   *John Trapp*

Discipline without direction is drudgery.
Donald S. Whitney

In my own personal and pastoral experience, I can say I have never known a man or woman who came to spiritual maturity except through discipline.
Donald S. Whitney

DISCONTENT

The poorest man in the world is the one who is always wanting more than he has.
Anon.

Discontent is one of the most satanic of all sins, and to indulge in it is to rebel against God just as Satan did.
Jerry Bridges

The contented man is never poor, the discontented never rich.   *George Eliot*

Discontent follows ambition like a shadow.   *Henry H. Haskins*

A man's discontent is his worst evil.
George Herbert

DISCOURAGEMENT — See Despair; Depression

DISHONESTY
(See also: Lying)

Dishonesty is moral suicide, a disintegration of the moral self.   *Anon.*

One of the marks of spiritual rebellion is deviousness.   *Jan Barclay*

There are people so addicted to exaggeration that they cannot tell the truth without lying.   *John Billings*

Truth exists, only falsehood has to he invented.   *Georges Braque*

A lie stands on one leg, truth on two.
Benjamin Franklin

Nothing is more offensive to God than deceit in commerce.   *Matthew Henry*

That which is won ill will never wear well.   *Matthew Henry*

You can fool some of the people all of the time, and all of the people some of the time, but you cannot fool all of the people all of the time.   *Abraham Lincoln*

A lie is the refuge of weakness. The man of courage is not afraid of the truth.
J. C. MacAulay

No wickedness on earth is more common than the various forms of deceit.
William S. Plumer

To depart from the truth affords a testimony that one first despises God and then fears man.   *Plutarch*

He who tells a lie is forced to invent twenty more to sustain it. *Alexander Pope*

If there were no law against thieving most of us would be thieves. *Bertrand Russell*

Every time a Christian cheats on his Income Tax he perverts and obscures the gospel. *John Sanderson*

Oh! what a tangled web we weave
When first we practise to deceive!
Walter Scott

Money dishonestly acquired is never worth its cost, while a good conscience never costs as much as it is worth.
J. P. Senn

An honest death is better than a dishonest life. *Socrates*

What a poor thing is the temporary triumph of falsehood! *C. H. Spurgeon*

DIVORCE

Divorce is always a bombshell. However much it has been anticipated and even thought through, it almost invariably turns out to be much harder for both partners than either ever imagined.
Andrew Comes

So many people who think divorce a panacea for every ill find out when they try it that the remedy is worse than the disease. *Dorothy Dix*

It is not marriage that fails, it is people that fail. *Harry Emerson Fosdick*

Divorce tells us the truth about man. It tells us nothing about marriage.
Terence Kelshaw

Divorce is always a tragedy no matter how civilized the handling of it may be. It is always a confession of human failure, even when it is the better of sorry alternatives. *Lawrence S. Kubie*

I have such hatred of divorce that I prefer bigamy to divorce. *Martin Luther*

DOCTRINE
(See also: Theology)

The life of Christian doctrine is its practical application. *Anon.*

The question is not whether a doctrine is beautiful, but whether it is true. *Anon.*

The doctrines of Christianity have just as much right to be believed as its duties have to be practised. *M. Arnaud*

If you believe what you like in the gospel, and reject what you like, it is not the gospel you believe, but yourself.
Augustine

Doctrinal indifference is no solution to the problem of doctrinal differences.
John Blanchard

Every Christian should have an insatiable appetite for sound doctrine.
John Blanchard

Doctrine is practical, for it is that that stirs up the heart. *Andrew Bonar*

Doctrine is not an affair of the tongue but of the life … It is received only when it possesses the whole soul. *John Calvin*

Purity of doctrine is the soul of the church.
John Calvin

The design of Christian doctrine is that believers should exercise themselves in good works. *John Calvin*

Doctrine

Zeal without doctrine is like a sword in the hand of a lunatic. *John Calvin*

A church with a little creed is a church with a little life. *B. H. Carroll*

The modern cry 'Less creed and more liberty' is a degeneration from the vertebrate to the jellyfish. *B. H. Carroll*

How humbling it is to all learning when a man is made to know that his doctrine has outrun his experiences! *Thomas Chalmers*

Doctrine without duty is a tree without fruits; duty without doctrine is a tree without roots. *Talbot W. Chambers*

Every doctrine that is not embedded in the cross of Jesus will lead astray. *Oswald Chambers*

Some who demonstrate a passion for accurate doctrine place a question mark over their love for God by evidencing no active love for lost sinners. *Walter J. Chantry*

The conduct of our lives is the true mirror of our doctrine. *Michel de Montaigne*

Biblical truth has been given to change lives, not simply to stimulate discussion. *Dick Dowsett*

Doctrine is the necessary foundation of duty. *Tryon Edwards*

Invariably when a great doctrine is misused there is a tendency for it to be devalued. *Sinclair Ferguson*

As seed is made for soil and soil for seed, so the heart is made for God's truth and God's truth for the heart. *Richard Glover*

God hath but three things dear unto him in this world, his saints, his worship and his truth; and it is hard to say which of these is dearest unto him. *Thomas Goodwin*

Doctrine is the framework of life — the skeleton of truth, to be clothed and rounded out by the living grace of a holy life. *A. J. Gordon*

Some things we trust God with, some things God trusts us with … That which God trusts us chiefly with is his truth. *William Gurnall*

The New Testament always ties up prophetic doctrine with practical duty. *Vance Havner*

The plainest truths are sometimes the strongest arguments for the hardest duties. *Matthew Henry*

The doctrines of the Bible are not isolated but interlaced; and the view of one doctrine must necessarily affect the view taken of another. *A. A. Hodge*

True doctrine is a master key to all the world's problems. With it the world can be taken apart and put together. *Eric Hoffer*

Let us embrace the whole truth, or renounce Christianity altogether. *Joseph Irons*

You cannot drop the big themes and create great saints. *John Henry Jowett*

He who attempts to stress Christian living by disparaging Christian doctrine is guilty of a most serious blunder. He neglects the important fact that Christian living is rooted in Christian doctrine. *R. B. Kuiper*

Middle-of-the-road pacifism in significant doctrinal controversy has ruined many a church. *R. B. Kuiper*

The church is where the truth is. Sound doctrine always has been, is today, and ever will be the foremost mark of the true church. *R. B. Kuiper*

Today's church … has no more solemn duty than to maintain purity of doctrine. *R. B. Kuiper*

Doctrines are not God: they are only a kind of map. But that map is based on the experience of hundreds of people who were really in touch with God. *C. S. Lewis*

To say, 'Never mind doctrine, let's get on with evangelism' is as ridiculous as a football team saying, 'Never mind about a ball, let's get on with the game.' *Peter Lewis*

I always find that those who are driven with every wind of doctrine are those who are too lazy to study doctrine. *D. Martyn Lloyd-Jones*

If your knowledge of doctrine does not make you a great man of prayer, you had better examine yourself again. *D. Martyn Lloyd-Jones*

The man whose doctrine is shaky will be shaky in his whole life. *D. Martyn Lloyd-Jones*

There is nothing so fatuous as the view that Christian doctrine is removed from life. There is nothing which is more practical. *D. Martyn Lloyd-Jones*

Any teaching which does not square with the Scriptures is to be rejected even if it snows miracles every day. *Martin Luther*

Nothing is to be introduced as doctrine which is not according to revelation. *Henry T. Mahan*

The end for which God instructs the mind is that he might transform the life. *Al Martin*

Doctrine and life have been married by God. *Will Metzger*

A creed is the road or street. It is very good as far as it goes, but if it doesn't take us to Christ it is worthless. *D. L Moody*

In Christianity, creed has always to do with Christ. *G. Campbell Morgan*

Doctrinal Christianity is not a pastime for intellectuals. It involves life and death. *Iain H. Murray*

Real doctrine Christianity has an obstinacy about it which no amount of modern opinion or religious excitement can change. *Iain H. Murray*

Christian doctrine is grace, and Christian conduct is gratitude. *J. I. Packer*

Miracles enable us to judge of doctrine, and doctrine enables us to judge of miracles. *Blaise Pascal*

Doctrine is never meant merely to make us knowledgeable, but to make us godly. *James Philip*

We are far more concerned about the results of the gospel than we are about the purity of it. *A. W. Pink*

Weak doctrines will not be a match for powerful temptations. *William S. Plumer*

True holiness flows from the soundness of a man's doctrine.　*Robert A. Richey*

You can talk about religious experiences all you wish, but if it does not have doctrinal roots, it is like cut flowers stuck into the ground. They will soon wither and die.　*J. C. Ryle*

The Christian faith is the most exciting drama that ever staggered the imagination — and the dogma is the drama.
Dorothy L. Sayers

If we do not make clear by word and by practice our position *for* truth and *against* false doctrine we are building a wall between the next generation and the gospel.　*Francis Schaeffer*

Say what men say, it is doctrine that moves the world. He who takes no position will not sway the human intellect.
W. G. T. Shedd

It is a positive and very hurtful sin to magnify liberty at the expense of doctrine.
Walter Shurden

He that believes ill can never live well, for he hath no foundation. *Richard Sibbes*

To separate doctrine from life or life from doctrine is to sue for a groundless divorce. God has joined them together, and what he has joined together we must never put asunder.　*R. C. Sproul*

A dead creed is of no use; we must have our creed baptized with the Holy Ghost.
C. H. Spurgeon

Certain doctrines would not make a mouse stir its ears; the grand old doctrines of grace stir our blood, quicken our pulse,

and fill our whole being with enthusiasm.
C. H. Spurgeon

Men to be truly won must be won by truth.　*C. H. Spurgeon*

Those who do away with Christian doctrine are ... the worst enemies of Christian living.　*C. H. Spurgeon*

The best theology is rather a divine life than a divine knowledge. *Jeremy Taylor*

A doctrine has practical value only as far as it is prominent in our thoughts and makes a difference in our lives.
A. W. Tozer

Christianity has been watered down until the solution is so weak that if it were poison it would not hurt anyone and if it were medicine it would not cure anyone!
A. W. Tozer

The purpose behind all doctrine is to secure moral action.　*A. W. Tozer*

The unattended garden will soon be overrun with weeds; the heart that fails to cultivate truth and root out error will shortly be a theological wilderness.
A. W. Tozer

There is scarcely anything so dull and meaningless as Bible doctrine taught for its own sake. Truth divorced from life is not truth in its biblical sense, but something else and something less. *A. W. Tozer*

Orthodoxy is my doxy; heterodoxy is another man's doxy. *William Warburton*

Doctrine won't make you happy unless it is translated into life. *Henry Van Dyke*

DOGMATISM — See Convictions

DOUBT
(See also: Uncertainty)

For too many Christians vagueness is the vogue; all they have is the courage of their confusions.   *Anon.*

All doubts are not honest. *Victor Budgen*

Doubt is not always a sign that a man is wrong; it may be a sign that he is thinking.   *Oswald Chambers*

The truth, however dreadful it is, is not so dreadful as uncertainty. *Anton Chekov*

The doubter can't find God for the same reason that a thief can't find a policeman.
Robert Cleath

Believe your beliefs and doubt your doubts; do not make the mistake of doubting your beliefs and believing your doubts.   *Charles F. Deems*

Christ distinguished between doubt and unbelief. Doubt says, 'I can't believe.' Unbelief says, 'I won't believe.' Doubt is honest. Unbelief is obstinate.
Henry Drummond

Never doubt in the dark what God told you in the light.   *V. Raymond Edman*

Either Jesus is who he says he is, in which case Christianity is true in a way no other religion is; or else Jesus is not who he says he is, in which case the very essence of Christianity is not true at all.
C. Stephen Evans

Doubters invert the metaphor and insist that they need faith as big as a mountain in order to move a mustard seed.
Webb B. Garrison

No alcoholic was ever more in bondage to his habit of drink than many Christians are to their habit of doubting. In fact, many Christians have settled down under their doubts as though they had contracted an incurable disease.
Billy Graham

The inescapable presence of doubt is a constant reminder of our responsibility to truth in a twilight world of truth and half-truth.   *Os Guinness*

Doubt indulged soon becomes doubt realized.   *Frances Ridley Havergal*

He is a fool who leaves a certainty to pursue an uncertainty.   *Hesiod*

Clouds of doubt are created when the warm, moist air of our expectations meets the cold air of God's silence. The problem is not as much in God's silence as it is in your ability to hear.   *Max Lucado*

The art of doubting is easy, for it is an ability that is born with us. *Martin Luther*

Doubt is brother devil to despair.
John Boyle O'Reilly

Doubt cramps energy.   *F. W. Robertson*

Satan loves to fish in muddy water.
William S. Plumer

Chronic doubt is a sin that is not to be tolerated.   *C. H. Spurgeon*

Doubt breeds distress but trust means joy in the long run.   *C. H. Spurgeon*

The teachers of doubt are doubtful teachers.   *C. H. Spurgeon*

Give me the benefit of your convictions, if you have any. Keep your doubts to yourself; I have enough of my own.
Johann Wolfgang von Goethe

Men who wrap themselves in question marks cannot crusade. *David K. Wachtel*

Man is not made to question, but adore.
Edward Young

DRESS — See Clothing

DRUNKENNESS
(See also: Alcohol)

Drunkenness unmans the man.
Thomas Brooks

The drunken man is a living corpse.
Chrysostom

A drinker has a hole under his nose that all his money runs into. *Thomas Fuller*

The drunkard is a walking quagmire.
William Jenkyn

Drinking is the refuge of the weak; it is crutches for lame ducks. *E. Stanley Jones*

Drunkenness is temporary suicide.
Bertrand Russell

The sight of a drunkard is a better sermon against that vice than the best sermon that was ever preached on that subject. *Sarah E. Saville*

Drunkenness is nothing else but a voluntary madness. *Seneca*

Drunkenness places man as much below the level of the brutes as reason elevates him above them. *John Sinclair*

Drunken porters keep open gates.
Henry Smith

DUTY
(See also: Actions; Good Deeds; Responsibility; Service)

Do what you know to be your present duty and God will acquaint you with your future duty as it comes to be present.
Samuel Annesley

Duties delayed are the devil's delight.
Anon.

Duties may be good crutches to go upon, but they are bad Christs to lean upon.
Anon.

Everyone must row with the oars he has.
Anon.

If God gives himself to us in promises, we must give ourselves to him in duties.
Anon.

The Christian's privileges lie in pronouns; but his duty in adverbs. *Anon.*

In doing what we ought we deserve no praise. *Augustine*

Your daily duties are a part of your religious life just as much as your devotions are. *Henry Ward Beecher*

Faith does not set aside natural duties, but perfects and strengthens them.
J. A. Bengel

Duty makes us do things well, but love makes us do them beautifully.
Phillips Brooks

It is your duty and glory to do that every day that you would willingly do on a dying day. *Thomas Brooks*

Neglect of duty will never get guilt off the conscience. *Thomas Brooks*

He who disregards his calling will never keep the straight path in the duties of his work. *John Calvin*

Men do less than they ought unless they do all that they can. *Thomas Carlyle*

Our grand business is not to see what lies dimly at a distance, but to do what lies clearly at hand. *Thomas Carlyle*

Doctrine without duty is a tree without fruits; duty without doctrine is a tree without roots. *Talbot W. Chambers*

Eternity cannot free us from duty. *Stephen Charnock*

If we once become listless to duty, we shall quickly become lifeless in it. *Stephen Charnock*

No duty can be spiritual that has a carnal aim. *Stephen Charnock*

There is not a moment without some duty. *Cicero*

The reward of one duty done is the power to do another. *George Eliot*

Those who give to God only the shadow of duty can never expect from him a real reward. *John Flavel*

He that leaves a duty may soon be left to commit a crime. *William Gurnall*

Never did the holy God give a privilege where he did not expect a duty. *Joseph Hall*

Do not let not being able to do it any better keep you from doing what you can. *Vance Havner*

Duty is ours, events are God's. *Matthew Henry*

No pretence of humility must make us decline our duty. *Matthew Henry*

Our rule is not to go a step out of the way of duty, either to meet a cross or to miss one. *Matthew Henry*

When the law of God is written on our hearts, our duty will be our delight. *Matthew Henry*

The consciousness of a duty performed gives us music at midnight. *George Herbert*

Let us not run out of the path of duty lest we run into the way of danger. *Rowland Hill*

Without duty, life is soft and boneless; it cannot hold itself together. *Joseph Joubert*

I ought, therefore I can. *Immanuel Kant*

Duty is the sublimest word in the English language. *Robert F. Lee*

Every duty is a religious duty, and our obligation to perform every duty is therefore absolute. *C. S. Lewis*

The world might stop in ten minutes; meanwhile, we are to go on doing our duty. The great thing is to be found at one's post as a child of God, living each day as though it were our last, but planning as though the world might last a hundred years. *C. S. Lewis*

Believe in Christ and do your duty in that state of life to which God has called you.
Martin Luther

There is nothing in the universe I fear but that I shall not know all my duty, or shall fail to do it. *Mary Lyon*

You would not think any duty small if you yourself were great.
George Macdonald

Ability involves responsibility. Power to its last participle is duty.
Alexander MacLaren

There are no great principles for great duties and little ones for little duties.
Alexander MacLaren

There are two things which are indispensable to true Christian life: first, a clear knowledge of duty: and, second, an obedience coordinate with that knowledge.
Douglas Macmillan

Duty is the greatest liberty, and sin the greatest bondage. *Thomas Manton*

The best motive to present duty is to be drawn from future destiny.
Thomas V. Moore

Perish discretion when it interferes with duty. *Hannah More*

Who escapes a duty, avoids a gain.
Theodore Parker

The gracious operations of the Spirit were never designed to be a substitute for the Christian's discharge of duty. *A. W. Pink*

Do what you can, with what you have, where you are. *Theodore Roosevelt*

Faithfulness knows no difference between small and great duties.
John Ruskin

God never imposes a duty without giving time to do it. *John Ruskin*

Duties can never have too much of our diligence or too little of our confidence.
William Secker

If God should call me into judgement before him, according to the strictness of his perfect law, for the best duty I have ever performed, and for nothing else, I must be condemned as a transgressor; for when weighed in these exact balances, it would be found wanting. *Thomas Scott*

Duties come from doctrines.
Richard Seume

Consequences and usefulness are nothing to us. Duty and right — these are to be our guides. *C. H. Spurgeon*

Duty fits the heart for duty.
George Swinnock

EARNESTNESS
(See also. Enthusiasm; Zeal)

Execute every act of thy life as if it were thy last. *Marcus Aurelius*

Earnestness is the devotion of all the faculties. *C. N. Bovee*

It is your duty and glory to do that every day that you would willingly do on a dying day. *Thomas Brooks*

The kingdom of God is not for the well meaning, but for the desperate.
James Denney

Don't touch Christianity unless you mean business. I promise you a miserable existence if you do. *Henry Drummond*

Earnestness is the salt of eloquence.
Victor Hugo

Earnestness is enthusiasm tempered by reason. *Blaise Pascal*

ECUMENISM — See Church Unity

EDUCATION
(See also: Knowledge; Mind; Reason)

Anyone who stops learning is old, whether at twenty or eighty. *Anon.*

Education is never as expensive as ignorance. *Anon.*

Education is what is left over when you subtract what you have forgotten from what you have learned. *Anon.*

Education is a progressive discovery of our own ignorance. *Will Durant*

Many learned men, with all the rich furniture of their brain, live and die slaves to the spirit of this world. *William Law*

Education without religion, as useful as it is, seems rather to make man a more clever devil. *C. S. Lewis*

One of the reasons why it needs no special education to be a Christian is that Christianity is an education in itself.
C. S. Lewis

When you educate a man in mind and not in morals you educate a menace to society. *Franklin D. Roosevelt*

The great aim of education is not knowledge but action. *Herbert Spencer*

It is better to learn late than never.
Publilius Syrus

Education is useless without the Bible.
Noah Webster

EGOTISM
(See also: Boasting; Conceit; Pride; Vanity)

An egotist is a man whose self-importance makes his mind shrink while his head swells. *Anon.*

An egotist is a person who is his own best friend. *Anon.*

Egotism is an odd disease. It makes everybody sick but the one who has it. *Anon.*

Egotism is obesity of the head. *Anon.*

The egotist is an 'I' specialist. *Anon.*

Most of the trouble in the world is caused by people wanting to be important.
T. S. Eliot

An egotist is a man who talks about himself so much that you don't have a chance to talk about yourself. *Vance Havner*

ELECTION — and Calling

In whatever dunghill God's jewels be hid, election will both find them out there and fetch them out from hence.
John Arrowsmith

Thou didst seek us when we sought thee not; didst seek us indeed that we might seek thee. *Augustine*

As Christians we ought always to remember that the Lord called us to himself not because of our virtues, but in spite of our vices. *John Blanchard*

Election — and Calling

Christians are a select minority and God has made the selection. *John Blanchard*

God never chooses on merit.
John Blanchard

God prepares his elect for hearing, and gives them ears for that purpose.
John Calvin

At the heart of the election doctrine throbs God's freedom. *Carl F. H. Henry*

What election means in simple terms is this: God chooses us before we choose him; God does not choose us because we deserve it; and God does not choose us to be his favourites but to be his servants. *A. M. Hunter*

When God chose certain persons unto eternal life he did not do so in order that they might be in Christ, but he viewed them from eternity as being in Christ.
R. B. Kuiper

Amiable agnostics will talk cheerfully about man's search for God. For me, they might as well talk about the mouse's search for a cat … God closed in on me.
C. S. Lewis

Better to be the elect of God than the elect of a whole nation. *C. H. Spurgeon*

We are chosen as an afflicted people and not as a prosperous people, chosen not in the palace but in the furnace.
C. H. Spurgeon

Election is the cause of our vocation and vocation is the sign of our election.
Thomas Watson

It is only as God seeks us that we can be found of him. God is seeker rather than sought. *Arthur Skevington Wood*

ELECTION — and Conversion
(See also: Predestination)

You begin at the wrong end if you first dispute about your election. Prove your conversion, and then never doubt your election. *Joseph Alleine*

Grace and election are the essence and mystery of history. *Augustine*

Man is not converted because he wills to be, but he wills to be because he is ordained to election. *Augustine*

Election kills at the roots salvation by merits and works. *George S. Bishop*

A Christian has been selected to live; to live essentially in Christ, to live effectively for Christ and to live eternally with Christ. *John Blanchard*

Election is … the parent of faith.
John Calvin

None believe but those whom God, of free grace, enlightens for his own good pleasure. *John Calvin*

When God elects us, it is not because we are handsome. *John Calvin*

Every departure from the doctrine of election in any degree has been a departure from the gospel, for such departure always involves the introduction of some obligation on man's part to make a contribution towards his own salvation, a contribution he simply cannot make.
Arthur C. Custance

Oh, happy day, that fixed my choice
On thee, my Saviour and my God!
Well may this glowing heart rejoice,
And tell its raptures all abroad.
Philip Doddridge

160

Until we have come to the place where we can sing about election with a full heart we have not grasped the spirit of the New Testament teaching.
Sinclair Ferguson

Election, while it places no bar in the way of any man which would not have been there without it, resolves the salvation of the saved into mere grace. *Andrew Fuller*

Election is the holy and loving choice by God of those who are to receive his grace.
Ernest F. Kevan

Nobody ever came to Christ because he knew he was one of the elect: he came because he needed Christ and because he wanted Christ. *Ernest F. Kevan*

Election is salvation. *R. B. Kuiper*

God's choices are without human precedent. *R. C. Lucas*

The saved are singled out not by their own merits, but by the grace of the Mediator.
Martin Luther

Election is ascribed to God the Father, sanctification to the Spirit, and reconciliation to Jesus Christ … The Son cannot die for them whom the Father never elected, and the Spirit will never sanctify them whom the Father hath not elected nor the Son redeemed. *Thomas Manton*

This doctrine affords comfort: thy unworthiness may dismay thee, but remember that thy election depends not upon thy worthiness but upon the will of God.
Elnathan Parr

Let us understand that we live in a day of election, and not of universal conversion.
J. C. Ryle

The believer who knows his own heart will ever bless God for election. *J. C. Ryle*

To either deny sovereign election or to store it away in some theological closet on shelves labelled 'good for nothing' or 'harmful' is to rob the people of God of the fullest view of God's glory and to limit the church's worship to the realms of human logic. *Robert B. Selph*

Election shapes everything.
C. H. Spurgeon

From the Word of God I gather that damnation is all of man, from top to bottom, and salvation is all of grace, from first to last. He that perishes chooses to perish; but he that is saved is saved because God has chosen to save him.
C. H. Spurgeon

It is no mean thing to be chosen of God. God's choice makes chosen men choice men. *C. H. Spurgeon*

It is one of the axioms of theology that if a man be lost God must not be blamed for it; and it is also an axiom of theology that if a man be saved God must have the glory for it. *C. H. Spurgeon*

At the heart of election is a particular and passionate love that was the cause of God sending his Son to be the Saviour of his people. *G. Steveson*

Election and sovereignty are only sources of good. Election is not a decree to destroy, it is a decree to save. When we elect a president, we do not need to hold a second election to determine that the remaining millions shall be non-presidents. *Augustus H. Strong*

Election — and Conversion

Election keeps no one out of heaven who would otherwise have been there, but it keeps a whole multitude of sinners out of hell who would otherwise have been there. *Mark Webb*

Let a man go to the grammar school of faith and repentance before he goes to the university of election and predestination. *George Whitefield*

ELECTION — and Eternal Security
(See also: Eternal Security)

We do despite to the doctrines of election and predestination when we use them as a kind of theological hand grenade to throw at each other. They are not given to us for that purpose; they are given as mighty stabilizers. *Eric Alexander*

The Christian's eternal security is rooted not in what he has done, but in where he has been placed. *John Blanchard*

The doctrine of election is not meant to confuse the Christian but to comfort him. *John Blanchard*

God watches over the scattered dust of his own children, gathers it again, and will suffer nothing of them to perish. *John Calvin*

There is no better assurance of salvation to he found anywhere than can be gained from the decree of God. *John Calvin*

As God did not at first choose you because you were high, so he will not forsake you because you are low. *John Flavel*

Our spiritual estate standeth upon a sure bottom; the beginning is from God the Father, the dispensation from the Son and the application from the Holy Ghost ... It is free in the Father, sure in the Son, ours in the Spirit. *Thomas Manton*

God's plans reach from an eternity past to an eternity to come. Let him take his own time. *William S. Plumer*

God will never cast away his jewels, but gather them into his cabinet of just men made perfect. *William S. Plumer*

Should any man be fully persuaded that God had decreed his eternal happiness, however groundless that persuasion might be, he would find his aversion to the doctrine of election exceedingly abated by it. *Thomas Scott*

Salvation is no precarious half-measure but a foundation laid in heaven. *E. K. Simpson*

Candles which are lit by God the devil can never blow out. *C. H. Spurgeon*

They are well kept whom the Lord keeps. *William Tiptaft*

God never repents of his electing love. *Thomas Watson*

God's call is founded upon his decree, and his decree is immutable. *Thomas Watson*

If once God's electing love rises upon the soul, it never sets. *Thomas Watson*

Who shall the Lord's elect condemn?
'Tis God that justifies their souls,
And mercy like a mighty stream
O'er all their sins divinely rolls. *Isaac Watts*

Election — and Holiness

ELECTION — and Evangelism — See Evangelism and Election

ELECTION — and Faith

It is God who causes faith in the believer by prompting his will and enlightening his intellect. *Thomas Aquinas*

God chooses us, not because we believe, but that we may believe. *Augustine*

If God did not choose some men without any conditions, no man would ever choose God under any conditions.
John Blanchard

Election depends on the promise of God.
John Calvin

Election is not in consequence of faith, but faith is in consequence of election.
C. J. Ellicott

Election, in the Scriptures, is something for which we worship God because in it he reveals the greatness and the freeness of his love for sinful men.
Sinclair Ferguson

Faith as the fruit of election is also the proof of election. *R. B. Kuiper*

Christ did not die for any upon condition, if they do believe; but he died for all God's elect, that they should believe.
John Owen

No man believes with a true and saving faith unless God inclines his heart; and no man when God does incline his heart can refrain from believing.
Blaise Pascal

We are not elected … either for our faith, or according to our faith, but to our faith;

that is, elected that we might believe.
William Perkins

God alone can make a man a believer. Our part is to accept or reject his initiative. *John Powell*

God does not choose us for faith but to faith. *Thomas Watson*

ELECTION — and Forgiveness

Those who deny election deny that God can have mercy.
Robert Murray M'Cheyne

Who shall the Lord's elect condemn?
'Tis God that justifies their souls,
And mercy like a mighty stream
O'er all their sins divinely rolls.
Isaac Watts

ELECTION — and Holiness

No man can prove that he is a child of God without showing the family likeness.
John Blanchard

The end of our election is that we might show forth the glory of God in every way.
John Calvin

Nothing could be further from the truth than the suggestion that God's choice destroys moral effort on our part.
Sinclair Ferguson

The doctrine of God's electing purposes reveals his character. *Sinclair Ferguson*

Thou mayest know thou art elect as surely by a work of grace in thee as if thou hadst stood by God's elbow when he writ thy name in the book of life. *William Gurnall*

The calling of God never leaves men where it finds them. *Joseph Hall*

None can know their election but by their conformity to Christ; for all that are chosen are chosen to sanctification.
Matthew Henry

Holiness is the only evidence of election.
Charles Hodge

The doctrines of grace humble a man without degrading him and exalt a man without inflating him. *Charles Hodge*

The only certain proof of my election is that today I am following the Lord.
R. C. Lucas

The Holy Spirit does *something more in* each of God's elect than he does in the non-elect. He works in them 'both to will and to do of God's good pleasure'.
A. W. Pink

The proof of our election is always and only to be found in a holy life.
William S. Plumer

Election is always to sanctification. Those whom Christ chooses out of mankind, he chooses not only that they may be saved, but that they may bear fruit, and fruit that can be seen. All other election beside this is a mere vain delusion, and a miserable invention of man. *J. C. Ryle*

The Bible speaks of election through sanctification, and predestination to be conformed to the image of the Son of God. If these are lacking, it is a waste of time to speak of election. *J. C. Ryle*

The names and number of the elect are a secret thing, no doubt ... But if there is one thing clearly and plainly laid down about election, it is this — that elect men and women may be known and distinguished by holy lives. *J. C. Ryle*

God has not chosen us because we were holy, or because he foresaw we should become holy, but in order that we might be holy. *Charles Simeon*

Our election is not based on our wills but on the purposes of the will of God.
R. C. Sproul

The realization that we are predestined and elected to life is one of the mightiest incentives to Christian living.
W. H. Griffith Thomas

It is idle to seek assurance of election outside of holiness of life.
Benjamin B. Warfield

We are not chosen because we are good; we are chosen that we may be good.
Benjamin B. Warfield

We can never know that we are elected of God to eternal life except by manifesting in our lives the fruits of election.
Benjamin B. Warfield

As chastity distinguishes a virtuous woman from a harlot, so sanctification distinguishes God's people from others.
Thomas Watson

Purity is the end of our election.
Thomas Watson

Sanctification is the earmark of Christ's elect sheep. *Thomas Watson*

ELECTION — Mystery

Grace and election are the essence and mystery of history. *Augustine*

The elect are whosoever will; the non-elect are whosoever won't.
Henry Ward Beecher

God's sovereign election is the mould into which the whole universe is poured.
John Blanchard

In the election of man to Salvation, God has the only vote. *John Blanchard*

Take away the glorious truth of God's unconditional election and not only would every Christian fall out of the church, but every star would fall out of the sky and every page out of the Bible!
John Blanchard

The difference which exists between the elect and the rest of the world is the mere good pleasure of God. *John Calvin*

The election of God is anterior to Adam's fall. *John Calvin*

The ground of the discrimination that exists among men is the sovereign will of God and that alone; but the ground of damnation to which the reprobate are consigned is sin and sin alone.
John Calvin

When we come to election, we see nothing but mercy on every side. *John Calvin*

Either God is sovereign and election is an expression of God's will, or man is sovereign and election is an expression of God's foreknowledge.
Arthur C. Custance

God graciously elected some to salvation, and he decreed justly to leave others to their deserts. *R. B. Kuiper*

Eternal love devised the plan; eternal wisdom drew the model; eternal grace comes down to build it. *Henry Law*

The doctrine of election does not … exist in a vacuum. It must be seen in the context of the divine sovereignty, the depravity of man and the givenness of faith. *Donald MacLeod*

The Son cannot die for them whom the Father never elected, and the Spirit will never sanctify them whom the Father hath not elected nor the Son redeemed.
Thomas Manton

Election is a divine choice of individuals, unto salvation, made in connection with Christ the Redeemer, in eternity, based upon the mere good pleasure of God's will. *Al Martin*

Nothing gives such offence, and stirs up such bitter feeling among the wicked, as the idea of God making any distinction between man and man, and loving one person more than another. *J. C. Ryle*

We had a Saviour before we were born.
Richard Sibbes

I believe the doctrine of election, because I am quite sure that if God had not chosen me I would never have chosen him; and I am sure he chose me before I was born, or else he never would have chosen me afterward. *C. H. Spurgeon*

You must first deny the authenticity and full inspiration of the Holy Scripture before you can legitimately and truly deny election. *C. H. Spurgeon*

We may better praise God that he saves any than charge him with injustice because he saves so few. *Augustus H. Strong*

The marvel of marvels is not that God, in his infinite love, has not elected all of this guilty race to be saved, but that he has elected any.　　*Benjamin B. Warfield*

ELOQUENCE
(See also: Speech)

Eloquence is logic on fire.
Lyman Beecher

Eloquence and ignorance sometimes go together.　　*John Blanchard*

True eloquence is vehement simplicity.
Richard Cecil

One of the best definitions of eloquence is 'to have something to say and to *burn* to say it'.　　*Henry C. Fish*

True eloquence is the transference of thought and emotion from one heart to another, no matter how it is done.
John B. Gough

EMOTIONS

It is certainly true that our faith is not to be based on our feelings — but equally true that if our faith is not accompanied by feelings it is suspect. *John Blanchard*

If you resolve to make sense and feeling the judge of your conditions, you must resolve to live in fears and lie down in tears.　　*Thomas Brooks*

If you are limping around on the crutches of feelings, throw them away and walk on the legs of faith.　　*Ronald Dunn*

When Christ comes in, the wonder is not that one has emotion, but the wonder is that one can be so restrained!
E. Stanley Jones

Don't bother much about your feelings. When they are humble, loving, brave, give thanks for them; when they are conceited, selfish, cowardly, ask to have them altered.　　*C. S. Lewis*

Feelings come and go, and when they come a good use can be made of them; they cannot be our regular spiritual diet.
C. S. Lewis

Emotion arises out of the truth; emotionalism is poured on to it.　*W. R. Maltby*

Confidence that one's impressions are God-given is no guarantee that this is really so, even when they persist and grow stronger through long seasons of prayer. Bible-based wisdom must judge them.　　*J. I. Packer*

There is no great Christianity where there is no great feeling.　*Maurice Roberts*

The man who screams at a football game, but is distressed when he hears of a sinner weeping at the cross, and murmurs about the dangers of emotionalism, hardly merits intelligent respect. *W. E. Sangster*

God is more concerned with the state of people's hearts than with the state of their feelings.　　*A. W. Tozer*

I believe that in any setting, the tendency to place personal feeling above the Scriptures is always an insult to God.
A. W. Tozer

EMPATHY — See Sympathy

ENCOURAGEMENT

Encouragement is oxygen to the soul.
George M. Adams

A good word costs no more than a bad one. *Anon.*

If you wish to be disappointed look at others; if you wish to be disheartened, look at yourself; if you wish to be encouraged, look to Jesus. *Anon.*

More people fail for lack of encouragement than for any other reason. *Anon.*

Nothing succeeds like encouragement.
Anon.

The church should be a community of encouragement. *Fred Catherwood*

The faintest whisper of support and encouragement uttered by a Christian in the ears of his fellow believer is heard in heaven. *John J. Murray*

A compliment is verbal sunshine.
Robert Orben

We cannot hold a torch to another's path without brightening our own.
Ben Sweetland

Correction does much, but encouragement does more. Encouragement after censure is as the sun after a shower.
Johann Wolfgang von Goethe

ENDURANCE — See Perseverance

ENTHUSIASM
(See also: Earnestness; Zeal)

Enthusiasm is essential to the triumph of truth. *Anon.*

Most great men and women are not perfectly rounded in their personalities, but are instead people whose one driving enthusiasm is so great it makes their faults seem insignificant. *Charles A. Cerami*

Wherever you be, be all there. Live to the hilt every situation you believe to be the will of God. *Jim Elliot*

Nothing great was ever achieved without enthusiasm. *Ralph Waldo Emerson*

Enthusiasm is easier than obedience.
Michael Griffiths

We have stage fire and strange fire and satanic fire, but not much Spirit fire.
Vance Havner

Enthusiasm finds the opportunities and energy makes the most of them.
Henry S. Huskins

A man can succeed at almost anything for which he has unlimited enthusiasm.
Charles M. Schwab

Enthusiasm, like fire, must not only burn, but must be controlled.
Augustus H. Strong

If there is any reality within the whole sphere of human experience that is by its very nature worthy to challenge the mind, charm the heart and bring the total life to a burning focus, it is the reality that revolves around the person of Christ.
A. W. Tozer

Only encouragement with God can maintain perpetual spiritual enthusiasm, because only God can supply everlasting novelty. *A. W. Tozer*

Enthusiasm and persistence can make an average person superior; indifference and lethargy can make a superior person average. *William A. Ward*

Envy

ENVY
(See also: Jealously)

He that looks through a green glass sees no other colour. *Thomas Adams*

Envy eats nothing but its own heart. *Anon.*

Envy never enriched any man. *Anon.*

Envy provides the mud that failure throws at success. *Anon.*

Every time you turn green with envy you are ripe for trouble. *Anon.*

If envy were a fever, all the world would be ill. *Anon.*

As rust corrupts iron, so envy corrupts man. *Antisthenes*

If there is any sin more deadly than envy, it is being pleased at being envied. *Richard Armour*

Envy is a coal that comes hissing hot from hell. *Philip James Baily*

Love looks through a telescope, envy through a microscope. *John Billings*

An envious man is a squinty-eyed fool. *H. C. Bohn*

Envy, it tortures the affections, it vexes the mind, it inflames the blood, it corrupts the heart, it wastes the spirits; and so it becomes man's tormentor and man's executioner at once. *Thomas Brooks*

Envy is a denial of providence. *Stephen Charnock*

As a moth gnaws a garment, so doth envy consume a man. *Chrysostom*

Envy is the sign of a nature that is altogether evil. *Demosthenes*

Envy is the greatest of all diseases among men. *Euripides*

Envy shoots at others and wounds herself. *Thomas Fuller*

It is as hard to keep our hearts and envy asunder as it is to hinder two lovers from meeting together. *William Gurnall*

If we love our neighbour we shall be so far from envying his welfare, or being displeased with it, that we shall share in it and rejoice at it. *Matthew Henry*

The prosperity of those to whom we wish well can never grieve us; and the mind which is bent on doing good to all can never wish ill to any. *Matthew Henry*

Envy is its own punishment. *William Jenkyn*

Too many Christians envy the sinners their pleasure and the saints their joy because they don't have either one. *Martin Luther*

Envy is a rebellion against God himself, and the liberty and pleasure of his dispensations. *Thomas Manton*

Envy is a settled, crooked malice. *Thomas Manton*

There are two sins which were Christ's sorest enemies, covetousness and envy. Covetousness sold Christ and envy delivered him. *Thomas Manton*

The envious man is an enemy to himself, for his mind is always spontaneously occupied with his own unhappy thoughts. *Menander*

Envy of another man's calling can work havoc in our own.   *Watchman Nee*

Envy always implies inferiority, wherever it resides.   *Pliny*

There is no worse passion than envy.
William S. Plumer

There is not a passion so strongly rooted in the human heart as envy.
Richard Brinsley Sheridan

Envy and malice are quicksighted.
Richard Sibbes

In spiritual things there is no envy.
Richard Sibbes

The cure for envy lies in living under a constant sense of the divine presence, worshipping God and communing with him all the day long, however long the day may seem.   *C. H. Spurgeon*

Envy does nothing with reason.
John Trapp

Envy is a self-murder, a fretting canker.
Thomas Watson

ERROR — See Heresy

ESCHATOLOGY — See Judgement; Second Coming of Christ

ETERNAL LIFE
(See also: Destiny; Eternity; Heaven; Immortality; The Christian's Eternal Home)

Everlasting life is a jewel of too great a value to be purchased by the wealth of this world.   *Matthew Henry*

Eternal life does not begin with death; it begins with faith.   *Samuel Shoemaker*

All who die in faith are firmly grasped by Christ's love, and will not be conscious of any passage of time until the moment when Christ returns — any more than we are conscious of time passing between our going to sleep and waking up in the morning.   *Stephen Travis*

ETERNAL SECURITY
(See also: Election — and Eternal Security; Eternal Life; Heaven — The Christian's Eternal Home)

God never promises us an easy time, only a safe arrival.   *Anon.*

We do believe in eternal security, but we do not believe in eternal presumption. Let a man examine himself.
Donald Grey Barnhouse

Glory for the Christian is more certain than the grave.   *John Blanchard*

God has never torn up a Christian's birth certificate.   *John Blanchard*

It is possible to fall in grace, but not to fall from grace.   *John Blanchard*

The Christian can be as certain of arriving in heaven as he is that Christ has already ascended there.   *John Blanchard*

The Christian's place in heaven was assured before there was a single angel there to help in arranging his accommodation.   *John Blanchard*

The fact that a Christian is uncertain does not mean that he is insecure.
John Blanchard

The reason no Christian can be snatched out of the Father's hand is that it was the Father who placed him there.
John Blanchard

Christ is to be answerable for all those that are given to him, at the last day, and therefore we need not doubt but that he will certainly employ all the powers of his Godhead to secure and save all those that he must be accountable for.

Thomas Brooks

Earthly jewels sometimes get separated from their owner, Christ's jewels, never … Earthly jewels are sometimes lost, Christ's jewels, never … Earthly jewels are sometimes stolen, Christ's jewels, never! *Thomas Brooks*

We have not the slightest cause to fear that our integrity will make us a prey to the ungodly when God promises us safety under his hand. *John Calvin*

According to Scripture, there is no salvation purposed, offered, or under-taken under grace which is not infinitely perfect and that does not abide for ever.

Lewis Sperry Chafer

The ultimate answer to the insecurity or security of the believer rests on the ques-tion of who does the work of salvation.

Lewis Sperry Chafer

It may be that we are sinful; but God did not love us for our goodness, neither will he cast us off for our wickedness.

John Cotton

Did Christ finish his work *for* us? Then there can be no doubt but he will also finish his work *in* us. *John Flavel*

The life of Christ's own glory is bound up in the eternal life of his saints.

William Gurnall

If the elect should perish then Jesus Christ should be very unfaithful to his Father, because God the Father hath given this charge to Christ, that whomsoever he elected Christ should preserve them safe, to bring them to heaven.

Christopher Love

God never finally forsakes his people.

Martin Luther

Whoever falls from God's right hand is caught into his left. *Edwin Markham*

If God maintains sun and planets in bright and ordered beauty he can keep us.

F. B. Meyer

We can afford to walk in the dark now if we are assured of eternal light hereafter.

Thomas V. Moore

The perseverance of the saints reminds us very forcefully that only those who persevere to the end are truly saints.

John Murray

The earth shall soon dissolve like snow,
The sun forbear to shine;
But God, who called me here below,
Will be for ever mine. *John Newton*

Perseverance is the rope that ties the soul to the doorpost of heaven.

Frances J. Roberts

He that formed me in the womb,
He shall guide me to the tomb;
All my times shall ever be
Ordered by his wise decree.

John Ryland

God's seed will come to God's harvest.

Samuel Rutherford

No soldiers of Christ are ever lost, miss-ing or left dead on the battlefield.

J. C. Ryle

The perseverance of the saints is only possible because of the perseverance of God.   *J. Oswald Sanders*

Christianity is the world's monumental fraud if there be no future life.
    Martin J. Scott

As God numbers the hairs of his people, he must needs preserve their heads.
    William Secker

Though Christians be not kept altogether from falling, yet they are kept from falling altogether.   *William Secker*

An inheritance is not only kept for us, but we are kept for it.   *Richard Sibbes*

He that keeps heaven for us will give us necessary graces to bring us thither.
    Richard Sibbes

When we die, we have not a place to seek. Our house is provided beforehand … We had a place in heaven before we were born.   *Richard Sibbes*

As we are under the covenant of grace, we are secured against departing from the living God by the sure declaration of the covenant.   *C. H. Spurgeon*

Child of God, you cost Christ too much for him to forget you.   *C. H. Spurgeon*

God promises to keep his people, and he will keep his promises.   *C. H. Spurgeon*

He that takes care of our times will take care of our eternity.   *C. H. Spurgeon*

If God lights the candle, none can blow it out.   *C. H. Spurgeon*

It is a glorious truth that God will keep his people, but it is an abominable falsehood that sin will do them no harm.
    C. H. Spurgeon

Jesus has made the life of his people as eternal as his own.   *C. H. Spurgeon*

None can find out a single person whom God has forsaken after having revealed himself savingly to him.   *C. H. Spurgeon*

The doctrine of final perseverance of believers seems to me to be written as with a beam of sunlight throughout the whole of Scripture.   *C. H. Spurgeon*

The Lord Jesus has paid too high a price for our redemption to leave us in the enemy's hand.   *C. H. Spurgeon*

The Lord's trees are all evergreen.
    C H. Spurgeon

Until God can be unjust, and demand two payments for one debt, he cannot destroy the soul for whom Jesus died.
    C. H. Spurgeon

When Christ can die, then can the believer perish.   *C. H. Spurgeon*

We can call out even to the demons in hell, 'Which of you is going to condemn me?' And there will be no answer.
    John R. W. Stott

My name from the palms of his hands
Eternity will not erase;
Impressed on his heart it remains,
In marks of indelible grace;
Yes, I to the end shall endure,
As sure as the earnest is given;
More happy, but not more secure,
The glorified spirits in heaven.
    Augustus M. Toplady

Payment God cannot twice demand;
First at my bleeding Saviour's hand,
And then again at mine.
Augustus M. Toplady

The work which his goodness began,
The arm of his strength will complete;
His promise is Yea and Amen
And never was forfeited yet;
Things future, nor things that are now,
Nor all things below nor above,
Can make him his purpose forgo,
Or sever my soul from his love.
Augustus M. Toplady

Never did a believer in Jesus die or drown in his voyage to heaven.   *Robert Traill*

The soul that is shaped into the image of Christ will remain for ever.
Takesaburo Uzaki

God never repents of his electing love.
Thomas Watson

God's decree is the very pillar and basis on which the saints' perseverance depends. That decree ties the knot of adoption so fast that neither sin, death nor hell can break it asunder. *Thomas Watson*

God may for a time desert his children, but he will not disinherit them.
Thomas Watson

If one justified person may fall away from Christ, all may; and so Christ would be a head without a body.   *Thomas Watson*

When God calls a man, he does not repent of it ... This is the blessedness of a saint; his condition admits of no alteration.   *Thomas Watson*

The question is not one of the retention of salvation based upon a persistence of faith, but of the possession of salvation as evidenced by a continuation of faith.
Kenneth Wuest

ETERNITY
(See also: Destiny; Eternal Life; Heaven; Hell; Judgement)

Alas! that the farthest end of all our thoughts should be thought of our ends.
Thomas Adams

Eternity is the lifetime of the Almighty.
Anon.

Life, if properly viewed in any aspect, is great, but mainly great when viewed in its relation to the world to come.
Albert Barnes

The thought of eternity particularly delights those assured of grace, while it terrifies others.   *J. A. Bengel*

The great weight of eternity hangs upon the small wire of time.   *Thomas Brooks*

We do all for eternity.   *Thomas Brooks*

The created world is but a small parenthesis in eternity.   *Thomas Browne*

He who has no vision of eternity will never get a true hold of time.
Thomas Carlyle

We treat sensible and present things as realities, and future and eternal things as fables: whereas the reverse should be our habit.   *Richard Cecil*

The sum and substance of the preparation needed for a coming eternity is that you believe what the Bible tells you and do what the Bible bids you.
Thomas Chalmers

Whatsoever is eternal is immutable.
Stephen Charnock

None but a theology that came out of eternity can carry you and me safely to and through eternity. *T. L. Cuyler*

If God exists, then it is possible for me confidently to affirm that my existence does not end with my death.
Stephen T. Davies

O God, stamp eternity on my eyeballs!
Jonathan Edwards

All the world's ends, arrangements, changes, disappointments, hopes and fears are without meaning if not seen and estimated by eternity. *Tryon Edwards*

Eternity shall be at one and the same time a great eye-opener and a great mouth-shutter. *Jim Elliot*

Without a belief in the hereafter, the moral case against God is overwhelming.
Rod Garner

If you look past the world, you put your head up into eternity. *Thomas Goodwin*

Any philosophy which deals only with the here and now is not adequate for man.
Billy Graham

I've read the last page of the Bible. It's going to turn out all right. *Billy Graham*

Eternity will be too short to exhaust our learning of God or to end our enjoyment of him. *Peter Green*

Do not so contemplate eternity that you waste today. *Vance Havner*

The crosses and comforts of this present time would not make such an impression upon us as they do if we did but believe the things of eternity as we ought.
Matthew Henry

This world is our passage not our portion. *Matthew Henry*

Men that believe not another world are the ready actors of any imaginable mischiefs and tragedies in this. *John Howe*

The thirst for infinity proves infinity.
Victor Hugo

Life is only lived wisely to the extent that it is spent in preparation for the eternity which follows. *Dave Hunt*

As meditation on this word, 'eternity', has been so beneficial to my own soul, I would advise others to make the same experiment. *Thomas Jones*

All that is not eternal is eternally out of date. *C. S. Lewis*

In our sad condition, our only consolation is the expectancy of another life. Here below all is incomprehensible.
Martin Luther

Live near to God, and all things will appear little to you in comparison with eternal realities. *Robert Murray M'Cheyne*

Eternity depends upon this moment.
Thomas Manton

Eternity is an everlasting now.
Christopher Nesse

Learn to hold loosely all that is not eternal. *Agnes Maude Royden*

'For ever' is the most solemn saying in the Bible. *J. C. Ryle*

After our death a gate will open; it could be called 'the gate of reality'.
Basilea Schlink

One thought of eternity makes all earthly sorrows fade away. *Basilea Schlink*

This word 'eternal', it is a heavy word.
Richard Sibbes

Belief in the immortality of the soul and belief in the accountability of the soul are fundamental beliefs in all religion.
O. J. Smith

Christ's resurrection is not only the best proof of immortality, but we have no certain evidence of immortality without it. *Augustus H. Strong*

Science tells us that nothing in nature, not even the tiniest particle, can disappear without a trace. Nature does not know extinction, only transformation. If God applies this fundamental principle to the most minute part of his universe, doesn't it make sense to assume that he applies it also to the soul of man?
Wernher Von Braun

Those who hope for no other life are dead even for this. *Johann Wolfgang von Goethe*

An eternity past puzzles all human comprehension. *Daniel Waterland*

Eternity is a jewel of the saints' crown.
Thomas Watson

Eternity to the godly is a day that has no sunset: eternity to the godless is a night that has no sunrise. *Thomas Watson*

Ever is a short word but it has no end.
Thomas Watson

The wicked have a never-dying worm and the godly a never-fading crown.
Thomas Watson

I desire to have both heaven and hell ever in my eye, while I stand on this isthmus of life, between two boundless oceans.
John Wesley

The real value of a thing is the price it will bring in eternity. *John Wesley*

The future life only brings to fruition the seed sown here. *Geoffrey B. Wilson*

Eternity is duration without beginning and without end. *Thomas Wilson*

The solution of the riddle of life in space and time lies outside space and time.
Ludwig Wittgenstein

Praise God for eternity to come, when the order of things shall be reversed.
Spiros Zodhiates

ETHICS
(See also: Goodness: Morality; Virtue)

The Christian must recognize that there are no degrees in right or wrong.
Donald Grey Barnhouse

Without transcendent norms, laws are either established by social elites or are merely bargains struck by competing forces in society. *Charles Colson*

Science does not of itself provide us with an ethical system, yet it raises many ethical issues. *Rodney D. Holder*

All men stand condemned, not by alien codes of ethics, but by their own, and all men therefore are conscious of guilt.
C. S. Lewis

Let us very clearly understand that, in a certain sense, it is no more possible to invent a new ethic than to place a new sun in the sky. *C. S. Lewis*

There are no pastel shades in the Christian ethic. *Arnold H. Lowe*

For the person who has encountered Jesus, ethics is grounded not in philosophical abstraction but in adoration and relationship. *Pete Lowman*

Situation ethics is actually blasphemy because it pictures God as being either ignorant or stupid. *Robert A. Morey*

Christian ethics are eschatological ethics, that is to say that they derive strength from what God will do in Christ at the last day.
J. A. Motyer

Christian ethics do not contain a particle of chaff — all is pure wheat.
E. G. Robinson

Every human being has some ethical sense within him, a light of nature by which he can distinguish right from wrong. *R. C. Sproul*

The essence of Christian ethics is gratitude. *R. C. Sproul*

True ethical absolutes can only be grounded in the fear of a living God.
R. C. Sproul

The basis of ethics is simple. It is the specification of those basic intrinsic values that all rational beings would desire.
Keith Ward

To say that 'God is good' is to say that God is the origin and standard of our ethical judgements, and is himself consistent with those judgements. *Peter S. Williams*

We are not in need merely of a superior ethic, we are in need of a transformed heart and will that seek to do the will of God. *Ravi Zacharias*

Without a transcendent order, ethics is unjustifiable, and without ethics, life is unliveable. *Ravi Zacharias*

EVANGELISM — Cost

The church is not a yachting club but a fleet of fishing boats. *Anon.*

When a Christian presents the good news about Jesus he is preaching treason in the devil's kingdom. *Doug Barnett*

Anyone who witnesses to the grace of God revealed in Christ is undertaking a direct assault against Satan's dominion.
Thomas Cosmades

The gospel is for lifeboats not showboats, and a man must make up his mind which he is going to operate. *Vance Havner*

When Christians evangelize, they are not engaging in some harmless and pleasant pastime. They are engaging in a fearful struggle, the issues of which are eternal.
Leon Morris

There is a tremendous price to be paid for winning men and women to Jesus Christ. After all, the price to God ... was a cross on a hill. *Alan Walker*

It is impossible to save a life from burning and avoid the heat of the fire.
Mary S. Wood

EVANGELISM — Definition and Aim

Evangelism is the redistribution of spiritual wealth. *John Blanchard*

Evangelism is truth demanding a verdict. *Lionel Fletcher*

Evangelism's highest and ultimate end is not the welfare of men, not even their eternal bliss, but the glorification of God. *R. B. Kuiper*

You can have evangelism without revival, but you cannot have revival without evangelism. *Brian Mills*

Evangelism is one beggar telling another beggar where to get bread. *D. T. Niles*

Evangelism that does not lead to purity of life and purity of doctrine is just as faulty and incomplete as an orthodoxy which does not lead to a concern for, and communication with, the lost. *Francis Schaeffer*

EVANGELISM — Divine Initiative

The gospel does not fall from the clouds like rain, by accident, *but* is brought by the hands of men to where God has sent it. *John Calvin*

God is a communicating being. *Jonathan Edwards*

When our Lord sends us out to witness for him, he does not send us out against a wall. Rather, he gives us an open door for personal evangelism, an open door that no man can shut. *Josip Horak*

God had only one Son and he made him an evangelist. *R. C. Lucas*

The Spirit of Christ is the spirit of missions, and the nearer we get to him the more intensely missionary we must become. *Henry Martyn*

There is not a better evangelist in the world than the Holy Spirit. *D. L. Moody*

Evangelism is still God's Word for this hour. *Alan Walker*

Our God is a missionary God. *William J. C. White*

Evangelism is not a human enterprise; it is a divine operation. *Arthur Skevington Wood*

EVANGELISM — and Doctrine

You cannot evangelize in a doctrinal vacuum. *Anon.*

I have not the slightest interest in a theology which doesn't evangelize. *James Denney*

The fashionable doctrine 'God loves you, Christ died for you, believe that and be happy', is but daubing immortal souls with 'untempered mortar'. *John Kennedy*

Evangelism must be trinitarian if it is to be biblical. *Harold J. Ockenga*

All true theology has an evangelistic thrust, and all true evangelism is theology in action. *J. I. Packer*

In the last analysis there is only one means of evangelism: namely, the gospel of Christ, explained and applied. *J. I. Packer*

In all evangelism, the primacy of the Bible is essential. *Douglas Webster*

Evangelism is not primarily a matter of method. It is a channel of the Word.
Arthur Skevington Wood

No refinements of technique can make up for any failure to recognize that the Word of God itself is the true method of evangelism. *Arthur Skevington Wood*

EVANGELISM — and Election

Election is a doctrine I am called upon to believe; evangelism is a command I am called upon to obey. *John Blanchard*

In the Bible, election and evangelism meet with joined hands, not clenched fists. *John Blanchard*

Election demands evangelism. All of God's elect must be saved. Not one of them may perish. And the gospel is the means by which God bestows saving faith upon them. *R. B. Kuiper*

Election, so far from undermining evangelism, undergirds it, for it provides the only hope of its succeeding in its aim.
J. I. Packer

EVANGELISM — Message

Sinners must be caught with the gospel, not with sugary morsels of worldly wisdom. *Fred A. Malone*

If we think wrongly about our definition of evangelism, we are likely to act wrongly in our methods of evangelism.
Will Metzer

We are not to try to entice people by methods appealing to their desires. *Will Metzer*

The evangel is not denunciatory of sin. It is not pronunciatory of judgement. It is annunciatory of salvation.
G. Campbell Morgan

We may boldly tell the chief of sinners that Christ loves him. Salvation is ready for the worst of men, if they will only come to Christ. If men are lost, it is not because Jesus does not love them and is not ready to save. *J. C. Ryle*

What is the first hypothesis for evangelism? That God is there, and is the kind of God that the Bible says he is, and that he has not been silent but has given us propositional truth. *Francis Schaeffer*

Cling to the great truth of electing love and divine sovereignty, but let not these bind you in fetters when, in the power of the Holy Ghost, you become fishers of men. *C. H. Spurgeon*

The driving force of the early Christian mission was not propaganda of beautiful ideals of the brotherhood of man. It was proclamation of the mighty acts of God.
James S. Stewart

The medicine of the gospel has been prescribed by the Good Physician; we may neither dilute it nor add ingredients to make it more palatable; we must serve it neat. *John R. W. Stott*

When social action is mistaken for evangelism the church has ceased to manufacture its own blood cells and is dying of leukemia. *Sherwood Wirt*

EVANGELISM — Principles

When telling thy salvation free,
Let all absorbing thoughts of thee
My heart and soul engross.
And when all hearts are bowed and stirred
Beneath the influence of thy Word
Hide me behind thy cross. *Anon.*

Many of us cannot reach the mission fields on our feet, but we can reach them on our knees.   *T. J. Bach*

The evangelist must be as bold in denouncing sin as others are in committing it.   *John Blanchard*

The true glory of evangelism is rooted not in our own nervous claims to success, but in the eternal covenant of a sovereign God.   *John Blanchard*

You cannot evangelize and entertain at the same time.   *John Blanchard*

The incarnation is the pattern for all evangelism. Jesus Christ was totally in the world yet wholly uncontaminated by it.
                    Everett L. Cattell

The skill of the evangelist, or the pastor who would do the work of an evangelist, is seen in the ability to present the limited body of redemptive truth repeatedly, yet with freshness and variety.
                    Lewis Sperry Chafer

Our Lord's first obedience was to the will of his Father, not to the needs of men; the saving of men was the natural outcome of his obedience to the Father.
                    Oswald Chambers

You can never give another person that which you have found, but you can make him homesick for what you have.
                    Oswald Chambers

Why should we fear that the arm of God should be short for others that could reach us?   *Thomas Fuller*

The way from God to a human heart is through a human heart. *Samuel Gordon*

I just want to lobby for God. *Billy Graham*

Sinners are not pelted into Christ with stones of hard provoking language, but wooed into Christ by heartmelting exhortations.   *William Gurnall*

The person who is unconcerned about those who are perishing may well wonder whether he is a Christian.
                    William Hendriksen

We ought carefully to distinguish between the sinner and the sin, so as not to love the sin for the sake of the person, nor to hate the person for the sake of the sin.   *Matthew Henry*

Christ owes the unevangelized nothing, absolutely nothing.   *A. A. Hodge*

The unfinished task which lies before us is no greater than the unlimited power of God behind us.   *Fred D. Jarvis*

Every gospel imperative is full of the divine power of grace to effect what it demands. If it counted on even the least power in the sinner it would never secure the least effect.   *R. C. H. Lenski*

When we are spreading the gospel we must follow God's providential indications as to where we ought to work.
                    R. C. H. Lenski

We cannot evangelize unless we understand the Word; and we cannot evangelize unless we understand the world.
                    Donald MacLeod

Since the Lord saved *me,* I have despaired of no man living.   *Henry T. Mahan*

It is our privilege to have world evangelism as a passion, not our responsibility to have as a burden.   *Mary Nordstrom*

Most people are brought to faith in Christ, not by argument for it, but by exposure to it. *Samuel Shoemaker*

Christian labourers disconnected from the church are like sowing and reaping without having any barn in which to store the fruits of the harvest; they are useful but incomplete. *C. H. Spurgeon*

The only New Testament precedents for spreading the gospel are godly living, praying and boldly speaking.
Geoffrey Thomas

God has never indicated that proclamation of the gospel is to become dependent upon human performances.
A. W. Tozer

EVANGELISM — Responsibility for
(See also: Soul-Winning; Witnessing)

Evangelism in the New Testament sense is the vocation of every believer and there is therefore something radically wrong when we imply that personal evangelism is the province of those who have the time and/or inclination to take special courses and learn special techniques. *Roland Allen*

In making a person a Christian, God takes a burden off the heart and places another on the shoulders. *Anon.*

Missions are a must, not a maybe. *Anon.*

No church has the right to send out missionaries. God alone sends missionaries. The church's part is simply to release them as soon as God's plan is revealed. *Derek Bigg*

Evangelism is morally right — it is the payment of a debt. *John Blanchard*

Every Christian who is not called to preach is called to send other Christians to do so. *John Blanchard*

No church is obedient that is not evangelistic. *John Blanchard*

To refuse to evangelize is as sinful as to commit adultery or murder.
John Blanchard

We do not evangelize because we expect results. We evangelize because we are sent men. *Joe Blinco*

The whole world is assigned to be reduced under the obedience of Christ.
John Calvin

Evangelism is the perpetual task of the whole church, and not the peculiar hobby of certain of its members.
E. Wilson Carlisle

The gospel is not to be preserved like the Crown Jewels, locked in our ecclesiastical strong room. It is to be spread locally, and to the ends of the earth.
Herbert M. Carson

The special person called to do missionary work is every person who is a member of the church of Christ. The call does not come to a chosen few, it is to every one of us. *Oswald Chambers*

Evangelism is the disinterested interest of the comparative few. *James Denney*

The church that ceases to be evangelistic will soon cease to be evangelical.
Alexander Duff

We are to evangelize not because it is pleasant, not because it is easy, not because we may be successful, but because Christ has called us. He is our Lord. We have no other choice but to obey him.   *Leighton Ford*

The Word of God is not just for domestic consumption; it is also for export.
William Freel

There is but one question of the hour: how to bring the truth of God's Word into vital contact with the minds and hearts of all classes of people.
William E. Gladstone

There is no hint among ancient records that the early church saw evangelism as the task of the leadership alone. It was too good to leave to the professionals.
Michael Green

Every Christian is a postmaster for God. His duty is to pass out good news from above.   *Vance Havner*

The gospel is not a secret to be hoarded but a story to be heralded.   *Vance Havner*

Too many are missionaries by proxy but not in person.   *Vance Havner*

Too many Christians are stuffing themselves with gospel blessings while millions have never had a taste.
Vance Havner

No Christian is outside our Lord's last command.   *A. W. Goodwin Hudson*

Every single believer is a God-ordained agent of evangelism.   *R. B. Kuiper*

What above all else makes Christian evangelism urgent is its contribution to the hastening of the day when God shall receive all the glory due to his great and holy name.   *R. B. Kuiper*

The greatest charity in the world is the communication of divine truth to the ignorant.   *Alexander Maclaren*

We must consider it an honour that the gospel of salvation has been committed to the church.   *Shuichi Matsumura*

Christian mission is the only reason for our being on earth.   *Andrew Murray*

Always and everywhere the servants of Christ are under order to evangelize.
J. I. Packer

Holy Writ is to be kept not under a bushel, but under men's noses. Its message is to be held forth as diligently as it is held fast.   *J. I. Packer*

The command to evangelize is a part of God's law. It belongs to God's revealed will for his people.   *J. I. Packer*

The gospel is nothing but a frozen asset unless it is communicated. *J. B. Phillips*

If a church does not evangelize it will fossilize.   *A. W. Pink*

Vision is not enough, or even resolution; it is action that is required in the work of evangelism.   *W. T. H. Richards*

No candle which God lights was ever meant to burn alone.   *J. C. Ryle*

The highest form of selfishness is that of the man who is content to go to heaven alone.   *J. C. Ryle*

Every age is an age for evangelism. God has no grandchildren.   *Eugene L. Smith*

Every Christian is either a missionary or an impostor.   *C. H. Spurgeon*

If sinners will be damned, at least let them leap to hell over our bodies.
C. H. Spurgeon

It will not matter whether I live or die if you all become ministers. *C. H. Spurgeon*

No man is truly awake today who has not developed a supra-national horizon to his thinking. No church is anything more than a pathetic pietistic backwater unless it is first and fundamentally and all the time a world missionary church.
James S. Stewart

In the last resort, we engage in evangelism today not because we want to or because we choose to or because we like to, but because we have been told to.
John R. W. Stott

Evangelism is always dangerous, though it is not so dangerous as the lack of evangelism. *George Sweazey*

The Great Commission is not an option to be considered, but a command to be obeyed. *J. Hudson Taylor*

The church has nothing to do but to save souls; therefore spend and be spent in this work. It is not your business to speak so many times, but to save souls as you can; to bring as many sinners as you possibly can to repentance. *John Wesley*

EVANGELISM — Scope

We cannot bring the whole world to Christ, but we must bring Christ to the whole world. *John Blanchard*

In the offer of the gospel we must make no limitation whatever, because 'God commandeth all men everywhere to repent.' *Thomas Chalmers*

Evangelism is not a spare-time activity.
Thomas Cosmades

Our task is a world task. It cannot longer be divided into the artificial and geographical compartments of home and foreign. *John W. Decker*

The world will never be Christianized, but it should be evangelized.
Vance Havner

Evangelism, like charity, begins at home.
Arthur Skevington Wood

EVANGELISM — Spontaneity

What we read in the New Testament is not anxious appeal to Christians to spread the gospel, but a note here and there which suggests how the gospel was being spread abroad ... for centuries the Christian church continued to expand by its own inherent grace and threw up an unceasing supply of missionaries without any direct exhortation. *Roland Allen*

The great need in the church is for a spirit of evangelism, not just a spurt of evangelism. *John Blanchard*

When our hearts are filled with Christ's presence, evangelism is as inevitable as it is contagious. *Robert E. Coleman*

Evangelism should be an attitude permeating all the activities of the Christian.
Bryan Green

Evangelism never seemed to be an 'issue' in the New Testament. That is to say, one does not find the apostles urging, exhorting, scolding, planning and organizing for evangelistic programmes ... Evangelism happened! Issuing effortlessly from the community of believers

as light from the sun, it was automatic, spontaneous, continuous, contagious.
Richard C. Halverson

Evangelism for the early Christians was not something they isolated from other aspects of Christian living in order to specialize, analyse, theorize and organize. They just did it! *Roy Joslin*

EVIL — See Sin; Satan

EVIL SPIRIT — See Demons

EVOLUTION
(See also: Creation; Nature)

Evolution appeals to the operation of physical, chemical and mathematical laws to explain its processes, but remains forever silent on how these laws came to be or why they are as they are and not otherwise. *E. H. Andrews*

The theory of evolution has not grown, and is never likely to grow, out of the infant hypothetical form. *E. H. Andrews*

If you search the scientific literature on evolution, and if you focus your search on the question of how molecular machines — the basis of life — developed, you find an eerie and complete silence.
Michael Behe

The theory of evolution is a stab in the dark that has acquired the status of a dogma. *John Blanchard*

There is no more reason to believe that man descended from an inferior animal than there is to believe that a stately mansion has descended from a small cottage. *William Jennings Bryan*

What shall we say of the intelligence ...

of those who distinguish between fishes and reptiles and birds, but put a man with an immortal soul in the same circle with the wolf, the hyena and the skunk?
William Jennings Bryan

Evolution is a good example of that modern intelligence which, if it destroys anything, destroys itself. *G. K. Chesterton*

The evolutionists seem to know everything about the missing link except the fact that it is missing. *G. K. Chesterton*

Science is the chance to discover something that no man has known before, but God has known all along. In some ways you can almost think of it as a form of worship. *Francis Collins*

We are not a chance collision of atoms in an indifferent universe or islands amid cold currents of modern culture.
Charles Colson

It was because Darwinian theory broke man's link with God and set him adrift in a cosmos without purpose or end that its impact was so fundamental.
Michael Denton

The failure to give a plausible explanation for the origin of life casts a number of shadows over the whole field of evolutionary speculation. *Michael Denton*

The origin of a new species from a pre-existing species has never been directly observed. *Michael Denton*

If evolution works, how come mothers still have only two hands? *Ed Dussault*

Nobody has the slightest idea how genuine moral laws, genuine 'oughts', could be explained by evolution.
C. Stephen Evans

The theory of evolution is totally inadequate to explain the origin and manifestation of the inorganic world.

Ambrose Fleming

Why should I assume that chance has equipped me with eyes and a brain so that I can actually see what I am doing? Isn't it equally possible that when I think I'm a seminary professor typing at my desk in California, I am really a cockroach running around the New York City subway? *John M. Frame*

Nothing yet even scratches at an explanation of how a transformed ape could produce the magnificence of Beethoven's *Choral Symphony*. *Rob Frost*

Take the human body alone — the chance that all the functions of the individual could just happen is a statistical monstrosity. *George Gallup*

The sheer improbability of the cosmos evolving in the way it has — so finely tuned, so constant in its governing laws — should induce in us a sense of wonder. *Rod Garner*

Evolution, in the sense of causal proofs, is not an explanation, but rather it needs an explanation. *John H. Gerstner*

Evolution has been postulated, but it has never been observed. *Duane Gish*

Man is not making his way up through animism, fetishism, totemism, polytheism and monotheism to a knowledge of God. He started with knowledge of God and has been going the other way ever since. *Vance Havner*

The evolutionary record leaks like a sieve. *Fred Hoyle*

The basic premise of the 'molecule-to-man' theory is that hydrogen gas, given enough time, will eventually turn into people. *Scott M. Huse*

The doctrine of evolution, if consistently accepted, makes it impossible to believe the Bible. *T. H. Huxley*

So far, evolution has been nothing but staggering from one error to the other.

Henrik Ibsen

'Evolution' is a concept broad enough to encompass just about any alternative to instantaneous creation. *Phillip E. Johnson*

Evolution is not a fact, it is a philosophy.

Phillip E. Johnson

The doctrine that some known process of evolution turned a protozoan into a human is a philosophical assumption, not something that can be confirmed by experiment or by historical studies of the fossil record. *Phillip E. Johnson*

Evolutionism begins with impersonal material and energy, and is never able to answer the question of how it got there nor what it means once it is there.

Douglas F. Kelly

It seems at times as if many of our modern writers on evolution have had their views by some sort of revelation.

G. A. Kerkut

Scripture answers three basic questions to which the evolutionary theory has no answer whatever. These questions concern the origin of matter, the origin of life and the origin of man as a religious being. *R. B. Kuiper*

Evolution

Our faith in the idea of evolution depends on our reluctance to accept the antagonistic doctrine of special creation.
L. T. More

Evolution is the greatest hoax ever foisted on human minds. *Malcolm Muggeridge*

The mind cannot evolve from matter, neither can spirit evolve from flesh.
Edgar Powell

Blithely to accept that evolution succeeded against all odds is to believe in a long series of miracles. *George Roche*

How do we celebrate our emergence from chaos of chance without undermining the validity of human thought?
George Roche

The odds against random life would swallow the history of the universe as the oceans swallow a raindrop.
George Roche

There is no 'fact' of evolution, Insisting on the 'fact' is simply the anti-hero's way of saying he believes in evolution, regardless of the evidence. *George Roche*

A number of materialist thinkers have ascribed to blind evolution more miracles, more improbable coincidences and wonders, than all those who believe in God's purpose and design could ever devise. *Isaac Bashevis Singer*

Modern evolutionary secularism provides no foundation for valuing human life.
R. C. Sproul

A straight line of evolution from amino acids all the way through to Shakespeare's sonnets — that strikes me as possible, but a very long shot. Why back such an outsider? *Tom Stoppard*

Evolution cannot account for ultimate origins or the existence of order, because its operation requires the existence of entities with certain possible behaviours in an environment that works upon those entities in an ordered way.
Peter S. Williams

What cannot be explained scientifically is the origin of the information encoded in DNA. *Peter S. Williams*

EXAMPLE
(See also: Influence)

Example is the best precept. *Æsop*

Conduct is an unspoken sermon.
Henri Amiel

A good example is the best sermon. *Anon.*

Precepts may lead, but examples draw.
Anon.

The example of good men is visible philosophy. *Anon.*

If both horse and mare trot, the colt will not amble. *John Boys*

A person who lives right, and is right, has more power in his words. *Phillips Brooks*

Be such a man and live such a life that if every man were such as you and every life a life like yours, this earth would be a paradise. *Phillips Brooks*

Example is the most powerful rhetoric.
Thomas Brooks

One example is worth a thousand arguments. *Thomas Carlyle*

Example is more forceful than precept. People look at me six days a week to see what I mean on the seventh day.
Richard Cecil

The light of a holy example is the gospel's main argument.   *R. L. Dabney*

Of all commentaries upon the Scriptures, good examples are the best and the liveliest.   *John Donne*

Well done is better than well said.
Benjamin Franklin

We can do more good by being good than in any other way.   *Rowland Hill*

No man is so insignificant as to be sure his example can do no harm. *Edward Hyde*

Nothing is so infectious as example.
Charles Kingsley

The world takes its notions of God from the people who say they belong to God's family.   *Alexander Maclaren*

More depends on my walk than talk.
D. L. Moody

Live to explain thy doctrine by thy life.
Matthew Prior

Example is not the main thing in influencing others; it is the only thing.
Albert Schweitzer

Great men's vices are more imitated than poor men's graces.   *William Secker*

Let him that would move the world first move himself.   *Socrates*

Our lives should be such as men may safely copy.   *C. H. Spurgeon*

Man is a creature that is led more by patterns than by precepts. *George Swinnock*

Truth in propositions is powerful; truth in example is more powerful.
David Thomas

Good example is a language and an argument which everybody understands.
Thomas Wilson

EXCESS — See Luxury

EXCUSES

There is a vast difference between an excuse and a reason. There may be some validity in the latter, but not in the former.
Donald Grey Barnhouse

He that is good at making excuses is seldom good at anything else.
Benjamin Franklin

Bad excuses are worse than none.
Thomas Fuller

An excuse is only the skin of a reason, stuffed with a lie.   *Vance Havner*

He who wants to know people should study their excuses.   *Friedrich Hebbel*

He who excuses himself accuses himself.
Gabriel Meurier

An excuse is a lie guarded.
Alexander Pope

It is easy to make excuses when we ought to be making opportunities.
Warren Wiersbe

EXPERIENCE

A man with an experience is never at the mercy of a man with an argument. *Anon.*

Experience is not always the kindest of teachers, but it is the best. *Anon.*

Unused experience is a dead loss. *Anon.*

We are not to make our experience the rule of Scripture, but Scripture the rule of our experience. *Anon.*

The experience of Christians is not necessarily Christian experience.
Donald Grey Barnhouse

Experience is the best of schoolmasters, only the school fees are heavy.
Thomas Carlyle

How humbling it is to all learning when a man is made to know that his doctrine has outrun his experiences!
Thomas Chalmers

Never make a principle out of your experience; let God be as original with other people as he is with you.
Oswald Chambers

Do not confuse great experiences with great grace. *Sinclair Ferguson*

Many spiritual experiences are possible which do not in and of themselves produce maturity. Rather, it is our response to experience which will determine our progress in maturity. *Sinclair Ferguson*

Experience is a costly school, yet some learn no other way. *Benjamin Franklin*

Today is yesterday's pupil. *Thomas Fuller*

One man with a glowing experience of God is worth a library full of arguments.
Vance Havner

All experience must be subservient to the discipline of Scripture. *Erroll Hulse*

Experience is not what happens to you; it is what you do with what happens to you. *Aldous Huxley*

Experience is the great schoolmaster.
A. W. Pink

Nothing shuts the mouth, seals the lips, ties the tongue, like the poverty of our own spiritual experience. We do not bear witness for the simple reason that we have no witness to bear. *John R. W. Stott*

Practice is the best of all instructors.
Publilius Syrus

Every experience God gives us, every person he puts in our lives, is the perfect preparation for the future that only he can see. *Corrie ten Boom*

Experience is the one thing you can't get for nothing. *Oscar Wilde*

FAILURE

Half the failures of life arise from pulling in one's horse as he is leaping.
J. C. Hare

No amount of falls will really undo us if we keep picking ourselves up each time.
C. S. Lewis

It is very difficult to be humble if you are always successful, so God chastises us with failure at times in order to humble us, to keep us in a state of humility.
D. Martyn Lloyd-Jones

Failure is an invitation to have recourse to God. *Antonin Sertillanges*

The greatest failure is the failure to try. *William A. Ward*

FAITH — and Deeds
(See also: Faith — Saving; Good Deeds; Holiness — and Justification)

Moral virtue may wash the outside, but faith washes the inside. *Thomas Adams*

Faith and works are like the light and heat of a candle; they cannot be separated. *Anon.*

Faith does not set aside natural duties, but perfects and strengthens them. *J. A. Bengel*

Idle faith is as useless as idle words. *John Blanchard*

Only he who believes is obedient; only he who is obedient believes. *Dietrich Bonhoeffer*

The saints of God are sealed inwardly with faith, but outwardly with good works. *John Boys*

Till men have faith in Christ, their best services are but glorious sins. *Thomas Brooks*

Faith and love must be inseparable companions. There is a necessary connection between them. Faith without love is no living grace, and love without faith is no saving faith. *Francis Burkitt*

It is faith alone that justifies, but the faith that justifies is not alone. *John Calvin*

Faith is the starting-post of obedience. *Thomas Chalmers*

Faith justifies the person and works justify his faith. *Elisha Coles*

Practice is the incarnation of faith. *John Donne*

He does not believe that does not live according to his belief. *Thomas Fuller*

The only saving faith is following faith. *Richard Glover*

Faith that saves has one distinguishing quality; saving faith is a faith that produces obedience, it is a faith that brings about a way of life. *Billy Graham*

We must come to good works by faith, and not to faith by good works. *William Gurnall*

Man fell by a desire to be independent of God, and now man wishes to be equally independent of God in returning to him. *T. C. Hammond*

Works without faith are like a suit of clothes without a body, empty. Faith without works is a body without clothes; no warmth. *John P. K. Henshaw*

Faith must have adequate evidence, else it is mere superstition. *A. A. Hodge*

Let your practice praise your creed, and your lives do honour to your heads. *William Jay*

Faith is a living, restless thing. It cannot be inoperative. *Martin Luther*

Good works do not make a good man, but a good man makes the works to be good. *Martin Luther*

The true, living faith, which the Holy

Spirit instils into the heart, simply cannot be idle. *Martin Luther*

Faith is not an idle grace. *Thomas Manton*

Wherever there is genuine faith it must blossom into works. *Joseph B. Mayor*

A life of faith involves hard work, courage and discipline. *Philip Nunn*

To live by faith is to live a reasonable life based on God's Word, a life which reflects God's values and priorities. *Philip Nunn*

What saves is faith alone, but the faith that saves is never alone. *J. I. Packer*

To assume that a holy God winks at sin and grants eternal life on the basis of our performance is the greatest deception plaguing mankind. *R. C. Sproul*

Believing and obeying always run side by side. *C. H. Spurgeon*

Faith and obedience are bound up in the same bundle. He that obeys God, trusts God; and he that trusts God, obeys God. *C. H. Spurgeon*

Obedience is the hallmark of faith. *C. H. Spurgeon*

There is never a doubt in our heart about the experience of faith while it is in action. *C. H. Spurgeon*

If God gives you St Paul's faith, you will soon have St James's works. *Augustus M. Toplady*

The Bible recognizes no faith that does not lead to obedience, nor does it recognize any obedience that does not spring from faith. The two are opposite sides of the same coin. *A. W Tozer*

Faith believes as if it did not work, and it works as if it did not believe. *Thomas Watson*

You may as well separate weight from lead or heat from fire as works from faith. *Thomas Watson*

No more, my God, I boast no more
Of all the duties I have done:
I quit the hopes I held before,
To trust the merits of thy Son. *Isaac Watts*

Faith can neither be stationary nor complete. *Brooke Foss Westcott*

Works? Works? A man get to heaven by works? I would as soon think of climbing to the moon on a rope of sand. *George Whitefield*

All right believing in God is visibly reflected in right behaviour towards men. *Geoffrey B. Wilson*

FAITH — Definition
(See also: Faith — Saving)

Faith is in the spiritual realm what money is in the commercial realm. *Anon.*

Faith is to the soul what a mainspring is to a watch. *Anon.*

Trusting means drawing on the inexhaustible resources of God. *Anon.*

What is faith, unless it is to believe what you do not see? *Augustine*

At the end of the day, faith means letting God be God. *John Blanchard*

Faith is the means by which the infirmity of man lays hold on the infinity of God.
John Blanchard

Walking by faith means being prepared to trust where we are not permitted to see.
John Blanchard

Faith is the soul's ear. *John Boys*

Faith is the resurrection of the soul.
John Calvin

Faith is like the hand of the beggar that takes the gift while adding nothing to it.
Thomas Chalmers

Faith is more than assent, but it is never *less* than assent. *Sinclair Ferguson*

Belief is not faith without evidence but commitment without reservation.
Leighton Ford

Faith is to the Christian what Nehemiah was to Artaxerxes. Of all the graces this is the Christian's cupbearer.
William Gurnall

Faith is an activity of the whole soul bringing into movement the intellect, the emotions and the will, and anything less than this is not biblical faith. *Iain Inglis*

Faith is the capacity to trust God while not being able to make sense out of everything. *James Kok*

Faith is a humble, self-effacing grace; it makes the Christian nothing in himself and all in God. *Robert Leighton*

Faith is a living, daring confidence in God's grace. It is so sure and certain that a man could stake his life on it a thousand times. *Martin Luther*

Faith is the sight of the inward eye.
Alexander MacLaren

Faith is the instinct of the spiritual world; it is the sixth sense, the sense of the unseen. *Ian Maclaren*

Faith is the open hand of the soul to receive all the bounteous supplies of God.
Thomas Manton

Faith is the power of putting self aside that God may work unhindered.
F. B. Meyer

Faith is knowledge passing into conviction, and it is conviction passing into confidence. *John Murray*

Faith is our seal; assurance of faith is God's seal. *Christopher Nesse*

Faith, to put it simply, is the conviction that God does not tell lies. *Frank Retief*

Faith is our acceptance of God's acceptance of us. *Adrian Rogers*

What is faith but obedience to the commands of Christ? *Salvianus*

Faith is the soul riding at anchor.
H. W. Shaw

Faith is the marriage of the soul to Christ.
Richard Sibbes

Faith is reason at rest in God.
C. H. Spurgeon

Faith is the silver thread upon which the pearls of the graces are strung.
C. H. Spurgeon

Faith is a knowledge conditioned by holy affection. *Augustus H. Strong*

Faith is the grip which connects us with the moving energy of God.
Augustus H. Strong

Faith is self-surrender to the great Physician, a leaving of our case in his hands. But it is also the taking of his prescriptions and the active following of his directions.
Augustus H. Strong

Faith is not shelter against difficulties, but belief in the face of all contradictions.
Paul Tournier

The faith that saves is not a conclusion drawn from evidence; it is a moral thing, a thing of the spirit, a supernatural infusion of confidence in Jesus Christ, a very gift of God. *A. W. Tozer*

The faith that saves reposes in the person of Christ; it leads at once to a committal of the total being to Christ, an act impossible to natural man. To believe rightly is as much a miracle as was the coming forth of dead Lazarus at the command of Christ. *A. W. Tozer*

FAITH — Essence

Faith has no merit with God when it is not the testimony of divine authority that leads us to it, but the evidence of human reason. *Peter Abelard*

Faith builds a bridge from this world to the next. *Anon.*

Faith follows God implicitly, albeit with trembling on occasion; while sight calculates, considers, cautions and cringes.
Anon.

Faith is dead to doubt, dumb to discouragement, blind to impossibilities. *Anon.*

Faith never fears that it will overdraw its account at the bank of heaven. *Anon.*

Some people think they need faith as big as a mountain to remove a mustard seed.
Anon.

Faith is to believe what we do not see, and the reward of this faith is to see what we believe. *Augustine*

Faith is not an achievement. It is a gift.
Roland Bainton

Faith forces its way to Christ through every obstacle. *J. A. Bengel*

Grace is not a reward for faith; faith is the result of grace. *John Blanchard*

Repentance and faith are graces we have received, not goals we have achieved.
John Blanchard

When Abraham went out, he was not sure of his destination, but he was sure of his company. *John Blanchard*

'My' is the handle of faith. *Andrew Bonar*

Faith in the heart of a Christian is like the salt that was thrown into the corrupt fountain, that made the naughty waters good and the barren land fruitful. *John Bunyan*

Faith brings a man empty to God, that he may be filled with the blessings of God.
John Calvin

True faith is ever connected with hope.
John Calvin

Faith is the daring of the soul to go farther than it can see. *William N. Clarke*

Faith ascribes all that is good to the grace of God, even its own existence.
J. C. P. Cockerton

Believe your beliefs and doubt your doubts; do not make the mistake of doubting your beliefs and believing your doubts. *Charles F. Deems*

The best hold that faith can have of God is to take him by his word. *David Dickson*

Biblical faith is more than simply transferring our natural faith to spiritual objects. *Ronald Dunn*

Faith is not idle; it works while it waits. *Ronald Dunn*

Faith will give you a positive attitude; but a positive attitude is not necessarily faith. *Ronald Dunn*

God wants to bring us to the place where we trust in him and him alone, without the aid of emotional crutches.
Ronald Dunn

If we truly believe in Christ it must be penitently; if we repent of sin it must be believingly. *Sinclair Ferguson*

There are three acts of faith; assent, acceptance and assurance. *John Flavel*

The world will offer God almost anything but this one all-important element of belief. ... belief is too humbling.
Frank Gabelein

Faith is the only receiving grace.
William Gurnall

We must not confide in the armour of God, but in the God of the armour.
William Gurnall

Faith does not look at itself. *Vance Havner*

Faith has no value save as it links us with God. *Vance Havner*

We make faith more difficult than God ever made it. *Vance Havner*

Faith is the trunk of the tree whose roots represent grace and whose fruit symbolizes good works. *William Hendriksen*

It is the business of faith to resolve doubts. *Matthew Henry*

There is no merit in believing. It is only the act of receiving a proffered favour.
Charles Hodge

Saving faith is not creative, but receptive. It does not make our salvation, it accepts it gratefully. *Robert M. Horn*

If your faith isn't contagious it must be contaminated. *Chester Johnson*

Faith is not a question of majorities.
Auguste Lecerf

Faith is always an obedience.
D. Martyn Lloyd-Jones

Faith is a refusal to panic.
D. Martyn Lloyd-Jones

Faith is not an achievement; it is a gift. Yet it comes only through the hearing and study of the Word. *Martin Luther*

The property of faith is not to be proud of what the eye sees, but to rely on what the Word reveals. *Martin Luther*

Faith has no back door. *Paul Madsen*

Faith is the life of our lives, the soul that

animates the whole body of obedience.
Thomas Manton

Learn to put your hand on all spiritual blessings in Christ and say, 'Mine'.
F. B. Meyer

Some people are always telegraphing to heaven for God to send a cargo of blessings to them; but they are not at the wharfside to unload the cargo when it comes. *F. B. Meyer*

Seeing is not believing. Seeing is seeing. Believing is being confident without seeing. *G. Campbell Morgan*

Faith does not operate in the realm of the possible. There is no glory for God in that which is humanly possible. Faith begins where man's power ends. *George Muller*

The broken spirit and the contrite heart are the abiding marks of the believing soul. *John Murray*

True faith is suffused with penitence.
John Murray

Faith abandons hope in man's own accomplishments, leaves all works behind, and comes to Christ alone and empty-handed, to cast itself on his mercy.
J. I. Packer

Faith is a principle of life by which the Christian lives unto God; a principle of motion, by which he walks to heaven along the highway of holiness; a principle of strength, by which he opposes the flesh, the world and the devil. *A. W. Pink*

Faith always anticipates. *David C. Potter*

In faith two characteristics are inherent: it is worked by God and willed by man.
Adolf Schlatter

The walk of faith is not getting a series of jerks from God. *David Shepherd*

A believer sees invisible things.
Richard Sibbes

To trust God in matters of things unseen is not a matter of blind faith. It is not credulity. It is a reasonable faith. *R. C. Sproul*

Faith always sees the bow of covenant promise whenever sense sees the cloud of affliction. *C. H. Spurgeon*

Faith and obedience are bound up in the same bundle. He that obeys God, trusts God; and he that trusts God, obeys God.
C. H. Spurgeon

The essence of faith lies in the heart's choice of Christ. *C. H. Spurgeon*

To many, faith seems a hard thing. The truth is, it is only hard because it is easy.
C. H. Spurgeon

Faith affects the whole of man's nature. It commences with the conviction of the mind based on adequate evidence; it continues in the confidence of the heart or emotions based on conviction, and it is crowned in the consent of the will, by means of which the conviction and confidence are expressed in conduct.
W. H. Griffith Thomas

It is the peculiar business of faith's eye to see in the dark. *Augustus M. Toplady*

Faith in faith is faith astray. *A. W. Tozer*

Faith is a gift of God to a penitent soul and has nothing whatsoever to do with the senses or the data they afford.
A. W. Tozer

Faith is a quickening grace, the vital artery of the soul.   *Thomas Watson*

Repentance and faith are both humbling graces; by repentance a man abhors himself, by faith he goes out of himself.
Thomas Watson

The steps of faith fall on the seeming void, but find the rock beneath.
John Greenleaf Whittier

Faith tries God and God tries the faith he gives.   *Mary Winslow*

Faith means believing in advance what will only make sense in reverse.
Philip Yancey

Faith in Jesus Christ is a cognitive, passionate and moral commitment to that which stands up under the scrutiny of the mind, the heart and the conscience.
Ravi Zacharias

FAITH — Ground

Lack of faith is such a waste of time when there is God.   *Larry Burner*

Faith cannot stand unless it be founded on the promises of God.   *John Calvin*

Faith does not depend on miracles, or on any extraordinary sign, but is the peculiar gift of the Spirit, and is produced by means of the Word.   *John Calvin*

Faith does not proceed from ourselves, but is the fruit of spiritual regeneration.
John Calvin

Faith should fix its whole attention on the power of God alone.   *John Calvin*

There is no faith without God's Word.
John Calvin

No faith is genuine faith which believes that something extra needs to be added to the death of Jesus to make me acceptable to God.   *John C. Chapman*

Faith is not on this side of knowledge but beyond it.   *John Donne*

The character of God is the foundation of faith.   *Ronald Dunn*

You will never understand why God does what he does, but if you believe him, that is all that is necessary. Let us learn to trust him for who he is.   *Elisabeth Elliot*

Faith which is built on emotion is resting on a very changeable foundation.
François Fenelon

True faith takes its character and quality from its object and not from itself.
Sinclair Ferguson

The authority for faith is the revelation of God.   *G. B. Foster*

The true Christian should not seek proofs for his faith, but rather be firmly content with Scripture.   *John Hus*

Those who need miracles are men of little faith.   *John Hus*

Faith rests on the naked Word of God; that Word believed gives full assurance.
H. A. Ironside

Real true faith is man's weakness leaning on God's strength.   *D. L Moody*

My hope is built on nothing less
Than Jesus' blood and righteousness;
I dare not trust the sweetest frame,
But wholly lean on Jesus' name.
On Christ the solid rock I stand;

All other ground is sinking sand.
Edward Mote

Why are we so slow to trust an infinite God? *William S. Plumer*

My faith has no bed to sleep on but omnipotency. *Samuel Rutherford*

Faith brings with it to Christ nothing but a sinful man's soul. *J. C. Ryle*

If our faith were as strong as our security is good, we need fear no combination of enemies, no revolutions in kingdoms, and no convulsions in nature. *Thomas Scott*

At the root of the Christian life lies belief in the invisible. The object of the Christian's faith is unseen reality. *A. W. Tozer*

Faith rests upon the character of God, not upon the demonstration of laboratory or logic. *A. W. Tozer*

FAITH — Importance

Faith in God is never out of season. *Anon.*

We can choose what to believe, but not whether to believe. *Anon.*

I believe in order that I might understand.
Anselm

If you do not believe you will not understand. *Augustine*

Trust the past to the mercy of God, the present to his love and the future to his providence. *Augustine*

Without faith it would be impossible for us to live in a meaningful way and as what we believe radically affects how we behave, faith is the engine driving all our actions. *John Blanchard*

You can do a great deal without faith, but nothing that is pleasing to God.
John Blanchard

If we love Christ much, surely we shall trust him much. *Thomas Brooks*

Strike from mankind the principle of faith and men would have no more history than a flock of sheep. *John Bulwer*

Faith is the identifying mark of the Christian. *Ronald Dunn*

To believe is our chief duty and the fountain from which all other duties flow.
Ronald Dunn

The one who has come to trust in the salvation of Jesus for his soul will be content to rest in the revelation of Jesus for his mind. *H. Enoch*

Through union with Christ all that is his by incarnation becomes ours through faith. *Sinclair Ferguson*

The man who prays without faith has a radical defect in his character.
H. W. Fulford

Where there is no hope, there is no faith.
William Gouge

Nothing is more disastrous than to study faith, analyse faith, make noble resolves of faith, but never actually to make the leap of faith. *Vance Havner*

Of all graces faith honours Christ most; therefore of all graces Christ honours faith most. *Matthew Henry*

We must rejoice in God when we have nothing else to rejoice in and cleave to him … though we cannot for the present find comfort in him. *Matthew Henry*

There can be no hope without faith in Christ, for hope is rooted in him alone. Faith without hope would, by itself, be empty and futile.   *Ernst Hoffmann*

Christian life consists in faith and charity.   *Martin Luther*

The time of fear is the time to trust.
    John MacBeath

Faith is the mother of obedience.
    Thomas Manton

Be careful for nothing, prayerful for everything, thankful for anything. *D. L Moody*

However little we see or feel, let us believe.   *Andrew Murray*

We shall never believe with a vigorous and unquestioning faith unless God touches our hearts; and we shall believe as soon as he does so.   *Blaise Pascal*

Panic is possible only when God is obscured from our thoughts by visible circumstances.   *Maurice Roberts*

The question is not whether we believe so much as what we believe and why we believe it.   *Martin Robinson*

Whatever our trust is most in, that is our God.   *Richard Sibbes*

Everything I do is predicated on belief.
    James W. Sire

If you are not seeking the Lord, judgement is at your heels.   *C. H. Spurgeon*

When you have nothing but God, see all in God.   *C. H. Spurgeon*

Faith is God's measure of a man.
    Augustus H. Strong

The Christian, like a net, must have both the lead of a godly fear and the cork of a lively faith.   *George Swinnock*

Every man lives by faith, the non-believer as well as the saint; the one by faith in natural laws and the other by faith in God.
    A. W. Tozer

What we believe about God is the most important thing about us.   *A. W. Tozer*

The devil labours to put out the right eye of faith and to leave us only the left eye of reason.   *John Trapp*

Faith is the vital artery of the soul.
    Thomas Watson

Our limitless trust in God seems to satisfy him as nothing else can do, because it corresponds with his eternal faithfulness, it honours his veracity, and is a constant, silent worship of all his perfections.   *G. D. Watson*

Our reliance upon reason is ultimately an act of faith.   *Peter S. Williams*

FAITH — Increase

If we desire an increase of faith we must consent to its testings.   *Anon.*

So many Christians badly need a faith lift!
    John Blanchard

Let faith have elbow room.
    Thomas Brooks

Our faith is never perfect ... we are partly unbelievers.   *John Calvin*

Unless our faith be now and then raised up, it will lie prostrate; unless it is warmed, it will be frozen; unless it be roused, it will grow torpid. *John Calvin*

Faith does not grow by being pulled up by the roots time and again to see how it is getting on. Faith grows when we look steadily towards God for the supply of all our needs and concentrate on him. There is little point in becoming engrossed with our faith as if that were the thing we believed in! *J. C. P. Cockerton*

We learn to trust by trusting. *Ronald Dunn*

Faith grows as it feeds on facts, not on feelings nor on fancies. *Geoffrey Grogan*

We live by faith and faith lives by exercise. *William Gurnall*

Faith rises or falls according to the measure in which we remember the things which are unseen. *Maurice Roberts*

Labour to have large faith, answerable to our large riches. *Richard Sibbes*

The larger the God we know, the larger will be our faith. The secret of power in our lives is to know God and expect great things from him. *A. B. Simpson*

Faith is fostered by prayer, is fortified by the study of the Word, and is fulfilled by our yielding moment by moment to the Lord Jesus himself. *J. Charles Stern*

FAITH — and Knowledge
(See also: Reason)

I do not seek to understand that I may believe, but I believe that I may understand: for this I also believe, that unless I believe I will not understand. *Anselm*

God does not expect us to submit our faith to him without reason, but the very limits of our reason make faith a necessity. *Augustine*

Understanding is the reward of faith. Therefore seek not to understand that you may believe, but believe that you may understand. *Augustine*

Faith does not mean believing without evidence. It means believing in realities that go beyond sense and sight — for which a totally different sort of evidence is required. *John Baillie*

Faith that goes no farther than the head can never bring peace to the heart. *John Blanchard*

Where reason fails, faith can rest. *John Blanchard*

Faith requires no surrender of the intellect. *Charles Colson*

It is not a very robust faith which in order to survive must distort or ignore the facts. *Elisabeth Elliot*

All I have seen teaches me to trust the Creator for all I have not seen. *Ralph Waldo Emerson*

Faith is not anti-intellectual. It is an act of man that reaches beyond the limits of our five senses. *Billy Graham*

One grain of faith is more precious than a pound of knowledge. *Joseph Hall*

Faith must have adequate evidence, else it is mere superstition. *A. A. Hodge*

A Christian with faith has nothing to fear from the facts. *Paul Johnson*

Faith is greater than learning. *Martin Luther*

The more we know of God, the more unreservedly we will trust him; the greater our progress in theology, the simpler and more childlike will be our faith.

J. Gresham Machen

The faith that does not come from reason is to be doubted, and the reason that does not lead to faith is to be feared.

G. Campbell Morgan

Faith is a … form of knowledge which transforms the intellect.

Malcolm Muggeridge

Belief is a truth held in the mind. Faith is a fire in the heart.   *Joseph Fort Newton*

It is poor philosophy to say we will believe nothing unless we can understand everything!   *J. C. Ryle*

True faith and saving knowledge go together.   *George Swinnock*

The natural man must know in order to believe; the spiritual man must believe in order to know.   *A. W. Tozer*

Faith is seated in the understanding as well as in the will. It has an eye to see Christ as well as a wing to fly to Christ.

Thomas Watson

To those who believe, no explanation is necessary. To those who do not believe, no explanation is possible. *Franz Werfel*

We are as much obliged to believe God with reluctance to our understanding as to obey him with reluctance to our will.

Thomas Wilson

Faith often outreaches reason, but it does not outrage it.   *Verna Wright*

FAITH — Power

Faith makes things possible — it does not make them easy.   *Anon.*

He who feeds his faith will starve his doubts to death.   *Anon.*

Life asks no questions that faith cannot answer.   *Anon.*

Faith opens every gateway of the soul.

George Barlow

Faith keeps us, but God keeps our faith.

Andrew Bonar

Faith deadens a man's heart to the things of this world.   *Thomas Brooks*

Faith is an appropriating grace.

Thomas Brooks

Faith makes invisible things visible, absent things present, and things that are very far off to be very near to the soul.

Thomas Brooks

Faith does the same against the devil as unbelief does against God. *John Bunyan*

As he that fears God fears nothing else, so, he that sees God sees nothing else.

John Donne

Faith is the master key of the Christian life.   *Ronald Dunn*

If only a soul can believe in God, to the extent to which it believes it can obtain anything that is in the heart of God to bestow.   *Ronald Dunn*

We persevere through faith and never apart from it.   *Sinclair Ferguson*

Faith — Power

Faith is blind — except upward. It is blind to impossibilities and deaf to doubt. It listens only to God.   *S. D. Gordon*

Faith and a good conscience are hope's two wings.   *William Gurnall*

Faith is a plant that can grow in the shade, a grace that can find the way to heaven in a dark night.   *William Gurnall*

Faith will not always get for us what we want, but it will get what God wants us to have.   *Vance Havner*

A man at his wit's end is not at his faith's end.   *Matthew Henry*

As we must not trust to an arm of flesh when it is engaged for us, so we must not be afraid of an arm of flesh when it is stretched out against us.   *Matthew Henry*

The crosses and comforts of the present time would not make such an impression upon us as they do if we did but believe the things of eternity as we ought.
     Matthew Henry

We look with an eye of faith farther than we can see with an eye of sense.
     Matthew Henry

Faith draws the poison from every grief, takes the sting from every loss, and quenches the fire of every pain; and only faith can do it.   *Josiah Holland*

Faith will lead you where you cannot walk. Reason has never been a mountain climber.   *E. W. Kenyon*

Faith is the life of our lives, the soul that animates the whole body of obedience.
     Thomas Manton

Faith instructs us in the depths of God.
     Jacques Maritain

The man who measures things by the circumstances of the hour is filled with fear; the man who sees Jehovah enthroned and governing has no panic.
     G. Campbell Morgan

Faith can rest in what it cannot comprehend.   *John Owen*

Nothing but faith will ever rectify the mistakes of reason on divine things.
     William S. Plumer

Faith can place a candle in the darkest night.   *Margaret E. Sangster*

Faith enables us so to rejoice in the Lord that our infirmities become platforms for the display of his grace.   *C. H. Spurgeon*

Faith, having God with her, is in a clear majority.   *C. H. Spurgeon*

Faith is the soul's mouth, whereby the hunger of the heart is removed.
     C. H. Spurgeon

Faith is the surest of all sin-killers.
     C. H. Spurgeon

Faith may be simple, but its effect is sublime.   *J. Charles Stern*

Faith in Jesus laughs at impossibilities.
     C. T. Studd

All God's giants have been weak men who did great things for God because they reckoned on God being with them.
     J. Hudson Taylor

Faith sees the invisible, believes the unbelievable, and receives the impossible.   *Corrie ten Boom*

The poor man's hand is Christ's bank.
John Trapp

A little faith is faith as a spark off fire is fire. *Thomas Watson*

Faith fetches Christ's strength into the soul. *Thomas Watson*

Faith gives a true map of the world.
Thomas Watson

Faith paves a causeway to heaven.
Thomas Watson

Faith reconciles providences and promises. *Thomas Watson*

Faith, mighty faith, the promise sees,
And looks to that alone;
Laughs at impossibilities,
And cries it shall be done.
Charles Wesley

Faith is a mighty, living thing, producing wonderful results in the conscience, heart, will, mind and life of the recipient.
A. Paget Wilkes

Faith builds a bridge across the gulf of death. *Edward Young*

FAITH — and Prayer
See also: Prayer — and Faith)

The door is closed to prayer unless it is opened with the key of trust. *John Calvin*

The true proof of faith is the assurance when we pray that God will really perform what he has promised us.
John Calvin

Faith cannot grow outside of the environment of prayer. Prayer is its natural habitat. *J. C. P. Cockerton*

Let's keep our chins up and our knees down — we're on the victory side!
Alan Redpath

Faith is to prayer what the feather is to the arrow. *Thomas Watson*

Prayer is the key of heaven; faith is the hand that turns it. *Thomas Watson*

Mature faith does not live by answers to prayer, but by prayer. *R. E. O. White*

FAITH — Rewards

Faith sees God and God sees faith. *Anon.*

Weave in faith and God will find thread.
Anon.

Faith is to believe what we do not see, and the reward of this faith is to see what we believe. *Augustine*

Hope is never ill when faith is well.
John Bunyan

Faith makes the uplook good, the outlook bright, the inlook favourable and the future glorious. *V. Raymond Edman*

God is most glorified in the faith of his servants. *William Gouge*

Faith sucks peace from the promise.
William Gurnall

The Christian faith is not a way to explain, enjoy or endure this world, but to overcome it. *Vance Havner*

Those that are acquainted with God and Christ are already in the suburbs of life eternal. *Matthew Henry*

How blest thy saints! how safely led!
How surely kept! how richly fed!
Saviour of all in earth and sea,
How happy they who rest in thee!
Henry Francis Lyte

Take any class of society, the highest or
the lowest, and there is not an instance of
one who trusted in the Lord and was
confounded. *William Pennefather*

It is because God has promised certain
things that we can ask for them with the
full assurance of faith. *A. W. Pink*

Faith in God will always be crowned.
William S. Plumer

Have faith in God, my heart,
Trust and be unafraid;
God will fulfil in every part
Each promise he has made.
Bryn Austin Rees

A clear faith should produce a light heart.
J. C. Ryle

The function of faith is to turn God's
promises into facts. *J. Oswald Sanders*

The larger faith we bring, the larger measure we carry from Christ. *Richard Sibbes*

Doubt breeds distress, but trust means joy
in the long run. *C. H. Spurgeon*

The outlook may be dark, but if we know
the secret of the uplook . . . we shall find
our God is able to deliver. *J. C. Stern*

Upon the two hinges of faith and repentance do all the promises of the Bible
stand. *George Swinnock*

Every benefit flowing from the atonement
of Christ comes to the individual through
the gateway of faith. *A. W. Tozer*

Faith and the promise make a happy mixture, a precious confection. *John Trapp*

Faith unlocks the divine storehouse, but
unbelief bars its doors. *Curtis Vaughan*

FAITH — Saving
(See also: Conversion; Faith — Definition; Regeneration; Repentance)

Saving faith is grasping God with the
heart. *Anon.*

Saving faith is repentant faith. *Anon.*

Repentance and faith are twins.
John Blanchard

Saving faith is not consent to a proposition, but commitment to a person.
John Blanchard

The evidence of saving faith is not how
much you believe but how well you
behave. *John Blanchard*

Upon a life I did not live,
Upon a death I did not die;
Another's life, another's death,
I stake my whole eternity.
Horatius Bonar

Faith is nothing else but the soul's venture. It ventures *to* Christ, in opposition
to all legal terrors. It ventures *upon* Christ,
in opposition to our guiltiness. It ventures
for Christ, in opposition to all difficulties
and discouragements. *W. Bridge*

Faith wraps itself in the righteousness of
Christ. *Thomas Brooks*

Faith is not a distant view, but a warm
embrace of Christ. *John Calvin*

Faith is the evidence of divine adoption.
John Calvin

The gospel can be understood by faith alone — not by reason, nor by the perspicacity of the human understanding.
John Calvin

The seat of faith is not in the brain but in the heart. *John Calvin*

Repentance and faith are Siamese twins.
Walter J. Chantry

Saving faith is not *offered* to man by God: it is *conferred* upon him.
Arthur C. Custance

Saving faith is not the human contribution of a sinner seeking salvation, but the divine contribution of the gracious God seeking a sinner. *Arthur C. Custance*

Faith and repentance must be seen as marriage partners and never separated.
Sinclair Ferguson

The faith with which we believe and trust is only ours because God has created it within our hearts. *Sinclair Ferguson*

Saving faith is confidence in Jesus; a direct confidential transaction with him.
Richard Fuller

I am not skilled to understand
What God hath willed, what God hath
    planned;
I only know at his right hand
Stands one who is my Saviour.
Dorothy Greenwell

Faith hath two hands; with one it pulls off its own righteousness and throws it away . . . with the other it puts on Christ's.
William Gurnall

Without faith we are not fit to desire mercy. *William Gurnall*

Faith is not a work which Christ condescends in the gospel to accept instead of perfect obedience as the ground of salvation — it is only the hand whereby we clasp the person and work of our Redeemer, which is the true ground of salvation. *A. A. Hodge*

The very act of faith by which we receive Christ is an act of utter renunciation of self and all its works, as a ground of salvation. *Mark Hopkins*

Saving faith is not creative, but receptive. It does not make our salvation, it takes it gratefully. *Robert M. Horn*

That faith can save a man, and that nothing else can, is written throughout the Scriptures as with a pencil of light.
Robert Johnstone

Before faith and obedience become acts of man they are gifts of God. *R. B. Kuiper*

Conviction of sin is an indispensable prerequisite of faith in Christ. *R. B. Kuiper*

Faith as the fruit of election is also the proof of election. *R. B. Kuiper*

Nowhere does the Bible tell us that salvation is by a faith that does not work.
R. B. Kuiper

Salvation is only by a working faith. In short, good works are the fruit of saving faith. They are also the proof of saving faith. *R. B. Kuiper*

Saving faith is a gift of the electing God to his elect by which their election is realized. Instead of being the *ground* of election, it is one of its consequences.
R. B. Kuiper

Faith — Saving

True faith is never found alone; it is accompanied by expectation. *C. S. Lewis*

We cannot *force* ourselves to have faith. We are as much in need of this as everything. Faith can only originate in the soul of man by the gift of God. *Marcus Loane*

Faith lays hold of Christ and grasps him as a present possession, just as the ring holds the jewel. *Martin Luther*

Let us conclude that faith alone justifies and that faith alone fulfils the law. *Martin Luther*

The only saving faith is that which casts itself on God for life or death. *Martin Luther*

Be as holy as you can, as if there were no gospel to save you. Yet … believe in Christ as if there were no law at all to condemn you. *Thomas Lye*

Men who are dead in trespasses and sins are utterly unable to have saving faith, just as completely unable as a dead man lying in the tomb is unable to contribute the slightest bit to his resurrection. *J. Gresham Machen*

True saving faith clings to Christ and his Word, regardless of the consequences caused by that faith. *Henry T. Mahan*

Faith settles the soul. *Thomas Manton*

We must not close with Christ because we *feel* him, but because God has *said* it, and we must take God's word *even in the dark*. *Robert Murray M'Cheyne*

It is impossible to disentangle faith and repentance. Saving faith is permeated with repentance and repentance is permeated with faith. *John Murray*

Regeneration is inseparable from its effects and one of its effects is faith. *John Murray*

The embrace of Christ in faith is the first evidence of regeneration and only thus may we know that we have been regenerated. *John Murray*

The faith that is unto salvation is a penitent faith and the repentance that is unto life is a believing repentance. *John Murray*

Faith is not of some good work which God must reward with salvation. Faith is not the cause of salvation, but the means through which we receive it. *Philip Nunn*

In the Bible, faith … involves both credence and commitment. *J. I. Packer*

Coming to Christ not only involves the abandoning of every false object of confidence, it also includes and entails the forsaking of all other competitors for my heart. *A. W. Pink*

Saving faith is not only the heart being weaned from every other object of confidence as the ground of my acceptance before God, but it is also the heart being weaned from every other object that competes with him for my affections. *A. W. Pink*

Saving faith not only historically credits the truths of God, but with the heart believes them. *William S. Plumer*

It is not the strength of our faith that saves but the truth of our faith. *John Rogers*

If we would know whether our faith is genuine, we do well to ask ourselves how we are living. *J. C. Ryle*

Saving faith is the hand of the soul ... the eye of the soul ... the mouth of the soul ... the foot of the soul.   *J. C Ryle*

Most people are brought to faith in Christ, not by argument for it, but by exposure to it.   *Samuel Shoemaker*

It requires not only a power, but an almighty power, to raise the heart of man to believe.   *Richard Sibbes*

It is not a brave thing to trust God: for true believers it is a simple matter of sweet necessity.   *C. H. Spurgeon*

It will not save me to know that Christ is a Saviour; but it will save me to trust him to be my Saviour.   *C. H. Spurgeon*

Little faith will bring your soul to heaven; great faith will bring heaven to your soul.
C. H. Spurgeon

Never make a Christ out of your faith, nor think of it as if it were the independent source of your salvation.
C. H. Spurgeon

There is no sin that shall damn the man who believes, and nothing shall save the man who will not believe. *C. H. Spurgeon*

Saving faith is resting faith, the trust which relies entirely on the Saviour.
John R. W. Stott

What saves us is faith in *Christ,* not faith in our *faith,* or faith in *the* faith.
Augustus H. Strong

Spurious faith has no saving power.
R. V. G. Tasker

We are not saved for believing but by believing.   *Thomas Taylor*

Nothing in my hand I bring,
Simply to thy cross I cling;
Naked, come to thee for dress;
Helpless, look to thee for grace;
Foul, I to the fountain fly;
Wash me, Saviour, or I die.
Augustus M. Toplady

Faith is not a once-done act, but a continuous gaze of the heart at the triune God.
A. W. Tozer

God is never never found accidentally.
A. W. Tozer

True faith commits us to obedience.
A. W. Tozer

Faith in Jesus Christ ... in the office of justification, is neither condition nor qualification, ... but in its very act a renouncing of all such pretences.
Robert Traill

Right faith is a thing wrought in us by the Holy Ghost, which changes us, turns us into a new nature, and begets us anew in God, and makes us sons of God ... and makes us altogether new in the heart, mind, will, desire, and in all the other affections and powers of the soul — the Holy Ghost ever accompanying it and ruling the heart.   *William Tyndale*

No man's salvation depends on his *believing that he believes;* but it does depend on his seeing and receiving Jesus Christ as his Saviour.
M. R. Vincent

A weak faith may receive a strong Christ.
Thomas Watson

Simple faith honours God and God honours simple faith.   *Mary Winslow*

FAITH — Supremacy

Faith is the grace of graces.
Thomas Brooks

To believe is our chief duty and the fountain from which all other duties flow.
Ronald Dunn

All other graces, like birds in the nest, depend on what faith brings in to them.
John Flavel

Men and brethren, a simple trust in God is the most essential ingredient in moral sublimity of character. *Richard Fuller*

No one can occupy higher spiritual ground than that of simply being a believer. *Frank Gabelein*

Faith is a mother grace, a breeding grace.
William Gouge

One grain of faith is more precious than a pound of knowledge. *Joseph Hall*

Faith always shows itself in the whole personality. *D. Martyn Lloyd-Jones*

The errors of faith are better than the best thoughts of unbelief. *Thomas Russell*

Justifying faith is that act of the soul by which a man lays hold on Christ and has peace with God. *J. C. Ryle*

What is the life of saving faith, when once begun, but a continual leaning on an unseen Saviour's word? *J. C. Ryle*

Get the queen bee of faith and all the other virtues will attend her. *C. H. Spurgeon*

It is very well to rest on God when you have other props, but it is best of all to rest on him when every prop is knocked away. *C. H. Spurgeon*

To live by faith is a far surer and happier thing than to live by feelings or by works.
C. H. Spurgeon

Faith is the mother-grace, the womb wherein love and all the rest of the heavenly offspring are conceived. *John Trapp*

Faith is a stooping grace. *Thomas Watson*

Faith is the master-wheel; it sets all the other graces running. *Thomas Watson*

Love is the crowning grace in heaven, but faith is the conquering grace upon earth. *Thomas Watson*

Where reason cannot wade, there faith may swim. *Thomas Watson*

FAITH — Testing

Faith is demonstrated by Christians who refuse to accept failure as final. *Anon.*

If our faith is not in the present tense it will never be able to stand the test of the days in which we live. *Anon.*

The proof of real saving faith is a persistent mindset to obey what Jesus has taught us in his Word, the Bible. *Anon.*

That faith which is never assaulted with doubting is but a fancy. Assuredly that assurance which is ever secure is but a dream. *Robert Bolton*

Our faith is really and truly tested only when we are brought into very severe conflicts, and when even hell itself seems opened to swallow us up. *John Calvin*

Judge not the Lord by feeble sense,
But trust him for his grace;
Behind a frowning providence
He hides a smiling face.
William Cowper

When Satan borrows sense to speak one thing, let faith borrow Scripture to speak the contrary. *David Dickson*

Faith must be tested and it is of the essence of the testing that no escape seems possible. *Edward Donnelly*

An untried faith is a worthless faith.
Ronald Dunn

God ... often reveals himself to the souls of the elect only in the deep night of pure faith. *Françis Fenelon*

The Christian must trust in a withdrawing God. *William Gurnall*

When God's way is in the sea, so that he cannot be traced, yet we are sure his way is in the sanctuary, so that he may be trusted. *Matthew Henry*

When I cannot live by the faith of assurance I live by the faith of adherence.
Matthew Henry

Trust God even when the pieces don't seem to fit. *John Hercus*

You don't know what faith you have until it is tested. *Rees Howells*

Better a baffled faith than no faith at all.
Albert Knudson

He who would believe, let him reconcile himself to the fact that his faith will not stay untempted. *Martin Luther*

There may be a time when God will not be found, but no time wherein he must not be trusted. *Thomas Lye*

Faith is such a vital matter to the children of God that it must needs be put to the test, first in order to prove that it is genuine, and second to purge and strengthen it. *Philip Mauro*

We never test the resources of God until we attempt the impossible. *F. B. Meyer*

Faith, like a muscle, grows by stretching.
A. W. Tozer

Pray for a faith that will not shrink when washed in the waters of affliction.
Ernest Wadsworth

Faith tries God and God tries the faith he gives. *Mary Winslow*

FAITH — Weak

The faith that will shut the mouth of lions must be more than a pious hope that they will not bite. *Anon.*

In the gospels, Jesus often rebukes weak faith, but never rejects it. *John Berridge*

To believe only possibilities is not faith but philosophy. *Thomas Browne*

Distrust is cured by meditating upon the promises of God. *John Calvin*

Waverings where faith is are like the tossings of a ship fast at anchor.
Stephen Charnock

A fellow shouldn't abandon his faith when it weakens, any more than he would throw away a suit because it needs pressing. *Frank A. Clark*

If we are spiritually impoverished, it is not because the hand of grace is tight-fisted; it is because the hand of faith is too weak.   *Ronald Dunn*

Even those of us who have weak faith have the same strong Christ as others!
Sinclair Ferguson

True faith may be weak faith, and weak faith true faith.   *Richard Glover*

Better to be slow of head to understand than slow of heart to believe!
Vance Havner

Faith is not always alike lively; but where it is true it is always living.
Thomas Manton

The Lord Jesus does not cast off his believing people because of failures and imperfections.   *J. C. Ryle*

A weak hand may receive a rich jewel.
Richard Sibbes

The promises are not made to strong faith but to true.   *Thomas Watson*

FAITHFULNESS
(See also: God — Faithfulness)

God has no larger field for the man who is not faithfully doing his work where he is.   *Anon.*

One thing you can give and still keep is your word.   *Anon.*

When faithfulness is most difficult it is most necessary.   *Anon.*

Without consistency there is no moral strength.   *Anon.*

Faithfulness in little things is a big thing.
Chrysostom

God requires no more than faithfulness in our place.   *William Gurnall*

How can there be great faith where is little faithfulness?   *William Gurnall*

Christians do not have to live; they have only to be faithful to Jesus Christ, not only *until* death but *unto* death if necessary.
Vance Havner

If God's goodness to us be like the morning light, which shines more and more to the perfect day, let not ours to him be like the morning cloud and the early dew that pass away.   *Matthew Henry*

Religion is not a matter of fits, starts and stops, but an everyday affair.
David Livingstone

Faithfulness to God is our *first* obligation in all that we are called to do in the service of the gospel.   *Iain H. Murray*

There is no guarantee that men faithful to God will be recognizable by their numbers, their talents or their success.
Iain H. Murray

Faithfulness is our business; fruitfulness is an issue that we must be content to leave with God.   *J. I. Packer*

Consistency is a jewel. *William S. Plumer*

Reverent fear of God is the key to faithfulness in any situation.   *Alan Redpath*

Faithfulness knows no difference between small and great duties.
John Ruskin

I know of nothing which I would choose to have as the subject of my ambition for life than to be kept faithful to my God till death. *C. H. Spurgeon*

It is impossible to be faithful to Jesus Christ and not incur the opposition of the world. *William Still*

FAME
(See also: Popularity)

He is genuinely great who considers himself small and cares nothing about high honours. *Thomas à Kempis*

The honours of this world: what are they but puff, and emptiness, and peril of falling? *Augustine*

Fame is a fickle food
Upon a shifting plate. *Emily E. Dickinson*

Men think highly of those who rise rapidly in the world; whereas nothing rises quicker than dust, straw and feathers. *August W Hare*

Seeking to perpetuate one's name on earth is like writing on the sand by the seashore. *D. L. Moody*

It is better to be faithful than famous. *Theodore D. Roosevelt*

For a man to spend his life in pursuit of a trifle that serves only when he dies to furnish out an epitaph is below a wise man's business. *Seneca*

FAMILY LIFE — Importance

Woman takes her being from man, man takes his well-being from woman. *Thomas Adams*

Many a fine house is something else — and less — than a home. *Anon.*

The atmosphere of a Christian home should be eloquent. *Anon.*

Holy families must be the chief preservers of the interest of religion in the world. *Richard Baxter*

If family religion were duly attended to and properly discharged, I think the preaching of the Word would not be the common instrument of conversion. *Richard Baxter*

Help us O Lord our homes to make
Thy Holy Spirit's dwelling place;
Our hands and hearts' devotion takes
To be the servants of thy grace. *A. F. Bayley*

A home with no head is a disaster, one with two is a monstrosity. *John Blanchard*

A happy family is but an earlier heaven. *John Bowring*

The greatest benefits conferred on human life, fatherhood, motherhood, childhood, home, become the greatest curse if Jesus Christ is not the Head. *Oswald Chambers*

Home is the seminary of all other institutions. *E. H. Chapin*

No other structure can replace the family. *Charles Colson*

The family circle is the supreme conductor of Christianity. *Henry Drummond*

The Christian is supposed to love his neighbour, and since his wife is his nearest neighbour, she should be his deepest love. *Martin Luther*

Family Life — Importance

I believe the family was established long before the church, and my duty is to my family first. *D. L. Moody*

If Christ is in your house your neighbours will soon know it. *D. L. Moody*

A home is not a building; it is a relational structure. *Stephen Olford*

Bringing up a family should be an adventure, not an anxious discipline in which everybody is constantly graded for performance. *Milton R. Sapirstein*

He that loves not his wife and children breeds a lioness at home and broods a nest of sorrows. *Jeremy Taylor*

FAMILY LIFE — Influence on Children

The religion of a child depends on what its father and mother are, and not on what they say. *Henri Amiel*

A pat on the back is all right provided it is administered early enough, hard enough and low enough. *Anon.*

Children need to he trained, not just in the facts of life, but in the ways of life. *Anon.*

Every word and deed of a parent is a fibre woven into the character of a child that ultimately determines how that child fits into the fabric of society. *Anon.*

Many parents give their children everything except themselves. *Anon.*

The best thing to spend on your children is your time. *Anon.*

The best time to tackle a minor problem is before he grows up. *Anon.*

The child's first school is the family. *Anon.*

The mother who spoils her child fattens a serpent. *Anon.*

The surest way to make it hard for your children is to make it soft for them. *Anon.*

Whatever parent gives his children good instruction, and sets them at the same time a bad example, may be considered as bringing them food in one hand and poison in the other. *John Balguy*

For parents to see a child grow up without Christ is a far greater dereliction of duty than for parents to have children who grow up without learning to read or write. *Donald Grey Barnhouse*

Our children need our presence more than our presents. *John Blanchard*

There is little hope of children who are educated wickedly. If the dye have been in the wool, it is hard to get it out of the cloth. *Jeremiah Burroughs*

A child, like your stomach, doesn't need all you can afford to give it. *Frank A. Clark*

What we desire our children to be we must endeavour to be before them. *Andrew Combe*

Ideal parenting is modelled after the relationship between God and man. *James C. Dobson*

No job can compete with the responsibility of shaping and moulding a new human being. *James C. Dobson*

The father is a debtor to his child, and owes him love, provision and nurture.

The child is a debtor to his parent, and owes him honour and obedience.
William Gurnall

If a parent does not punish his sons, his sons will be sure to punish him.
Thomas Guthrie

A permissive home is a home where you don't love enough to exercise the authority that Christ gave you. *Ben Haden*

No man or woman ever had a nobler challenge or a higher privilege than to bring up a child for God, and whenever we slight that privilege or neglect that ministry for anything else, we live to mourn it in heartache and grief. *Vance Havner*

Do not handicap your children by making their lives easy. *Robert Heinlein*

It is emphatically not a Christian duty to let a child 'make up its own mind' without first informing, guiding and encouraging him. *Paul Helm*

Godly parents do not inflict upon their children the cruelty of telling them that they should do 'just as they please'.
William Hendriksen

The cure of crime is not the electric chair, but the high chair. *J. Edgar Hoover*

Children need love, especially when they do not deserve it. *Harold S. Hulbert*

It is common sense to put the seal to the wax while it is soft. *Arthur Jackson*

Children have more need of models than of critics. *Joseph Joubert*

Fathering is a marathon, not a sprint.
Paul L. Lewis

Parents wonder why the streams are bitter, when they themselves have poisoned the fountain. *John Locke*

Let us not fool ourselves — without Christianity, without Christian education, without the principles of Christ inculcated into young life, we are simply rearing pagans. *Peter Marshall*

How many careless parents does God's pure eye see among you who will one day, if you turn not, meet your neglected children in an eternal hell!
Robert Murray M'Cheyne

The parent's life is the child's copybook.
John Partridge

A parent must respect the spiritual person of his child, and approach it with reverence. *George Macdonald*

If we teach good things, it is hopeful that they will be learned. If our lives exemplify virtue, it is hopeful that they will be imitated. *Cotton Mather*

The secret of home rule is self rule, first being ourselves what we want our children to be. *Andrew Murray*

One of the greatest means of grace in the life of a child is the biblical implementation of discipline. *Al Martin*

If you would train your children rightly, train them in the way they *should* go and not in the way they *would*. *J. C. Ryle*

Better a little chiding than a great deal of heartache. *William Shakespeare*

Every child has a right to be both well fed and well led. *Ruth Smelter*

A father's holy life is a rich legacy for his sons. *C. H. Spurgeon*

If we walk before the Lord in integrity, we shall do more to bless our descendants than if we bequeathed them large estates. *C. H. Spurgeon*

One of the best legacies a father can leave his children is to love their mother. *C. Neil Strait*

The best way to beat the devil is to hit him over the head with a cradle. *Billy Sunday*

The most influential of all educational factors is the conversation in a child's home. *William Temple*

The mistaken kindness of parents has ever proved the greatest curse to children. *David Thomas*

I learned more about Christianity from my mother than from all the theologians of England. *John Wesley*

FAMILY LIFE — Love
(See also: Marriage)

Love is the master key to a happy home. *Anon.*

Money can build a house, but it takes love to make it a home. *Anon.*

When hugging and kissing end in any home, trouble is on the way. *Stephen Olford*

FAMILY LIFE — a Test of Character

A Christian should so live that he would not be afraid to sell the family parrot to the town gossip. *Anon.*

He that has not rest at home is in the world's hell. *Anon.*

Holiness begins at home and sanctification at the sink. *W. F. Batt*

A severe test of a man's essential nature is how he appears to the members of his own family. *Maldwyn Edwards*

A home is no home unless it contains food and fire for the mind as well as for the body. *Margaret Fuller*

Can he be a good Christian that spends all his religion abroad and leaves none for his nearest relations at home …? *William Gurnall*

He that walketh not uprightly in his house is but a hypocrite at church. *William Gurnall*

It is a poor light that is made to shine brighter in the distance than close at hand. *Vance Havner*

The real test of your Christianity is not how pious you look at the Lord's table on Sunday, but how you act at the breakfast table at home. *Vance Havner*

I would give nothing for that man's religion whose very dog and cat are not the better for it. *Rowland Hill*

Family life is a school for character. *Martin Luther*

It is the mark of a hypocrite to be a Christian everywhere except at home. *Robert Murray M'Cheyne*

No service for God is of any value which is contradicted by the life at home. *G. Campbell Morgan*

A man has no right to stand and preach if his home is not in alignment with the Word of God. *Stephen Olford*

If we serve the church or serve the Lord at the expense of our duty to our loved ones and the responsibilities of our home, there is something wrong with the balance of our Christian lives. *Alan Redpath*

Praise will transform the humblest dwelling to a hallowed heaven. *Frances J. Roberts*

The easiest place in which to be spiritual is in public; the most difficult is at home. *Charles Caldwell Ryrie*

When home is ruled according to God's Word, angels might be asked to stay with us, and they would not find themselves out of their element. *C. H. Spurgeon*

The best test of a sanctified man is to ask his family about him. *C. T. Studd*

Home is a mighty test of character. What you are at home you are everywhere, whether you demonstrate it or not. *Thomas Dewitt Talmadge*

FAMILY LIFE — Worship

Families that pray together stay together. *Anon.*

The family altar would alter many a family. *Anon.*

If family religion were duly attended to and properly discharged, I think the preaching of the Word would not be the common instrument of conversion. *Richard Baxter*

Let family worship be short, savoury, simple, plain, tender, heavenly. *Richard Cecil*

Where we have a tent God must have an altar. *Matthew Henry*

A house without family worship has neither foundation nor covering *J. M. Mason*

FASHION — See Clothing

FASTING — See Prayer and Fasting

FAULTFINDING
(See also: Criticism of Others)

Faultfinding is a trade that can be carried on with very little capital. *Anon.*

Faultfinding is one talent that ought to be buried. *Anon.*

People who are out to find fault seldom find anything else. *Anon.*

The easiest thing to find is fault. *Anon.*

When you are looking for faults to correct, look in the mirror. *Anon.*

FEAR
(See also: Anxiety; Worry)

Fear is the beginning of defeat. *Anon.*

God can secure us from fear, either by removing the thing feared, or by subduing the fear of the thing. *William Beveridge*

No passion so effectually robs the mind of all its powers of acting and reasoning as fear. *Edmund Burke*

Fear is generated by unbelief, and

unbelief strengthened by fear. Nothing can cure us of fear till God cures us of unbelief. *Francis Burkitt*

The right fear is the fear of losing God. *Meister Eckhart*

Let none but the servants of sin be the slaves of fear. *John Flavel*

The chains of love are stronger than the chains of fear. *William Gurnall*

We fear men so much because we fear God so little. *William Gurnall*

We are so afraid of being offensive that we are not effective. *Vance Havner*

Those who would be fearless must keep themselves guiltless. *Matthew Henry*

We need not look upon those enemies with fear whom God looks upon with contempt. *Matthew Henry*

Who lives in fear will never be a free man. *Horace*

Fear is the sand in the machinery of life. *E. Stanley Jones*

If you stood alone, it would be presumption to hope. Because you are not alone, it is offence to tremble. *Henry Law*

I know not the way he leads me, but well do I know my Guide. What have I to fear? *Martin Luther*

The time of fear is the time to trust. *John MacBeath*

Fear is faithlessness. *George Macdonald*

Only he who can say, 'The Lord is the strength of my life' can say, 'Of whom shall I be afraid?' *Alexander MacLaren*

A good life is a good fence against fear. *Edward Marbury*

Panic is the sinful failure to apply our knowledge of God to particular problems. *Maurice Roberts*

Where fear is, happiness is not. *Seneca*

Fear is the tax that conscience pays to guilt. *George Sewell*

Half our fears are the result of ignorance. *C. H. Spurgeon*

There is nothing in the world more ridiculous than unbelieving fears. *C. H. Spurgeon*

This only can my fears control,
And bid my sorrows fly;
What harm can ever reach my soul
Beneath my Father's eye? *Anne Steele*

Fear is of the flesh and panic is of the devil. *A. W. Tozer*

Fear enfeebles. *Thomas Watson*

Fear is the root of apostasy. *Thomas Watson*

It is only the fear of God that can deliver us from the fear of man. *John Witherspoon*

FEAR OF GOD
(See also Awe; Worship)

He who knows what it is to enjoy God will dread his loss. He who has seen his face will fear to see his back. *Richard Alleine*

He who does not fear God has need to fear everything else. *Anon.*

The fear of God is the greatest antidote against the fear of man. *Anon.*

Godly fear shrinks from sin, worldly fear from punishment; the one influences our thoughts, the other only our actions.
Ayguan

But what is this fear of the Lord? It is that affectionate reverence, by which the child of God bends himself humbly and carefully to his Father's law.
Charles Bridges

If Jesus in his humanity delighted in the fear of God, surely we need to give serious thought to cultivating this attitude in our lives. *Jerry Bridges*

Just as obedience to the Lord is an indication of our love for him, so is it also a proof of our fear of God. *Jerry Bridges*

I fear God, yet am not afraid of him.
Thomas Browne

The fear of God is the beginning of wisdom, and they that lack the beginning have neither middle nor end. *John Bunyan*

Though there is not always grace where there is fear of hell, yet, to be sure, there is no grace where there is no fear of God.
John Bunyan

He that fears God fears nothing else.
Edmund Burke

Nothing is more powerful to overcome temptation than the fear of God.
John Calvin

Righteousness flows from only one principle — the fear of God. *John Calvin*

The fear of God is the root and origin of all righteousness. *John Calvin*

There is no wisdom but that which is founded on the fear of God. *John Calvin*

The remarkable thing about fearing God is that when you fear God you fear nothing else. *Oswald Chambers*

The fear of the Lord is not just the end of wisdom but its beginning.
Edmund P. Clowney

The learning of the Christian man ought to begin with the fear of God.
Thomas Cranmer

Let us familiarize our minds with the fear due to Christ the Judge, and a new power will enter into our service, making it at once more urgent and more wholesome than it could otherwise be. *James Denney*

As he that fears God fears nothing else, so, he that sees God sees nothing else.
John Donne

The fear of the Lord was a lovely grace in the perfect humanity of Jesus. Let it be the test of our 'predestination to be conformed to his image' *Sinclair Ferguson*

The essential ingredients of the fear of God are correct concepts of the character of God, a pervasive sense of the presence of God and a constant awareness of our obligation to God. *Al Martin*

The fear of God is the soul of godliness.
John Murray

No man acts with true wisdom till he fears God and hopes in his mercy.
William S. Plumer

True piety is never separate from the fear of God. *William S. Plumer*

Reverent fear of God is the key to faithfulness in any situation.   *Alan Redpath*

The fear of men weakens, but the fear of the Lord strengthens.   *Remigius*

As faith is a grace that feeds all the rest, so fear is a grace that guards all the rest.
William Secker

True ethical absolutes can only be grounded in the fear of a living God. *R. C. Sproul*

It is a blessed fear which drives us to trust.
C. H. Spurgeon

Unregenerate fear drives from God, gracious fear drives to him. *C. H. Spurgeon*

The Christian, like a net, must have both the lead of a godly fear and the cork of a lively faith.   *George Swinnock*

The height of God must lay man low.
George Swinnock

No one can know the true grace of God who has not first known the fear of God.
A. W. Tozer

The fear of God is both a virtue and a keeper of other virtues.   *John Trapp*

As the embankment keeps out the water, so the fear of the Lord keeps out uncleanness.   *Thomas Watson*

The fear of God promotes spiritual joy; it is the morning star that ushers in the sunlight of comfort.   *Thomas Watson*

It is only the fear of God that can deliver us from the fear of man. *John Witherspoon*

FEELINGS — See Emotions

FELLOWSHIP
(See also: Church — Fellowship; Friendship)

Keep such company as God keeps. *Anon.*

There is danger of losing the spiritual fellowship by thinking that our social fellowship is the climax of all fellowship.
Donald Grey Barnhouse

Keep company with the soundest Christians that have most experience of Christ.
John Bunyan

Man is made for society and Christians for the communion of saints.
Matthew Henry

We ought not to make any conditions of our brethren's acceptance with us but such as God has made the conditions of their acceptance with him. *Matthew Henry*

Fellowship with Christians is for the sake of fellowship with God.   *J. I. Packer*

The fact that we share social activities with other Christians does not of itself imply that we have fellowship with them.
J. I. Packer

For the early Christians *koinonia* was not the frilly 'fellowship' of church-sponsored bi-weekly outings. It was not tea, biscuits and sophisticated small talk in the Fellowship Hall after the sermon. It was an unconditional sharing of their lives with the other members of Christ's body.   *Ronald J. Sider*

Genuine fellowship comes when Christians stop relating to one another as righteous saints and accept one another as unrighteous sinners.   *David Watson*

As the communion of saints is in our creed, so it should be in our company.
Thomas Watson

FELLOWSHIP WITH GOD — See Communion with God

FLATTERY

Flattery has turned more heads than garlic. *Anon.*

Flattery is the art of telling a person exactly what he thinks of himself. *Anon.*

Like a bee, the flatterer has honey in his mouth and a sting in his tail. *Anon.*

Many men know how to flatter; few know how to praise. *Anon.*

Praise undeserved is poison in disguise.
Anon.

How can we conquer the world when it rages, if we cannot vanquish it when it flatters? *Augustine*

It is better to be persecuted for having said the truth than to be favoured for having flattered. *Augustine*

You would not fear reproof if you did not love flattery. *Augustine*

Flattery is praise insincerely given for an interested purpose. *Henry Ward Beecher*

Flatterers are the very worst of sinners.
Thomas Brooks

Flattery is the devil's invisible net.
Thomas Brooks

Whilst an ass is stroked under the belly you may lay on his back what burden you please. *Thomas Brooks*

Flattery is a juggler, and no kin unto sincerity. *Thomas Browne*

Flattery corrupts both the receiver and giver. *Edmund Burke*

Everyone flatters himself and carries a kingdom in his breast. *John Calvin*

Flatterers look like friends as wolves look like dogs. *George Chapman*

Flattery pleases those who wish to appear more virtuous than they are.
Cicero

Talk to a man about himself and he will listen for hours. *Benjamin Disraeli*

It is a dangerous crisis when a proud heart meets with flattering lips. *John Flavel*

Flatterers are the worst of tame beasts.
Thomas Fuller

Flattery sits in the parlour when plain dealing is kicked out of doors.
Thomas Fuller

As pressing irons can smooth the greatest wrinkles in cloth, so can flattering tongues do as to the most deformed actions. *Thomas Goodwin*

Be as much troubled by unjust praises as by unjust slanders. *Philip Henry*

Spiritual flatterers are commonly more respected than spiritual fathers.
William Jenkyn

Flattery is a device for getting somebody to pay attention to what you're saying.
Franklin P. Jones

There is nothing so shabby and mean and nauseating as the spirit of flattery because

its motives are always of the lowest.
James Philip

All other flattery would be harmless if we did not flatter ourselves.
William S. Plumer

Did we not flatter ourselves, the flattery of others would not hurt us.
François Rochefoucauld

Flattery is a sort of bad money, to which our vanity gives currency.
Françis Rochefoucauld

The voice of the flatterer stays long in the ear.
Seneca

What really flatters a man is that you think him worth flattering.
George Bernard Shaw

Flattery and friendship never go together.
C. H. Spurgeon

None but the silliest of geese would go to the fox's sermon.
C. H. Spurgeon

Flatterers are the worst kind of enemies.
Tacitus

FORGIVENESS BY GOD
(See also: Atonement; Cross; Jesus Christ — Death)

Sins are so remitted as if they had never been committed.
Thomas Adams

I will not glory because I am righteous, but because I am redeemed; not because I am clear of sin, but because my sins are forgiven.
Ambrose

Jesus freely forgives sinners, but never when they have no desire to seek holiness.
Anon.

Forgiveness from others is charity; from God, grace; from oneself, wisdom.
Anon.

If God were not willing to forgive sin heaven would be empty.
Anon.

Sin forsaken is the best evidence of sin forgiven.
Anon.

The cross is the cost of my forgiveness.
Anon.

If anybody imagines that God could simply forgive us in the same way that we forgive one another, he has not yet considered the seriousness of sin.
Anselm

It would tire the hands of an angel to write down all the pardons God bestows upon true penitent believers.
William Bates

God has never promised to forgive a single sin that man is not willing to forsake.
John Blanchard

What man uncovers, God will cover; what man covers, God will uncover.
John Blanchard

God does not wish us to remember what he is willing to forget.
George A. Buttrick

When God designs to forgive us he changes our hearts and turns us to obedience by his Spirit.
John Calvin

It is shallow nonsense to say God forgives us because he is love. The only ground upon which God can forgive us is the cross.
Oswald Chambers

Those who are most conscious of forgiveness are invariably those who have been most acutely convicted of their sin.
Sinclair Ferguson

In these days of guilt complexes, perhaps the most glorious word in the English language is 'forgiveness'. *Billy Graham*

Be careful to keep the old receipts which you have from God for the pardon of your sins. *William Gurnall*

The sin which is not too great to be forsaken is not too great to be forgiven.
Thomas Horton

Do you think that you deserve forgiveness? If you do, you are not a Christian.
D. Martyn Lloyd-Jones

To divorce forgiveness of sins from the actual living of the Christian life is nothing but rank heresy! *D. Martyn Lloyd-Jones*

True forgiveness breaks a man, and he must forgive. *D. Martyn Lloyd-Jones*

Forgiveness forms the church. *R. C. Lucas*

When is your life more fragrant than when the kiss of forgiveness is most fresh upon your cheek? *Al Martin*

The pleasures of being forgiven are as superior to the pleasures of an unforgiven man as heaven is higher than hell.
Robert Murray M'Cheyne

Nothing will make you want to give up sinning more than knowing that Christ has actually taken and remitted all your sin, past, present and future. *John Metcalfe*

Forgiveness is to be set loose from sins.
G. Campbell Morgan

God never forgives sin without at the same time changing the nature of the sinner. *Iain H. Murray*

Should we leave this world unforgiven, it will be a dire event. *J. I. Packer*

The basic fact of biblical religion is that God pardons and accepts believing sinners. *J. I. Packer*

Christ comes with a blessing in each hand; forgiveness in one, holiness in the other. *A. W. Pink*

Sinners need nothing more than pardon.
William S. Plumer

We cannot experience God's forgiveness until our sins have been dealt with.
Frank Retief

When God pardons, he consigns the offence to everlasting forgetfulness.
Merv Rosell

Where we went with our vicious sins, there we must go with our soiled virtues.
W. E. Sangster

God is as sternly and inflexibly just towards sin as if he never forgave iniquity, and yet he forgives sinners through Christ Jesus as freely and fully as if he never punished a transgression. *C. H. Spurgeon*

You can have forgiven all your sin in half the tick of the clock, and pass from death to life more swiftly than I can utter the words. *C. H. Spurgeon*

Release! Signed in tears, sealed in blood, written on heavenly parchment, recorded in eternal archives. The black ink of the indictment is written all over with the red ink of the cross: 'the blood of Jesus Christ cleanseth us from all sin.'
T. De Witt Talmage

Forgiveness is a golden thread spun out

of the bowels of free grace.
Thomas Watson

Our guilty spirits dread
To meet the wrath of heaven;
But in his righteousness arrayed,
We see our sins forgiven.   *Isaac Watts*

Ours is the religion of the forgiven.
Theodore Williams

No man is rich enough to buy back his
past.   *Oscar Wilde*

As unforgiven sin presents an insuper-
able barrier to blessing, so the forgiveness of sins is the priceless boon which
opens the door to every other spiritual
blessing.   *Geoffrey B. Wilson*

The Bible knows nothing of mere
pardon. There can be no pardon except
on the ground of satisfaction of justice.
Geoffrey B. Wilson

The magnitude of the sacrifice which *our*
sins called forth manifests the supreme
folly of looking elsewhere for their
forgiveness.   *Geoffrey B. Wilson*

There can be no thought of 'cheap'
forgiveness when we remember that our
redemption cost God the life of his
beloved Son.   *Geoffrey B. Wilson*

Our God has a big eraser.   *Billy Zeoli*

FORGIVENESS OF OTHERS

There is no revenge so complete as forgiveness.   *Anon.*

We are most like beasts when we kill. We
are most like men when we judge. We
are most like God when we forgive. *Anon.*

If you are suffering from a bad man's
injustice, forgive him lest there be two
bad men.   *Augustine*

It is the person who most knows himself
liable to fall that will be most ready to
overlook any offences from his fellow
men.   *Alexander Auld*

You should forgive many things in
others, but nothing in yourself. *Ausonius*

Every man should have a fair-sized cemetery in which to bury the faults of his
friends.   *Henry Ward Beecher*

The glory of Christianity is to conquer
by forgiveness.   *William Blake*

The Christian can always afford to
forgive — and can never afford not to!
John Blanchard

Nothing causes us to so nearly resemble
God as the forgiveness of injuries.
Chrysostom

Nothing in this low and ruined world
bears the meek impress of the Son of God
so surely as forgiveness.   *Alice Clay*

The unforgiving spirit as a pride form is
the number one killer of spiritual life.
James Coulter

We are not finished with the need of
forgiveness when we become Christians.
G. B. Duncan

The noblest revenge is to forgive.
Thomas Fuller

There's no point in burying a hatchet if
you're going to put up a marker on the
site.   *Sydney Harris*

Forgiveness is not an occasional act, it is a permanent attitude. *Martin Luther King*

Everyone says forgiveness is a lovely idea until he has something to forgive.. *C. S. Lewis*

If God forgives us, we must forgive others. Otherwise it is almost like setting up ourselves as a higher tribunal than him. *C. S. Lewis*

I say to the glory of God and in utter humility that whenever I see myself before God and realize even something of what my blessed Lord has done for me, I am ready to forgive anybody anything. *D. Martyn Lloyd-Jones*

If we really know Christ as our Saviour our hearts are broken and cannot be hard, and we cannot refuse forgiveness *D. Martyn Lloyd-Jones*

Those who say they will forgive but can't forget, simply bury the hatchet but leave the handle out for immediate use. *D. L. Moody*

A Christian will find it cheaper to pardon than to resent. Forgiveness saves us the expense of anger, the cost of hatred, the waste of spirits. *Hannah More*

If you have a thing to pardon, pardon it quickly. Slow forgiveness is little better than no forgiveness. *Arthur W Pinero*

To err is human, to forgive divine. *Alexander Pope*

Humanity is never so beautiful as when praying for forgiveness, or else when forgiving another. *Jean Paul Richter*

It is a melancholy fact that there are few Christian duties so little practised as that of forgiveness. *J. C. Ryle*

No prayers can be heard which do not come from a forgiving heart. *J. C. Ryle*

Forgive and forget. When you bury a mad dog, don't leave his tail above the ground. *C. H. Spurgeon*

You never so touch the ocean of God's love as when you forgive and love your enemies. *Corrie Ten Boom*

Forgiveness is a funny thing — it warms the heart and cools the sting. *William A. Ward*

Friendship flourishes at the fountain of forgiveness. *William A. Ward*

A man may as well go to hell for not forgiving as for not believing. *Thomas Watson*

FORMALISM
(See also: Hypocrisy; Ritulism

It is a poor worship to move our hats, not our hearts. *Thomas Adams*

Dead devotion is a living mockery. *Anon.*

Ordinances without the Spirit are cisterns without water. *Anon.*

Orthodoxy of words is atheism unless backed up by excellent character. *Anon.*

It is no advantage to be near the light if the eyes are closed. *Augustine*

God hates the sanctimonious hallelujah more than he hates the godless curse. *Donald Grey Barnhouse*

No one can thrive spiritually on mere

church membership, sacraments, ritual or formality.   *Donald Grey Barnhouse*

God requires an inward purity as well as an outward performance. *John Blanchard*

The house of a formalist is as empty of religion as the white of an egg is of savour.   *John Bunyan*

God is not taken with the cabinet but the jewel.   *Stephen Charnock*

Many pray with their lips for that for which their hearts have no desire.
    Jonathan Edwards

Many a Christian, many a church, has everything in the showcase and nothing on the shelves.   *Vance Havner*

Our heads are travelling by fast express these days, and our hearts follow by slow freight.   *Vance Havner*

Sunday-morning Christianity is the greatest hindrance to true revival.
    Vance Havner

Using Christian terminology means nothing if one is not a Christian. Having a case of athlete's foot doesn't make you an athlete!   *Vance Havner*

Nothing is more destructive to Christianity than placing it in modes and forms and circumstantials which eat out the essentials.   *Matthew Henry*

Justification is totally against formal religion. God has no room for those who persist in relying on forms or ceremonies.
    Robert M. Horn

The more exalted pomp there be of men's devising, there will be the less spiritual truth.   *George Hutcheson*

Formal religion always makes fertile soil for false religion.   *Gilbert W. Kirby*

Men may hasten to perdition with the name of Jesus upon their lips.
    Friedrich W. Krummacher

Solemn prayers, rapturous devotions, are but repeated hypocrisies unless the heart and mind be conformable to them.
    William Law

God is not deceived by externals.
    C. S. Lewis

Painted fire needs no fuel; a dead, formal profession is easily kept up.
    Thomas Manton

Many of us who profess to be Christians are so busy with the mechanics of our religion that we have no time left for the spiritual part of it.   *William B. Martin*

Ministers are but the pole; it is to the brazen serpent you are to look.
    Robert Murray M'Cheyne

External observances alone feed no consciences and sanctify no hearts. *J. C. Ryle*

It must not content us to take our bodies to church if we leave our hearts at home.
    J. C. Ryle

Men have only to go on hearing without believing, listening without repenting, going to church without going to Christ, and by and by they will find themselves in hell!   *J. C. Ryle*

That man must famish at last who always feeds upon the dish instead of the meat.
    William Secker

Religion that is merely ritual and ceremonial can never satisfy. Neither can we be

satisfied by a religion that is merely humanitarian or serviceable to mankind. Man's craving is for the spiritual.
Samuel Shoemaker

Outward things will do no more good than a fair shoe to a gouty foot.
Richard Sibbes

A dead creed is of no use; we must have our creed baptized with the Holy Ghost.
C. H. Spurgeon

I would sooner risk the dangers of a tornado of religious excitement than see the air grow stagnant with a deadly formality.
C. H. Spurgeon

One can grasp orthodox religion while having no grasp of the Saviour.
Geoff Thomas

You can be as straight as a gun barrel theologically — and as empty as one spiritually.
A. W. Tozer

Blessedness does not lie in externals.
Thomas Watson

God's name is not hallowed when worship becomes an excuse for focussing upon human personalities, or exercising spiritual gifts for our own enjoyment.
Thomas Watson

Posture in worship is too often imposture.
Thomas Watson

No matter how spiritual the song you are singing, no matter how poetic the prayer you are praying, if it isn't sincere then it isn't worship, it's hypocrisy.
Donald S. Whitney

FORTITUDE — See Patience

FREE WILL
(See also: Will)

A dog is free to be a dog; a sinner is free to be a sinner.
Andrew Anderson

It was by the evil use of his free will that man destroyed both it and himself.
Augustine

The sinner, apart from grace, is unable to be willing and unwilling to be able.
W. E. Best

If a man could will himself to be saved, he could just as easily change his mind and will himself to become unsaved.
John Blanchard

The myth of man's free will is exploded by the simple statistic that all men by nature decide against God.
John Blanchard

When the will is enchained as the slave of sin, it cannot make a movement towards goodness, far less steadily pursue it.
John Calvin

Because we are conscious of volition, we suppose our volition is free. What we discover by experience is that our freedom of will is unidirectional. We are truly free only when we sin, for we are then acting according to our nature, a fact which accounts for the pleasures of sin.
Arthur C. Custance

If Christ came to save that which is lost, free will has no place.
J. N. Darby

The phrase 'free will' is only used by the Bible in the context of stewardship. It is never used in the context of coming to Christ in faith.
Sinclair Ferguson

Free will without God's grace is not free

will at all, but is the permanent prisoner and bondslave of evil, since it cannot turn itself to good. *Martin Luther*

A man's choices are free in the sense that they are not just determined by external compulsion. But they are not free if by freedom is meant freedom from determination by the man's own character. *J. Gresham Machen*

Sinners are free in working their own destruction, notwithstanding the divine work on them; just as the saints are free in working out their own salvation, while God works in them to will and to do of his good pleasure. *Basil Manly*

The will is not free ... the affections love as they do and the will chooses as it does because of the state of the heart, and ... the heart is deceitful above all things and desperately wicked. *A. W. Pink*

The will is not sovereign; it is a servant, because influenced and controlled by the other faculties of man's being. The will is not free because *the man* is the slave of sin. *A. W. Pink*

Any view of the human will that destroys the biblical view of human responsibility is seriously defective. Any view of the human will that destroys the biblical view of God's character is even worse. *R. C. Sproul*

Man's will is free to follow his inclinations, but fallen man's inclinations are always and invariably away from God. *R. C. Sproul*

Free will I have often heard of, but I have never seen it. I have met with will, and plenty of it, but it has either been led captive by sin or held in blessed bonds of grace. *C. H. Spurgeon*

The friends of free will are the enemies of free grace. *John Trapp*

FREEDOM — See Liberty

FRIENDSHIP
(See also: Fellowship)

A friend is one who comes in when the world goes out. *Anon.*

A real friend warms you up by his presence, trusts you with his secrets, and remembers you in his prayers. *Anon.*

Christians may not see eye to eye, but they can walk arm in arm. *Anon.*

Friendship doubles our joy and divides our grief. *Anon.*

There are not many things in life so beautiful as true friendship, and there are not many things more uncommon. *Anon.*

There is no better proof of friendship than to help our friends with their burdens. *Augustine*

A friend is someone with whom you dare to be yourself. *C. Raymond Beran*

Friendship is like money, easier to make than to keep. *Samuel Butler*

Nothing is more dangerous than associating with the ungodly. *John Calvin*

The firmest friendships have been formed in mutual adversity, as iron is most strongly united by the fiercest flame. *C. C. Colton*

A friend is a person with whom I may be sincere. Before him I may think aloud. *Ralph Waldo Emerson*

Every man passes his life in the search after friendship.   *Ralph Waldo Emerson*

The only way to have a friend is to be one.   *Ralph Waldo Emerson*

It is best to be with those in time we hope to be with in eternity.   *Thomas Fuller*

Nothing is more stimulating than friends who speak the truth in love. *Os Guinness*

There may be those with whom we cannot fall in and yet with whom we need not fall out.   *Matthew Henry*

A friend is never known until a man has need.   *John Heywood*

One should keep his friendships in constant repair.   *Samuel Johnson*

It is the best and truest friend who honestly tells us the truth about ourselves even when he knows we shall not like it. False friends are the ones who hide such truth from us and do so in order to remain in our favour.   *R. C. H. Lenski*

Friendship is the greatest of worldly goods. Certainly to me it is the chief happiness of life.   *C. S. Lewis*

Better it is to go with a few to heaven, than with a multitude to hell, and be damned for the sake of company.
Elnathan Parr

In friendship there is one soul in two bodies.   *Richard Sibbes*

A man is known by the company he shuns as well as by the company he keeps.
C. H. Spurgeon

Show me a man's books and show me a man's companions and I will tell you what sort of man he is.   *William Tiptaft*

Friendship flourishes at the fountain of forgiveness.   *William A. Ward*

Association begets assimilation.
Thomas Watson

Counterfeiting friendship is worse than counterfeiting money.   *Thomas Watson*

Friendship is the marriage of affections.
Thomas Watson

Tell me with whom thou art found and I will tell thee who thou art.
Johann Wolfgang von Goethe

FRUITFULNESS

A fruitless person is not a failed Christian, but a false one — in other words, not a Christian at all.   *John Blanchard*

Fruit is evidence of the root.
John Blanchard

If I were fruitless, it mattered not who commended me; but if I were fruitful, I cared not who did condemn. *John Bunyan*

The fruit of the Spirit is not push, drive, climb, grasp and trample ... Life is more that a climb to the top of the heap.
Richard J. Foster

Our Lord never thought of a relationship to him that does not issue in fruitfulness for him.   *Vance Havner*

Have you ever noticed the difference in the Christian life between work and fruit? A machine can do work; only a life can bear fruit.   *Andrew Murray*

Judge a tree by its fruits, not by its leaves.
Phaedrus

The Christian should resemble a fruit tree, not a Christmas tree.   *John R. W. Stott*

FULNESS OF LIFE

Fulness of the Spirit is not a press-button panacea; it is the growing experience of those who hunger and thirst after right-eousness.   *John Blanchard*

We will never crave to be filled until we are convinced that we are empty.
John Blanchard

There is one thing we cannot imitate; we cannot imitate being full of the Holy Ghost.   *Oswald Chambers*

The Spirit-filled life is no mystery re-vealed to a select few, no goal difficult of attainment. To trust and to obey is the sub-stance of the whole matter. *Victor Edman*

I've never known a person whom I thought was truly filled with the Holy Spirit who went out and bragged about it or sought to draw attention to himself.
Billy Graham

The whole secret of abundant living can be summed up in this sentence: 'Not your responsibility but your response to God's ability.'   *Carl F. H. Henry*

God commands us to be filled with the Spirit, and if we are not filled it is because we are living beneath our privi-leges.   *D. L. Moody*

Christians should have ... such abundant life that in poverty they are rich, in sick-ness they are in spiritual health, in contempt they are full of triumph and in death full of glory.   *C. H. Spurgeon*

The Spirit-filled life is not a special, deluxe edition of Christianity. It is part and parcel of the total plan of God for his people.   *A. W. Tozer*

FUTURE
(See also: Hope)

We should all be concerned about the future because we will have to spend the rest of our lives there. *Charles Kettering*

Belief in a future life is the appetite of reason.   *Walter Landor*

The future belongs to those who belong to God. This is hope.   *W. T. Purkiser*

We know not what the future holds, but we do know who holds the future.
Willis J. Ray

God assures us of a future that is better than all our past.   *J. Charles Stern*

Never be afraid to trust an unknown future to a known God. *Corrie ten Boom*

We have come to a wretched emphasis in the Christian church, so that when we talk about the future we talk about 'eschatology' instead of heaven!
A. W. Tozer

GAMBLING

Gambling is stealing by mutual consent.
Anon.

The specific indictment of betting, gambling and lotteries is that they are a means, or device, or stratagem for attempting to appropriate other people's money ... a person can only win if others lose. Success in gambling depends entirely on the failure of others ... this is that which makes the practice so sordid and contemptible. *Fred Caddick*

In essence, gambling is a sin against charity; for the gambler hopes to gain at the expense of the total loss of the other competitors. *Kenneth F. W. Prior*

GENEROSITY
(See also: Charity; Giving; Kindness)

The quickest generosity is the best. *Anon.*

When it comes to generosity, some people stop at nothing. *Anon.*

Stretch your purse to the utmost, and do all the good you can. *Richard Baxter*

Watch lest prosperity destroy generosity. *Henry Ward Beecher*

Those who give the most have most left. *George F. Burba*

Without the rich heart, wealth is an ugly beggar. *Ralph Waldo Emerson*

Liberality was formerly called honesty, as if to imply that unless we are liberal we are not honest, either toward God or man. *Tryon Edwards*

It is much better to have your gold in the hand than in the heart. *Thomas Fuller*

Not possession, but use, is the only riches. *Thomas Fuller*

As the purse is emptied the heart is filled. *Victor Hugo*

A holy life and a bounteous heart are ornaments to the gospel. *Thomas Manton*

He who is not liberal with what he has, does but deceive himself when he thinks he would be liberal if he had more. *William S. Plumer*

A generous action is its own reward. *William Walsh*

True liberality is the spontaneous expression of love. *Geoffrey Wilson*

GENTLENESS

There is nothing stronger than gentleness. *Anon.*

Perhaps no grace is less prayed for or less cultivated than gentleness. *George Bethune*

Seldom do we reflect that not to be gentle is sin. *George Bethune*

Gentle words fall lightly, but they have great weight. *Derick Bingham*

Only the truly strong and great can be truly tender. Tenderness is a mark of nobility, not of weakness. *James Philip*

Nothing is so strong as gentleness; nothing so gentle as real strength. *François de Sales*

We need power for gentleness. *W. Graham Scroggie*

GIFTS — Spiritual — See Spiritual Gifts

GIVING
(See also Charity; Generosity; Kindness; Tithing)

Are you giving God what is right, or what is left? *Anon.*

225

Giving

Give from the bottom of your heart, not from the top of your purse. *Anon.*

He who gives only when he is asked has waited too long. *Anon.*

If you don't give away anything God wants you to give, you don't own it — it owns you. *Anon.*

Let us give according to our incomes lest God make our incomes match our gifts. *Anon.*

Seeking empties a life; giving fills it. *Anon.*

The hand that gives gathers. *Anon.*

Give to all, lest the one you pass over should be Christ himself. *Augustine*

Nearly half the parables Jesus told have the use of money as their main subject. It is sometimes said that we should give until it hurts. But Jesus teaches that it should hurt when we cease to give! *Ian Barclay*

If men do not give according to their means, they must answer for it to God. *Albert Barnes*

In this world it is not what we take up but what we give up that makes us rich. *Henry Ward Beecher*

They who in giving think, not how little they can give, as they would if self-enrichment were the aim, but of benefits to be conferred, will receive back on the same principle. As they do to others, so God will act to them. *J. A. Beet*

Christian giving is not a matter of finance, it is a matter of faith. The church treasurer counts what we give; God counts what we keep. *John Blanchard*

When we give to God we are taking the gift out of one of his hands and putting it into the other. *John Blanchard*

Your money can make you an overseas missionary without ever leaving your home town, an evangelist without ever mounting a platform, a broadcaster without ever entering a studio, a Bible teacher without ever writing a book. *John Blanchard*

It is possible to give without loving, but it is impossible to love without giving. *Richard Braunstein*

From what curses and degradations should we be delivered if Christian people gave as the Scriptures direct! *Samuel Chadwick*

I am persuaded that there is nothing upon which the Christian conscience is so ill-informed as the subject of Christian giving. *Samuel Chadwick*

Spirit-directed giving is depending only on the Spirit of God to direct the gifts in the case of every person, and then being willing to abide by the results of this confidence and trust. *Lewis Sperry Chafer*

He who receives a benefit should never forget it; he who bestows should never remember it. *Pierre Charron*

Not how much we give, but how much we do not give, is the test of our Christianity. *Oswald Chambers*

What we spend in piety and charity is not tribute paid to a tyrant, but the response of gratitude to our Redeemer. *James Denney*

The world is composed of takers and givers. The takers *eat* better but the givers *sleep* better.   *Byron Frederick*

God has given us two hands — one to receive with and the other to give with. We are not cisterns made for hoarding; we are channels made for sharing.
                                    Billy Graham

Labour hard, consume little, give much — and all to Christ. *Anthony Norris Groves*

God hates a false economy that is out to reduce a budget instead of to receive a blessing.   *Vance Havner*

By practising the grace of sharing, a person is storing up treasure for himself. Gifts are investments. *William Hendriksen*

Whatever we part with for God's sake shall be made up to us in kind or kindness.   *Matthew Henry*

Unless we feel it is an honour and a joy to give, God does not accept the offering.   *Charles Hodge*

We make a living by what we get. We make a life by what we give. *Duane Hulse*

God's greatest desire is to give. When man follows God's example, he receives a divine blessing because he demonstrates that he is one of God's children.
                                    Simon Kistemaker

The manner of giving shows the character of the giver, more than the gift itself.
                                    J. C. Lavater

The limit of giving is to be the limit of our ability to give.   *C. S. Lewis*

The only safe rule is to give more than we can spare. Our charities should pinch and hamper us. If we live at the same level of affluence as other people who have our level of income, we are probably giving away too little.   *C. S. Lewis*

God gave us riches as a means to escape wrath, by a liberal and charitable distribution of them to his glory.
                                    Thomas Manton

He gives twice who gives quickly.
                                    Publius Mimus

If we would have God open his treasury, we must open ours.   *Thomas V. Moore*

The secret of true giving is the joy of the Holy Ghost.   *Andrew Murray*

We ask how much a man *gives;* Christ asks how much he *keeps. Andrew Murray*

When a man gives, the world still asks, '*What* does he give?' Christ asks, '*How* does he give?'   *Andrew Murray*

The only valid and virtuous motive in our giving is to give God pleasure.
                                    Arthur Neil

I shall not value his prayers at all, be he never so earnest and frequent in them, who gives not alms according to his ability.   *John Owen*

When we have given God all we have and are, we have simply given him his own.   *William S. Plumer*

There are three kinds of giving: grudge giving, duty giving and thanksgiving. Grudge giving says, 'I have to'; duty giving says, 'I ought to'; thanksgiving says, 'I want to'.   *Robert Rodenmayer*

When a man dies he clutches in his hands only that which he has given away in his lifetime. *Jean-Jacques Rousseau*

A giving Saviour should have giving disciples. *J. C. Ryle*

Grace does not make giving optional. *Charles Caldwell Ryrie*

The only way to have more than enough to spare is to give God more than you can spare. *Oswald J. Smith*

We expect our young people to lay down their lives for God, but most of us are not willing to lay down our bank accounts. *Paul B. Smith*

As you have done unto others, so will the Lord do unto you. Empty your pockets! *C. H. Spurgeon*

Faith's way of gaining is giving. *C. H. Spurgeon*

Giving is true having. *C. H. Spurgeon*

I may expect that as much of prosperity as will be good for me will come to me as a gracious reward for a liberal course of action. *C. H. Spurgeon*

Many a man becomes empty-handed because he does not know the art of distribution. *C. H. Spurgeon*

Many people will always be poor because they never give to the cause of God. *C. H. Spurgeon*

We are to give to the poor out of pity. Not to be seen and applauded, much less to get influence over them; but out of pure sympathy and compassion we must give them help. *C. H. Spurgeon*

All believers are taught to give — but there is such a thing as a special gift of giving. *A. W. Tozer*

Mercy is not miserly; charity is no churl. *John Trapp*

The way to lay up is to lay out. *Thomas Watson*

If I leave more than £10, you and all mankind bear witness that I lived and died a thief and a robber. *John Wesley*

Arrogant giving can turn the best of gifts to ashes. *Kenneth L. Wilson*

GLOOM — See Despair

GLORY — See God — Glory

GLUTTONY
(See also: Covetousness; Greed)

Gluttons dig their graves with their teeth. *Anon.*

Gluttony kills more than the sword. *Anon.*

The minutes spent at the dinner table won't make you fat — but the seconds will. *Anon.*

Bridle the appetite of gluttony and thou wilt with less difficulty restrain all other inordinate desires of animal nature. *Thomas à Kempis*

Those who eat too much are just as guilty of sin as those who drink too much. *Joseph Caryl*

Meat kills as many as the musket; the board as the sword. *Chrysostom*

Gluttony is an emotional escape, a sign that something is eating us. *Peter Devries*

Gluttony is the sepulchre of the living, and a kind of spiritual drowning of a man.
William Jenkyn

GOAL — See Purpose

GOD — Condescension

God never plays philosopher with a washer-women. *C. S. Lewis*

God's condescension is nowhere more conspicuous than in his hearing of prayer.
Austin Phelps

God's condescension is equal to his majesty. *Henry Scott*

GOD — Eternality

God is not the great 'I WAS'; he is the great 'I AM'. *Eric Alexander*

Eternity is the lifetime of the Almighty.
Anon.

Time writes no wrinkle on the brow of the Eternal. *Anon.*

God can as well and as soon cease to be, as he can cease to be holy. *Thomas Brooks*

God can neither die nor lie.
Thomas Brooks

Time is nothing to God.
Oswald Chambers

God is his own eternity.
Stephen Charnock

The eternity of God is nothing else but the duration of God, and the duration of God is nothing else but his existence enduring. *Stephen Charnock*

God doesn't rush men; he owns time.
John Hercus

All but God is changing day by day.
Charles Kingsley

God is not hurried along in the time-stream of this universe any more than an author is hurried along in the imaginary time of his own novel. *C. S. Lewis*

To accept that God exists outside the time and space framework as we know it renders any question of where he came from and what he was doing before he created what we know as the universe totally meaningless. *John McDowell*

God is beyond origin. *Novation of Rome*

There is no higher mystery than God's eternity. *William S. Plumer*

It is not for us to set an hour-glass to the Creator of time. *Samuel Rutherford*

God is not subject to time.
Dorothy L Sayers

God's duration is without succession.
George Swinnock

Our life is scarcely the twinkle of a star in God's eternal day. *Bayard Taylor*

In God there is no was or will be, but a continuous and unbroken is. In him history and prophecy are one and the same. *A. W. Tozer*

Whatever God is he is infinitely.
A. W. Tozer

Unlike mortal man, God is incorruptible and so immortal. *Geoffrey B. Wilson*

GOD — Existence

A dead God is the creation of men; a living God is the Creator of men.   *Anon.*

God is his own best evidence.   *Anon.*

He who leaves God out of his reasoning does not know how to count.   *Anon.*

God is more truly imagined than expressed, and he exists more truly than is imagined.   *Augustine*

Not one word in the Bible seeks to explain God; God is assumed.
John Blanchard

The truth of God is immortal. *John Calvin*

The being of a God is the guard of the world.   *Stephen Charnock*

The existence of God is the foundation of all religion.   *Stephen Charnock*

If every gnat that flies were an archangel, all that could but tell me that there is a God; and the poorest worm that creeps tells me that.   *John Donne*

I could prove God statistically. Take the human body alone — the chance that all the functions of the individual would just happen is a statistical monstrosity.
George Gallup

God's existence not only *cannot* be proved, it *should not* be attempted.
Os Guinness

God is not for proof but proclamation; not for argument but acceptance.
Robert M. Horn

God is not human writ large: he is GOD, a being totally different. *Robert M. Horn*

We trust not because 'a god' exists, but because *this* God exists.   *C. S. Lewis*

You have to go outside the sequence of engines, into the world of men, to find the real originator of the rocket. Is it not equally reasonable to look outside nature for the real Originator of the natural order?   *C. S. Lewis*

Belief in God is an instinct as natural to man as walking on two legs.
G. C. Lichtenberg

One of the great needs of today is a profound conviction that God is.
W. Holloway Main

The ultimate fact about the universe is a personal God.   *Peter C. Moore*

Let us weigh the gain and the loss in wagering that God is. If you win, you win all; if you lose, you lose nothing. Do not hesitate, then, to wager that he is.
Blaise Pascal

God is the great reality.   *J. B. Phillips*

Men and women who refuse to acknowledge God's existence do so, in the final analysis, because it is contrary to their manner of living. They do not want to bow to the moral claims of a holy God on their lives.   *R. C. Sproul*

Who … has ever seen an idea? … Who has ever seen love? … Who has ever seen faith? … The real things in the world are the invisible spiritual realities. Is it so difficult, then, to believe in God?
Charles Templeton

What we believe about God is the most important thing about us.   *A. W. Tozer*

If God did not exist, it would be necessary to invent him.   *Voltaire*

To grasp the idea of God is to grasp an idea of the only reality that could form a completely adequate explanation of the existence of the universe, for God is the only reality which, in being supremely intelligible or comprehensible to itself, explains itself.   *Keith Ward*

Until a man has found God he begins at no beginning and ends at no end.
H. G. Wells

The existence of God does not just face us with something to be believed or rejected, but someone to be accepted or rejected.   *Peter S. Williams*

The existence of God means that human existence is not absurd. *Peter S. Williams*

GOD — Faithfulness

A man were better to say there is no God than say that God is unfaithful.
Thomas Brooks

God is always like himself. *John Calvin*

What more powerful consideration can be thought on to make us true to God, than the faithfulness and truth of God to us?   *William Gurnall*

Divine faithfulness is a wonderful comfort to those who are loyal. It is a very earnest warning for those who might be inclined to become disloyal.
William Hendriksen

Though men are false, God is faithful.
Matthew Henry

Believing prayer takes its stand upon the faithfulness of God. *D. Edmond Hiebert*

What God is to one saint he is to all saints.
William S. Plumer

You can never understand the faithfulness of God by taking the short view.
Paul S. Rees

The quality of faithfulness is essential to God's being.   *Frank Retief*

GOD — Forgiveness — See Forgiveness by God

GOD — Glory

A concern for the glory of God is the ultimate motive for Christian living.
Anon.

We should give God the same place in our hearts that he holds in the universe.
Anon.

God's greatest glory is his grace.
Donald Grey Barnhouse

The reverent, godly Christian sees God first in his transcendent glory, majesty and holiness before he sees him in his love, mercy and grace.   *Jerry Bridges*

This is, indeed, the proper business of the whole life, in which men should daily exercise themselves, to consider the infinite goodness, justice, power and wisdom of God, in this magnificent theatre of God.
John Calvin

As no place can be without God, so no place can compass and contain him.
Stephen Charnock

The most perfect idea of God that we can form in this life is that of an independent, unique, infinite, eternal, omnipotent, immutable, intelligent and free First Cause, whose power extends over all things. *E. B. De Condillac*

Perish each thought of human pride,
Let God alone be magnified;
His glory let the heavens resound,
Shouted from earth's remotest bound.
Philip Doddridge

Outside of God there is nothing but nothing. *Meister Eckhart*

My God, how wonderful thou art!
Thy majesty how bright!
How beautiful thy mercy seat,
In depths of burning light!
Frederick W. Faber

The Lord's presence is infinite, his brightness insupportable, his majesty awful, his dominion boundless and his sovereignty incontestable. *Matthew Henry*

We cannot make God greater or higher than he is; but if we adore him as infinitely great, and higher than the highest, he is pleased to reckon this magnifying and exalting him. *Matthew Henry*

A man can no more diminish God's glory by refusing to worship him than a lunatic can put out the sun by scribbling the word 'darkness' on the walls of his cell.
C. S. Lewis

In commanding us to glorify him, God is inviting us to enjoy him. *C. S. Lewis*

The ultimate end of all things that come to pass, including the ultimate end of the great drama of redemption, is found in the glory of the eternal God.
J. Gresham Machen

God's overriding goal is to glorify himself. *J. I. Packer*

The only thing that God is bound to do is the very thing that he requires of us — to glorify himself. *J. I. Packer*

God cannot allow another to be partaker of honours due to him without denying himself. It is as much his prerogative to be God alone as to be God at all.
William S. Plumer

God is as incomparable as he is immutable. He is infinitely farther above the tallest archangel than that archangel is above a worm. *William S. Plumer*

What is the glory of God? It is the manifestation of any or all of his attributes. In other words, it is the displaying of God to the world. Thus, things which glorify God are things which show the characteristics of his being to the world.
Charles Caldwell Ryrie

God, and all that he has made, is not more than God without anything that he has made. *William Secker*

The glory of God refers to who God is, not what he does. *R. C. Sproul*

There is nothing little in God.
C. H. Spurgeon

Creation can add nothing to the essential wealth or worthiness of God.
Augustus H. Strong

God will get glory out of every human life. Man may glorify God voluntarily by love and obedience, but if he will not do this he will be compelled to glorify God by his rejection and punishment.
Augustus H. Strong

God's glory is that which makes him glorious.   *Augustus H. Strong*

His own glory is the only end which consists with God's independence and sovereignty.   *Augustus H. Strong*

If the universe were God, theology would be the only science. *Augustus H. Strong*

God is transcendent above all his works even while he is immanent within them. He is here and the whole universe is alive with his life!   *A. W. Tozer*

God is the source of all truth, and every discovery is a means of glorifying him.
Gene Veith

God is simple in a very special sense, as being the one self-explanatory and supremely integrating reality. *Keith Ward*

A sight of God's glory humbles. The stars vanish when the sun appears.
Thomas Watson

Glory is the sparkling of the Deity.
Thomas Watson

The glory of God is more worth than the salvation of all men's souls.
Thomas Watson

We may see God's glory blazing in the sun and twinkling in the stars.
Thomas Watson

The Lord Jehovah reigns;
His throne is built on high,
The garments he assumes
Are light and majesty:
His glories shine with beams so bright,
No mortal eye can bear the sight.
Isaac Watts

As the light of the moon is swallowed up by the brightness of the sun, so the shining achievements of men and women are swallowed up by the glory of God.
Janice Wise

GOD — Goodness

God's giving deserves our thanksgiving.
Anon.

Because he is all-powerful and good, he made everything exceedingly good.
Augustine

The Lord's goodness surrounds us at every moment. I walk through it almost with difficulty, as through thick grass and flowers.   *R. W Barbour*

God's goodness is equal to his greatness.
Richard Baxter

God gives not only generously but genuinely, not only with an open hand but with a full heart.   *John Blanchard*

God is never less than generous, even when we are less than grateful.
John Blanchard

God's riches are never lessened by his generosity.   *John Blanchard*

Nothing good comes except from God and nothing except good comes from God.   *John Blanchard*

God's goodness is the pre-eminent expression of his glory.   *Jerry Bridges*

God's gifts put man's best dreams to shame.   *Elizabeth Barrett Browning*

God's judgements are always founded on his goodness.   *John Calvin*

For those who have everything, as well as for those who have nothing, there is only one single good — God himself.
J. H. Merle d'Aubigné

God has two sheepdogs: Goodness and Mercy. He sends them to us from his throne of grace; sometimes to bark at us, to badger us; sometimes to woo us by persuading us that his will is good and perfect for our lives. *Sinclair Ferguson*

His love has no limit, his grace has no
measure,
His power has no boundary known unto
men;
For out of *his* infinite riches in Jesus
He giveth, and giveth, and giveth again!
Annie Johnson Flint

If I could write as I would about the goodness of God to me, the ink would boil in my pen! *Frances Ridley Havergal*

God is just, and he is good, and he is solvent. *Matthew Henry*

He who feeds his birds will not starve his babes. *Matthew Henry*

We cannot look for too little from the creature nor too much from the Creator.
Matthew Henry

Good when he gives, supremely good,
Nor less when he denies,
E'en crosses from his sovereign hand
Are blessings in disguise.
James Hervey

The goodness of God is as curious as his disappointments. *J. A. Motyer*

The works of a good Creator can only be good. *Novation of Rome*

When we declare that God is good we are saying that he is in every way all that he as God should be, something that marks him out as altogether different from us. *Derek Prime*

Putting our trust in God and depending on his intrinsic goodness frees us from the need to find explanations for everything. *Frank Relief*

There are no days when God's fountain does not flow. *Richard Owen Roberts*

Times are bad; God is good.
Richard Sibbes

The treasury of the church is the liberality of God. *C. H. Spurgeon*

We cannot always trace God's hand but we can always trust God's heart.
C. H. Spurgeon

God never tires of giving. *William Still*

It is not enough that we acknowledge God's infinite resources; we must believe also that he is infinitely generous to bestow them. *A. W. Tozer*

God's goodness is the root of all goodness; and our goodness, if we have any, springs out of his goodness.
William Tyndale

God is ever giving to his children, yet has not less. *Thomas Watson*

God is patron of all the graces.
Thomas Watson

High in the heavens, eternal God,
Thy goodness in full glory shines;
Thy truth shall break through every cloud
That veils and darkens thy designs.
Isaac Watts

To say that 'God is good' is to say that God is the origin and standard of our ethical judgements, and is himself consistent with those judgements.
Peter S. Williams

GOD — Holiness

God's holiness and his nature are not two things, they are but one. God's holiness is his nature, and God's nature is his holiness. *Thomas Brooks*

Holiness in angels and saints is but a quality, but in God it is his essence.
Thomas Brooks

Holiness is the glory of every perfection in the Godhead. *Stephen Charnock*

If every attribute of the Deity were a distinct member, purity would be the form, the soul, the spirit to animate them. Without holiness, his patience would be an indulgence to sin, his mercy a fondness, his wrath a madness, his power a tyranny, his wisdom an unworthy subtlety. Holiness gives decorum to them all.
Stephen Charnock

The holiness of God is his glory, as his grace is his riches. *Stephen Charnock*

A true love to God must begin with a delight in his holiness, and not with a delight in any other attribute.
Jonathan Edwards

No attribute of God is more dreadful to sinners than his holiness. *Matthew Henry*

We only learn to behave ourselves in the presence of God, and if the sense of that presence weakens, humanity tends to lark about. *C. S. Lewis*

No attribute of God is more rejoiced in by unfallen angels and redeemed men than his holiness. *William S. Plumer*

The holiness of God is the 'Godness' of God. It is what sets him apart from everyone else — his moral perfection.
Vaughan Roberts

If we stress the love of God without the holiness of God, it turns out to be only compromise. *Francis Schaeffer*

Holiness is a dimension of God that consumes his very essence. *R. C. Sproul*

Holiness is not just an attribute, it is God's very essence. *R. C. Sproul*

When we see even a small glimpse of God's holiness, we will bow in worship.
R. C. Sproul

God cannot have more holiness, because he is perfectly holy; so he cannot have less holiness, because he is unchangeably holy. *Thomas Watson*

God permits sin but does not promote it.
Thomas Watson

GOD — Immanence

Although he is distinct from the entire universe, God is not an 'absentee landlord', but is everywhere present and active in it. *John Blanchard*

Rebellious man is like someone who tries all the buttons on a transistor radio but always gets the same message — he can never entirely turn off God's voice.
John Campbell

God is not just over and above the creation, he is also powerfully in it.
Martin Robinson

There is no greater probability of laws existing without God than of God existing as the creator of the laws of nature.
Keith Ward

GOD — Immutability

God is where he was.   *Anon.*

God may change our circumstances, but our circumstances never change God.
John Blanchard

God never 'becomes'; God is.
John Blanchard

If God could be proved there would be no need for faith.   *Rob Frost*

The unchangeableness of the divine purposes is a necessary consequence of the unchangeableness of the divine nature.   *Johann Keil*

To deny the immutability of God is to deny that he is God.   *R. B. Kuiper*

God is the most obligated being that there is. He is obligated by his own nature. He is infinite in his wisdom; therefore he can never do anything that is unwise. He is infinite in his justice; therefore he can never do anything that is unjust. He is infinite in his goodness; therefore he can never do anything that is not good. He is infinite in his truth; therefore it is impossible that he should lie.
J. Gresham Machen

Nothing created can ever alter the Creator.   *Stuart Olyott*

God cannot change for the better, for he is perfect; and being perfect, he cannot change for the worse.   *A. W. Pink*

With God the only difference between the future and the past is that certain truths which are as eternal as God himself have not yet become part of human history.
W. Ian Thomas

All God's reasons come from within his uncreated being. Nothing has entered the being of God from eternity, nothing has been removed and nothing has been changed.   *A. W. Tozer*

Human unbelief cannot alter the character of God.   *A. W. Tozer*

Since God is self-existent, he is not composed. There are in him no parts to be altered.   *A. W. Tozer*

The immutability of God appears in its most perfect beauty when viewed against the mutability of men. In God no change is possible; in men change is impossible to escape.   *A. W. Tozer*

Still restless nature dies and grows,
From change to change the creatures run:
Thy being no succession knows,
And all thy vast designs are one.
Isaac Watts

GOD — Independence

God is not in need of anything, but all things are in need of God.
Marcianus Aristides

God without man is still God; man without God is nothing.   *John Blanchard*

God has no need of his creatures, but everything created has need of him.
Meister Eckhart

Not everything must have a cause, but every *effect* must have a cause. Because every effect must have a cause, there must ultimately be one cause that is not an effect but pure cause, or how, indeed, can one explain effect?   *John H. Gerstner*

Being self-existent, God cannot but be self-sufficient, and therefore all sufficient, and the inexhaustible fountain of being and bliss.   *Matthew Henry*

The greatest and best man in the world must say, 'By the grace of God I am what I am'; but God says absolutely — and that is more than any creature, man or angel, can say — 'I am that I am.'
Matthew Henry

Even if God did have needs we could not supply them, for we have only what he has first given us.   *Robert M. Horn*

God has no needs.   *C. S. Lewis*

God does not stop to consult us.
D. Martyn Lloyd-Jones

God is the cause of causes.
Christopher Nesse

God exists independently of our needs, and the universe was not created in order to fulfil them.   *Edward Norman*

He who is over all and in all is yet distinct from all.   *G. D. B. Pepper*

God is a law unto himself, and ... he is under no obligation to give an account of his matters to any.   *A. W. Pink*

God is; if he were not, nothing could be.
Richard Sibbes

God cannot be limited by anything outside of himself, because he created all that exists outside of himself.   *R. C. Sproul*

Dear me, the Lord got on very well before I was born, and I'm sure he will when I am dead.   *C. H. Spurgeon*

God is the cause of all causes, the soul of all souls.   *Augustus H. Strong*

When we think of anything that has origin, we are not thinking of God. God is self-existent, while all created things necessarily originated somewhere at some time. Aside from God, nothing is self-caused.   *A. W. Tozer*

GOD — Inscrutability

Were the works of God really understandable by human reason, they would be neither wonderful nor unspeakable.
Thomas à Kempis

The utmost that we know of God is nothing in respect of that which he is.
Thomas Aquinas

God is more truly imagined than expressed, and he exists more truly than he is imagined.   *Augustine*

The Almighty does nothing without reason, though the frail mind of man cannot explain the reason.   *Augustine*

Though we can know that God is, we cannot know what God is.   *Augustine*

God is at work in the world in ways far beyond our power to comprehend.
Nancy B. Barcus

God's decrees, impossible to be resisted, and leaving us in the dark as to what may come next, are calculated to fill the mind with holy awe.   *Albert Barnes*

You may know God, but not comprehend him.   *Richard Baxter*

A cockle-fish may as soon crowd the ocean into its narrow shell as vain man ever comprehend the decrees of God.
William Beveridge

Man can find God but never fathom him.
John Blanchard

To confess the fathomlessness of God's glory is perfectly compatible with knowing him. *John Blanchard*

The Christian who is truly spiritual revels as much in his ignorance of God as in his knowledge of him. *John Blanchard*

There is infinitely more in God than the tongues of men or angels can express.
Thomas Brooks

We demand proof of God, forgetting that if we could prove God we would be within the compass of our rationalities, and then our logical mind would be our own grotesque God. *George A. Buttrick*

God, to keep us sober, speaks sparingly of his essence. *John Calvin*

The wisdom of the flesh is always exclaiming against the mysteries of God.
John Calvin

The mystery of providence defies our attempt to tame it by reason. I do not mean it is illogical; I mean that we do not know enough about it to be able to unpack it.
D. A. Carson

It is visible that God is; it is invisible what he is. *Stephen Charnock*

We better understand what God is not than what he is. *Stephen Charnock*

God knows the way that you take; you don't know his. *Elisabeth Elliot*

God ... cannot be fitted into a diagram.
Empedocles

Were I fully able to describe God, I should be God myself, or God must cease to be what he is. *Epictetus*

It is part of God's wise providence that he will not be apprehended by intellectual speculation. *T. S. Evans*

God's works are never above right, though often above reason. *Thomas Fuller*

With God there are mysteries, but no mistakes. *Michael Griffiths*

We must believe God great without quantity, everlasting without time, and containing all things without extent; and when our thoughts are come to their highest, let us stop, wonder and adore.
Joseph Hall

Our safest eloquence concerning God is silence, when we confess without confession that his glory is inexplicable, his greatness above our capacity and reach.
Richard Hooker

We cannot know all about God for the obvious reason that the finite cannot comprehend the infinite. *R. B. Kuiper*

All that which we call the attributes of God are only so many human ways of our conceiving that abyssal All which can neither be spoken nor conceived by us.
William Law

The very being of God is so transcendent and eternal that all our efforts to arrive at an understanding are doomed at the very outset to failure. *D. Martyn Lloyd-Jones*

God's actual divine essence and his will, administration and works are absolutely beyond all human thought, human understanding or wisdom; in short, they are and ever will be incomprehensible, inscrutable, and altogether hidden to human reason. *Martin Luther*

We know God but as men born blind know the fire. They know that there is such a thing as fire, for they feel it warm them, but what it is they know not. So, that there is a God we know, but what he is we know little, and indeed we can never search him out to perfection; a finite creature can never fully comprehend that which is infinite. *Thomas Manton*

Whenever God is at work there is the inexplicable. *Ralph R. Martin*

We must never imagine that the existence of love and wrath in the same nature is evidence of a split personality, but only evidence that God is greater than can be grasped in our finite logic. *J. A. Motyer*

Exposition fails to fathom that before which sanctified understanding is affixed with amazement. *John Murray*

Incomprehensible? But because you cannot understand a thing, it does not cease to exist. *Blaise Pascal*

God is not discoverable or demonstrable by purely scientific means, unfortunately for the scientifically-minded. But that really proves nothing. It simply means that the wrong instruments are being used for the job. *J. B. Phillips*

We must not judge the Lord by any rules we would apply to men, or even to angels. *William S. Plumer*

What we can know about God is so great and glorious that we can confidently trust what we do not know about him. Our God is a good God. *Frank Retief*

The infinity of God is not mysterious, it is only unfathomable — not concealed but incomprehensible. It is a clear infinity — the darkness of the pure, unsearchable sea. *John Ruskin*

The more I learn about God, the more aware I become of what I don't know about him. *R. C. Sproul*

We will never understand God exhaustively, but what we do understand about him is real, not myth. *R. C. Sproul*

Instinctively we know that we cannot box God up in any conceptual framework of our own devising, and that if we think we have succeeded in doing so, then what we have in our box is not God.
John R. W. Stott

A comprehended God is no God at all.
Gerhard Tersteegen

Do not try to imagine God, or you will have an imaginary God. *A. W. Tozer*

God is spirit and to him magnitude and distance have no meaning. *A. W. Tozer*

If God can be understood and comprehended by any of our human means, then I cannot worship him. *A. W. Tozer*

Our concepts of measurement embrace mountains and men, atoms and stars, gravity, energy, numbers, speed, but never God. We cannot speak of measure or amount or size or weight and at the same time be speaking of God, for these tell of degrees and there are no degrees in God.

All that he is he is without growth or addition or development. *A. W. Tozer*

There is in the awful and mysterious depths of the triune God neither limit nor end. *A. W. Tozer*

In vain our haughty reason swells,
For nothing's found in thee
But boundless inconceivables
And vast eternity.
Isaac Watts

God is beyond human examination and can be known only by those to whom he chooses to reveal himself.
Geoffrey Wilson

God would not be God if he could be fully known to us, and God would not be God, if he could not be known at all.
H. G. Wood

GOD — Jealousy

God is jealous for the good of his redeemed people — but he can never be jealous of anything or anyone.
John Blanchard

The jealousy of God is one of the Christian's greatest challenges — and comforts. *John Blanchard*

God, as a jealous God, is filled with a burning desire for our holiness, for our righteousness, for our goodness.
Donald Grey Barnhouse

The jealousy of God is nothing else but the vehemence and ardour of his paternal love. *John Calvin*

GOD — Justice

God is not always a God of immediate justice, but he is a God of ultimate justice. *John Blanchard*

There is nothing that can stand the touchstone of God's justice. Christ is my all, and I am nothing. *John Bunyan*

Whenever you hear the glory of God mentioned, think of his justice.
John Calvin

Belief in a just God is not optional.
John Rowland

As long as there is eternity, God has time enough to reckon with his enemies.
Thomas Watson

God of all mercy is a God unjust.
Edward Young

GOD — Kingdom— See Kingdom of God

GOD — Law — See Law of God

GOD — Love

God loves his people when he strikes them as well as when he strokes them.
Anon.

The true measure of God's love is that he loves without measure. *Anon.*

God's love is not lazy good nature, as a great many think it to be and so drag it in the mud; it is rigidly righteous, and therefore Christ died. *Donald Grey Barnhouse*

Our great matters are little to God's infinite power, and our little matters are great to his Father love.
Donald Grey Barnhouse

It is but right that our hearts should be on

God, when the heart of God is so much on us. *Richard Baxter*

There is no parental abuse in the character of God's fatherhood. *Alistair Begg*

God was love long before he had made any creatures to be the objects of his love, even from all eternity. *George Bethune*

God looks over us but never overlooks us. *John Blanchard*

God loved us when there was nothing good to be seen in us and nothing good to be said for us. *John Blanchard*

God loves each one of his people as if there was only one of them to love. *John Blanchard*

God's hand is sometimes turned against his people, but never his heart. *John Blanchard*

There is nothing the Christian can do to make God love him more, or love him less. God's love for his people is infinite and unconditional. *John Blanchard*

O love of God, how strong and true!
Eternal and yet ever new;
Uncomprehended and unbought,
Beyond all knowledge and all thought. *Horatius Bonar*

We must see our circumstances through God's love instead of, as we are prone to do, seeing God's love through our circumstances. *Jerry Bridges*

God loves to smile most upon his people when the world frowns most. *Thomas Brooks*

God's love is a free love, having no motive or foundation but within itself. *Thomas Brooks*

The only ground of God's love is his love. *Thomas Brooks*

To believers a persuasion of God's fatherly love is more delightful than all earthly enjoyments. *John Calvin*

The springs of love are in God, not in us. *Oswald Chambers*

God would not be holy if he were not love, and could not be love if he were not holy. *William Newton Clarke*

God is holy love. *P. T. Forsyth*

Divine love is no abstract theory; it is a living Person. *Harry Foster*

God in his love pitcheth upon persons ... Christ died not for propositions only, but for persons. He loved *us,* not ours. *Thomas Goodwin*

How good is the God we adore,
Our faithful, unchangeable Friend!
His love is as great as his power,
And knows neither measure nor end! *Joseph Hart*

God can be described as a heavenly Father, a caring parent who brings human persons into existence and continues to watch over them. Part of that caring is shown in God's desire to communicate with us. *Walter R. Hearn*

God's love is always supernatural, always a miracle, always the last thing we deserve. *Robert M. Horn*

God did not make us because he stood to gain for the making. He made us out of sheer love. *T. G. Jalland*

241

There is no human wreckage, lying in the ooze of the deepest sea of iniquity, that God's deep love cannot reach and redeem. *John Henry Jowett*

Divine love, unlike human love, is not dependent on its object. *R. B. Kuiper*

Rather than find fault with God for his altogether righteous dealings with certain hell-deserving sinners, let us adore him for his eternal, gracious, saving love for others just as deserving of damnation. *R. B. Kuiper*

The point ... is not that the world is so big that it takes a great deal of love to embrace it, but that the world is so bad that it takes an exceedingly great kind of love to love it at all. *R. B. Kuiper*

God is love, and law is the way he loves us. But it is also true that God is law, and love is the way he rules us. *G. S. Lee*

God loves us; not because we are loveable but because he is love; not because he needs to receive but because he delights to give. *C. S. Lewis*

God, who needs nothing, loves into existence wholly superfluous creatures in order that he may love and perfect them. *C. S. Lewis*

Though our feelings for (God) come and go, his love for us does not. It is not wearied by our sins, or our indifference; and, therefore, it is quite relentless in its determination that we shall be cured of those sins, at whatever cost to us, at whatever cost to him. *C. S. Lewis*

To ask that God's love should be content with us as we are is to ask that God should cease to be God. *C. S. Lewis*

God does not love us because we are valuable, but we are valuable because God loves us. *Martin Luther*

God's love is not drawn out by our lovableness, but wells up, like an artesian spring, from the depths of his nature. *Alexander MacLaren*

Eternal love means that the redeemed were never objects of divine hatred, but it does not mean that they were never objects of God's anger. *Donald MacLeod*

God smothers repenting sinners in forgiving and redemptive love. *Al Martin*

That God should pity the world I understand, because when I walk down a hospital and see a sick child, I pity the child ... but that God should *love* the world — the more I think about it, the more staggered I am. *F. B. Meyer*

I know of no truth in the whole Bible that ought to come home to us with such power and tenderness as that of the love of God. *D. L. Moody*

It is the love of God that makes him the sworn enemy of sin. *G. Campbell Morgan*

The love of God is anchored to his character. He can only love in ways that are suitable to the sort of person he is. *J. A. Motyer*

The Supreme Disposer of all things is the friend of sinners; it is the truth at the heart of the message of Christ. *Edward Norman*

Even though there is no final answer to the mystery of evil prospering in the world, the overriding consideration that more than offsets everything else is God's unchanging love and care. *James Philip*

'God so loved that he gave . . .' And the giving — with Calvary at its heart, was not a trickle but a torrent. *Paul S. Rees*

God is far more willing to save sinners than sinners are to be saved. *J. C. Ryle*

There is an infinite willingness in God to save man, if man is only willing to be saved. *J. C. Ryle*

The love of God does not measure you by eyesight. *Frederick Sampson*

God has a holy love and a holy wrath, but not a loving wrath or a wrathful love. *R. C. Sproul*

God soon turns from his wrath, but he never turns from his love. *C. H. Spurgeon*

Lord, send us such a floodtide of thy love that we shall be washed beyond the mire of doubt and fear. *C. H. Spurgeon*

Nothing binds me to my Lord like a strong belief in his changeless love. *C. H. Spurgeon*

There are no changes in Jehovah's love, though there may be changes in the ways of showing it. *C. H. Spurgeon*

It is God's love which, all unseen outwardly, supplies our life inwardly. *J. Charles Stern*

God's favourite word is —come! *Robert L. Sterner*

At the heart of election is a particular and passionate love that was the cause of God sending his Son to be the Saviour of his people. *G. Steveson*

Divine love can admit no rival. *Johann Tauler*

God chose us for his love, and now loves us for his choice. *John Trapp*

God keeps open house for hungry sinners. *Thomas Watson*

God loves his children as well in adversity as in prosperity. *Thomas Watson*

God never repents of his electing love. *Thomas Watson*

Thy providence is kind and large,
Both man and beast thy bounty share;
The whole creation is thy charge,
But saints are thy peculiar care.
Isaac Watts

Our total welfare is the constant concern of God's loving heart. *W. J. C. White*

Immortal love, for ever full,
For ever flowing free,
For ever shared, for ever whole,
A never-ebbing sea!
John Greenleaf Whittier

God has never been casual about the condition of the lost. *Thomas Zimmerman*

GOD — Mercy — See Mercy from God

GOD — Name

God's name is his revealed character. *John Blanchard*

To know God's name is to know something of his nature. *John Blanchard*

The titles of God are virtually promises. *David Clarkson*

God's name is God himself in his revealed holiness. *F. J. Delitzsch*

God's name, as it is set out in the Word, is both a glorious name, full of majesty; and also a gracious name, full of mercy.
William Gourge

That God should be kindly disposed to a world that hates, so as to bring the gospel of good news to them all is gracious, and that he should go further and actually apply that gospel in such a way as to rescue men and transform them is marvellous. *Erroll Hulse*

The greatest argument of Scripture is the glory of God's own name.
Charles Simeon

The name Jehovah carries majesty in it; the name Father carries mercy in it.
Thomas Watson

GOD — Omnipotence

What is impossible to God? Not that which is difficult to his power, but that which is contrary to his nature. *Ambrose*

Man's requirements are not a drain on God's resources. *Anon.*

Marvel not that God does great things. Marvel that he stoops to do such little things. *Anon.*

There are some things which God cannot do, and that because of the very reason of his omnipotence. *Augustine*

We should never tire of the thought of God's power. *Donald Grey Barnhouse*

God can do more in a moment than man in a millennium. *John Blanchard*

If God is against us, who can be for us?
John Blanchard

God hath in himself all power to defend you, all wisdom to direct you, all mercy to pardon you, all grace to enrich you, all righteousness to clothe you, all goodness to supply you, and all happiness to crown you. *Thomas Brooks*

Water is stronger than earth, fire stronger than water, angels stronger than men, and God stronger than them all.
Thomas Brooks

There is power in God to lay prostrate the whole world, and to tread it under his feet, whenever it may please him.
John Calvin

One with God is a majority. *William Carey*

We are not to think that, where we see no possibility, God sees none. *Marcus Dods*

We must learn to cease from measuring the power of God by our own, and reasoning from one to the other.
Marcus Dods

When God is about to do something great, he starts with a difficulty. When he is about to do something truly magnificent, he starts with an impossibility.
Armin Gessivein

God's power is the best guard, the safest convoy and surest castle that any can have. *William Gouge*

One Almighty is more than all mighties.
William Gurnall

God is not waiting to show us strong in his behalf, but himself strong in our behalf. That makes a lot of difference. He is not out to demonstrate what we can do but what he can do. *Vance Havner*

When a man makes alliance with the Almighty, giants look like grasshoppers.
Vance Havner

Man's extremity is God's opportunity of helping and saving. *Matthew Henry*

A man with God on his side is always in the majority. *John Knox*

God can do without any exception what he wills to do. *R. B. Kuiper*

The power of God is not diminished when it is said that he cannot die and cannot sin; for if he could do these things, his power would be less. *R. B. Kuiper*

God is not wasted by bestowing.
Thomas Manton

There is an Arm that never tires,
When human strength gives way.
George Matheson

God cannot be withstood by man's incompetence or by Satan's enmity.
Watchman Nee

You will never need more than God can supply. *J. I. Packer*

God works without labour.
William S. Plumer

Our theology is never right till in our hearts we invest God with infinite power and perfections. *William S. Plumer*

If God be God, then no insoluble problems exist. And if God be *my* God, then no problem of mine is without its appropriate solution. *Maurice Roberts*

When we have nothing left but God, then we become aware that God is enough.
Agnes M. Royden

My faith has no bed to sleep upon but omnipotency. *Samuel Rutherford*

It is the glory of Omnipotence to work by improbabilities. *C. H. Spurgeon*

The presence of God in the flood is better than a ferry boat. *C. H. Spurgeon*

God has all the power that is consistent with infinite perfection.
Augustus H. Strong

God raises the level of the impossible.
Corrie ten Boom

The power of God is identified with his will; what he cannot do is what he will not do. *Tertullian*

In the New Testament it is not believers who tremble at the power of Satan, but demons who tremble at the power of God.
Stephen Travis

God's riches are imparted, not impaired.
Thomas Watson

GOD — Omnipresence

From every point of earth we are equally near to heaven and the infinite.
Henri Amiel

God is ultimately unavoidable. *Anon.*

God is an infinite circle whose centre is everywhere and whose circumference is nowhere. *Augustine*

Though heaven be God's palace, yet it is not his prison. *Thomas Brooks*

We cannot get away from God, though we can ignore him. *James Cabot*

If God is not everywhere, he is not true God anywhere.   *William Newton Clarke*

There is a God in science, a God in history, and a God in conscience, and these three are one.   *Joseph Cook*

Nature is too thin a screen; the glory of the omnipresent God bursts through everywhere.   *Ralph Waldo Emerson*

God is as present as the air.
Michael Hollings

We may ignore, but we can nowhere evade, the presence of God. The world is crowded with him.   *C. S. Lewis*

This is the fundamental thing, the most serious thing of all, that we are always in the presence of God.
D. Martyn Lloyd-Jones

He is not eternity and infinity, but eternal and infinite; he is not duration or space, but he endures and is present. He endures forever and is everywhere present; and by existing always and everywhere he constitutes duration and space.
Isaac Newton

A man may hide God from himself, and yet he cannot hide himself from God.
William Secker

God is neither shut up in nor shut up out of any place.   *George Swinnock*

Begin where we will, God is there first.
A. W. Tozer

The notion that there is a God but that he is comfortably far away is not embodied in the doctrinal statement of any Christian church.   *A. W. Tozer*

Within thy circling power I stand;
On every side I find thy hand;
Awake, asleep, at home, abroad,
I am surrounded still with God.
Isaac Watts

GOD — Omniscience

Anyone can count the seeds in one apple, but only God can count the apples in one seed.   *Anon.*

You cannot too often think there is a never-sleeping eye, which reads the heart and registers our thoughts.
Francis Bacon

As a Christian is never out of the reach of God's hand, so he is never out of the view of God's eye.   *Thomas Brooks*

There is comfort in the fact that God can never be taken by surprise.
Frank Gabelein

God not only sees men, he sees through them.   *Matthew Henry*

Omniscience cannot be separated from omnipotence.   *Matthew Henry*

Though the Lord is out of sight, we are not out of his.   *Matthew Henry*

Do not let us deceive ourselves. No possible complexity which we can give to our picture of the universe can hide us from God: there is no copse, no forest, no jungle thick enough to provide cover.
C. S. Lewis

If one thing lies at the basis of the whole biblical teaching about God it is that God knows all things.   *J. Gresham Machen*

If there is ever any one thought, full, distinct, vivid, thoroughly comprehended by yourself, then, just what that is to you, *all* knowledge is to God.   *Basil Manly*

Is it not clear that God foreknows what will be because he has decreed what shall be? God's foreknowledge is not the cause of events, rather are events the effects of his eternal purpose.   *A. W. Pink*

God looks most where man looks least.
     William Secker

He that fills all must needs see and know all.   *Richard Sibbes*

God does not learn things; he knows them from the beginning.   *R. C. Sproul*

God knows us altogether and cares for us in spite of that knowledge.
     J. Charles Stern

There is nothing round the corner which is beyond God's view.   *J. Charles Stern*

There is not a moment of privacy from God.   *Geoff Thomas*

Because God knows all things perfectly, he knows no thing better than any other thing, but all things equally well. He never discovers anything, he is never surprised, never amazed.   *A. W. Tozer*

We can never sin but there will be two witnesses present to observe and register it: our own selves and God.
     Ralph Venning

We never do anything so secretly but that it is in the presence of two witnesses: God and our own conscience.
     Benjamin Whichcote

GOD — Patience

God is patient because he is eternal.
     Augustine

There is no divine attribute more wonderful than the patience of God.
     John Benton

Many have been reprieved that were never forgiven.   *Stephen Charnock*

God's love for sinners is very wonderful, but God's patience with ill-natured saints is a deeper mystery.   *Henry Drummond*

Though the patience of God be lasting, yet it is not everlasting.   *William Secker*

The Almighty is working on a great scale and will not be hustled by our peevish impetuosity.   *W. Graham Scroggie*

God's forbearance is no acquittance.
     John Trapp

The deep and due consideration of the infinite patience of God towards us will greatly promote the patience of our spirits, and transform us into the same image.   *John Trapp*

GOD — Perfection

God writes with a pen that never blots, speaks with a tongue that never skips, and acts with a hand that never fails.   *Anon.*

God's attributes coincide with his being.
     Herman Bavnick

God is self-centred — and rightly so.
     John Blanchard

God is equal to each of his attributes, whereas he 'possesses' each attribute in an infinite degree.   *William Hendriksen*

God is unsusceptible to evil; evil never has any appeal to him.
D. Edmond Hiebert

The fact that God is untemptable of evil is the foundation for the Christian belief in a moral universe. *D. Edmond Hiebert*

Righteousness infills all that he does because that is what he is. *J. A. Motyer*

Doubting any perfection of God is tantamount to robbing him of his glory.
William S. Plumer

The character of God is a perfect and glorious whole. *William S. Plumer*

God stands in such a relationship to evil that it is not outside of his rule yet he cannot be held responsible for it.
Frank Retief

If God is not just, he is not righteous; if he is not righteous, he is not holy; if he is not holy, he is not good. *John Rowland*

Those who lose faith in God's perfection increasingly believe in the perfection of all kinds of false messiahs and their promises. *Isaac Bashevis Singer*

Scripture says that the one thing God cannot do, and cannot because he will not, is to contradict himself. *John R. W. Stott*

The harmony of God's being is the result not of a perfect balance of parts but of the absence of parts. *A. W. Tozer*

God can neither deceive, nor be deceived; he cannot deceive because he is truth, nor be deceived because he is wisdom.
Thomas Watson

Our love of God will always be according to our knowledge of him and his perfections. *Thomas Wilson*

GOD — Promises — See Promises of God

GOD — Purposes

God's purposes always have God's provision. *John Blanchard*

God's purposes are sometimes delayed but they are never abandoned.
John Blanchard

God is in control of every atom in his universe, and even those things which seem a direct contradiction of his love will one day be seen to be a dynamic confirmation of his power.
John Blanchard

If it pleases God's purposes, he can bring a millionaire to the breadline and set up a pauper in a palace. *John Blanchard*

God knows what he is going to make of us. *James Montgomery Boice*

All a believer's present happiness, and all his future happiness springs from the eternal purposes of God. *Thomas Brooks*

God is less interested in answering our questions than in other things: securing our allegiance, establishing our faith, nurturing a desire for holiness.
D. A. Carson

Any attempt to justify God's ways is arrogant and childish. Any attempt to seize on what we regard as evidence that he was right after all is fatuous.
Elisabeth Elliot

God knows what he is doing and he is not under any obligation to make us any explanation. *Elisabeth Elliot*

The most crooked tree will make timber for the temple, if God be pleased to hew it. *Thomas Fuller*

God is not running an antique shop! He is making all things new! *Vance Havner*

God never needs to change his counsels. *Matthew Henry*

The purposes of God are his concealed promises; the promises — his revealed purposes! *Philip Henry*

Though God has many things in his purposes, he has nothing in his prophecies but what are in his purposes. *Matthew Henry*

Nothing whatever surprises God; all things that happen are absolutely certain from all eternity because they are all embraced in God's eternal plan. *J. Gresham Machen*

The many decrees all constitute just one purpose or one plan. They are not without relation to one another, but form a mighty unity as God himself is one. *J. Gresham Machen*

God is his own motive. *Alexander Maclaren*

The whole world is ordered and arranged to match and meet the needs of the people of God. *J. A. Motyer*

God is working out his eternal purpose, not only in spite of human and satanic opposition, but by means of them. *A. W. Pink*

What God is and has, he is and has for all his people's good. *William S. Plumer*

All the events that take place in the world carry on the same work — the story of the Father and the salvation of his children. *Daniel Rowlands*

God watches and weeds us, and continues his labour upon us, till he brings us to the end of his promise. *Richard Sibbes*

God's whole purpose, conceived in past eternity, being worked out for and in his people in history, to be completed in the glory to come, may be encapsulated in this single concept: God intends to make us like Christ. *John R. W. Stott*

If we had to sum up in a single brief sentence what life is all about, why Jesus Christ came into this world to live and die and rise, and what God is up to in the long-drawn-out historical process both BC and AD, it would be difficult to find a more succinct explanation than this: God is making human beings more human by making them more like Christ. *John R. W. Stott*

To suppose that God has a multitude of plans, and that he changes his plan with the exigencies of the situation, is to make him infinitely dependent upon the varying wills of his creatures, and to deny him one necessary element of perfection, namely, immutability. *Augustus H. Strong*

What God does, he always purposed to do. *Augustus H. Strong*

God has no problems, only plans. *Corrie ten Boom*

In spite of all appearances to the contrary, God has a plan for this bankrupt world. *Helmut Thielicke*

God's cause is never in danger; what he has begun in the soul or in the world he will complete unto the end. *B. B. Warfield*

GOD — Sovereignty

God is never in a hurry, but he is always on time. *Anon.*

Man drives, but it is God who holds the reins. *Anon.*

God is so powerful that he can direct any evil to a good end. *Thomas Aquinas*

Man proposes, God disposes.
Ludovic Aristo

The devil's way of extinguishing goodness is God's way of advancing it.
George Barlow

God is the first cause, he is the final cause, but he uses other causes to accomplish his cause. *Wilson Benton*

If anything in this world is the result of chance then God is not sovereign over all. *Wilson Benton*

We do not arrive at a proper understanding of God by reasoning from specific events to the nature of God; on the contrary we understand specific events by reasoning from the nature of God to those events. *Wilson Benton*

God has no 'no-go' areas. *John Blanchard*

God is never taken by surprise.
John Blanchard

God's cause is never in any danger.
John Blanchard

Nothing that happens to the Christian is accidental or incidental. *John Blanchard*

To speak of the sovereignty of God is nothing less than to speak of his Godhood. *John Blanchard*

God's sovereignty does not negate our responsibility to pray, but rather makes it possible for us to pray with confidence.
Jerry Bridges

God has in himself all power to defend you, all wisdom to direct you, all mercy to pardon you, all grace to enrich you, all righteousness to clothe you, all goodness to supply you, and all happiness to crown you. *Thomas Brooks*

The conclave of hell can do nothing without a commission from heaven.
Thomas Brooks

The sovereignty of God is that golden sceptre in his hand by which he will make all bow, either by his word or by his works, by his mercies or by his judgements. *Thomas Brooks*

God does not deliberate or consult, but has once for all decreed before the creation of the world what he will do.
John Calvin

Nothing that is attempted in opposition to God can ever be successful. *John Calvin*

Satan ... can do nothing without the command of God, to whose dominion he is subject. *John Calvin*

God has sovereign right to dispose of us as he pleases. We ought to acquiesce in all that God does with us and to us.
William Carey

God is absolutely sovereign, but his sovereignty never functions in such a way that human responsibility is curtailed, minimized or mitigated. *D. A. Carson*

When the Bible speaks of God's permission of evil, there is still no escape from his sovereignty.   *D. A. Carson*

God is the world's Sovereign, but a good man's Father. He rules heaven and earth, but he loves his holy ones. Other things are the objects of his providence, and a good man is the end of it.
Stephen Charnock

To be God and sovereign are inseparable.   *Stephen Charnock*

There can be but one Infinite. *Elisha Coles*

The Lord is King! Who then shall dare
Resist his will, distrust his care,
Or murmur at his wise decrees,
Or doubt his royal promises?
Josiah Conder

Events of all sorts creep and fly exactly as God pleases.   *William Cowper*

Men, like stars, appear on the horizon at the command of God.
J. H. Merle d'Aubigné

God's ways are behind the scenes, but he moves all the scenes which he is behind.
John Nelson Darby

Without a doubt, what helps us most in accepting and dealing with suffering is an adequate view of God — learning who he is and knowing he is in control.
Joni Eareckson Tada

God casts the die, not the dice.
Albert Einstein

Appearances can be deceptive. The fact that we cannot see what God is doing does not mean that he is doing nothing.
Sinclair Ferguson

God has the sovereign right to do what he wishes, and no other explanation is necessary.   *John M. Frame*

God never foreordains an evil event without a good purpose.   *John M. Frame*

There is no question of God's trying to do anything and failing.   *Peter Geach*

That my times are in God's hand is a fact whether I realize and experience it or not.
E. F. Hallock

The title deed to this world does not belong to dictators, to Communism, nor to the devil, but to God.   *Vance Havner*

Things do not happen in this world — they are brought about.   *Will Hays*

Whatever point of compass the wind is in, it is fulfilling God's word, and turns about by his counsel.   *Matthew Henry*

Whatever you do, begin with God.
Matthew Henry

To admit universal providence and deny special is nonsense. You might as well talk of a chain without any links.
A. A. Hodge

If our view of God is different from or smaller than the Bible's, we shall be astray in all our thinking and living.
Robert M. Horn

God does all that he does because he is who he is.   *R. B. Kuiper*

God is a totalitarian Ruler who demands full allegiance from his subjects.
R. B. Kuiper

If God were less than sovereign, man

would be less than responsible. Since God is absolutely sovereign, man is wholly responsible to him.   *R. B. Kuiper*

The sovereignty of God may be defined as his absolute right to govern and dispose of all his creatures according to his good pleasure.   *R. B. Kuiper*

God is in the facts of history as surely as he is in the march of the seasons.
John Lanahan

There is no question of a compromise between the claims of God and the claims of culture, or politics, or anything else.
C. S. Lewis

Where a God who is totally purposive and totally foreseeing acts upon a nature which is totally interlocked, there can be no accidents or loose ends, nothing whatever of which we can safely use the word 'merely'. Nothing is 'merely a by-product' of anything else.   *C. S. Lewis*

God does not stop to consult us.
D. Martyn Lloyd-Jones

Let God be God!   *Martin Luther*

The devil is God's devil. *Martin Luther*

All nature, including the nature of man, is a wondrous instrument of many strings, delicately tuned to work God's will and upon which he plays with a master hand.
J. Gresham Machen

Even the wicked actions of men serve God's purposes and it is by his works of providence that he permits those wicked actions to be done. *J. Gresham Machen*

Wicked men may not think they are serving God's purposes; but they are serving

his purposes all the same, even by the most wicked of their acts.
J. Gresham Machen

The sovereignty of God never excuses us from responsibility.   *Will Metzger*

God is not just the Lord of creation, the one who starts everything going in accordance with a grand plan. He is also the Lord of history. History is 'his story', and in some unfathomable combination of divine sovereignty and human will, God is the master chess player moving his chessmen forward and back in anticipation of the final moment when all that opposes him will be checkmated and his reign will be universally recognized.
Peter C. Moore

The fixed point in the universe, the unalterable fact, is the throne of God.
G. Campbell Morgan

The man who measures things by the circumstances of the hour is filled with fear; the man who sees Jehovah enthroned and governing has no panic.
G. Campbell Morgan

God is too great to be knocked off course by the malpractice of wicked men.
J. A. Motyer

There is no situation so chaotic that God cannot from that situation create something that is surpassingly good.
Handley C. G. Moule

God is the great Unanswerable.
Stuart Olyott

To deny the sovereignty of God is to deny God.   *T. P. Osborne*

Once for all, let us rid our minds of the

idea that things are as they are because God cannot help it. *J. I. Packer*

To know that nothing happens in God's world apart from God's will may frighten the godless, but it stabilizes the saints. *J. I. Packer*

The Christ who rules us rules all things for us. *J. I. Packer*

The world dwarfs us all, but God dwarfs the world. *J. I. Packer*

The world belongs to God and he wants it back. *David Pawson*

God always has the last word. *James Philip*

Alternatives confront us, and between them we are obliged to choose; either God governs, or he is governed; either God rules, or he is ruled; either God has his way, or men have theirs. And is our choice between these alternatives hard to make? *A. W. Pink*

God is a law unto himself, and … he is under no obligation to give an account of his matters to any. *A. W. Pink*

God is working out his eternal purpose, not only in spite of human and satanic opposition, but by means of them. *A. W. Pink*

If then we see the sovereignty of God displayed throughout all creation why should it be thought a strange thing if we behold it operating in the midst of the human family? *A. W. Pink*

Sovereignty characterizes the whole being of God. He is sovereign in all his attributes. *A. W. Pink*

We read the Scriptures in vain if we fail to discover that the actions of men, evil men as well as good, are governed by the Lord God. *A. W. Pink*

Where the sovereignty of God is denied there will be no holy awe of him. *A. W. Pink*

God acts as he does because he is what he is. *William S. Plumer*

God is choice in keeping the keys of time at his own girdle. *Matthew Poole*

Man does what he can, and God what he will. *John Ray*

In the saving of individuals, as well as in the calling of nations, God acts as a sovereign, and gives no account of his matters. *J. C. Ryle*

Of all the doctrines of the Bible none is so offensive to human nature as the doctrine of God's sovereignty. *J. C. Ryle*

The hands of the wicked cannot stir one moment before God allows them to begin, and cannot stir one moment after God commands them to stop. *J. C. Ryle*

The wickedest enemies of God are only axes and saws and hammers in his hands, and are ignorantly his instruments for doing his work in the world. *J. C. Ryle*

God can never be outmanoeuvred, taken by surprise, or caught at a disadvantage. He is a God who knows no crisis. Before an emergency arises, God in his providence has made adequately and perfectly timed provision to meet it. *J. Oswald Sanders*

The evil desires of men's hearts cannot

thwart God's sovereignty. Indeed they are subject to it. *R. C. Sproul*

The kingdom of God is not a democracy. When the Lord speaks … he utters his law unilaterally. He does not rule by referendum. *R. C. Sproul*

If God lights the candle, none can blow it out. *C. H. Spurgeon*

If the Lord will not suffer it, neither men nor devils can do it. *C. H. Spurgeon*

No doctrine in the whole Word of God has more excited the hatred of mankind than the truth of the absolute sovereignty of God. *C. H. Spurgeon*

Opposition to divine sovereignty is essentially atheism. *C. H. Spurgeon*

The devices of the wicked are overruled for their defeat. *C. H. Spurgeon*

There is no attribute of God more comforting to his children than the doctrine of divine sovereignty. *C. H. Spurgeon*

Whether you shall live to reach home today or not, depends absolutely upon God's will. *C. H. Spurgeon*

We must believe in the grace of sovereignty as well as the sovereignty of grace. *Augustus H. Strong*

God does not do many things that he can, but he does all things that he will. *George Swinnock*

God in his wisdom is making evil men as well as good men; adverse things as well as favourable things work for the bringing forth of his glory in the day when all shall be fulfilled in him. *A. W. Tozer*

God's plan will continue on God's schedule. *A. W. Tozer*

The whole history of the world is discovered to be but a contest between the wisdom of God and the cunning of Satan and fallen men. The outcome of the contest is not in doubt. *A. W. Tozer*

Whatever God did and was able to do and willing to do at any time, God is able and willing to do again, within the framework of his will. *A. W. Tozer*

Monarchs have their times and their turns, their rises and their ruin. *John Trapp*

God can make a straight stroke with a crooked stick. *Thomas Watson*

God would never permit any evil if he could not bring good out of evil. *Thomas Watson*

There's not a plant or flower below
But makes his glories known;
And clouds arise, and tempests blow
By order from his throne. *Isaac Watts*

Absolutely nothing lies outside the scope of God's sovereignty. *Geoffrey B. Wilson*

Satan's malice is always frustrated by God and made to minister a blessing to his people. The 'all things' of Romans 8:28 admits of no exceptions. *Geoffrey B. Wilson*

The work of Satan is overruled so that it assists in bringing to pass the divine purpose, though Satan on his part uses his utmost powers to thwart that purpose. *Geoffrey B. Wilson*

God's sovereignty is not arbitrariness, as some misunderstand it, for God has his reasons, based on his infinite wisdom, which he does not always choose to reveal to us.   *Spiros Zodhiates*

GOD — Will — See Will of God

GOD — Wisdom

God knows best what is best. Why then should we question him?   *Anon.*

If God would concede me his omnipotence for twenty-four hours, you would see how many changes I would make in the world. But if he gave me his wisdom, too, I would leave things as they are.
          J. M. L. Monsabre

The truth is that God *in* his wisdom, to make and keep us humble and to teach us to walk by faith, has hidden from us almost everything that we should like to know about the providential purposes which he is working out in the churches and in our own lives.   *J. I. Packer*

God is not in the slightest degree baffled or bewildered by what baffles and bewilders us ... he is either a present help, or he is not much help at all.   *J. B. Phillips*

God's wisdom is that attribute of God whereby he produces the best possible results with the best possible means.
          H. B. Smith

None of us has the ability to fool God.
          A. W. Tozer

He formed the stars, those heavenly
    flames,
He counts their numbers, calls their
    names;
His wisdom's vast, and knows no bound,
A deep where all our thoughts are
    drowned.   *Isaac Watts*

GOD — Wrath

The real horror of being outside of Christ is that there is no shelter from the wrath of God.   *Eric Alexander*

If sin is man's contradiction of God and his expressed will, God cannot be complacent about sin and still be God.
          Saphir P. Athyal

There is terror in the Bible as well as comfort.   *Donald Grey Barnhouse*

No cloud can ever hang over a Christian's life that is darker than a cloud of anger on the face of God.   *John Blanchard*

The wrath of God is not ignoble. Rather, it is too noble, too just, too perfect — it is this that bothers us.
          James Montgomery Boice

The love of God has no meaning apart from Calvary. And Calvary has no meaning apart from the holy and just wrath of God.   *Jerry Bridges*

The wrath of God is as pure as the holiness of God. When angry he is perfectly angry. When he is displeased there is every reason he should be. *Stuart Briscoe*

There is nothing impersonal about God's wrath; it is the necessary response of his holiness to persistent wickedness.
          F. F. Bruce

God has an endless variety of scourges for punishing the wicked.   *John Calvin*

Though the Lord should damn us eternally, he should do us no wrong, but only that which our nature deserveth.
          Daniel Cawdray

The reality of God's wrath is as much a part of the biblical message as is God's grace.   *Leighton Ford*

God giveth his wrath by weight, but his mercy without measure.   *Thomas Fuller*

At every door where sin sets its foot, there the wrath of God meets us.
               William Gurnall

As God's mercies are new every morning toward his people, so his anger is new every morning against the wicked.
               Matthew Henry

When we merely *say* that we are bad, the 'wrath' of God seems a barbarous doctrine; as soon as we *perceive* our badness, it appears inevitable, a mere corollary from God's goodness.   *C. S. Lewis*

The doctrine of the wrath of God is not a popular doctrine, but there is no doctrine that is more utterly pervasive in the Bible.   *J. Gresham Machen*

Just as sin belongs to persons, so the wrath rests upon the persons who are the agents of sin.   *John Murray*

God's wrath is his righteousness reacting against unrighteousness. *J. I. Packer*

The essence of God's action in wrath is to *give men what they choose,* in all its implications: nothing more, and equally nothing less.   *J. I. Packer*

The fact is that the subject of divine wrath has become taboo in modern society, and Christians by and large have accepted the taboo and conditioned themselves never to raise the matter.   *J. I. Packer*

Those who are under the rule of sin are also under the wrath of God. *J. I. Packer*

A God who cannot be angry is a God who cannot love.   *James Philip*

There are more references (in the Bible) to the anger, fury and wrath of God than there are to his love and tenderness.
                 A. W. Pink

A God of love who has no wrath is no God. He is an idol of our own making as much as if we carved him out of stone.
               R. C. Sproul

It is the cross ... that reveals the most violent and mysterious outpouring of the wrath of God that we find anywhere in Scripture.   *R. C. Sproul*

If God be against you, who can be for you?   *C. H. Spurgeon*

The God of the Bible is as severe as if he were unmerciful, and just as if he were not gracious; and yet he is as gracious and as merciful as if he were not just.
               C. H. Spurgeon

The most terrible warning to impenitent men in all the world is the death of Christ. For if God spared not his own Son, on whom was only laid *imputed* sin, will he spare sinners whose sins are their own?
               C. H. Spurgeon

The wrath of God does not end with death.   *C. H. Spurgeon*

Every wrathful judgement of God in the history of the world has been a holy act of preservation.   *A. W. Tozer*

Not only is it right for God to display anger against sin, I find it impossible to understand how he could do otherwise.
                 A. W. Tozer

God is as faithful in his menaces as in his promises. *John Trapp*

Sinners may oppose God's ways, but not his wrath. *Thomas Watson*

Wrath … is the expression of God's holy, loving displeasure with sin.
Arthur Skevington Wood

GODHEAD

If asked to define the Trinity, we can only say that it is not this or that. *Augustine*

The Trinity is (not *are*) God the Father, God the Son, God the Holy Spirit.
Donald Grey Barnhouse

The word 'Trinity' is not found in the Bible, but the truth of this doctrine is in every part of the book.
Donald Grey Barnhouse

No wonder that the doctrine of the Trinity is inexplicable, seeing that the nature of God is incomprehensible. Our faith must assent to what our reason cannot comprehend, otherwise we can never be Christians. *Francis Burkitt*

The doctrine of the Trinity is basic to the Christian religion. It is no exaggeration to assert that the whole of Christianity stands or falls with it. *R. B. Kuiper*

Thousands of the ablest minds of the centuries have pondered this problem and no man has been able to explain it; who then invented it? What man can invent, man can explain: what man cannot explain, man cannot have. It must be a revelation. *G. H. Lang*

The doctrine of the Trinity is the differentiating doctrine of the Christian faith.
D. Martyn Lloyd-Jones

It needs to be stressed that the eternal relationship between the Father and the Son in no way suggests that one is senior and the other junior. *Stuart Olyott*

The Trinity is the basis of the gospel, and the gospel is a declaration of the Trinity in action. *J. I. Packer*

Nothing will so enlarge the intellect and magnify the whole soul of man as a devout, earnest, continued investigation of the whole subject of the Trinity.
C. H. Spurgeon

The proper study of the Christian is the Godhead. The highest science, the loftiest speculation, the mightiest philosophy, which can ever engage the attention of a child of God is the name, the nature, the person, the work, the doings, and the existence of the great God whom he calls the Father. *C. H. Spurgeon*

Love and faith are at home in the mystery of the Godhead. Let reason kneel in reverence outside. *A. W. Tozer*

Our sincerest effort to grasp the incomprehensible mystery of the Trinity must remain for ever futile, and only by deepest reverence can it be saved from actual presumption. *A. W. Tozer*

Our narrow thoughts can no more comprehend the Trinity in Unity than a nutshell will hold all the water in the sea.
Thomas Watson

Tell me how it is that in this room there are three candles and but one light, and I will explain to you the mode of the divine existence. *John Wesley*

GODLINESS
(See also: Christlikeness; Holiness)

The rich are not always godly, but the godly are always rich.
Anon.

God is never more properly thanked for his goodness than by our godliness.
John Blanchard

Godliness … is devotion to God which results in a life that is pleasing to him.
Jerry Bridges

It is impossible to practice godliness without a constant, consistent and balanced intake of the Word of God in our lives.
Jerry Bridges

The truly godly person is not interested in becoming rich. He possesses inner resources which furnish riches far beyond that which earth can offer. *Jerry Bridges*

The words 'godly' and 'godliness' actually appear only a few times in the New Testament; yet the entire book is a book on godliness. *Jerry Bridges*

There is no higher compliment that can be paid to a Christian than to call him godly. *Jerry Bridges*

Godliness separates us from the pollutions of the world, and by true holiness unites us to God. *John Calvin*

Righteousness flows from only one principle – the fear of God. *John Calvin*

There is a certain secret majesty in holy discipline and in sincere godliness.
John Calvin

True godliness is that which breeds the

quarrel between God's children and the wicked. *John Dod*

Godliness is the child of truth, and it must be nursed … with no other milk than of its own mother. *William Gurnall*

We are transformed into the image of the Lord by beholding it, not by reflecting it.
Charles Hodge

Godliness is living to the glory of the Lord from the heart out of gratitude.
R. T. Kendall

He who attempts to stress Christian living by disparaging Christian doctrine is guilty of a most serious blunder. He neglects the important fact that Christian living is rooted in Christian doctrine.
R. B. Kuiper

The difference between worldliness and godliness is a renewed mind.
Erwin W. Lutzer

Sincerity is of the essence of the life of godliness. *Iain H. Murray*

The fear of God is the soul of godliness.
John Murray

The godly man's dearest wish is to exalt God with all that he is in all that he does.
J. I. Packer

The way to be truly happy is to be truly human, and the way to be truly human is to be truly godly. *J. I. Packer*

If society is to be awakened one day from its deep slumber, it will only be done by Christians who have first woken up themselves to the full splendour of their privilege and who have taken seriously the call to live wholly and entirely for God.
Maurice Roberts

Godliness is nothing but God-likeness.
George Swinnock

Godliness is the constitution of a real Christian. *George Swinnock*

A godly life is always the best advertisement for Christianity. *Geoffrey B. Wilson*

GOOD DEEDS
(See also; Faith — and Deeds; Fruitfulness; Holiness — and Justification)

Good deeds are such things that no man is saved for them nor without them.
Thomas Adams

Better do it than wish it done. *Anon.*

Deeds are fruit, words are leaves. *Anon.*

Duties may be good crutches to go upon, but they are bad christs to lean upon.
Anon.

Justification never results from good deeds; justification always results in good deeds. *John Blanchard*

Our good deeds are to be scattered upon all men, Christian and non-Christian.
Jerry Bridges

In our good works nothing is our own.
John Calvin

We are saved not by our deeds but by Christ's sacrifice for our misdeeds.
Fred Catherwood

Do good until it is an unconscious habit of life and you do not know you are doing it. *Oswald Chambers*

The gospel teaches us that while believers are not rewarded on account of their works, they are rewarded according to their works. *R. L. Dabney*

While our works are naught as a ground of merit for justification, they are all-important as evidences that we are justified. *R. L. Dabney*

I have taken my good deeds and bad deeds and thrown them together in a heap and fled from them both to Christ, and in him I have peace. *David Dickson*

I count all that part of my life lost which I spent not in communion with God or in doing good. *John Donne*

If there be ground for you to trust in your own righteousness, then all that Christ did to purchase salvation, and all that God did to prepare the way for it, is in vain.
Jonathan Edwards

The luxury of doing good surpasses every other personal enjoyment. *John Gay*

Learn the luxury of doing good.
Oliver Goldsmith

When we take least notice of our good deeds ourselves, God takes most notice of them. *Matthew Henry*

We are not justified by doing good works, but being justified we then do good.
William Jenkyn

Although … disciples are to be seen doing good works, they must not do good works in order to be seen.
Paul B. Levertoff

Even if I knew the world would be destroyed tomorrow I would plant a tree today. *Martin Luther*

We no more earn heaven by good works than babies earn their food and drink by crying and howling.   *Martin Luther*

It is not enough to do good. One must do it in the right way.   *John Morley*

No amount of good deeds can make us good persons. We must be good before we can do good. *Chester A. Pennington*

Do what you can with what you have where you are.   *Theodore D. Roosevelt*

I believe that the root of almost every schism and heresy from which the Christian church has ever suffered has been the effort of men to earn, rather than to receive, their salvation.   *John Ruskin*

Our best works before we are justified are little better than splendid sins.
J. C. Ryle

If you be found in your own righteousness you will be lost in your own righteousness.   *William Secker*

It is our bounden duty to live *in* obedience, but it would prove our utter ruin to live *on* obedience.   *William Secker*

The reward of a good action lies in having done it.   *Seneca*

Good works, as they are called, in sinners are nothing but splendid sins.
C. H. Spurgeon

I would not give much for your religion unless it can be seen. Lamps do not talk, but they do shine.   *C. H. Spurgeon*

If you can save yourselves by your works, go and do so, fools that you are, for you might as well hope to drink dry the Atlantic.   *C. H. Spurgeon*

Unpractical religion is unscriptural religion.   *James Wolfendale*

GOOD WORKS — See Good Deeds

GOODNESS
(See also: Ethics; Morality; Virtue)

Don't compare your goodness with that of other men; compare it with the goodness of the Man of Galilee.   *Anon.*

Good in the heart works its way up into the face and prints its own beauty there.
Anon.

Goodness is like praise to God.   *Anon.*

He that is good is free, though he be a slave; he that is evil is a slave, though he be a king.   *Augustine*

A man is only as good as what he loves.
Saul Bellow

The best practical definition of goodness is given in the life and character of Jesus Christ. 'Jesus of Nazareth, who went about doing good'.   *George Bethune*

Goodness is kindness in action.
Jerry Bridges

When you are alone, think of good things; and when you are in company, speak of good things.   *William Bridge*

When we speak of goodness, it is only as a reflection of divine goodness.
William Dembski

Goodness that preaches undoes it.
Ralph Waldo Emerson

A good life fears not life nor death.
Thomas Fuller

We can circumvent a lot of our worries by giving our attention to the good. Most of our ailments will die from neglect.
Vance Havner

We can do more good by being good than in any other way. *Rowland Hill*

No man knows how bad he is until he has tried to be good. *C. S. Lewis*

Every man has far more knowledge of good than he uses. *Alexander Maclaren*

A good life is a good fence against fear.
Edward Marbury

The good have no need of an advocate.
Phocion

A musician is commended not that he played so long, but that he played so well. And thus it is not the days of our life, but the goodness of our life … that is acceptable unto God Almighty. *Josias Shute*

Naturalists who deny the existence of any transcendent, personal God cannot successfully solve the problem of good. They cannot explain why there is a difference between right and wrong. *James W. Sire*

Goodness is the only investment that never fails. *Henry D. Thoreau*

When the mists have cleared away and all things appear in their proper light I think it will be revealed that goodness and greatness are synonymous. I do not see how it could be otherwise in a moral world. *A. W. Tozer*

It is chiefly in being good persons ourselves that we help others.
Elton Trueblood

God's goodness is the root of all goodness; and our goodness, if we have any, springs out of his goodness.
William Tyndale

GOSPEL
(See also: Evangelism; Soul-Winning)

The law gives menaces, the gospel gives promises. *Thomas Adams*

The Christian message is for those who have done their best *and failed!* *Anon.*

If you believe what you like in the gospel, and reject what you don't like, it is not the gospel you believe, but yourself. *Augustine*

The gospel is not so much a miracle as a marvel, and every line is suffused with wonder. *Roland Bainton*

The gospel is a glorious declaration of the mighty acts of God when he invaded this earth in the person of his eternal Son, the Lord Jesus Christ. *John Blanchard*

The gospel is not a human plan for reaching up to God, but a divine plan for reaching down to man. *John Blanchard*

The gospel is who Jesus is and what Jesus did. *John Blanchard*

The law sends us to the gospel, that we may be justified, and the gospel sends us to the law again to enquire what is our duty, being justified. *Samuel Bolton*

Christ's gospel is the sceptre of his kingdom. *John Calvin*

The blindness of unbelievers in no way detracts from the clarity of the gospel; the sun is no less bright because blind men do not perceive its light. *John Calvin*

The gospel is an anvil that has broken many a hammer, and will break many hammers yet. *John Calvin*

The gospel is not a doctrine of the tongue, but of life. *John Calvin*

The gospel is the clear manifestation of the mystery of Christ. *John Calvin*

The Spirit of God, from whom the doctrine of the gospel comes, is its only true interpreter. *John Calvin*

The whole gospel is contained in Christ. *John Calvin*

Whenever the gospel is preached it is as if God himself came into the midst of us. *John Calvin*

There is nothing attractive about the gospel to the natural man; the only man who finds the gospel attractive is the man who is convicted of sin. *Oswald Chambers*

The law and the gospel are allies, not enemies. *Walter J. Chantry*

The gospel is the ground of the believer's assurance, while the Holy Spirit is its cause. *J. C. P. Cockerton*

The gospel is good news. But Jesus never said it was easy news. *Charles Colson*

The gospel cannot stand in part and fall in part. *Cyprian*

As there is only one God, so there can be only one gospel. *James Denney*

The law was for the *condemnation* of sinners; the gospel was for the *saving* of sinners and the ministration of forgiveness. *C. J. Ellicott*

The gospel is the gospel of a happy God, because he now has an ever-growing family of those who by faith share the perfect life of his perfect Son.
Harry Foster

God will not allow the light of his truth to be covered up indefinitely.
David F. Gardner

The gospel is the chariot wherein the Spirit rides victoriously when he makes his entrance into the hearts of men.
William Gurnall

Religion is the story of what a sinful man tries to do for a holy God; the gospel is the story of what a holy God has done for sinful men. *Roy Gustafson*

Any man touched by Jesus Christ is good publicity for the gospel. *Vance Havner*

The gospel makes some people sad, some mad and some glad. It is better that people should go out of church mad than merely go out, neither sad, mad, nor glad. *Vance Havner*

The gospel reminds all men of an inescapable personal destiny in eternity, based on a conclusive decision in time.
Carl F. H. Henry

The success of the gospel exasperates its enemies. *Matthew Henry*

The gospel makes husbands better husbands, wives better wives, parents better parents, masters better masters and servants better servants; in a word, I would not give a farthing for that man's religion whose cat and dog were not the better for it. *Rowland Hill*

The rejection of the gospel is as clear

proof of moral depravity as inability to see the sun at noon is proof of blindness.
Charles Hodge

The gospel begins and ends with what God is, not with what we want or think we need. *Tom Houston*

That God should be kindly disposed to a world that hates him so as to bring the gospel of good news to them all is gracious, and that he should go further and actually apply that gospel in such a way as to rescue men and transform them is marvellous. *Erroll Hulse*

The church is the fruit of the gospel.
Hywel R. Jones

The vitality of the heavenly seed is not dependent upon the feelings of the sower, but upon the perpetual energy of the Spirit of truth. *G. H. Lang*

The gospel is not so much a miracle as a marvel, and every line is suffused with wonder. *Martin Luther*

The law is what we must do; the gospel is what God will give. *Martin Luther*

The gospel does not abrogate God's law, but it makes men love it with all their hearts. *J. Gresham Machen*

The gospel is not speculation but fact. It is truth, because it is the record of a person who is the Truth. *Alexander Maclaren*

Apart from the bright hope of the gospel everything would be meaningless.
Poul Madsen

The gospel no more excuses sin than the law does. What is repugnant to the moral law of God is also contrary to the gospel of Christ. *Henry T. Mahan*

God and his truth cannot be changed; the gospel is not negotiable. *John Marshall*

A gospel that elevates man and dethrones God is not the gospel. *Will Metzger*

In a God-centred gospel, grace is central — God is exalted at every point.
Will Metzger

The gospel is true not just in this or that part, but rather true in its completeness, so that all other truths must be tested by it. *Peter C. Moore*

The gospel will never be fashionable at any period of history or in any country.
Jules-Marcel Nicole

The world has many religions; it has but one gospel. *George Owen*

The Trinity is the basis of the gospel, and the gospel is a declaration of the Trinity in action. *J. I. Packer*

We are far more concerned about the results of the gospel than we are about the purity of it. *A. W. Pink*

The annals of the world tell us not of one instance where a sinner was converted, sanctified, filled with pious hopes, made willing to suffer in the cause of God and enabled mightily to triumph over the world, the flesh and the devil, over fears, temptations and death itself, except by the gospel of Christ. *William S. Plumer*

The gospel is neither a discussion nor a debate. It is an announcement.
Paul S. Rees

The nature of the gospel is that it divides.
Richard Owen Roberts

The light which men got from Moses and the law was at best only starlight compared to noonday. *J. C. Ryle*

The man who does not glory in the gospel can surely know little of the plague of sin that is within him. *J. C. Ryle*

There are no incurable cases under the gospel. Any sinner may be healed if he will only come to Christ. *J. C. Ryle*

The revelation of the gospel is to a world that is already under indictment for its universal rejection of God the Father.
R. C. Sproul

I bless my Lord and Master he has given me a gospel which I can take to *dead* sinners, a gospel which is available for the vilest of the vile. *C. H. Spurgeon*

If our Lord's bearing our sin for us is not the gospel, I have no gospel to preach.
C. H. Spurgeon

The heart of the gospel is redemption, and the essence of redemption is the substitutionary sacrifice of Christ.
C. H. Spurgeon

We have an unchanging gospel, which is not today green grass and tomorrow dry hay; but always the abiding truth of the immutable Jehovah. *C. H. Spurgeon*

When we preach Christ crucified, we have no reason to stammer, or stutter, or hesitate, or apologize; there is nothing in the gospel of which we have any cause to be ashamed. *C. H. Spurgeon*

The gospel is a declaration, not a debate.
James S. Stewart

There are two things to do about the gospel — believe it and behave it.
Susannah Wesley

The gospel has the hallmark of heaven upon it. *William J. C. White*

The ethical demand for holy living is inseparable from what is freely given in the gospel. *Geoffrey B. Wilson*

GOSSIP
(See also: Rumour; Slander; Speech)

Gossip is nature's telephone.
Sholem Aleichem

A gossip's mouth is the devil's mailbag.
Anon.

A gossip usually makes a mountain out of a molehill by adding some dirt. *Anon.*

Gossip is halitosis of the brain. *Anon.*

Gossip is like mud thrown against a clean wall; it may not stick, but it leaves a mark.
Anon.

Gossip is something that goes in the ear and comes out of the mouth greatly enlarged. *Anon.*

Gossip is the art of confessing other people's sins. *Anon.*

No one can have a gossiping tongue unless he has gossiping ears. *Anon.*

Whoever gossips to you will gossip of you. *Anon.*

Gossip is what no one claims to like but what everybody enjoys. *Joseph Conrad*

A lie has no leg, but a scandal has wings.
Thomas Fuller

There would not be so many open mouths if there were not so many open ears.
Joseph Hall

Gossip is the lack of a worthy theme.
Elbert Green Hubbard

A gossip is one who talks to you about others; a bore is one who talks to you about himself; and a brilliant conversationalist is one who talks to you about yourself. *Lisa Kirk*

Never report what may hurt another unless it be a greater hurt to conceal it.
William Penn

I hold it to be a fact, that if all persons knew what each said of the other, there would not be four friends in the world.
Blaise Pascal

When tempted to gossip, breathe through your nose. *T. N. Tiemeyer*

GRACE — The Christian's Indebtedness to

Anything this side of hell is pure grace.
Anon.

He who is graceless in the day of grace will be speechless in the Day of Judgement. *Anon.*

There is no reason for grace but grace.
Anon.

Every day we are objects of the grace of God. *Donald Grey Barnhouse*

Perfection demands perfection; that is why salvation must be by grace, and why works are not sufficient.
Donald Grey Barnhouse

All the Christian's rewards in heaven are his by the sovereign grace of a loving Father. *John Blanchard*

God owes us nothing. *John Blanchard*

All that I was, my sin, my guilt,
My death, was all my own;
All that I am I owe to thee,
My gracious God, alone.
Horatius Bonar

True grace always produces vigilance rather than complacency; it always produces perseverance rather than indolence.
Jerry Bridges

A man may find out many ways to hide his sin, but he will never find out any way to subdue his sin, but by the exercise of grace. *Thomas Brooks*

The more grace thrives in the soul, the more sin dies in the soul. *Thomas Brooks*

Men may fall by sin, but cannot raise up themselves without the help of grace.
John Bunyan

There is not a day, nor a duty; not a day that you live, nor a duty that you do, but will need that mercy should come after to take away your iniquity. *John Bunyan*

As by the grace of God we are what we are, so by his grace it is we are not what we are not. *Francis Burkitt*

God's grace turns out men and women with a strong family likeness to Jesus Christ, not milksops. *Oswald Chambers*

The marvel of God's grace is that he will not take 'No' for an answer from some men. *Walter Chantry*

Grace, 'tis a charming sound,
Harmonious to my ear;
Heaven with the echo shall resound
And all the earth shall hear.
Philip Doddridge

A Christian never lacks what he needs when he possesses in Christ the unsearchable riches of God's grace.
G. B. Duncan

A supply of grace is in store for believers against all exigencies; but they are only supplied with it as the need arises.
A. R. Fausset

All grace comes from the God of grace.
William Gurnall

There is a greater gulf between grace and no grace than between weak grace and strong.
William Gurnall

God's grace is not only amazing grace, it is abounding grace.
Vance Havner

We can never be blessed until we learn that we can bring nothing to Christ but our need.
Vance Havner

All the Christian's rights are his by grace.
William Hendriksen

We have a constant dependence upon God. All our natural actions depend upon his providence, all our spiritual actions upon his grace.
Matthew Henry

Knowledge is but folly unless it is guided by grace.
George Herbert

It takes grace to accept grace.
Robert M. Horn

Nature without grace is as Samson without his guide when his eyes were out.
John King

In all the Word of God there is no doctrine which, if properly applied, is more conducive to godly living than is the doctrine of salvation by grace, and by grace alone.
R. B. Kuiper

Whatever contribution men make to their salvation they make by the grace of God. And that makes salvation the work of grace a hundred per cent.
R. B. Kuiper

Every gospel imperative is full of the divine power of grace to effect what it demands. If it counted on even the least power in the sinner it would never secure the least effect.
R. C. H. Lenski

A man is not a Christian unless he can say with Paul, 'I am what I am by the grace of God.'
D. Martyn Lloyd-Jones

Everything is of grace in the Christian life from the very beginning to the very end.
D. Martyn Lloyd-Jones

Were it not for the grace of God there would be no such thing as a Christian.
D. Martyn Lloyd-Jones

The saved are singled out not by their own merits, but by the grace of the Mediator.
Martin Luther

When I stand before the throne,
Dressed in beauty not my own,
When I see thee as thou art,
Love thee with unsinning heart,
Then, Lord, shall I fully know
Not till' then, how much I owe.
Robert Murray M'Cheyne

Always distinguish between the words 'attain' and 'obtain'. We can never attain or earn God's gracious help by prayer or service, but we can obtain, appropriate and take it.
F. B. Meyer

All the Christian's rewards in heaven are his by the sovereign grace of a loving heavenly Father. *J. A. Motyer*

There is no grace unless God bestows it, and there is no real peace unless it flows forth from God's reconciliation with sinful man. *J. J. Muller*

I am not what I might be, I am not what I ought to be, I am not what I wish to be, I am not what I hope to be; but I thank God I am not what I once was, and I can say with the great apostle, 'By the grace of God I am what I am.' *John Newton*

The human mind without grace is a nest of wickedness swarming with thoughts of evil. *William S. Plumer*

Oh, to grace how great a debtor
Daily I'm constrained to be!
Let that grace, Lord, like a fetter,
Bind my wandering heart to thee.
Prone to wander, Lord, I feel it,
Prone to leave the God I love;
Take my heart, Oh, take and seal it
Seal it from thy courts above!
Robert Robinson

The church of Christ is little better than a great hospital. We ourselves are all, more or less, weak, and all daily need the skilful treatment of the heavenly Physician. There will be no complete cures until the resurrection day. *J. C. Ryle*

I know Christ and I shall never be even; I shall die in his debt. *Samuel Rutherford*

Grace is not like the tide, that ebbs and flows, that we know when it will come again when we see it go. *Richard Sibbes*

Any blessing which is bestowed by the Father upon his undeserving children

must be considered to be an act of grace. *David Smith*

God never owes us grace. *R. C. Sproul*

The God of the Bible is as severe as if he were unmerciful, and just as if he were not gracious; and yet he is as gracious and as merciful as if he were not just. *C. H. Spurgeon*

If there is to be in our celestial garment but one stitch of our own making we are all of us lost. *C. H. Spurgeon*

The greatest, highest and most practical truth of our life is that we are *recipients*. *William Still*

God does not owe you salvation. You deserve damnation, but he provides salvation. *Billy Sunday*

Grace finds us beggars but leaves us debtors. *Augustus Toplady*

Our salvation is a pure gratuity from God. *Benjamin B. Warfield,*

Behold, what wondrous grace
The Father hath bestowed
On sinners of a mortal race,
To call them sons of God *Isaac Watts*

GRACE — Common Grace

Common grace places everyone continually in God's debt — and the debt grows with every moment of life. *John Blanchard*

God, by the seasonable weeping of heaven, has caused plentiful laughter of the earth. *Thomas Fuller*

Grace is a universal principle. *William Gurnall*

The common grace of God enables us to interpret world history.   *Erroll Hulse*

Common grace is an omnipresent operation of divine mercy, which reveals itself everywhere where human hearts are found to beat, and which spreads its blessing upon these human hearts.
Abraham Kuyper

We need to thank God that there is such a thing as common grace; were it not so, we would have a taste of what hell would be like here and now.   *Al Martin*

There is nothing but God's grace. We walk upon it; we breathe it; we live and die by it; it makes the nails and axles of the universe.   *Robert Louis Stevenson*

All common grace is earlier grace. Its commonness lies in its earliness. It pertains not merely to the lower dimensions of life. It pertains to all dimensions, and to these dimensions in the same way at all stages of history. *Cornelius Van Til*

The essence of common grace is the restraint of the process of sin.
Cornelius Van Til

Every time you draw your breath you suck in mercy.   *Thomas Watson*

GRACE — Daily

They travel lightly whom God's grace carries.   *Thomas à Kempis*

God's grace is sufficient for us anywhere his providence places us.   *Anon.*

Grace is something more than 'unmerited favour' ... grace is favour shown where there is positive *demerit* in the one receiving it.   *Anon.*

Temptations are everywhere, *and so is the grace of God.*   *Anon.*

The will of God can never lead you where the grace of God cannot keep you. *Anon.*

Yesterday's hits won't win today's game.
Anon.

Grace grows by exercise and decays by disuse.   *Thomas Brooks*

No folly is greater than to suppose that God is optional for daily living.
Edmund P. Clowney

As grace is first from God, so it is continually from him, as much as light is all day long from the sun, as well at first dawn or at sun rising. *Jonathan Edwards*

He giveth more grace when the burdens
  grow greater,
He sendeth more strength when the
  labours increase;
To added affliction he addeth his mercy,
To multiplied trials, his multiplied peace.
Annie Johnson Flint

I would rather make bricks without straw than try to live the Sermon on the Mount in my own strength.
D. Martyn Lloyd-Jones

A man can no more take in a supply of grace for the future than he can eat enough for the next six months or take sufficient air into his lungs at one time to sustain life for a week. We must draw upon God's boundless store of grace from day to day, as we need it.   *D. L. Moody*

The sanctifying grace of God is appropriated by the obedient and unrelenting activity of the regenerate man.
J. A. Motyer

Grace is stronger than circumstances.
J. C. Ryle

God crowns grace with grace.
Richard Sibbes

The Lord may not give gold, but he will give grace; he may not give gain, but he will give grace. *C. H. Spurgeon*

There is within our nature that which would send the best saint to hell if sovereign grace did not prevent. *C. H. Spurgeon*

We need restraining grace as well as saving grace. *William Tiptaft*

No human frailty need be a hindrance to God's infinite grace. *David Watson*

GRACE — Essence

In the Bible there are three distinctive meanings of grace; it means the mercy and active love of God; it means the winsome attractiveness of God; it means the strength of God to overcome.
Charles L. Allen

Grace is a certain beginning of glory in us. *Thomas Aquinas*

God gives where he finds empty hands.
Augustine

Mercy is God's favour that holds back from us what we deserve. Grace is God's favour that gives us what we do not deserve. *Rolfe Barnard*

Grace is incapable of explanation.
John Blanchard

Grace has long arms. *John Blanchard*

Sin and grace are like two buckets at a well; when one is up the other is down.
Thomas Brooks

Grace … turns lions into lambs, wolves into sheep, monsters into men and men into angels. *Thomas Brooks*

Grace … turns counters into gold, pebbles into pearls, sickness into health, weakness into strength and wants into abundance. *Thomas Brooks*

Grace is but glory begun, and glory is but grace perfected. *Jonathan Edwards*

Grace often grows strongest where conviction of sin has pierced deepest.
Sinclair Ferguson

Grace is the freeness of love.
Thomas Goodwin

Grace is the free favour of God; peace is the condition which results from its reception. *H. L. Goudge*

The doctrines of grace humble a man without degrading him, and exalt him without inflating him. *Charles Hodge*

Grace is love that gives, that loves the unlovely and the unlovable.
Oswald C. Hoffman

From what the Bible says it seems to me that we shall not know the full explanation of grace even in heaven.
Robert M. Horn

Grace is not native but donative.
William Jenkyn

God gives his gifts where he finds the vessel empty enough to receive them.
C. S. Lewis

Grace is nothing but an introduction of the virtues of God into the soul.
Thomas Manton

Grace is love in action.
G. Campbell Morgan

Grace in God is his compassion on the unworthy.
Andrew Murray

Grace in the New Testament is not . . . an impersonal energy automatically switched on by prayer and sacraments, but the heart and hand of the living almighty God.
J. I. Packer

The essence of the doctrine of grace is that God is *for us*.
T. H. L. Parker

God's grace cannot stand with man's merit.
William Perkins

We cannot seek grace through gadgets.
J. B. Priestley

Grace and nature can no more amalgamate than oil and water.
J. C. Ryle

Grace that cannot be seen, like light, and tasted, like salt, is not grace but hypocrisy.
J. C. Ryle

Grace is God's contradiction of human pride.
David Silversides

Grace is love that cares and stoops and rescues.
John R. W. Stott

Grace is the oil of gladness; and the more of this oil, the more of gladness.
George Swinnock

Grace is omnipotence acting redemptively.
Geoff Thomas

No one can know the true grace of God who has not first known the fear of God.
A. W. Tozer

Grace is both a grace and a vessel to receive grace.
John Trapp

True grace is operative and will not lie dormant.
John Trapp

There is no reason to be given for grace but grace.
Ralph Venning

GRACE — and Heaven

Death *shortens* our way to heaven, but grace *sweetens* our way to heaven.
Anon.

Grace is glory militant and glory is grace triumphant.
Thomas Brooks

Grace is glory begun, and glory is grace consummated. Grace is glory in the bud, and glory is grace in the fruits. Grace is the lowest degree of glory, and glory the highest degree of grace.
Francis Burkitt

Grace in the soul is heaven in that soul.
Matthew Henry

Grace and glory are one and the same thing in a different print, in a smaller and greater letter. Glory lies couched and compacted in grace, as the beauty of a flower lies couched and eclipsed in the seed.
Thomas Hopkins

If you would lay up a treasure of glory in heaven, lay up a treasure of grace in your hearts.
John Mason

The least grace is a better security for heaven than the greatest gifts or privileges whatsoever.
John Owen

Grace is young glory.
Alexander Peden

Grace tried is better than grace, it is glory in its infancy. *Samuel Rutherford*

Grace shall always lead to glory.
J. C. Ryle

Glory must begin in grace.
Richard Sibbes

There are many who are barely Christians and have scarcely enough grace to float them into heaven, the keel of their vessel grating on the gravel all the way.
C. H. Spurgeon

Grace is glory inchoate; glory is grace consummate. *George Swinnock*

If you have one grain of grace, you must die to know how rich you are.
William Tiptaft

What a mercy to have a religion that will do to die by. *William Tiptaft*

The way to heaven lies not over a toll bridge, but over a free bridge.
Augustus Toplady

The more we grow in grace the more we shall flourish in glory. *Thomas Watson*

GRACE — Means — See Means of Grace

GRACE — and Salvation

Grace is especially associated with men in their sins: mercy is usually associated with men in their misery. *Anon.*

Grace and election are the essence and mystery of history. *Augustine*

The grace of God does not find men fit for salvation, but makes them so.
Augustine

Grace is what all need, what none can merit and what God alone can give.
George Barlow

God's grace can save souls without preaching; but all the preaching in the world cannot save souls without God's grace. *Benjamin Beddome*

The sinner, apart from grace, is unable to be willing and unwilling to be able.
W. E. Best

Grace is not a reward for faith; faith is the result of grace. *John Blanchard*

Justice is getting what you deserve; mercy is not getting what you deserve; grace is getting what you do not deserve.
Stuart Briscoe

Saving grace makes a man as willing to leave his lusts as a slave is willing to leave his galley, or a prisoner his dungeon, or a thief his bolts, or a beggar his rags.
Thomas Brooks

Law and love have no quarrel. The conflict arises between law and grace as a way of salvation. *Walter J. Chantry*

Grace first inscribed my name
In God's eternal book:
'Twas grace that gave me to the Lamb,
Who all my sorrows took.
Philip Doddridge

Grace comes not to take away a man's affections, but to take them up.
William Fenner

The first step to grace is to see they have no grace; the first degree of grace is the desire of grace. *William Fenner*

Our salvation is all of grace. The one thing

necessary is the one thing we ourselves cannot perform! *Sinclair Ferguson*

We will never properly understand the work of God which takes place in the Christian life unless we first of all have some kind of grasp of why we need the grace of God. *Sinclair Ferguson*

Grace is to corruption as water is to fire. *John Flavel*

In God's economy, emptying comes before filling, confession before forgiveness and poverty before riches. *Billy Graham*

God excludes none if they do not exclude themselves. *William Guthrie*

We are born with our backs upon God and heaven, and our faces upon sin and hell, till grace comes and that converts — turns us. *Philip Henry*

Nothing is sure for sinners that is not gratuitous. Unless we are saved by grace, we cannot be saved at all. *Charles Hodge*

Efficacious grace is invincible. *Ernest F. Kevan*

If the 'grace' you have received does not help you to keep the law, you have not received grace. *D. Martyn Lloyd-Jones*

A man must completely despair of himself in order to become fit to obtain the grace of Christ. *Martin Luther*

They have no grace that can be content with a little grace. *Thomas Manton*

It is a sure mark of grace to desire more. *Robert Murray M'Cheyne*

In a God-centred gospel, grace is central. *Will Metzger*

The law tells me how crooked I am. Grace comes along and straightens me out. *D. L. Moody*

The whole point about the divine redemption of humanity was that humanity did not deserve it. *Edward Norman*

There is nothing more offensive to man's self-esteem than a gospel of salvation by the grace of God, and by that grace alone. *T. P. Osborne*

No man ever believes with a true and saving faith unless God inclines his heart; and no man when God does incline his heart can refrain from believing. *Blaise Pascal*

Grace that cannot be seen is no grace at all. *J. C. Ryle*

It is grace, not place, which makes people believers. *J. C. Ryle*

To come to the end of your resources is a happy state, for then you grow desperate, and desperate men find God. *Hugh Silvester*

Sovereign grace can make strangers into sons. *C. H. Spurgeon*

The first link between my soul and Christ is not my goodness but my badness, not my merit but my misery, not my riches but my need. *C. H. Spurgeon*

It is a greater work of God to bring men to grace than, being in the state of grace, to bring them to glory; because sin is far more distant from grace than grace is from glory. *John Trapp*

Grace is power. It does not instruct, it energizes; and what dead men need is energizing, such energizing as raises the dead. *Benjamin B. Warfield*

Man does not 'secure' the grace of God: the grace of God 'secures' the activities of man. *Benjamin B. Warfield*

My God, how excellent thy grace,
Whence all our hope and comfort spring!
The sons of Adam in distress
Fly to the shadow of thy wing.
Isaac Watts

GRACE — Supremacy

Grace comes into the world as the morning sun into the world; first a dawning, then a light; and at last the sun in his full and excellent brightness. *Thomas Adams*

Grace is richer than prayer, for God always gives more than is asked of him. *Ambrose*

God's greatest glory is in his grace. *Donald Grey Barnhouse*

It is only by the grace of God that man can obey the law of God. *John Blanchard*

As heat is opposed to cold, and light to darkness, so grace is opposed to sin. Fire and water may as well agree in the same vessel as grace and sin in the same heart. *Thomas Brooks*

Grace is a ring of gold, and Christ is the sparkling diamond in that ring. *Thomas Brooks*

The life of grace is the death of sin, and the growth of grace the decay of sin. *Thomas Brooks*

Grace is the most important word in the Protestant vocabulary. *Robert Macafee Brown*

Nothing can be done aright without grace. *John Bunyan*

Faith and prayer may be means for procuring us an interest in the grace of God, but the source whence it flows is not within but without us. *John Calvin*

Whatever is laudable in our works proceeds from the grace of God. *John Calvin*

Grace is as large in renewing us as sin was in defacing. *Stephen Charnock*

Great God of wonders! All thy ways
Are matchless, Godlike, and divine;
But the fair glories of thy grace,
More Godlike and unrivalled shine.
Samuel Davies

With the doctrine of prevenient grace the evangelical doctrine stands or falls. *John Foster*

The ocean will hold a boat or a battleship, and God's grace will stand any weight you put on it. *Vance Havner*

The stream of grace and righteousness is deeper and broader than the stream of guilt. *Matthew Henry*

Knowledge is but folly unless it is guided by grace. *George Herbert*

A drop of grace is worth a sea of gifts. *William Jenkyn*

The word 'grace' is unquestionably the most significant single word in the Bible. *Ilion T. Jones*

God's grace can never break down. *Ernest F. Kevan*

The grace of God ... is a much higher

thing than the grace of a king to his dutiful subjects; it has its inspiration not in the worthiness of those to whom it is shown but entirely in the heart of God himself. *Ernest F. Kevan*

The ultimate test of our spirituality is the measure of our amazement at the grace of God. *D. Martyn Lloyd-Jones*

There is no chemistry like to that of grace. *Thomas Manton*

The religion of the Bible is a religion of grace or it is nothing. *James Moffatt*

Grace is the sum and substance of New Testament faith. *J. I. Packer*

Grace is what the New Testament is about. *J. I. Packer*

This one word 'grace' contains within itself the whole of New Testament theology. *J. I. Packer*

Where grace exists it reigns; it is the dominant factor in the situation. *J. I. Packer*

A little grace is better than many gifts. *J. C. Ryle*

Grace in the heart of man is an exotic. It is a new principle from without, sent down from heaven and implanted in his soul. *J. C. Ryle*

Grace is stronger than circumstances. *J. C. Ryle*

Grace is above all conditions. *Richard Sibbes*

Abounding sin is the terror of the world, but abounding grace is the hope of mankind. *A. W. Tozer*

God is always previous, God is always there first, and if you have any desire for God, and for the things of God, it is God himself who put it there. *A. W. Tozer*

GRACES

A man's true spiritual quality is to be judged by his graces, not his gifts. *John Blanchard*

Jewels are to wear, not hide; so are our graces. *Thomas Brooks*

The richest pearl in the Christian's crown of graces is humility. *John Mason Good*

Gifts are but as dead graces, but graces are living gifts. *Christopher Nesse*

Love is the queen of all the Christian graces. *A. W. Pink*

The strength of every grace lies in the sincerity of it. *A. W. Pink*

Gifts are what a man has but graces are what a man is. *F. W. Robertson*

Some graces grow best in winter. *Samuel Rutherford*

No grace is stronger than humility. *Richard Sibbes*

There are some of your graces which would never be discovered if it were not for your trials. *C. H. Spurgeon*

It is better to grow in grace than gifts. *Thomas Watson*

GRATITUDE
(See also: Thanksgiving)

Don't grumble because you don't get

what you want; be grateful that you don't get what you deserve. *Anon.*

The greatest sufferer that lives in this world of redeeming love, and who has the offer of heaven before him, has cause of gratitude. *Albert Barnes*

How strange that the Lord must plead with those whom he has saved from the pit to show gratitude to him!
Donald Grey Barnhouse

God is never more properly thanked for his goodness than by our godliness.
John Blanchard

It is only with gratitude that life becomes rich. *Dietrich Bonhoeffer*

Christians should have a gratitude attitude. *Stuart Briscoe*

He who receives a benefit should never forget it; he who bestows should never remember it. *Pierre Charron*

The finest test of character is seen in the amount and the power of gratitude we have. *Milo H. Gates*

There is nothing quite so stirring in the matter of moving us to pray as being thankful to God for what he has done for us and with us. *E. F. Hallock*

So much has been given to me, I have no time to ponder over that which has been denied. *Helen Keller*

Gratitude is the most exquisite form of courtesy. *Jacques Maritain*

Gratitude to God makes even a temporal blessing a taste of heaven.
William Romaine

Gratitude is a duty which ought to be paid, but which none have a right to expect.
Jean Jacques Rousseau

A grateful mind is both a great and happy mind. *William Secker*

Where God becomes a donor man becomes a debtor. *William Secker*

The essence of Christian ethics is gratitude. *R. C. Sproul*

It ought to be as habitual to us to thank as to ask. *C. H. Spurgeon*

The man who forgets to be grateful has fallen asleep in life. *Robert Louis Stevenson*

He who forgets the language of gratitude can never be on speaking terms with happiness. *C. Neil Strait*

God is pleased with gratitude; he gets so little of it. *William Tiptaft*

GREATNESS

He is genuinely great who considers himself small and cares nothing about high honours. *Thomas à Kempis*

Great men never know they are great; small men never know they are small.
Anon.

Kindness is the true revealer of a person's greatness. *Anon.*

Greatness is a matter, not of size, but of quality, and it is within the reach of every one of us. *Sidney Greenberg*

Nothing can make a man truly great but being truly good and partaking of God's holiness. *Matthew Henry*

Greatness

The man who disciplines himself stands out and has the mark of greatness upon him.   *D. Martyn Lloyd-Jones*

The true hallmark of greatness is simplicity. It is little minds that are complicated and involved.   *D. Martyn Lloyd-Jones*

One of the marks of true greatness is the ability to develop greatness in others.
                                J. C. MacAulay

Seek not greatness, but seek truth, and you will find both.   *Horace Mann*

Really great men have a curious feeling that the greatness is not in them but through them.   *John Ruskin*

All greatness is unconscious. *Walter Scott*

The great of this world are those who simply loved God more than others did.
                                A. W. Tozer

GREED
(See also: Covetousness; Gluttony)

Big mouthfuls often choke.   *Anon.*

No gain satisfies a greedy mind.   *Anon.*

Greed of gain is nothing less than the deification of self, and if our minds are set on hoarding wealth we are being idolatrous.   *John Blanchard*

Greed and ambition … the two sources from which stems the corruption of the whole of the ministry.   *John Calvin*

The lack of faith is the source of greed.
                                John Calvin

Somehow, for all the wondrous glimpses of 'goodness' I see in society, there remains the unmistakable stain of selfishness, violence and greed. *John Dickson*

Greed is a bottomless pit which exhausts the person in an endless effort to satisfy the need without ever reaching satisfaction.   *Erich Fromm*

If your desires be endless, your cares and fears will be so too.   *Thomas Fuller*

Riches have made more covetousness than covetousness has made rich men.
                                Thomas Fuller

The world provides enough for every man's need but not for every man's greed.
                            Mohandas Gandhi

That we shall carry nothing out of this world is a sentence better known than trusted, otherwise I think men would take more care to live well than to die rich.
                            John P. K. Henshaw

Whereas other vices grow as a man advances in life, avarice alone grows young.   *Jerome*

Avarice increases with the increasing pile of gold.   *Juvenal*

Nearly all those evils in the world which people put down to greed or selfishness are really far more the result of pride.
                                C. S. Lewis

Avarice is as destitute of what it has as poverty of what it has not. *Publilius Syrus*

Poverty wants much; greed everything.
                            Publilius Syrus

Most men pray more for full purses than for pure hearts.   *Thomas Watson*

GRIEF — See Sorrow

GROWTH

A sculptor can leave his work and come back to it another day, and take it up where he left off. But it is not so with the growth of the soul. The work of grace in us either waxes or wanes, flows or ebbs.
Andrew Anderson

God will do everything that we cannot do in order that we may live, but will do nothing that we can do in order that we may grow. *Anon.*

The biggest room in the world is the room for improvement. *Anon.*

The soul of all improvement is the improvement of the soul. *Anon.*

You may not be the best judge of the distance you have travelled, but you ought to have a good idea of the direction in which you are travelling. *Anon.*

There is no progress possible to the man who does not see and mourn over his defects. *George Barlow*

Moving in the right circles is not the same as making progress. *John Blanchard*

The Christian who has stopped repenting has stopped growing. *John Blanchard*

There is a world of difference between activity and progress. *John Blanchard*

Everywhere, everything in apostolic times was on the stretch ... No premium was given to dwarfs, no encouragement to an old babyhood. *E. M. Bounds*

Why stay we on earth except to grow?
Robert Browning

All our progress and perseverance are from God. *John Calvin*

Let us not cease to do the utmost, that we may incessantly go forward in the way of the Lord; and let us not despair because of the smallness of our accomplishments. *John Calvin*

We Christians are miserable indeed if we grow old in making no improvement.
John Calvin

Measure your growth in grace by your sensitiveness to sin. *Oswald Chambers*

It is only when men begin to worship that they begin to grow. *Calvin Coolidge*

If I cease becoming better, I shall soon cease to be good. *Oliver Cromwell*

Progress towards maturity is not to be measured by victory over the sins we are aware of; but by hatred of the sins which we had overlooked and which we now see all too clearly. *Arthur C. Custance*

You can't do anything about the length of your life, but you can do something about its width and depth. *Evan Esar*

Many spiritual experiences are possible which do not in and of themselves produce maturity. Rather, it is our response to experiences which will determine our progress in maturity. *Sinclair Ferguson*

We discern the growth of grace as the growth of plants, which we perceive rather to have grown than to grow.
John Flavel

Growth

The more a Christian grows in grace the more aware he becomes of the need for purity of heart. *Owen French*

There is no formula to teach us how to arrive at maturity, and there is no grammar for the language of the inner life. *Dag Hammarskjold*

God would have us not merely 'take a stand', he would have us walk. Too many have taken a stand and are still standing; for years they have made no progress. *Vance Havner*

Spiritual growth consists most in the growth of the root, which is out of sight. *Matthew Henry*

Some people's religion reminds me of a rockinghorse, which has motion without progress. *Rowland Hill*

Happy is he who makes daily progress and who considers not what he did yesterday but what advance he can make today. *Jerome*

The business of life is to go forward. *Samuel Johnson*

The perfect Christian is the one who, having a sense of his own failure, is minded to press towards the mark. *Ernest F. Kevan*

Spiritual maturity comes not by erudition, but by compliance with the known will of God. *D. W. Lambert*

The best of all tests of growth is a man's attitude to God. *D. Martyn Lloyd-Jones*

There is no better test of growth than that a man desires God because he is God. *D. Martyn Lloyd-Jones*

The quest for excellence is a mark of maturity. The quest for power is childish. *Max Lucado*

A Christian is never in a state of completion but always in a process of becoming. *Martin Luther*

There are no short cuts to spiritual maturity. It takes time to be holy. *Erwin W. Lutzer*

All growth that is not towards God is growing to decay. *George MacDonald*

Maturity begins to grow when you can sense your concern for others outweighing your concern for yourself. *John MacNaughton*

Progress is a tide. If we stand still we will surely be drowned. *Harold Mayfield*

I am persuaded that nothing is thriving in my soul unless it is growing. *Robert Murray M'Cheyne*

God never put anyone in a place too small to grow in. *Henrietta Mears*

The progressing Christian must cultivate the concentrated gaze of a person living in the future. *J. A. Motyer*

We grow in proportion as we know. *J. A. Motyer*

Growth is the only evidence of life. *John Henry Newman*

If I have observed anything by experience it is this: a man may take the measure of his growth and decay in grace according to his thoughts and meditations upon the person of Christ and the glory of Christ's kingdom and of his love. *John Owen*

We may lay it down as an elemental principle of religion that no large growth in holiness was ever gained by one who did not take time to be often alone with God.
Austin Phelps

Just as the sinner's despair of any help from himself is the first prerequisite of a sound conversion, so the loss of all confidence in himself is the first essential in the believer's growth in grace. *A. W. Pink*

The mature believer is a searching believer. *John Powell*

When a Christian ceases to grow he begins to decay. *Clate Risley*

Sanctification is always a progressive work. *J. C. Ryle*

In this life we never ascend to a plateau above and beyond which there is no further ground to gain.
Charles Caldwell Ryrie

There is a state of grace which *can* be enjoyed by Christians demonstrably higher than that which is commonly enjoyed. *W. F. Sangster*

None of us can come to the highest maturity without enduring the summer heat of trials. *C. H. Spurgeon*

However holy or Christlike a Christian may become, he is still in the condition of 'being changed'. *John R. W. Stott*

Growth is not the product of effort, but of life. *Augustus H. Strong*

Refuse to be average. *A. W. Tozer*

God wants us to be victors, not victims; to grow, not grovel; to soar, not sink; to overcome, not to be overwhelmed.
William A. Ward

We shall never graduate this side of heaven. *David Watson*

A good Christian is not like Hezekiah's sun that went backwards, nor Joshua's sun that stood still, but is always advancing in holiness, and increasing with the increase of God. *Thomas Watson*

It is better to grow in grace than gifts.
Thomas Watson

The growth of grace is the best evidence of the truth of it; things that have no life will not grow. *Thomas Watson*

The right manner of growth is to grow less in one's own eyes. *Thomas Watson*

When we stop growing we stop living and start existing. *Warren Wiersbe*

Progress is the only alternative to falling. We must advance or we shall decline. To prevent decay we must grow.
John Wilmot

GUIDANCE
(See also: Will of God)

God always provides a light through every one of his tunnels. *Anon.*

Listen to no man who fails to listen to God. *Anon.*

God leads his people out of sin by faith; through the world by hope; into heaven by love. *Michael Ayguan*

I can say from experience that 95% of knowing the will of God consists in being prepared to do it before you know what it is. *Donald Grey Barnhouse*

279

Christ leads me through no darker rooms than he went through before.
Richard Baxter

I dare not choose my lot;
I would not if I might;
Choose thou for me, my God,
So shall I walk aright.   *Horatius Bonar*

The Lord does not shine upon us, except when we take his Word as our light.
John Calvin

Unless God's Word illumine the way, the whole life of men is wrapped in darkness and mist, so that they cannot but miserably stray.   *John Calvin*

The answer to decision-making is not putting the Lord to the test by ascribing arbitrary significance to events in his providence ... God has not authorized us to make oracles of events.
Edmund P. Clowney

While providence supports,
Let saints securely dwell;
That hand which bears all nature up
Shall guide his children well.
Philip Doddridge

Always try the suggestions or impressions that you may at any time feel by the unerring rule of God's most holy Word.
Jonathan Edwards

One erroneous principle, than which scarce any has proved more mischievous to the present glorious work of God, is a notion that it is God's manner in these days to guide his saints, at least some that are more eminent, by inspiration, or immediate revelation.   *Jonathan Edwards*

Guidance is not normally ecstatic or mystical. It is always ethical and intensely practical.   *Sinclair Ferguson*

Guidance, knowing God's will for our lives, is much more a matter of thinking than of feeling.   *Sinclair Ferguson*

Very often when young people say they are having problems about guidance, what they are really faced with is a problem about obedience. *Sinclair Ferguson*

Take God into thy counsel. Heaven overlooks hell. God at any time can tell thee what plots are hatching there against thee.
William Gurnall

Where God guides he provides. He is responsible for our upkeep if we follow his directions. He is not responsible for expenses not on his schedule. *Vance Havner*

God is an ever-present Spirit guiding all that happens to a wise and holy end.
David Hume

A glimpse of the next three feet of road is more important than a view of the horizon.   *C. S. Lewis*

The devil can give you remarkable guidance … There are powers that can counterfeit almost anything in the Christian life.   *D. Martyn Lloyd-Jones*

However you define guidance you must resist anything that moves it in the direction of new revelation from God.
Sam Logan

I know not the way God leads me, but well do I know my guide. *Martin Luther*

The life of the believer is a conducted tour, and the skilful guide is Abraham's guide and ours. He knows the end of the journey which is in view, and he knows the best way to arrive there. *Fred Mitchell*

Where God's glory rests we need not ask the way. *Watchman Nee*

All the biblical narratives of God's direct communications with men are on the face of it exceptional, and the biblical method of personal guidance is quite different.
J. I. Packer

Be prepared for God to direct you to something you do not like, and teach you to like it! *J. I. Packer*

If God restored David after his adultery with Bathsheba and murder of Uriah, and Peter after his threefold denial of Christ, we should have no doubt that he can and will restore Christians who err through making honest mistakes about his guidance. *J. I. Packer*

Scripture gives us no more warrant constantly to expect 'hotline', 'voice-from-the control-tower' guidance than to expect new authoritative revelations to come our way for the guidance of the whole church. *J. I. Packer*

The fundamental mode whereby our rational Creator guides his rational creatures is by rational understanding and application of his written Word.
J. I. Packer

The truth is that God in his wisdom, to make and keep us humble and to teach us to walk by faith, has hidden from us almost everything that we should like to know about the providential purposes which he is working out in the churches and in our own lives. *J. I. Packer*

God Almighty, to reserve to himself the sole right of instructing us, and to prevent our solving the difficulties of our own being, has hid the knot so high, or, to speak more properly, so low, that we cannot reach it. *Blaise Pascal*

In the light of God, human vision clears.
James Philip

Men give advice; God gives guidance.
Leonard Ravenhill

If disappointment, trouble, frustration or failure have influenced our decision, we should be doubly careful before acting on it. Had Paul and Silas allowed their reception in Philippi to sway them in their guidance Europe might still have been without the gospel. *J. Oswald Sanders*

God's promises of guidance are not given to save us the bother of thinking.
John R. W. Stott

The Bible is not a kind of horoscope by which to tell your fortune … I do not deny that God sometimes reveals his particular will by lighting up a verse of Scripture. But this is not his usual method, and it is highly dangerous to follow such supposed guidance without checking and confirming it. *John R. W. Stott*

It is my deliberate conviction that the only way of arriving at a knowledge of the divine will, in regard to us, is by simplicity of purpose and earnest prayer.
J. H. Thornwell

In some ways I find guidance, if anything, gets harder rather than easier the longer I am a Christian. Perhaps God allows this so that we have to go on relying on him and not on ourselves. *David Watson*

God made the moon as well as the sun; and when he does not see fit to grant us the sunlight, he means us to guide our steps by moonlight. *Richard Whately*

Deep in your heart it is not guidance that you want so much as a guide. *John White*

GUILT
(See also: Depravity; Man; Sin; Sinful Nature)

A guilty conscience needs no accuser.
Anon.

Guilt is the very nerve of sorrow.
Horace Bushnell

Man falls according as God's providence ordains, but he falls by his own fault.
John Calvin

The terrors of God are the effects of guilt.
Stephen Charnock

Guilt is to danger what fire is to gunpowder.
John Flavel

Who was the guilty? Who brought this
upon thee?
Alas, my treason, Lord Jesus, hath
undone thee.
'Twas I, Lord Jesus, I it was denied thee;
I crucified thee! *Johann Heermann*

There smites nothing so sharp, nor smelleth so sour, as shame.
William Langland

All men stand condemned, not by alien codes of ethics, but by their own, and all men therefore are conscious of guilt.
C. S. Lewis

We have no choice but to be guilty. God is unthinkable if we are innocent.
Archibald MacLeish

Nothing is more personal than guilt.
Donald MacLeod

The burden of sin is the wrath of God.
Edward Marbury

We need not be ashamed of that now, which we are sure we shall not repent of when we come to die. *John Mason*

Every guilty person is his own hangman.
Seneca

Guilt is related to sin as the burnt spot to the blaze. *Augustus H. Strong*

It is guilt, which makes us shy of God.
George Swinnock

Guilt is present universally in the human soul, and we cannot deal with guilt without dealing with the religious questions it poses. *Paul Tournier*

GULLIBILITY

You can have such an open mind that it is too porous to hold a conviction.
George Crane

A dog that follows everybody is no good to anybody. *Vance Havner*

Incredible as it may seem, there are still people who believe what they read in the newspapers. *D. Martyn Lloyd-Jones*

HABIT

Habit is overcome by habit.
Thomas à Kempis

Habits are like cork or lead. They tend to keep you up or hold you down. *Anon.*

Habit is a shirt made of iron. *Anon.*

Habit, if not resisted, soon becomes necessity. *Augustine*

It is but a step from companionship to slavery when one associates with vice.
Hosea Ballou

Habits that begin as cobwebs sometimes end as cables. *John Blanchard*

All acts strengthen habits. *Thomas Brooks*

Every man has his besetting sin. *Cicero*

Habits, like fish-hooks, are lots easier to get caught than uncaught. *Frank A. Clark*

The second half of a man's life is made up of the habits he acquired during the first half. *Fyodor Dostoyevski*

We first make our habits, then our habits make us. *John Dryden*

An old dog can't alter his way of barking. *Thomas Fuller*

A young sinner will be an old devil.
William Gurnall

The chains of habit are generally too small to be felt until they are too strong to be broken. *Samuel Johnson*

I never knew a man to overcome a bad habit gradually. *John R. Mott*

Custom of sinning takes away the sense of it; the course of the world takes away the shame of it. *John Owen*

The strength of a man's virtues should not be measured by his special exertions, but by his habitual acts. *Blaise Pascal*

The best way to stop a bad habit is never to begin it. *J. C. Penney*

Habit is stronger than reason.
George Santayana

Beware of the habits we learn in controversy. *Francis Schaeffer*

The miller does not observe the noise of his own mill. *C. H. Spurgeon*

Custom in sin takes away all conscience of sin. *George Swinnock*

Powerful indeed is the empire of habit.
Publilius Syrus

How hard it is to pray against besetting sins! *William Tiptaft*

The best way to break a bad habit is to drop it. *D. S. Yoder*

HAPPINESS
(See also: Humour; Joy)

Happiness is the art of making a bouquet of those flowers within reach. *Anon.*

Man wishes to be happy even when he lives so as to make happiness impossible.
Augustine

To seek God is to desire happiness; to find him *is* that happiness. *Augustine*

Happiness is not the end of life; character is. *Henry Ward Beecher*

A man may be satisfied but not sanctified, contented but not converted, happy but not holy. *John Blanchard*

Superficial happiness without spiritual holiness is one of hell's major exports.
John Blanchard

The way of holiness that leads to happiness is a narrow way; there is but just room enough for a holy God and a holy soul to walk together. *Thomas Brooks*

When our holiness is perfect, our happiness shall be perfect; and if this were attainable on earth, there would be but little reason for men to long to be in heaven. *Thomas Brooks*

A happy life depends on a good conscience. *John Calvin*

To live happily the evils of ambition and self-love must be plucked from our hearts by the roots. *John Calvin*

While all men seek after happiness, scarcely one in a hundred looks for it from God. *John Calvin*

The secret of happiness is renunciation. *Andrew Carnegie*

Happiness can be built only on virtue, and must of necessity have truth for its foundation. *Samuel Taylor Coleridge*

The enjoyment of God is the only happiness with which our souls can be satisfied. *Jonathan Edwards*

A happy man is he that knows the world and cares not for it. *Joseph Hall*

God did not save us to make us happy but to make us holy. *Vance Havner*

The world's happiness should be spelled 'happeness', because it depends on what happens. *Vance Havner*

The search for happiness is one of the chief sources of unhappiness. *Eric Hoffer*

True happiness is not attained through self-gratification, but through fidelity to a worthy purpose. *Helen Keller*

The end of life is not to be happy, nor to achieve pleasure and avoid pain, but to do the will of God, come what may. *Martin Luther King*

A right to happiness doesn't, for me, make much more sense than a right to be six feet tall, or to have a millionaire for your father, or to get good weather whenever you want to have a picnic. *C. S. Lewis*

God cannot give us happiness and peace apart from himself, because it is not there. There is no such thing. *C. S. Lewis*

Seek for happiness and you will never find it. Seek righteousness and you will discover you are happy. It will be there without your knowing it, without your seeking it. *D. Martyn Lloyd-Jones*

If you're not allowed to laugh in heaven, I don't want to go there. *Martin Luther*

A man should look after a happiness that will last as long as his soul lasts. *Thomas Manton*

My true happiness is to go and sin no more. *Robert Murray M'Cheyne*

Pleasure-seeking is a barren business; happiness is never found till we have the grace to stop looking for it, and to give our attention to persons and matters external to ourselves. *J. I. Packer*

Happiness is neither within us only, or without us; it is the union of ourselves with God. *Blaise Pascal*

Searching for true happiness in the context of a godless life is like looking for a needle in a haystack that doesn't have any. *W. T. Purkiser*

It is a barren life that holds only happiness. *Frances J. Roberts*

God has linked together holiness and happiness; and what God has joined together we must not think to put asunder. *J. C. Ryle*

Never was there a greater mistake than to suppose that vital Christianity interferes with human happiness. *J. C. Ryle*

Those who fancy that true religion has any tendency to make men unhappy are greatly mistaken. It is the absence of it that does this, not the presence. *J. C. Ryle*

The greatest happiness you can have is knowing that you do not necessarily require happiness. *William Saroyan*

We must love our happiness no further than we can have it with God's leave and liking. *Richard Sibbes*

Wise men and women in every major culture have maintained that the secret of happiness is not in getting more but in wanting less. *Philip Slater*

Happiness does not depend on the actual number of blessings we manage to scratch from life, but on our attitude towards them. *Alexandr Solzhenitsyn*

Happier to be chained in a dungeon with a Paul than reign in the palace with an Ahab. *C. H. Spurgeon*

There can be no happiness if the things we believe in are different from the things we do. *Treya Stark*

He who forgets the language of gratitude can never be on speaking terms with happiness. *C. Neil Strait*

Happiness is nothing but the sabbath of our thoughts. *George Swinnock*

Sow holiness and reap happiness. *George Swinnock*

Whoever thinks of finding happiness in this world will be a day's march behind. *William Tiptaft*

Christians have every right to be the happiest people in the world. We do not have to look to other sources — for we look to the Word of God and discover how we can know the faithful God above and draw from his resources. *A. W. Tozer*

The reason we have to search for so many things to cheer us up is the fact that we are not really joyful and contentedly happy within. *A. W. Tozer*

Happiness is the spiritual experience of living every minute with love, grace and gratitude. *Denis Waitley*

There is no happiness out of GOD. *John Wesley*

HATRED
(See also: Anger; Passion)

Violent hatred sinks us below those we hate. *Anon.*

Hatred is self-punishment. *Hosea Ballou*

Hate no one; hate their vices, not themselves. *John Gardiner Brainard*

Hatred is nothing more than inveterate anger. *John Calvin*

The price of hating other human beings is loving oneself less. *Eldridge Cleaver*

Hatred is like fire — it makes even light rubbish deadly. *George Eliot*

Hatred

Hatred is blind as well as love.
Thomas Fuller

Hate, like love, picks up every shred of evidence to justify itself.   *Os Guinness*

Hate is too great a burden to bear.
Martin Luther King

Animosity cloaked in piety is a demon even if it sits in church praising the Creator.   *Calvin Miller*

Life is too short for hate. *George Peppard*

I will not permit any man to narrow and degrade my soul by making me hate him.
Bokker T. Washington

HEART
(See also: Soul)

A man's heart is right when he wills what God wills.   *Thomas Aquinas*

To my fellow men a heart of love; to my friends a heart of loyalty; to my God a heart of flame; to myself a heart of steel.
Augustine

No man is conquered until his heart is conquered.   *George Barlow*

The recesses of the heart are so hidden that no judgement can be formed by any human being.   *John Calvin*

The essence of the virtue and vice of dispositions of the heart and acts of the will lies not in their cause but in their nature.   *Jonathan Edwards*

The keeping and right managing of the heart in every condition is the great business of the Christian's life. *John Flavel*

The more a Christian grows in grace the more aware he becomes of the need for purity of heart.   *Owen French*

As seed is made for soil and soil for seed, so the heart is made for God's truth and God's truth for the heart. *Richard Glover*

Our hearts are slippery commodities.
Thomas Goodwin

The basic needs of the human heart never change. The answers to that need never change.   *William G. Hughes*

If your heart does not want a world of moral reality, your head will assuredly never make you believe in one.
William James

A man's heart is what he is. *R. B. Kuiper*

I am more afraid of my own heart than of the pope and all his cardinals.
Martin Luther

God alone sees the heart; the heart alone sees God.   *Thomas Manton*

If you would have the life holy before men, let the heart be pure before God.
Thomas Manton

There is nothing in the life but what was first in the heart.   *Thomas Manton*

Rather look to the cleansing of thine heart than to the cleansing of thy well; rather look to the feeding of thine heart than to the feeding of thy flock; rather look to the defending of thine heart than to the defending of thine house; rather look to the keeping of thine heart than to the keeping of thy money.   *Peter Moffat*

The heart in the Scriptures is variously used; sometimes for the mind and understanding, sometimes for the will, sometimes for the affection, sometimes for the conscience ... *Generally,* it denotes the whole soul of man and all the faculties of it. *John Owen*

It is the heart which experiences God and not the reason. *Blaise Pascal*

If the keeping of the heart be the great work of the Christian, then how few *real* Christians are there in the world! *A. W. Pink*

The heart is the warehouse, the hand and tongue are but the shops; what is in *these* is from *thence* — the heart contrives and the members execute. *A. W. Pink*

Sin and the devil will always find helpers in our hearts. *J. C. Ryle*

The seeds of every wickedness lie hidden in our hearts. They only need the convenient season to spring forth into a mischievous vitality. *J. C. Ryle*

There is far more wickedness in all our hearts than we know. *J. C. Ryle*

There is a concert of all the members when the heart is in tune. *Henry Smith*

The heart is the metal of the bell, the tongue but the clapper. *George Swinnock*

God is more concerned with the state of people's hearts than with the state of their feelings. *A. W. Tozer*

Keep your heart with all diligence and God will look after the universe. *A. W. Tozer*

The heart of man is like a musical instrument and may be played upon by the Holy Spirit, by an evil spirit or by the spirit of man himself. *A. W. Tozer*

The heart is a triangle which only the Trinity can fill. *Thomas Watson*

HEAVEN — the Christian's Eternal Home
(See also: Eternal Security; Eternity)

In heaven to be even the least is a great thing, for all will be great.
Thomas à Kempis

Heaven is a reality, not seen by eyes of flesh, but made known by revelation and received by faith. *Archibald Alexander*

Christ is preparing saints for heaven and heaven for saints. *Anon.*

Everyone will get to heaven who could live there. *Anon.*

Heaven is a prepared place for prepared people. *Anon.*

If God were not willing to forgive sin heaven would be empty. *Anon.*

Our earthly life is merely the preface to the book. Life in heaven will be the text — a text without end. *Anon.*

Saints are never far from home. *Anon.*

Those who live in the Lord never see each other for the last time. *Anon.*

The saint's enduring riches are in the future, locked up in the heavenly casket.
George Barlow

Heaven — the Christian's Eternal Home

In our first paradise in Eden there was a way to go out but no way to go in again. But as for the heavenly paradise, there is a way to go in, but no way to go out again.
Richard Baxter

All the Christian's rewards in heaven are his by the sovereign grace of a loving Father. *John Blanchard*

All the places in heaven and hell are reserved. *John Blanchard*

If knowing God here can mean so much, how much more will it mean in heaven?
John Blanchard

There are no tourists in heaven.
John Blanchard

We were born on the earth, we live on the earth, we cling to the earth as long as we can — yet as Christians we do not actually belong here at all. Our legal domicile is in heaven. *John Blanchard*

Heaven would be no heaven were there any strangers there. *Thomas Brooks*

If we look around us, a moment can seem a long time, but when we lift up our hearts heavenwards, a thousand years begin to be like a moment. *John Calvin*

I've wrestled on towards heaven,
'Gainst storm and wind and tide;
Now, like a weary traveller
That leans upon his guide,
Amid the shades of evening,
While sinks life's lingering sand,
I hail the glory dawning
From Immanuel's land.
Anne Ross Cousin

This world is the land of the dying; the next is the land of the living.
Tryon Edwards

Heaven's number of glorified saints is made up of justified sinners.
William Gurnall

A dog is at home in this world because this is the only one a dog will ever live in. We are not at home in this world because we are made for a better one.
Vance Havner

Christians are not citizens of earth trying to get to heaven, but citizens of heaven making their way through this world.
Vance Havner

Those that are acquainted with God and Christ are already in the suburbs of life eternal. *Matthew Henry*

The Christian's heaven is to be with Christ, for we shall be like him when we see him as he is. *Charles Hodge*

It is the gospel alone which connects us with the era to come. *R. C. H. Lenski*

The church will out live the universe; in it the individual person will out live the universe. Everything that is joined to the immortal Head will share his immortality. *C. S. Lewis*

We must ... I'm afraid recognize that, as we grow older, we become like old cars — more and more repairs and replacements are necessary. We must look forward to the fine new machines (latest resurrection model) which are waiting for us, we hope, in the Divine garage!
C. S. Lewis

You must not only *seek heaven;* you must also *think heaven.* *J. B. Lightfoot*

My whole outlook upon everything that happens to me should be governed by these three things: my realization of who

I am, my consciousness of where I am going, and my knowledge of what awaits me when I get there.
D. Martyn Lloyd-Jones

We shall not rest from our work but from our labours. There will be no toil, no pain in our work. *Robert Murray M'Cheyne*

When I get to heaven, I shall see three wonders there — the first wonder will be to see many people there whom I did not expect to see; the second wonder will be to miss many people whom I did expect to see; and the third and greatest wonder of all will be to find myself there.
John Newton

Heaven will not fully be heaven to Christ till he has all his redeemed with himself.
A. W. Pink

Worship alone of all the activities of the believer will continue in heaven and will occupy the redeemed host for ever.
Robert G. Rayburn

I wonder, many times, that ever a child of God should have a sad heart, considering what his Lord is preparing for him.
Samuel Rutherford

As surely as God is eternal, so surely is heaven an endless day without night and hell an endless night without day.
J. C. Ryle

Grace shall always lead to glory.
J. C. Ryle

They that enter heaven will find that they are neither unknown nor unexpected.
J. C. Ryle

Eternal life does not begin with death, it begins with faith. *Samuel Shoemaker*

He is sure of heaven who is sure of Christ.
C. H. Spurgeon

I have a strong appetite for heaven.
C. H. Spurgeon

Heaven is not all rest. On the door is inscribed: 'No admission except on business.' *Augustus H. Strong*

Heaven is not a lease which soon expires, but an inheritance. *Thomas Watson*

Many may outlive me on earth, but they cannot outlive me in heaven.
George Whitefield

HEAVEN — Glory

Heaven will pay for any loss we may suffer to gain it; but nothing can pay for the loss of heaven. *Richard Baxter*

There is nothing but heaven worth setting our hearts upon. *Richard Baxter*

Heaven would be hardly be heaven if we could define it. *W. E. Biederwoif*

Heaven is not a conditional reward, but a consummated relationship.
John Blanchard

If one man should suffer all the sorrows of all the saints in the world, yet they are not worth one hour's glory in heaven.
Chrysostom

If the fire of hell is not literal, it is worse than actual fire; and if the gates of the Celestial City are not actual gold, they are far finer. *Vance Havner*

Heaven is not a state of mind. Heaven is reality itself. *C. S. Lewis*

Joy is the serious business of heaven.
C. S. Lewis

I would not give one moment of heaven for all the joy and riches of the world, even if it lasted for thousands and thousands of years. *Martin Luther*

It is not death to close
The eye long dimmed by tears,
And wake in glorious repose
To spend eternal years.
Henri Abraham Cesar Malan

If it be sweet to be the growing corn of the Lord here, how much better to be gathered into his barn!
Robert Murray M'Cheyne

Earth has no sorrow that heaven cannot heal. *Thomas V. Moore*

One breath of paradise will extinguish all the adverse winds of earth. *A. W. Pink*

Heaven will be a world of sanctified excitement. *Maurice Roberts*

If sin or evil could ever enter into heaven we could never truly enjoy a moment's peace there. *Maurice Roberts*

I suspect that every saved soul in heaven is a great wonder, and that heaven is a vast museum of wonders of grace and mercy, a palace of miracles, in which everything will surprise everyone who gets there. *C. H. Spurgeon*

If this world with its fading pleasures is so much admired, what must heaven be, which God praises! *William Tiptaft*

There is a land of pure delight,
Where saints immortal reign;
Infinite day excludes the night,
And pleasures banish pain.
Isaac Watts

All here are but shadows; all above is substance. *Andrew Welwood*

HEAVEN — God's Presence

Christ is the centre of attraction in heaven.
Archibald Alexander

In heaven, God will never hide his face and Satan will never show his.
John Blanchard

Heaven is the perfectly ordered and harmonious enjoyment of God and of one another in God. *Augustine*

I do not go to heaven to be advanced, but to give honour to God. *David Brainerd*

It is God alone who makes heaven to be heaven. *Thomas Brooks*

Hell is to be eternally in the presence of God. Heaven is to *be* eternally *in* the presence of God, *with a Mediator.*
R. A. Finlayson

Would you know what makes heaven heaven? It is communion with God. And would you know what makes hell hell? It is to be forsaken of God. *R. B. Kuiper*

How can we expect to live with God in heaven if we love not to live with him on earth? *John Mason*

The heavenly state is so organized as to express visibly what God thinks of the cross of Christ. *J. A. Motyer*

Heaven will chiefly consist in the enjoyment of God. *William S. Plumer*

Without God, heaven would be no heaven.   *William S. Plumer*

The humble heart is God's throne in regard to his gracious presence; and heaven is his throne as to his glorious presence.
Thomas Watson

HEAVEN — Perfection

Heaven begins where sin ends.
Thomas Adams

Who can measure the happiness of heaven, where no evil at all can touch us, no good will be out of reach; where life is to one long laud extolling God, who will be all in all; where there will be no weariness to call for rest, no need to call for toil, no place for any energy but praise.
Augustine

No line in Scripture indicates any sorrow or grief in heaven.
Donald Grey Barnhouse

No one will ever be bored in heaven.
John Benton

Heaven's riches are moth-proof, rust-proof, and burglar-proof. *John Blanchard*

Nothing that has ruined man's life on earth will be allowed to do so in heaven.
John Blanchard

There are no furrowed brows in heaven.
John Blanchard

There are no regrets in heaven, no remorseful tears, no second thoughts, no lost causes.   *John Blanchard*

How soon shall the present night be forgotten in the brightness of endless day! How quickly shall the curse give place to the blessing, barrenness be exchanged for fruitfulness, and all pollution be swept clean away!   *Horatius Bonar*

Believers will swim for ever in an ocean of joy.   *Thomas Boston*

In heaven is no warfare but all well-fare.
John Boys

Heaven would be a very hell to an unholy person.   *Thomas Brooks*

In the streets of that new Jerusalem above, none shall ever complain that others have too much, or that themselves have too little.   *Thomas Brooks*

We shall have everything we desire and desire everything we have.
Richard Brooks

There are three things which the true Christian desires in respect to sin: justification, that it might not condemn; sanctification, that it may not reign; and glorification, that it may not be.
Richard Cecil

In heaven it is always autumn. God's mercies are ever in their maturity.
John Donne

There is no misbelief in heaven.
Andrew Gray

One hour in heaven and we shall be ashamed we ever grumbled.
Vance Havner

If an unholy man were to get to heaven he would feel like a hog in a flower garden.   *Rowland Hill*

Heaven is reserved for heaven.
James Janeway

Heaven will mean the realization of all the things for which man was made and the satisfaction of all the outreachings of his heart.   *Ernest F. Kevan*

I would not give one moment of heaven for all the joys and riches of the world, even if it lasted for thousands and thousands of years.   *Martin Luther*

Heaven is a day without a cloud to darken it and without a night to end it.
John Mason

In heaven there is the presence of all good and the absence of all evil. *John Mason*

It will be one of the felicities of heaven that saints shall no longer misunderstand each other.   *Isaac Milner*

Beyond this vale of tears
There is a life above;
Unmeasured by the flight of years,
And all that life is love.
James Montgomery

Earth has no sorrow that heaven cannot heal.   *Thomas V. Moore*

The road is not to be complained of; as it leads to such a home.   *John Newton*

Heaven is a state of holiness, which only persons with holy tastes will appreciate, and into which only persons of holy character can enter.   *J. I. Packer*

There will be no sin in heaven, for those who are in heaven will not have it in them to sin any more.   *J. I. Packer*

Christ and his cross are not separable in this life; howbeit, they part at heaven's door. There is no storage place for crosses in heaven.   *Samuel Rutherford*

If contentment were here, heaven were not heaven.   *Samuel Rutherford*

Nothing but glory will make tight and fast our leaking and rifty vessels.
Samuel Rutherford

Heaven makes amends for all. *J. C. Ryle*

When an eagle is happy in an iron cage, when a sheep is happy in water, when an owl is happy in the blaze of the noonday sun, when a fish is happy on dry land then, and not till then, will I admit that the unsanctified man could be happy in heaven.
J. C. Ryle

Heaven is a kingdom where there are no perils to brave, no loneliness to face, no wants to suffer, no crosses to bear.
Basilea Schlink

'Difficulty' is not a word to be found in the dictionary of heaven. *C. H. Spurgeon*

If a thief should get into heaven unchanged, he would begin by picking the angels' pockets.   *C. H. Spurgeon*

The Lamb's wedding is a time for boundless pleasure, and tears would be out of place.   *C. H. Spurgeon*

Heaven is the proper place for comfort, earth for grace.   *George Swinnock*

Here, joy begins to enter into us; there, we enter into joy.   *Thomas Watson*

There can be no grief in heaven any more than there can be joy in hell.
Thomas Watson

HEAVEN —— Preparation for

The more of heaven we cherish, the less of earth we covert.   *Anon.*

Christ brings the heart to heaven first, and then the person.   *Richard Baxter*

The Christian should never look ahead without looking up.   *John Blanchard*

To believe in heaven is not to run away from life; it is to run towards it.
                    Joseph D. Blinco

Grace is glory begun, and glory is grace consummated. Grace is glory in the bud, and glory is grace in the fruits. Grace is the lowest degree of glory, and glory the highest degree of grace. *Francis Burkitt*

Make it the business of life to prepare for heaven.   *Esther Burr*

We ought to apply our minds to meditation upon a future life, so that this world may become cheap to us.   *John Calvin*

All the way to heaven is heaven.
                Catherine of Siena

When we learn to hold the world with a loose grip we are learning to take hold of the world to come with a firm grip.
                Sinclair Ferguson

The child is willing who calls to be put to bed.   *William Gurnall*

It is certain that all that will go to heaven hereafter begin their heaven now, and have their hearts there. *Matthew Henry*

Our duty as Christians is always to keep heaven in our eye and earth under our feet.   *Matthew Henry*

Those who have the new Jerusalem in their eye must have the ways that lead to it in their heart.   *Matthew Henry*

Grace and glory are one and the same thing in a different print, in a smaller and greater letter. Glory lies couched and compacted in grace, as the beauty of a flower lies couched and eclipsed in the seed.   *Thomas Hopkins*

A continual looking forward to the eternal world is not a form of escapism or wishful thinking, but one of the things a Christian is meant to do.   *C. S. Lewis*

The more spiritual we are, the more we shall think about heaven.
            D. Martyn Lloyd-Jones

Christians are the more cold and careless in the spiritual life because they do not oftener think of heaven. *Thomas Manton*

Holiness indeed is perfected in heaven: but the beginning of it is invariably confined to this world.   *John Owen*

The Lord Christ leads none to heaven but whom he sanctifies on earth. This living Head will not admit of dead members.
                    John Owen

Basic to New Testament ethics is the belief that Christians should live on earth in the light of heaven, should make decisions in the present with their eye on the future, and should avoid behaving here in a way that would jeopardize their hope of glory hereafter.   *J. I. Packer*

There is a difference between being willing to go to heaven and wanting to stay on earth — and wanting to go to heaven while being willing to stay on earth.
                    David Pawson

Grace is young glory.   *Alexander Peden*

The highway of holiness is the only path which leads to heaven.   *A. W. Pink*

There is only one attitude possible for us if we mean to get to heaven. We must wage a ceaseless warfare against sin within us all the days of our life.
Maurice Roberts

Heaven itself would be no heaven if we entered it with an unsanctified character.
J. C. Ryle

It does seem clear that heaven would be a miserable place to an unholy man. It cannot be otherwise. *J. C. Ryle*

Our hearts must be in tune for heaven if we are to enjoy it. *J. C. Ryle*

We must be saints on earth if we ever mean to be saints in heaven. *J. C. Ryle*

Eternal life does not begin with death; it begins with faith. *Samuel Shoemaker*

Glory must begin in grace.
Richard Sibbes

The person who cannot look forward to God's dessert will have a tough time munching his way through the turnip greens and the rolled oats porridge now.
Paul B. Smith

Heaven must be in thee before thou canst be in heaven. *George Swinnock*

No man may go to heaven who hath not sent his heart thither before.
Thomas Wilson

HEDONISM — See Pleasures and Headonism

HELL
(See also: Destiny; Eternity; Judgement; Satan)

The most awful fact in the world is the fact of hell and that some of our dearest relations and friends with whom we have lived, worked and worshipped will spend an eternity of anguish, away from God, eternally unforgiven, eternally doomed.
Isaac H. A. Ababio

Hell is truth seen too late. *H. G. Adams*

He shall have hell as a debt who will not have heaven as a gift. *Anon.*

'Too late' is written on the gates of hell.
Anon.

Each man's sin is the instrument of his punishment, and his iniquity is turned into his torment. *Augustine*

God will give the rebel what he chooses and what he deserves. *Simon Austen*

All the roads that lead to hell are one way streets. *John Blanchard*

At the end of the day, hell is anywhere outside of heaven. *John Blanchard*

In hell, even the gospel is bad news.
John Blanchard

It is never true to say that something 'hurts like hell'. Nothing hurts like hell.
John Blanchard

The roads to hell are all downhill.
John Blanchard

There are no quiet corners in hell.
John Blanchard

Those who demand nothing more than a God of justice get precisely what they ask; the Bible calls it hell. *John Blanchard*

To believe in heaven but not in hell is to declare that there were times when Jesus was telling the truth and times when he was lying.   *John Blanchard*

Could every damned sinner weep a whole ocean, yet all those oceans together would never extinguish one spark of eternal fire.
Thomas Brooks

Eternity of eternity is the hell of hell.
Thomas Brooks

God has but one hell, and that is for those to whom sin has been commonly a heaven in this world.   *Thomas Brooks*

The damned in hell may weep their eyes out of their heads, but they can never weep sin out of their souls.
Thomas Brooks

The damned shall live as long in hell as God himself shall live in heaven.
Thomas Brooks

The greatest and the hottest fires that ever were on earth are but ice in comparison of the fire of hell.   *Thomas Brooks*

The truth is, were there the least real joy in sin, there could be no perfect hell, where men shall most perfectly sin, and be most perfectly tormented with their sin.
Thomas Brooks

The wicked have the seeds of hell in their own hearts.   *John Calvin*

Sure I am, that if hell can be disproved in any way that is solid and true, and consistent with God's honour and man's good, there is not a trembling sinner in this land that would hail the demonstration with more joy than I would. *Robert L. Dabney*

To appreciate justly and fully the gospel of eternal salvation we must believe, the doctrine of eternal damnation. *J. L. Dagg*

Vain are the dreams of infatuated mortals who suppose that the only punishment to be endured for sin is in the present life.
J. L. Dagg

Damnation: continual dying. *John Donne*

There is many a learned head in hell.
John Flavel

If there is no belief in hell the concept of judgement also becomes meaningless; and then all that is left of Christianity is a system of ethics.   *Geoffrey Gorer*

Christ needs take no other revenge on a soul for refusing him … than to condemn such a one to have its own desire.
William Gurnall

Were the fire out as to positive torments, yet a hell would be left in the dismal darkness which the soul would sit under for want of God's presence. *William Gurnall*

Eternal death is not the cessation of existence, but rather the loss of that life of fellowship with God which alone is worthy of the name. *D. Edmond Hiebert*

If I am afraid of sin I need not be afraid of hell.   *Rowland Hill*

A man who realizes in any measure the awful force of the words *eternal hell* won't shout about it, but will speak with all tenderness.   *A. A. Hodge*

Men may hasten to perdition with the name of Jesus on their lips.
Friedrich W. Krummacher

Would you know what makes heaven heaven? It is communion with God. And would you know what makes hell hell? It is to be forsaken of God. *R. B. Kuiper*

Men are not in hell because God is angry with them: they are in wrath and darkness because they have done to the light, which infinitely flows forth from God, as that man does to the light who puts out his own eyes. *William Law*

Exit is not a word found in the vocabulary of hell. *Robert G. Lee*

I willingly believe that the damned are, in one sense, successful, rebels to the end; that the doors of hell are locked on the *inside.* *C. S. Lewis*

The safest road to hell is the gradual one — the gentle slope, soft underfoot, without sudden turnings, without milestones, without sign posts. *C. S. Lewis*

There are no personal relationships in hell. *C. S. Lewis*

Let not anyone who thinks that fear of hell should be put out of the mind of unregenerate men ever suppose that he has the slightest understanding of what Jesus came into the world to say and do.
J. Gresham Machen

When the world dissolves, all places will be hell that are not heaven.
Christopher Marlowe

The reason why so many fall into hell is because so few think of it. *John Mason*

They that will not feel the punishment in the threatening shall feel the threatening in the punishment. *John Mason*

Hell is full of God's glory, as well as heaven, and the sinner shall show it forth in his perdition no less truly than the saint in his salvation. *Thomas V. Moore*

Sin is but hell in embryo; hell is but sin in fulfilment. *Thomas V. Moore*

If you are still unconverted, thank God that you are still not in hell.
Andrew Murray

The lost will eternally suffer in the satisfaction of justice, but they will never satisfy it. *John Murray*

You will be a believer some day. If you never believe on earth, you will believe in hell. *Brownlow North*

An endless hell can no more be removed from the New Testament than an endless heaven can. *J. I. Packer*

Those who regard the whole idea of hell as completely repulsive betray the fact that they think that their moral sense is more acute than that of Jesus.
Edgar Powell

The second death is the continuance of spiritual death in another and timeless existence. *E. G. Robinson*

As surely as God is eternal, so surely is heaven an endless day without night and hell an endless night without day.
J. C. Ryle

Hell itself would be endurable if after millions of ages there was a hope of freedom and of heaven. But universal salvation will find no foothold in Scripture.
J. C. Ryle

Once let the old doctrine about hell be

overthrown and the whole system of Christianity is unsettled, unscrewed, unpinned and thrown into disorder.
J. C. Ryle

The darkness endured by our blessed Surety on the cross was only for three hours. The chains of darkness which shall bind all who reject his atonement and die in sin shall be for evermore. *J. C. Ryle*

The saddest road to hell is that which runs under the pulpit, past the Bible and through the midst of warnings and invitations. *J. C. Ryle*

There are two ways of going to hell; one is to walk into it with your eyes open . . . the other is to go down by the steps of little sins. *J. C. Ryle*

Suffering that is penal can never come to an end, because guilt is the reason for its infliction, and guilt once incurred never ceases to be ... One sin makes guilt, and guilt makes hell. *W. G. T. Shedd*

The existing demoralization in society and politics ... is due, mainly, to a disbelief of the doctrine of endless punishment.
W. G. T. Shedd

I do not know if there is a more dreadful word in the English language than that word 'lost'. *C. H. Spurgeon*

I greatly fear that the denial of the eternity of future punishment is one wave of an incoming sea of infidelity.
C. H. Spurgeon

In hell there is no hope. They have not even the hope of dying. *C. H. Spurgeon*

It will be hell to a man to have his own voluntary choice confirmed, and made unchangeable. *C. H. Spurgeon*

The wrath of God does not end with death. *C. H. Spurgeon*

Think lightly of hell and you will think lightly of the cross. *C. H. Spurgeon*

Hell is the highest reward that the devil can offer you for being a servant of his.
Billy Sunday

If there is no hell, a good many preachers are obtaining money under false pretences! *Billy Sunday*

If you in any way abate the doctrine of hell it will abate your zeal. *R. A. Torrey*

Hell will be seen to be hell all the way through. *A. W. Tozer*

Hell will be the ugliest place in all of creation. *A. W. Tozer*

Hell is an abiding place, but no resting place. *Thomas Watson*

Hell is full of hard hearts; there is not one soft heart there. *Thomas Watson*

Many a man goes to hell in the sweat of his brow. *Thomas Watson*

The breath of the Lord kindles the infernal lake, and where shall we have engines or buckets to quench that fire?
Thomas Watson

The wicked in hell shall be always dying but never dead. *Thomas Watson*

There are no agnostics in hell.
Geoffrey B. Wilson

Hell is the penitentiary of the moral universe. *J. S. Wrightnour*

HERESY

They that will give God a new tongue shall feel his old hand.   *Thomas Adams*

An error is the more dangerous the more truth it contains.   *Henri Amiel*

An error no wider than a hair will lead a hundred miles away from the goal. *Anon.*

The most dangerous of all false doctrine is the one seasoned with a little truth.
Anon.

The wind of error does not blow long in the same direction.   *Anon.*

Heresy flourishes when those who know the truth fail to maintain it resolutely.
Brian Beevers

Almost all the corruptions of doctrines flow from the pride of men. *John Calvin*

When a half truth is presented as a whole truth it becomes an untruth.
Walter J. Chantry

The passion for ruling is the mother of heresy.   *Chrysostom*

Unless your vision of Christ is as large as it can possibly be, you will always be in danger of heresy.   *Donald English*

False doctrine always uses a plausible gimmick to get its foot in the door — and it is always the back door!
Vance Havner

When Bible believers take a stand against false doctrine, they are accused of 'rocking the boat'. It is better that belief should rock the boat than that unbelief should wreck the boat.   *Vance Havner*

Heresy is the school of pride.
George Herbert

One error is a bridge to another.
William Jenkyn

Whom God intends to destroy, he gives them leave to play with Scripture.
Martin Luther

Error, preached as truth, has contributed to the delusion of multitudes who are lost.
Iain H. Murray

It is the oldest stratagem of Satan to disfigure the truth by misrepresentation.
Iain H. Murray

Truth lives in the cellar, error on the door-step.   *Austin O'Malley*

We constantly flirt with heresies that are not new but old.   *Roger C. Palms*

Error does not advertise its coming to the soul. It sidles in, and breeds inward and secret infidelity for long before it becomes evident to others. *James Philip*

I believe that the root of almost every schism and heresy from which the Christian church has ever suffered has been the effort of men to earn, rather than to receive, their salvation.   *John Ruskin*

Ignorance of the Scriptures is the root of all error.   *J. C. Ryle*

There is no mercy in keeping back from men the subject of hell.   *J. C. Ryle*

To commit theological error is to commit sin.   *R. C. Sproul*

Fellowship with known and vital error is participation in sin.   *C. H. Spurgeon*

The faculty of inventing false doctrine is ruinous. *C. H. Spurgeon*

Heresy is picking out what you want to believe and rejecting, or at least ignoring, the rest. *A. W. Tozer*

No heresy is ever entertained with impunity. *A. W. Tozer*

The human heart is heretical by nature. *A. W. Tozer*

Heresy is the leprosy of the head. *John Trapp*

Orthodoxy is my doxy; heterodoxy is another man's doxy. *William Warburton*

A man may go to hell as well for heresy as for adultery. *Thomas Watson*

Error damns as well as vice. *Thomas Watson*

Serious piety is the best defence against wicked doctrine. *Thomas Watson*

Anyone who burdens the church with false teaching shall not escape being burdened with a crushing judgement. *Geoffrey B. Wilson*

A truncated Christology forms the foundation of all false teaching. *Geoffrey B. Wilson*

False teaching not only poisons the mind, but also demoralizes the life. *Geoffrey B. Wilson*

HISTORY

History teaches us the mistakes we are going to make. *Anon.*

The biblical view of history is not cyclical, it is linear. It has a definite beginning, with God's creation of the universe, and it is building to a final climax. *John Benton*

What history does is to uncover man's universal sin. *Herbert Butterfield*

The farther back you look, the farther forward you are likely to see. *Winston Churchill*

To test the present you must appeal to history. *Winston Churchill*

Human history is the sad result of everyone looking out for himself. *Julio Cortazar*

What are all histories but God manifesting himself? *Oliver Cromwell*

The history of the world should purport to be the annals of the government of the great King. *J. H. Merle d'Aubigné*

History is little more than the crimes, follies and misfortunes of mankind. *Edward Gibbon*

History as men see it is a Punch and Judy show manipulated by unseen hands behind the scenes ... but God will dispose of both manikins and manipulators one of these days. *Vance Havner*

History is the long story of man trying to be God. *Vance Havner*

If you know how to read between the lines of secular history, you will see that God is writing another history, and some people who are very important in secular history are only incidental in God's history. If they have any importance at all, it depends on how they relate to Jesus Christ. *Vance Havner*

We learn from history that we do not learn from history. *Georg Hegal*

History is just the accumulated stories of how God is working in the lives of all the individual people on earth. *John Hercus*

The whole course of history is represented (in Scripture) as the development of the plan and purpose of God; and yet human history is little else than the history of sin. *Charles Hodge*

God is in the facts of history as truly as he is in the march of the seasons, the revolutions of the planets, or the architecture of the worlds. *John Lanahan*

History is a story written by the finger of God. *C. S. Lewis*

History can be understood only in terms of God's kingdom.
D. Martyn Lloyd-Jones

The key to the history of the world is the kingdom of God. *D. Martyn Lloyd-Jones*

Consciousness of the past alone makes us understand the present. *Herbert Luethy*

God is not just the Lord of creation, the one who starts everything going in accordance with a grand plan. He is also the Lord of history. History is 'his story', and in some unfathomable combination of divine sovereignty and human will, God is the master chess player moving his chessmen forward and back in anticipation of the final moment when all that opposes him will be checkmated and his reign will be universally recognized.
Peter C. Moore

Pondering the past is often the best way of providing for the future.
Thomas V. Moore

God orders history for the good of the elect. *Robert A. Morey*

The whole of Bible history exists to tell us that history turns upon the hinge of sinfulness, not upon the hinge of polities.
J. A. Motyer

The history of man is his attempt to escape his own corruption. *Daniel Mullis*

Jesus Christ is the one to whom the whole alphabet of history points.
Lesslie Newbigin

Learning from history and basking in nostalgia are two different things.
Roger C. Palms

Blessed is he who sees God in history and in nature as well as in revelation.
William S. Plumer

All history is incomprehensible without Christ. *Ernest Renan*

No history ought to receive so much of our attention as the past and future history of the church of Christ. The rise and fall of worldly empires are events of comparatively small importance in the sight of God. *J. C. Ryle*

Those who cannot remember the past are condemned to repeat it.
George Santanaya

The purpose of the historian is not to construct a history from preconceived notions and to adjust it to his own liking, but to reproduce it from the best evidence and to let it speak for itself. *Philip Schaff*

The hinge of history is on the door of a Bethlehem stable.   *Ralph W. Sockman*

We must never set theology and history over against each other, since Scripture refuses to do so.   *John R. W. Stott*

Basic to the biblical view is that all events are God's events.   *David Wilkinson*

HOLINESS — Definition
(See also: Christlikeness; Godliness)

Holiness is that perspective through which we must see God.   *Thomas Adams*

Holiness is the habit of being of one mind with God.   *Anon.*

Sanctification is that gracious and continuous operation of the Holy Spirit by which he delivers the justified sinner from the pollution of sin, renews his whole nature in the image of God, and enables him to perform good works.
Louis Berkhof

Do you know what holiness is? It is pure love.   *Samuel Logan Brengle*

God's will is the rule of righteousness, and his righteousness is the rule of his will.   *Elisha Coles*

A holy life is not an ascetic, or gloomy, or solitary life, but a life regulated by divine truth and faithful in Christian duty. It is living above the world while we are still in it.   *Tryon Edwards*

Holiness is an unselfing of ourselves.
Frederick W. Faber

What health is to the heart, that holiness is to the soul.   *John Flavel*

A holy life is the life of God.
William Gurnall

Holiness in us is the copy or transcript of the holiness that is in Christ. *Philip Henry*

Holiness is the symmetry of the soul.
Philip Henry

Righteousness is obedience to law, observance of duty and fidelity to conscience.   *J. P. Hopps*

Holiness is not an experience you have; holiness is keeping the law of God.
D. Martyn Lloyd-Jones

We in Christ = justification; Christ in us = sanctification.   *Martin Luther*

Holiness is not an optional extra to the process of creation, but rather the whole point of it.   *Donald Nicholl*

To know what holiness is you have to be holy.   *Donald Nicholl*

If regeneration is a work of new creation, sanctification is a work of new formation. If regeneration is a new birth, sanctification is a new growth.   *J. I. Packer*

Sanctification is the progressive restoration of a man's rationality so that he becomes a man.   *J. I. Packer*

Sanctification is a process by which, because we love God, we become like him.   *Joseph Pipa*

Holiness in man is the image of God's.
E. G. Robinson

Wrong views about holiness are generally traceable to wrong views about human corruption.   *J. C. Ryle*

Holiness is the visible side of salvation.
C. H. Spurgeon

What is holiness except Christlikeness?
John R. W. Stott

HOLINESS — Essence

Show me someone who hates sin and I will show you someone who loves holiness. *Richard Alderson*

Holiness does not produce cranks.
John Benton

Morally, a Christian is called to holiness; dynamically, he is called to service.
John Blanchard

Never be tempted to think that you can achieve in a moment's crisis what God has said can only happen by a lifetime's process. *John Blanchard*

Holiness is a constellation of graces.
Thomas Boston

A holy heart is always attended with a holy life. *Thomas Brooks*

A holy person looks upon his sins as the crucifiers of his Saviour. *Thomas Brooks*

A man that is really holy will be holy among the holy and he will be holy among the unholy. *Thomas Brooks*

The most holy men are always the most humble men. *Thomas Brooks*

True holiness makes a man divinely covetous. *Thomas Brooks*

Holiness does not consist in mystic speculations, enthusiastic fervours, or uncommanded austerities; it consists in thinking as God thinks and willing as God wills. *John Brown*

Holiness is not a merit by which we can attain communion with God, but a gift of Christ which enables us to cling to him and to follow him. *John Calvin*

Perfect holiness is the *aim* of the saints on earth and it is the *reward* of the saints in heaven. *Joseph Caryl*

The holiest person is ... one who is most conscious of what sin is.
Oswald Chambers

Holiness can no more approve of sin than it can commit it. *Stephen Charnock*

Holiness is much more than a set of rules against sin. Holiness must be seen as the opposite of sin. *Charles Colson*

Holiness is the only possible response to God's grace. *Charles Colson*

Holy living is loving God.
Charles Colson

Holiness has love for its essence, humility for its clothing, the good of others as its employment, and the honour of God as its end. *Nathanael Emmons*

Holiness depends less upon what we do than how we do it. *Frederick W. Faber*

Holiness can only be attained by living by the revealed Word of God.
C. Tom Fincher

What health is to the heart, that holiness is to the soul. *John Flavel*

There is no true holiness without humility. *Thomas Fuller*

The secret of Christian holiness is heart occupation with Christ himself.
H. A. Ironside

My mind is the central control area of my personality, and sanctification is the mind coming more and more under the Holy Spirit's control. *David Jackman*

There is nothing destroyed by sanctification but that which would destroy us.
William Jenkyn

How little people know who think that holiness is dull. *C. S. Lewis*

The essence of true holiness is conformity to the nature and will of God.
Samuel Lucas

To be holy is to be like Jesus.
C. H. McIntosh

Holiness is not freedom from temptation, but power to overcome temptation.
G. Campbell Morgan

The Christian life is not applied like make-up to the outside of our personalities, but is an outgrowth from an inner transformation. *J. A. Motyer*

The life of sanctification is the life of obedience. *J. A. Motyer*

Holiness is exemplified in obedience to the commandments of God. *John Murray*

Sanctification is not mystical passivity, as our use of the slogan 'let go and let God' has too often implied, but it is active moral effort energized by prayerful and expectant faith. *J. I. Packer*

The greatest wisdom on this earth is holiness. *William S. Plumer*

Unless grace has radically altered my behaviour it cannot possibly alter my destiny. *Alan Redpath*

The trouble with too many Christians is that they are more concerned about their doctrine of holiness than they are about being clothed with the beauty of Christ's purity. *Paul S. Rees*

Sanctification is the immediate work of the Spirit of God upon our whole nature, by which we are being changed into Christ's likeness. *Ernest C. Reisinger*

We must aim to have a Christianity which, like the sap of a tree, runs through twig and leaf of our character and sanctifies all. *J. C. Ryle*

Holiness is persevering obedience.
C. H. Spurgeon

The secret of holy living is in the mind.
John R. W. Stott

There is a beauty in holiness as well as a beauty of holiness. *George Swinnock*

The first rule in holy living is 'Don't lie to God'. *Jeremy Taylor*

I am the little servant of an illustrious Master. *J. Hudson Taylor*

Sanctification is progressive; if it does not grow it is because it does not live.
Thomas Watson

HOLINESS — God's Work

God does not expect any good in us but what he has wrought in us. *Anon.*

He who gave his image to us must of necessity wish to see his image in us.
Anon.

303

Holiness is offered to every believer.
Donald Grey Barnhouse

Holiness is to be measured not in terms of man's ecstasy but of God's energy.
John Blanchard

I am one of those who do not think that the beauty of holiness consists in beauty but rather in holiness, in that holiness which is God and which comes from God and in which alone there is strength to live and work and pray. *John R. De Witt*

Whatever good we do, God does in us.
A. R. Fausset

So in love is Christ with holiness that he will buy it with his blood for us.
John Flavel

A holiness which is the device of our heart is not the holiness after God's heart.
William Gurnall

As God makes use of all the seasons of the year for the harvest – the frost and cold of the winter, as well as the heat of the summer — so doth he, of fair and foul, pleasing and unpleasing providences, for promoting holiness. *William Gurnall*

God loves purity so well that he had rather see a hole than a spot in his child's garments. *William Gurnall*

This is the great design of God, to have his people holy. It runs like a silver thread through all God's other designs.
William Gurnall

God saved us to make us holy, not happy. Some experiences may not contribute to our happiness, but all can be made to contribute to our holiness. *Vance Havner*

What God requires of us he himself works in us, or it is not done. *Matthew Henry*

God useth many a moving persuasion to draw us to holiness, not a hint to encourage us to sin. *Thomas Manton*

I often pray, 'Lord make me as holy as a pardoned sinner can be.'
Robert Murray M'Cheyne

Holiness is not something we do or attain; it is the communication of the divine life, the inbreathing of the divine nature; the power of the divine presence resting on us. *Andrew Murray*

God works in us and with us, not against us or without us. *John Owen*

We may lay it down as an elemental principle of religion that no large growth in holiness was ever gained by one who did not take time to be often long alone with God. *Austin Phelps*

Christ comes with a blessing in each hand; forgiveness in one, holiness in the other. *A. W. Pink*

The regenerate have a spiritual nature within that fits them for holy action, otherwise there would be no difference between them and the unregenerate.
A. W. Pink

There is no way that we by ourselves can generate sanctification. Our sanctification is Christ. There is no way we can be good. Our goodness is Christ. There is no way we can be holy. Our holiness is Christ.
A. W. Pink

Holiness is not only commanded by God's law, but it is made available to men by his grace. *Kenneth F. W. Prior*

Sanctification, in Scripture, is always something that God does.
Kenneth F. W. Prior

The greatest miracle that God can do today is to take an unholy man out of an unholy world, and make that man holy and put him back into that unholy world and keep him holy in it.
Leonard Ravenhill

Holiness is not the way to Christ; Christ is the way to holiness.   *Adrian Rogers*

Holiness is not the laborious acquisition of virtue from without, but the expression of the Christ-life from within.
J. W. C. Wand

HOLINESS — Importance

Christ comes with a blessing in each hand — forgiveness in one and holiness other; and never gives either to any who will not take both.   *Anon.*

Holiness is the preparation for the presence of God.   *Anon.*

Live so that the preacher can tell the truth at your funeral.   *Anon.*

Holiness is to be the touchstone of the Christian life.   *Donald Grey Barnhouse*

No subject which ever engages the thought of Christian believers can be more sacredly commanding than that of personal holiness.   *J. Sidlow Baxter*

Regeneration is the fountain; sanctification is the river.   *J. Sidlow Baxter*

A holy God calls his people to holy living. It is inconceivable that it should be otherwise.   *John Blanchard*

An unholy Christian is a contradiction of everything the Bible teaches.
John Blanchard

God is much more concerned about our holiness than our happiness, much more about our character than our comfort.
John Blanchard

Holiness is to be the driving ambition of the Christian.   *John Blanchard*

Without holiness there is no wholeness, no spiritual happiness — and no heaven.
John Blanchard

Prayer and a holy life are one. They mutually act and react. Neither can survive alone. The absence of the one is the absence of the other.   *E. M. Bounds*

There was nothing of any importance to me but holiness of heart and life and the conversion of the Indians to God.
David Brainerd

Assurance makes most for your comfort, but holiness makes most for God's honour.   *Thomas Brooks*

A baptism of holiness, a demonstration of godly living, is the crying need of our day.   *Duncan Campbell*

The destined end of man is not happiness, nor health, but holiness. God's one aim is the production of saints.
Oswald Chambers

Holiness is the everyday business of every Christian.   *Charles Colson*

There is no detour to holiness. Jesus came to the resurrection through the cross, not around it.   *Leighton Ford*

A sanctified heart is better than a silver tongue. *Thomas Goodwin*

God saved us to make us holy, not happy. Some experiences may not contribute to our happiness, but all can be made to contribute to our holiness. *Vance Havner*

'Be ye holy' is the great and fundamental law of our religion. *Matthew Henry*

The beauty of holiness needs no paint. *Matthew Henry*

Holiness is the distinguishing mark of the Christian. *Michael Howell*

Holiness is necessary to present peace and future glory. *William Jay*

Christianity has the only true morality; no other religion conduces to true holiness. *R. B. Kuiper*

Fully aware that he will not reach the goal of moral perfection in this life, the Christian must yet press on with might and main towards that very mark. *R. B. Kuiper*

A redeemed flock should live in redemption's pastures. *Henry Law*

Christianity is a universal holiness in every part of life. *William Law*

If you do not desire to be holy I do not see that you have any right to think that you are a Christian. *D. Martyn Lloyd-Jones*

The New Testament way of handling sanctification is never an appeal, it is a command. *D. Martyn Lloyd-Jones*

A holy life and a bounteous heart are ornaments to the gospel. *Thomas Manton*

Holiness is a Christian's ornament, and peaceableness is the ornament of holiness. *Thomas Manton*

I feel there are two things it is impossible to desire with sufficient ardour — personal holiness and the honour of Christ in the salvation of souls. *Robert Murray M'Cheyne*

There is no argument like a holy life. *Robert Murray M'Cheyne*

A holy life will produce the deepest impression. Lighthouses blow no horns; they only shine. *D. L. Moody*

'Holiness' is the most intimately divine word the Bible possesses. *J. A. Motyer*

All through the New Testament, when God's work in human lives is spoken of, the ethical takes priority over the charismatic. *J. I. Packer*

Scriptural holiness is in fact the most positive, potent and often passionate quality of life that is ever seen. *J. I. Packer*

The New Testament does not say that Christians must lead holy lives in order to become saints; instead, it tells Christians that, because they are saints, they must henceforth lead holy lives! *J. I. Packer*

The serene beauty of a holy life is the most powerful influence in the world next to the power of God. *Blaise Pascal*

Everything in Scripture has in view the promotion of holiness. *A. W. Pink*

The highway of holiness is the only path which leads to heaven. *A. W. Pink*

Nothing can set aside the evidence of a holy life. It is better than a revelation from heaven. *William S. Plumer*

Sanctification is the main course of the Christian life. *Joseph Pipa*

Sanctification will not get us to heaven but we cannot go to heaven without it. *Joseph Pipa*

True holiness flows from the soundness of a man's doctrine. *Robert A. Richey*

God has linked together holiness and happiness; and what God has joined together we must not think to put asunder. *J. C. Ryle*

The names and number of the elect are a secret thing, no doubt … But if there is one thing clearly and plainly laid down about election, it is this — that elect men and women may be known and distinguished by holy lives. *J. C. Ryle*

We must be saints on earth if ever we mean to be saints in heaven. *J. C. Ryle*

It is better to be innocent than penitent. *William Secker*

Those that look to be happy must first look to be holy. *Richard Sibbes*

Holiness is better than morality. It goes beyond it. Holiness affects the heart. Holiness respects the motive. Holiness regards the whole nature of man. *C. H. Spurgeon*

Holiness is the best sabbath dress — but it is equally suitable for everyday wear. *C. H. Spurgeon*

Only sanctified souls are satisfied souls. *C. H. Spurgeon*

Regeneration is a change which is known and felt: known by works of holiness and felt by a gracious experience. *C. H. Spurgeon*

The gift which I feel I should crave beyond every other boon is holiness, pure and immaculate holiness. *C. H. Spurgeon*

The serene, silent beauty of a holy life is the most powerful influence in the world, next to the might of the Spirit of God. *C. H. Spurgeon*

Heaven must be in thee before thou canst be in heaven. *George Swinnock*

The best theology is rather a divine life than a divine knowledge. *Jeremy Taylor*

The true Christian ideal is not to be happy but to be holy. *A. W. Tozer*

We can never know that we are elected of God to eternal life except by manifesting in our lives the fruits of election. *Benjamin B. Warfield*

The important point is where you are *today* in terms of holiness. *George Verwer*

HOLINESS — and Justification
(See also: Faith — and Deeds; Good Deeds)

The God who declares us righteous in Christ by imputation will make us holy by imparting that righteousness. *Richard Alderson*

Any attempt to make *justification* dependent upon sanctification is to rob grace of its freeness and to add 'works' to saving grace. *Donald Grey Barnhouse*

Justification never results from good

works; justification always results in good works. *John Blanchard*

Any Christian who is not earnestly pursuing holiness in every aspect of his life is flying in the face of God's purpose in saving him. *Jerry Bridges*

Justification and sanctification are inseparable companions; distinguished they *must* be, *but* divided they can never be. *Thomas Brooks*

While our works are naught as a ground of merit for justification, they are all-important as evidences that we are justified. *R. L. Dabney*

God did not save us to make us happy but to make us holy. *Vance Havner*

Any man who thinks that he is a Christian, and that he has accepted Christ for justification, when he did not at the same time accept him for sanctification, is miserably deluded in that very experience. *A. A. Hodge*

We must first be made good before we can do good; we must first be made just before our works can please God — for when we are justified by faith in Christ, then come good works. *Hugh Latimer*

Be as holy as you can, as if there were no gospel to save you. Yet ... believe in Christ as if there were no law at all to condemn you. *Thomas Lye*

If Christ justifies you he will sanctify you! He will not save you and leave you in your sins. *Robert Murray M'Cheyne*

According to Scripture it is quite impossible to be justified by faith and not to experience the commencement of true sanctification, because the spiritual life communicated by the Spirit in the act of regeneration (which introduces the new power to believe) is morally akin to the character of God and contains within it the germ of all holiness. *Iain H. Murray*

While justification and sanctification are to be sharply distinguished they must not be divorced. *A. W. Pink*

It is as dangerous to rest on a justification unattended with holiness as it is to rest on a justification that has works for its basis. *William S. Plumer*

Justification and sanctification are distinguishable but not separable.
William S. Plumer

I fear it is sometimes forgotten that God has married together justification and sanctification. *J. C. Ryle*

There are none justified who are not sanctified and there are none sanctified who are not justified. *J. C. Ryle*

By grace we are what we are in justification, and work what we work in sanctification. *Richard Sibbes*

In the court of justification merits are nothing worth, insufficient; but in the court of sanctification, they are jewels and ornaments. *Richard Sibbes*

There is no time lapse between our justification and the beginning of our sanctification ... As soon as we truly believe, at that very instant, the process of becoming pure and holy is under way, and its future completion is certain. *R. C. Sproul*

Christ promises to save his people from their sins, not in their sins. *C. H. Spurgeon*

When God declares a man righteous he instantly sets about to make him righteous.   *A. W. Tozer*

Sanctification is so involved in justification that the justification can never be real unless it be followed by sanctification.
Benjamin B. Warfield

Grace can be no more concealed than fire.
Thomas Watson

If God should justify a people and not sanctify them, he would justify a people whom he could not glorify.
Thomas Watson

Purity is the end of our election.
Thomas Watson

Those who are unwilling to cleanse themselves from every stain of sin only show that they have not been cleansed from the guilt of sin. The unsanctified are the unjustified.   *Geoffrey B. Wilson*

HOLINESS — Man's Part

The renewed heart has within it the desire to glorify God by presenting a moral life.   *Donald Grey Barnhouse*

We do not strive to be holy in order to be saved; that is legalism. We do not strive to be holy in order to prove we are saved; that is bondage. We seek to be holy because that is God's purpose in saving us and because we have come to be thankful to him.   *John Benton*

All we have to do is to be holy; and we are to be holy in all we do.
John Blanchard

The best way to prepare for tomorrow is to seek God's kingdom and righteousness first today.   *John Blanchard*

The holiness which can only be accomplished by the power of God will only be accomplished by the care of man.
John Blanchard

We do not suddenly become holy in one moment by making Christ Lord; we are to be holy moment by moment because he is Lord.   *John Blanchard*

The way of holiness that leads to happiness is a narrow way; there is but just room enough for a holy God and a holy soul to walk together.   *Thomas Brooks*

Men make more haste to get their afflictions removed than their hearts sanctified; but this is not the work God looks for.
Thomas Case

I went on with my eager pursuit after more holiness and conformity to Christ. The heaven I desired was a heaven of holiness.   *Jonathan Edwards*

We ought to behave ourselves every day as though we had no dependence on any other.   *Jonathan Edwards*

There is no detour to holiness. Jesus came to the resurrection through the cross, not around it.   *Leighton Ford*

There is no true holiness without humility.   *Thomas Fuller*

Righteousness is a commitment to a relationship.   *Don Garlington*

The old mystics tried to make themselves holier by hiding from society; but living in a hole does not make you holier!
Vance Havner

It is not enough to wish to be good unless we *hunger* after it.   *Jerome*

Holiness is not something to be received in a meeting; it is a life to be lived and to be lived in detail. *D. Martyn Lloyd-Jones*

The trouble with much holiness teaching is that it leaves out the Sermon on the Mount and asks us to experience sanctification. That is not the biblical method.
D. Martyn Lloyd-Jones

If you cannot make the world completely pious, then do what you can.
Martin Luther

It is a great deal better to live a holy life than to talk about it. Lighthouses do not ring bells and fire cannon to call attention to their shining — they just shine!
D. L Moody

The sanctifying grace of God is appropriated by the obedient and unrelenting activity of the regenerate man.
J. A. Motyer

Let not men deceive themselves. Sanctification is a qualification indispensably necessary unto those who will be under the conduct of the Lord Christ unto salvation. He leads none to heaven but whom he sanctifies on earth. *John Owen*

Holiness is no more by faith without effort than it is by effort without faith.
J. I. Packer

To live in the light of eternity and the coming day of God is the surest way of promoting the work of sanctification in our hearts. *James Philip*

I am convinced that the first step towards attaining a higher standard of holiness is to realize more fully the amazing sinfulness of sin. *J. C. Ryle*

Sanctification is always a progressive work. *J. C. Ryle*

There is no holiness without a warfare.
J. C. Ryle

The grace of God will do very little for us if we resolve to do nothing for ourselves. God calls us to co-operate with him in the perfecting of character.
W. Graham Scroggie

Brethren, we can be much more holy than we are. Let us attain first to that holiness about which there is no controversy.
C. H. Spurgeon

The secret of clean living is clear thinking. *John R. W. Stott*

There is no short cut to sanctity.
A. W. Tozer

So let our lips and lives express
The holy gospel we profess;
So let our works and virtues shine,
To prove the doctrine all divine.
Isaac Watts

HOLINESS — Motive

The thought of the great nobility God has conferred upon us ought to whet our desire for holiness and purity. *John Calvin*

The ethical demand for holy living is inseparable from what is freely given in the gospel. *Geoffrey B. Wilson*

HOLINESS — Rewards

Holiness in the seed shall have happiness in the harvest. *Thomas Adams*

Holiness is its own reward.
Thomas Brooks

Man's holiness is now his greatest happiness, and in heaven man's greatest happiness will be his perfect holiness.
Thomas Brooks

When our holiness is perfect, our happiness shall be perfect; and if this were attainable on earth, there would be but little reason for men to long to be in heaven.   *Thomas Brooks*

The holy person is the only contented man in the world.   *William Gurnall*

Nothing can make a man truly great but being truly good and partaking of God's holiness.   *Matthew Henry*

It is the tendency of righteousness to produce blessings, as it is the tendency of evil to produce misery. *Charles Hodge*

When there shall be universal holiness there shall also be universal happiness.
Thomas V. Moore

Many of us would pursue holiness with far greater zeal and eagerness if we were convinced that the way of holiness is the way of life and peace. And that is precisely what it is; there is life and peace no other way.   *J. I. Packer*

The Christian who has the smile of God needs no status symbols.
Leonard Ravenhill

The way of uprightness is the way of heavenly wealth.   *C. H. Spurgeon*

Sow holiness and reap happiness.
George Swinnock

We are becoming what we shall be eternally.   *Samuel E. Waldron*

The Lord has two heavens to dwell in,
and the holy heart is one of them.
Thomas Watson

HOLY SPIRIT
(See also: Godhead)

Before Pentecost, the disciples were like rabbits; after Pentecost, they were like ferrets!   *Anon.*

No one may ask a believer whether he has been baptized with the Spirit. The very fact that a man is in the body of Christ demonstrates that he has been baptized with the Spirit, for there is no other way of entering the body.
Donald Grey Barnhouse

A Christian may not always be conscious of the Holy Spirit's presence, but he would not even be a Christian in his absence.   *John Blanchard*

Fullness of the Spirit is not a press-button panacea; it is the growing experience of those who hunger and thirst after righteousness.   *John Blanchard*

It is the Spirit's ministry to bring the sinner to the Saviour and to make the sinner like the Saviour. *John Blanchard*

The fruit of the Spirit is active, not just academic.   *John Blanchard*

The Holy Ghost does not flow through methods but through men. He does not come on machinery but on men. He does not anoint plans but men — men of prayer.   *E. M. Bounds*

He never sins against the Holy Ghost that fears he has sinned against the Holy Ghost.   *William Bridge*

The first work of the Spirit is to make a man look upon sin as an enemy and to

Holy Spirit

deal with sin as an enemy, to hate it as an enemy, to loathe it as an enemy and to arm against it as an enemy. *Thomas Brooks*

The Spirit never loosens where the Word binds; the Spirit never justifies where the Word condemns; the Spirit never approves where the Word disapproves; the Spirit never blesses where the Word curses. *Thomas Brooks*

What the Spirit does is exactly what the Lord does; the Spirit's work is not an additional or special work *beyond* the Lord's; the Spirit is the Lord at work.
F. D. Bruner

Seamen cannot create the wind, but they can hoist their sails to welcome it; neither can we create the breath of the Spirit, but are we to miss it when it comes through failure to keep our sails unfurled?
John Bunyan

As the soul does not live idly in the body, but gives motion and vigour to every member and part, so the Spirit of God cannot dwell in us without manifesting himself by the outward effects.
John Calvin

God does not bestow his Spirit on his people in order to set aside the use of his Word, but rather to render it fruitful.
John Calvin

The gift of the Spirit was a fruit of the resurrection of Christ. *John Calvin*

The Spirit of God, from whom the doctrine of the gospel comes, is its only true interpreter. *John Calvin*

To be filled with the Spirit is to have the Spirit fulfilling in us all that God intended him to do when he placed him there.
Lewis Sperry Chafer

There is one thing we cannot imitate; we cannot imitate being full of the Holy Ghost. *Oswald Chambers*

A great part of your prayer work should be imploring the Almighty for a greater measure of his Spirit. *Walter Chantry*

The gospel is the ground of the believer's assurance, while the Holy Spirit is its cause. *J. C. P. Cockerton*

Spirit of God, descend upon my heart;
Wean it from earth; through all its pulses move;
Stoop to my weakness, mighty as thou art,
And make me love thee as I ought to love.
George Croly

The fruit of the Spirit is not excitement or orthodoxy: it is *character.*
G. B. Duncan

The Spirit-filled life is no mystery revealed to a select few, no goal difficult of attainment. To trust and to obey is the substance of the whole matter.
Victor Edman

The Christian's birthright is the power of the Holy Ghost. *Lionel Fletcher*

Unless there is that which is above us, we shall soon yield to that which is about us. *P. T. Forsyth*

We may take it as a rule of the Christian life that the more we are filled with the Holy Spirit, the more we shall glorify the Lord Jesus. *Frank Gabelein*

Before Pentecost the disciples found it hard to do easy things; after Pentecost they found it easy to do hard things.
A. J. Gordon

312

The Holy Spirit is the heavenly Lover's engagement ring given to us.
Michael Green

One might as well try to catch sunbeams with a fishhook as to lay hold of God's revelation unassisted by God's Holy Spirit. *Vance Havner*

Paul speaks of being absent from the body and present with the Lord. But being present in the body does not mean being absent from the Lord; for he lives in all who believe, and these bodies are the temples of the Holy Spirit. *Vance Havner*

Satan has scored a point in making us so afraid of extremism about the Holy Spirit — which abounds indeed — that we may miss the true in our fear of the false. We can be so wary of getting out on a limb that we never go up the tree!
Vance Havner

All the Holy Spirit's influences are heaven begun, glory in the seed and bud.
Matthew Henry

The Spirit of God knows the things of God because he is one with God.
Matthew Henry

The Holy Spirit is the only authenticator of Christianity. *Arthur P. Johnson*

The Holy Spirit may be had for the asking. *R. B. Kuiper*

If it were possible to put the Holy Spirit into a textbook of pharmacology I would put him under the stimulants, for that is where he belongs. *D. Martyn Lloyd-Jones*

We could not pray at all were it not for the Holy Spirit. *D. Martyn Lloyd-Jones*

Come, Holy Spirit, God and Lord!
Be all thy graces now out-poured
On the believer's mind and soul,
To strengthen, save, and make us whole.
Martin Luther

Proper understanding of the Scriptures comes only through the Holy Spirit.
Martin Luther

He who has the Holy Spirit in his heart and the Scriptures in his hands has all he needs. *Alexander MacLaren*

The Spirit is the source of all our natural gifts. *Donald MacLeod*

The work of the Holy Spirit is as needful as that of Christ. *William MacLeod*

God's mind is revealed in Scripture, but we can see nothing without the spectacles of the Holy Ghost. *Thomas Manton*

Remember, we may grieve the Spirit as truly by not joyfully acknowledging his wonders, as by not praying to him.
Robert Murray M'Cheyne

God commands us to be filled with the Spirit, and if we are not filled it is because we are living beneath our privileges. *D. L. Moody*

There is not a better evangelist in the world than the Holy Spirit. *D. L. Moody*

If the Holy Spirit guides us at all, he will do it according to the Scriptures, and never contrary to them. *George Muller*

As all the Word of God is given by the Spirit of God, so each word must be interpreted to us by that same Spirit.
Andrew Murray

Scripture places no limitation upon the Spirit's work of glorifying Christ and extending his kingdom. *lain H. Murray*

If Pentecost is not repeated, neither is it retracted. This is the era of the Holy Spirit.
John Murray

(The Holy Spirit) has not promised to reveal new truths, but to enable us to understand what we read in the Bible; and if we venture beyond the pale of Scripture we are upon enchanted ground and exposed to all the illusions of imagination and enthusiasm. *John Newton*

The Holy Spirit is the great beautifier of souls. *John Owen*

With a perversity as pathetic as it is impoverishing we have become preoccupied today with the sporadic extraordinary and non-universal ministries of the Spirit to the neglect of the more general ones. *J. I. Packer*

The gracious operations of the Spirit were never designed to be a substitute for the Christian's discharge of duty. *A. W. Pink*

The mind of the unregenerate man can easily hear and mentally comprehend the facts set forth in the gospel, but only the Spirit of God can make the inward man experience the spiritual power of those truths. *John G. Reisinger*

We may depend upon it as a certainty that where there is no holy living there is no Holy Ghost. *J. C. Ryle*

The gift of the Holy Spirit made the apostles at home with the miraculous.
Adolph Schlatter

The Holy Spirit is always in, with and by the Word. *Philipp Spener*

A dead creed is of no use; we must have our creed baptized with the Holy Ghost.
C. H. Spurgeon

He is your credentials as a Christian: he is your life as a believer. *C. H. Spurgeon*

If you could pray the best prayer in the world without the Holy Spirit, God would have nothing to do with it. *C. H. Spurgeon*

The Spirit who convicts us is also the Spirit who consoles. *C. H. Spurgeon*

Unless the Spirit of God convinces the judgement and constrains the will, man has no heart to believe in Jesus unto eternal life. *C. H. Spurgeon*

Before Christ sent the church into the world, he sent the Spirit into the church. The same order must be observed today.
John R. W. Stott

The only way to arrive at faith in the Holy Spirit is along the road of self-despair.
John R. W. Stott

I do not believe in a repetition of Pentecost, but I do believe in a perpetuation of Pentecost — and there is a vast difference between the two. *A. W. Tozer*

The filling of the Holy Spirit brings a sharp separation between the believer and the world. *A. W. Tozer*

The gospel is light but only the Spirit can give sight. *A. W. Tozer*

The Holy Spirit is God's imperative of life. *A. W. Tozer*

The Spirit-filled life is not a special, deluxe edition of Christianity. It is part and parcel of the total plan of God for his people. *A. W. Tozer*

To possess a Spirit-indwelt mind is the Christian's privilege under grace.
A. W. Tozer

We have a Celebrity in our midst.
A. W. Tozer

Why should the children of a King
Go mourning all their days?
Great Comforter, descend, and bring
Some tokens of thy grace. *Isaac Watts*

Without the Spirit of God we can do nothing but add sin to sin. *John Wesley*

The Holy Spirit loves so to arrange men's circumstances that they are brought within the sphere of God's influence.
Maurice A. P. Wood

HOLY TRINITY — See Godhead

HOME — See Family Life; Marriage

HONESTY
(See also: Truth)

Honesty is a question of right and wrong, not a matter of policy. *Anon.*

No honest man ever repented of his honesty. *Anon.*

One thing you can give and still keep is your word. *Anon.*

There are no degrees of honesty. *Anon.*

No man is really honest; none of us is above the influence of gain. *Aristophanes*

For the Christian, honesty is not the best policy it is the only one. *John Blanchard*

Where is there dignity unless there is honesty? *Cicero*

Honesty is a fine jewel, but much out of fashion. *Thomas Fuller*

The only basis for real fellowship with God and man is to live out in the open with both. *Roy Hession*

Honesty is the first chapter in the book of wisdom. *Thomas Jefferson*

I have not observed men's honesty to increase with their riches. *Thomas Jefferson*

The more honesty a man has, the less he affects the air of a saint. *J. C. Lavater*

A straight line is shortest in morals as well as in geometry. *I. Rahel*

The life of an honest man is an oath.
Richard Sibbes

If faith does not make a man honest, it is not an honest faith *C. H. Spurgeon*

Honesty that can be trusted and respected is a very fragrant flower in the life of the Christian. *A. W. Tozer*

One's mere word should be as trustworthy as a signed agreement attested by legal witnesses. *Curtis Vaughan*

HOPE
(See also: Eternal Life; Eternal Security; Future; Heaven)

Hope is faith in the future tense.
Peter Anderson

Christ is our hope of glory and the glory of our hope. *Anon.*

Hope is grief's best music. *Anon.*

Our hope lies not in the man we put on

the moon, but in the man we put on the cross. *Don Basham*

'Hope' is biblical shorthand for unconditional certainty. *John Blanchard*

The Christian's hope of glory is not the fact that Christ is in him, but the Christ who is in him as a fact. *John Blanchard*

Bless God that there is *in* us resurrection life, and that there *awaits us* a resurrection morn! *J. J. Bonar*

A man full of hope will be full of action. *Thomas Brooks*

Hope can see heaven through the thickest clouds. *Thomas Brooks*

We are refugees from the sinking ship of this present world order, so soon to disappear; our hope is fixed in the eternal order, where the promises of God are made good to his people in perpetuity. *F. F. Bruce*

Hope is never ill when faith is well. *John Bunyan*

Hope is the foundation of patience. *John Calvin*

The word hope I take for faith; and indeed hope is nothing else but the constancy of faith. *John Calvin*

When hope animates us there is a vigour in the whole body. *John Calvin*

Hope means expectancy when things are otherwise hopeless. *G. K. Chesterton*

When you stop hoping you are on the vestibule of hell, for there is no hope there. *A. J. Cronin*

Hope is the only tie which keeps the heart from breaking. *Thomas Fuller*

If it were not for hopes, the heart would break. *Thomas Fuller*

Where there is no hope, there is no faith. *William Gouge*

Faith and a good conscience are hope's two wings. *William Gurnall*

Hope is the saint's covering wherein he wraps himself when he lays his body down to sleep in the grave. *William Gurnall*

The nearer to heaven in hopes, the farther from earth in desires. *William Gurnall*

The Christian's hope is like a rainbow. It is essentially one, yet made up of the most glorious colours which, though they merge together to form an exquisite whole, may each be admired individually. *Graham Heaps*

He that was our help from our birth ought to be our hope from our youth. *Matthew Henry*

Our fear must save our hope from swelling into presumption, and our hope must save our fear from sinking into despair. *Matthew Henry*

The ground of our hope is Christ in the world, but the evidence of our hope is Christ in the heart. *Matthew Henry*

Hoping is disciplined waiting. *Ernst Hoffmann*

Like faith, New Testament hope carries unconditional certainty within itself. *Ernst Hoffmann*

There can be no hope without faith in Christ, for hope is rooted in him alone. Faith without hope would, by itself, be empty and futile.   *Ernst Hoffmann*

Hope is the mother of patience.
William Jenkyn

My future is as bright as the promises of God.   *Adoniram Judson*

Hope teaches endurance and an eager anticipation of that which will become reality.   *Simon J. Kistemaker*

True faith is never found alone; it is accompanied by expectation. *C. S. Lewis*

The Christian hope is the hope of a time when even the possibility of our sinning will be over. It is not the hope then of a return to the condition of Adam before the Fall but the hope of an entrance into a far higher condition. *J. Gresham Machen*

Apart from the bright hope of the gospel everything would be meaningless.
Poul Madsen

What an excellent ground of hope and confidence we have when we reflect upon these three things in prayer — the Father's love, the Son's merit and the Spirit's power!   *Thomas Manton*

I am walking toward a bright light and the nearer I get the brighter it is.
D. L. Moody

The future belongs to those who belong to God. This is hope.   *W. T. Purkiser*

From Christ's death flow all our hopes.
J. C. Ryle

The nature of hope is to expect that which faith believes.   *Richard Sibbes*

The Christian hope is not a matter for tickling our minds but for changing our lives and for influencing society.
Stephen Travis

The world hopes for the best, but Jesus Christ offers the best hope.
John Wesley White

As God is the author of our salvation, so Christ is the embodiment of our hope.
Geoffrey B. Wilson

Our risen and glorified Lord is himself our hope, because his triumph over sin and death provides the objective pledge of our final redemption.
Geoffrey B. Wilson

HUMAN NATURE — See Man; Sinful Nature

HUMANISM

The strange thing is that while on the one hand man cries for help in his desperate sickness, on the other hand he refuses to consider even the possibility of a panacea beyond the range of his ability.
Akbar Abdul-Haqq

Christians need to recognize the solemn fact that humanism is not an ally in making the world a better place in which to live. It is a deadly enemy, for it is a religion without God and without hope in this world or the next. *L. Nelson Bell*

By ruling God out, humanism presents a picture in which the universe serves no purpose, humanity has no lasting meaning, ethics has no transcendent basis and morality has no fixed reference point.
John Blanchard

Human doctrines have no humbling power in them.   *Thomas Brooks*

Humanism

He builds too low who builds below the skies. *Richard Cecil*

Humanism can motivate neither morality nor life itself. *Gordon H. Clark*

The very first temptation that ever came to man and woman was to be a humanist. *Brian H. Edwards*

Humanism cannot, in any fair sense, apply to one who still believes in God. *Paul Kurtz*

The humanist counsellor cannot give the assurance of sin forgiven, guilt assuaged, life beyond death, a loving God, or a caring Jesus. *Gerald Larue*

Humanism does not solve problems; it creates them. *Josh McDowell*

Man operating by himself cannot set up true standards of justice or values in the world without God. If one man decides his view of human values is correct, while another man decides differently, who will decide between them? *Josh McDowell*

Everything that humanism teaches is a development or an application of the non-existence of God. *Robert A. Morey*

For the optimistic humanist, life has no objective value or purpose; it offers only subjective satisfaction. *J. P. Moreland*

So long as we cling to the idea that we live in a closed-world system, the most we can do is to adjust and rearrange existing forces. *J. B. Phillips*

The most a thoroughgoing humanist can do is to express his own opinion about what is 'good' and 'right' and there may be a hundred different views about that! *J. B. Phillips*

The weakness of nice people without faith is that they have nothing to offer the 'not nice people'. *J. B. Phillips*

Humanism is caught in an inescapable relativism. If we are ever to discover the clue to the meaning of reality, history, and life itself, it must come to us from beyond the flux of the human situation. *Clark H. Pinnock*

Humanism is not wrong in its cry for sociological healing, but humanism is not producing it. *Francis Schaeffer*

Humanism is the defiant denial of the God who is there, with man defiantly set up in the place of God as the measure of all things. *Francis Schaeffer*

Naturalistic humanism leads to a diminishing of man and eventually to a zeroing of man. *Francis Schaeffer*

The concept that the final reality is energy which has existed forever in some form and takes its present form by chance has totally destructive consequences for life. *Francis Schaeffer*

The humanist has both feet firmly planted in midair. *Francis Schaeffer*

When one accepts the secular world view that the final reality is only material or energy shaped by chance, then human life is lowered to the level of animal existence. *Francis Schaeffer*

Humanism logically leads to relativism. *Gary Scott Smith*

If secular humanism were widely accepted, would people enjoy a better life on earth? *Gary Scott Smith*

Humanism is fundamentally irrational. Once its values are stripped from their theological foundation they have no platform upon which to rest except sentiment.
R. C. Sproul

Humanism is intellectually untenable, but it is emotionally attractive ... because we want to believe that life has some meaning for us.
R. C. Sproul

Modern humanism celebrates the importance of man while whistling in the dark.
R. C. Sproul

Modern secular humanism is one of the stupidest beliefs ever concocted.
R. C. Sproul

We must remember that humanism is a worldview. It shares the scepticism and agnosticism with respect to God found in secularism.
R. C. Sproul

If you mix humanism with Christian truths, the basic message of Christianity is destroyed.
John W. Whitehead

HUMANITY — See Man

HUMILITY — Blessings

He that will be knighted must kneel for it.
Thomas Adams

Humility is to the Christian what ballast is to the ship; it keeps him in his proper position and regulates all his thoughts and feelings.
Archibald Alexander

God is closest to those whose hearts are broken.
Anon.

Swallowing of pride seldom leads to indigestion.
Anon.

The easiest way to dignity is humility.
Anon.

The lowliest Christian is the loveliest Christian.
Anon.

It was pride that changed angels into devils; it is humility that makes men as angels.
Augustine

The proud hilltops let the rain run off; the lowly valleys are richly watered.
Augustine

God thinks most of the man who thinks himself least.
John Blanchard

If you lay yourself at Christ's feet he will take you into his arms.
William Bridge

The most holy men are always the most humble men.
Thomas Brooks

He that is down needs fear no fall;
He that is low, no pride.
He that is humble ever shall
Have God to be his Guide.
John Bunyan

Humility is the beginning of true intelligence.
John Calvin

Humility is the root, mother, nurse, foundation and bond of all virtue.
Chrysostom

Humility is the hallmark of wisdom.
Jeremy Collier

It is with men as with wheat; the light heads are erect even in the presence of Omnipotence, but the full heads bow in reverence before him.
Joseph Cook

As rivers flow through valleys and low countries, so the root of all holy actions is nourished by humility.
Thomas De Villanova

319

Nothing sets a person so much out of the devil's reach as humility.
Jonathan Edwards

When God intends to fill a soul, he first makes it empty. When he intends to enrich a soul, he first makes it poor. When he intends to exalt a soul, he first makes it sensible to its own miseries, wants and nothingness. *John Flavel*

If we learned humility it might spare us humiliation. *Vance Havner*

When we take least notice of our good deeds ourselves, God takes most notice of them. *Matthew Henry*

God can only fill valleys, not mountains.
Roy Hession

If you want to see the height of the hill of God's eternal love you must go down into the valley of humility. *Rowland Hill*

God's choice acquaintances are humble men. *Robert Leighton*

Humility, after the *first* shock, is cheerful virtue. *C. S. Lewis*

Only those who see themselves as utterly destitute can fully appreciate the grace of God. *Erwin W. Lutzer*

The way to rise is to fall. *Thomas Manton*

All God's thrones are reached by going downstairs. *C. Campbell Morgan*

Not until we have become humble and teachable, standing in awe of God's holiness and sovereignty ... acknowledging our own littleness, distrusting our own thoughts, and willing to have our minds turned upside down, can divine wisdom become ours. *J. I. Packer*

Just as the sinner's despair of any help from himself is the first prerequisite of a sound conversion, so the loss of all confidence in himself is the first essential in the believer's growth in grace. *A. W. Pink*

The humble Christian is far happier in a cottage than the wicked in a palace.
A. W. Pink

The best way to see divine light is to put out thine own candle. *Francis Quarles*

Humble hearts lie in the valleys where streams of grace are flowing, and hence they drink of them. *C. H. Spurgeon*

The more we are humbled in grace, the more we shall be exalted in glory.
C. H. Spurgeon

The less a person strives for himself, the more God will be his champion.
John Trapp

Humility solders Christians together in peace. *Thomas Watson*

The right manner of growth is to grow less in one's own eyes. *Thomas Watson*

The lowest parts of the land are warm and fertile; the lofty mountains are cold and barren. *Spiros Zodhiates*

HUMILITY — Characteristics

He is genuinely great who considers himself small and cares nothing about high honours. *Thomas á Kempis*

If you know Hebrew, Greek and Latin, do not put them where Pilate did, at the head of Christ; put them at his feet. *Anon.*

The sufficiency of my merit is to know that my merit is not sufficient. *Augustine*

I did nothing that I might not have done better. *Richard Baxter*

I have written about one hundred and twenty-eight books, but I would commend to the poor but a few. *Richard Baxter*

I was but a pen in God's hands, and what praise is due to a pen? *Richard Baxter*

If there is one thing I would like to have said of me by those who are left behind when I have gone into the glory land, it would be just this that the overflow hid the vessel! *A. Lindsay Glegg*

A humble spirit loves a low seat. *William Gurnall*

Humility is a necessary veil to all other graces. *William Gurnall*

The Christian is like the ripening corn; the riper he grows, the more lowly bends his head. *Thomas Guthrie*

Humility is not thinking meanly of oneself, but rather it means not thinking of oneself at all. *Vance Havner*

Better be a humble worm than a proud angel. *William Jenkyn*

I sometimes think that the very essence of the whole Christian position and the secret of a successful spiritual life is just to realize two things … I must have complete, absolute confidence in God and no confidence in myself. *D. Martyn Lloyd-Jones*

Humility is not only a clothing, but also an ornament. *Thomas Manton*

Men frequently admire me; but I abhor the pleasure that I feel. *Henry Martyn*

True humility makes way for Christ and throws the soul at his feet. *J. Mason*

Humility is an invisible virtue. *Thomas Philippe*

Of all garments, none is so graceful, none wears so well, and none is so rare, as humility. *J. C. Ryle*

Oh for true, unfeigned humility! I know I have cause to be humble; and yet I do not know one half of that cause. I know I am proud; and yet I do not know the half of that pride. *Robert Murray M'Cheyne*

The fullest and best ears of corn hang lowest towards the ground. *Edward Reynolds*

He whose garments are the whitest will best perceive the spots upon them. *C. H. Spurgeon*

The higher a man is in grace, the lower he will be in his own esteem. *C. H. Spurgeon*

If pride and madness go together, so do humility and sanity. *John R. W. Stott*

Let my name be forgotten, let me be trodden under the feet of all men, if Jesus may thereby be glorified. *George Whitefield*

Lord, give me humility or I perish. *George Whitefield*

Think as little as possible about yourself. Turn your eyes resolutely from any view of your influence, your success, your following. Above all speak as little as possible about yourself. *Samuel Wilberforce*

HUMILITY — Essence

Humility is the knees of the soul.
Thomas Adams

Great men never think they are great —
small men never think they are small.
Anon.

Humility is to have a just estimate of oneself.
Anon.

If you sincerely desire to hide your good
actions, pride will not harm you.
Augustine

The true way to be humble is not to stoop
until you are smaller than yourself, but
to stand at your real height against some
higher nature that will show you what the
real smallness of your greatness is.
Phillips Brooks

It is one of the hardest matters under the
sun to become nothing in ourselves.
Elisha Coles

Humility is not simply feeling small and
useless — like an inferiority complex. It
is sensing how great and glorious God
is, and seeing myself in that light.
Sinclair Ferguson

By humility I mean not the abjectness of
a base mind; but a prudent care not to
over-value ourselves upon any account.
Obadiah Grew

Humility is the grace which lies prostrate
at God's footstool, self-abasing and self
disparaging, amazed at God's mercy and
abhorring its own vileness.
James Hamilton

Humility is the ability to see ourselves as
God describes us. *Henry Jacobsen*

Humility is the ornament of angels and
the deformity of devils. *William Jenkyn*

If anyone would like to acquire humility,
I can, I think, tell him the first step. The
first step is to realize that one is proud.
C. S. Lewis

The way to become poor in spirit is to
look at God. *D. Martyn Lloyd-Jones*

The best of God's people have abhorred
themselves. Like the spire of a steeple,
we are least at the highest.
Thomas Manton

Humility is not diffidence. Humility is
that disposition of honest recognition: He
is God, I am but a creature. *Al Martin*

Humility is pure honesty. *Jack McAlister*

Humility is a most strange thing. The
moment that you think you have acquired
it is just the moment you have lost it.
Bernard Meltzer

Humility is simply the sense of entire
nothingness. *Andrew Murray*

Humility is that grace that, when you
know you have it, you have lost it.
Andrew Murray

Humility is the repentance of pride.
Nehemiah Rogers

The true secret of spiritual strength is self-
distrust and deep humility. *J. C. Ryle*

Humility is not a Sunday frock, but a
workaday smock. *J. Oswald Sanders*

Pride is a sinner's torment, but humility
is a saint's ornament. *William Secker*

Humility is to make a right estimate of oneself. *C. H. Spurgeon*

Poverty of spirit is a kind of self-annihilation. *Thomas Watson*

The humble heart is God's throne in regard to his gracious presence; and heaven is his throne as to his glorious presence. *Thomas Watson*

The poor in spirit are divorced from themselves. *Thomas Watson*

Let my name be forgotten, let me be trodden under the feet of all men, if Jesus may thereby be glorified. *George Whitefield*

O heavenly Father, for thy dear Son's sake, keep me from climbing.
George Whitefield

HUMILITY — False

He who brags of his humility loses it.
John Boys

There is nothing more awful than conscious humility; it is the most satanic type of pride. *Oswald Chambers*

To see a man humble under prosperity is one of the greatest rarities in the world.
John Flavel

No pretence of humility must make us decline our duty. *Matthew Henry*

You can have no greater sign of a confirmed pride than when you think you are humble enough. *William Law*

If our humility is not unconsciousness it is exhibitionism. *D. Martyn Lloyd-Jones*

We can be proud of our humility, indeed I think we always are if we try to give the impression of humility.
D. Martyn Lloyd-Jones

False humility is really a lie, and cannot be acceptable to a God of truth.
William S. Plumer

If any man tells me that he is humble, I know him to be profoundly proud.
C. H. Spurgeon

Our humility serves us falsely when it leads us to shrink from any duty. The plea of unfitness or inability is utterly insufficient to excuse us. *Spiros Zodhiates*

HUMILITY — Importance

He who has other graces without humility is like one who carries a box of precious powder without a cover on a windy day. *Anon.*

Many would be scantily clad if clothed in their humility. *Anon.*

One test of a person's strength is his knowledge of his weakness. *Anon.*

There is no limit to the good a man can do if he doesn't care who gets the credit.
Anon.

As pride was the beginning of sin, so humility must be the beginning of the Christian discipline. *Augustine*

For those who would learn God's ways, humility is the first thing, humility is the second, humility is the third. *Augustine*

Life is a long lesson in humility.
James M. Barrie

He who knows himself best esteems himself least. *Henry G. Bohn*

Much more of true religion consists in deep humility, brokenness of heart and an abasing sense of barrenness and want of grace and holiness than most who are called Christians imagine.
David Brainerd

Humility in every area of life, in every relationship with other people, begins with a right concept of God as the one who is infinite and eternal in his majesty and holiness. *Jerry Bridges*

Show when you are tempted to hide, and hide when you are tempted to show.
A. B. Bruce

God will never come to his right unless we are totally reduced to nothing, so that it may be clearly seen that all that is laudable in us comes from elsewhere.
John Calvin

Nothing but the pure knowledge of God can teach us humility. *John Calvin*

How easy it is to reason out man's humility, but how hard to reason man into it. *Stephen Charnock*

Christ demands a humility which is foolishness to the world. *J. N. Figgis*

They that know God will be humble; they that know themselves cannot be proud.
John Flavel

There is no true holiness without humility. *Thomas Fuller*

The richest pearl in the Christian's crown of graces is humility. *John Mason Good*

The greatest men are those who are humble before God. The tallest men are those who bend before God. *Richard Halverson*

God grant us the beatitude of the background, that only he may be seen!
Vance Havner

Those whom God will employ are first struck with a sense of their unworthiness to be employed. *Matthew Henry*

No garment is more becoming to a child of God than the cloak of humility.
Cyril M. Jackson

Humility is one of the chief of all the Christian virtues; it is the hallmark of the child of God. *D. Martyn Lloyd-Jones*

In order to make us trust him, God works hard to make us lose trust in ourselves.
Dick Lucas

Until a man is nothing God can make nothing of him. *Martin Luther*

The great secret of a right waiting upon God is to be brought down to utter impotence. *Andrew Murray*

There is no need for us to devise means to draw attention to our work. God in his sovereign providence can well bear that responsibility. *Watchman Nee*

There walks not this earth a man who is too humble in the sight of God.
William S. Plumer

I believe the first test of a truly great man is his humility. *John Ruskin*

Humility is the very first letter in the alphabet of Christianity. *J. C. Ryle*

The surest mark of true conversion is humility. *J. C. Ryle*

If God has made us men, let us not make ourselves gods. *Richard Sibbes*

No grace is stronger than humility. *Richard Sibbes*

I believe every Christian man has a choice between being humble and being humbled. *C. H. Spurgeon*

Let us be humble that we may not need to be humbled, but may be exalted by the grace of God. *C. H. Spurgeon*

Humility neither falls far, or heavily. *Publilius Syrus*

Esteem thyself not to have profited by religion unless thou thinkest well of others and meanly of thyself. *Jeremy Taylor*

Knowledge without humility is vanity. *A. W. Tozer*

They are quite mistaken that faith and humility are inconsistent; they not only agree well together, but they cannot be parted. *Robert Traill*

Humility is the sweet spice that grows from poverty of spirit. *Thomas Watson*

Till we are poor in spirit we are not capable of receiving grace. *Thomas Watson*

HUMOUR
(See also: Happiness; Joy)

If you want to know whether a man's life is made up of frivolous or serious things, watch what he laughs at. *Anon.*

There ain't much fun in medicine, but there's a good deal of medicine in fun. *Josh Billings*

Genuine laughing is the vent of the soul, the nostrils of the heart, and it is just as necessary for health and happiness as spring water is for a trout. *Josh Billings*

I have never understood why it should be considered derogatory to the Creator to suppose that he has a sense of humour. *William Ralph Inge*

Nothing is so insipid as indiscriminate good humour. *J. Gresham Machen*

Few things are as useful in the Christian life as a gentle sense of humour and few things are as deadly as a sense of humour out of control. *A. W. Tozer*

There's plenty to laugh at in the world — but be sure you don't laugh at something that God takes seriously. *A. W. Tozer*

We should all be aware by this time that one way the devil has of getting rid of something is to make jokes about it. *A. W. Tozer*

Whenever humour takes a holy thing as its object that humour is devilish at once. *A. W. Tozer*

Nothing shows a man's character more than what he laughs at. *Johann Wolfgang von Goethe*

HUNGER — Spiritual — See Spiritual Hunger

HURRY

Rush is destructive of rest, and pace of peace. *Thomas Adams*

The hurrier I go, the behinder I get! *Anon.*

There are no deadlines against which God must work. Only to know this is to quiet our spirits and relax our nerves.
A. W. Tozer

Though I am always in haste, I am never in a hurry. *John Wesley*

HUSBAND — See Family Life

HYPOCRISY
(See also. Formalism; Ritualism)

Hypocrites are like pictures on canvas: they show fairest *at* farthest.
Thomas Adams

The hypocrite fries in words, freezes in works. *Thomas Adams*

The hypocrite has much angel without, more devil within. *Thomas Adams*

The hypocrite is like Hosea's dough-baked cake, only hot on the visible side.
Thomas Adams

Nothing is more amiable than true modesty, and nothing more contemptible than false. The one guards virtue, the other betrays it. *Joseph Addison*

I will have nought to do with a man who can blow hot and cold with the same breath. *Aesop*

The hypocrite desires holiness only as a bridge to heaven. *Joseph Alleine*

A clean glove often hides a dirty hand.
Anon.

A hypocrite is a man who lets his light so shine before men that they can't tell what is going on behind! *Anon.*

A hypocrite preaches by the yard but practises by the inch. *Anon.*

Many wear God's livery but are not his servants. *Anon.*

To profess to love God while leading an unholy life is the worst of falsehoods.
Augustine

The hypocrite's bellows blow out the candle under pretence of kindling the fire.
Richard Baxter

Keeping up appearances is the most expensive thing in the world.
A. C. Benson

A man who hides behind the hypocrite is smaller than the hypocrite.
W. E. Biederwolf

If the world despises a hypocrite, what must they think of him in heaven?
Josh Billings

Hypocrisy is nothing better than skin-deep holiness. *John Blanchard*

It is possible to be back-slapping and backsliding at the same time.
John Blanchard

Spoken faith is not necessarily saving faith. *John Blanchard*

What you are in public will never blind God to what you are in private.
John Blanchard

A man who does not practise what he preaches destroys what he builds.
Bonaventura

An apple, if it be rotten at the core, though it have a fair and shining outside, yet rottenness will not stay long, but will taint the outside also ... hypocrisy will discover itself in the end.   *John Bond*

God will not be put off with the shell while we give the devil the kernel.
Thomas Brooks

Self-ends are the operative ingredients in all a hypocrite does.   *Thomas Brooks*

The hypocrite is a cloud without rain, a blossoming tree without fruit, a star without light, a shell without a kernel.
Thomas Brooks

The hypocrite is only constant in inconstancy.   *Thomas Brooks*

There is not more counterfeit coin this day in the world than there is counterfeit holiness in the world.   *Thomas Brooks*

Do not seek to cover up your sins with the varnish of hypocrisy, the fine gloss that pleases men.   *William C. Burns*

Hypocrites are so stupid that they do not feel their sores.   *John Calvin*

A bad man is worse when he pretends to be a saint.   *Oswald Chambers*

A hypocrite may well be termed a religious atheist, an atheist masked with religion.   *Stephen Charnock*

A running sore may lie under a purple robe.   *Stephen Charnock*

If the devil ever laughs, it must be at hypocrites; they are the greatest dupes he has.   *C. C. Colton*

Men defend nothing more violently than the pretensions they live by. *Allen Drury*

A man can be outwardly conformed to the Christian way of life while he is inwardly conformed to the spirit of this world.   *Sinclair Ferguson*

A man may have the tongue of an angel and the heart of a devil.   *John Flavel*

Religion is the best armour in the world, but the worst cloak.   *Thomas Fuller*

There is nothing worse than being something on the outside that you are not on the inside.   *Mohandas Gandhi*

There are three things I don't like — they are liver, kidneys and hypocrisy.
A. Lindsay Glegg

Hypocrisy not only covers faults, but swiftly eats out of the soul every remnant of truth and honour left in it.
Richard Glover

Piety outside and corruption inside is a revolting mixture.   *Michael Green*

Hypocrisy is a lie with a fair cover over it.   *William Gurnall*

Hypocrisy is a sin that offers violence to the very light of nature. *William Gurnall*

Hypocrisy is too thin a veil to blind the eyes of the Almighty.   *William Gurnall*

We must not spread our sails of profession in a calm and furl them up when the wind rises.   *William Gurnall*

Many a Christian, many a church, has everything in the showcase and nothing on the shelves.   *Vance Havner*

There is no use singing of milk and honey, figs and pomegranates, if all we have to show is crab apples!   *Vance Havner*

Hypocrisy

Hypocrites and betrayers of Christ are no better than devils.   *Matthew Henry*

Hypocrites do the devil's drudgery in Christ's livery.   *Matthew Henry*

Piety from the teeth outward is an easy thing.   *Matthew Henry*

The day is coming when hypocrites will be stripped of their fig-leaves.
      Matthew Henry

Where the hypocrite's work ends, there the true Christian's work begins.
      Matthew Henry

A good name upon an unchanged nature is but white feathers upon a black skin.
      William Jenkyn

A rotten apple discovers itself in a windy day.   *William Jenkyn*

Hereafter all paint must fall off which is not laid in the oil of sincerity.
      William Jenkyn

There are many who are lip-servants but not life-servants.   *William Jenkyn*

How difficult it is to avoid having a special standard for oneself! *C. S. Lewis*

Of all bad men religious bad men are the worst.   *C. S. Lewis*

The most exhausting thing in life is being insincere. *Anne Morrow Lindbergh*

We play the game; God keeps the score.
      Erwin W. Lutzer

There are over many who have much knowledge and little virtue, and who often speak of God while rarely speaking to him.   *Malaval*

It is the mark of a hypocrite to be a Christian everywhere except at home.
      Robert Murray M'Cheyne

Whitewashing the pump won't make the water pure.   *D. L. Moody*

There is something of the hypocrite in us all.   *Derek Prime*

There are many who agree with God in principle but not in practice.
      Richard Owen Roberts

The hypocrite will have the lowest place in hell.   *J. C. Ryle*

Whatever we are in our religion, let us resolve never to wear a cloak. Let us by all means be honest and real. *J. C. Ryle*

A painted harlot is less dangerous than a painted hypocrite is. *William Secker*

No hypocrite can bear the cross.
      Henry Smith

Nothing devalues the truth more quickly than the counterfeit.   *R. C. Sproul*

Conviction of ignorance is the doorstep to the temple of wisdom. *C. H. Spurgeon*

Nothing is more to be despised than a mere painted fire, the simulation of earnestness. Sooner let us have an honest death than a counterfeit life.
      C. H. Spurgeon

Of all things in the world that stink in the nostrils of men, hypocrisy is the worst.
      C. H. Spurgeon

Religion which is begun in hypocrisy will certainly end in apostasy.
      William Spurstowe

How few of us live one life and live it in the open! We are tempted to wear a different mask and play a different role according to each occasion. This is not reality but play-acting, which is the essence of hypocrisy.   *John R. W. Stott*

Some people weave around them such a tissue of lies that they can no longer tell which part of them is real and which is make-believe.   *John R. W. Stott*

Ignorance is the mother of superstition, not of devotion.   *Augustus H. Strong*

Hypocrisy is the loudest lie.
George Swinnock

Ignorance and confidence are often twins.
George Swinnock

To be proud of learning is the greatest ignorance.   *Jeremy Taylor*

I cannot believe that a man is on the road to heaven when he is habitually performing the kind of deeds that would logically indicate that he ought to be on his way to hell.   *A. W. Tozer*

When hypocrites ran up against Jesus it was like a cat running into a mowing machine.   *A. W. Tozer*

We must not think to dine with the devil all day and sup with Christ at night.
John Trapp

The righteous man hath grace beyond expression; the hypocrite hath expression beyond grace.   *Ralph Venning*

Hypocrites cannot sail in stormy weather.
Thomas Watson

Hypocrites love a cheap religion.
Thomas Watson

The hypocrite hath a squint eye, for he looks more to his own glory than God's.
Thomas Watson

The hypocrite's tongue may be silver, yet his heart stone.   *Thomas Watson*

The white devil is the worst.
Thomas Watson

Not ignorance, but the ignorance of ignorance, is the death of knowledge.
Alfred North Whitehead

IDLENESS — see Indolence

IDOLATRY

We are all born idolaters.   *Thomas Adams*

Inordinate affections bring extraordinary affliction.   *Anon.*

All who forsake the Word fall into idolatry.   *John Calvin*

Every one of us is, from his mother's womb, expert in inventing idols.
John Calvin

Man's mind is like a store of idolatry and superstition; so much so that if a man believes his own mind it is certain that he will forsake God and forge some idol in his own brain.   *John Calvin*

Idolatry is anything which cooleth thy desires after Christ.   *Oliver Cromwell*

A made God is no God.   *Matthew Henry*

Idols are called lies because they belie God, as if he had a body, whereas he is a spirit.   *Matthew Henry*

Idolatry is everywhere represented in Scripture as the greatest insult the creature can offer the Creator. *Charles Hodge*

Where idolatry ends, there Christianity begins; and where idolatry begins, there Christianity ends. *Friedrich H. Jacobi*

All idols are the product of human imagination. *R. B. Kuiper*

Ever since man ruined the image of God in which he had been created he has been fashioning gods in his own image. *R. B. Kuiper*

Ultimately, all idolatry amounts to worship by the idolater of himself. *R. B. Kuiper*

We easily fall into idolatry, for we are inclined to it by nature; and coming to us by inheritance, it seems pleasant. *Martin Luther*

Satan doesn't care what we worship, as long as we don't worship God. *D. L. Moody*

The method of the evil one is to obscure himself behind some other object of worship. *G. Campbell Morgan*

In all this ordered universe there is no reality corresponding to idols. *Leon Morris*

You do not have to make a graven image picturing God as a man to be an idolater; a false mental image is all that is needed to break the second commandment. *J. I. Packer*

All idolatry is stupid, though not all equally indecent. *William S. Plumer*

When we invent our own ideas of God, we simply create him in our own image. *Kenneth F. W. Prior*

Anything above God is idolatry. *Richard Sibbes*

Whatsoever our trust is most in, that is our god. *Richard Sibbes*

The most basic sin found in the world is that of idolatry. *R. C. Sproul*

While it is intimidating to bow down in awe before the powerful God of the Bible, it is utterly pointless to bow politely to false gods of our own making. *R. C. Sproul*

An idol of the mind is as offensive to God as an idol of the hand. *A. W. Tozer*

The essence of idolatry is the entertainment of thoughts about God that are unworthy of him. *A. W. Tozer*

Whatever a man seeks, honours, or exalts more than God, this is the god of idolatry. *William Ullathorne*

An idol may be defined as any person or thing that has usurped in the heart the place of pre-eminence that belongs to the Lord. *Arthur Wallis*

An image lover is a God hater. *Thomas Watson*

God made man of the dust of the earth and man makes a god of the dust of the earth. *Thomas Watson*

In his natural state, every man born into the world is a rank idolater. *John Wesley*

Man in his rebellion against the Creator remains incurably religious, and he seeks to satisfy this instinct by making his own deities. He much prefers these lifeless puppets to the one true living God, because they allow him to pull the strings.
Geoffrey B. Wilson

IGNORANCE

An empty sack cannot stand upright.
Anon.

Education is never as expensive as ignorance.
Anon.

It is unlikely in the foreseeable future that there will be a serious shortage of ignorance.
Anon.

To be aware that you are ignorant is a great step to knowledge.
Anon.

Ignorance is your disease; knowledge must be your cure.
Richard Baxter

Atheism is the ultimate ignorance.
John Blanchard

By comparison with God's perfect understanding, we are like a man inside a barrel looking through a bunghole.
R. R. Brown

It is a common fault, that ignorance is closely followed by obstinacy.
John Calvin

The mind is never so enlightened that there are no remains of ignorance, nor the heart so established that there are no misgivings.
John Calvin

Passion does not compensate for ignorance.
Samuel Chadwick

He who would be cured of ignorance must confess it.
Michel de Montaigne

We do not know a millionth part of one per cent about anything.
Thomas Edison

I feel like a man chained. I get a glimpse of reality and then it flees. If only I could be free from the shackles of my intellectual smallness, then I could understand the universe in which I live.
Albert Einstein

You cannot find knowledge by rearranging your ignorance.
Ronald Eyre

He that knows nothing will believe anything.
Thomas Fuller

I am still searching for the truth.
Buddha Siddhartha Gautama

Every natural man is a fool.
Thomas Granger

Ignorance is the mother of mischief.
Thomas Hall

It is debatable which is causing us more harm — hot-headed ignorance or cold-hearted intellectualism.
Vance Havner

The opposite of ignorance in the spiritual realm is not knowledge but obedience.
Howard Hendricks

The more we know, the more we see of our own ignorance.
Matthew Henry

Ignorance is the beaten path to hell.
William Jenkyn

We know things about God, but our real trouble is our ignorance about God himself — what he really is, and what he is to his people.
D. Martyn Lloyd-Jones

The ultimate proof of the sinner is that he does not know his own sin.
Martin Luther

Nothing in the world is more dangerous than sincere ignorance and conscientious stupidity. *Martin Luther King*

There is nothing so costly as ignorance.
Horace Mann

The more I advance, the more clearly I perceive that the greatest human knowledge amounts to a more pompous proof of our ignorance, by showing us how little we know about anything.
John Newton

As creatures, we have no right or reason to expect that at every point we shall be able to comprehend the wisdom of our Creator. *J. I. Packer*

Can we not be persuaded to believe that specks of consciousness on this little planet cannot, in all reasonableness, be thought of as accurate critics of the total purpose behind creation? *J. B. Phillips*

Everybody is ignorant — only on different subjects. *Will Rogers*

The worst ignorance in the world is not to know ourselves. *J. C. Ryle*

To feel that we are ignorant is the first beginning of all saving knowledge.
J. C. Ryle

The only thing I know certainly is that I am ignorant. *Socrates*

Because of our ignorance we are not fully aware of our sins of ignorance.
C. H. Spurgeon

Conviction of ignorance is the doorstep to the temple of wisdom. *C. H. Spurgeon*

Half our fears are the result of ignorance.
C. H. Spurgeon

Ignorance is the mother of superstition, not of devotion. *Augustus H. Strong*

Ignorance and confidence are often twins.
George Swinnock

To be proud of learning is the greatest ignorance. *Jeremy Taylor*

There is nothing so frightful as an active ignorance. *Johann Wolfgang von Goethe*

Ignorance is not the mother of religion, but of irreligion. *Benjamin B. Warfield*

Grace cannot reign where ignorance reigns. *Thomas Watson*

Ignorance is Satan's strong-hold.
Thomas Watson

Not ignorance, but the ignorance of ignorance, is the death of knowledge.
Alfred North Whitehead

IMAGINATION
(See also: Mind; Thought)

The devil would have us continually crossing streams that do not exist. *Anon.*

You should no more allow sinful imaginations to accumulate in your mind and soul than you would allow garbage to collect in your living-room. *Anon.*

The soul without imagination is what an observatory would be without a telescope. *Henry Ward Beecher*

Modern psychologists tell us that in any battle between the imagination and the will, the imagination always wins.
E. Stanley-Jones

IMMORALITY — See Sex

IMMORTALITY
(See also: Destiny; Eternity; Eternal Life; Heaven)

The human body is formed for immortality … By sinking into death it does not utterly perish.
John Calvin

Immortal souls were not created for merely mortal ends.
C. H. Spurgeon

He sins against this life who slights the next.
Edward Young

IMPATIENCE

Ignorance of the providence of God is the cause of all impatience. *John Calvin*

Adversity borrows its sharpest sting from our impatience.
George Home

The nicest people are often the most impatient.
D. Martyn Lloyd-Jones

The Almighty is working on a great scale and will not be hustled by our peevish impetuosity.
W. Graham Scroggie

IMPENITENCE

Hardening of the heart ages people more quickly than hardening of the arteries.
Anon.

To those whom God finds impenitent sinners he will be found to be an implacable Judge.
Matthew Henry

A stone in the heart is worse than in the kidneys.
Thomas Watson

IMPIETY
(See also: Atheism; Unbelief)

How many are there like children who play till their candle be out, and then they go to bed in the dark!
Thomas Brooks

There is no stupidity more brutish than forgetfulness of God.
John Calvin

Forgetfulness of God is at the bottom of all the wickedness of the wicked.
Matthew Henry

The carnal mind sees God in nothing, not even in spiritual things. The spiritual mind sees him in everything, even in natural things.
Robert Leighton

Mocking God is life's great impossibility.
W. T. Purkiser

INCARNATION — Jesus Christ
(See also: Virgin Birth)

The incarnation of Christ is the clearest affirmation of the truth that man is created in the image of God.
Lawrence Adams

Christ veiled his deity but he did not void it.
Anon.

The Son came out from the Father to help us to come out from the world; he descended to us to enable us to ascend to him.
Anthony of Padua

Christ became what we are that he might make us what he is.
Athanasius

Filling the world he lies in a manger!
Augustine

The Son of God became the Son of Man in order that the sons of men might become the sons of God. *John Blanchard*

When Jesus came to earth, it was not his Godhood he laid aside, but his glory.
John Blanchard

In the creation, the Lord made man like himself; but in the redemption he made himself like man. *John Boys*

Christ voluntarily took upon him everything that is inseparable from human nature. *John Calvin*

The incarnation is the pattern for all evangelism. Jesus Christ was totally in the world yet wholly uncontaminated by it.
Everett L. Cattell

The earth wondered, at Christ's nativity, to see a new star in Heaven; but heaven might rather wonder to see a new sun on earth. *Richard Clerke*

Jesus Christ is perennial and he who makes his boast in him stays fresh for ever. *Vance Havner*

He took the form of a servant while he retained the form of God! It is exactly that which makes our salvation possible and achieves it. *William Hendriksen*

It was to save sinners that Christ Jesus came into the world. He did not come to help them to save themselves, nor to induce them to save themselves, nor even to enable them to save themselves. He came to save them! *William Hendriksen*

The early Christians did not say in dismay, 'Look what the world has come to,' but in delight, 'Look what has come to the world!' *Carl F. H. Henry*

The incarnation was a necessary means to an end, and the end was the putting away of the sin of the world by the offering of the body of Christ. *Thomas Hewitt*

Rejoice that the immortal God is born that mortal men may live in eternity. *Jan Hus*

God became man to turn creatures into sons; not simply to produce better men of the old kind but to produce a new kind of man. *C. S. Lewis*

The Christian story is precisely the story of one grand miracle. *C. S. Lewis*

The mystery of the humanity of Christ, that he sunk himself into our flesh, is beyond all human understanding.
Martin Luther

To the human mind there is something almost illogical in the assertion that God became a man. It is like speaking about a square circle. Yet this is what Christmas says — and we take refuge from our bewilderment not in explanation but in adoration. *Ralph P. Martin*

The Incarnation is not an event; but an institution. What Jesus once took up he never laid down. *Vincent McNabb*

The divine Son became a Jew; the Almighty appeared on earth as a helpless human baby, unable to do more than lie and stare and wriggle and make noises, needing to be fed and changed and taught to talk like any other child. The more you think about it, the more staggering it gets. *J. I. Packer*

The Son of God . . . came to seek us where we are in order that he might bring us to be with him where he is. *J. I. Packer*

Before Christ could marry us he must be born in our nature, for the husband and the wife must be of one nature.
Richard Sibbes

Christmas is the day that holds all time together. *Alexander Smith*

The hinge of history is on the door of a Bethlehem stable. *Ralph W. Sockman*

He that made man was made man.
C. H. Spurgeon

The awful majesty of the Godhead was mercifully sheathed in the soft envelope of human nature to protect mankind.
A. W. Tozer

The glory of the incarnation is that it presents to our adoring gaze not a humanized God or a deified man, but a true God-man — one who is all that God is and at the same time all that man is: one on whose almighty arm we can rest, and to whose human sympathy we can appeal.
Benjamin B. Warfield

Christ took our flesh upon him that he might take our sins upon him.
Thomas Watson

Let earth and heaven combine,
Angels and men agree,
To praise in songs divine
The incarnate Deity,
Our God contracted to a span,
Incomprehensibly made man.
Charles Wesley

INCONSISTENCY

No seal can be set on running water.
Thomas Adams

The damage of the sin of inconsistency in the life of the Christian is that it sours even our worship of God. *J. A. Motyer*

The natural man cannot be expected to love the gospel, but let us not disgust him by inconsistency. *J. C. Ryle*

The glaring disparity between theology and practice among professing Christians is a more destructive evil in its effect upon the Christian religion than Communism, Romanism and liberalism combined.
A. W. Tozer

How many by the wind of popular breath have been blown to hell! *Thomas Watson*

INDIFFERENCE
(See also: Apathy; Complacency)

Doctrinal indifference is no solution to the problems of doctrinal differences.
John Blanchard

Men boast of their tolerance who should be ashamed of their indifference.
Will H. Houghton

I believe that if there is one thing which pierces the Master's heart with unutterable grief it is not the world's iniquity but the church's indifference.
F. B. Meyer

The refusal to be committed and the attitude of indifference can in fact never be neutral. *J. B. Phillips*

Indifference in religion is the first step to apostasy from religion. *William Seeker*

INDOLENCE
An idle brain is the devil's workshop.
Anon.

Between the great things we cannot do and the little things we will not do, we are in danger of doing nothing.   *Anon.*

Footprints on the sands of time are never made by sitting down.   *Anon.*

God's biggest problem with labourers in his vineyard is absenteeism.   *Anon.*

He who kills time kills opportunities.   *Anon.*

Idleness is the nest in which mischief lays its eggs.   *Anon.*

It costs the devil little trouble to catch the lazy man.   *Anon.*

No farmer ever ploughed a field by turning it over in his mind.   *Anon.*

No one ever climbed the ladder of success with his hands in his pockets. *Anon.*

Our idle days are Satan's busy days.   *Anon.*

Rust wastes more than use.   *Anon.*

Satan selects his disciples when they are idle; but Christ chose his when they were busy at their work, either mending their nets, or casting them into the sea. *Anon.*

The devil does most when men are doing least.   *Anon.*

The devil tempts all, but the idle man tempts the devil.   *Anon.*

The lazier a man is the more he plans to do tomorrow.   *Anon.*

An idle man and a Christian are names which do not harmonize. *Albert Barnes*

Laziness breeds a love of amusement.   *Richard Baxter*

If you are idle, you are on the road to ruin, and there are few stopping-places upon it. It is rather a precipice than a road.   *Henry Ward Beecher*

Idleness is the enemy of the soul. *Benedict*

All our activity is sowing; and so is our inactivity.   *John Blanchard*

Inaction speaks louder than words.   *John Blanchard*

It is often said that it is difficult to get the sinners in — but it is often just as difficult to get the saints out. *John Blanchard*

Wasting time is a kind of unarmed robbery.   *John Blanchard*

We must not seek rest or ease in a world where he whom we love had none.   *Horatius Bonar*

Our laziness after God is our crying sin . . . No man gets God who does not follow hard after him.   *E. M. Bounds*

A lazy Christian will always lack four things: comfort, content, confidence and assurance.   *Thomas Brooks*

A lazy spirit is always a losing spirit.   *Thomas Brooks*

An idle life and a holy heart is a contradiction.   *Thomas Brooks*

Idleness is the very source of sin.   *Thomas Brooks*

The only thing necessary to the triumph of evil is for good men to do nothing.   *Edmund Burke*

Lose an hour in the morning and you will be looking for it the rest of the day.
Philip Chesterfield

To do nothing is nothing less than to do some harm. *Chrysostom*

It is better to wear out than to rust out.
Richard Cumberland

While God assists our weakness, he does not intend to encourage our laziness.
Henry Dove

Despise an idle mind. *Jim Elliff*

No temptation is more frequently before us than that of easing up.
Sinclair Ferguson

The man who does things makes many mistakes, but he never makes the biggest mistake of all — doing nothing.
Benjamin Franklin

An idle man does none good, and himself most harm. *William Gurnall*

Laziness grows on people; it begins in cobwebs and ends in iron chains. *M. Hale*

Do not so contemplate eternity that you waste today. *Vance Havner*

Idleness is the devil's work-shop.
Vance Havner

The field left idle returns to weeds and thorns. *Vance Havner*

Salvation is a helmet, not a nightcap.
Vance Havner

Idleness tempts God instead of trusting him. *Matthew Henry*

The slothful desire the gains which the diligent get, but they hate the pains which the diligent take. *Matthew Henry*

Whom God sends he employs, for he sends none to be idle. *Matthew Henry*

Not to serve God is to serve Satan.
Charles Hodge

The way to be nothing is to do nothing.
Nathaniel Howe

Determine never to be idle ... It is wonderful how much may be done if we are always doing. *Thomas Jefferson*

The man who tries to do something and fails is infinitely better than the man who tries to do nothing and succeeds.
D. Martyn Lloyd-Jones

When the hands are idle, the tongue is usually very active. *Henry T. Mahan*

Activity may lead to evil, but inactivity cannot lead to good. *Hannah More*

Ease is never good for the people of God.
Alexander Peden

There has never yet been a man in our history who led a life of ease whose name is worth remembering.
Theodore Roosevelt

Idle Christians are not tempted of the devil so much as they tempt the devil to tempt them. *C. H. Spurgeon*

Idleness is the key of beggary.
C. H. Spurgeon

It is an abomination to let the grass grow up to your knees and do nothing towards making it into hay. God never sent a man into the world to be idle. *C. H. Spurgeon*

Indolence

Some temptations come to the industrious, but all temptations attack the idle.
C. H. Spurgeon

Some people seem to me to have three hands: a right hand, a left hand, and a little behind hand. *C. H. Spurgeon*

He is not only idle who does nothing, but he is idle who might be better employed.
Socrates

Idleness is the burial of our persons, and negligence is the burial of our actions.
George Swinnock

The idle man may call the prodigal brother. *George Swinnock*

Idleness is the burial of a living man.
Jeremy Taylor

An idle man is the devil's tennis ball.
John Trapp

Idleness is a kind of business. *John Trapp*

Not to do what we ought to do is as bad as doing what we ought not to do.
George W Truett

Jesus has never slept for an hour while one of his disciples watched and prayed in agony. *H. Clay Trumbull*

God has given no man a dispensation to be idle. *Ralph Venning*

Enthusiasm and persistence can make an average person superior; indifference and lethargy can make a superior person average. *William A. Ward*

The greatest failure is the failure to try.
William A. Ward

Beware of idleness. Satan sows most of his seed in fallow ground.
Thomas Watson

The great God never sealed any warrants for idleness. *Thomas Watson*

Idleness tempts the devil to tempt.
Thomas Watson

Religion gives no warrant for idleness ... a Christian must mind not only heaven, but his calling. *Thomas Watson*

Satan finds some mischief still for idle hands to do. *Isaac Watts*

INFIDELITY — see Unbelief

INFLUENCE
(See also: Example)

Every life is a profession of faith, and exercises an inevitable and silent influence. *Henri Amiel*

A crooked stick will have a crooked shadow. *Anon.*

A good man does good merely by living.
Anon.

Every hair makes its shadow on the ground. *Anon.*

There is little we touch but we leave the print of our fingers behind.
Richard Baxter

No man is an island, entire of itself; every man is a piece of the continent.
John Donne

The tiniest post office can bear a letter that may wreck or bless a nation. And the simplest life can relay blessings that may

rock a continent toward God.
Vance Havner

We are the salt of the earth, not the sugar, and our ministry is truly to cleanse and not just to change the taste. *Vance Havner*

We are called to be thermostats, not thermometers — affecting our environment, not reflecting it. *Charles R. Hembree*

To be a Christian is to be a key personality in the world situation today.
Geoffrey King

When I think of those who have influenced my life the most, I think not of the great but of the good. *John Knox*

Your influence is negative or positive, never neutral. *Henrietta Mears*

A holy life will produce the deepest impression. Lighthouses blow no horns; they only shine. *D. L. Moody*

There is no such person as a person without influence. *J. A. Motyer*

The entire ocean is affected by a pebble.
Blaise Pascal

The serene beauty of a holy life is the most powerful influence in the world next to the power of God. *Blaise Pascal*

No one is a light unto himself, not even the sun. *Antonio Porchia*

A little man may cast a long shadow.
C. H. Spurgeon

The serene, silent beauty of a holy life is the most powerful influence in the world, next to the might of the Spirit of God.
C. H. Spurgeon

Influence is the exhalation of character.
W. M. Taylor

One live coal may set a whole stack on fire. *John Trapp*

The most serious thing in all the world is this matter of personal influence.
George Truett

INGRATITUDE

The vast majority of mankind never gives a thought of gratitude towards God for all his care and blessings.
Donald Grey Barnhouse

Unthankfulness is the devil's text.
John Boys

Forgetfulness of God's benefits is a sort of madness. *John Calvin*

Ingratitude is very frequently the reason why we are deprived of the light of the gospel, as well as of other divine favours.
John Calvin

Thankless men are like swine feeding on acorns, which, though they fall upon their heads, never make them look up to the tree from which they come. *Jean Daille*

I believe that the best definition of man is the ungrateful biped.
Feodor Dostoevsky

When we become thankless we become sinners against God and man.
E. F. Hallock

Every virtue, divorced from thankfulness is maimed and limps along the spiritual road. *John Henry Jowett*

Alas for that capital crime of the Lord's people, — barrenness in praises!
John Livingstone

I fear that what will surprise us most, when we see our Lord, will be the extent of our own ingratitude.   *E. B. Pusey*

It must make the devils themselves marvel to see us able to receive a pardon and a title to everlasting glory with scarcely more than a few cold syllables of gratitude to God.   *Maurice Roberts*

Ingratitude is not only the basest and meanest of sins, but it is the most frequent.
Wilton Merle Smith

It is sad when there is nothing for which we feel grateful to God, but it is serious when there is something and we fail to show gratitude, and it is tragic when we are so busy asking for more that we forget to thank him for what we have received.
William Still

INJUSTICE

If you are suffering from a bad man's injustice, forgive him lest there be two bad men.   *Augustine*

Those who commit injustice bear the greatest burden.   *Hosea Ballou*

Injustice anywhere is a threat to justice everywhere.   *Martin Luther King*

Injustice never rules for ever.   *Seneca*

INSECURITY

There is nothing so characteristic of our world as its instability and uncertainty.
D. Martyn Lloyd-Jones

This age is a gadget-filled paradise suspended in a hell of insecurity.
Foy Valentine

INSPIRATION — See Bible

INTEGRITY
(See also: Honesty; Truth)

It is better to go straight than to move in the best of circles.   *John Blanchard*

Integrity of heart is indispensable.
John Calvin

The three most important ingredients in Christian work are integrity, integrity, integrity.   *Charles Colson*

Integrity without knowledge is weak and useless, and knowledge without integrity is dangerous and dreadful.
Samuel Johnson

Integrity is the first step to true greatness.
Charles Sommons

If we cannot be believed on our word, we are surely not to be trusted on our oath.
C. H. Spurgeon

A guileless mind is a great treasure; it is worth any price.   *A. W. Tozer*

The plainer the diamond the more it sparkles; the plainer the heart is the more it sparkles in God's eyes. *Thomas Watson*

INTOLERANCE

God is the only being in the world who has a right to be intolerant.
Donald Grey Barnhouse

Nothing dies so hard or rallies so often as intolerance.   *Henry Ward Beecher*

Intolerance has been the curse of every age and state. *Samuel Davies*

The devil loves nothing better than the intolerance of reformers, and dreads nothing so much as their charity and patience. *J. R. Lowell*

JEALOUSY
(See also: Envy)

Jealousy is a blister on the heels of friendship. *Anon.*

Jealousy is the raw material of murder. *Anon.*

Jealousy sees too much. *Anon.*

Many lovely things pass out of life when jealousy comes in. *Anon.*

Jealousy never thinks itself strong enough. *John Bunyan*

JESUS CHRIST — Ascension

When Jesus came to earth he did not cease to be God; when he returned to heaven he did not cease to be man. *John Blanchard*

When Jesus went back to heaven his desk was clear. *John Blanchard*

Christ's ascension into heaven was the real commencement of his reign. *John Calvin*

Christ was taken up into heaven, not to enjoy blessed rest at a distance from us, but to govern the world for the salvation of all believers. *John Calvin*

Since Christ, our Head, has ascended to heaven, we should leave our carnal desires behind and lift our hearts upward to him. *John Calvin*

If Christ had not ascended he could not have interceded, as he now does in heaven for us. And do but take away Christ's intercession and you starve the hope of the saints. *John Flavel*

Astronauts sink into insignificance beside this ascension! *Vance Havner*

The head that once was crowned with thorns
Is crowned with glory now;
A royal diadem adorns
The mighty Victor's brow.
Thomas Kelly

Triumphant, Christ ascends on high,
The glorious work complete;
Sin, death and hell low vanquished lie
Beneath his awful feet. *Anne Steele*

He hath left with us the earnest of the Spirit, and taken from us the earnest of our flesh, which he hath carried into heaven as a pledge that the whole shall follow after. *Tertullian*

Our Lord is risen from the dead!
Our Jesus is gone up on high!
The powers of hell are captive led,
Dragged to the portals of the sky.
Charles Wesley

JESUS CHRIST — Birth — see Incarnation

JESUS CHRIST — Death
(See also: Atonement; Cross; Forgiveness by God)

He died that we might be forgiven,
He died to make us good,
That we might go at last to heaven,
Saved by his precious blood.
Cecil Frances Alexander

He gave up his life *because* he willed it, *when* he willed it and *as* he willed it.
Augustine

In taking the sinner's place on the cross, Jesus became as totally accountable for sin as if he was totally responsible for it.
John Blanchard

Jesus is not a substitute for the symptoms — he is the cure for the cause.
John Blanchard

The death of Christ not only demonstrates something, it demands everything.
John Blanchard

The death of Jesus was not a proposition for sinners but a plan of salvation.
John Blanchard

That tiny hill in that tiny land is the centre of all history, not only of this world, but of all the countless galaxies and island universes of outer space from eternity to eternity. *Paul E. Billheimer*

Jesus did not die just to give us peace and a purpose in life; he died to save us from the wrath of God. *Jerry Bridges*

Christ's blood is heaven's key.
Thomas Brooks

Jesus Christ, the condescension of divinity, and the exaltation of humanity.
Phillips Brooks

Christ suffered in his soul the dreadful torments of a person condemned and irretrievably lost. *John Calvin*

If Christ's soul had experienced no punishment he would have been only a Redeemer for the body. *John Calvin*

There is no tribunal so magnificent, no throne so stately, no show of triumph so distinguished, no chariot so elevated, as is the gibbet on which Christ hath subdued death and the devil. *John Calvin*

The doctrine of the death of Christ is the substance of the gospel.
Stephen Charnock

There is a fountain filled with blood
Drawn from Immanuel's veins;
And sinners plunged beneath that flood
Lose all their guilty stains.
William Cowper

When Jesus bowed his head,
And dying took our place,
The veil was rent, a way was found
To that pure home of grace. *John Elias*

Though God loved Christ as a Son he frowned upon him as a Surety.
Matthew Henry

The cross is the key. If I lose this key I fumble. The universe will not open to me. But with the key in my hand I know I hold its secret. *E. Stanley Jones*

It does not follow that because the death of Christ has a special application to the elect that it has no reference to the whole world. It is the ground on which salvation is offered to all who hear. The merit of Christ's death is immeasurable.
E. F. Kevan

The dying of the Lord Jesus rescues us from eternal death, whilst the doing of the Lord Jesus obtains for us eternal life.
J. M. Killen

The whole world in comparison with the cross of Christ is one grand impertinence.
Robert Leighton

Jesus Christ never died for our good works. They were not worth dying for. But he gave himself for our sins, according to the Scriptures.   *Martin Luther*

One drop of Christ's blood is worth more than heaven and earth.   *Martin Luther*

The wounds of Christ were the greatest outlets of his glory that ever were. The divine glory shone more out of his wounds than out of all his life before.
Robert Murray M'Cheyne

He humbled himself to the accursed death of the cross. There were no lower depths possible, for the cross bespeaks the whole curse of God upon sin. It is humiliation inimitable, unrepeated, unrepeatable.
John Murray

If I would appreciate the blood of Christ I must accept God's valuation of it, for the blood is not primarily for me but for God.   *Watchman Nee*

This precious Lamb of God gave up his precious fleece for us. *Christopher Nesse*

He suffered not as God, but he who suffered was God.   *John Owen*

The death of Christ was the most dreadful blow ever given to the empire of darkness.   *William S. Plumer*

Death stung himself to death when he stung Christ.   *William Romaine*

From Christ's death flow all our hopes.
J. C. Ryle

The blood of Christ is the seal of the testament.   *Henry Smith*

A dying Christ is the last resort of the believer.   *C. H. Spurgeon*

God had condemned sin before, but never so efficiently as in the death of his Son.
C. H. Spurgeon

If we would live aright it must be by the contemplation of Christ's death.
C. H. Spurgeon

Christ's death, as it were, uncovered God so that man might have a vision of the glory that shone upon his face.
R. V. G. Tasker

Christ assumed every consequence of sin which was not itself sinful. *S. P. Tregelles*

He himself was forsaken that none of his children might ever need to utter his cry of loneliness.   *J. H. Vincent*

Was it for crimes that I had done,
He groaned upon the tree?
Amazing pity! grace unknown!
And love beyond degree!   *Isaac Watts*

The magnitude of the sacrifice which our sins called forth manifests the supreme folly of looking elsewhere for their forgiveness.   *Geoffrey B. Wilson*

Who delivered up Jesus to die? Not Judas, for money; not Pilate, for fear; not the Jews, for envy; but the Father, for love!   *Octavius Winslow*

JESUS CHRIST — Deity and Humanity

As the print of the seal on the wax is the express image of the seal itself, so Christ is the express image — the perfect representation — of God.   *Ambrose*

He who made man was made man. *Anon.*

Christ was a complete man.   *Augustine*

343

Jesus Christ is God in the form of man; as completely God as if he were not man; as completely man as if he were not God.
A. J. F. Behrends

He who sees the Son sees the Father in the face of Christ. The Son exactly represents and reflects the Father.
J. A. Bengel

A man who can read the New Testament and not see that Christ claims to be more than a man can look all over the sky at high noon on a cloudless day and will not see the sun. *W. E. Biederwolf*

Jesus neither laid aside his deity when he came to earth nor his humanity when he returned to heaven. *John Blanchard*

When Jesus came to earth he did not cease to be God; when he returned to heaven he did not cease to be man.
John Blanchard

With the exception of being sinful, everything that can be said about a man can be said about Jesus Christ.
James Montgomery Boice

The nature of Christ's existence is mysterious, I admit; but this mystery meets the wants of man. Reject it and the world is an inexplicable riddle; believe it, and the history of our race is satisfactorily explained. *Napoleon Bonaparte*

If Jesus Christ is not true God, how could he help us? If he is not true man, how could he help us? *Dietrich Bonhoeffer*

God has taken the attributes of his being — his love, his mercy, his holiness, his justice, his power — and has translated them into a form that men can understand, believe and respond to. *Richard Bube*

The climax of God's revelation of himself is the person of Jesus Christ. In him the ultimate and the unconditional are wed to the transient and the conditioned in such a way that a human being can respond with his or her own personality.
Richard Bube

He who ... does not perceive Christ to be God ... is blind amidst the brightness of noon-day. *John Calvin*

The characteristics of God Almighty are mirrored for us in Jesus Christ. Therefore if we want to know what God is like we must study Jesus Christ.
Oswald Chambers

As to his deity he had no mother, and as to his humanity he had no father.
Robert Clarke

Christ was God, not because he was virgin born. He was virgin born because he was God. *Robert Clarke*

Christ uncrowned himself to crown us, and put off his robes to put on our rags, and came down from heaven to keep us out of hell. He fasted forty days that he might feast us to all eternity; he came from heaven to earth that he might send us from earth to heaven. *W. Dyer*

Christ is the image of God — no feature absent, none misplaced and none impaired in fullness or dimmed in lustre.
John Eadie

Jesus became as like us as God can be.
Donald English

Jesus did not become identical to us; he did become identified with us.
Donald English

344

Jesus is the human form of the original Word through whom the worlds were brought into being.   *Donald English*

Either Jesus is who is says he is, in which case Christianity is true in a way no other religion is; or else Jesus is not who he says he is, in which case the very essence of Christianity is not true at all.
C. Stephen Evans

It pleases the Father that all fullness should be in Christ; therefore there is nothing but emptiness anywhere else.
W. Gadsby

The miracles as such do not directly prove Jesus to be the Son of God; this power could have been given to him as a mere man. But indirectly they prove him to be the Son of God because they prove him to be a truthful messenger, and this truthful messenger says that he is God.
John H .Gerstner

Christ's humanity is the great hem of the garment, through which we can touch his Godhead.   *Richard Glover*

Jesus is God spelling himself out in a language that man can understand.
S. D. Gordon

All that Jesus was and taught and did is but a revealing of the eternal God.
E. F. Hallock

Christ is our temple, in whom by faith all believers meet.   *Matthew Henry*

It was great condescension that he who was God should be made in the likeness of flesh; but much greater that he who was holy should be made in the likeness of sinful flesh!   *Matthew Henry*

The Son of God did not unite himself with a human person, but with a human nature.
Charles Hodge

In Christ Jesus heaven meets earth and earth ascends to heaven.   *Henry Law*

Surely royalty in rags, angels in cells, is not descent compared to Deity in flesh!
Henry Law

Jesus did not cease to be the Son of God when he became man. He did not drop his deity, which is an impossible thought. He remained what he was and added what he had not had, namely a human nature, derived out of a woman, a human mother. He became the God-man. *R. C. H. Lenski*

A man who was merely a man and said the sort of things Jesus said wouldn't be a great moral teacher. He'd be either a lunatic — on a level with a man who says he's a poached egg — or else he'd be the devil of hell. You must make your choice. Either this man was and is the Son of God, or else a madman or something worse … But don't let us come up with any patronizing nonsense about his being a great human teacher. He hasn't left that open to us. He didn't intend to. *C. S. Lewis*

Christians believe that Jesus Christ is the Son of God because he said so. The other evidence about him has convinced them that he was neither a lunatic nor a quack.
C. S. Lewis

The union between God and nature in the person of Christ admits no divorce.
C. S. Lewis

Anything that one imagines of God apart from Christ is only useless thinking and vain idolatry.   *Martin Luther*

I have had so many experiences of Christ's divinity, that I must say: either there is no God, or he is God.

Martin Luther

If Christ is divested of his deity, there remains no help against God's wrath and no rescue from his judgement.

Martin Luther

The doctrine that Jesus Christ had a true human nature is probably the single most important article of the Christian faith.

Donald MacLeod

If Christ is only man, then I am an idolater. If he is very God, then the man who denies it is a blasphemer. There can be no union between those who hold his deity and those who deny it.

G. Campbell Morgan

We do not believe that God has added, or ever will add, anything to his revelation in his Son.

C. B. Moss

Jesus was man in guise, not in disguise.

Handley C. G. Moule

The fact that Jesus will sit upon the throne of judgement will be the consternation of his enemies and the consolation of his people.

John Murray

The eternal generation of the Son in no way implies inferiority.

Stuart Olyott

He suffered not as God, but he suffered who was God.

John Owen

The impression of Jesus which the gospels give ... is not so much one of deity reduced as of divine capacities restrained.

J. I. Packer

Christ is the aperture through which the immensity and magnificence of God can be seen.

J. B. Phillips

In becoming man Christ took upon him a nature that was capable of dying. This the angels were not; and in this respect he was, for a season, made lower than they.

A. W. Pink

If the life and death of Socrates are those of a philosopher, the life and death of Jesus Christ are those of a God.

Jean Jacques Rousseau

The Saviour of sinners knows what it is to be poor.

J. C. Ryle

Unless our Lord Jesus is very God of very God, there is an end of his mediation, his atonement, his advocacy, his priesthood, his whole work of redemption.

J. C. Ryle

Christ stands ... solitary and alone among all the heroes of history and presents to us an unsolvable problem, unless we admit him to be more than man, even the eternal Son of God.

Philip Schaff

Christ assumed both body and soul; and he offered both in our room, as was necessary to expiate guilt incurred in both and by both.

G. Smeaton

Let us come to Jesus — the person of Christ is the centre of theology.

H. B. Smith

If you want to know what God has to say to you, see what Christ was and is.

C. H. Spurgeon

It is an infallible proof of our Lord's divinity that he may be addressed in prayer.

C. H. Spurgeon

Jesus is not the child of eternity, but the Father of it.

C. H. Spurgeon

Remember, Christ was not a deified man, neither was he a humanized God. He was perfectly God and at the same time perfectly man. *C. H. Spurgeon*

Christ was not half a God and half a man; he was perfectly God and perfectly man. *James Stalker*

Because Christ was God, did he pass unscorched through the fires of Gethsemane and Calvary? Rather let us say, because Christ was God he underwent a suffering that was absolutely infinite. *Augustus H. Strong*

If Jesus Christ was a product of evolution, how is it that no better man has since appeared, after nineteen centuries? *W. H. Griffith Thomas*

All that man can know of God and his love in this life is revealed in Jesus Christ. *A. W. Tozer*

We know how God would act if he were in our place — he has been in our place. *A. W. Tozer*

Christ's consciousness of deity was not suspended during his earthly life. *Marvin R. Vincent*

If ever the Divine appeared on earth, it was in the person of Christ. *Johann Wolfgang von Goethe*

He was like a king who temporarily puts on the garments of a peasant while at the same time remaining king. *John F. Walvoord*

A cloud over the sun makes no change in the body of the sun; so, though the divine nature be covered with the human, it makes no change in the divine nature. *Thomas Watson*

He who was the Son by nature willingly took the form of a servant so that we who were by nature the servants of sin might become sons by the adoption of grace! *Geoffrey B. Wilson*

The incarnation of the Son of God was not a diminishing of his deity, but an acquiring of manhood. *Verna Wright*

JESUS CHRIST — Glory

Christ is our hope of glory and the glory of our hope. *Anon.*

The Word of God became flesh;
The Son of God became Man;
The Lord of all became a servant;
The Righteous One was made sin;
The Eternal One tasted death;
The Risen One now lives in men;
The Seated One is coming again! *Anon.*

Christ contains in himself the totality of divine powers and excellencies. *George Barlow*

If Socrates would enter the room, we should rise and do him honour. But if Jesus Christ came into the room, we should fall down on our knees and worship him. *Napoleon Bonaparte*

Christ is lovely, Christ is very lovely, Christ is most lovely, Christ is always lovely, Christ is altogether lovely. *Thomas Brooks*

Christ is the most sparkling diamond in the ring of glory. *Thomas Brooks*

The name of Christ excludes all merit of our own. *John Calvin*

The whole gospel is contained in Christ. *John Calvin*

Who can deny that Jesus of Nazareth, the incarnate Son of the Most High God, is the eternal glory of the human race?
Benjamin Disraeli

Unless your vision of Christ is as large as it can possibly be, you will always be in danger of heresy.   *Donald English*

When the sun is up, the moon seems to have no light.   *George Estey*

The excellencies of Christ are perfectly exclusive of all their opposites.
John Flavel

Christ is the ocean, in which every drop is infinite compassion. He is the mountain towering above the mountains, in which every grain is God's own goodness.   *Henry Law*

In his life Christ is an example, showing us how to live; in his death he is a sacrifice, satisfying for our sin; in his resurrection, a conqueror; in his ascension, a king; in his intercession, a high priest.
Martin Luther

The Jesus of the New Testament has at least one advantage over the Jesus of modern reconstruction — he is real.
J. Gresham Machen

Without the miracles, you would have in Jesus a teacher and an example; but with the miracles you have a Saviour from your sins.   *J. Gresham Machen*

Jesus Christ is the one to whom the whole alphabet of history points.
Leslie Newbigin

Jesus Christ is the centre of everything and the object of everything, and he who does not know him knows nothing of the order of nature and nothing of himself.
Blaise Pascal

Jesus is the cornerstone of humanity. If he were taken away, it would shake the world to its foundations.   *Ernest Renan*

They lose nothing who gain Christ.
Samuel Rutherford

No man ever errs on the side of giving too much honour to God the Son.
J. C. Ryle

No man ever thought too much of Christ.
J. C. Ryle

There is an infinite fullness in Jesus Christ.   *J. C. Ryle*

No physician like the Lord, no tonic like his promise, no wine like his love.
C. H. Spurgeon

Christ has outlasted the empire that crucified him nineteen centuries ago. He will outlast the dictators who defy him now.   *Ralph W. Sockman*

God is more glorified in the person of his Son than he would have been by an unfallen world.   *C. H. Spurgeon*

The glory of Jesus and of the Father are so wrapped up together that the grace which magnifies the one magnifies the other.   *C. H. Spurgeon*

There was never a sinner half as big as Christ is as a Saviour.   *C. H. Spurgeon*

We have much more to receive, but God has no more to give than he has given in Jesus Christ.   *John R. W. Stott*

The world cannot bury Christ. The earth is not deep enough for his tomb, the clouds are not wide enough for his winding-sheet.   *Edward Thomson*

The more you think about Christ, the more you think of him.   *H.C. Trumbul*

The act of incarnation was not a temporary arrangement which ended with Christ's death and resurrection but, as the Scriptures make evident, his human nature continues for ever. *John F. Walvoord*

To rob the divine nature of God of a single attribute would destroy his deity, and to rob man of a single attribute would result in the destruction of a true humanity. It is for this reason that the two natures of Christ cannot lose or transfer a single attribute.   *John F. Walvoord*

Without question the crucial issue in biblical theology is the deity of Christ, and disregard or question of this central doctrine of the Bible leads to inevitable chaos in theology as a whole.
John F. Walvoord

All that man as man is, that Christ is to eternity.   *Benjamin B. Warfield*

Join all the glorious names
Of wisdom, love and power,
That ever mortals knew,
That angels ever bore;
All are too mean to speak his worth,
Too mean to set my Saviour forth.
Isaac Watts

Christ is the fulfiller and fulfilment of all the promises of God because he is the sum and substance of them.
Geoffrey B. Wilson

JESUS CHRIST — Holiness

The Lord Jesus Christ would have the whole world to know that though he pardons sin he will not protect it.
Joseph Alleine

Jesus was never guarding himself, but always invading the lives of others with his holiness.   *Phillips Brooks*

JESUS CHRIST — Humility

No other man has ever humbled himself so greatly; and no man has ever been more exalted as a result. *John Blanchard*

Nothing is so sweet and beautiful, yet to ambitious men so surprising, as the humility of the Lord Jesus.*Walter Chantry*

JESUS CHRIST — Intercession

I change, he changes not,
The Christ can never die;
His love, not mine, the resting-place,
His truth, not mine, the tie.
Horatius Bonar

Christ's purse is always full, though he be always giving.   *Thomas Brooks*

He who for men their surety stood,
And poured on earth his precious blood,
Pursues in heaven his mighty plan,
The Saviour and the Friend of man.
Michael Bruce

Where high the heavenly temple stands,
The house of God not made with hands,
A great High Priest our nature wears,
The Saviour of mankind appears.
Michael Bruce

God can listen to no prayers without the intercession of Christ.   *John Calvin*

There is no way of obtaining favour from God but through the intercession of Christ.   *John Calvin*

Christ is the still point of the turning world.   *T. S. Eliot*

Faith asks no signal from the skies
To show that prayers accepted rise;
Our Priest is in the holy place
And answers from the throne of grace.
Josiah Fonder

Before the throne of God above
I have a strong, a perfect plea,
A great High Priest, whose name is love,
Who ever lives and pleads for me.
Charitie Lees de Chenze

If I could hear Christ praying for me in the next room, I would not fear a million of enemies. Yet the distance makes no difference; he is praying for me!
Robert Murray M'Cheyne

The sea ebbs and flows, but the rock remains unmoved.
Robert Murray M'Cheyne

Christ has taken our nature into heaven to represent us, and has left us on earth with his nature to represent him.
John Newton

Prayer as it comes from the saint is weak and languid; but when the arrow of a saint's prayer is put into the bow of Christ's intercession it pierces the throne of grace.   *Thomas Watson*

See where before the throne he stands,
And pours the all-prevailing prayer,
Points to his side, and lifts his hands,
And shows that I am graven there.
Charles Wesley

JESUS CHRIST — Life and Influence

All the armies that ever marched, and all the navies that ever were built, and all the parliaments that ever sat, and all the kings that ever reigned, put together, have not affected the life of mankind on this earth as powerfully as has that one solitary life.   *Anon.*

Christ's actions are our patterns.   *Anon.*

This man changed history. Our dating, our culture, our legal system, our educational system and the belief that has dominated vast amounts of the world for the last 2,000 years, all stem from this one individual who died as a young man after a short time in the public eye. *Simon Austen*

The example of Christ is supreme in its authority.   *George Barlow*

Jesus Christ disturbs everything he confronts.   *Rolfe Barnard*

The sublimest virtue according to philosophy is to live the life of nature, but Scripture points us to the perfect Christ as our example.   *John Calvin*

The name of Jesus is not so much written as ploughed into the history of the world.
Ralph Waldo Emerson

The fear of the Lord was a lovely grace in the perfect humanity of Jesus. Let it be the test of our 'predestination to be conformed to his image'. *Sinclair Ferguson*

It is more significant that God walked on earth than that man walked on the moon.
Rob Frost

We must not heed what others did who were before us, but what Christ did who was before all.   *Thomas Fuller*

Jesus was the most disturbing person in history. *Vance Havner*

No revolution that has ever taken place in society can be compared to that which has been produced by the words of Jesus Christ. *Mark Hopkins*

Jesus walking on the earth is far more important than man walking on the moon. *James Irwin*

He produced mainly three effects: hatred, terror, adoration. There was no trace of people expressing mild approval. *C. S. Lewis*

Christ is the only character in all history who has four contemporary biographers and historians, every one of whom suffered persecution (and martyrdom) in attestation of the truth of his narrative. *Irwin Linton*

Jesus' miracles are decisive evidence for all time of who he is and what power he has. *J. I. Packer*

After reading the doctrine of Plato, Socrates, or Aristotle, we feel that the specific difference between their words and Christ's is the difference between an inquiry and a revelation. *Joseph Parker*

Jesus was the very King of meekness. *A. W. Pink*

Our Lord's life was ordered by his objective. *Ken Robins*

I cannot think of even one lonely passage in the New Testament which speaks of Christ's revelation, manifestation, appearing or coming that is not directly linked with moral conduct, faith and spiritual holiness. *A. W. Tozer*

If there is any reality within the whole sphere of human experience that is by its very nature worthy to challenge the mind, charm the heart and bring the total life to a burning focus, it is the reality that revolves around the person of Christ. *A. W. Tozer*

Jesus Christ left us an example for our daily conduct and from it there can be no appeal. *A. W. Tozer*

Jesus Christ himself was a do-gooder from the beginning of his public ministry to the end of it. There is a sense in which he did nothing else. *Foy Valentine*

Christ lived what he preached and preached what he lived. *Fernando Vangioni*

My dear Redeemer and my Lord,
I read my duty in thy Word;
But in thy life the law appears
Drawn out in living characters. *Isaac Watts*

Christ's deed and examples are commandments of what we should do. *John Wycliffe*

JESUS CHRIST — Lordship

As Christ is the root by which a saint grows, so is he the rule by which a saint walks. *Anon.*

He values not Christ at all who does not value Christ above all. *Augustine*

The Lord who vacated his tomb has not vacated his throne. *G. R. Beasley Murray*

Christ will either be a whole Saviour or none at all. *John Berridge*

The lordship of Christ is neither optional nor negotiable. *John Blanchard*

There is never a day when the Lord could love his people more — or less.
John Blanchard

Christ with anything would have satisfied me; nothing without Christ could do it. *Thomas Boston*

The command of authority is an invitation of love. *Charles Bridges*

Miss Christ and you miss all.
Thomas Brooks

The rattle without the breast will not satisfy the child; the house without the husband will not satisfy the wife; the cabinet without the jewel will not satisfy the virgin; the world without Christ will not satisfy the soul. *Thomas Brooks*

They do not love Christ who love anything more than Christ. *Thomas Brooks*

Jesus cannot be our Saviour unless he is first our Lord. *Hugh C. Burr*

Certainly if we are to believe what our eyes see, then the kingdom of Christ seems to be on the verge of ruin. But [the] promise that Christ will never be dragged from his throne but that rather he will lay low all his enemies banishes from us all fear. *John Calvin*

The whole of Satan's kingdom is subject to the authority of Christ. *John Calvin*

There is nothing holier, or better, or safer, than to content ourselves with the authority of Christ alone. *John Calvin*

The system of human mediation falls away in the advent to our souls of the living Christ. Who wants stars, or even the moon, after the sun is up? *A. B. Cave*

Jesus will not be a Saviour to any man who refuses to bow to him as Lord.
Walter J. Chantry

No repentance is true repentance which does not recognize Jesus as Lord over every area of life. *John C. Chapman*

If Christ is Lord of all, Christians must recapture their sense of moral outrage.
Charles Colson

If Christ's lordship does not disrupt our own lordship, then the reality of our conversion must be questioned.
Charles Colson

Christ is either both Saviour and Lord, or he is neither Saviour nor Lord.
John R. De Witt

Every blessing God has for man is in and through Jesus Christ. *A. Lindsay Glegg*

You cannot have the gifts of Christ apart from the government of Christ.
A. Lindsay Glegg

Christ is now creation's sceptre-bearer, as he was once creation's burden-bearer.
A. J. Gordon

Jesus Christ demands more complete allegiance than any dictator who ever lived. The difference is, he has the right to.
Vance Havner

Salvation is not a cafeteria where you take what you want and leave the rest. You cannot take Christ as Saviour and refuse him as Lord and be saved. *Vance Havner*

A Christ supplemented is a Christ supplanted. *William Hendriksen*

Tomorrow's history has already been written ... at the name of Jesus every knee must bow. *Paul E. Kauffman*

The beginning of self-mastery is to be mastered by Christ, to yield to his lordship. *D. G. Kehl*

There is not an inch of secular life of which Christ does not say, 'It belongs to me.' *Abraham Kuyper*

There's not a thumb's breadth of this universe about which Jesus Christ does not say, 'It is mine.' *Abraham Kuyper*

Seek Christ, and you will find him, and with him everything else thrown in. *C. S. Lewis*

How divinely supreme is our Lord above all others! *D. Martyn Lloyd-Jones*

You cannot receive Christ in bits and pieces. *D. Martyn Lloyd-Jones*

When Jesus Christ utters a word, he opens his mouth so wide that it embraces all heaven and earth, even though that word be but in a whisper. *Martin Luther*

When we come to Jesus for salvation, we come to the one who is Lord over all. Any message omitting this truth cannot be called the gospel according to Jesus. *John F. MacArthur Jr*

Jesus Christ is everywhere; he is behind everything we see if only we have eyes to see him; and he is the Lord of history if only we penetrate deep enough beneath the surface. *Charles Malik*

Where Christ does not rule, sin does. *J. I. Packer*

The early Christians would have been quite surprised to hear 'Jesus is Lord' as a second experience. For them it was a baptismal confession! *Kenneth F. W. Prior*

All history is incomprehensible without Christ. *Ernest Renan*

Whatever may be the surprises of the future, Jesus will never be surpassed. *Ernest Renan*

Christ is the great central fact in the world's history. To him everything looks forward or backward. All the lines of history converge upon him. *C. H. Spurgeon*

I have a great need for Christ; I have a great Christ for my need. *C. H. Spurgeon*

The keys of providence swing at the girdle of Christ. *C. H. Spurgeon*

It is as unbiblical as it is unrealistic to divorce the lordship from the Saviourhood of Jesus Christ. *John R. W. Stott*

Nobody can call himself a Christian who does not worship Jesus. *John R. W. Stott*

For the true Christian the one supreme test for the present soundness and ultimate worth of everything religious must be the place our Lord occupies in it. *A. W. Tozer*

To present Christ's lordship as an option leaves it squarely in the category of stereo equipment for a new car. *Dallas Willard*

JESUS CHRIST — Love

Christ's love to his people is not a lip-love, from the teeth outwardly, but a real love, from the heart inwardly.   *W. Dyer.*

I stand amazed in the presence
Of Jesus the Nazarene,
And wonder how he could love me,
A sinner, condemned, unclean.
                    Charles Homer Gabriel

We are never nearer Christ than when we find ourselves lost in a holy amazement at his unspeakable love.   *John Owen*

Though our Saviour's passion is over, his compassion is not.   *William Penn*

Every day we may see some new thing in Christ. His love has neither brim nor bottom.   *Samuel Rutherford*

In our fluctuations of feeling, it is well to remember that Jesus admits no change in his affections; your heart is not the compass Jesus saileth by.
                    Samuel Rutherford

The man who knows the love of Christ in his heart can do more in one hour than the busy type of man can do in a century.
                    D. Martyn Lloyd-Jones

There is no higher priority in the believer's life than to delight himself in the love of Christ.   *Maurice Roberts*

The distinguishing mark of a Christian is his confidence in the love of Christ, and the yielding of his affections to Christ in return.   *C. H. Spurgeon*

JESUS CHRIST — Perfection

Fallen human nature has neither grace nor truth in it, but the human nature of Christ was full of grace and truth.   *W. E. Best*

Only a perfect righteousness can stand in the judgement, and the Christian can have such righteousness only outside himself and in the perfection of Christ.
                    John Calvin

Every virtue known to man is found in Jesus.   *Michael Green*

Jesus perfectly lived what he perfectly taught.   *Herman H. Horne*

The most destructive criticsm has not been able to dethrone Christ as the incarnation of perfect holiness.
                    Herrick Johnson

Christ was made sin, but never a sinner. Sinner means one who is personally affected by sin; Christ's person never was. He never had any fellowship with sin other than that of love and compassion, to bear it as our High Priest and Substitute.   *Abraham Kuiper*

It is a lovely sight to see man treading earth and no mire clinging to his feet; and breathing our polluted air without infection's taint.   *Henry Law*

We can say that Christ was 'made sin' but we cannot say that he was made sinful.   *Donald MacLeod*

The one person a relativist cannot relativize is Jesus Christ.   *Peter C. Moore*

While always in contact with sin, Christ continued sinless, for the infection never spread to him.   *G. Smeaton*

There was not a particle of evil in any one of the Redeemer's tears. Salt there may have been, but not fault.
C. H. Spurgeon

Christ, if not good, is not God.
Augustus H. Strong

The heavenly perfection of Jesus discloses to us the greatness of our own possible being, while at the same time it reveals our infinite shortcoming and the source from which all restoration must come. *Augustus H. Strong*

Our Lord Jesus Christ called himself the Truth, not the Custom. *Tertullian*

Jesus Christ is both the most absolute grace and the most perfect law; so that to believe in him is to embrace at once both law and grace. *Alexandre Viret*

Jesus Christ is made up of all sweets and delights. He himself is all that is desirable. He is light to the eye, honey to the taste, joy to the heart. *Thomas Watson*

JESUS CHRIST — Power

Jesus' life was a blaze of miracles.
Karl Adam

The power of Christ manifests to the full its irresistible energy and attains its highest results by performing works of power with powerless instruments. *J. A. Beet*

Christ himself is the dynamic of all his demands. *John Blanchard*

We marvel, not that Christ performed miracles, but rather that he performed so few. He who could have stormed the citadels of men with mighty battalions of angels let men spit on him and crucify him. *Oswald Chambers*

Jesus Christ is God's everything for man's total need. *Richard Halverson*

Jesus Christ is the divine Physician and Pharmacist, and his prescriptions are never out of balance. *Vance Havner*

Jesus Christ is no security against life's storms, but he is perfect security in life's storms. *Wendell Loveless*

Christ's performances outstrip his promises. *Nehemiah Rogers*

It is not your hold of Christ that saves, but his hold of you! *C. H. Spurgeon*

The highest sin and the deepest despair together cannot baffle the power of Jesus. *C. H. Spurgeon*

The maker of the will is alive to carry out his own intentions. *C. H. Spurgeon*

There is no pit so deep that Jesus is not deeper still. *Corrie Ten Boom*

JESUS CHRIST — Resurrection —
See Resurrection of Christ

JESUS CHRIST — Second Coming —
See Second Coming of Christ

JESUS CHRIST — Sympathy

Christ's statements are either cosmic or comic. *John Blanchard*

How is it that nobody has dreamed up any moral advances since Christ's teaching? What was there in his heredity and his environment to account for this unique teacher, and the remarkable fact that no greater has ever looked like emerging?
Michael Green

Jesus takes to heart the sufferings of his friends. *William Hendriksen*

Certainly, no revolution that has ever taken place in society can be compared to that which has been produced by the words of Jesus Christ. *Mark Hopkins*

The discrepancy between the depth, sincerity and, may I say, shrewdness of Christ's moral teaching and the rampant megalomania which must lie behind his theological teaching unless he is indeed God, has never been got over. *C. S. Lewis*

The essential teachings of Jesus … were literally revolutionary and will always remain so if they are taken seriously.
Herbert J. Miller

Jesus Christ is not only the Son of God mighty to save, but the Son of man able to feel. *J. C. Ryle*

O Saviour Christ, thou too art man;
Thou hast been troubled, tempted, tried;
Thy kind but searching glance can scan
The very wounds that shame would hide.
Henry Twells

Touched with a sympathy within,
He knows our feeble frame;
He knows what sore temptations mean,
For he has felt the same.
Isaac Watts

We shall never understand anything of our Lord's preaching and ministry unless we continually keep in mind what exactly and exclusively his errand was in this world. *Alexander Whyte*

JESUS CHRIST — Teaching

Standing back and looking at the teaching of Jesus about God's love, compassion and provision, we find a fitness in his actions, be they ordinary or miraculous, which gives credence to his teaching.
John Houghton

The personality and teachings of Jesus are not inherited from the collective spirit of his time, but stand out in contrast to it. Their very uniqueness is a testimony to the reality of his personhood.
John A. Sanford

JESUS CHRIST — Uniqueness

Jesus Christ is light to the eye, honey to the taste, music to the ear, joy to the heart.
Anon.

Religion without Christ is a lamp without oil. *Anon.*

The strange thing about Jesus is that you can never get away from him. *Anon.*

Jesus was not the first Christian; he was and is the Christ. *Herman Bavinck*

Between Jesus and whomsoever else in the world there is no possible comparison.
Napoleon Bonaparte

To search for wisdom apart from Christ means not simply foolhardiness but utter insanity. *John Calvin*

Christ is wisdom for your ignorance, strength for your weakness, righteousness for your guilt, sanctification for your corruption, redemption from all the thraldom of your apostasy. *Richard Fuller*

Christ is not only the Saviour but the salvation itself. *Matthew Henry*

There is more of power to sanctify, elevate, strengthen and cheer in the word

Jesus (Jehovah - Saviour) than in all the utterances of man since the world began.
Charles Hodge

In a civilization like ours, I feel that everyone has to come to terms with the claims of Jesus Christ upon his life, or else be guilty of inattention or of evading the question.   *C. S. Lewis*

In his life Christ is an example showing us how to live; in his death, he is a sacrifice satisfying for our sins; in his resurrection, a conqueror; in his ascension, a king; in his intercession, a high priest.
Martin Luther

All is loss that comes between us and Christ.   *George Macdonald*

Jesus Christ cannot be adequately understood in terms of any category applicable to man ... He is a category by himself.
Donald MacLeod

He who thinks he hath no need of Christ hath too high thoughts of himself. He who thinks Christ cannot help him hath too low thoughts of Christ.   *J. M. Mason*

Everything that is really worth while in the morality of today has come to the world through Christ. Dismiss his standards of right and wrong and try to draw up your own ethical code, and see where you will be!   *G. Campbell Morgan*

When God spoke to humanity in Jesus, he said the last thing he has to say.
G. Campbell Morgan

Jesus was the greatest religious genius that ever lived. His beauty is eternal and his reign will never end. He is in every respect unique and nothing can be compared with him.   *Ernest Renan*

Christ is the meeting-point between the Trinity and the sinner's soul.   *J. C. Ryle*

He is not the Great — he is the Only!
Carnegie Simpson

The more you know about Christ, the less you will be satisfied with superficial views of him.   *C. H. Spurgeon*

Christ is the most unique person in history. No man can write a history of the human race without giving first and foremost place to the penniless teacher of Nazareth.   *H. G. Wells*

JOY
(See also: Happiness; Humour)

A cheerful countenance has a lot of face value.   *Anon.*

It is a poor heart that never rejoices. *Anon.*

Joys are our wings; sorrows are our spurs.
Anon.

Joy is the flag that is flown from the citadel of the heart when the King is in residence.   *Anon.*

Nothing will stop your song quicker than your sin.   *Anon.*

The Christian should be an alleluia from head to foot.   *Augustine*

Keep company with the more cheerful sort of the godly; there is no mirth like the mirth of believers.   *Richard Baxter*

God is a God of joy and the human desire for happiness is a legitimate desire.
John Benton

Joy is the natural outcome of the Christian's obedience to the revealed will of God. *John Blanchard*

True joy glows in the dark. *John Blanchard*

We are meant to enjoy our salvation, not endure it. *John Blanchard*

True Christian joy is both a privilege and a duty. *Jerry Bridges*

There is nothing in afflictions which ought to disturb our joy. *John Calvin*

Lord, take away from me all joy which does not come directly from the Lord Jesus. *Oswald Chambers*

The joy that Jesus gives is the result of our disposition being at one with his own disposition. *Oswald Chambers*

There may be joy in God when there is little joy from God. *Stephen Charnock*

Joy is the gigantic secret of the Christian. *G. K. Chesterton*

Take a saint, and put him in any condition, and he knows how to rejoice in the Lord. *Walter Cradock*

A joyless Christian is a libel on his Master. *Northcote Deck*

Only in obedience can we discover the great joy of the will of God. *Sinclair Ferguson*

Job was a happier man on the dunghill than Adam was in paradise. *John Flavel*

Laughter adds richness, texture and colour to otherwise ordinary days. It is a gift, a choice, a discipline and an art. *Tim Hansel*

'Pleasure' and 'joy' not only are not synonymous, but may be as profoundly different as heaven and hell. *Sidney J. Harris*

The joy of the Lord is not to be confused with the religious levity that has no root or depth. *Vance Havner*

Holy joy is the oil to the wheels of our obedience. *Matthew Henry*

There are more believers who have peace than have joy, because there are more whose evidences are dark and weak — and it is their own fault. *Philip Henry*

Joy is the serious business of heaven. *C. S. Lewis*

Sorrows and joys alike are temporary. In a moment all may be changed. Therefore to one who judges rightly, earthly grief is not over grievous and earthly joy not over joyous. *J. B. Lightfoot*

The joy of the Christian is a holy joy; the happiness of the Christian is a serious happiness. *D. Martyn Lloyd-Jones*

The Christian ought to be a living doxology. *Martin Luther*

Great joys, like griefs, are silent. *Shackerley Marmion*

Joy ceases to be joy when it ceases to be 'in the Lord'. *J. A. Motyer*

Laughter is the music of life. *William Osier*

Joy is a condition that is experienced, but it is more than a feeling; it is, primarily, a state of mind. *J. I. Packer*

Joy is at the heart of satisfied living. *J. I. Packer*

Joy is not an accident of temperament or an unpredictable providence; joy is a matter of choice. *J. I. Packer*

The secret of joy for believers lies in the fine art of Christian thinking. *J. I. Packer*

The word 'joy' is too great and grand to be confused with the superficial things we call happiness. *Kirby Page*

Next to Christ I have one joy, to preach Christ my Lord. *Samuel Rutherford*

It is an unrealistic concept of spirituality to think that joy and heaviness cannot go together. Indeed, it is unbiblical. *Charles Caldwell Ryrie*

Joy is delight at God's grace which enables us to endure our trials. *George Seevers*

Carnal joy is always outward, and easy to express. *Richard Sibbes*

We can do nothing well without joy, and a good conscience which is the ground of joy. *Richard Sibbes*

Nothing gives believers more joy than to see God glorified. *R. C. Sproul*

Better to have a Christian's days of sorrows than a wordling's joys. *C. H. Spurgeon*

Joy in God is the happiest of all joys. *C. H. Spurgeon*

People really full of joy do not usually talk much. *C. H. Spurgeon*

Sorrow for sin should be the keenest sorrow; joy in the Lord should be the loftiest joy. *C. H. Spurgeon*

The greatest joy of a Christian is to give joy to Christ. *C. H. Spurgeon*

If you have no joy in your religion, there's a leak in your Christianity somewhere. *Billy Sunday*

Joy is a great therapeutic for the mind. *A. W. Tozer*

Here, joy begins to enter into us; there, we enter into joy. *Thomas Watson*

There is as much difference between spiritual joys and earthly as between a banquet that is eaten and one that is painted on the wall. *Thomas Watson*

We never better enjoy ourselves than when we most enjoy God. *Benjamin Whichcote*

JUDGEMENT
(See also: Destiny; Eternity; Eternal Life; Heaven; Hell; Punishment)

That which a man spits against heaven shall fall back on his own face. *Thomas Adams*

God does not pay weekly, but he pays at the end. *Anon.*

God is ultimately unavoidable. *Anon.*

The day of judgement is remote; thy day of judgement is at hand. *Anon.*

No one is redeemed except through unmerited mercy, and no one is condemned except through merited judgement.
Augustine

Nothing has contributed more powerfully to wean me from all that held me down to earth than the thought, constantly dwelt upon, of death and of the last judgement.
Augustine

God will give the rebel what he chooses and what he deserves.   *Simon Austen*

Condemnation will always be in exact proportion to guilt; and guilt is in proportion to abused light and privileges.
Albert Barnes

The fact that the Christian can face the day of judgement secure in the knowledge that he will not be rejected does not mean that he is to think of it in terms of a glorified prize-giving.   *John Blanchard*

We shall stand before the judgement seat of Christ on the basis of our performance, not our profession.   *John Blanchard*

We will go past the judgement seat of Christ in single file.   *John Blanchard*

All men's secret sins are printed in heaven, and God will at last read them aloud in the ears of all the world.
Thomas Brooks

As death leaves us, so judgement will find us.   *Thomas Brooks*

Those whose hearts are not pierced by the sword of God's justice shall certainly be cut down and destroyed by the axe of his judgements.   *Francis Burkitt*

It is no inconsiderable security that we shall stand before no other tribunal than that of our Redeemer.   *John Calvin*

Mortal man, however, however inimical he may be, cannot carry his enmity beyond death, but the power of God is not confined to such narrow limits. We often escape from men; we cannot escape the judgement of God.   *John Calvin*

There is nothing that tends more to check a foolish eagerness for display than to reflect that we have to deal with God.
John Calvin

Man cannot cover what God would reveal.   *Thomas Campbell*

Let me ask every day what reference it has to the Day of Judgement and cultivate a disposition to be reminded of that day.   *Richard Cecil*

He whose throne is built on justice and righteousness will see that righteousness prevails. That is why sin must, and will, be punished.   *John C. Chapman*

Secular sanctions do not work. Morality needs the divine sanction of a judgement day.   *Gordon H. Clark*

The gospel teaches us that while believers are not rewarded on account of their works, they are rewarded according to their works.   *R. L. Dabney*

The hours which come fresh to you out of the mercy of your heavenly Father will carry for ever the imprint which your life leaves on them, until all accounts are closed at his Last Assize.
Sinclair Ferguson

When every human being comes face to face with their Creator, no one will be able to compain that they got a raw deal.
Stephen Gaukroger

If we are believers in Jesus Christ we have already come through the storm of judgement. It happened at the cross.
Billy Graham

Heaven will be filled with such as have done good works, and hell with such as intended to do them.   *Antonio Guevasa*

Absolute evil calls for absolute judgement.   *Os Guinness*

God's fork follows the wicked's rake.
William Gurnall

Those that love darkness rather than light shall have their doom accordingly.
Matthew Henry

Those that will not hear the comfortable voice of God's Word shall be made to hear the dreadful voice of his rod.
Matthew Henry

Those who will not deliver themselves into the hand of God's mercy cannot be delivered out of the hand of his justice.
Matthew Henry

Those who will not observe the judgements of God's mouth shall not escape the judgements of his hand.
Matthew Henry

As the king of terrors leaves us, so the day of terror will find us.   *John Mason*

We must fall into the arms of Christ or into the flames of hell.   *John Mason*

God will be glorified in the punishment of sin as well as in the reward of obedience.   *Thomas V. Moore*

Men must choose between an exceeding great and eternal weight of glory and an exceeding great and eternal weight of wrath.   *Thomas V. Moore*

The power of man can never reverse the sentence of God.   *Thomas V. Moore*

The punishment of the sinner is not an arbitrary vengeance, but the due process of moral providence.   *J. A. Motyer*

Those who hated God here will hate him there; the morally careless in daily life will be morally careless still; the defiant will continue defiant, and the unclean will remain uncleansed and unrepentant.
J. A. Motyer

God's will is done no less in the condemnation of unbelievers than in the salvation of those who put faith in the Lord Jesus.   *J. I. Packer*

No man is entirely without inklings of judgement to come.   *J. I. Packer*

Human tribunals deal with crime; they have punishments but no rewards. The divine tribunal has both.   *A. Plummer*

It is character rather than separate acts that will be rewarded or punished.
A. Plummer

The coming day of judgement is a doctrine that has been abused, misunderstood and often used to manipulate people. But correctly understood in the context of God's character and justice, it is a doctrine full of comfort for Christians.
Frank Retief

There are simply too many atrocities in the history of our world for there to be no day of judgement. *Frank Retief*

The judgement seat of Christ lends a seriousness to all life.
William Childs Robinson

We shall have to render an account of every privilege that was granted to us and of every ray of light that we enjoyed.
J. C. Ryle

There will be no possibility of standing before Christ but by standing in Christ.
William Secker

In God's ultimate judgement he gives sinners over to their sins. *R. C. Sproul*

If you are not seeking the Lord, judgement is at your heels. *C. H. Spurgeon*

It is shocking to reflect that a change in the weather has more effect on some men's lives than the dread alternative of heaven or hell. *C. H. Spurgeon*

Time shall be no more when judgement comes, and when time is no more change is impossible. *C. H. Spurgeon*

The instinct of retribution is the strongest instinct of the human heart.
Augustus H. Strong

Sin is the weight on the clock which makes the hammer to strike.
George Swinnock

The resurrection and the judgement will demonstrate before all worlds who won and who lost. We can wait! *A. W. Tozer*

Two stimuli are necessary to make man endeavour to conform with accepted moral standards: belief in an ultimate judgement and belief in the immortality of the soul. *Wernher von Braun*

In this liberal age we tend naturally to avoid any thought of God's judgement.
David Watson

The Lord has a golden sceptre and an iron rod. Those who will not bow to the one shall be broken by the other.
Thomas Watson

Just as the tree cut down, that falls to
North or southward, there it lies;
So man departs to heav'n or hell,
Fix'd in the state wherein he dies.
Isaac Watts

JUSTICE

Let justice be done though the world perish. *Augustine*

Without justice, what are kingdoms but great banditries. *Augustine*

Justice always makes mercy dumb when sin has made the sinner deaf.
Thomas Brooks

The world is a ring, and justice is the diamond in that ring; the world is a body, and justice is the soul in that body.
Thomas Brooks

The Bible insists that God is entirely just, and that therefore ultimately justice will be done, and will be seen to be done.
D. A. Carson

Indeed, I tremble for my country when I reflect that God is just. *Thomas Jefferson*

When we speak of justice in the biblical sense we ... are talking about meeting

need wherever it exists and particularly where it exists most helplessly.
Jay Poppinga

Belief in a just God is not optional.
John Rowland

A God who could pardon without justice might one day pardon without reason.
C. H. Spurgeon

Justice is the greatest interest of man on earth. *Daniel Webster*

JUSTIFICATION
(See also: Faith — and Deeds; Holiness — and Justification)

Christ's righteousness, pleaded in the court of justice, is our full and final discharge. *Anon.*

In justification, the sinner is not only pardoned, he is promoted. *John Blanchard*

Justification does mean that we are right with God, but it does not imply that we are equal with him. *John Blanchard*

God hath two hands, a right hand of mercy and a left hand of justice.
John Boys

Justification by faith is the hinge on which all true religion turns. *John Calvin*

If there be ground for you to trust in your own righteousness, then all that Christ did to purchase salvation, and all that God did to prepare the way for it, is in vain.
Jonathan Edwards

The scriptural doctrine of justification by faith alone, without any manner of goodness or excellency of ours, does in no wise diminish either the necessity or benefit

of a sincere evangelical obedience.
Jonathan Edwards

Faith alone justifies, through Christ alone. Assurance is the enjoyment of that justification. *Sinclair Ferguson*

If justification depended on works it would be unobtainable.
Sinclair Ferguson

In justification we are not only told that Christ has paid the debt of our sins. We receive Christ's righteousness!
Sinclair Ferguson

The stream of grace and righteousness is deeper and broader than the stream of guilt. *Matthew Henry*

In every period when God has awakened his people, the gospel of justification has come to the fore. *Robert M. Horn*

Justification is totally against formal religion. God has no room for those who persist in relying on forms or ceremonies.
Robert M. Horn

Remove justification and the church begins to crumble. *Robert M. Horn*

We need to get such a hold on justification that in the dark day we shall find it holding us. *Robert M. Horn*

When we lack the peace of God, we should turn to our peace with God.
Robert M. Horn

Justification does not make the sinner any different: it declares him just in the eyes of the law. *Ernest F. Kevan*

Justification has to do not with our state, but with our standing: it refers to our position before God. *Ernest F. Kevan*

Justification supplies the only efficient motive to obedience.   *Ernest F. Kevan*

When God justifies the ungodly, he does not declare that the sinner is innocent, but that satisfaction for his sins has been made, and that, as a believer in the Lord Jesus Christ, he has a title to eternal life — a title which is founded in justice.
Ernest F. Kevan

Evangelical obedience is fully a condition of justification but not a cause of justification.   *Sam Logan*

A Christian man is free from all things; he needs no works in order to be justified and saved, but receives these gifts in abundance from his faith alone.
Martin Luther

I have preached justification by faith so often, and I feel sometimes that you are so slow to receive it that I could almost take the Bible and bang it about your heads.   *Martin Luther*

Justification is still the article of the standing or falling church.   *John Murray*

I had rather learn what some men really judge about their own justification from their prayers than their writings.
John Owen

Justification is God's act of remitting the sins of guilty men, and accounting them righteous, freely, by his grace, through faith in Christ, on the ground, not of their own works, but of the representative lawkeeping and redemptive blood-shedding of the Lord Jesus Christ on their behalf.   *J. I. Packer*

No amount of good deeds can make us good persons. We must be good before we can do good. *Chester A. Pennington*

We may rest assured that we are in the domain of error if we in any way divorce justification and sanctification.
William S. Plumer

Justification takes place in the mind of God and not in the nervous system of the believer.   *C. I. Schofield*

There is a double degree of justification: one in our conscience now, another at the Day of Judgement.   *Richard Sibbes*

Christ hides our unrighteousness with his righteousness, he covers our disobedience with his obedience, he shadows our death with his death, that the wrath of God cannot find us.   *Henry Smith*

Nobody has understood Christianity who does not understand ... the word 'justified'.   *John R. W. Stott*

The real reason why the doctrine of justification by grace alone through faith alone is unpopular is that it is grievously wounding to our pride. *John R. W. Stott*

The doctrine of justification by faith ... is a blessed relief from sterile legalism and unavailing self-effort.   *A. W. Tozer*

Justification is through faith, not on account of faith.   *Benjamin B. Warfield*

God does not justify us because we are worthy, but justifying makes us worthy.
Thomas Watson

KINDNESS
(See also: Compassion; Love for others; Mercy to others)

He is too busy who is too busy to be kind.
James W. Alexander

Every moment is the right one to be kind.
Anon.

If we are not very kind we are not very holy. *Anon.*

Kindness is the truest revealer of a person's greatness. *Anon.*

Speak your kind words soon, for you never know how soon it will be too late.
Anon.

Kindness is a language that the deaf can hear and the blind can see.
John Blanchard

The best exercise for strengthening the heart is reaching down and lifting people up. *Ernest Blevins*

Kind words are the music of the world.
Frederick W. Faber

Kindness has converted more sinners than zeal, eloquence or learning.
Frederick W. Faber

If you're naturally kind you attract a lot of people you don't like. *William Feather*

As perfume to the flower, so is kindness to speech. *Katherine Francke*

The disposition to give a cup of cold water to a disciple is a far nobler property than the finest intellect. *William Dean Howells*

A part of kindness consists in loving people more than they deserve.
Joseph Joubert

Kindness in ourselves is the honey that blunts the sting of unkindness in another.
Walter Savage Landor

Be kind; everyone you meet is fighting a hard battle. *Ian MacLaren*

Kindness always brings its own reward. The kind person will seldom be without friends. *J. C. Ryle*

Kindness is a grace that all can understand. *J.C. Ryle*

Constant kindness can accomplish much. As the sun makes ice melt, kindness causes misunderstanding, mistrust and hostility to evaporate. *Albert Schweitzer*

Kindness is a hard thing to give away. It keeps coming back to the giver.
Ralph Scott

Fidelity to God does not require any to act uncharitably to his servants.
C. H. Spurgeon

You can accomplish by kindness what you cannot do by force. *Publilius Syrus*

God has a secret method by which he recompenses his saints: he sees to it that they become the prime beneficiaries of their own benefactions! *I. D. E. Thomas*

Be kind. Remember that everyone you meet is fighting a hard battle.
Harry Thompson

KINGDOM OF GOD

The only kingdom that will prevail in this world is the kingdom that is not of this world. *Anon.*

Ten million roots are pumping in the streets: do you hear them? Ten million buds are forming in the axles of the leaves: do you hear the sound of the saw or the hammer? All next summer is at work in the world: but it is unseen by us. And so 'the kingdom of God comes not with observation'. *Henry Ward Beecher*

365

The throne of God outlives the dissolution of the world.   *Stephen Charnock*

The entrance fee into the kingdom of God is nothing; the annual subscription is all we possess.   *Henry Drummond*

The principles of the kingdom of God cannot be woven by unregenerated men into the pattern of our pagan society. The blueprints of the age to come cannot be forced upon this present world.
Vance Havner

He who is the King of the kingdom of heaven is at the same time the Father of its citizens.   *William Hendriksen*

The Bible is the statute-book of God's kingdom.   *Ezekiel Hopkins*

The kingdom of God does not exist because of your effort or mine. It exists because God reigns. Our part is to enter this kingdom and bring our life under his sovereign will.   *T. Z. Koo*

The kingdom of God has come into the world and the powers of the age to come are operative even in the age that now is.
Peter Lewis

The key to the history of the world is the kingdom of God.   *D. Martyn Lloyd-Jones*

The kingdom of God is not a value system.   *Donald MacLeod*

The kingdom of God is like a grain of mustard seed, not like a can of nitro-glycerine.   *J. B. Thomas*

Everyone wants the kingdom of God, but few want it first.   *Charles L. Venable*

KNOWLEDGE
(See also: Education; Mind; Reason)

He who is proud of his knowledge ... has gout in the wrong end.   *Thomas Adams*

Knowledge directs conscience; conscience perfects knowledge.
Thomas Adams

Practice is the soul of knowledge.
Thomas Adams

All men naturally desire to know, but what doth knowledge avail without the fear of God?   *Thomas á Kempis*

To be aware that you are ignorant is a great step to knowledge.   *Anon.*

Knowledge fills a large brain; it merely inflates a small one.   *Anon.*

Knowledge humbles the great man, astonishes the common man, puffs up the little man.   *Anon.*

Knowledge is folly, except grace guide it.   *Anon.*

Zeal without knowledge is the sister of folly.   *Anon.*

All men by nature desire to know.
Aristotle

Ignorance is your disease; knowledge must be your cure.   *Richard Baxter*

It is not good to know more unless we do more with what we already know.
R. K. Bergethon

Wisdom has never made a bigot, but learning has.   *John Billings*

There is no fear of knowing too much, but there is much fear of practising too little. *Thomas Brooks*

We can never hear too often that we can never learn too well. *Thomas Brooks*

Knowledge of nature and atheism are incompatible. To know nature is to know that there must be a God.
Edward G. Bulwer-Lytton

Almost all men are infected with the disease of desiring to obtain useless knowledge. *John Calvin*

God is less interested in answering our questions than in other things: securing our allegiance, establishing our faith, nurturing a desire for holiness.
D. A. Carson

That knowledge which puffs up will at last puff down. *Joseph Caryl*

A man may be theologically knowing and spiritually ignorant. *Stephen Charnock*

Knowledge is the foundation of wisdom.
Stephen Charnock

Knowledge in the head is as money in the purse; knowledge in the heart is as money for our use. *Stephen Charnock*

All knowledge must come from him who made us in his image. *Edmund P. Clowney*

Knowledge cannot save us, but we cannot be saved without knowledge. *John Donne*

You cannot find knowledge by rearranging your ignorance. *Ronald Eyre*

However paradoxical it seems to our natural minds, it is one of the facts of spiritual reality that practical Christian living is based on understanding and knowledge. *Sinclair Ferguson*

Action is the proper fruit of knowledge.
Thomas Fuller

If you have knowledge, let others light their candles at it. *Thomas Fuller*

Knowledge is to be the usher of grace; information in the understanding must go before reformation in the will and affections. *Thomas Fuller*

One grain of faith is more precious than a pound of knowledge. *Joseph Hall*

Seldom was ever any knowledge given to keep, but to impart. *Joseph Hall*

Because some things do not make sense to us now does not mean they will never make sense. *Vance Havner*

It is debatable which is causing us more harm — hot-headed ignorance or cold-hearted intellectualism. *Vance Havner*

Things which don't make sense to our ordinary reasoning can make sense to our spiritual understanding. *Vance Havner*

You can have a head full of Scripture and a heart full of sin. *Vance Havner*

Knowledge is but folly unless it is guided by grace. *George Herbert*

All means of knowing rest on premises outside themselves. *W. Andrew Hoffecker*

Without God we cannot trust reason, sense experience, intuition, or any other methods purported to give knowledge.
W. Andrew Hoffecker

Knowledge

Knowledge without integrity is dangerous and dreadful.   *Samuel Johnson*

One of the things that distinguishes man from the other animals is that he wants to know things, wants to find out what reality is like, simply for the sake of knowing.   *C. S. Lewis*

To the Christian, all knowledge is, in the long run, revelation; and it is almighty God, not us, who ensures that we are able to know what we need to know.
Pete Lowman

Every man has far more knowledge of good than he uses. *Alexander Maclaren*

Let me always remember that it is not the amount of religious knowledge which I have, but the amount which I use, that determines my religious position and character.   *Alexander Maclaren*

There are over many who have much knowledge and little virtue, and who often speak of God while rarely speaking to him.   *Malaval*

Sins of omission are aggravated by knowledge.   *Thomas Manton*

The more I advance, the more clearly I perceive that the greatest human knowledge amounts to a more pompous proof of our ignorance, by showing us how little we know about anything.
John Newton

Not only do we know God through Jesus Christ, we only know ourselves through Jesus Christ.   *Blaise Pascal*

What use is deeper knowledge if we have shallower hearts?   *Leonard Ravenhill*

The devil has more knowledge than any of us, and yet is no better for it. *J. C. Ryle*

Since the tree of knowledge has been tasted, the key of knowledge has been rusted.   *William Secker*

What a lamentable condition is that man in whose knowledge is only sufficient to damn his own soul!   *Richard Sibbes*

Knowledge is indispensable to Christian life and service ... Knowledge is given us to be used, to lead us to higher worship, greater faith, deeper holiness, better service.   *John R. W. Stott*

There may be a clear head without a clean heart.   *George Swinnock*

True faith and saving knowledge go together.   *George Swinnock*

To be proud of learning is the greatest ignorance.   *Jeremy Taylor*

Knowledge without humility is vanity.
A. W. Tozer

The natural man must know in order to believe; the spiritual man must believe in order to know.   *A. W. Tozer*

All human knowledge is only fragmentary. All of us who call ourselves students of nature possess only portions of natural science.   *Rudolph Virchow*

Knowledge is the eye that must direct the foot of obedience.   *Thomas Watson*

Many a man's knowledge is a torch to light him to hell.   *Thomas Watson*

What is a knowing head without a fruitful heart?   *Thomas Watson*

Not ignorance, but the ignorance of ignorance, is the death of knowledge.
Alfred North Whitehead

The knowledge of which we make no use will only serve to condemn us.
Thomas Wilson

KNOWLEDGE OF GOD
(See also: Revelation)

The evidence of knowing God is obeying God. *Eric Alexander*

Who has God has all; who has him not has less than nothing. *Anon.*

There is but one thing in the world really worth pursuing — the knowledge of God.
Robert H. Benson

The Christian who is truly spiritual revels as much in his ignorance of God as in his knowledge of him. *John Blanchard*

To many people, God is no more than an upright blur. *John Blanchard*

That knowledge of God that does not produce a love to him and a desire to be like him is not true knowledge. *Esther Burr*

Knowledge of God can no more connect a man with God than the sight of the sun can carry him to heaven. *John Calvin*

Nearly all the wisdom we possess, that is to say, true and sound wisdom, consists of two parts: the knowledge of God and of ourselves. *John Calvin*

The true knowledge of God corresponds to what faith discovers in the written Word. *John Calvin*

Faith is not on this side of knowledge but beyond it. *John Donne*

Everything in the Christian life depends upon an adequate understanding of who God is. *Ronald Dunn*

If we seek God for our own good and profit, we are not seeking God.
Meister Eckhart

The recognition of who God is is a life-long process. *Elizabeth Elliot*

Knowing God is your single greatest privilege as a Christian. *Sinclair Ferguson*

There is no such thing as genuine knowledge of God that does not show itself in obedience to his Word and will.
Sinclair Ferguson

One would have to be God to know God exhaustively. Finite man can only have a finite knowledge of the Infinite.
Norman Geisler

Man is not making his way up through animism, fetishism, totemism, polytheism and monotheism to a knowledge of God. He started with a knowledge of God and has been going the other way ever since.
Vance Havner

When you come to knowing God, the initiative lies on his side. If he does not show himself, nothing you can do will enable you to find him. *C. S. Lewis*

If we want to know God and to be blessed of God, we must start by worshipping him. *D. Martyn Lloyd-Jones*

He that is made in the image of God must know him or be desolate.
George MacDonald

'To know' is not a mere exercise of the head. Nothing is 'known' until it has also passed over into obedience. *J. A. Motyer*

We grow in proportion as we know.
J. A. Motyer

If ever man is to come to a knowledge of God ... two veils must be taken away: that which hides God's mind and that which clouds our heart. God in his mercy removes both. Thus our knowledge of God, first to last, is his gracious gift.
J. I. Packer

Little knowledge of God is worth a lot more than a great deal of knowledge about him. *J. I. Packer*

Once you become aware that the main business that you are here for is to know God, most of life's problems fall into place of their own accord. *J. I. Packer*

One can know a great deal about godliness without much knowledge of God.
J. I. Packer

To affirm, as some do, that man can discover and know God without God speaking to him is really to deny that God is personal. *J. I. Packer*

The knowledge of God is very far from the love of him. *Blaise Pascal*

What a vast difference there is between knowing God and loving him!
Blaise Pascal

The fact beats ceaselessly into my brain these days that there is a world of difference between knowing the Word of God and knowing the God of the Word.
Leonard Ravenhill

To feel that we are ignorant is the first beginning of all saving knowledge.
J. C. Ryle

Divine knowledge leaves no man stationary. *W. Graham Scroggie*

Divine knowledge is not as the light of the moon to sleep by, but as the light of the sun to work by. *William Seeker*

The larger the God we know, the larger will be our faith. The secret of power in our lives is to know God and expect great things from him. *A. B. Simpson*

If you wish to know God you must know his Word. *C. H. Spurgeon*

The knowledge of God is the great hope of sinners. *C. H. Spurgeon*

Our greatest claim to nobility is our created capacity to know God, to be in personal relationship with him, to love him and to worship him. Indeed, we are most truly human when we are on our knees before our Creator. *John R. W. Stott*

We cannot seek God till we have found him. *George Swinnock*

God is never found accidentally.
A. W. Tozer

The Christian is strong or weak depending upon how closely he has cultivated the knowledge of God.
A. W. Tozer

The heart that knows God can find God anywhere. *A. W. Tozer*

The wisest person in the world is the person who knows the most about God.
A. W. Tozer

To know God is at once the easiest and the most difficult thing in the world.
A. W. Tozer

We can never know who or what we are till we know at least something of what God is. *A. W. Tozer*

We can seek God and find him! God is knowable, touchable, hearable, seeable, with the mind, the hands, the ears and the eyes of the inner man. *A. W. Tozer*

The Christian is a God-explorer.
Tom Wells

LAW OF GOD

The law gives menaces; the gospel gives promises. *Thomas Adams*

The law may *express sin* but it cannot *suppress* sin. *Thomas Adams*

The law, though it has no power to condemn us, has power to command us.
Thomas Adams

The law can pursue a man to Calvary, but no farther. *Anon.*

Those who go against the grain of God's laws shouldn't complain when they get splinters. *Anon.*

Man everywhere is under law, written or unwritten; and he is morally obligated to obey it. *George Barlow*

Love is not perfected, except as the fulfilling of the law. *Theodore Beza*

Christ abolished the law as a means of justification not by destroying it but by fulfilling it. *John Blanchard*

God forbids sin not to prevent us enjoying ourselves, but to prevent us destroying ourselves. *John Blanchard*

God's law was given to reveal sin, not to remove it. *John Blanchard*

God's law is a reflection of his own character. *John Blanchard*

Not only does God's law open my eyes to my guilt, it shuts my mouth when I try to excuse myself. *John Blanchard*

The law of God is like a mirror; it can reveal flaws, but not remove them.
John Blanchard

The man who does not set himself under the law of God sets himself above it.
John Blanchard

The law sends us to the gospel for our justification; the gospel sends us to the law to frame our way of life … Christ has freed us from the *manner of* our obedience, but not from the *matter of* our obedience. *Samuel Bolton*

Without law, love is blind.
Samuel Bolton

The Bible's God, and none other, can satisfy human needs. His moral code for centuries has passed through the flames of controversy, but it does not even have the smell of fire upon it. *D. J. Burrell*

Just as the moon and the stars, though they are themselves bright and spread their light over all the earth, yet vanish before the greater brightness of the sun, so the law, however glorious in itself, has no glory in face of the gospel's grandeur.
John Calvin

371

Only *if* we walk in the beauty *of* God's law do we become sure of our adoption as children of the Father.   *John Calvin*

Those only are worthy students of the law who come to it with a cheerful mind, and are so delighted with its instruction as to account nothing more desirable or delicious than to make progress therein.
John Calvin

Law and love have no quarrel. The conflict arises between law and grace as a way of salvation.   *Walter J. Chantry*

Law makes love practical. Love which is unexpressed will die.   *Walter J. Chantry*

Love makes the law enjoyable. Anyone who loves God delights in keeping his precepts.   *Walter J. Chantry*

Moral law imposes no heavy bondage. It points to the glorious liberty of love, joy and peace. All its ways are good for a man.
Walter J. Chantry

The cross means nothing apart from the law.   *Walter J. Chantry*

The law and the gospel are allies, not enemies.   *Walter J. Chantry*

The law is a hammer to break us, the gospel God's oil to cure us.
Stephen Charnock

No man can break any of the Ten Commandments; he can only break himself against them.   *G. K. Chesterton*

We cannot understand the Ten Commandments apart from Jesus Christ. If we view them as a list of 'don'ts' from which we may infer a corresponding list of 'dos', we forget the Lord who spoke the words from Sinai and the context in which he spoke them. God's commandments call his people to acknowledge him as their Saviour and Lord.   *Edmund P. Clowney*

All the decrees of God are harmonious.
Jonathan Edwards

The law was for the *condemnation* of sinners, the gospel was for the *saving* of sinners and the ministration of forgiveness.   *C. J. Ellicott*

The law sends us to Christ to be justified, and Christ sends us to the law to be regulated.   *John Flavel*

Actually you cannot break the law of God. If you jump off a skyscraper you do not break the law of gravitation, you break your neck.   *Vance Havner*

One might as well attack Gibraltar with a popgun as to attack the moral law of the universe and the God who reigns in righteousness.   *Vance Havner*

There is a universe of moral law, whether we like it or not, and when we disregard it we pull down the house on ourselves and our generation.   *Vance Havner*

We have not learned the commandments until we have learned to do them.
Vance Havner

When the law of God is written in our hearts, our duty will be our delight.
Matthew Henry

If God had wanted us to have a permissive society he would have given us the Ten Suggestions instead of the Ten Commandments.   *M. M. Hershman*

The divine law, as seen by the Christian, exhibits liberty, gives liberty, is liberty.
Robert Johnstone

Law says 'Do', grace says 'Done'.
John Henry Jowett

The Ten Commandments are not a set of do's and don'ts; rather, for the Christian, they are rules for thankful living.
Simon J. Kistemaker

The strongest inducement for a Christian to obey the divine law is the fact that he has been graciously pardoned for having broken it.
Ernest F. Kevan

God is love, and law is the way he loves us. But it is also true that God is law, and love is the way he rules us.
G. S. Lee

People make excuses for not keeping the law of God, which is proof how deeply they believe in the law.
C. S. Lewis

The law was not meant to be praised, it was meant to be practised.
D. Martyn Lloyd-Jones

The law discovers the disease. The gospel gives the remedy. *Martin Luther*

The law is what we must do; the gospel is what God will give. *Martin Luther*

A low view of law leads to legalism in religion; a high view makes man a seeker after grace. *J. Gresham Machen*

At the heart of everything that the Bible says are two great truths, which belong inseparably together — the majesty of the law of God, and sin as an offence against that law. *J. Gresham Machen*

The consciousness of sin alone leads men to turn to the Saviour from sin, and the consciousness of sin comes only when men are brought face to face with the law of God. *J. Gresham Machen*

The gospel does not abrogate God's law, but it makes men love it with all their hearts. *J. Gresham Machen*

The giving of the law is part of the dispensation of the covenant of grace.
Donald MacLeod

In the Ten Commandments we have a transcript of the moral constitution of Deity. *Douglas Macmillan*

The law reflects the nature and character of God just as surely as does the gospel.
Douglas Macmillan

The gospel no more excuses sin than the law does. What is repugnant to the moral law of God is also contrary to the gospel of Christ. *Henry T. Mahan*

God's law was once impressed upon our natures, and we are obliged to all that was written upon Adam's heart.
Thomas Manton

The law sends us to the gospel so that we may be justified. The gospel sends us to the law to find out what our duty is now that we are justified. *Will Metzger*

The law tells me how crooked I am. Grace comes along and straightens me out.
D. L. Moody

The Christian must remember that he is called not only to believe revealed doctrine but to obey revealed law.
J. A. Motyer

The law of God is the royal law of liberty, and liberty consists in being captive to the Word and law of God. All other liberty is not liberty but the thraldom of servitude to sin.   *John Murray*

Law is needed as love's eyes; love is needed as law's heart-beat. Law without love is Pharisaism; love without law is antinomianism.   *J. I. Packer*

The law demands what it cannot give; grace gives all it demands. *Blaise Pascal*

Law and order are infinitely important because they are the expression of the character of God.   *James Philip*

Avoid as you would a deadly snake any man who denies the law of God is the Christian's rule of life.   *A. W. Pink*

Christ has redeemed his people from the curse of the law and not from the command of it; he has saved them from the wrath of God, but not from his government.   *A. W. Pink*

The law of God is no other than a transcript of his most holy mind, and ... whoever loves one must love the other.
Thomas Robinson

I cannot find a syllable in [the Apostle's] writings which teach that any one of the Ten Commandments is done away ... I believe that the coming of Christ's gospel did not alter the position of the Ten Commandments one hair's breadth.
J. C. Ryle

The light which men got from Moses and the law was at best only starlight compared to noonday.   *J. C. Ryle*

There was grace under law and there is law under grace. *Charles Caldwell Ryrie*

The law by which God rules us is as dear to him as the gospel by which he saves us.   *William Secker*

The law of God will not take ninety-nine for a hundred.   *William Secker*

He who really, and in good faith, preaches the cross, never opposes the preaching of the law.   *W. G. T. Shedd*

The law is meant to lead the sinner to faith in Christ by showing the impossibility of any other way.   *C. H. Spurgeon*

The law stirs the mud at the bottom of the pool and proves how foul the waters are.   *C. H. Spurgeon*

The needle of the law must precede the thread of the gospel.   *C. H. Spurgeon*

There is no healing a man till the law has wounded him, no making him alive till the law has slain him.   *C. H. Spurgeon*

To convince and condemn is all the law can do.   *C. H. Spurgeon*

The law is a court of justice, but the gospel is a throne of grace. *George Swinnock*

Keep close to the law if thou wilt keep close to Christ.   *John Wesley*

The law is not opposed to grace by preparing for it; it is only opposed to it if we stay in it after grace has come.
A. Lukyn Williams

It is the function of the law to convict men of their sin and drive them to faith in the promise. Consequently even the Old Testament saints were saved by their faith in the promise, and not by their obedience to the law. *Geoffrey B. Wilson*

The commands of God are all designed to make us more happy than we can possibly be without them. *Thomas Wilson*

LAZINESS — See Indolence

LEADERSHIP

A bad servant will not make a good master. *Anon.*

A leader has been defined as one who knows the way, goes the way and shows the way. *Anon.*

The pursuit of power can separate the most resolute of Christians from the true nature of Christian leadership.
Charles Colson

Leadership is a serving relationship that has the effect of facilitating human development. *Ted Ward*

LEGALISM

The believer mortifies because God is pacified towards him; the legalist mortifies that he may pacify God by his mortification … that he may have whereof to glory. *Ralph Erskine*

Legalism is always unloving.
Robert M. Horn

Legalism is man's misuse of God's law.
Robert M. Horn

Legalism is an abuse of the law; it is a reliance on law-keeping for acceptance with God, and the proud observance of laws is no part of the grace of God.
Ernest F. Kevan

Christian morality differs radically from legalism. Legalism is obedience to the letter of the law to the neglect of the spirit; Christian morality is obedience to the spirit of the law as well as the letter.
R. B. Kuiper

Legalism is self-righteousness. It is the belief that God is satisfied with our attempt to obey a moral code.
Erwin W. Lutzer

Legalism is bound to produce pride of heart. *Watchman Nee*

What is legalism? It is a wrong attitude towards the code of laws under which a person lives … Thus legalism may be defined as 'a fleshly attitude which conforms to a code for the purpose of exalting self'. *Charles Caldwell Ryrie*

LEISURE

It is what you do when you have nothing to do that reveals what you are. *Anon.*

Leisure is a beautiful garment, but it will not do for constant wear. *Anon.*

Tell me how a young person spends his leisure time and I will tell you the kind of person he is. *Billy Graham*

Temptation rarely comes in working hours. It is in their leisure time that men are made or marred. *W. T. Taylor*

LIBERALISM

A liberal is one who transforms biblical terms into theological bubble gum. *Anon.*

Liberalism is a miscarriage of truth.
John Blanchard

Those who preach liberal theology are robbers; they rob God of his sovereignty,

Jesus of his divinity, the Holy Spirit of his ministry, the miracles of their credibility, Mary of her virginity, the apostles of their authority, the church of its history and the new birth of its necessity.
John Blanchard

Ecumenical advocates appear to have forgotten that the more important question to be asked today is not what will fill the churches but what emptied them in the first place ... When the critics emptied the Bible of its meaning they emptied the churches of their members.
Brian H. Edwards

This is exactly where a liberal attitude to the Bible leads us: there is no final authority, no reliable words of Christ, no test by which we shall be judged, and nothing to obey. *Brian H. Edwards*

Liberalism is not the answer to a heart longing for a vital faith. We must look in some other direction. *Vance Havner*

Modernism is politically a volcano and theologically a windbag. *Carl F. H. Henry*

Modernism is not a brand of Christianity, but a denial of it. *R. B. Kuiper*

Theological liberalism, in spite of all its clamour for ecumenism and church union, is working more effectively towards the disruption of the church of Christ than is any other force. *R. B. Kuiper*

Liberalism has been described as a system in which you can believe whatever you like so long as you don't believe it's true. *Pete Lowman*

A cardinal doctrine of modern liberalism is that the world's evil may be overcome by the world's good; no help is thought to be needed from outside the world.
J. Gresham Machen

An examination of the teachings of liberalism in comparison with those of Christianity will show that at every point the two movements are in direct opposition. *J. Gresham Machen*

Liberalism is totally different from Christianity, for the foundation is different. Christianity is founded upon the Bible ... liberalism on the other hand is founded upon the shifting emotions of sinful men.
J. Gresham Machen

The grace of God is rejected by modern liberalism. And the result is slavery — the slavery of the law, the wretched bondage by which man undertakes the impossible task of establishing his own righteousness as a ground of acceptance with God. *J. Gresham Machen*

Historic Christianity and either the old or the new liberal theology are two separate religions with nothing in common except certain terms which they use with totally different meanings.
Francis Schaeffer

Liberalism ... is unfaithfulness; it is spiritual adultery towards the divine Bridegroom. *Francis Schaeffer*

The real difference between liberalism and biblical Christianity is not a matter of scholarship but of presumptions.
Francis Schaeffer

Many modem critics are to the Word of God what blow-flies are to the food of men: they cannot do any good, and unless relentlessly driven away they do great harm. *C. H. Spurgeon*

LIBERALITY — See Generosity; Giving

LIBERTY

Better starve free than be a fat slave.
Aesop

Freedom is not the right to do as you please; it is the liberty to do as you ought.
Anon.

No man has a right to do as he pleases unless he pleases to do right. *Anon.*

Man is most free when controlled by God alone. *Augustine*

There is no true liberty except the liberty of the happy who cleave to the eternal law. *Augustine*

Liberty is not the same as licence; to be free is not to be free and easy; the Christian is not free to please himself but to please God. *John Blanchard*

The modern cry 'Less creed and more liberty' is a degeneration from the vertebrate to the jellyfish. *B. H. Carroll*

Liberty means ability not to violate the law of God. Licence means personal insistence on doing what I like.
Oswald Chambers

Liberty is turned to licence by self.
Walter Chantry

The Bible ... presupposes that only in so far as a man is free *for* God can he be truly free *from* all those things which would prevent him from being his best.
J. C. P. Cockerton

He is the freeman whom the truth makes free, and all are slaves beside.
William Cowper

Perfect conformity to the will of God is the sole sovereign and complete liberty.
J. H. Merle D'Aubigne

True liberty consists only in the power of doing what we ought to will, and in not being constrained to do what we ought not to will. *Jonathan Edwards*

True freedom is only to be found when one escapes from oneself and enters into the liberty of the children of God.
François Fenelon

Liberty unregulated by law degenerates into anarchy. *Lowell Fillmore*

Gospel liberty is a liberty *from* sin, not *to* sin. *Thomas Hall*

This is liberty: to know that God alone matters. *Donald Haukey*

The truth makes us free *from* our spiritual enemies, free *in* the service of God, free to the privileges of sons.
Matthew Henry

My liberty is controlled by my love for my brothers and sisters. *Jan Kaleta*

Freedom comes by filling your mind with God's thoughts. *Erwin W. Lutzer*

What then is the nature of true liberty? Not being free to do anything you want to do, but in coming to the place where you delight in the performance of what you ought to do. *Al Martin*

The only perfect freedom is serving God.
Malcolm Muggeridge

Happy is the man who can use Christian liberty without abusing it.　　*J. C. Ryle*

Liberty has brought us the freedom to be the slaves of righteousness.
Charles Caldwell Ryrie

To obey God is perfect liberty.　*Seneca*

We have been born under a monarchy; to obey God is freedom.　　　*Seneca*

We find freedom when we find God; we lose it when we lose him.　*Paul Sherer*

It is a positive and very hurtful sin to magnify liberty at the expense of doctrine.
Walter Shurden

A Christian is the greatest freeman in the world ... yet in regard of love he is the greatest servant.　　*Richard Sibbes*

The only freedom that man ever has is when he becomes a slave to Jesus Christ.
R. C. Sproul

The freedom of the Christian is freedom *in* the law.　　*Augustus H. Strong*

We need to be delivered from the freedom which is absolute bondage into the bondage which is perfect freedom.
William Temple

True freedom consists with the observance of law.　　*W. L. Thornton*

The important thing about a man is not where he goes when he is compelled to go, but where he goes when he is free to go where he will.　　*A. W. Tozer*

Where we go when we are free to go where we will is a near-infallible index of character.　　*A. W. Tozer*

Our real freedom from sin and the bondage to sin is found in our enslavement, both body and soul, to Christ, the Lord of all.　　*Spiros Zodhiates*

We are free to choose, but not free to choose the consequences of our choice, for those are determined by the eternal purpose and laws of God.
Spiros Zodhiates

LIFE

Every life without Christ is a mission field; every life with Christ is a missionary.　　*Anon.*

How frail is human life! A thin texture of living flesh is the only screen between never-dying souls and their eternal condition.　　*Anon.*

It is not how long but how well we live that matters.　　*Anon.*

Life asks no questions that faith cannot answer.　　*Anon.*

Life is measured by its depth, not its duration.　　*Anon.*

Life is not a solo but a chorus. We live in relationships from cradle to grave. *Anon.*

Life is worth living better than most men live it.　　*Anon.*

Live your best, and act your best, and think your best each day, for there may be no tomorrows.　　*Anon.*

Live your own life, and you will die your own death.　　*Anon.*

The world is only a passage-room to eternity; the world is to us as the wilderness was to Israel, not to rest in but to travel through. *Anon.*

This life is all the heaven the worldling has, and all the hell the saint ever sees. *Anon.*

Today is the first day of the rest of your life. *Anon.*

As soon as man is born he begins to sicken; he only terminates his sickness by his death. *Augustine*

Life, if properly viewed in any aspect, is great, but mainly great when viewed in its relation to the world to come. *Albert Barnes*

A person who really wishes to learn to know how to live more successfully must first know whether he has life to live, or whether he possesses nothing more than mere existence. *Donald Grey Barnhouse*

Life is a long lesson in humility. *James M. Barrie*

Age and youth look upon life from the opposite ends of the telescope; to the one it is exceedingly long, to the other exceedingly short. *Henry Ward Beecher*

Life is a one-way street. *Bernard Berenson*

Live your life and forget your age. *Frank Bering*

All living is preparation for dying. *John Blanchard*

Everything in life is a test of character. *John Blanchard*

If life is an accident, it cannot conceivably have any purpose, for accidents and purpose are mutually exclusive. *John Blanchard*

Life at its best means putting God first. *John Blanchard*

Life ought not merely to contain acts of worship, it should be an act of worship. *John Blanchard*

The two greatest facts in life are sin and death. *John Blanchard*

If human life is not sacred it is expendable. *Joe Boot*

Be such a man, and live such a life, that if every man were such as you, and every life a life like yours, this earth would be God's paradise. *Phillips Brooks*

Life is but a day at most. *Robert Burns*

If it were not that ingratitude had blinded our eyes, every birth would fill us with amazement. *John Calvin*

The meaning of life is the most urgent of questions. *Albert Camus*

One life — a little gleam of time between two eternities. *Thomas Carlyle*

The quality of life is more important than life itself. *Alexis Carrel*

Life in itself is neither good nor evil; it is the scene of good or evil, as you make it. *Michel de Montaigne*

The failure to give a plausible explanation for the origin of life casts a number of shadows over the whole field of evolutionary speculation. *Michael Denton*

Life is too short to be small.
Benjamin Disraeli

The man who regards his own life and that of his fellow creatures as meaningless is not merely unfortunate but almost disqualified for life. *Albert Einstein*

What makes life dreary is absence of motive. What makes life complicated is multiplicity of motive. What makes life victorious is singleness of motive.
George Eliot

Life with its joys and griefs, business, the use of the world, must be carried on as under notice to quit, by men prepared to cast loose from the shores of time.
G. G. Findlay

Life is a path trodden by all men, *and but once.* *John Gill*

Life is not measured by length but by depth. Birthdays tell us how long we have been on the road, not how far we have travelled. *Vance Havner*

Nothing is trivial here if heaven looks on.
Vance Havner

Every man's life is his opportunity of doing that which will make for him in eternity. *Matthew Henry*

The business of our lives is not to please ourselves but to please God.
Matthew Henry

This world is our passage not our portion. *Matthew Henry*

Life in worldly pleasure is only life in appearance. *H. J. Holtzmann*

Of what does life essentially consist? ...
the Bible answers that life is composed of relationships. *Robert Horn*

Life is only lived wisely to the extent that it is spent in preparation for the eternity which follows. *Dave Hunt*

It is not possible to set out in the Christian profession with a more instructive or impressive idea than this — *life is the seed-time for eternity.* *John Angell James*

Sow an action and you reap a habit; sow a habit and you reap a character; sow a character and you reap a destiny.
William James

The great use of life is to spend it for something that outlasts it. *William James*

The most important thing in life is to live your life for something more important than your life. *William James*

The end of life is not to be happy, nor to achieve pleasure and avoid pain, but to do the will of God, come what may.
Martin Luther King

Actually it seems to me that one can hardly say anything either bad enough or good enough about life. *C. S. Lewis*

Life, according to the Bible, is not just existence, but it is existence in the presence and with the favour of God; and death is not just the death of the body but it is separation from God and a doom that should fill the heart of man with a nameless dread. *J. Gresham Machen*

Whatever we do in this life is seed.
Thomas Manton

The longest life is a lingering death.
John Mason

Make sure the thing you are living for is worth dying for.　*Charles Mayes*

One can live on less when he has more to live for.　*S. S. McKenny*

If life be short, then moderate your worldly cares and projects; do not cumber yourselves with too much provision for a short voyage.　*Thomas Manton*

Live so as to be missed.
　Robert Murray M'Cheyne

Let God have your life; he can do more with it than you can.　*D. L. Moody*

How short is human life!
The very breath
Which frames my words
accelerates my death.　*Hannah More*

Life must be filled with life.
　Andrew Murray

The seven ages of man: spills, drills, thrills, bills, ills, pills, wills.
　Richard J. Needham

We are here to add what we can to life, not to get what we can from it.
　William Osler

God alone made life, and God alone can tell us its meaning.　*J. I. Packer*

Plan your life, budgeting for seventy years … and understand that if your time proves shorter that will not be unfair deprivation but rapid promotion.　*J. I. Packer*

Between us and heaven or hell there is only life, which is the frailest thing in the world.　*Blaise Pascal*

The whole of life is a test, a trial of what is in us, so arranged by God himself.
　William S. Plumer

All the care in the world will not make us continue a minute beyond the time God has appointed.　*J. C. Ryle*

We are not so to live as if we had nothing but a body.　*J. C. Ryle*

Man, made in the image of God, has a purpose — to be in relationship to God, who is there. Man forgets his purpose and thus he forgets who he is and what life means.　*Francis Schaeffer*

We must not live only to live.
　Richard Sibbes

For the Christian, all of life is sacred.
　Paul B. Smith

The meaning of earthly existence is not, as we have grown used to thinking, in prosperity, but in the development of the soul.　*Alexandr Solzhenitsyn*

We should employ our passions in the service of life, not spend life in the service of our passions.　*Richard Steele*

Let us live as people who are prepared to die, and die as people who are prepared to live.　*James S. Stewart*

The primary test of life is not service but love, both for man and for God.
　William Still

The secret of life is theological and the key to heaven as well.　*A. W. Tozer*

Let us endeavour so to live that when we come to die even the undertaker will be sorry.　*Mark Twain*

A useless life is only an early death.
Johann Wolfgang von Goethe

Life is the childhood of our immortality.
Johann Wolfgang von Goethe

No one can live well until they can die well. *David Watson*

O Lord, let me not live to be useless!
John Wesley

Take care of your life and the Lord will take care of your death.
George Whitefield

We are immortal till our work is done.
George Whitefield

There is nothing that arises more spontaneously from man's nature than the question about life's meaning.
Rheinallt Nantlais Williams

Ask the Lord to make your life a glory to him, a menace to the devil, a strength to your church and a witness to the world.
Frederick P. Wood

Life can only be enjoyed as one acquires a true perspective of life and death and of the real purpose of life.
Spiros Zodhiates

LITERATURE

The printed page is a visitor who gets inside the home and stays there; it always catches a man in the right mood, for it speaks to him only when he is reading it.
Anon.

If I might control the literature of the household, I would guarantee the well-being of the church and state.
Francis Bacon

The oldest books in the world are still only just out to those who have not read them. *Samuel Butler*

Books may preach when the author cannot, when the author may not, when the author dares not, yea, and which is more, when the author is not.
Thomas Brooks

Next to acquiring good friends, the best acquisition is that of a good book.
C. C. Colton

Literature can be our most effective medium of mass communication of the gospel. In terms of the price paid for it, the number of people reached and the fact that the message can be read over and over again until it is understood, there is no other method than can compare with literature. *Harold Cook*

If the crowns of all the kingdoms were laid down at my feet in exchange for my books and my love of reading, I would spurn them all. *François Fenelon*

The worst thing about new books is that they keep us from reading the old ones.
Joseph Joubert

You really lose a lot by never reading books again. *C. S. Lewis*

The devil hates goose quills.
Martin Luther

We must throw the printer's inkpot at the devil. *Martin Luther*

Nothing substitutes for what can be found when we master books.
Gordon MacDonald

The smallest tract may be the stone in

David's sling. In the hands of Christ it may bring down a giant soul.
Robert Murray M'Cheyne

We become what we read.
Matilda Nordtved

I divide all readers into two classes: those who read to remember and those who read to forget. *Willia Lyons Phelps*

The printed page never flinches, it never shows cowardice; it is never tempted to compromise. The printed page never gets tired; it never gets disheartened.
Ernest C. Reisinger

The printed page travels cheaply — you can be a missionary for the price of a stamp. *Ernest C. Reisinger*

Everything in this modern world is somehow inexplicably geared to inducing sleep in our souls ... This is one reason why the modern Christian must keep up his spiritual and theological reading. We need to read for dear life. *Maurice Roberts*

I read for eternity. *John C. Ryland*

Literature is the immortality of speech.
August Schlegel

A man may usually be known by the books he reads as well as by the company he keeps. *Samuel Smiles*

Reading is to the mind what exercise is to the body. *Richard Steele*

Books are the treasured wealth of the world, the fit inheritance of generations and actions. *Henry David Thoreau*

The things you read will fashion you by slowly conditioning your mind.
A. W. Tozer

Be careful what books you read; for as water tastes of the soil it runs through, so does the soul of the authors that a man reads. *John Trapp*

The man who does not read good books has no advantage over the man who cannot read at all. *Mark Twain*

The value of a book is not determined by its cost but by its use. *Jerry Walker*

The most effective political and religious movements have always known the power of the printed page. What men think is largely determined by what they read. *David Watson*

No other agency can penetrate so deeply, witness so daringly, abide so persistently and influence so irresistibly as the printed page. *Samuel Zwemmer*

LONELINESS

When Christ saves a man, he not only saves him from his sin, he also saves him from his solitude. *Frank Colquhoun*

There is none more lonely than the man who loves only himself.
Abraham Ibn Esra

Walking with our divine Lord we should never feel lonely and never feel lost.
Frank Farley

Loneliness is inner emptiness. Solitude is inner fulfilment. *Richard Foster*

One of the worst things about loneliness is that you can't run away from it.
Vance Havner

Loneliness is the first thing which God's eye named not good. *John Milton*

Christ understands loneliness; he's been through it.   *Paul S. Rees*

The soul hardly ever realizes it, but whether he is a believer or not, his loneliness is really a homesickness for God.
Hubert Van Zeller

The world is filled with rootless people. So many cannot say the lovely, necessary little phrase 'I belong'.   *Alan Walker*

LONGSUFFERING — See Patience

LORD'S DAY

Sunday clears away the rust of the whole week.   *Joseph Addison*

Sunday is the summer of the week. *Anon.*

In the absence of any divine instruction to the contrary, we may assume that the fourth commandment is still binding on us.   *Gleason Archer*

He keeps the Sunday badly who does no good works. Rest from bad works ought to be perpetual.   *Augustine*

See that the Lord's day be spent in holy preparation for eternity. *Richard Baxter*

I never knew one man or woman who steadily avoided the house of prayer and public worship on the Lord's day, who did not come to grief, and bring other people to grief. *Henry Whitney Bellows*

The sabbath is God's special present to the working man, and one of its chief objects is to prolong his life, and preserve efficient his working tone. The savings bank of human existence is the weekly sabbath.   *William G. Blaikie*

Profaning of the Lord's Sabbath is as great an argument of a profane heart as any that can be found in the whole book of God.   *Thomas Brooks*

Make the Lord's day the market for thy soul.   *John Bunyan*

Sunday should strike the keynote for the week.   *J. Wilbur Chapman*

Sunday is a divine and priceless institution.   *Winston Churchill*

God, by giving the sabbath, has given fifty-two springs in every year.
Samuel Taylor Coleridge

Sunday is the core of our civilization, dedicated to thought and reverence. It invites to the noblest solitude and to the noblest society. *Ralph Waldo Emerson*

Make not that wearisome that should always be welcome.   *Thomas Fuller*

The sabbath is not only a blessing and privilege for those who keep it. In an increasingly despairing and restless world, its observance is a sign and witness of the hope God's people have.
Richard B. Gaffin

It would be as difficult to take an inventory of the benefits the world receives from the sunshine as to enumerate the blessings we derive from the Christian sabbath.   *Hervey Doddridge Ganse*

The law of the sabbath is still binding on us today.   *Matthew Henry*

Where sabbaths are neglected all religion sensibly goes to decay. *Matthew Henry*

The essence of the sabbath could not be

changed without changing the nature of man. *A. A. Hodge*

The sabbath is the golden clasp that binds together the volume of the week. *J. C. MacAuley*

A well-spent sabbath we feel to be a day of heaven upon earth ... we love to rise early on that morning, and to sit up late, that we may have a long day with God. *Robert Murray M'Cheyne*

The murderer who is dragged to the gibbet and the polished Sabbath-breaker are one in the sight of God. *Robert Murray M'Cheyne*

You show me a nation that has given up the sabbath and I will show you a nation that has got the seed of decay. *D. L. Moody*

When a nation remembers Sunday as the Lord's day and keeps it holy unto him this is both pleasing to God and beneficial to the country. *W. R. Mohon*

Man was made to worship every day, but work is eliminated on the sabbath to show its proper perspective in God's divine plan. *Clyde Narramore*

A weekly sabbath walls in our wild nature. *Christopher Nesse*

I never knew a man escape failures in either mind or body who worked seven days a week. *Robert Peel*

Common sense, reason, conscience, will combine, I think, to say that if we cannot spare God one day in a week we cannot be living as those ought to live who must die one day. *J. C. Ryle*

Holiness is the best sabbath dress — but it is equally suitable for everyday wear. *C. H. Spurgeon*

The day of the Lord is likely to be a dreadful day to them that despise the Lord's day. *George Swinnock*

The Jews' seventh day was buried in Christ's grave. *George Swinnock*

If you want to kill Christianity you must abolish Sunday. *Voltaire*

Break down Sunday, close the churches, open the bars and the theatres on that day, and where would values be? What was real estate worth in Sodom? *H. L. Wayland*

Oh, what a blessing is Sunday, interposed between the waves of worldly business like the divine path of the Israelites through Jordan! There is nothing in which I would advise you to be more strictly conscientious than in keeping the sabbath day holy. *William Wilberforce*

He that would prepare for heaven must honour the sabbath upon earth. *Daniel Wilson*

LOVE FOR CHRIST
(See also: Communion with Christ; Meditation; Prayer)

If we love Christ our devotion will not remain a secret. *Anon.*

True love for Christ will mean hatred of sin. *John Benton*

If we love Christ much, surely we shall trust him much. *Thomas Brooks*

The church has no greater need today than to fall in love with Jesus all over again. *Vance Havner*

The question is still the same: Do you love Jesus? Affection is the answer to apathy. *Vance Havner*

The surest evidence of our love to Christ is obedience to the laws of Christ ... Love is the root, obedience is the fruit.
Matthew Henry

If you claim to love Christ and yet are living an unholy life, there is only one thing to say about you. You are a bare-faced liar! *D. Martyn Lloyd-Jones*

You must love Christ with a sincere love, with a new love, with an entire love, with a superlative love; and you must love him for himself, and not anything you get from him. *James Renwick*

Of all the things that will surprise us in the resurrection morning, this, I believe, will surprise us most: that we did not love Christ more before we died. *J. C. Ryle*

A man who loves his wife will love her letters and her photographs because they speak to him of her. So if we love the Lord Jesus, we shall love the Bible because it speaks to us of him.
John R. W. Stott

Christ's lovers prove their love by their obedience. *John R. W. Stott*

No man can be a true disciple of Christ who gives his friends a preference to Christ in the affections of his heart.
Kennedy Sunkuthu

LOVE FOR GOD
(See also: Communion with God; Meditation; Prayer)

The greatest and best thing that can be said of a man is that he loved the Lord.
Anon.

I would hate my own soul if I did not find it loving God. *Augustine*

It is but right that our hearts should be on God, when the heart of God is so much on us. *Richard Baxter*

Love for God is not love for him at all unless it expresses itself in a practical way. *John Benton*

Just as obedience to the Lord is an indication of our love for him, so is it also a proof of our fear of God. *Jerry Bridges*

Love to God and obedience to God are so completely involved in each other that any one of them implies the other too.
F. F. Bruce

We ought to love our Maker for his own sake, without either hope of good or fear of pain. *Miguel de Cervantes*

Obedience to God is the most infallible evidence of sincere and supreme love to him. *Nathaniel Emmons*

A true love to God must begin with a delight in his holiness, and not with a delight in any other attribute.
Jonathan Edwards

O Jesus, Jesus, dearest Lord!
Forgive me if I say,
For very love, thy sacred name
A thousand times a day.
Frederick W. Faber

God cares not for phrases but for affections. *Joseph Hall*

Our love to the Lord is not worth speaking of but his to us can never be enough spoken of. *Matthew Henry*

Even the heart of God thirsts after love.
Abraham Kuyper

To cherish true love for God is to be constrained by love to yield one's ego with all that it is and has, and to let God be God again. *Abraham Kuyper*

Christian love, either towards God or towards man, is an affair of the will.
C. S. Lewis

Every Christian would agree that a man's spiritual health is exactly proportional to his love for God. *C. S. Lewis*

There is no better test of growth than that a man desires God because he is God.
D. Martyn Lloyd-Jones

Don't throw God a bone of your love unless there's the meat of obedience on it. *John MacArthur*

Self-love may lead us to prayers, but love to God excites us to praises.
Thomas Manton

I ought to have loved God always. It is of his mere mercy that I love him now.
Handley C. G. Moule

What a vast difference there is between knowing God and loving him!
Blaise Pascal

The man who loves God is in an unassailable position. *J. B. Phillips*

The severest self-denials and the most lavish gifts are of no value in God's esteem unless they are prompted by love.
A. W. Pink

Love of the creature toward the Creator must include obedience or it is meaningless. *Francis Schaeffer*

Our love for God is tested by the question of whether we seek him or his gifts.
Ralph W. Sockman

Love to God is the indelible token of the chosen seed; by this secret seal the election of grace is certified to the believer.
C. H. Spurgeon

We must give our Lord our love or that love will go somewhere else. We are so created that we must love something or other. *C. H. Spurgeon*

You may rest quite certain that if you love God it is a fruit, not a root. *C. H. Spurgeon*

The primary test of life is not service but love, both for man and for God.
William Still

Love to God is the essence of all virtue.
Augustus H. Strong

The great of this world are those who simply loved God more than others did.
A. W. Tozer

To adore God means we love him with all the powers within us. *A. W. Tozer*

As the sunbeams united in a burning glass burn the hotter, so all our affections should be united, that our love to God may be more ardent. *Thomas Watson*

Love is the only thing in which we can retaliate with God ... We must not give him word for word, but we must give him love for love. *Thomas Watson*

Our love of God will always be according to our knowledge of him and his perfections. *Daniel Wilson*

LOVE FOR OTHERS — Definition
(See also: Kindness; Mercy to others)

The loneliest place in the world is the human heart when love is absent. *Anon.*

To have the heart glow with mutual love is vastly better than to glare with the most pompous titles, offices or powers.
Matthew Henry

Love is not affectionate feeling, but a steady wish for the loved person's ultimate good as far as it can be obtained.
C. S. Lewis

Every man feels instinctively that all the beautiful sentiments in the world weigh less than a single lovely action.
J. R. Lowell

Jealousy, properly considered, is an essential element of true love: it is … an unceasing longing for the loved one's welfare. *J. A. Motyer*

Love is that jewel of human nature which commands a valuation wherever it is found. *John Owen*

Love = to live for. *Mary Slessor*

Love is service rather than sentiment.
John R. W. Stott

Love is the outgoing of the entire nature in self-sacrificing service.
W. H. Griffith Thomas

LOVE FOR OTHERS — Effects

Love is the master key to a happy home.
Anon.

One loving heart sets another on fire.
Augustine

Duty makes us do things well, but love makes us do them beautifully.
Phillips Brooks

If you work at love, you will find love at work. *Peter Jackson*

Suspicions subtract, faith adds, but love multiplies. It blesses twice — him who gives it and him who gets it. *C. T. Studd*

LOVE FOR OTHERS — Importance

Christian love is the distinguishing mark of Christian life. *John Blanchard*

Faith and love must be inseparable companions. There is a necessary connection between them. Faith without love is no living grace, and love without faith is no saving grace. *Francis Burkitt*

Whatever is devoid of love is of no account in the sight of God. *John Calvin*

You can give without loving, but you cannot love without giving.
Amy Carmichael

There is no greater opportunity to influence our fellowman for Christ than to respond with love when we have been unmistakably wronged. *James C. Dobson*

If God should have no more mercy on us than we have charity one to another, what would become of us? *Thomas Fuller*

Not tongues nor faith nor prophecy nor knowledge nor martyrdom nor philanthropy, but love is the Christian's mark of distinction. *Vance Havner*

Brotherly love is the badge of Christ's disciples. *Matthew Henry*

Love is the leading affection of the soul.
Matthew Henry

Love is the very essence and life of the Christian religion. *Matthew Henry*

Whatever of outward service or obedience we render to God or man, if love is withheld, the law is not fulfilled.
F. B. Meyer

A man may be a good doctor without loving his patients; a good lawyer without loving his clients; a good geologist without loving science; but he cannot be a good Christian without love. *D. L. Moody*

Love is the binding power which holds the body of the Christian church together.
Stephen Olford

Love is the oxygen of the kingdom.
Juan Carlos Ortiz

Love is the hardest lesson in Christianity; but for that reason it should be our most care to learn it. *William Penn*

Love is the queen of all the Christian graces. *A. W. Pink*

Love should be the silver thread that runs through all your conduct. *J. C. Ryle*

Nothing will be intentionally lacking where there is love. *J. C. Ryle*

All men are our neighbours, and we are to love them as ourselves. We are to do this on the basis of creation, even if they are not redeemed, for all men have value because they are made in the image of God. Therefore they are to be loved even at great cost. *Francis Schaeffer*

Love — and the unity it attests to — is the mark Christ gave Christians to wear before the world. Only with this mark may the world know that Christians are indeed Christians and that Jesus was sent by the Father. *Francis Schaeffer*

We are as we love, not as we know.
Richard Sibbes

Our understanding of what it means to be human affects how we treat other people. *R. C. Sproul*

You never so touch the ocean of God's love as when you forgive and love your enemies. *Corrie Ten Boom*

If a man says he is a Christian but has no love he is simply deluding himself.
Geoffrey Thomas

We are shaped and fashioned by what we love. *Johann Wolfgang von Goethe*

He who is not filled with love is necessarily small, withered, shrivelled in his outlook on life and things.
Benjamin B. Warfield

LOVE FOR OTHERS — Measure

The proof of love is its capacity to suffer for the object of its affection. *Anon.*

Of love there be two principal offices, one to give, another to forgive. *John Boys*

Love's mantle is very large.
Thomas Brooks

If my heart is right with God, every human being is my neighbour.
Oswald Chambers

Love must love even when it gets nothing out of it. *Roger Forster*

Religion that does not glow with love is unsatisfactory.   *Richard Glover*

The chains of love are stronger than the chains of fear.   *William Gurnall*

Love rules his kingdom without a sword.
          Robert Herrick

Love seeks one thing only: the good of the one loved. It leaves all the other secondary effects to take care of themselves.   *Thomas Merton*

Love never reasons, but profusely gives; gives, like a thoughtless prodigal, its all, and trembles then lest it has done too little.   *Hannah Moore*

The measure of our love for others can largely be determined by the frequency and earnestness of our prayers for them.
          A. W. Pink

Love feels no loads.   *William S. Plummer*

Love is its own evidence.
          William S. Plummer

Love goes beyond safety.
          Frederick Sampson

No man can love a saint, as a saint, but a saint.   *Richard Sibbes*

Love is the livery of Christ.
          C. H. Spurgeon

I am so determined that I am going to love everybody, even if it kills me! I have to set my heart on it. I am going to do it.
          A. W. Tozer

Perfect love knows no *because.*
          A. W. Tozer

As soon as the love of God was shed abroad in my soul; I loved all, of whatsoever denomination, who loved the Lord Jesus in sincerity of heart.
          George Whitefield

LOVE FOR OTHERS — Practical

Love never asks, 'How much must I do?', but 'How much can I do?' *Frederick Agar*

Many love at their tongue's end, but the godly love at their fingers' end.   *Anon.*

People will not care what you know until they know that you care.   *Anon.*

Respect is what we owe; love is what we give.   *Philip James Bailey*

Love not merely does seek that which does not belong to it; it is prepared to give up for the sake of others even what it is entitled to.   *C. K. Barrett*

Of love there be two principal offices; one to give, another to forgive. *John Boys*

Love does not say, 'Give me', but 'Let me give you'.   *Jill Briscoe*

Love rolls up its sleeves.   *Robert Cook*

True love is always costly. *Billy Graham*

Love is practical or it is not love at all.
          P. W. Heward

Nobody will know what you mean by saying that 'God is Love' unless you act it as well.   *Lawrence Pearsall Jacks*

Love will stammer rather than be dumb.
          Robert Leighton

Love for the brethren is far more than an agreeable society whose views are the same. *A. W. Pink*

Whereas obedience is righteousness in relation to God, love is righteousness in relation to others. *A. Plummer*

Whatever else love is, it is not passive. *Frederick Sampson*

He who does not love sinners cannot pray aright for them. *C. H. Spurgeon*

Christian love is not the victim of our emotions but the servant of our will. *John R. W. Stott*

Love is not only full of benevolence but beneficence. Love which enlarges the heart never straitens the hand. *Thomas Watson*

Love without obedience is a satanic substitute for God's plan. *John C. Whitcomb*

LUCK — See Chance

LUKEWARMNESS — See Apathy; Complacency, Indifference

LUST
(See also Desire; Sex)

Lust is like rot in the bones. *Anon.*

The world is littered with the debris of what *eros* has promised but been unable to provide. *Jill Briscoe*

A little will satisfy nature; less will satisfy grace; nothing will satisfy men's lusts. *Thomas Brooks*

Lust and lucre follow one another as closely akin, both seducing the heart from the Creator to the creature. *A. R. Fausset*

Our eyes, when gazing on sinful objects, are out of their calling and God's keeping. *Thomas Fuller*

Lust and reason are enemies. *Solomon Ben Gabirol*

What lust is so sweet or profitable that is worth burning in hell for? *William Gurnall*

Natural desires are at rest when that which is desired is obtained, but corrupt desires are insatiable. Nature is content with little, grace with less, but lust with nothing. *Matthew Henry*

The right way to put out the fire of lust is to withdraw the fuel of excess. *William Jenkyn*

Lust is felt even by fleas and lice. *Martin Luther*

Intemperance is odious to God. *Thomas Manton*

Love can wait to give; it is lust that can't wait to get. *Josh McDowell*

Lust is appetite run wild. *F. B. Meyer*

Love is not blind. Lust is blind. If love is blind, God is blind. *Gordon Palmer*

It is the difference betwixt lust and love, that this is fixed, that volatile. Love grows, lust wastes, by enjoyment; and the reason is that one springs from a union of souls, and the other springs from a union of sense. *William Penn*

The expression 'free love' is a contradiction in terms. If it's free, it's not love; if it's love, it's not free. *David Watson*

LUXURY
(See also: Materialism; Money; Possessions; Prosperity; Riches; Wealth)

Christ did not die to purchase this world for us.   *Thomas Adams*

Comfort comes as a guest, lingers to become a host, and stays to enslave us.
Anon.

Luxury is a sin that never goes alone.
Thomas Brooks

Many are so devoted to luxury in all their senses that their mind lies buried.
John Calvin

Luxury is more deadly than any foe.
Juvenal

God rarely seems to use a man who pampers himself with luxury.
Kenneth F. W. Prior

On the soft bed of luxury most of the kingdoms have died.   *Edward Young*

LYING
(See also: Dishonesty)

Nothing is rarer than a solitary lie; for lies breed like toads; you cannot tell one but out it comes with a hundred young ones on its back.   *Washington Allston*

A clean glove often hides a dirty hand.
Anon.

A good memory is needed once you have lied.   *Anon.*

A lie is a poor substitute for the truth, but the only one discovered so far.   *Anon.*

The ability to lie is always a liability.
Anon.

Those who are given to white lies soon become colour blind.   *Anon.*

All that one gains by falsehood is not to be believed when he speaks the truth.
Aristotle

It is easy to tell one lie, but not easy to tell just one lie.   *John Blanchard*

Better to die than to lie.   *Thomas Brooks*

Liars pervert the end for which God created speech.   *Thomas Brooks*

Certainly falsehood and calumnies are more deadly than swords and all other kinds of weapons.   *John Calvin*

There are three kinds of lies; a lie told, a lie taught, a lie acted out.   *Joseph Caryl*

When a half truth is presented as a whole truth it becomes an untruth.
Walter J. Chantry

There is no form of sin in which we act more satanically than when we indulge in telling a lie.   *Frank Gabelein*

We lie loudest when we lie to ourselves.
Eric Hoffer

The cruellest lies are often told in silence.
John Hus

Sin has many tools, but a lie is the handle that fits them all. *Oliver Wendell Holmes*

Calumny would soon starve and die of itself if nobody took it in and gave it lodging.   *Robert Leighton*

No man has a good enough memory to be a successful liar.   *Abraham Lincoln*

A lie is a snowball. The longer it is rolled on the ground, the larger it becomes.
Martin Luther

None but cowards lie.   *Arthur Murphy*

One lie must be thatched with another or it will soon rain through.
John Jason Owen

Lies and false reports are among Satan's choicest weapons.   *J. C. Ryle*

False words are not only evil in themselves, but they infect the soul with evil.   *Socrates*

Lying is a certain mark of cowardice.
Thomas Southern

Every liar is a child of the devil, and will be sent home to his father. *C. H. Spurgeon*

One of the most striking differences between a cat and a lie is that a cat has only nine lives.   *Mark Twain*

Falsehoods not only disagree with truths, but they usually quarrel among themselves.   *Daniel Webster*

MALICE

Malice is anger long cherished, until it becomes a settled habit of mind.
George Barlow

Malice never spoke well.
William Camden

Malice has a strong memory.
Thomas Fuller

The malicious have a dark happiness.
Victor Hugo

Nothing on earth consumes a man more quickly than resentment.
Friedrich Neitzsche

Malice and envy are quick-sighted.
Richard Sibbes

Malice can always find a mark to shoot at, and a pretence to fire. *Charles Simmons*

Malice is mental murder. *Thomas Watson*

MAN — Dignity

Man is indeed lost, but that does not mean he is nothing.   *Francis Schaeffer*

Man's dignity is derived and dependent, not intrinsic.   *R. C. Sproul*

We are not autonomous czars over slime; we are vice-regents over a divine creation.   *R. C. Sproul*

Our greatest claim to nobility is our created capacity to know God, to be in personal relationship with him, to love him and to worship him. Indeed, we are most truly human when we are on our knees before our Creator. *John R. W. Stott*

I am greater than the stars, for I know that they are up there, and they do not know that I am down here.
William Temple

If this is God's world, there are no unimportant people.   *George Thomas*

When we speak about 'human rights' we are not speaking about some purely personal preferences which vary from one country to another. We are speaking about giving everyone access to some share in the intrinsic values that make human life worthwhile.   *Keith Ward*

MAN — a Failure

Man, in his fallen nature, is a dissatisfied and frustrated rainbow-chaser.   *Anon.*

What shadows we are, and what shadows we pursue!   *Edmund Burke*

The whole life of man until he is converted to Christ is a ruinous labyrinth of wanderings.   *John Calvin*

Whatever else is or is not true, this one thing is certain — man is not what he was meant to be.   *G. K. Chesterton*

Man is a disaster.   *Cicero*

Our world is filled with self-absorbed, frightened, hollow people.
Charles Colson

Man is a jewel robbed of its precious stone, with only the costly setting left, and even of that we must exclaim, 'How is the gold become dim and the most fine gold changed!'   *Henry Gill*

Every natural man is a fool.
Thomas Granger

It is becoming more and more obvious that it is not starvation, not microbes, not cancer, but man himself who is mankind's greatest danger.   *Carl Gustav Jung*

For the first time I examined myself with a serious purpose. And there I found what appalled me: a zoo of lusts, a bedlam of ambitions, a nursery of fear, a harem of fondled hatreds. My name was Legion.
C. S. Lewis

I haven't any language weak enough to depict the weakness of my spiritual life. If I weakened it enough it would cease to be language at all. As when you try to turn the gas-ring a little lower still, it merely goes out.   *C. S. Lewis*

Never, never pin your whole faith on any human being; not if he is the best and wisest in the whole world. There are lots of nice things you can do with sand; but do not try building a house on it.
C. S. Lewis

The real trouble about fallen man is not the strength of his pleasure but the weakness of his reason.   *C. S. Lewis*

Man in sin is a pygmy fighting against Almighty God — like a fly pitting itself against atomic power!
D. Martyn Lloyd-Jones

The state of the world today is nothing but an appalling monument to human failure.   *D. Martyn Lloyd-Jones*

Never is a man in his right mind till he is converted, or in his right place till he sits by faith at the feet of Jesus, or rightly clothed till he has put on the Lord Jesus Christ.   *J. C. Ryle*

Made in God's image, man was made to be great, he was made to be beautiful and he was made to be creative in life and art. But his rebellion has led him into making himself into nothing but a machine.   *Francis Schaeffer*

Man, made in the image of God, has a purpose — to be in relationship to God, who is there. Man forgets his purpose and thus he forgets who he is and what life means.   *Francis Schaeffer*

If God should call me into judgement before him, according to the strictness of his perfect law, for the best duty I ever performed, and for nothing else, I must be condemned as a transgressor; for when weighed in these exact balances, it would be found wanting. *Thomas Scott*

Man was created to know God but he chose the gutter. That is why he is like a bird shut away in a cage or like a fish taken from the water. *A. W. Tozer*

Man was created for an empire but is living in a pit. *H. G. Wells*

The weakness of man sets the stage for the display of God's strength. *Janice Wise*

MAN — God's Creation and Concern

The incarnation of Christ is the clearest affirmation of the truth that man is created in the image of God.
Lawrence Adams

God made man to be somebody — not just to have things. *Anon.*

The yearning of man's heart is homesickness for God. *Anon.*

The most profound essence of my nature is that I am capable of receiving God.
Augustine

Man without God ceases to be a man.
Nicolas Berdyaev

His creation by God is man's only claim to dignity, importance or value.
John Blanchard

If man was not created by God in God's image, he has no more inherent dignity than a donkey. *John Blanchard*

If human life is not sacred it is expendable. *Joe Boot*

Godly self-respect is possible when we realize that we are created in the image of God, that we are accepted by God solely on the merits of Jesus Christ.
Jerry Bridges

It is only an infinite God, and an infinite good, that can fill and satisfy the precious and immortal soul of man. *Thomas Brooks*

A circle cannot fill a triangle; no more can the whole world fill the heart of man.
Thomas Brooks

Of all God's creatures, man alone is able to think immortality. *S. Parkes Cadman*

God is less interested in answering our questions than in other things: securing our allegiance, establishing our faith, nurturing a desire for holiness.
D. A. Carson

We are here for God's designs, not for our own. *Oswald Chambers*

Man is born to have connection with God.
Clement of Alexandria

Man is a creature, because he is made by God. But he is a unique creature, because he is made like God. *Edmund P. Clowney*

Jesus Christ never met an unimportant person. That is why God sent his Son to die for us. If someone dies for you, you must be important. *M. C. Cleveland*

I cannot believe that our existence in this universe is a mere quirk of fate, an accident of history, an incidental blip in the great cosmic drama…We are truly meant to be here. *Paul Davies*

Meditate on our making, that we may fall in love with our Maker. *David Dickson*

God defend me from ever looking at a man as an animal. *Ralph Waldo Emerson*

Man can only find meaning for his existence in something outside himself.
Viktor Frankl

Humankind is given the very specific task of caring for the created world on God's behalf. He is to be a steward, a caretaker, of the created order. The issue of morality, of man's relationship with his fellow man and with the created world, flow from this central declaration of the meaning and purpose of life.
Martin Robinson

In God's sight there are two men —Adam and Jesus Christ — and these two men have all other men hanging at their girdle strings. *Thomas Goodwin*

Because he is made in the image of God, man is inviolable. *Os Guinness*

Historic Christianity sees man as distinct, but not divorced, from nature.
Os Guinness

If God is God and man is made in his image, then *each* man is significant.
Os Guinness

If the universe was created we can view ourselves as purposeful creatures bearing the stamp of God's intentions. Human life takes on a sacred dimension. We become obligated to treat each other with dignity and respect. *John Halver*

God can be described as a heavenly Father, a caring parent who brings human persons into existence and continues to watch over them. Part of that caring is shown in God's desire to communicate with us. *Walter R. Hearn*

The image of God describes not just something that man has, but something man is. It means that human beings both mirror and represent God.
Anthony Hoekema

Our father was Adam, our grandfather dust, our great-grandfather nothing.
William Jenkyn

Mankind has the highest possible spiritual, transcendent reference: likeness to God himself. *Douglas K. Kelly*

Man was shaped or formed to fit into the image of God. He was created in such an exalted fashion that he and she would fit into fellowship with God, in a way totally surpassing that of any other earthly being. *Douglas K. Kelly*

We are not begotten by God, only made by him: in our natural state we are not sons of God, only (so to speak) statues.
C. S. Lewis

If every least scrawl of a Picasso has tremendous value because Picasso made it, so we too as God's creations each have unimaginable, intrinsic worth.
Pete Lowman

If there is no God, what else is there to celebrate and believe in as a source of significance? *Pete Lowman*

God does not love us because we are valuable, but we are valuable because God loves us. *Martin Luther*

Man was not, as created, morally neutral — indeed the whole notion of a morally neutral person is a monstrosity — but his nature was positively directed to the right and opposed to the wrong.
J. Gresham Machen

Man was made of earth which was made of nothing. *Edward Marbury*

We have come from somewhere and are going somewhere. The great Architect of the universe never built a stairway that leads to nowhere. *Robert Milkman*

Man can be truly understood only in the light of God and his purpose for mankind. *Bruce Milne*

All men are by nature equal, made of the same earth by the same Creator, and however we deceive ourselves, as dear to God is the poor peasant as the mighty prince. *Plato*

Man is heaven's masterpiece. *Francis Quarles*

Humankind is given the very specific task of caring for the created world on God's behalf. He is to be a steward, a caretaker of the created order. The issue of morality, of man's relationship with his fellow man and with the created world, flow from this central declaration of the meaning and purpose of life. *Martin Robinson*

Although man says he is no more than a machine, his whole life denies it. *Francis Schaeffer*

Man, made in the image of God, has a purpose — to be in relationship to God, who is there. Man forgets his purpose and thus he forgets who he is and what life means. *Francis Schaeffer*

Man is not just a chance configuration of atoms in the slipstream of meaningless, chance history. No, man, in the image of God, has a purpose — to be in relationship to the God who is there. *Francis Schaeffer*

Man still stands in the image of God — twisted, broken abnormal, but still the image-bearer of God. *Francis Schaeffer*

No matter who I look at, no matter where he is, every man is created in the image of God as much as I am. *Francis Schaeffer*

It is because man is made in the image of God that Christians hold human life in such high esteem. *R. C. Sproul*

Man's dignity rests in God, who assigns an inestimable worth to every person. Man's origin is not an accident, but a profoundly intelligent act by One who has eternal value; by One who stamps his image on each person. *R. C. Sproul*

Immortal souls were not created for merely mortal ends. *C. H. Spurgeon*

We human beings have both a unique dignity as creatures made in God's image and a unique depravity as sinners under his judgement. *John R. W. Stott*

My worth is what I am worth to God, and that is a marvellous great deal, for Christ died for me. *William Temple*

Because we are the handiwork of God it follows that all our problems and their solutions are theological. *A. W. Tozer*

God has made us a little lower than the angels, but he has made us a little higher than the animals. *A. W. Tozer*

God is not greater for our being, nor would he be less if we did not exist. That we do exist is altogether of God's free determination, not by our desert nor by divine necessity. *A. W. Tozer*

God made us for himself: that is the first and last thing that can be said about human existence and whatever more we add is but commentary.   *A. W. Tozer*

God made us to be worshippers. That was the purpose of God in bringing us into the world.   *A. W. Tozer*

I know that I take a chance of being misunderstood and perhaps of being misjudged when I state that man was more like God than any other creature ever created. Because of the nature of man's creation there is nothing in the universe so much like God as the human soul.   *A. W. Tozer*

Man's only claim to importance is that he was created in the divine image; in himself he is nothing.   *A. W. Tozer*

The man who denies that fallen man bears upon him something of the ruined relic of what he once was is no true friend of the Bible.   *A. W. Tozer*

The existence of God means that human existence is not absurd. *Peter S. Williams*

MAN — a Paradox

Man is harder than rock, and more fragile than an egg.   *Anon.*

I have become a puzzle to myself.
Augustine

Although modern man zestfully explores outer space, he seems quite content to live in a spiritual kindergarten and to play in a moral wilderness.   *Carl F. H. Henry*

Man is an enigma to himself.
Carl Gustav Jung

Man's conquest of nature has been astonishing. His failure to conquer human nature has been tragic.
Julius Mark

All the evidence of history suggests that man is indeed a rational animal, but with a nearly infinite capacity for folly ... He draws blueprints for Utopia but never quite gets it built.   *Robert McNamara*

What a chimera, then, is man! What a novelty! What a chaos, what a contradiction, what a prodigy! Judge of all things, imbecile worm of the earth; depository of truth; a sink of uncertainty and error; the pride and refuse of the universe.
Blaise Pascal

We human beings have both a unique dignity as creatures made in God's image and a unique depravity as sinners under his judgement.   *John R. W. Stott*

Man is a peculiar, puzzling paradox, groping for God and hoping to hide from him at the selfsame time. *William A. Ward*

MAN — a Religious Being
(See also: Religion)

I want to understand something of the truth which my heart believes and loves.
Anselm

You made us for yourself, O Lord, and our hearts are restless till they rest in you.
Augustine

Man does not have a soul, he is a soul.
James Barr

Man must and will have some religion. If he has not the religion of Jesus he will have the religion of Satan. *William Blake*

A human being is more than information and data. *John Blanchard*

Man is by his constitution a religious animal. *Edmund Burke*

That there exists in the human mind, and indeed by natural instinct, some sense of Deity, we hold to be beyond dispute, since God himself, to prevent any man pretending ignorance, has endued all men with some idea of his Godhead. *John Calvin*

The idea of a Deity impressed upon the mind of man is indelible. *John Calvin*

The soul is a never-ending sigh after God. *Theodore Christlieb*

The story of religious movements is the story of man's search for God. *Stephen Gaukroger*

Animals can eat, drink and be contented, but man cannot. *John H. Gerstner*

The human self was never created for *any* other purpose than to manifest the divine Self. *Norman P. Grubb*

Men are religious beings. Religion can't be got rid of by seeking to ignore it. *A. A. Hodge*

There is general evidence that most human beings, from whatever part of the world and from the earliest times, have exhibited a fundamental belief in a divine being or beings, and in some sort of spiritual world. *John Houghton*

Man is constitutionally religious. *R. B. Kuiper*

God designed the human machine to run on himself. He himself is the fuel our spirits were designed to burn, or the food our spirits were designed to feed on. There is no other. *C. S. Lewis*

If I find in myself a desire which no experience in this world can satisfy, the most probable explanation is that I was made for another world. *C. S. Lewis*

Our whole being by its very nature is one vast need: incomplete, preparatory, empty yet cluttered, crying out for him who can untie things that are now knotted together and tie up things that are still dangling loose. *C. S. Lewis*

Belief in God is an instinct as natural to man as walking on two legs. *G. C. V. Lichtenberg*

Man must have a God or an idol. *Martin Luther*

There can be no greater glory for man than to glorify God. *J. I. Packer*

There is a God-shaped vacuum in the heart of every man, and only God can fill it. *Blaise Pascal*

Man is incurably religious. *Paul Sabatier*

God is silent and that I cannot possibly deny — everything in me calls for God and that I cannot forget. *Jean-Paul Sartre*

That God does not exist I cannot deny, but that my whole being cries out for God I cannot forget. *Jean-Paul Sartre*

I could not bear to be an 'ignoramus' or an 'agnostic' about God! I must have a God. I cannot do without him. *C. H. Spurgeon*

Man is a worshipper and only in the spirit

of worship does he find release for all the powers of his amazing intellect.

A. W. Tozer

None but God can satisfy the longings of the immortal soul; as the heart was made for him, he only can fill it.

Richard C. Trench

Man is so made that he cannot ignore God. If he cannot love him he will hate him. His face is such that it haunts.

Mary Whitehouse

The religious thirst of humanity can only be quenched in the worship of a transcendent, all-good personal being.

Peter S. Williams

The theory that God exists predicts that, as man's highest good, humanity will have a natural desire to know God which will not be answered by any other object.

Peter S. Williams

Man in his rebellion against his Creator remains incurably religious, and he seeks to satisfy this instinct by making his own deities. He much prefers these lifeless puppets to the one true living God, because they allow him to pull the strings.

Geoffrey B. Wilson

MAN — a Sinner
(See also: Depravity; Guilt; Sin; Sinful Nature)

Civilized man is psychologically sick, and the more cultured and civilized he becomes, the more sick he will be, for modern man is seeking to feel at home in the world without any reference to God.

Akbar Abdul-Haqq

Modern man wants to be treated as an invalid rather than a sinner. *Eric Alexander*

It was by the evil use of his free will that man destroyed both it and himself.

Augustine

Man is a good thing spoiled. *Augustine*

Not only the worst of my sins, but the best of my duties speak of me as a child of Adam. *William Beveridge*

Man was made to dwell in a garden, but his sin has turned it into a wilderness.

John Blanchard

The Bible does not picture man as a risen creature but as a fallen one.

John Blanchard

There are no reluctant rebels against God's will. We are sinners not merely by birth, but by choice. *John Blanchard*

The natural man's affections are wretchedly misplaced; he is a spiritual monster. His heart is where his feet should be, fixed on earth; his heels are lifted up against heaven, where his heart should be set.

Thomas Boston

We are of the world, and until Christ rescues us from it, the world reigns in us and we live unto it. *John Calvin*

The sovereign and utterly good God created a good universe. We human beings rebelled; rebellion is now so much a part of our make-up that we are all enmeshed in it. Every scrap of suffering we face turns on this fact. *D. A. Carson*

By obeying the serpent, Adam and Eve made themselves the friends of Satan and the enemies of God. *Edmund P. Clowney*

Somehow, for all the wondrous glimpses of 'goodness' I see in society, there

remains the unmistakable stain of self-ishness, violence and greed.
John Dickson

God created man in mint condition, but sin has seriously defaced him. Satan vandalized man. *Brian Edwards*

I have never yet met any parents who admit that their child was such a perfect angel that they actually taught it one or two naughty things to make it normal!
Brian Edwards

Man lost his freedom in the garden of Eden. He is free to sin, but he is not free not to sin. *Brian Edwards*

Sin is a matter of what we are, not what we learn. *Brian Edwards*

Man is God's natural enemy.
Jonathan Edwards

The real problem is in the hearts and minds of men. It is not a problem of physics but of ethics. It is easier to denature plutonium than to denature the evil spirit of man. *Albert Einstein*

Even when Scripture specifically mention's God's foreordination of an evil event, the blame for the evil rests exclusively with the human perpetrators.
John M. Frame

That every person should grow up and do evil can be no coincidence. It calls for an explanation. *John H. Gerstner*

The nature of man became corrupt by the transgression of the first parents of mankind. Reflection reveals that this is indeed the only tenable explanation of what has become a recognized fact: universal sin.
John H. Gerstner

The dilemma for man is not who he is but what he has done. His predicament is not that he is small but that he is sinful.
Os Guinness

Everything man touches he perverts.
Philip E. Hughes

Man is by nature more inclined to one sin than to another. *John Hus*

If your heart does not want a world of moral reality, your head will assuredly never make you believe in one.
William James

Sin has left a deep and disfiguring mark on man: his life is now a moral discord.
Ernest F. Kevan

We are all murderers and prostitutes — no matter to what culture, society, class, nation one belongs; no matter how normal, moral or mature one takes oneself to be. *R. D. Laing*

Fallen man is not simply an imperfect creature who needs improvement: he is a rebel who must lay down his arms.
C. S. Lewis

I look forward with horror to contact with the other inhabited planets, if there are such. We would only transport to them all of our sin and our acquisitiveness, and establish a new colonialism. I can't bear to think of it. *C. S. Lewis*

We are members of a spoiled species.
C. S. Lewis

Even if we never did anything wrong, we should still be sinners.
D. Martyn Lloyd-Jones

Everything in creation manifests the glory of God by obeying the law of its nature; man alone does not do so.
D. Martyn Lloyd-Jones

The natural man is always play-acting, always looking at himself and admiring himself. *D. Martyn Lloyd-Jones*

The whole case of the Bible is that the trouble with man is not intellectual (in the mind) but moral (in the heart).
D. Martyn Lloyd-Jones

Fallen man is curved in on himself.
Martin Luther

Sin is not the brute in us; it is, rather, the man in us. *J. Gresham Machen*

Man is born with a fractured will. He wants to go his own way.
John E. Marshall

The disposition of every human heart by nature can be visually pictured as a clenched fist raised against the living God. *Al Martin*

The history of man is his attempt to escape his own corruption. *Daniel Mullis*

Sin has so degraded man that from what he is now we can form no conception of what he was meant to be. *Andrew Murray*

The world is beautiful, but has a disease called man. *Friedrich Nietzsche*

A man who is not a Christian is Satan's prisoner: Satan has him where he wants him. *J. I. Packer*

It is the most damnable and pernicious heresy (and I use those words very carefully) that has ever plagued the mind of man that we can somehow make ourselves good enough to deserve to live with an almighty, all-holy God.
Bernard Palmer

Men may be changed by divine grace, but *man* is unchanged. *William S. Plumer*

The evil that is in us is all our own.
J. C. Ryle

We need no bad company to teach us, and no devil to tempt us, in order to run into sin. We have within us the beginning of every sin under heaven. *J. C. Ryle*

Man is the greatest miracle and the greatest problem on this earth. *David Sarnoff*

Any natural man, he is iron to God and wax to the devil. *Richard Sibbes*

The problem is not that there is insufficient evidence to convince rational beings that there is a God, but that rational beings have a natural hostility to the being of God. *R. C. Sproul*

It is one of the axioms of theology that if a man be lost God must not be blamed for it; and it is also an axiom of theology that if a man be saved, God must have the glory for it. *C. H. Spurgeon*

Man is a reeking mass of corruption.
C. H. Spurgeon

Man is a suicide. Our sin slays the race. We die because we have sinned. How this should make us hate sin! *C. H. Spurgeon*

The best of men are men at the best; and, apart from the work of the Holy Spirit, and the power of divine grace, hell itself does not contain greater monsters than you and I might become. *C. H. Spurgeon*

Every man, so far as he is apart from God, is morally insane.   *Augustus H. Strong*

The lostness of man is not a dogma, it is a fact.   *A. W. Tozer*

We are a bad lot, we sons of Adam.
A. W. Tozer

Man is the only animal that blushes — and the only animal that needs to!
Mark Twain

If man could be crossed with the cat, it would improve man, but it would deteriorate the cat.   *Mark Twain*

A wicked man may search the records of hell for his pedigree.   *Thomas Watson*

By nature we are strangers to God, swine not sons.   *Thomas Watson*

Man is a skin-encapsulated ego.
Alan Watts

There is no evidence that humans have become more moral.   *Peter S. Williams*

MARRIAGE
(See also: Family Life)

As God by creation made two of one, so again by marriage he made one of two.
Thomas Adams

Don't look around for a life partner, look *up*. Any other choice than God's will mean disaster.   *Anon.*

Marriage is a perpetual test of character.
Anon.

Marriage is more than finding the right person; it is being the right person.   *Anon.*

Marriages may be made in heaven, but man is responsible for the maintenance work.   *Anon.*

Never be yoked to one who refuses the yoke of Christ.   *Anon.*

When a woman rules the marriage roost, she is sitting on the wrong perch! *Anon.*

The Christian married couple can be a powerful weapon in the hand of Jesus.
John Benton

All the troubles men find in marriage they ought to impute to sin.   *John Calvin*

Marriage is a covenant consecrated by God.   *John Calvin*

A pledge to take a woman for his wife commits a man to sharing life in its entirety.   *Walter J. Chantry*

Each instance of a wife failing to defer to known wishes of her husband (unless those wishes oppose the moral law of God) subverts the divinely appointed order.   *Walter J. Chantry*

How soon marriage counselling sessions would end if husbands and wives were competing in thoughtful self-denial!
Walter J. Chantry

Marriage, and the process of coming to it, is not heaven! It is the bonding together of two needy sinners in order to make a partnership which is substantially greater than either of them alone.
Sinclair Ferguson

The powerful sexual drives which are built in to man's relationship with woman are not seen in Scripture as the foundation of marriage, but the consummation

and physical expression of it.
Sinclair Ferguson

It is not marriage that fails, it is people that fail. *Harry Emerson Fosdick*

A successful marriage demands a divorce: a divorce from your own self-love.
Paul Frost

Choose a wife rather by your ear than your eye. *Thomas Fuller*

It is not evil to marry but good to be wary.
Thomas Gataker

A pertinent question for millions would be: 'Is there a *home* in your house?'
Vance Havner

The cause of broken marriages is self-ishness in one form or another.
Vance Havner

God made the human pair in such a manner that it is natural for the husband to lead, for the wife to follow.
William Hendriksen

A man's children are pieces of himself, but his wife *is* himself. *Matthew Henry*

The woman was made of a rib out of the side of Adam; not made out of his head to rule over him, nor out of his feet to be trampled on by him; but out of his side to be equal to him, under his arm to be protected, and near his heart to be loved.
Matthew Henry

Sexual desire is natural and marriage is provided for its fulfilment.
Norman Hillyer

Anyone can build a house; we need the Lord for the creation of a home.
John Henry Jowett

The woman was made for the man, yet not as his slave-girl, but his queen.
Meredith Kline

There is no estate to which Satan is more opposed as to marriage. *Martin Luther*

One plus one equals one may not be an accurate mathematical concept, but it is an accurate description of God's intention for the marriage relationship.
Wayne Mack

A successful marriage requires falling in love many times — always with the same person. *Mignon McLaughlin*

God is the witness to every marriage ceremony, and will be the witness to every violation of its vows. *Thomas V. Moore*

Marriage is not a concession to our sinfulness; marriage is a provision for our holiness. *J. A. Motyer*

Successful marriage is always a triangle: a man, a woman and God. *Cecil Myers*

A happy marriage is the union of two good forgivers. *Robert Quillen*

In no relation is so much earthly happiness to be found, if it be entered upon discreetly, advisedly and in the fear of God. In none is so much misery seen to follow, if it be taken in hand unadvisedly, lightly, wantonly and without thought.
J. C. Ryle

The marriage relation lies at the very root of the social system of nations. *J. C. Ryle*

The nearer a nation's laws about marriage approach to the law of Christ, the higher has the moral tone of that nation always proved to be. *J. C. Ryle*

God did not create woman to be a competitor but to be a companion.
Frederick Sampson

It takes two to make a marriage a success and only one to make it a failure.
Herbert Samuel

The heart of marriage is its communication system. It can be said that the success and happiness of any married pair is measurable in terms of the deepening dialogue which characterizes their union.
Dwight Small

Before man had any other calling he was called to be a husband. *Henry Smith*

First man must choose his love, and then he must love his choice. *Henry Smith*

The man and wife are partners, like two oars in a boat. *Henry Smith*

There is always a danger of marriage taking the razor edge off the passion for Jesus and souls. *C. T. Studd*

Try praising your wife, even if it does frighten her at first. *Billy Sunday*

A gracious wife satisfies a good husband and silences a bad one. *George Swinnock*

Marriage is both honourable and onerable. *George Swinnock*

God's love ties the marriage knot so fast that neither death nor hell can break it.
Thomas Watson

MARTYRDOM
(See also: Persecution)

The martyrs were bound, imprisoned, scourged, racked, burnt, rent, butchered — and they multiplied. *Augustine*

If there be glory laid up for them that die in the Lord, much more shall they be glorified that die for the Lord. *Richard Baxter*

Divine presence made the martyrs as willing to die as to dine. *Thomas Brooks*

It is not the blood but the cause that makes a martyr. *Thomas Brooks*

The martyr is made by his cause, not by his punishment. *John Calvin*

The Lord knows I go up this ladder [to be hung as a martyr] with less fear, confusion or perturbation of mind than ever I entered a pulpit to preach.
Donald Cargill

Christianity has made martyrdom sublime and sorrow triumphant. *E. H. Chapin*

A man may give his life for something that is trifling indeed, but he cannot give his life for something that seems trifling to him. To do so would prove him to be a non-rational being, or something other than he is. *John H. Gerstner*

A martyr is a person who holds the truth and dies for it. If he holds the truth and does not die for it, he is a hypocrite; if he dies for something other than the truth, he is a fool. A martyr is a person who dies for truth, the truth of God.
John H. Gerstner

Nothing proves a man's attachment to a thing so surely as his readiness to die for it. *John H. Gerstner*

Martyrs are the eldest sons of blessedness among all the sons of adoption.
Thomas Goodwin

God sometimes raises up many faithful ministers out of the ashes of one.
Matthew Henry

Most joyfully will I confirm with my blood that truth which I have written and preached. *Jan Hus*

It is better for me to be a martyr than a monarch. *Ignatius*

Martyrdom came into the world early; the first man that died died for religion.
William Jenkyn

The blood of the martyrs is the seed of the church. *Jerome*

You may kill us, but you can never hurt us. *Justyn Martyr*

The martyrs shook the powers of darkness with the irresistible power of weakness. *John Milton*

It is a small matter to die once for Christ; if it might be, I could wish I might die a thousand deaths for him. *Lewis Paschalis*

Weak grace may *do* for God, but it must be strong grace that will *die* for God.
William Secker

Martyrdom has always been a proof of the intensity, never of the correctness of a belief. *Arthur Schnitzler*

It is far less important to die the martyr's death than to live the martyr's life.
Robert E. Speer

If they are blessed who die in the Lord, are they not blessed who die for the Lord?
Thomas Watson

Never have any princes been so famous for their victories as the martyrs were for their sufferings. *Thomas Watson*

The hypocrite makes faith a cloak; the martyr makes it a shield. *Thomas Watson*

MATERIALISM
(See also: Possessions; Prosperity; Riches; Wealth)

Materialism and self-centredness are forms of idolatry. *John Benton*

A man caught up with this world is not ready for the next one. Materialism is no preparation for judgement or for heaven.
John Blanchard

In the world in which we live today it takes a miracle for a man not to be a materialist. *John Blanchard*

Materialism is every bit as dangerous as modernism. *John Blanchard*

Materialists know the price of everything but the value of nothing. *John Blanchard*

It is a very high point of Christian wisdom and prudence always to look upon the good things and the great things of this world as a man will certainly look upon them when he comes to die.
Thomas Brooks

Death is the final mockery of materialism. We brought nothing into this world and it is certain we can carry nothing out. If a man has lived to accumulate good, how indescribably tragic his dying!
Herbert M. Carson

A simple materialistic explanation for all that man is and does will not fit with human experience or with what we know about the human brain. *Michael Cosgrove*

While we rightly recoil from materialistic Communism, pervading our society is an even more insidious materialism which makes Christians short of breath through prosperity and ill-equipped to run the race that is set before them.
J. D. Douglas

Materialism is suicidal. *Michael Griffiths*

Materialism is wrong because it does not do justice to the mental life, in terms of imagination, belief and memory, and to its social implications. *Stuart Hampshire*

The more you have to live *for,* the less you need to live *on.* Those who make acquisition their goal never have enough.
Sydney Harris

Lives based on having are less free than lives based either on doing or on being.
William James

The biologists have to tell us candidly whether they are asking us to believe in materialism because of what they know from studying the facts or whether they are so devoted to the philosophy that they are willing to disregard evidence that doesn't fit. *Phillip E. Johnson*

May God pity a nation whose factory chimneys rise higher than her church steeples. *John Kelman*

The most vicious aspect of the tyranny of materialism is its ability to produce merely earth-bound aspirations.
Harold B. Kuhn

The simplicity of materialism is a baneful simplicity. It is the simplicity which is arrived at by an ignoring of some of the facts. *J. Gresham Machen*

There is not a vice which more effectually contracts and deadens the feelings, which more completely makes a man's affections centre in himself and excludes all others from partaking in them, than the desire of accumulating possessions.
Thomas Manton

Materialism leads to the denial of all the social values and ethics which have formed the basis of human worth, freedom and democracy. *Robert A. Morey*

Materialism, open or disguised, is the logical result of thinking that above and beyond this world there is nothing else.
Stephen Olford

The genius of modern civilization, if it is allowed to run its present course to perfection, will bring mankind to the point at which there is everything to live with and nothing to live for.
Maurice Roberts

Materialism is not a faith to live by or to die for. It is unliveable because it is merely a philosophy of negation, denying anything that is worth living or dying for. *Martin Robinson*

Build your nest in no tree here ... for the Lord of the forest has condemned the whole woods to be demolished.
Samuel Rutherford

No oriental monarch ever ruled his cowering subjects with any more cruel tyranny than things, visible things, audible things, tangible things, rule mankind.
A. W. Tozer

The possessive clinging to things ... must be torn for our souls in violence as Christ expelled the money changers from the temple. *A. W. Tozer*

Materialism is organized emptiness of the spirit. *Franz Werfel*

MATURITY — See Growth

MEANING — See Purpose

MEANNESS

The miser deprives himself of this world and God will deprive him of the next.
Thomas Adams

A miser is ever in want. *Anon.*

Some people don't let the left hand know what the right hand is giving because they don't want to embarrass the right hand.
Anon.

The only time a miser puts his hand in his pocket is during cold weather. *Anon..*

When it comes to helping others some people stop at nothing. *Anon.*

A tight fist means a shrivelled soul.
Samuel Chadwick

Many people will always be poor because they never give to the cause of God.
C. H. Spurgeon

The miser does no one any good, but he treats himself worst of all. *Publilius Syrus*

MEANS OF GRACE

Without the diligent use of means a lazy Christian has no right to expect to receive assurance. *Thomas Brooks*

It is far easier to speak to others than it is constantly to use and improve all holy means and duties to preserve the soul from sin and maintain it in a sweet and free communion with God. *A. W. Pink*

Neither be idle in the means, nor make an idol of the means. *William Secker*

Many live all their days under the means of grace that never get one dram of grace in the use of the means. *George Swinnock*

Means must be neither trusted nor neglected. *John Trapp*

MEDITATION
(See also: Communion with God; Love for God; Prayer)

Meditation fits a man for supplication.
Anon.

Meditation has a digesting power and turns special truth into nourishment.
Anon.

The hearer of God's Word ought to be like those animals that chew the cud; he ought not only to feed upon it, but to ruminate upon it. *Augustine*

The vessels are fullest of grace which are nearest its spring. The more Christ's glory is beheld, the more men are changed.
William Bagshawe

Meditation is the acting of all the powers of the soul. *Richard Baxter*

Meditation is the life of most other duties. *Richard Baxter*

A man may think on God every day and meditate on God no day. *William Bridge*

Memorization is the first step to meditation. *Jerry Bridges*

Continual meditation on the Word is not ineffectual; ... God, by one and another promise, establishes our faith.
John Calvin

Merely having an open mind is nothing. The object of opening the mind, as of opening the mouth, is to shut it again on something solid.   *G. K. Chesterton*

Meditate on our making, that we may fall in love with our Maker.   *David Dickson*

There is no place like the feet of Jesus for resolving the problems that perplex our hearts.   *G. B. Duncan*

If we hope to move beyond the superficialities of our culture ... we must be willing to go down into the recreating silences.   *Richard Foster*

Meditation is the soul's chewing.
William Grimshaw

Speed-reading may be a good thing, but it was never meant for the Bible. It takes calm, thoughtful, prayerful meditation on the Word to extract its deepest nourishment.   *Vance Havner*

When we are too busy to sharpen the axe, we are too busy.   *Vance Havner*

Meditation is the best help to memory.
Matthew Henry

It is easier to go six miles to hear a sermon, than to spend one quarter of an hour in meditating on it when I come home.   *Philip Henry*

Meditation keeps out Satan. It increases knowledge, it inflames love, it works patience, it promotes prayer, it evidences sincerity.   *Philip Henry*

The mind grows by what it feeds on.
Josiah Holland

Meditation is a serious intention of the mind whereby we come to search out the truth and settle it effectively upon the heart.   *Thomas Hooker*

There is such a thing as sacred idleness.
George MacDonald

If it is the will of the Holy Ghost that we attend to the soul, certainly it is not his will that we neglect the mind.
Charles Malik

Truths are concocted and ripened by meditation.   *Thomas Manton*

True contemplation is not a psychological trick but a theological grace.
Thomas Merton

Meditation is a scriptural duty ... as binding as Bible reading and prayer.
John J. Murray

If I have observed anything by experience it is this: a man may take the measure of his growth and decay in grace according to his thoughts and meditations upon the person of Christ, and the glory of Christ's kingdom, and of his love.
John Owen

Meditate on the Word in the Word.
John Owen

In meditation, the whole man is engaged in deep and prayerful thought on the true meaning and bearing of a particular biblical passage.   *J. I. Packer*

Meditation is not giving free rein to your imagination, nor is it reading your Bible for beautiful thoughts. Meditation is a discipline.   *J. I. Packer*

Meditation is the activity of calling to mind, and thinking over, and dwelling on,

and applying to oneself, the various things that one knows about the works and ways and purposes and promises of God.
J. I. Packer

Sustained imaginative reflection is, if I am not mistaken, so rare today that few of us understand its power to motivate, and are not ourselves motivated by it.
J. I. Packer

The minister who is to preach biblically can only do so as a result of much meditation.
J. I. Packer

Contemplation is a perspective glass to see our Saviour in; but examination is a looking-glass to see ourselves in.
William Secker

Meditation is the grand means of our growth in grace; without it, prayer itself is an empty service.
Charles Simeon

Our design in meditation must be rather to cleanse our hearts than to clear our minds.
George Swinnock

Whatever engages my attention when I should be meditating on God and things external does injury to my soul.
A. W. Tozer

Meditation is the bellows of the affections.
Thomas Watson

Reading and conversation may furnish us with many ideas of men and things, yet it is our own meditation that must form our judgement.
Isaac Watts

The heart is heated by meditation and cold truth is melted into passionate action.
Donald S. Whitney

MEEKNESS
(See also: Humility; Self-Crucifixion)

Meekness is a matter of grace, not genetics.
Anon.

Meekness is the bridle of anger.
Anon.

Poverty of spirit is the riches of the soul.
Anon.

A meek and quiet spirit is an incorruptible ornament, much more valuable than gold.
Thomas Books

The best way to outwit the devil is to be silent under the hand of God.
Thomas Brooks

The silent soul can bear a burden without a burden.
Thomas Brooks

You must have meekness stamped upon you. You assent to it today, but meekness is often forgotten when most needed.
Alfred Buxton

Meekness is a defining grace, produced by the Holy Spirit in the life of the Christian, which characterizes that person's response towards God and man.
John Calvin

Learn the blessedness of the unoffended in the face of the unexplainable.
Amy Carmichael

A meek person is not necessarily indecisive or timid. He is not so unsure of himself that he could be pushed over by a hard slap from a wet noodle! *D. A. Carson*

He who is without expectation cannot fret if nothing comes to him. The lowly man and the meek man dominate the world because they do not care for it.
Henry Drummond

Meekness is having a teachable spirit.
Ronald Dunn

Meekness is a jewel polished by grace.
Sinclair Ferguson

The meek man is the one who has stood before God's judgement and abdicated all his supposed 'rights'. He has learned, in gratitude for God's grace, to submit himself to the Lord and to be gentle with sinners. *Sinclair Ferguson*

Absolute resignation to divine will baffles a thousand temptations, and confidence in our Saviour will carry us through a thousand trials. *John Fletcher*

A lion in God's cause must be a lamb in his own. *Matthew Henry*

Poverty of spirit is the bag into which Christ puts the riches of his grace.
Rowland Hill

Keep thy heart in a soft and tractable state lest thou lose the imprints of God's hands.
Irenaeus

Meekness does not mean indolence.
D. Martyn Lloyd-Jones

Meekness is compatible with great strength. *D. Martyn Lloyd-Jones*

The most difficult thing in the world is to become poor in spirit.
D. Martyn Lloyd Jones

To be truly meek means we no longer protect ourselves because we see there is nothing worth defending.
D. Martyn Lloyd-Jones

Jesus was the very King of meekness.
A. W. Pink

Meekness is the opposite of self-will towards God and of ill-will towards men.
A. W. Pink

I have often made the observation that five minutes before I die it will not matter one whit to me who won the last argument. I will have other things of far greater importance on my mind.
Frank Retief

Meekness is the self-imposed restraint exercised by Christians so that Christ may be glorified in their lives. *Frank Retief*

Meekness is one of the brightest graces which can adorn the Christian character.
J. C. Ryle

The meek person has a preference for the will of God. *J. Oswald Sanders*

The purest gold is the most pliable.
William Secker

Meekness is looking to yourself in the light of God's law. *George Seevers*

A meek man is a good neighbour.
George Swinnock

The meek man is not a human mouse afflicted with a sense of his own inferiority. Rather, he may be in his moral life as bold as a lion and as strong as Samson; but he has stopped being fooled about himself. *A. W. Tozer*

Meekness is the mark of the man who has been mastered by God. His mildness towards others is the fruit of that divine discipline which brought him true self-knowledge. *Geoffrey B. Wilson*

MEMORY

God gave us memories that we might have roses in December. *James M. Barrie*

Each man's memory is his private literature. *Aldous Huxley*

The memory should be a storehouse, not a lumber-room. *John Jewel*

MERCY FROM GOD
(See also: Forgiveness by God)

When all thy mercies, O my God,
My rising soul surveys,
Transported with the view, I'm lost
In wonder, love and praise.
Joseph Addison

God's crumbs are better than the world's loaves. *Anon.*

God gives his anger by weight but his mercy without measure. *Anon.*

Grace is especially associated with men in their sins: mercy is usually associated with men in their misery. *Anon.*

Mercy is without price and beyond all price. *Anon.*

Sin's misery and God's mercy are beyond measure. *Anon.*

God leads us to eternal life not by our merits but according to his mercy.
Augustine

What a world this would be if God sat on a throne of justice only, and if no mercy were ever to be shown to men!
Albert Barnes

A Christian should always remember that his mercies are greater than his miseries.
John Blanchard

We are saved not by merit but by mercy.
John Blanchard

God hath two hands, a right hand of mercy and a left hand of justice.
John Boys

Remembrance of past mercies is a great stimulus to present faith. *Jerry Bridges*

As there is no mercy too great for God to give, so there is no mercy too little for us to crave. *Thomas Brooks*

God's mercies are above all his works, and above all ours too. *Thomas Brooks*

Mercy and punishment, they flow from God, as the honey and the sting from the bee. *Thomas Brooks*

The candle of mercy is set up not to play by but to work by. *Thomas Brooks*

When we come to election, we see nothing but mercy on every side. *John Calvin*

I have been a man of great sins, but he has been a God of great mercies, and now, through his mercies, I have a conscience as sound and quiet as if I had never sinned. *Donald Cargill*

Without faith we are not fit to desire mercy. *Stephen Charnock*

God has two sheepdogs: Goodness and Mercy. He sends them to us from his throne of grace; sometimes to bark at us, to badger us; sometimes to woo us by persuading us that his will is good and perfect for our lives. *Sinclair Ferguson*

Shall light troubles make you forget weighty mercies? *John Flavel*

God giveth his wrath by weight, but his mercy without measure. *Thomas Fuller*

If God should have no more mercy on us than we have charity one to another, what would become of us? *Thomas Fuller*

Mercy in the promise is as the apple in the seed. *William Gurnall*

If God dealt with people today as he did in the days of Ananias and Sapphira, every church would need a morgue in the basement. *Vance Havner*

All the compassions of all the tender fathers in the world compared with the tender mercies of our God would be but as a candle to the sun or a drop to the ocean. *Matthew Henry*

As God's mercies are new every morning toward his people, so his anger is new every morning against the wicked. *Matthew Henry*

God's reasons of mercy are all drawn from himself, not from anything in us. *Matthew Henry*

If the end of one mercy were not the beginning of another, we were undone. *Philip Henry*

Christ is the mine of mercy and the gold-ore of grace and salvation. *Thomas Hooker*

God's mercy is never given at the expense of his justice. *Gordon J. Keddie*

Mercy does not always express itself by withholding punishment. *Ernest M. Ligon*

Man has no more right to mercy than a murderer has to go free. *Fred A. Malone*

Mercy is an ocean that is ever full and ever flowing. *Thomas Manton*

Mercy is a treasure that cannot easily be spent. *Thomas Manton*

No man acts with true wisdom till he fears God and hopes in his mercy. *William S. Plumer*

One spiritual mercy is worth more than all temporal blessings. *William S. Plumer*

Clemency is one of the brightest diamonds in the crown of majesty. *William Secker*

Mercies are such gifts as advance our debts. *William Secker*

One ray of mercy is better than a sun of pleasure. *William Secker*

Everything that comes from God to his children, it is a mercy. *Richard Sibbes*

The depths of our misery can never fall below the depths of mercy. *Richard Sibbes*

All our past mercies are tokens of future mercies. *C. H. Spurgeon*

Mercy is God's Benjamin; the last born and best beloved of his attributes. *C. H. Spurgeon*

Mercy may seem slow, but it is sure. The Lord in unfailing wisdom has appointed a time for the outgoings of his gracious power, and God's time is the best time. *C. H. Spurgeon*

The God of the Bible is as severe as if he were unmerciful; and as just as if he were not gracious; and yet he is as gracious and as merciful as if he were not just.

C. H. Spurgeon

You never have to drag mercy out of Christ, as money from a miser.

C. H. Spurgeon

A debtor to mercy alone,
Of covenant mercy I sing;
Nor fear, with thy righteousness on,
My person and offering to bring;
The terrors of law and of God
With me can have nothing to do;
My Saviour's obedience and blood
Hide all my transgressions from view.

Augustus M. Toplady

Mercies are never so savoury as when they savour of a Saviour. *Ralph Venning*

Take notice not only of the mercies of God, but of God in the mercies.

Ralph Venning

There is no reason to be given for mercy but mercy. *Ralph Venning*

Every misery that I miss is a new mercy.

Izaac Walton

Every time you draw your breath you suck in mercy. *Thomas Watson*

God's mercy can drown great sins, as the sea covers great rocks. *Thomas Watson*

Mercy's clock does not strike at the sinner's beck. *Thomas Watson*

The diocese where mercy visits is very large. *Thomas Watson*

The tree of mercy will not drop its fruits unless shaken by the hand of prayer.

Thomas Watson

Those are the best prepared for the greatest mercies that see themselves unworthy of the least. *Thomas Watson*

God of all mercy is a God unjust.

Edward Young

MERCY TO OTHERS

(See also: Forgiveness of Others; Kindness; Love for Others)

He that demands mercy and shows none ruins the bridge over which he himself is to pass. *Thomas Adams*

In helping others we benefit ourselves; we heal our own wounds in binding up those of others. *Ambrose*

Nowhere do we imitate God more than in showing mercy. *Albert Barnes*

The more godly any man is, the more merciful that man will be. *Thomas Brooks*

Mercy imitates God and disappoints Satan. *Chrysostom*

Our presence in a place of need is more powerful than a thousand sermons.

Charles Colson

If God should have no more mercy on us than we have charity one to another, what would become of us? *Thomas Fuller*

Mercy prefers to deal with the needy in terms of what is needed rather than what is deserved. *D. Edmond Hiebert*

The merciful fall into the arms of mercy.

J. P. Lange

It will not bother me in the hour of death to reflect that I have been 'had for a sucker' by any number of impostors; but it would be a torment to know that one had refused even one person in need.
C. S. Lewis

Mercy in us is a sign of our interest in God's mercy. *Thomas Manton*

The right spring of mercy is a sense of God's mercy; it is a thank-offering, not a sin-offering. *Thomas Manton*

Mercy turns her back on the unmerciful.
Francis Quarles

Mercy is one end of patience. *Henry Smith*

If we refuse mercy here, we shall have justice in eternity. *Jeremy Taylor*

Show your piety by your pity.
Thomas Watson

MIND
(See also: Education; Imagination; Knowledge; Reason; Thoughts)

The head begins to swell when the mind stops growing. *Anon.*

It is good to have an open mind, provided it isn't open at both ends. *Doug Barnett*

If the mouth be bad, the mind is not good.
Thomas Brooks

If we have not quiet in our minds, outward comfort will do no more for us than a golden slipper on a gouty foot.
John Bunyan

Oh, how greatly has the man advanced who has learned not to be his own, not to be governed by his own reason, but to surrender his mind to God! *John Calvin*

Our minds are a beam from God.
Stephen Charnock

You can have such an open mind that it is too porous to hold a conviction.
George Crane

Despise an idle mind. *Jim Elliff*

The one who has come to trust in the salvation of Jesus for his soul will be content to rest in the revelation of Jesus for his mind. *H. Enoch*

The quiet mind is richer than a crown.
Robert Greene

Our greatest sins are those of the mind.
Thomas Goodwin

The human mind is like an umbrella — it functions best when open.
Walter Gropius

A mind at leisure from itself beats all rest cures. *Vance Havner*

The man is as the mind is. *Matthew Henry*

Rule your mind or it will rule you. *Horace*

In presenting the Christian gospel we must never, in the first place, make a direct approach either to the emotions or to the will. The emotions and the will should always be influenced through the mind. *D. Martyn Lloyd-Jones*

Let us never forget that the message of the Bible is addressed primarily to the mind, to the understanding.
D. Martyn Lloyd Jones

The difference between worldliness and godliness is a renewed mind.
Erwin W. Lutzer

The proper function of the mind is to think God's thoughts after him.
Will Metzger

All our minds are narrower than we think, and blind spots and obsessions abound in them like bees in clover. *J. I. Packer*

The human mind without grace is a nest of wickedness swarming with thoughts of evil. *William S. Plumer*

It doesn't take a great mind to be a Christian, but it takes all the mind a man has.
Richard C. Raines

There is a handle to every mind, and our chief aim must be to get hold of it.
J. C. Ryle

Speech is the index of the mind. *Seneca*

When filled with holy truth the mind rests.
C. H. Spurgeon

A Christian mind is a mind which thinks Christianly about everything.
John R. W. Stott

One of the highest and noblest functions of man's mind is to listen to God's Word, and so to read his mind and think his thoughts after him. *John R. W. Stott*

The secret of holy living is in the mind.
John R. W. Stott

The purpose of an open mind is to close it on something. *William Temple*

The mind of man is much wider than his mouth. *George Swinnock*

A guileless mind is a great treasure; it is worth any price. *A. W. Tozer*

The human intellect, even in its fallen state, is an awesome work of God, but it lies in darkness until it has been illuminated by the Holy Spirit. *A. W. Tozer*

The mind is good — God put it there. He gave us our heads and it was not his intention that our heads would function just as a place to hang a hat. *A. W. Tozer*

To possess a Spirit-indwelt mind is the Christian's privilege under grace.
A. W. Tozer

MINISTRY — See Preaching and Preachers

MIRACLES

Jesus' life was a blaze of miracle.
Karl Adam

If you start with the dogma that 'miracles are impossible' then clearly they are impossible. This is a statement, not an argument. *Denis Alexander*

Miracles represent God's unusual actions, detectable against a backcloth of uniformity. *Denis Alexander*

The Christian faith cannot stand without miracles. *E. H. Andrews*

The miraculous is absolutely basic to Christianity. *E. H. Andrews*

Miracles are not breaches of natural but revelations of spiritual law. *Anon.*

God never wrought miracles to convince atheism because his ordinary works convince it. *Francis Bacon*

The many signs that appear after Pentecost should make us the more careful not

to set limits, in our enlightened era, to the miraculous activity of God.
G. C. Berkouwer

A miracle is by definition beyond the ability of science to explain and must therefore also be beyond the ability of science to disprove.   *John Blanchard*

God is not in a rut, unable to do anything new or different.   *John Blanchard*

Miracles must never be separated from the Word.   *John Calvin*

That God normally operates the universe consistently makes science possible; that he does not always do so ought to keep science humble.   *D. A. Carson*

The church that does not work miracles is dead and ought to be buried.
Samuel Chadwick

We marvel, not that Christ performed miracles, but rather that he performed so few. He who could have stormed the citadels of men with mighty battalions of angels let men spit upon him and crucify him.   *Oswald Chambers*

It is not safe to define a miracle as something which cannot be understood; for, at that rate, what can be understood?
Francis Champneys

It is absurd for Christians to constantly seek new demonstrations of God's power, to expect a miraculous answer to every need, from curing ingrown toenails to finding parking spaces; this only leads to faith in miracles rather than the Maker.
Charles Colson

Only if atheism were proved to be true could one rationally deny the possibility of miracles.   *William Lane Craig*

The miracles of Jesus are signs of what lies ahead ... for the people of God.
James T. Dennison

A miracle is God doing what only God can do.   *Ronald Dunn*

Miracles, in both the Old and New Testaments, had only one main purpose, and that was to reveal God. *Brian H. Edwards*

Miracles are the great bell of the universe, which draws men to God's sermon.
John Foster

Scripture warns us against putting too much confidence in miracles to convert unbelieving hearts.   *John M. Frame*

Miracles are the swaddling-clothes of the infant church.   *Thomas Fuller*

The miracles as such do not directly prove Jesus to be the Son of God; this power could have been given to him as a mere man. But indirectly they prove him to be the Son of God because they prove him to be a truthful messenger, and this truthful messenger says that he is God.
John H. Gerstner

The miracles were to the gospel as seals are to a writing.   *William Gurnall*

Do not expect the supernatural when God would have you proceed in the normal, natural course of things.   *Vance Havner*

Some say that to believe the Bible miracles would mean intellectual suicide for them. If all who complain that way did commit such suicide, it would not be a major disaster!   *Vance Havner*

The average run-of-the-mill Christian today believes that God can do miracles,

but few think he will in any given case.
Vance Havner

The Christian life itself is a miracle, and every phase of it ought to bear the mark of the supernatural. *Vance Havner*

Grace will bring a man to heaven without working miracles, but working miracles will never bring a man to heaven without grace. *Matthew Henry*

Miracles are not to be expected when ordinary means are to be used.
Matthew Henry

Miracles don't break any genuine order if God wills everything. *A. J. Hoover*

No Christian would argue simply, 'Miracles prove the Christian faith.' Our evidence comes from many sources, miracles being only one of them. We don't think that isolated, naked miracles would prove any kind of worldview.
A. J. Hoover

You can no more understand a miracle torn from its context than you can understand a comet detached from the solar system in which it moves. *A. J. Hoover*

Miracles are only impossible if the universe is a closed system and all there is. *Dave Hunt*

Those who need miracles are men of little faith. *John Hus*

To strip Christianity of the supernatural is to destroy Christianity. *R. B. Kuiper*

By definition, miracles must of course interrupt the usual course of nature; but if they are real they must, in the very act of doing so, assert all the more the unity

and self-consistency of total reality at some deeper level. *C. S. Lewis*

Do not attempt to water Christianity down. There must be no pretence that you can have it with the supernatural left out. So far as I can see Christianity is precisely the one religion from which the miraculous cannot be separated. *C. S. Lewis*

I am in no way committed to the assertion that God has never worked miracles through and for pagans, or never permitted created supernatural beings to do so. *C. S. Lewis*

The Christian story is precisely the story of one grand miracle, the Christian assertion being that what is beyond all space and time, what is uncreated, eternal, came into nature, into human nature, descended into his own universe, and rose again, bringing nature up with him. It is precisely one great miracle. If you take that away there is nothing specifically Christian left. *C. S. Lewis*

The divine art of miracle is not an art of suspending the pattern to which events conform, but of feeding new events into that pattern. *C. S. Lewis*

The mind which asks for a non-miraculous Christianity is a mind in process of relapsing into mere 'religion'. *C. S. Lewis*

The miracles in fact are a retelling in small letters of the very same story which is written across the whole world in letters too large for some of us to see. *C. S. Lewis*

Miracles are not meant to be understood, they are meant to be believed.
D. Martyn Lloyd-Jones

If the ministry of Jesus had been merely signs and wonders, it would have been sterile within a generation. *R. C. Lucas*

The New Testament without the miracles would be far easier to believe. But the trouble is, would it be worth believing?
J. Gresham Machen

The miracles of Jesus were the ordinary works of his Father, wrought small and swift that we might take them in.
George Macdonald

A miracle is an event in the external world that is wrought by the immediate power of God. *J. Gresham Machen*

God is always the first cause, but there are truly second causes; and they are the means which God uses, in the ordinary course of the world, for the accomplishment of his ends. It is the exclusion of such second causes which makes an event a miracle. *J. Gresham Machen*

Without the miracles, you would have in Jesus a teacher and an example; but with the miracles you have a Saviour from your sins. *J. Gresham Machen*

We are not to require 'signs', but we are to regard signs. They are not given to produce faith, but to inform faith.
Ian MacPherson

We may define a miracle, then, as an event brought about by the immediate agency of God, in contrast with his ordinary method of working.
H. D. McDonald

The attempt to deny miracles in principle can succeed only by assuming the conclusion as one of the premises.
Bruce Milne

The only way we can know whether an event can occur is to see whether in fact it has occurred. The problem of 'miracles', then, must be solved in the realm of historical investigation, not in the realm of philosophical speculation.
John W. Montgomery

We rob Christianity of all excitement when we evacuate the miraculous.
Stephen Olford

Jesus' miracles are decisive evidence for all time of who he is and what power he has. *J. I. Packer*

It is impossible on reasonable grounds to disbelieve miracles. *Blaise Pascal*

Miracles enable us to judge of doctrine, and doctrine enables us to judge of miracles. *Blaise Pascal*

A religion without wonders is false. A theology without wonders is heretical.
William S. Plumer

A miracle would not be a miracle if it could be explained! *J. C. Ryle*

Even if no miracle had ever occurred at any time or place so far in the universe and we actually knew this to be true (which we don't and can't, but let's waive that) it would still be possible that miracles *could* occur. *James W. Sire*

There is no way we as human beings can *know* with absolute certainty that miracles cannot happen. We would have to know everything about the way the universe, reality itself, works. No one has that kind of knowledge. *James W. Sire*

It is more to God's glory that the world should be conquered by the force of truth

than by the blaze of miracles.
C. H. Spurgeon

The greatest of all miracles is the salvation of a soul. *C. H. Spurgeon*

Grant me God and miracles take care of themselves! *A. W. Tozer*

If God said that Jonah was swallowed by a whale, then the whale swallowed Jonah, and we do not need a scientist to measure the gullet of the whale. *A. W. Tozer*

Bare inexplicableness cannot be accepted as the sufficient criterion of the miraculous. *Benjamin B. Warfield*

No event can be really miraculous which has implications inconsistent with fundamental religious truth.
Benjamin B. Warfield

The connection of alleged miracles with erroneous doctrine invalidates their claim to be genuine works of God.
Benjamin B. Warfield

We believe in a wonder-working God, but not in a wonder-working church.
Benjamin B. Warfield

If God exists, miracles are not merely logically possible, but really and genuinely possible at every moment.
Merald Westphal

Because God exists miracles are possible and God might be expected to involve himself in human history as well as in the lives of individuals. *Peter S. Williams*

MISTAKES

The person who never makes a mistake never makes anything. *Anon.*

We must never overlook the untold benefits that can be derived from mistakes. A person should never hesitate to own he has been in the wrong, which is but saying in other words that he is wiser today than he was yesterday, because of his mistake. *Anon.*

The only real mistake is the one from which we learn nothing. *John Powell*

Many people would learn from their mistakes if they weren't so busy denying them. *Harold J. Smith*

Our mistakes won't irreparably damage our lives unless we let them.
James Sweaney

MODERNISM — See Liberalism

MODESTY

Nothing is more amiable than true modesty, and nothing more contemptible that the false. The one guards virtue, the other betrays it. *Joseph Addison*

Let us learn to lay upon ourselves the restraint of modesty. *John Calvin*

Modesty is the lifeguard of chastity.
Thomas Fuller

Modesty is the badge of wisdom.
Matthew Henry

The outward modesty which makes itself known in dress, is to be accompanied by inward purity and chastity, since the former would otherwise be of no account.
J. E. Hunter

All the rules of good behaviour are contained in that one word — modesty.
John C. Ryland

MONEY

(See also: Luxury; Materialism; Possessions; Prosperity; Riches; Wealth)

Money is like sea-water; the more a man drinks, the more thirsty he becomes.
Anon.

Money often unmakes the man who makes it. *Anon.*

Money really adds no more to the wise than clothes to the beautiful. *Anon.*

There are no pockets in a shroud. *Anon.*

When money speaks, the truth is silent.
Anon.

You can blot out the sun if you hold a penny close enough to your eye. *Anon.*

Money is like muck, no good unless it is spread. *Francis Bacon*

Nearly half the parables Jesus told have the use of money as their main subject. It is sometimes said that we should give until it hurts. But Jesus teaches that it should hurt when we cease to give!
Ian Barclay

Money is never more wisely used than in forwarding the cause of God.
George Barlow

Money is in some respects like fire; it is a very excellent servant, but a terrible master. *P. T. Barnum*

Money will buy a pretty good dog, but it won't buy the wag of his tail.
Josh Billings

Few things test a person's spirituality more accurately than the way he uses money. *John Blanchard*

We cannot serve God and mammon, for as the thoughts of the one rise up, the other goes down. *Donald Cargill*

The love of money is a greater curse to the church than the aggregate of all the other evils in the world. *Samuel Chadwick*

In the battle of faith, money is usually the last stronghold to fall. *Ronald Dunn*

To possess money is very well; it may be a most valuable servant; to be possessed by it is to be possessed by a devil, and one of the meanest and worst kind of devils. *Tryon Edwards*

Lust and lucre follow one another as closely akin, both seducing the heart from the Creator to the creature. *A. R. Fausset*

Make money your god, it will plague you like the devil. *Henry Fielding*

Money is a miraculous thing. It is a man's personal energy reduced to portable form and endowed with powers the man himself does not possess.
Harry Emerson Fosdick

A penny will hide the biggest star in the universe if you hold it close enough to your eye. *Samuel Grafton*

If a person gets his attitude towards money straight, it will help straighten out almost every other area in his life.
Billy Graham

Money is no defence against the arrests of death, nor any alleviation to the miseries of the damned. *Matthew Henry*

Money may be the husk of many things, but not the kernel. It brings you food, but not appetite; medicine, but not health;

acquaintance, but not friends; servants, but not loyalty; days of joy, but not peace or happiness. *Henrik Ibsen*

Time and money are the heaviest burdens of life, and the unhappiest of all mortals are those who have more of either than they know how to use. *Samuel Johnson*

The real measure of our wealth is how much we'd be worth if we lost all our money. *John Henry Jowett*

He that serves God for money will serve the devil for better wages.
Roger L'Estrange

If a man's religion does not affect his use of money, that man's religion is vain.
Hugh Martin

One of the ways of manifesting and maintaining the crucifixion of the flesh is never to use money to gratify it. *Andrew Murray*

Few things eat into the soul as devastatingly as the love of money.
James Philip

Some people are so poor they only have money! *Ivor Powell*

The key to our whole relationship to money lies in the attitude of our minds towards it. *Kenneth F. W. Prior*

The poorest man I know is the man who has nothing but money.
John D. Rockefeller

By doing good with his money a man, as it were, stamps the image of God upon it, and makes it pass current for the merchandise of heaven. *John Rutledge*

Although Christ's work does not depend on our money, yet Christ is pleased to test the reality of our grace by allowing us to help him. *J. C. Ryle*

It is possible to love money without having it, and it is possible to have it without loving it. *J. C. Ryle*

Money, in truth, is one of the most unsatisfying of possessions. It takes away some cares, no doubt; but it brings with it quite as many cares as it takes away. There is the trouble in the getting of it. There is anxiety in the keeping of it. There are temptations in the use of it. There is guilt in the abuse of it. There is sorrow in the losing of it. There is perplexity in the disposing of it. *J. C. Ryle*

Two-thirds of all the strifes, quarrels and lawsuits in the world arise from one simple cause — money! *J. C .Ryle*

How we use our money demonstrates the reality of our love for God. In some ways it proves our love more conclusively than depth of knowledge, length of prayers or prominence of service.
Charles Caldwell Ryrie

Mammon is the largest slave-holder in the world. *Frederick Saunders*

There are two ways in which a Christian may view his money — 'How much of my money shall I use for God?' or 'How much of God's money shall I use for myself?' *W. Graham Scroggie*

Money has never yet made anyone rich.
Seneca

I think that when Christians get to heaven and they speak of how much money they gave to missions, to build schools and so on, that the Lord is going to tell them it would have been better if they had had less money to give and had made their money with justice.   *Francis Shaeffer*

Money — the greatest god below the sky.
Herbert Spencer

A Christian making money fast is just like a man in a cloud of dust; it will fill his eyes if he is not careful.   *C. H. Spurgeon*

We need not covet money, for we shall always have our God, and God is better than gold, his favour is better than fortune.   *C. H. Spurgeon*

I fear money, Mother Hubbard's cupboard is safe; a full cupboard is very risky.
C. T. Studd

Money is an amoral instrument and like science serves good and evil alike. There is no such thing as dirty money; the stain is only on the hand that holds it as giver or taker.   *A. M. Sullivan*

Nothing that is God's is obtainable by money.   *Tertullian*

Money is not able to buy one single necessity of the soul. *Henry David Thoreau*

The two poles shall sooner meet than the love of God and the love of money.
John Trapp

When I have any money I get rid of it as quickly as possible, least it find a way into my heart.   *John Wesley*

MORALITY
(See also: Ethics; Goodness; Virtue)

Men are more accountable for their motives than for anything else; and primarily, morality consists in the motives, that is in the affections.   *Archibald Alexander*

Give ten thoughts to the question what will God think of it, before one to what men will think of it.   *J. W. Alexander*

No man can be a true member of the church of God who is a stranger to moral righteousness.   *Anon.*

If morality is just a matter of personal opinion, then we have no basis for a legal system. You can't send people to prison over differences in personal opinion.   *John Benton*

Our Creation by a holy God who placed us in a world subject to his perfect law and gave us moral discernment would explain our conviction that there is a radical difference between right and wrong.
John Blanchard

The Christian life is a moral marathon.
John Blanchard

The cost of putting a thing right can never be as great as the cost of leaving it wrong.
John Blanchard

We were not redeemed merely to be legally safe, but also to be morally sound.
John Blanchard

Moral honesty is not sufficient to keep a man out of eternal misery; all it can do is to help a man to one of the best rooms and easiest beds that hell affords.
Thomas Brooks

The Bible's God, and none other, can satisfy human needs. His moral code for centuries has passed through the flames of controversy, but it does not even have the smell of fire upon it.   *D. J. Burrell*

Morality, taken as apart from religion, is but another name for decency in sin.
Horace Bushnell

Morality

A breakdown in moral order leads to a breakdown in civil order.
Frederick Catherwood

Morality is not only correct conduct on the outside, but correct thinking within where only God can see.
Oswald Chambers

Morality without sanctions is a morality without obligations. *Gordon H. Clark*

If Christ is Lord of all, Christians must recapture their sense of moral outrage.
Charles Colson

Just as we are rational to assume that some objective moral order lies behind our sense perceptions, so we are rational to assume that some objective moral order lies behind our perceptions of value.
William Lane Craig

Without God there wouldn't be any foundation for calling anything evil.
William Lane Craig

If God exists, nothing is more natural than that we should experience a moral 'ought'. Without God the moral order would be a strange kind of inexplicable brute fact. How could there be an objective law with no lawgiver.
C. Stephen Evans

If there is a God, what better calling card could he have left in us than the consciousness of a moral order?
C. Stephen Evans

It is not guided missiles but guided morals that is our great need today.
George L. Ford

The immutability of God's holy character is itself the absolute and the final court of morality. *Os Guinness*

Nothing is ever settled until it is settled right; and nothing is ever settled right until it is settled with God. *Vance Havner*

Atheistic morality is not impossible, but it will never answer our purpose.
Roswell D. Hitchcock

All moral obligation resolves itself into the obligation of conformity to the will of God. *Charles Hodge*

Morality does not make us religious, but religion makes us moral. *Charles Hodge*

Even when a person asserts that all morality is relative, he thinks I ought to accept the proposition because it is true.
A. J. Hoover

You can't even discuss morality without assuming morality. *A. J. Hoover*

If your heart does not want a world of moral reality, your head will assuredly never make you believe in one.
William James

Men can be moral and godless.
R. T. Kendall

Christian morality differs radically from legalism. Legalism is obedience to the letter of the law to the neglect of the spirit; Christian morality is obedience to the spirit of the law as well as the letter.
R. B. Kuiper

Christianity has the only true morality; no other religion conduces to true holiness. *R. B. Kuiper*

However radically definitions of goodness may, and actually do, differ, there is not a religion on this globe which does not bid its adherents to be good after a

fashion and to do good of a kind.
R. B. Kuiper

If the God of the Bible is the one true and living God, the keeping of his precepts is the only true morality. *R. B. Kuiper*

Morality is rooted in religion ... True morality is rooted in true religion.
R. B. Kuiper

If [moral] truth is objective, if we live in a world we did not create and cannot change merely by thinking, if the world is not really a dream of our own, then the most destructive belief we could possibly believe would be the denial of this primary fact. It would be like closing your eyes while driving, or blissfully ignoring the doctor's warnings. *C. S. Lewis*

The human mind has no more power of inventing a new value than of planting a new sun in the sky or a new colour in the spectrum. *C. S. Lewis*

The moment you say that one set of moral ideas can be better than another, you are, in fact, measuring them both by a standard ... comparing them both with some Real Morality, admitting that there is such a thing. *C. S. Lewis*

If 'right' and 'wrong' are merely descriptions of what is best for others, and they do not happen to be what is best for me, why should I play the game?
Pete Lowman

The temptation to construct good and evil outside the context of loving trust in God constitutes precisely that fatal and unworkable snatching at independence that dooms the entire human race to misery. *Pete Lowman*

Man operating by himself cannot set up true standards of justice or values in the world without God. If one man decides his view of human values is correct, while another man decides differently, who will decide between them? *Josh McDowell*

Every time we make a moral judgement on someone else... we are assuming a moral order under which both we and they stand. *Peter C. Morey*

Everything that is really worth while in the morality of today has come to the world through Christ. Dismiss his standards of right and wrong and try to draw up your own ethical code, and see where you will be! *G. Campbell Morgan*

A straight line is shortest in morals as well as in geometry. *I. Rahel*

Morality is not just a social construct; it is rooted in the eternal character of God himself. *Vaughan Roberts*

Humankind is given the very specific task of caring for the created world on God's behalf. He is to be a steward, a caretaker of the created order. The issue of morality, of man's relationship with his fellow man and with the created world, flow from this central declaration of the meaning and purpose of life. *Martin Robinson*

Truth and morality are inextricably connected. *Martin Robinson*

Morality is not merely the purity patter of preachers — it is the law of God.
W. E. Sangster

Christian morality is not the product of an arbitrary God, but corresponds to the way we are made. The Ten Commandments . . . were given by a loving Creator who made us and best knows how we function. *Ian F. Shaw*

If society is uncoupled from a belief in God, who is our judge, we lose any basis for deciding what is right and what is wrong. *Jonathan Skinner*

Morality is always higher than law.
Alexandr Solzhenitsyn

No man's religion ever survives his morals. *Robert South*

If everything is relative including ethics and values then we are in deep weeds: the kind of deep weeds one finds in a jungle. *R. C. Sproul*

If everything is relative to everything else, then there is no ultimate reference point. There is no basis for truth. If everything is relative, then the statement, 'Everything is relative,' is also relative. *R. C. Sproul*

It is an undeniable fact that men hold that there is a difference between right and wrong; there are things which they ought to do and other things which they ought not to do. *A. E. Taylor*

The moral character of the soul depends upon its central object. *David Thomas*

As the sailor locates his position on the sea by 'shooting' the sun, so we may get our moral bearings by looking at God.
A. W. Tozer

All sects differ, because they come from men; morality is everywhere the same because it comes from God. *Voltaire*

Two stimuli are necessary to make man endeavour to conform with accepted moral standards: belief in an ultimate judgement and belief in the immortality of the soul. *Wernher von Braun*

Only he who knows God is truly moral.
Friedrich W. J. von Schelling

A man may be wonderfully moralized, yet but a tame devil. *Thomas Watson*

Morality may damn as well as vice. A vessel may be sunk with gold as well as with dung. *Thomas Watson*

There are plenty of moral dilemmas. What is not in question, however, is that there are some objective values which provide obviously good reasons for action. *Keith Ward*

If there is no God, to whom or what will we appeal for our moral outrage?
Peter S. Williams

Moral judgements are either true or false, and this truth or falsity is independent of human thought or belief or desire.
Peter S. Williams

Objective moral obligation must be grounded in a transcendent personal reality to whom we are objectively obligated. *Peter S. Williams*

The existence of an objective moral law leads us to recognize the existence of an objective moral lawgiver.
Peter S. Williams

The most plausible explanation of the existence of objective moral values, and our knowledge (however imperfect) of these values (most fundamentally of the objective distinction between right and wrong) is that there exists an all-good, personal, rational and eternal being who has made humans in his image.
Peter S. Williams

Morality does not make a Christian, yet no man can be a Christian without it.
Thomas Wilson

MORTIFICATION — See Self-Crucifixion

MOTIVATION — See Purpose

MOTIVE

God considers not the action, but the spirit of the action. *Peter Abelard*

Man sees your action, but God your motives. *Thomas à Kempis*

Men are more accountable for their motives than for anything else; and primarily, morality consists in the motives, that is in the affections. *Archibald Alexander*

A concern for the glory of God is the ultimate motive for Christian living.
Anon.

Devotion to God is the only acceptable motive for actions that are pleasing to God. *Jerry Bridges*

To be absolutely honest, I can't ever be certain what motivates me. Jeremiah tells us that nothing is more deceitful than the human heart — and he's right.
Charles Colson

It is not enough that our actions be good and praiseworthy, if our intentions are not pure and upright. It is to profane the good to do it with a bad end in view. *Jean Daille*

I cannot, by direct moral effort, give myself new motives. After the first few steps in the Christian life we realize that everything which really needs to be done in our souls can be done only by God.
C. S. Lewis

Actions speak louder than words, but, with God, motives speak louder than either. *Arthur Neil*

A good end cannot sanctify evil means; nor must we ever do evil that good may come of it. *William Penn*

We should often be ashamed of our best actions were the world witness to the motives which produce them.
Francois Rochefoucauld

It is universally recognized that *what* we do matters less than *why* we do it.
John R. W. Stott

As water cannot rise higher than its source, so the moral quality in an act can never be higher than the motive that inspires it. *A. W. Tozer*

It is not what a man does that determines whether his work is sacred or secular, it is why he does it. *A. W. Tozer*

The test by which all conduct must finally be judged is motive. *A. W. Tozer*

MURMURING

The frog and the murmurer, both of them are bred of the mud. *Thomas Adams*

A grouch always looks as if he were weaned on a pickle. *Anon.*

Discontent generally arises more from our desires than from our wants. *Anon.*

It is better to be mute than to murmur.
Thomas Brooks

Murmuring is a time-destroying sin.
Thomas Brooks

Murmuring uncrowns a man.
Thomas Brooks

Complain *to* God you may, but to complain *of* God, you may not.   *John Flavel*

If we growl all day we shouldn't be surprised if we end up dog tired at night!
Vance Havner

One hour in heaven and we shall be ashamed we ever grumbled.
Vance Havner

Those who complain most are most to be complained of.   *Matthew Henry*

Complaining about our lot in life might seem quite innocent in itself, but God takes it personally.   *Erwin W. Lutzer*

God's people may groan, but they may not grumble.   *C. H. Spurgeon*

Ten minutes' praying is better than a year's murmuring.   *C. H. Spurgeon*

The murmurer is his own martyr.
George Swinnock

Complain without cause and you will have cause to complain.   *Thomas Taylor*

Murmuring often ends in cursing.
Thomas Watson

Our murmuring is the devil's music.
Thomas Watson

MUSIC

The object of all music should be the glory of God and pleasant recreation.
Johann Sebastian Bach

Among other things adapted for man's pleasure and for giving them pleasure, music is either the foremost, or one of the principal; and we must esteem it as a gift from God designed for that purpose.
John Calvin

He who does not find (the great and perfect wisdom of God) in his wonderful work of music is truly a clod and is not worthy to be considered a man!
Martin Luther

Music is a means of giving form to our inner feelings without attaching them to events or objects in the world.
George Santayana

If you love and listen to the wrong kinds of music your inner life will wither and die.   *A. W. Tozer*

It is not overstating the case to insist that the kinds of music you enjoy will demonstrate pretty much what you are like inside.   *A. W. Tozer*

MYSTERY
(See also: God — Inscrutability)

A religion without mystery must be a religion without God.   *Anon.*

A religion that is small enough for our understanding is not great enough for our need.   *Arthur J. Balfour*

A science without mystery is unknown; a religion without mystery is absurd.
Henry Drummond

Mystery is but another name for our ignorance; if we were omniscient all would be perfectly plain.   *Tyron Edwards*

With God there are mysteries but no mistakes.   *Michael Griffiths*

Mystery is beyond human reason but it is not against reason.   *Os Guinness*

All the scriptural imagery (harps, crowns, gold, etc.) is, of course, a merely symbolic attempt to express the inexpressible ... People who take these symbols literally might as well think that when Christ told us to be like doves, he meant that we were to lay eggs.   *C. S. Lewis*

Reason's last step is the recognition that there are an infinite number of things that are beyond it.   *Blaise Pascal*

Even though there is no final answer to the mystery of evil prospering in the world, the overriding consideration that more than offsets everything else is God's unchanging love and care. *James Philip*

NATURALISM

Naturalists who deny the existence of any transcendent, personal God cannot successfully solve the problem of good. They cannot explain why there is a difference between right and wrong.
James W. Sire

NATURE
(See also: Creation; Evolution)

The world is the first Bible that God made for the instruction of man.
Clemens Alexandrinus

Nature is the art of God. *Dante Alighieri*

Let no man think or maintain that a man can search too far or be too well studied in the book of God's word or in the book of God's works.   *Francis Bacon*

Open your eyes, and the whole world is full of God.   *Jacob Boehme*

What are the heavens, the earth, the sea, but a sheet of royal paper, written all over with the wisdom and power of God?
Thomas Brooks

Knowledge of nature and atheism are incompatible. To know nature is to know that there must be a God.
Edward G. Bulwer-Lytton

If we would avoid a senseless natural philosophy we must always start with this principle, that everything in nature depends upon the will of God, and that the whole course of nature is only the prompt carrying into effect of his orders.
John Calvin

This is, indeed, the proper business of the whole life, in which men should daily exercise themselves, to consider the infinite goodness, justice, power and wisdom of God, in this magnificent theatre of God.
John Calvin

Nature is but a name for an effect whose cause is God.   *William Cowper*

The laws of nature are but the thoughts and agencies of God, the modes in which he works and carries out the designs of his providence and will. *Tryon Edwards*

Nature is too thin a screen; the glory of the omnipresent God bursts through everywhere.   *Ralph Waldo Emerson*

Nature does not despise art. It is the office of art to lead back to nature.
Henry C. Fish

All about us lies a world inviting some sort of explanation.   *Rod Garner*

Nature is a first volume, in itself incomplete, and demanding a second volume, which is Christ.   *Charles Gore*

Without consistent laws we would never know where we were; life would be a nightmare of confusion and unpredictability.   *Stephen Gaukroger*

All the powers of nature prove the greatness of the God of nature, from whom they are derived and on whom they depend.   *Matthew Henry*

The very existence of the world and the order within it comprise powerful evidence for the existence of God.
Rodney D. Holder

The world is charged with the grandeur of God.   *Gerard Manley Hopkins*

If nature is all there is, then nature had to have the ability to do its own creating.
Phillip E. Johnson

There are no laws of nature, only customs of God.   *C. Kingsley*

Because God created the natural — invented it out of his love and artistry — it demands our reverence.   *C. S. Lewis*

We find ourselves in a world of transporting pleasures, ravishing beauties, and tantalizing possibilities, but all constantly being destroyed, all coming to nothing. Nature has all the air of a good thing spoiled.   *C. S. Lewis*

All nature, including the nature of man, is a wondrous instrument of many strings, delicately tuned to work God's will and upon which he plays with a master hand.
J. Gresham Machen

As the star brought the wise men to Christ, so should all the stars in the world bring up your thoughts to God.
Thomas Manton

General revelation provides the point of contact for special revelation, this latter alone being saving knowledge of God.
Alister McGrath

Every formula which expresses a law of nature is a hymn of praise to God.
Maria Mitchell

The universe is centred on neither the earth nor the sun. It is centred on God.
Alfred Noyes

Everywhere I find the signature, the autograph of God.   *Joseph Parker*

Nature has some perfections in order to show that she is the image of God, and some defects to show that she is only his image.   *Blaise Pascal*

Those honour nature well who teach that she can speak on everything, even on theology.   *Blaise Pascal*

God's will is the law of universal nature.
William S. Plumer

Causes in nature do not obviate the necessity of a Cause in nature.
George John Romanes

It is not just that God spoke: but God is speaking! He is by his nature continuously articulate. He fills the world with his speaking voice.   *A. W. Tozer*

If a watch proves the existence of a watchmaker but the universe does not prove the existence of a great architect, then I consent to be called a fool.
François M. Voltaire

The concept of strict and generally valid laws of nature could hardly have arisen without the Christian concept of creation.
C. F. Vonwezacher

Nature with open volume stands
To spread her Maker's praise abroad,
And every labour of his hands
Shows something worthy of a God.
Isaac Watts

NEGLIGENCE
(See also: Sin of omission)

Negligence is the rust of the soul that corrodes through all her best resolves.
Owen Feltham

We can easily lose by negligence what we have laboured to acquire by grace.
Thomas à Kempis

Nothing offends God so much as neglect of privileges. *J. C. Ryle*

Neglect destroys men. *C. H. Spurgeon*

No talent can survive the blight of neglect.
Edgar A. Whitney

NEW BIRTH — See Regeneration

NOSTALGIA

Living in the past is no way to face the future. *John Blanchard*

Learning from history and basking in nostalgia are two different things.
Roger C. Palms

OBEDIENCE — Blessing

All heaven is waiting to help those who will discover the will of God and do it.
J. Robert Ashcroft

Obedience won't stop the decomposition of our physical lives but it will halt the decay of our spiritual lives. *Ian Barclay*

In the mysterious chemistry of God's mercy, a man's very obedience is made a blessing to him. *John Blanchard*

Joy is the natural out-come of the Christian's obedience to the revealed will of God. *John Blanchard*

Obedience changes things.
John Blanchard

To pay the price of obedience is to escape the cost of disobedience.
John Blanchard

It is not wrong to feel good about ourselves, but this should be a by-product of obedience which is motivated by a desire to please God. *Jerry Bridges*

By obeying Christ's commands you will gain more than you can give.
Thomas Brooks

Though no man merits assurance by his obedience, yet God usually crowns obedience with assurance. *Thomas Brooks*

It is only by obedience that we understand the teaching of God. *Oswald Chambers*

The Christian life begins with obedience, depends on obedience, and results in obedience. *Charles Colson*

Peace and comfort can be found nowhere except in simple obedience.
François Fenelon

Only in obedience can we discover the great joy of the will of God.
Sinclair Ferguson

Holy joy is the oil to the wheels of our obedience. *Matthew Henry*

Obedience is the key that unlocks the door to every profound spiritual experience. *Dorothy Kerin*

Obedience is the road to freedom. *C. S. Lewis*

Obedience is not only the touchstone of all progress in the Christian life, it is our only safe course. *James Philip*

Godly walking is the best aid to the digestion of godly truth. *Hugh Redwood*

To obey God is perfect liberty. *Seneca*

The reward of sin is more sin and the reward of obedience is the power to obey again. *David Shepherd*

The fundamental deception of Satan is the lie that obedience can never bring happiness. *R. C. Sproul*

The way of uprightness is the way of heavenly wealth. *C. H. Spurgeon*

To obey God's will is to find the fulfillment of our lives. *David Watson*

OBEDIENCE — Characteristics

True obedience has no lead at its heels. *Thomas Adams*

Wicked men obey from fear; good men from love. *Aristotle*

The difference between disobedience and obedience is marked by the individual's attitude toward the sin. *Donald Grey Barnhouse*

Christian obedience is not slavery to dominating legalism but it is submission to divine law. *John Blanchard*

It is only by the grace of God that a man can obey the law of God. *John Blanchard*

Obedience to God should never be conditioned by our convenience or comfort. *John Blanchard*

The beginning and perfection of lawful worship is readiness to obey. *John Calvin*

When God designs to forgive us he changes our hearts and turns us to obedience by his Spirit. *John Calvin*

Only when confidence wavers does obedience hesitate. *Ronald Dunn*

In all true obedience there is remembrance. *William Jenkyn*

Before faith and obedience become acts of man they are gifts of God. *R. B. Kuyper*

Obedience is counterfeit when it is not uniform. *Thomas Manton*

Doing the will of God leaves me no time for disputing about his plans. *George McDonald*

What is obedience? Giving up my will to the will of another. *Andrew Murray*

Obedience is submitting to the lover of our souls. *Ken Myers*

True obedience neither procrastinates nor questions. *Francis Quarles*

Christian obedience is unlike every other kind of obedience. It is not the obedience of slaves or soldiers, but essentially the obedience of lovers who know, love and trust the person who issues the commands. *John R. W. Stott*

The Lord is King! I own his power,
His right to rule each day and hour;
I own his claim on heart and will,
And his demands I would fulfil.
Darley Terry

The Bible recognizes no faith that does not lead to obedience, nor does it recognize any obedience that does not spring from faith. The two are opposite sides of the same coin. *A. W. Tozer*

Knowledge is the eye that must direct the foot of obedience. *Thomas Watson*

The true obedience of faith is a cheerful obedience. *Thomas Watson*

OBEDIENCE — Importance

Whoever strives to withdraw from obedience withdraws from grace.
Thomas à Kempis

Becoming a Christian does not alter the fact that I am still a created being under obligation to obey. *Richard Alderson*

The evidence of knowing God is obeying God. *Eric Alexander*

Christ's sheep are marked in the ear and the foot; they hear his voice and they follow him. *Anon.*

Christianity is obedience. *Anon.*

If God has called you, don't spend time looking over your shoulder to see who is following. *Anon.*

The proof of real saving faith is a persistent mindset to obey what Jesus has taught us in his Word, the Bible. *Anon.*

When Christ takes the burden of guilt off a sinner's shoulders he places the yoke of obedience upon his neck. *Anon.*

Christian obedience is to be the response to our acceptance, not the reason for it.
John Blanchard

Obedience is not the essence of a right relationship with God, but it is the evidence of it. *John Blanchard*

Obedience is the positive side of repentance. *John Blanchard*

The evidence of saving faith is not how much you believe but how well you behave. *John Blanchard*

Jesus has spoken; his is the Word, ours the obedience. *Dietrich Bonhoeffer*

One act of obedience is better than a hundred sermons. *Dietrich Bonhoeffer*

Only he who believes is obedient; only he who is obedient believes.
Dietrich Bonhoeffer

God does not give us his power so that we might feel good about ourselves; he gives us his power so that we can obey him for his sake, for his glory.
Jerry Bridges

Just as obedience to the Lord is an indication of our love for him, so is it also a proof of our fear of God. *Jerry Bridges*

Every man obeys Christ as he prizes Christ, and no otherwise. *Thomas Brooks*

He who obeys sincerely endeavours to obey thoroughly.   *Thomas Brooks*

No man obeys God truly who does not endeavour to obey God fully.
                              Thomas Brooks

The obedience that springs from faith is the obedience of a son, not of a slave.
                              Thomas Brooks

Love to God and obedience to God are so completely involved in each other that any one of them implies the other too.
                              F. F. Bruce

No man will actually obey God but he who loves him.   *John Calvin*

Nothing is more fatal to us than to refuse to give ourselves in obedience to God.
                              John Calvin

Obedience is the end of our calling.
                              John Calvin

The basis of true religion is obedience.
                              John Calvin

We cannot rely on God's promises without obeying his commandments.
                              John Calvin

God marks with sorrow the point in the history of any one of his servants where there is failure to yield him implicit, unquestioning, heroic obedience.
                              Leslie Carter

Faith is the starting-post of obedience.
                              Thomas Chalmers

The best measure of a spiritual life is not its ecstasies but its obedience.
                              Oswald Chambers

The golden rule for understanding in spiritual matters is not intellect, but obedience.   *Oswald Chambers*

The rugged obedience of the cross may still be seen in our creeds, but it is hard to find in our lives.   *Robert E. Coleman*

It is not what we do that matters, but what a sovereign God chooses to do through us. God doesn't want our success; he wants us. He doesn't demand our achievements; he demands our obedience.
                              Charles Colson

What God wants from his people is obedience, no matter what the circumstances, no matter how unknown the outcome.   *Charles Colson*

To obey is the proper office of a rational soul.   *Michel E. de Montaigne*

My gracious Lord, I own thy right
To every service I can pay;
And call it my supreme delight
To hear thy dictates and obey.
                              Philip Doddridge

The scriptural doctrine of justification by faith alone, without any manner of goodness or excellency of ours, does in no wise diminish either the necessity or benefit of a sincere evangelical obedience.   *Jonathan Edwards*

Obedience to God is the most infallible evidence of sincere and supreme love to him.   *Nathanael Emmons*

Be obedient even when you do not know where obedience may lead you.
                              Sinclair Ferguson

There is no such thing as genuine knowledge of God that does not show

itself in obedience to his Word and will.
Sinclair Ferguson

Faith that saves has one distinguishing quality: saving faith is a faith that produces obedience; it is a faith that brings about a way of life. *Billy Graham*

Understanding can wait. Obedience cannot. *Geoffrey Grogan*

One of the reasons people find it hard to be obedient to the commands of Christ is that they are uncomfortable taking orders from a stranger. *Gary Gulbranson*

Sacrifice without obedience is sacrilege.
William Gurnall

Perfect obedience is God's right as God.
Graham Heaps

God uses broken things: broken soil and broken clouds to produce rain; broken grain to produce bread; broken bread to feed our bodies. He wants our stubbornness broken into humble obedience.
Vance Havner

What our Lord said about cross-bearing and obedience is not in fine type. It is in bold print on the face of the contract.
Vance Havner

The opposite of ignorance in the spiritual realm is not knowledge but obedience.
Howard Hendricks

Love is the root, obedience is the fruit.
Matthew Henry

Those who would have the blessings of God's testimonies must come under the bonds of his statutes. *Matthew Henry*

God calls people to worship him with

their obedience, and instead they try to fob him off with their religion.
John Hercus

All moral obligation resolves itself into the obligation of conformity to the will of God. *Charles Hodge*

Obedience to legitimate authority is one of the fruits and evidences of Christian sincerity. *Charles Hodge*

God is not otherwise to be enjoyed than as he is obeyed. *John Howe*

Justification supplies the only efficient motive to obedience. *Ernest F. Kevan*

The strongest inducement for a Christian to obey the divine law is the fact that he has been graciously pardoned for having broken it. *Ernest F. Kevan*

God is a totalitarian Ruler who demands full allegiance from his subjects.
R. B. Kuiper

To know God is to know that our obedience is due to him. *C. S. Lewis*

Evangelical obedience is fully a condition of justification but not a cause of justification. *Sam Logan*

I had rather obey than work miracles.
Martin Luther

Obedience is the crown and honour of all virtue. *Martin Luther*

Don't throw God a bone of your love unless there's the meat of obedience on it. *John MacArthur*

Partial obedience is an argument of insincerity. *Thomas Manton*

There is no experience of sanctification which absolves us from the responsibility of day-to-day obedience. *David McKee*

Obedience is the best commentary on the Bible. *Theodore Monod*

The life of sanctification is the life of obedience. *J. A. Motyer*

The believer is not redeemed by obedience to the law but he is redeemed unto it. *John Murray*

Legal obedience was approved by *justice;* evangelical obedience is acceptable unto *mercy*. *A. W. Pink*

Not only does God require obedience, but an obedience which issues from, is animated by, and is an expression of, love. *A. W. Pink*

Sincere obedience, though it be not sinless, is acceptable unto God; if it were not, then it would be impossible for any of his children to perform a single act in this life which was pleasing in his sight. *A. W. Pink*

Love of the creature toward the Creator must include obedience or it is meaningless. *Francis Schaeffer*

It is our bounden duty to live *in* obedience, but it would prove our utter ruin to live *on* obedience. *William Secker*

We have been born under a monarchy; to obey God is freedom. *Seneca*

God's commands carry no RSVP — man indeed has the *power* to refuse the divine summons, but not the *right*. *R. C. Sproul*

A life under the rule of Christ can alone prove that we are the objects of our Lord's delight. *C. H. Spurgeon*

Believing and obeying always run side by side. *C. H. Spurgeon*

Faith and obedience are bound up in the same bundle. He that obeys God, trusts God; and he that trusts God, obeys God. *C. H. Spurgeon*

Obedience is the hallmark of faith. *C. H. Spurgeon*

Though the heavens should fall through our doing right, we are not to sin in order to keep them up. *C. H. Spurgeon*

It is the simplest things that are most difficult to understand and accept, and one of those which seems in my experience to have been most difficult for people to understand and accept has been the fact that the Lord demands of his servants, each and every one of them, to listen to him only and obey his will implicitly, irrespective of what it costs. *William Still*

Christ's lovers prove their love by their obedience. *John R. W. Stott*

Where the right is absolute, the obedience must not be conditional. *George Swinnock*

God being who he is must have obedience from his creatures. Man being who he is must render that obedience, and he owes God complete obedience whether or not he feels for him the slightest trace of love in his heart. *A. W. Tozer*

Theological truth is useless until it is obeyed. The purpose behind all doctrine is to secure moral action! *A. W. Tozer*

To escape the error of salvation by works we have fallen into the opposite error of salvation without obedience. *A. W. Tozer*

True faith commits us to obedience.
A. W. Tozer

Doers of the Word are the best hearers.
Thomas Watson

Love without obedience is a satanic substitute for God's plan. *John C. Whitcomb*

OBSTINACY — See Stubbornness

OLD AGE

Age: the only thing that comes to us without effort. *Anon.*

Don't resent growing old; many do not have the opportunity of doing so. *Anon.*

In old age life's shadows are meeting eternity's day. *Anon.*

Life's evening will take its character from the day that has preceded it. *Anon.*

It is not how many years we live, but what we do with them. *Evangeline Booth*

We Christians are miserable indeed if we grow old in making no improvement.
John Calvin

An aged Christian with the snow of time on his head may remind us that those points of earth are whitest that are nearest heaven. *E. H. Chapin*

Forty is the old age of youth; fifty is the youth of old age. *Victor Hugo*

When grace is joined with wrinkles, it is adorable. There is an unspeakable dawn in happy old age. *Victor Hugo*

The evening of a well-spent life brings its lamps with it. *Joseph Joubert*

The passions of the young are vices in the old. *Joseph Joubert*

The last ten years of life are the best, because we are freest from illusions and fullest of experience. *Benjamin Jowett*

If you will be cherished when you are old, be courteous while you are young.
John Lyly

Age is not all decay; it is the ripening, the swelling, of the fresh life within, that withers and bursts the husk.
George Macdonald

Old age is a blessed time. It gives us leisure to put off our earthly garments one by one and dress ourselves for heaven.
Ray Palmer

There is more felicity on the far side of baldness than young men can possibly imagine. *Logan Pearsall Smith*

No wise man ever wished to be younger.
Jonathan Swift

Seek that your last days be your best days, and so you may die in a good old age, which may be best done when you die good in old age. *Ralf Venning*

OPINION

Modesty in delivering our opinions leaves us the liberty of changing them without humiliation. *Anon.*

Only where there is no direct teaching in the Word of God on any matter may we hold opinions, subject to change.
Donald Grey Barnhouse

Opinion

Every man has a right to his opinion, but no man has a right to be wrong in his facts. *Bernard M. Baruch*

All too often we think we are standing on principle when in reality we may be only insisting on our opinion.
Jerry Bridges

Opinion is a mean between knowledge and ignorance. *Plato*

The number of people who believe a thing to be true does not even create a presumption about it one way or the other.
William G. Sumner

Every man has a right to his opinion, but his opinion may not be right.
Arthur H. Townsend

OPPORTUNITIES

The reason some people don't recognize opportunity is that it usually comes disguised as hard work. *Anon.*

A wise man will make more opportunities than he finds. *Francis Bacon*

Small opportunities are often the beginning of great enterprises. *Demosthenes*

ORTHODOXY

There is nothing more ugly than orthodoxy without understanding or compassion. *Anon.*

Orthodoxy of words is blasphemous unless it is backed up by superiority of character. *Blaise Pascal*

Biblical orthodoxy without compassion is surely the ugliest thing in the world.
Francis Schaeffer

There is no pride so insidious and yet so powerful as the pride of orthodoxy.
A. W. Tozer

Orthodoxy is my orthodoxy; heterodoxy is another man's orthodoxy.
William Warburton

You may be as orthodox as the devil, and just as wicked. *John Wesley*

PAIN
(See also: Sickness; Sufferings; Trials)

There is a pain that is productive of life itself. *Eric Alexander*

We cannot learn without pain. *Aristotle*

The existence of pain and evil is as much a threat to atheism as it is to faith.
Francis Bridger

Pain makes men think and forces us to ask questions. *Brian Edwards*

Pain is the body's early warning system. Without it, life would be unimaginably worse than it is now. *Stephen Gaukroger*

Pain can either make us better or bitter.
Tim Hansel

The experience of God's people shows that bodily pain has a special office to perform in the work of sanctification.
Charles Hodge

If anybody is not disturbed by the problem of pain, it is for one of two reasons: either because of hardening of the heart or else because of softening of the brain.
G. A. Studdert Kennedy

God whispers to us in our pleasures, speaks in our consciences, but shouts in our pains; it is his megaphone to rouse a deaf world.   *C. S. Lewis*

I'd rather hobble into heaven than walk into hell!   *D. Martyn Lloyd-Jones*

Even pain pricks to livelier living.
                                                        Amy Lowell

God uses chronic pain and weakness, along with other afflictions, as his chisel for sculpting our lives.   *J. I. Packer*

The weaker we feel, the harder we lean. And the harder we lean, the stronger we grow spiritually, even while our bodies waste away.   *J. I. Packer*

Pain makes man think.   *John Patrick*

I am trying, if I can, to find a joy in rheumatism, but I cannot get up to it yet. I have found a joy when it is over — I can reach that length — and I can and do bless God for any good result that may come of it; but when the pain is on me, it is difficult to be joyous about it, and so I conclude that my sanctification is very incomplete.   *C. H. Spurgeon*

Those who wear the shoe know best where it pinches.   *C. H. Spurgeon*

If I ever wonder about the appropriate 'spiritual' response to pain and suffering, I can note how Jesus responded to his own: with fear and trembling, with loud cries and tears.   *Philip Yancey*

PARDON — See Forgiveness by God; Forgiveness of Others

PARENTS — See Family Life

PASSION
(See also: Anger; Hatred; Zeal)

When your temper boils over, you are usually in hot water.   *Anon.*

Some men's passion is for gold. Some men's passion is for art. Some men's passion is for fame. My passion is for souls.
                                                        William Booth

Passion does not compensate for ignorance.   *Samuel Chadwick*

Fanaticism is the false fire of an overheated mind.   *William Cowper*

Serving one's own passions is the greatest slavery.   *Thomas Fuller*

Passions are spiritual rebels and raise rebellion against the understanding.
                                                        Ben Jonson

When passion is up, true zeal is usually asleep.   *Thomas Manton*

The ruling passion, be it what it will,
The ruling passion conquers reason still.
                                                        Alexander Pope

A frenzy is worse than a fever.
                                                        Thomas Watson

Passion unmans a man.   *Thomas Watson*

PATIENCE

Patience must not be an inch shorter than affliction.   *Thomas Adams*

A delay is better than a disaster.   *Anon.*

A handful of patience is worth more than a bushel of brains.   *Anon.*

439

Life is a symphony, and we lose a third of it by cutting out the slow movement.
Anon.

Patience is a quality that is most needed when it is exhausted. *Anon.*

Patience is a virtue that carries a lot of wait! *Anon.*

Patience is not passive: on the contrary it is active; it is concentrated strength. *Anon.*

Patience is the livery of Christ's servants.
Anon.

Patience is the companion of wisdom.
Augustine

Long-suffering is a grace of silence.
William Bagshawe

Biblical patience is not rooted in fatalism that says everything is out of control. It is rooted in faith that says everything is in God's control. *John Blanchard*

Waiting for an answer to prayer is often part of the answer. *John Blanchard*

Patience achieves more than force.
Edmund Burke

Hope is the foundation of patience.
John Calvin

Patience is the fruit and proof of faith.
John Calvin

There is no place for faith if we expect God to fulfil immediately what he promises. *John Calvin*

Where there is no patience, there is not even a spark of faith. *John Calvin*

Patient waiting is often the highest way of doing God's will. *Jeremy Collier*

The times we find ourselves having to wait on others may be the perfect opportunities to train ourselves to wait on the Lord. *Joni Eareckson Tada*

Though God take the sun out of heaven, yet we must have patience. *George Herbert*

Hope is the mother of patience.
William Jenkyn

Never cut what you can untie.
Joseph Joubert

Patience is the ballast of the soul that will keep it from rolling and tumbling in the greatest storms. *Ezekiel Hopkins*

Cheerful patience is a holy art and skill, which a man learns from God.
Thomas Manton

Teach us, O Lord, the discipline of patience, for to wait is often harder than to work. *Peter Marshall*

All true servants of Christ must be content to wait for their wages. *J. C. Ryle*

Our impatience only learns patience through the thorn of delay and darkness.
J. Charles Stem

To lengthen my patience is the best way to shorten my troubles. *George Swinnock*

The deep and due consideration of the infinite patience of God towards us will greatly promote the patience of *our* spirits, and transform us into the same image. *John Trapp*

A Christian without patience is like a soldier without arms. *Thomas Watson*

Patience in prayer is nothing but faith spun out. *Thomas Watson*

Patience makes a Christian invincible. *Thomas Watson*

PEACE
(See also: Peace-Making)

Peace is the establishment of harmonious relationships with that for which we are constituted. *Douglas Adam*

All men desire peace, but very few desire those things that make for peace. *Thomas à Kempis*

Great tranquillity of heart is his who cares for neither praise nor blame. *Thomas à Kempis*

Peace is rarely denied to the peaceful. *Anon.*

Peace is the conscious possession of adequate resources. *Anon.*

Peace is the deliberate adjustment of my life to the will of God. *Anon.*

Peace rules the day when Christ rules the mind. *Anon.*

Rest is not a hallowed feeling that comes over us in church; it is the response of a heart set deep in God. *Anon.*

The best tranquillizer is a clear conscience. *Anon.*

Where there is peace, God is. *Anon.*

Peace is to the soul what health is to the body: a sign of balance and order. *Guy Appere*

The peace of God means being grateful for his past mercies, conscious of his present mercies, and certain of his future mercies. *John Blanchard*

I hear the words of love,
I gaze upon the blood,
I see the mighty sacrifice,
And I have peace with God. *Horatius Bonar*

If we have not quiet in our minds, outward comfort will do no more for us than a golden slipper on a gouty foot. *John Bunyan*

Peace is a free gift and flows from the pure mercy of God. *John Calvin*

Peace is not to be purchased by the sacrifice of truth. *John Calvin*

I have taken my good deeds and bad deeds and thrown them together in a heap, and fled from them both to Christ, and in him I have peace. *David Dickson*

It is the religion of Jesus alone that can bring peace to a man. *François Fenelon*

Peace and comfort can be found nowhere except in simple obedience. *François Fenelon*

Peace does not dwell in outward things, but within the soul. *François Fenelon*

The peace of the soul consists in an absolute resignation to the will of God. *François Fenelon*

We sleep in peace in the arms of God when we yield ourselves up to his providence. *Fraçcois Fenelon*

Better a lean peace than a fat victory. *Thomas Fuller*

Grace is the free favour of God; peace is the condition which results from its reception. *H. L Goudge*

Peace is never to be obtained but by the rooting out of sin. *Francis Hall*

Stayed upon Jehovah
Hearts are fully blest,
Finding, as he promised,
Perfect peace and rest.
Frances Ridley Havergal

Peace is not packaged in pills.
Vance Havner

Peace is not real peace until it has been tested in the storm. *Eric Hayman*

Peace is the smile of God reflected in the soul of the believer. *William Hendriksen*

Peace is such a precious jewel that I would give anything for it but truth.
Matthew Henry

The peace of God will keep us from sinning under our troubles and from sinking under them. *Matthew Henry*

What peace can they have who are not at peace with God? *Matthew Henry*

When we lack the peace *of* God, we should turn to our peace *with* God.
Robert M. Horn

The mere absence of war is not peace.
John F. Kennedy

God is able to give us *peace* when our lives are going to pieces. *James F. Lewis*

Peace if possible, but truth at any rate.
Martin Luther

Peace comes not from the absence of trouble, but from the presence of God.
Alexander Maclaren

Peace without righteousness is but a sordid compliance; righteousness without peace is but a rough austerity.
Thomas Manton

There is no grace unless God bestows it, and there is no real peace unless it flows forth from God's reconciliation with sinful man. *J. J. Muller*

All peace with God is resolved into a purging atonement made for sin.
John Owen

Nothing can give perfect peace of conscience with God but what can make atonement for sin. And whoever attempts it in any other way but by virtue of that atonement will never attain it, in this world or hereafter. *John Owen*

Five great enemies to peace: greed, ambition, envy, anger and pride. *Petrarch*

I thank thee, Lord, that here our souls,
Though amply blest,
Can never find, although they seek,
A perfect rest,
Nor ever shall, until they lean
On Jesus' breast.
Adelaide Anne Proctor

There will be no universal peace till the Prince of peace appears. *J. C. Ryle*

You will never find peace and happiness until you are ready to commit yourself to something worth dying for.
Jean Paul Sartre

If you are to have peace with God there must be war with Satan. *C. H. Spurgeon*

If we lose inward peace, we lose more than a fortune can buy. *C. H. Spurgeon*

It is in the way of truth that real peace is found. *C. H. Spurgeon*

When filled with holy truth the mind rests. *C. H. Spurgeon*

Peace is the fruit of believing prayer. *M. R. Vincent*

Peace flows from purity. *Thomas Watson*

The seeming peace a sinner has is not from the knowledge of his happiness but the ignorance of his danger. *Thomas Watson*

We must not be so in love with the golden crown of peace as to pluck off the jewels of truth. *Thomas Watson*

There is no kind of peace that can be purchased on the bargain counter. *Carey Williams*

The fewer the desires, the more peace. *Joseph Wilson*

Peace of heart is the natural outcome of purity of heart. *Spiros Zodhiates*

PEACE-MAKING
(See also: Peace)

He that is not a son of peace is not a son of God. *Richard Baxter*

Labour mightily for a healing spirit. *Thomas Brooks*

The oilcan is mightier than the sword. *Everett Dirksen*

Few things more adorn and beautify a Christian profession than exercising and manifesting the spirit of peace. *A. W. Pink*

The peace-makers are those who are at peace with God and who show that they are truly children of God by striving to use every opportunity open to them to effect reconciliation between others who are at variance. *R. V. G. Tasker*

PENITENCE
(See also: Confession; Contrition; Conviction of Sin; Repentance)

A penitent's prayer is an undeniable ambassador. *Anon.*

He truly bewails the sins he has committed who never commits the sins he has bewailed. *Augustine*

Men never entertain a real hatred towards sin unless God illuminates their minds and changes their hearts. *John Calvin*

When the soul has laid down its faults at the feet of God, it feels as though it had wings. *Eugene de Guerin*

Holiness is a Christian's ornament, and a peaceableness is the ornament of holiness. *Thomas Manton*

Anything is good for us if it makes us loathe ourselves and penitently sue for mercy. *William S. Plumer*

Godly mourning is better than carnal rejoicing. *William S. Plumer*

It is with a true penitent as with a wounded man. He comes to the surgeon and shows him all his wounds. *Thomas Watson*

PERFECTION

This life was not intended to be the place of our perfection but the preparation for it. *Richard Baxter*

Perfection demands perfection; that is why salvation must be by grace, and why works are not sufficient.
Donald Grey Barnhouse

Those who aim at perfection, and persevere, will come much nearer to it than those whose laziness and despondency make them give it up as unattainable.
Philip D. S. Chesterfield

I would rather aim at perfection and fall short of it than aim at imperfection and fully attain it. *A. J. Gordon*

We shall never come to the perfect man till we come to the perfect world.
Matthew Henry

A great deal of perfectionism is rotten to the core. *A. A. Hodge*

The perfect Christian is the one who, having a sense of his own failure, is minded to press towards the mark.
Ernest F. Kevan

Fully aware that he will not reach the goal of moral perfection in this life, the Christian must yet press on with might and main towards that very mark. *R. B. Kuiper*

It is of the essence of Christianity to strive for the unattainable. *R. B. Kuiper*

The nearer men are to being sinless, the less they talk about it. *D. L. Moody*

As soon as I learn that a brother states that he has lived for months without sin … I feel sure that somewhere or other there is a leak in the ship. *C. H. Spurgeon*

I have met with some of these 'perfectly sanctified' gentlemen, but I could have spoilt their perfection simply by treading on their corns; and I believe I have done so, for they seem to be immensely cross when I have denied their proud boast.
C. H. Spurgeon

I met only one perfect man and he was a perfect nuisance! *C. H. Spurgeon*

Perfection in the flesh is a lie: I believe it to be one of the grossest falsehoods ever palmed on foolish minds. *C. H. Spurgeon*

All the perfection we can arrive at in this life is sincerity. *Thomas Watson*

What is Christian perfection? Loving God with all our heart, mind, soul and strength. *John Wesley*

PERMISSIVENESS

Permissiveness is man thinking he can take God's law into his own hands.
John Blanchard

Permissiveness is nothing less than moral mutiny. *John Blanchard*

If God did not exist, all would be permitted. *Feodor Dostoevsky*

A permissive home is a home where you don't love enough to exercise the authority that Christ gave you. *Ben Haden*

Permissiveness is not a policy; it is the abandonment of policy and its apparent advantages are illusory. *B. F. Skinner*

PERSECUTION
(See also: Martyrdom)

The purest church is the church under the cross.   *J. H. Merle d'Aubigne*

Persecutions are in a way seals of adoption to the children of God.   *John Calvin*

It is the suffering church that is the growing church.   *A. Jack Dain*

Never expect to find this world anything better than a wilderness.
    Jonathan Edwards

Persecution is one of the surest signs of the genuineness of our Christianity.
    Benjamin E. Fernando

Crushing the church is like smashing the atom: divine energy of high quality is released in enormous quantity and with miraculous effects. *Benjamin E. Fernando*

Who more innocent than Christ? And who more persecuted? The world is the world still.   *John Flavel*

It is unnatural for Christianity to be popular.   *Billy Graham*

If you are under any illusions about the attitude of this world towards Jesus Christ, try really living for him for a week and you will find out!   *Vance Havner*

Let a man really dare to be a New Testament Christian and take Christ seriously, beginning next Monday morning, and he will wake up to the fact that he is a sheep among wolves.   *Vance Havner*

Scars are the price which every believer pays for his loyalty to Christ.
    William Hendriksen

Christ's followers cannot expect better treatment in the world than their Master had.   *Matthew Henry*

Wherever you see persecution, there is more than a probability that truth is on the persecuted side.   *Hugh Latimer*

Persecution and opposition ought to encourage rather than discourage us, for we are faithfully warned by our Lord that the natural man and the religionist will not receive the gospel of the grace of God.
    Henry T. Mahan

When men try to extinguish the light of the gospel it burns more brightly.
    Henry T. Mahan

Storms cannot shipwreck the gospel; they waft it forward.   *F. B. Meyer*

Persecution often does in this life what the last great day will do completely — separate the wheat from the tares.
    James Milner

The Word of God never yet prospered in the world without opposition.
    Iain H. Murray

Persecution is no novelty … the offence of the cross will never cease till all flesh shall see the salvation of God.
    William S. Plumer

If you were not strangers here the hounds of the world would not bark at you.
    Samuel Rutherford

Persecution is like the goldsmith's hallmark on real silver and gold; it is one of the marks of a converted man.   *J. C. Ryle*

The assaults of persecution from without have never done half so much harm to the church as the rise of false doctrines within. *J. C. Ryle*

Take care if the world does hate you that it hates you without cause. *C. H. Spurgeon*

The wind of persecution often fans the torch of truth. *David Thomas*

The fire of God can't be damped out by the waters of man's persecution. *A. W. Tozer*

Suffering for Christ's sake is to be viewed as a privilege. As God has bestowed the gift of salvation so he has also bestowed the gift of suffering. *Howard F. Vos*

Persecution is the legacy bequeathed by Christ to his people. *Thomas Watson*

Put the cross in your creed. *Thomas Watson*

The weight of glory makes persecution light. *Thomas Watson*

To have two heavens is more than Christ had. Was the head crowned with thorns and do we think to be crowned with roses? *Thomas Watson*

PERSEVERANCE
(See also: Determination)

If you fall, don't give up, get up. *Anon.*

The difference between perseverance and obstinacy is that one often comes from a strong will and the other from a strong won't. *Henry Ward Beecher*

Endurance and perseverance are qualities we would all like to possess, but we are loath to go through the process that produces them. *Jerry Bridges*

Endurance is the ability to stand up under adversity; perseverance is the ability to progress in spite of it. *Jerry Bridges*

True grace always produces vigilance rather than complacency; it always produces perseverance rather than indolence. *Jerry Bridges*

All our progress and perseverance are from God. *John Calvin*

We persevere through faith and never apart from it. *Sinclair Ferguson*

He who gives over never truly begins. *William Jenkyn*

The root of all steadfastness is in consecration to God. *Alexander MacLauren*

The will to persevere is often the difference between failure and success. *Donald Sarnoff*

By perseverance the snail reached the ark. *C. H. Spurgeon*

Perseverance is the hallmark of a genuine interest in Christ. *Geoffrey B. Wilson*

PERSEVERANCE OF SAINTS — See Eternal Security

PHILOSOPHY

Any philosophy, though championed by the most brilliant intellects, that tends to lure the soul from Christ, that puts anything in the place of him, or depreciates in any way our estimate of his glorious character, is false and full of peril. *George Barlow*

Philosophy is the search for truth. In Jesus, the search ends. *John Blanchard*

The exhortations of the philosophers are cold and lifeless, if compared with the convictions, affections and boundless energy of the real believers.   *John Calvin*

The sublimest virtue according to philosophy is to live the life of nature, but Scripture points us to the perfect Christ as our example.   *John Calvin*

There is nothing so strange and so unbelievable that it has not been said by one philosopher or another.   *Rene Descartes*

The highest philosophy is often a judicious suspense of judgement.
Michael Faraday

Human philosophy, the wisdom of the world, has never converted a soul.
Henry C. Fish

Any philosophy which deals only with the here and now is not adequate for man.
Billy Graham

Whereas God's existence is the last or highest proof of philosophy, it is the *first* truth of theology.   *W. Andrew Hoffecker*

Good philosophy must exist … because bad philosophy needs to be answered.
C. S. Lewis

If a philosophy of life cannot help me to die, then in a sense it cannot help me to live.   *D. Martyn Lloyd-Jones*

The ordinary Christian knows and understands more about life than the greatest philosopher who is not a Christian.
D. Martyn Lloyd-Jones

I have looked into most philosophical systems, and I have seen that none will work without a God.   *Clerk Maxwell*

Philosophy has been a quest, and never a conquest.   *G. Campbell Morgan*

No philosophy that will not teach us how to master death is worth twopence to us.
J. I. Packer

What philosophy is striving to find, theology asserts has been found.
Augustus H. Strong

Philosophy is saying what everybody knows in language that no one can understand.   *J. F. Taviner*

It is poor philosophy to say we will believe nothing unless we can understand everything!   *J. C. Ryle*

Philosophy and science are good servants of Christ, but they are poor guides when they rule out the Son of God.
Augustus H. Strong

Philosophy and science have not always been friendly towards the idea of God, the reason being that they are dedicated to the task of accounting for things and are impatient with anything that refuses to give an account of itself.   *A. W. Tozer*

PIETY

Piety means letting God bend your will, not just your knees.   *Anon.*

Piety is the root of charity.   *John Calvin*

There is no solid wisdom but in true piety.
John Evelyn

The path of piety avoids ritualism and rationalism.   *Richard Glover*

Piety requires us to renounce no ways of life where we can act reasonably and

offer what we do to the glory of God.
William Law

Piety is God sensible to the heart.
Blaise Pascal

Practice is the very life of piety.
William S. Plumer

True piety is never separate from the fear of God. *William S. Plumer*

Piety is the best parentage. *William Secker*

True piety hath true plenty.
George Swinnock

Show your piety by your pity.
Thomas Watson

Serious piety is the best defence against wickedness. *Thomas Watson*

PLEASURES and HEDONISM

Consider pleasures as they depart, not as they come. *Aristotle*

He whose main pursuit is pleasure will never attain to righteousness.
Walter J. Chantry

Sinful and forbidden pleasures are like poisoned bread; they may satisfy appetite for the moment, but there is death in them at the end. *Tryon Edwards*

The difference between false pleasure and true is just this: for the true, the price is paid before you enjoy it; for the false, after you enjoy it. *John Foster*

There is no earthly pleasure whereof we may not surfeit; of the spiritual we can never have enough. *Joseph Hall*

'Pleasure' and 'joy' not only are not synonymous, but may be as profoundly different as heaven and hell.
Sidney J. Harris

A man never makes a bigger fool of himself than when he settles down in Sodom for personal advantage.
Vance Havner

The pleasures of sense are puddle-water; spiritual delights are rock water.
Matthew Henry

Let me rather have that fire which is rewarded with heaven than those pleasures which shall be rewarded with fire. *John P. K. Henshaw*

Fly the pleasure that bites tomorrow.
George Herbert

Life in worldly pleasure is only life in appearance. *H. J. Holtzmann*

The best cure for hedonism is the attempt to practice it. *John MacMurray*

All sins are rooted in love of pleasure. Therefore be watchful. *Thomas Manton*

All the pleasure that wicked men have is upon earth; here, and nowhere else.
Thomas Manton

God allows us to use pleasures, but not to live in them; to take delights, but not that they should take us. *Thomas Manton*

Pleasure seeking, as we learn from experience, is a barren business; happiness is never found until we have the grace to stop looking for it and to give our attention to persons and matters external to ourselves. *J. I. Packer*

The Christian tastes God in all his pleasures. *J. I. Packer*

That this world is a play-ground instead of a battle-field has now been accepted in practice by the vast majority of fundamentalist Christians. *A. W. Tozer*

Soft pleasures harden the heart. *Thomas Watson*

POPULARITY
(See also: Fame)

Popularity is fleeting, fickle and futile. *John Blanchard*

A dish around which I see too many people doesn't tempt me. *Julien Green*

Popularity has killed more prophets than persecution. *Vance Havner*

Avoid popularity; it has many snares, and no real benefits. *William Penn*

Nothing is so fickle and uncertain as popularity. It is here today and gone tomorrow. It is a sandy foundation, and sure to fail those who build upon it. *J. C. Ryle*

The more one pleases everybody, the less one pleases profoundly. *Stendhal*

POSSESSIONS
(See also: Luxury; Materialism; Money; Prosperity; Riches; Wealth)

If we have God in all things while they are ours, we shall have all things in God when they are taken away. *Anon.*

Worldly possessions, through human depravity, are often not helps but hindrances in the way of religion. *Anon.*

You actually possess everything you can see when you close your eyes. *Anon.*

Worldly possessions have ruined many people but redeemed none. *John Blanchard*

To be content with one's possessions is one of the most strongly worded exhortations in Scripture. *Jerry Bridges*

If we have not quiet in our minds, outward comfort will do no more for us than a golden slipper on a gouty foot. *John Bunyan*

To possess what Christ would not have us to possess is waste; to possess anything instead of Christ and his will is waste. *Sinclair Ferguson*

Possession pampers the mind. *William Hazlitt*

It is easier to renounce worldly possessions than it is to renounce the love of them. *Walter Hilton*

All the possessions of mortals are mortal. *Metrodorus*

Every possession is a trust. *Roy L. Smith*

All that we possess is qualified by what we are. *John Spalding*

Nothing influences a man so much as that which he calls his own. *C. H. Spurgeon*

That only is worth my having which I can have for ever. That only is worth my grasping which death cannot tear out of my hand. *C. H. Spurgeon*

One day we stand to lose everything except those qualities that have eternal value. *David Watson*

The real value of a thing is the price it will bring in eternity. *John Wesley*

POVERTY

Better to be poor than wicked. *Anon.*

It is good to run short, that we may be driven to Christ with our necessity. *Anon.*

The two great tests of character are wealth and poverty. *Anon.*

He who is not contented with a little will never be satisfied with much.
Thomas Brooks

There are worse things than poverty.
Vance Havner

Worry over poverty is as fatal to spiritual fruitfulness as is gloating over wealth.
A. W. Pink

There is no sin in poverty. *J. C. Ryle*

The Saviour of sinners knows what it is to be poor. *J. C. Ryle*

We never need be ashamed of our poverty unless our own sins have brought it upon us. *J. C. Ryle*

Wealth is no mark of God's favour. Poverty is no mark of God's displeasure.
J. C. Ryle

Poverty and affliction take away the fuel that feeds pride. *Richard Sibbes*

Whatever a man amasses by the way is in the nature of luggage, no part of his truest personality, but something he leaves behind at the toll-bar of death.
E. K. Simpson

Better to be a child of God in poverty than a child of Satan in riches.
C. H. Spurgeon

Poverty is a hard heritage; but those who trust in the Lord are made rich by faith.
C. H. Spurgeon

Poverty is a friend to prayer.
George Swinnock

We must lose things to know the value of them. It is a dry well which makes people know the value of water.
William Tiptaft

No one in this world has ever been saved and gone to heaven because he was poor. You can be as poor as a church mouse and still be as bad as a church rat.
A. W. Tozer

A piece of bread with God's love is angel's food. *Thomas Watson*

The pilgrim is not to despise the comforts which he may meet with by the way, but he is not to tarry among them, or leave them with regret. *Geoffrey B. Wilson*

I am mended by my sickness, enriched by my poverty, and strengthened by my weakness. *Abraham Wright*

POWER

Almighty must be that power whose sufficient strength is weakness. *Anon.*

Greatness lies not in being strong, but in the right use of strength. *Anon.*

The Christian needs won't power as well as will power. *Anon.*

When God is our strength, it is strength indeed; when our strength is our own, it is only weakness. *Augustine*

Power in the Christian life depends upon our communication with the source of power. *L. Nelson Bell*

The greater the power the more dangerous the abuse. *Edmund Burke*

Power intoxicates men. When a man is intoxicated by alcohol he can recover, but when intoxicated by power he seldom recovers. *James F. Byrnes*

Nothing will so avail to divide the church as love of power. *Chrysotom*

Power can corrupt us in Christian service as easily as it can corrupt those in political service. *Charles Colson*

The pursuit of power can separate the most resolute of Christians from the true nature of Christian leadership.
Charles Colson

Power will intoxicate the best hearts as wine the strongest heads. No man is wise enough, nor good enough, to be trusted with unlimited power. *C. C. Colton*

We are not to think that, where we see no possibility, God sees none. *Marcus Dods*

We must learn to cease from measuring the power of God by our own, and reasoning from the one to the other.
Marcus Dods

The power to live a new life depends upon daily communion with the living Lord. *John Eadie*

It is amazing how strong we become when we begin to understand what weaklings we are! *François Fenelon*

The lust for power is not rooted in strength but in weakness. *Erich Fromm*

Nearly all men can stand adversity, but if you want to test a man's character, give him power. *Abraham Lincoln*

The quest for excellence is a mark of maturity. The quest for power is childish. *Max Lucado*

Remember Jesus *for us* is all our righteousness before a holy God, and Jesus *in us* is all our strength in an ungodly world.
Robert Murray M'Cheyne

The same power that brought Christ back from the dead is operative within those who are Christ's. The resurrection is an ongoing thing. *Leon Morris*

Now that I am in Christ, God's moral demands have not altered, but it is no longer I who meets them. *Watchman Nee*

We have no power from God unless we live in the persuasion that we have none of our own. *John Owen*

Only those who do not desire power are fit to hold it. *Plato*

There is no stronger test of a man's character than power and authority.
Plutarch

He who has great power should use it lightly. *Seneca*

There is no telling how much power God can put into a man. *C. H. Spurgeon*

The greatest power today is not atomic but spiritual power; not Communism but communion; not the machinations of men but the might of God.   *J. Charles Stern*

We only lose our weaknesses through discovery of them.   *J. Charles Stern*

No power has such a commanding influence over us as the power of love.
David Thomas

PRAISE
(See also: Worship)

The best atmosphere for prayer is praise.
Peter Anderson

Be not hot in prayer and cold in praise.
Anon.

Bless God heartily though he afflict you heavily.   *Anon.*

Bless the Lord today; he blesses you every day.   *Anon.*

Hem your blessings with praise, lest they unravel.   *Anon.*

Praise ... decentralizes self.
Paul E. Billheimer

Had I a thousand tongues, I would praise God with them all.   *Peter Boehler*

I have never sufficiently praised the Lord, and never can.   *Andrew Bonar*

We should be always wearing the garment of praise, not just waving a palm-branch now and then.   *Andrew Bonar*

The servants of the Lord are to sing his praises in this life to the world's end; and in the next life world without end.
John Boys

God listens for nothing more tenderly as when his children help each other by their testimonies to his goodness and the way in which he has brought them deliverance.   *Horace Bushnell*

Men in general praise God in such a manner that he scarcely obtains the tenth part of his due.   *John Calvin*

Praise is the best of all sacrifices and the true evidence of godliness. *John Calvin*

The most holy service that we can render to God is to be employed in praising his name.   *John Calvin*

There is not a corner in heaven or on earth where God is not praised. *John Calvin*

It is a bad sign when a new-born babe has not lungs enough to make itself heard over the whole house. It is equally a bad symptom when the new convert is born dumb and cannot find his voice to praise God audibly.   *T. L. Cuyler*

In praising a creature, we may easily exceed the truth; but in praising God we have only to go on confessing what he really is to us. Hence it is impossible to exceed the truth: here is genuine praise.
A. R. Fausset

Be not afraid of saying too much in the praises of God; all the danger is of saying too little.   *Matthew Henry*

In thanking God, we fasten upon his favours to us; in praising and adoring God, we fasten upon his perfections in himself.   *Matthew Henry*

What we win by prayer we must wear with praise.   *Matthew Henry*

If Christians praised God more, the world would doubt him less. *Charles E. Jefferson*

Praise shall conclude that work which prayer began. *William Jenkyn*

Praise God, from whom all blessings flow,
Praise him, all creatures here below,
Praise him above, ye heavenly host,
Praise Father, Son and Holy Ghost.
Thomas Ken

In commanding us to glorify him, God is inviting us to enjoy him. *C. S. Lewis*

A line of praises is worth a leaf of prayer, and an hour of praises is worth a day of fasting and mourning! *John Livingstone*

The music of praise arises out of a fixed heart, a heart settled on God.
John MacArthur

Praise, to be acceptable to God, must come from a heart devoted to him.
Albertus Magnus

Self-love may lead us to prayers, but love to God excites us to praises.
Thomas Manton

Give unlimited credit to our God.
Robert Murray M'Cheyne

Praising energizes and renews praying.
J. I. Packer

Have we not more cause to praise God than to pray? Surely, for we have many things to thank him for, which we never ask for. *A. W. Pink*

Praising and adoring God is the noblest part of the saint's work on earth, as it will be his chief employ in heaven. *A. W. Pink*

Come, thou fount of every blessing,
Tune my heart to sing thy grace;
Streams of mercy, never ceasing,
Call for songs of loudest praise.
Teach me some melodious measure,
Sung by flaming tongues above;
Oh, the vast, the boundless treasure
Of my Lord's unchanging love!
Robert Robinson

A drop of praise is an unsuitable acknowledgement for an ocean of mercy.
William Secker

Let us keep a catalogue of God's blessings. *Richard Sibbes*

God deserves every imaginable praise from his creatures, whether heathens or Christians, and the more men praise him the greater will be their happiness.
Charles Simeon

God does not need praise by men, but he knows that when men cease to praise him they begin to praise one another excessively. *Isaac Bashevis Singer*

While we cannot comprehend God in his fulness, we can know enough about him through his revelation to praise him appropriately. *R. C. Sproul*

Praise is the rent which God requires for the use of his mercies. *C. H. Spurgeon*

The whole life of the Christian should be a psalm, of which the contents should be summed up in this sentence, 'Bless the Lord, O my soul: and all that is within me, bless his holy name.' *C. H. Spurgeon*

Our glorifying of God should be a good, loud brag about him. *Billy Strachan*

Praise

The water of saints' praises is drawn out of a deep spring, the heart.
George Swinnock

The concealment of praise is tantamount to depriving the Lord of half his glory.
Friedrich Tholuck

Oh, how I wish I could adequately set forth the glory of that One who is worthy to be the object of our worship!
A. W. Tozer

No duty almost is more pressed in both Testaments than this, of rejoicing in the Lord. It is no less a sin not to rejoice than not to repent. *John Trapp*

In prayer we act like men; in praise we act like angels. *Thomas Watson*

Praise is a soul in flower. *Thomas Watson*

The motion of our praise must be the motion of our pulse, which beats as long as life lasts. *Thomas Watson*

Though nothing can add to God's essential glory, yet praise exalts him in the eyes of others. *Thomas Watson*

I'll praise my Maker while I've breath,
And when my voice is lost in death,
Praise shall employ my nobler powers;
My days of praise shall ne'er be past,
While life, and thought, and being last
Or immortality endures. *Isaac Watts*

Praise, more divine than prayer; prayer points our ready way to heaven; praise is already there. *Edward Young*

PRAYER — Answers
(See also: Prayer — Unanswered)

Too often we forget to thank God for answered prayer. Praise is the proper punctuation mark for an answered prayer.
Anon.

To spend an hour worrying on our knees is not prayer. Indeed, there are times when it is our duty, having committed a problem to God in prayer, to stop praying and to trust and to do the necessary work to arrive at a solution. *Oliver Barclay*

No answer to prayer is an indication of our merit; every answer to prayer is an indication of God's mercy.
John Blanchard

Waiting for an answer to prayer is often part of the answer. *John Blanchard*

We dare not limit God in our asking, nor in his answering. *John Blanchard*

The hand of faith never knocked in vain at the door of heaven. Mercy is as surely ours as if we had it, if we have but faith and patience to wait for it. *Francis Burkitt*

God can no more divest himself of his attribute of hearing prayer than of being.
John Calvin

It is entirely of his free grace that God is propitious, and that our prayers are not wholly ineffectual. *John Calvin*

The answer of our prayers is secured by the fact that in rejecting them God would in a certain sense deny his own nature.
John Calvin

There is nothing meritorious in our prayers ... Whenever God hears them, it is in exercise of his free goodness.
John Calvin

Never make the blunder of trying to forecast the way God is going to answer your prayer. *Oswald Chambers*

Keep praying, but be thankful that God's answers are wiser than your prayers!
William Culbertson

Answered prayers cover the field of providential history as flowers cover western prairies. *T. L. Cuyler*

The firmament of the Bible is ablaze with answers to prayer. *T. L. Cuyler*

Pure prayers have pure blessings.
Thomas Goodwin

Those blessings are sweetest that are won with prayers and worn with thanks.
Thomas Goodwin

Never was a faithful prayer lost. Some prayers have a longer voyage than others, but then they return with their richer lading at last, so that the praying soul is a gainer by waiting for an answer.
William Gurnall

Good prayers never come weeping home. I am sure I shall receive either what I ask or what I should ask. *Joseph Hall*

Our prayer and God's mercy are like two buckets in a well; while the one ascends, the other descends. *Mark Hopkins*

Our prayers run along one road, and God's answers by another, and by and by they meet. God answers all true prayer, either in kind or in kindness.
Adoniram Judson

Surely he who feeds the ravens when they cry will not starve his children when they pray. *Joseph Hall*

We should be glad that God makes us wait for mercy. A great part of our sanctification is waiting for answer to our prayers.
Humphrey Mildred

Prayer is a serious thing. We may be taken at our words. *D. L. Moody*

If it were the case that whatever we ask God was pledged to give, then I for one would never pray again, because I would not have sufficient confidence in my own wisdom to ask God for anything.
J. A. Motyer

I live in the spirit of prayer. I pray as I walk about, when I lie down and when I rise up. And the answers are always coming. *George Muller*

All my discoveries have been made in answer to prayer. *Isaac Newton*

Beyond our utmost wants
His love and power can bless;
To praying souls he always grants
More than they can express.
John Newton

God's condescension is nowhere more conspicuous than in his hearing of prayer.
Austin Phelps

Genuine prayer will be looking out for answers. *William S. Plumer*

Those who trade with heaven by prayer grow rich by quick returns.
William S. Plumer

God's chief gift to those who seek him is himself. *E. B. Pusey*

Heaven finds an ear when sinners find a tongue. *Francis Quarles*

I seldom made an errand to God for another but I got something for myself.
Samuel Rutherford

We should believe that nothing is too small to be named before God. What should we think of the patient who told his doctor he was ill, but never went into particulars? *J. C. Ryle*

Prayer, among sane people, has never superseded practical efforts to secure the desired end. *George Santayana*

God can pick sense out of a confused prayer. *Richard Sibbes*

When we shoot an arrow, we look to the fall of it; when we send a ship to sea, we look for the return of it; and when we sow seed, we look for a harvest; and so when we sow our prayers into God's bosom, shall we not look for an answer? *Richard Sibbes*

Because God is the living God, he can hear; because he is a loving God, he will hear; because he is our covenant God, he has bound himself to hear. *C. H. Spurgeon*

Grass cannot call for dew as I do. Surely the Lord who visits the unpraying plant will answer to his pleading child. *C. H. Spurgeon*

If there be anything under heaven that I am as sure as I am of the demonstrations of mathematics, it is the fact that God answers prayer. *C. H. Spurgeon*

The granting of prayer, when offered in the name of Jesus, reveals the Father's love to him, and the honour which he has put upon him. *C. H. Spurgeon*

We must hear Jesus speak if we expect him to hear us speak. *C. H. Spurgeon*

When I pray coincidences happen, and when I do not, they don't. *William Temple*

I should not think lightly of that man's religion who gets answers to prayer. *William Tiptaft*

If God gives you a rose without giving you himself he is giving you a thorn. *A. W. Tozer*

God never denied that soul anything that went as far as heaven to ask it. *John Trapp*

PRAYER — and Christ's Intercession

Let not our prayers die while our Intercessor lives. *Anon.*

The impulse to prayer, within our hearts, is evidence that Christ is urging our claims in heaven. *Augustus H. Strong*

Prayer as it comes from the saint is weak and languid; but when the arrow of a saint's prayer is put into the bow of Christ's intercession it pierces the throne of grace. *Thomas Watson*

PRAYER — Earnestness

Do not pray *by* heart but *with* the heart. *Anon.*

Our prayers must mean something to us if they are to mean anything to God. *Maltbie D. Babcock*

Praying is much more difficult than saying words to God. *John Blanchard*

We need to agonize as well as organize. *John Blanchard*

To pray aright is right earnest work. *Jacob Boehm*

Work as if everything depended upon work and pray as if everything depended upon prayer. *William Booth*

456

God hears no more than the heart speaks, and if the heart be dumb God will certainly be deaf. *Thomas Brooks*

In prayer it is better to have a heart without words, than words without a heart. *John Bunyan*

That is but poor prayer which is only one of words. *John Bunyan*

The best prayers have often more groans than words. *John Bunyan*

Prayer requires more of the heart than of the tongue. *Adam Clarke*

The act of praying is the very highest energy of which the human mind is capable; praying, that is, with the total concentration of the faculties. *Samuel Taylor Coleridge*

In God's name I beseech you, let prayer nourish your soul as your meals nourish your body. *François Fenelon*

I am convinced that nothing in Christianity is so rarely attained as a praying heart. *Charles G. Finney*

Those prayers that awaken God must awaken us. *Thomas Goodwin*

We must pray with our hand at the pump, or the ship will sink in sight of our prayers. *William Gurnall*

Prayers not felt by us are seldom heard by God. *Philip Henry*

I like ejaculatory prayer; it reaches heaven before the devil can get a shot at it. *Rowland Hill*

There must be fired affections before our prayers will go up. *William Jenkyn*

Self-examination is the high road to prayer. *D. Martyn Lloyd-Jones*

Prayer is the sweat of the soul. *Martin Luther*

Let me burn out for God. After all, whatever God may appoint, prayer is the great thing. Oh, that I may be a man of prayer! *Henry Martyn*

Pray till you pray. *D. M. McIntyre*

Much of our praying is just asking God to bless some folks that are ill, and to keep us plugging along. But prayer is not merely prattle, it is warfare. *Alan Redpath*

We must wrestle earnestly in prayer, like men contending with a deadly enemy for life. *J. C. Ryle*

Do not reckon you have prayed until you have pleaded, for pleading is the very marrow of prayer. *C. H. Spurgeon*

He who prays without fervency does not pray at all. *C. H. Spurgeon*

I know of no better thermometer to your spiritual temperature than this, the measure of the intensity of your prayer. *C. H. Spurgeon*

Let your fleece lie on the threshing floor of supplication till it is wet with the dew of heaven. *C. H. Spurgeon*

Only that prayer which comes from our heart can get to God's heart. *C. H. Spurgeon*

The habit of prayer is good, but the spirit of prayer is better. *C. H. Spurgeon*

God the Father understands prayers which are sighed rather than said, because he searches our hearts and can read our thoughts.　　　　　*John R. W. Stott*

Do not work so hard for Christ that you have no strength to pray, for prayer requires strength.　　　*J. Hudson Taylor*

Prayer is the gun we shoot with, fervency is the fire that discharges it, and faith the bullet that pieces the throne of grace.
　　　　　　　　　　　John Trapp

Prayer is the most difficult and costly activity of the Christian.　　*Alan Walker*

Prayer is the gymnasium of the soul.
　　　　　　　Samuel M. Zwemer

PRAYER — Essence

Prayer is the wing where-with the soul flies to heaven and meditation the eye wherewith we see God.　　　*Ambrose*

Intercession is standing in other people's shoes and representing them before God.
　　　　　　　　　　　　Anon.

Prayer is something more than asking God to run errands for us.　　*Anon.*

When you kneel to pray, don't give orders — report for duty!　　*Anon.*

When you pray, there is a clash of arms in the heavenly sphere.　　*Anon.*

Between the humble and contrite heart and the majesty of heaven there are no barriers. The only password is prayer.
　　　　　　　　　　　H. Ballou

Effective prayer is a quartet — the Father, the Son, the Spirit and the Christian.　　　　　*John Blanchard*

Prayer is not so much submitting our needs to God but submitting ourselves to him.　　　　　*John Blanchard*

The real secret of prayer is secret prayer.
　　　　　　　　John Blanchard

Prayer is the language of a man burdened with a sense of need.　　*E. M. Bounds*

Prayer puts God's work in his hands and keeps it there.　　　*E. M. Bounds*

Talking to men for God is a great thing, but talking to God for men is greater still.
　　　　　　　　　E. M. Bounds

Prayer is weakness leaning on omnipotence.　　　　　*W. S. Bowden*

A prayer in its simplest definition is merely a wish turned Godward.
　　　　　　　　Phillips Brooks

Private prayer conscientiously performed is the privy key of heaven. *Thomas Brooks*

Prayer is a shield to the soul, a sacrifice to God, and a scourge to Satan.
　　　　　　　　　John Bunyan

Prayer is a sincere, sensible, affectionate pouring out of the soul to God, through Christ, in the strength and assistance of the Spirit, for such things as God has promised.　　　　　*John Bunyan*

When we present ourselves before God ... the finest rhetoric . . . is pure simplicity.
　　　　　　　　　John Calvin

True prayer is the attitude and resultant expression of one who has come to know God as Father.　　　*Herbert Carson*

As air is the breath of life, so prayer is the breath of faith.　*Paul Yonggi Cho*

He who wants anything from God must approach him with empty hands.
Robert Cunningham

He prays well who is so absorbed with God that he does not know he is praying.
Francois de Sales

God is still on the throne, we're still on his footstool, and there's only a knee's distance between. *Jim Elliot*

Prayer is not only our approach to God, but also his approach to us. *E. F. Hallock*

We can never be blessed until we learn that we can bring nothing to Christ but our need. *Vance Havner*

The Bible is a letter God has sent to us; prayer is a letter we send to him.
Matthew Henry

The greatest of men must turn beggars when they have to do with Christ.
Matthew Henry

Prayer is a summit meeting in the throne room of the universe. *Ralph A. Herring*

Prayer is a ladder on which thoughts mount to God. *Abraham J. Heschel*

Prayer is a time exposure of the soul to God. *E. Stanley Jones*

Prayer is exhaling the spirit of man and inhaling the spirit of God. *Edwin Keith*

When we seek the Lord, we soon discover that he has never been far away.
Chan Hie Kim

Prayer is the nearest approach to God and the highest enjoyment of him that we are capable of in this world. *William Law*

If you have never had any difficulty in prayer, it is absolutely certain that you have never prayed. *D. Martyn Lloyd-Jones*

For what is prayer in the last analysis? It is a conscious spreading out of my helplessness before God. *Al Martin*

Prayer is the simplest form of speech
That infant lips can try;
Prayer the sublimest strains that reach
The Majesty on high. *James Montgomery*

We talk about heaven being so far away. It is within speaking distance to those who belong there. *D. L. Moody*

Prayer is not eloquence, but earnestness; not the definition of helplessness, but the feeling of it. *Hannah More*

Prayer is not monologue but dialogue. God's voice in response to mine is its most essential part. *Andrew Murray*

Prayer is one hand with which we grasp the invisible; fasting the other, with which we let loose and cast away the visible.
Andrew Murray

The great secret of a right waiting upon God is to be brought down to utter impotence. *Andrew Murray*

Prayer is not some mystic reasoning after the unknown; it is response to the God who speaks in Scripture, the God who personally acts in the lives of his people. *Iain H. Murray*

Prayer is not designed for the furnishing of God with the knowledge of what we need, but it is designed as a confession to him of our sense of need. *A. W. Pink*

Prayer is a swift messenger, which in the twinkling of an eye can go and return with an answer from heaven. *William S. Plumer*

Real prayer seeks an audience and an answer. *William S. Plumer*

True prayer is born out of brokenness.
Frances J. Roberts

A prayer which only contains thanksgiving and profession and asks nothing, is essentially defective. It may be suitable for an angel, but it is not suitable for a sinner. *J. C. Ryle*

Prayer prompted by the Holy Spirit is the footfall of the divine decree.
C. H. Spurgeon

Prayer should be definite. What a lot of praying there is that prays for everything in general and nothing in particular!
C. H. Spurgeon

The goal of prayer is the ear of God.
C. H. Spurgeon

To pray is to expose the shores of the mind to the incoming tide of God.
Ralph W. Stockman

Could we be content to meet a loved one only in public? *J. Hudson Taylor*

The chief purpose of prayer is that God may be glorified in the answer.
R. A. Torrey

Praying is learnt by praying.
L. A. T. van Dooren

The pulse of prayer is praise. The heart of prayer is gratitude. The voice of prayer is obedience. The arm of prayer is service.
William A. Ward

Prayer is the key of heaven; faith is the hand that turns it. *Thomas Watson*

Prayer is the soul's breathing itself into the bosom of its heavenly Father.
Thomas Watson

Prayer is not something that I *do;* prayer is something that I am. *Warren Wiersbe*

Prayer is the pulse of the renewed soul; and the constancy of its beat is the test and measure of the spiritual life.
Octavius Winslow

PRAYER — and Faith
(See also: Faith — and Prayer)

God's ear lies close to the believer's lip.
Anon.

Prayer is possession by anticipation.
Anon.

There are no depths from which the prayer of faith cannot reach heaven.
John Blanchard

We are encouraged to come freely to God but not flippantly. *John Blanchard*

We dare not limit God in our asking, nor in his answering. *John Blanchard*

Pray not for crutches but for wings.
Phillip Brooks

Praying without faith is like shooting without a bullet; it makes a noise but does no execution. *Francis Burkitt*

The man who prays without faith has a radical defect in his character.
H. W. Fulford

Prayer, it is the very natural breath of faith.
William Gurnall

The prayer of faith is the only power in the universe to which the great Jehovah yields. *Robert Hall*

If we cannot go to the house of the Lord we can go by faith to the Lord of the house. *Matthew Henry*

Many a person is praying for rain with his tub the wrong side up. *Sam Jones*

We lie to God in prayer if we do not rely on him afterwards. *Robert Leighton*

Faith is the fountain of prayer, and prayer should be nothing else but faith exercised. *Thomas Manton*

What an excellent ground of hope and confidence we have when we reflect upon these three things in prayer — the Father's love, the Son's merit and the Spirit's power! *Thomas Manton*

All the storehouses of God are open to the voice of faith in prayer. *D. M. McIntyre*

The great thing in prayer is to feel that we are putting our supplications into the bosom of omnipotent love. *Andrew Murray*

When the Lord is to lead a soul to great faith he leaves its prayers unheard. *Andrew Murray*

An intrepid faith in prayer will always give it unction. *Austin Phelps*

Good prayers never come weeping home. I am sure I shall receive either what I ask or what I should ask. *Austin Phelps*

God may turn his ears from prattling prayers, or preaching prayers, but never from penitent, believing prayers. *William S. Plumer*

A saint is to put forth his faith in prayer, and after-wards follow his prayer with faith. *Vavasor Powell*

Dear Lord, never let me be afraid for the impossible. *Dorothy Shellenberger*

Believing supplications are forecasts of the future. *C. H. Spurgeon*

Large asking and large expectation on our part honour God. *A. L. Stone*

When faith sets prayer on work, prayer sets God on work. *Thomas Watson*

PRAYER — and Fasting

Since this is a holy exercise both for the humbling of men and for their confession of humility, why should we use it less than the ancients did? *John Calvin*

Fasting is the voluntary denial of a normal function for the sake of intense spiritual activity. *Richard Foster*

Prayer is one hand with which we grasp the invisible; fasting the other, with which we let loose and cast away the visible. *Andrew Murray*

By fasting, the body learns to obey the soul; by praying the soul learns to obey the body. *William Secker*

Fasting is calculated to bring a note of urgency and importance into our praying, and to give force to our pleading in the court of heaven. The man who prays with fasting is giving heaven notice that he is truly in earnest. *Arthur Wallis*

Few disciplines go against the flesh and the mainstream of culture as this one. *Donald S. Whitney*

Without a purpose, fasting can be a miserable, self-centred experience.
Donald S. Whitney

PRAYER — A Gift

The nature of the divine goodness is not only to open to those who knock, but also to *cause them* to knock and ask. *Augustine*

To pray rightly is a rare gift.   *John Calvin*

If you love God, you cannot be at a loss for something to say to him, something for your hearts to pour out before him, which his grace has already put there.
Matthew Henry

When God intends great mercy for his people, the first thing he does is set them a-praying.   *Matthew Henry*

Of all the blessings of Christian salvation none is greater than this, that we have access to God in prayer.
D. Martyn Lloyd-Jones

We could not pray at all if it were not for the Holy Spirit.   *D. Martyn Lloyd-Jones*

Prayer comes from God and . . . all the time God is training us to pray.
Iain H. Murray

Only the prayer which comes from God can go to God.   *C. H. Spurgeon*

True prayers are like those carrier pigeons which find their way so well; they cannot fail to go to heaven, for it is from heaven they came; they are only going home.
C. H. Spurgeon

The greatest and best talent that God gives to any man or woman in the world is the talent of prayer.   *Alexander Whyte*

PRAYER — Hindrances

Never tell me of a humble heart where I see a stubborn knee.   *Thomas Adams*

It is strange that in our praying we seldom ask for a change of character, but always a change in circumstances. *Anon.*

Nothing is discussed more and practised less than prayer.   *Anon.*

Prayer that costs nothing is worth nothing; it is simply a by-product of a cheap Christianity.   *Anon.*

Some people treat God as they do a lawyer; they go to him only when they are in trouble.   *Anon.*

The devil enjoys hearing a prayer that is addressed to an audience.   *Anon.*

Too many people pray like little boys who knock at doors, then run away.   *Anon.*

It is not well for a man to pray cream and live skim milk.   *Henry Ward Beecher*

No man can pray scripturally who prays selfishly.   *John Blanchard*

There is a great difference between praying to God about something and mentioning it to him in passing.   *John Blanchard*

Nothing whatever can atone for the neglect of praying.   *E. M. Bounds*

Other duties become pressing and absorbing and crowd out prayer. 'Choked to death' would be the coroner's verdict in many cases of dead praying if an inquest could be secured on this dire, spiritual calamity.   *E. M. Bounds*

Straight praying is never born of crooked conduct. *E. M. Bounds*

The little estimate we put on prayer is evident from the little time we give to it. *E. M. Bounds*

Most of modern man's troubles stem from too much time on his hands and not enough on his knees. *Ivern Boyett*

Cold prayers do always freeze before they reach to heaven. *Thomas Brooks*

Cold prayers shall never have any warm answers. *Thomas Brooks*

Look, as a painted man is no man, and as painted fire is no fire, so a cold prayer is no prayer. *Thomas Brooks*

He who runs from God in the morning will scarcely find him the rest of the day. *John Bunyan*

When thou prayest, rather let thy heart be without words than thy words without a heart. *John Bunyan*

Doubtful prayer is no prayer at all. *John Calvin*

Hurry is the death of prayer. *Samuel Chadwick*

What various hindrances we meet
In coming to the mercy-seat;
Yet who, that knows the worth of prayer,
But wishes to be often there? *William Cowper*

If you seek your own advantage or blessing through God you are not really seeking God at all. *Meister Eckhart*

Many pray with their lips for that for which their hearts have no desire. *Jonathan Edwards*

Cold prayers, like cold suitors, are seldom effective in their aims. *Jim Elliot*

Prayer as a means to effect a private end is theft and meanness. *Ralph Waldo Emerson*

Dealing in generalities is the death of prayer. *J. H. Evans*

Leave not off praying to God; for either praying will make thee leave off sinning, or continuing in sin will make thee desist from praying. *Thomas Fuller*

Prayer is never an excuse for laziness. *Gerald B. Griffiths*

Satan rocks the cradle when we sleep at our devotions. *Joseph Hall*

A heap of unmeaning words only smothers the words of devotion. *J. Hamilton*

It is not much *praying* that is condemned … but much *speaking;* the danger of this error is when we only *say* our prayers, not when we *pray* them. *Matthew Henry*

The sin of failing to come to God in prayer is one of the most common offences a Christian commits. *Simon J. Kistemaker*

I fancy we may sometimes be deterred from small prayers by a sense of our own dignity rather than of God's. *C. S. Lewis*

If I fail to spend two hours in prayer each morning, the devil gets the victory through the day. *Martin Luther*

What a fearful canopy the prayers that do not get beyond the atmosphere would make if they turned brown with age!
George MacDonald

God is not mocked. He does not answer prayers if he has already given us the answer and we are not willing to use it.
William Macdonald

If we be empty and poor, it is not because God's hand is straitened, but ours is not opened. *Thomas Manton*

When we make self the end of prayer, it is not worship but self-seeking.
Thomas Manton

Means without prayer is presumption. Prayer without means is tempting God.
Al Martin

As long as we just pour out our hearts in a multitude of petitions without taking time to see whether every petition is sent with the purpose and expectation of getting an answer, not many will reach the mark. *Andrew Murray*

Beware in your prayer above everything of limiting God, not only by unbelief but by fancying that you know what he can do. *Andrew Murray*

Saying prayers without praying is blasphemy. *Brownlow North*

Most Christians expect little from God, ask little and therefore receive little and are content with little. *A. W. Pink*

We may as well not pray at all as offer our prayers in a lifeless manner.
William S. Plumer

Satan is far more anxious to keep us off our knees than he is to keep us off our feet! *Ivor Powell*

The self-sufficient do not pray, the self-satisfied will not pray, the self-righteous cannot pray. *Leonard Ravenhill*

No prayers can be heard which do not come from a forgiving heart. *J. C. Ryle*

Many people pray for things that can only come by work and work for things that can only come by prayer. *W. E. Sangster*

Prayer without love has no suction. It does not draw the blessing down.
W. E. Sangster

Most commit the same mistake with God that they do with their friends: they do all the talking. *Fulton J. Sheen*

Prayer without faith! What sort of prayer is it? It is the prayer of a man who does not believe in God. *C. H. Spurgeon*

Public prayer is no evidence of piety. It is practised by an abundance of hypocrites. But private prayer is a thing for which the hypocrite has no heart.
C. H. Spurgeon

Prayer is good, but when used as a substitute for obedience, it is naught but a blatant hypocrisy, a despicable Pharisaism. *C. T. Studd*

Yank some of the groans out of your prayers, and shove in some shouts.
Billy Sunday

How hard it is to pray against besetting sins! *William Tiptaft*

Prayer is often conceived to be little more than a technique for self-advancement, a heavenly method for achieving earthly success. *A. W. Tozer*

Selfishness is never so exquisitely selfish as when it is on its knees ... Self turns what would otherwise be a pure and powerful prayer into a weak and ineffective one. *A. W. Tozer*

When we become too glib in prayer we are almost certainly talking to ourselves.
A. W. Tozer

It is foolish to pray against sin and then sin against prayer. *John Trapp*

A wicked man in prayer may lift up his hands, but he cannot lift up his face.
Thomas Watson

Lifeless prayer is no more prayer than the picture of a man is a man. *Thomas Watson*

The prayer that is faithless is fruitless.
Thomas Watson

Sincerity is the prime requisite in every approach to the God who requires 'truth in the inward parts' and who hates all hypocrisy, falsehood and deceit.
Geoffrey B. Wilson

PRAYER — and Holy Living

We cannot expect to live defectively and pray effectively. *John Blanchard*

A holy mouth is made by praying.
E. M. Bounds

Prayer and a holy life are one. They mutually act and react. Neither can survive alone. The absence of the one is the absence of the other. *E. M. Bounds*

Prayer is humbling work. It abases intellect and pride, crucifies vainglory and

signs our spiritual bankruptcy, and all these are hard for flesh and blood to bear.
E. M. Bounds

If you would have God hear you when you pray, you must hear him when he speaks. *Thomas Brooks*

Prayer will make a man cease from sin, or sin will entice a man to cease from prayer. *John Bunyan*

Pray, and then start answering your prayer. *Deane Edwards*

None can pray well but he that lives well.
Thomas Fuller

There is nothing that makes us love a man so much as praying for him. *William Law*

There is nothing that tells the truth about us as Christians so much as our prayer life. *D. Martyn Lloyd-Jones*

What a man is on his knees before God, that he is — and nothing more.
Robert Murray M'Cheyne

Honest dealing becomes us when we kneel in God's pure presence.
David McIntyre

The decisive preparation for prayer lies not in the prayer itself, but in the life prior to the prayer. *Handley C. G. Moule*

How our prayer avails depends upon what we are and what our life is.
Andrew Murray

Our lives must be as holy as our prayers.
Andrew Murray

He who prays as he ought will endeavour to live as he prays. *John Owen*

465

If we are not right, our prayers cannot be. *James Philip*

It is what we are when we pray our prayers that counts with God.
James Philip

The cardinal element in true prayer is no mere outward ritual but the inward, moral state of the one who prays. *James Philip*

Prayer is conditioned by one thing alone and that is spirituality. *Leonard Ravenhill*

Do not work so hard for Christ that you have no strength to pray, for prayer requires strength. *J. Hudson Taylor*

Every prayer should begin with the confession that our lips are unclean.
Friedrich Tholuck

Our prayers are only as powerful as our lives. In the long pull we pray only as well as we live. *A. W. Tozer*

Prayer at its best is the expression of the total life, for all things else being equal, our prayers are only as powerful as our lives. *A. W. Tozer*

Abandon the secret chamber and the spiritual life will decay. *Isaac Watts*

PRAYER — Importance

Kneel before you leap. *George H. Allen*

God tells us to burden him with whatever burdens us. *Anon.*

If your troubles are deep-seated or long-standing, try kneeling. *Anon.*

Mountains can only be climbed with the knees bent. *Anon.*

Prayer is the key of the morning and the bolt of the night. *Anon.*

When a good man falls, he falls on his knees. *Anon.*

When the knees are not often bent the feet soon slide. *Anon.*

Many of us cannot reach the mission fields on our feet, but we can reach them on our knees. *T. J. Bach*

To clasp the hands in prayer is the beginning of an uprising against the spirit of the world. *Karl Barth*

Let the day have a blessed baptism by giving your first waking thoughts into the bosom of God. The first hour of the morning is the rudder of the day.
Henry Ward Beecher

No heart thrives without much secret converse with God, and nothing will make amends for the want of it.
John Berridge

Prayer is not the least we can do; it is the most. *John Blanchard*

The secret of reaching men is to know the secret of reaching God.
John Blanchard

The place for prayer is everywhere.
John Blanchard

To attempt any work for God without prayer is as futile as trying to launch a space probe with a peashooter.
John Blanchard

We need more Christians for whom prayer is the first resort, not the last.
John Blanchard

When problems get Christians praying they do more good than harm.
John Blanchard

When we miss out on prayer we cause disappointment to Christ, defeat to ourselves and delight to the devil.
John Blanchard

Prayer honours God, acknowledges his being, exalts his power, adores his providence, secures his aid. *E. M. Bounds*

The prime need of the church is not men of money nor men of brains, but men of prayer. *E. M. Bounds*

To give prayer the secondary place is to make God secondary in life's affairs.
E. M. Bounds

If man is man and God is God, to live without prayer is not merely an awful thing, it is an infinitely foolish thing.
Phillips Brooks

The best Christian is he that is the greatest monopolizer of time for private prayer.
Thomas Brooks

What is the life of a Christian but a life of prayer? *David Brown*

Prayer is a shield to the soul, a sacrifice to God and a scourge for Satan.
John Bunyan

Prayer is the chief exercise of faith.
John Calvin

The Christian will find his parentheses for prayer even in the busiest hours of life. *Richard Cecil*

Prayer is the acid test of devotion.
Samuel Chadwick

Prayer does not enable us to do a greater work for God. Prayer is a greater work for God. *Thomas Chalmers*

To speak for God to men is a sacred and responsible task. To speak for men to God is not less responsible and is more solemn. *Robert Dabney*

Even if no command to pray had existed, our very weakness would have suggested it. *François Fenelon*

Time spent in prayer is never wasted.
François Fenelon

Prayer is the highest use to which speech can be put. *P. T. Forsyth*

Prayer should be the key of the day and the lock of the night. *Thomas Fuller*

The greatest thing anyone can do for God and for man is to pray. *S. D. Gordon*

You can do more than pray *after you* have prayed, but you cannot do more than pray *until you* have prayed. *S. D. Gordon*

What an awful place is the Christian's closet. The whole Trinity is about it every time he kneels. *Edward Griffin*

To pray without labouring is to mock God: to labour without prayer is to rob God of his glory. *Robert Haldane*

Prayer is a divine imperative because God desires fellowship with his redeemed children. *E. F. Hallock*

Prayerlessness is a sin against God and it is a sin that can find no excuse.
E. F. Hallock

The Bible is permeated by prayer.
E. F. Hallock

When we do not pray, we work against God. *E. F. Hallock*

If you can't pray as you want to, pray as you can. God knows what you mean. *Vance Havner*

The measure of any Christian is his prayer life. *Vance Havner*

As long as we continue living we must continue praying. *Matthew Henry*

Prayer-time must be kept up as duly as meal-time. *Matthew Henry*

Though we cannot by our prayers give God any information, yet we must by our prayers give him honour. *Matthew Henry*

We read of preaching the Word out of season, but we do not read of praying out of season, for that is never out of season. *Matthew Henry*

Prayer is the breath of the new-born soul, and there can be no Christian life without it. *Rowland Hill*

He who has learned to pray has learned the greatest secret of a holy and a happy life. *William Law*

I have many times been driven to my knees by the utter conviction that I had nowhere else to go. *Abraham Lincoln*

Everything we do in the Christian life is easier than prayer. *D. Martyn Lloyd-Jones*

Ultimately there is no better index of one's spiritual state and condition than one's prayers. *D. Martyn Lloyd-Jones*

We need less travelling by jet planes from congress to congress ... but more kneeling and praying and pleading to God to have mercy upon us, more crying to God to arise and scatter his enemies and make himself known. *D. Martyn Lloyd Jones*

As it is the business of tailors to make clothes and of cobblers to mend shoes, so it is the business of Christians to pray. *Martin Luther*

I have to hurry all day to get time to pray. *Martin Luther*

Prayer is a strong wall and fortress of the church; it is a goodly Christian's weapon. *Martin Luther*

To pray well is the better half of study. *Martin Luther*

Men of God are always men of prayer. *Henry T. Mahan*

Let us see God before man every day. *Robert Murray M'Cheyne*

There is nothing a natural man hates more than prayer. *Robert Murray M'Cheyne*

Prayer is the barometer of the church. *Thomas V. Moore*

Prayer is the pulse of life. *Andrew Murray*

To know how to speak to God is more important than knowing how to speak to men. *Andrew Murray*

The spirit of prayer is the fruit and token of the Spirit of adoption. *John Newton*

Prayer is to religion what thinking is to philosophy. *Novalis*

I am only as tall as I am on my knees. *Stephen Olford*

I had rather learn what some men really judge about their own justification from their prayers than their writings.
John Owen

Men who know their God are before anything else men who pray. *J. I. Packer*

We are never more like Christ than in prayers of intercession. *Austin Phelps*

The measure of our love for others can largely be determined by the frequency and earnestness of our prayers for them.
A. W. Pink

If we can bring our woes before God in prayer we have done the best possible thing. *William S. Plumer*

Satan is far more anxious to keep us off our knees than he is to keep us off our feet. *Ivor Powell*

No man is greater than his prayer life.
Leonard Ravenhill

A man's state before God may always be measured by his prayers. *J. C. Ryle*

Never, never may we forget that if we would do good to the world, our first duty is to pray! *J. C. Ryle*

No time is so well spent in every day as that which we spend upon our knees.
J. C. Ryle

Prayer is the very life-breath of true Christianity. *J. C. Ryle*

Whatever else you make a business of, make a business of prayer. *J. C. Ryle*

If you are too busy to pray then you are too busy. *W. E. Sangster*

One cannot get deep into religion until one gets deep into prayer. *W. E. Sangster*

Anything is a blessing which makes us pray. *C. H. Spurgeon*

As artists give themselves to their models, and poets to their classical pursuits, so must we addict ourselves to prayer.
C. H. Spurgeon

God has no dumb children. *C. H. Spurgeon*

He that is never on his knees on earth shall never stand upon his feet in heaven.
C. H. Spurgeon

I always feel that there is something wrong if I go without prayer for even half an hour in the day. *C. H. Spurgeon*

If you cannot go to the house of the Lord, go to the Lord of the house.
C. H. Spurgeon

It is a good rule never to look into the face of man in the morning till you have looked into the face of God.
C. H. Spurgeon

Neglect of private prayer is the locust which devours the strength of the church.
C. H. Spurgeon

Prayer has become as essential to me as the heaving of my lungs and the beating of my pulse. *C. H. Spurgeon*

Prayer is the breath of faith. Prayer meetings are the lungs of the church.
C. H. Spurgeon

Prayer meetings are the throbbing machinery of the church. *C. H. Spurgeon*

Remember that prayer is your best means of study. *C. H. Spurgeon*

Sometimes we think we are too busy to pray. That is a great mistake, for praying is a saving of time.   *C. H. Spurgeon*

We shall never see much change for the better in our churches in general till the prayer meeting occupies a higher place in the esteem of Christians. *C. H. Spurgeon*

Whether we like it or not, asking is the rule of the Kingdom.   *C. H. Spurgeon*

If we ever forget our basic charter — 'My house is a house of prayer' — we might as well shut the church doors.
James S. Stewart

A prayerless man is a careless man.
William W. Tiptaft

I want to be begging mercy every hour.
William Tiptaft

A prayerless Christian should be a non-existent species.   *Geoff Treasure*

It is significant that there is no record of the Lord teaching his disciples how to preach; but he took time to teach them how to pray and how not to pray.
L. A. T. Van Dooren

Do with your hearts as you do with your watches, wind them up every morning by prayer, and at night examine whether your hearts have gone true all that day.
Thomas Watson

God does nothing but in answer to prayer.
John Wesley

Prayer should be fundamental, not supplemental.   *William J. C. White*

Of all things, guard against neglecting God in the secret place of prayer.
William Wilberforce

Surely the experience of all good men confirms the proposition that without a due measure of private devotions the soul will grow lean.   *William Wilberforce*

PRAYER — Length

God looks not at the pomp of words and variety of expression, but at the sincerity and devotion of the heart. The key opens the door, not because it is gilt but because it fits the lock.   *Anon.*

We may pray when we say least, and we may pray least when we say most.
Augustine

Lay no weight on the quantity of your prayers; that is to say, how long or how many they are. These things avail nothing with God, by whom prayers are not measured, but weighed. *Thomas Boston*

The worth of a prayer is not gauged by its dimensions. *Robert Murray M'Cheyne*

Some people's prayers need to be cut off at both ends and set on fire in the middle.
D. L. Moody

It is better ... that the hearers should wish the prayer had been longer, than spend half or a considerable part of the time in wishing it was over.   *John Newton*

God does not, it seems to us, frequently yield up his blessing to us till we have spent a reasonable length of time in his presence.   *Maurice Roberts*

Time spent with God in the secret place is never the cause of spiritual inefficiency.
Maurice Roberts

It is necessary to draw near unto God, but it is not required of you to prolong your speech till everyone is longing to hear the word 'Amen'.   *C. H. Spurgeon*

PRAYER — Power

He stands best who kneels most.   *Anon.*

If your day is hemmed with prayer it is less likely to become unravelled.   *Anon.*

Prayers are the leeches of care.   *Anon.*

The Holy Spirit turns prayer from activity into energy.   *John Blanchard*

Prayer can do anything that God can do.
E. M. Bounds

The church upon its knees would bring heaven upon the earth.   *E. M. Bounds*

The men who have done the most for God in this world have been early on their knees.   *E. M. Bounds*

Units of prayer combined, like drops of water, make an ocean which defies resistance.   *E. M. Bounds*

The one concern of the devil is to keep the saints from praying. He fears nothing from prayerless studies, prayerless work, prayerless religion. He laughs at our toil, he mocks at our wisdom, but he trembles when we pray.   *Samuel Chadwick*

Restraining prayer we cease to fight;
Prayer makes the Christian's armour
    bright;
And Satan trembles when he sees
The weakest saint upon his knees.
William Cowper

Prayer is the rope up in the belfry; we pull it, and it rings the bell up in heaven.
Christmas Evans

The man who kneels to God can stand up to anything.   *Louis H. Evans*

Prayer is the key to heaven's treasures.
John Gerhard

Prayer is striking the winning blow ... service is gathering up the results.
S. D. Gordon

Prayer is the sovereign remedy.
Robert Hall

Within God's limitations prayer is unlimited.   *E. F. Hallock*

Prayer is the slender sinew that moves the muscle of omnipotence.
J. Edwin Hartill

Prayer may not get us what we want, but it will teach us to want what we need.
Vance Havner

When a man makes alliance with the Almighty, giants look like grasshoppers.
Vance Havner

I judge that my prayer is more than the devil himself; if it were otherwise, Luther would have fared differently long before this.   *Martin Luther*

Prayer is that mightiest of all weapons that created natures can wield.
Martin Luther

I had rather stand against the cannons of the wicked than against the prayers of the righteous.   *Thomas Lye*

There is no burden of the spirit but is lighter by kneeling under it.   *F. B. Meyer*

Most churches don't know that God rules the world by the prayers of his saints.
Andrew Murray

I can take my telescope and look millions of miles into space; but I can go away to my room and in prayer get nearer to God and heaven than I can when assisted by all the telescopes of earth. *Isaac Newton*

Prayer is the great engine to overthrow and rout my spiritual enemies, the great means to procure the graces of which I stand in hourly need. *John Newton*

Thou art coming to a King;
Large petitions with thee bring;
For his grace and power are such,
None can ever ask too much.
John Newton

When prayers are strongest, mercies are nearest. *Edward Reynolds*

The prayers of the Christian are secret, but their effect cannot be hidden.
Howard Chandler Robbins

I know no blessing so small as to be reasonably expected without prayer, nor any so great but may be obtained by it.
Robert South

All our perils are as nothing, so long as we have prayer. *C. H. Spurgeon*

I could no more doubt the efficacy of prayer than I could disbelieve in the law of gravity. *C. H. Spurgeon*

Time spent on the knees in prayer will do more to remedy heart strain and nerve worry than anything else.
George D. Stewart

When I pray coincidences happen, and when I do not, they don't. *William Temple*

The power of prayer consists in the knowledge that God is *our* God.
Friedrich Tholuck

The Christian on his knees sees more than the philosopher on tiptoe.
Augustus M. Toplady

The strongest knees are those which bend most easily. *Mary S. Wood*

PRAYER — and the Promises of God
(See also: Promises of God)

Theology and prayer are inextricably intertwined. *Richard Bewes*

Prayer is not wrestling with God's reluctance to bless us; it is laying hold on his willingness to do so. *John Blanchard*

God loves to be consulted.
Charles Bridges

Prayer is a sincere, sensible, affectionate pouring out of the soul to God, through Christ, in the strength and assistance of the Spirit, for such things as God has promised. *John Bunyan*

Prayer is only true when it is within the compass of God's Word. *John Bunyan*

Prayer flows from doctrine. *John Calvin*

All the prayers in the Scripture you will find to be reasoning with God, not a multitude of words heaped together.
Stephen Charnock

True prayer is rooted in the promises and covenants of God, in his past achievements, in his ability to do immeasurably more than all we ask or imagine.
Bob Cotton

That which God abundantly makes the subject of his promises, God's people should abundantly make the subject of their prayers. *Jonathan Edwards*

The mightier any is in the Word, the more mighty he will be in prayer.
William Gurnall

Prayer is receiving what God has promised.
E. F. Hallock

God's promises are to be our pleas in prayer.
Matthew Henry

We cannot expect too little from man, nor too much from God.
Matthew Henry

Turn the Bible into prayer.
Robert Murray M'Cheyne

We are to pray only for what God has promised, and for the communication of it unto us in that way whereby he will work it and effect it.
John Owen

The Scriptures make prayer a reality and not a reverie.
Austin Phelps

Believing prayer never asks more than is promised.
William S. Plumer

Every prayer is an inverted promise ... If God teaches us to pray for any good thing, we may gather by implication the assurance that he means to give it.
C. H. Spurgeon

God does not keep office hours.
A. W. Tozer

God's promises are the cork to keep faith from sinking in prayer.
Thomas Watson

PRAYER — Unanswered
(See also: Prayer — Answers)

The reason why we obtain no more in prayer is because we expect no more. God usually answers us according to our own hearts.
Richard Alleine

If you do not get all you ask, it is because the Saviour intends to give you something better.
Anon.

We ask for silver and God sometimes sends his denials wrapped in gold.
Anon.

In reality, the denial of prayer is a denial of God himself.
E. M. Bounds

God can never be expected to undertake a cause which is unworthy of defence.
John Calvin

Prayer's perplexities are most often camouflaged discoveries, there for the making.
Donald Cranefield

I have learned that God's silence to my questions is not a door slammed in my face. I may not have the answers — but I do have him.
Dave Dravecky

God is not a cosmic bellboy for whom we can press a button to get things.
Harry Emerson Fosdick

God has not always answered my prayers. If he had, I would have married the wrong man — *several times! Ruth Bell Graham*

I have lived to thank God that all my prayers have not been answered.
Jean Ingelow

How good is God to deny us mercies in mercy!
William Jenkyn

If God had granted all the silly prayers I've made in my life, where would I be now?
C. S. Lewis

It is quite useless knocking at the door of heaven for earthly comfort; it's not the sort of comfort they supply there.
C. S. Lewis

Prayer is request. The essence of request, as distinct from compulsion, is that it may or may not be granted. And if an infinitely wise Being listens to the requests of finite and foolish creatures, of course he will sometimes refuse them.   *C. S. Lewis*

The great tragedy of life is not unanswered prayer but unoffered prayer.
F. B. Meyer

When the Lord is to lead a soul to great faith he leaves its prayers unheard.
Andrew Murray

If you can't pray a door open, don't pry it open.   *Lyell Rader*

Patience in prayer is nothing but faith spun out.   *Thomas Watson*

PRAYER — and the Will of God

What God sovereignly decrees in eternity, men will always demand in time. *Anon.*

Nothing lies outside the reach of prayer except that which lies outside the will of God.   *John Blanchard*

God likes to see his people shut up to this, that there is no hope but in prayer. Herein lies the church's power against the world.
Andrew Bonar

God shapes the world by prayer.
E. M. Bounds

God's sovereignty does not negate our responsibility to pray, but rather makes it possible to pray with confidence.
Jerry Bridges

We ask what we think to be best; God gives what he knows to be best.
William Burkitt

We are not at liberty in calling upon God to follow the suggestions of our own mind and will, but must seek God only in so far as he has invited us to approach him.
John Calvin

When we disclose our wants in prayer,
May we our wills resign;
That not a thought may enter there
Which is not wholly thine.
Joseph Dacre Carlyle

God always answers us in the deeps, never in the shallows of our soul.
Amy Carmichael

God answers only the requests which he inspires.   *Ralph A. Herring*

Prayer is a mighty instrument, not for getting man's will done in heaven, but for getting God's will done in earth.
Robert Law

The marvellous and supernatural power of prayer consists not in bringing God's will down to us, but in lifting our will up to his.   *Robert Law*

Did not God sometimes withhold in mercy what we ask, we should be ruined at our own request.   *Hannah More*

Prayer is not monologue, but dialogue; God's voice in response to mine is its most essential part. Listening to God's voice is the secret of the assurance that he will listen to mine.   *Andrew Murray*

In prayer, while we seek in appearance to bend God's will to ours, we are in reality bringing our will to his. *J. M. Neale*

To ask in the name of Christ is … to set aside our own will and bow to the perfect will of God.   *A. W. Pink*

Don't pray to escape trouble. Don't pray to be comfortable in your emotions. Pray to do the will of God in every situation. Nothing else is worth praying for.
Samuel Shoemaker

Every true prayer is a variation on the theme 'Thy will be done.' *John R. W. Stott*

Prayer is not a convenient device for imposing our will upon God, or bending his will to ours, but the prescribed way of subordinating our will to his.
John R. W. Stott

To pray effectively we must want what God wants — that and that only is to pray in the will of God. *A. W. Tozer*

Father, I wait thy daily will;
Thou shalt divide my portion still;
Grant me on earth what seems thee best,
Till death and heaven reveal the rest.
Isaac Watts

PREACHING AND PREACHERS — Aim

A sheep must be fed on the ground. *Anon.*

It is no easy matter to speak so plain that the ignorant may understand us, so seriously that the deadest hearts may feel us and so convincingly that contradictory cavaliers may be silenced. *Richard Baxter*

Jesus told Peter to feed his sheep, not to flog them. *John Blanchard*

The purpose of preaching must always be the first condition that decrees its character … and what is preaching for? The answer comes without hesitation. It is for man's salvation. *Phillips Brooks*

He is the best preacher, not that tickles the ear, but that breaks the heart.
Thomas Brooks

The job of a pastor is to gather the people in his arms and draw them near to God. *Michael Buss*

If ministers wish to do any good, let them labour to form Christ, not to form themselves, in their hearers. *John Calvin*

The skill of the evangelist, or the pastor who would do the work of an evangelist, is seen in the ability to present the limited body of redemptive truth repeatedly, yet with freshness and vitality.
Lewis Sperry Chafer

Put the hay down where the sheep can reach it. *Clovis Chappell*

Preachers should never forget that preaching is destined for *immediate* effect. We always miss the mark when we preach with the idea of doing good at some other time. *Samuel Cook*

Let the preacher hold before him, through the whole preparation of the sermon, the one practical effect intended to be produced upon the hearer's will.
R. L. Dabney

Ministers are not cooks but physicians, and therefore should not study to delight the palate but to recover the patient; they must not provide sauce but physic.
Jean Daille

If you shoot over the heads of your congregation, you don't prove anything except that you don't know how to shoot.
James Denney

Christ is the native subject, upon which all preaching should run. *James Durham*

Our people do not so much have their heads stored as to have their hearts touched, and they stand in the greatest need of that sort of preaching which has the tendency to do this.

Jonathan Edwards

Jesus said, 'Feed my sheep', not 'Feed my giraffes'. *William Evans*

My pulpit work must go from law to grace. It must never rush at grace as if, to unconvicted men, grace can ever be a 'harmonious sound'. *Guy R. Finnie*

All ministers should be revival ministers, and all preaching should be revival preaching. *Charles G. Finney*

The excellency of a sermon lies in the plainest discoveries and liveliest applications of Jesus Christ. *John Flavel*

A true pastor must not only feed the flock, he must warn the flock. He must not only be zealous but jealous. *Vance Havner*

It is a mark of a prophet to make men face sin. *Vance Havner*

The task of the preacher is to comfort the afflicted and afflict the comfortable.

Vance Havner

We are here to preach sin black, hell hot, judgement certain, eternity long and salvation free. *Vance Havner*

Ministers are but interpreters; they cannot make the thing otherwise than it is.

Matthew Henry

Preach nothing down but the devil, and nothing up but Jesus Christ. *Rowland Hill*

The minister's task is not to coddle the saints but to collar the sinners.

Hugh Price Hughes

Aim at pricking the heart, not stroking the skin. *Jerome*

The history of ministers proves that the Saviour has never withheld his blessing from the labours of those whose supreme object, whose first, last, and absorbing desire has been the salvation of their fellow-men. *D. P. Kidder*

The charge to Peter was 'Feed my sheep'; not 'Try experiments on my rats', or even 'Teach my performing dogs new tricks'.

C. S. Lewis

I can forgive the preacher almost anything if he gives me a sense of God.

D. Martyn Lloyd-Jones

What is the chief end of preaching? I like to think it is this: it is to give men and women a sense of God and his presence.

D. Martyn Lloyd-Jones

A preacher must be both soldier and shepherd. *Martin Luther*

When I preach, I regard neither doctors nor magistrates, of whom I have above forty in my congregation. My eyes are on the servant maids and the children.

Martin Luther

I see a man cannot be a faithful minister until he preaches Christ for Christ's sake.

Robert Murray M'Cheyne

Every preacher must come come to his people with the mind of Christ.

Donald MacLeod

Ministers are not managing directors, administrators or counsellors. They are heralds of God. *Donald MacLeod*

476

Preaching is not a specific form or method of proclamation. Preaching is verbalizing the gospel. Beyond that we cannot be more specific.   *Donald MacLeod*

The Christian ministry exists for the promotion of holiness. *Donald MacLeod*

We are not called upon to invent the message, nor to decorate the message, but to proclaim God's Word.
Donald MacLeod

We must tell men to embrace Christ as prophet, priest and king and as preachers we need to work hard to attain a theological vocabulary that is both accurate and contemporary.   *Donald MacLeod*

Those who make comfort the great subject of their preaching seem to mistake the end of their ministry. Holiness is the great end.   *John Henry Newman*

Aim at the conscience. Soldiers aim at the faces.   *John Newton*

My grand point in preaching is to break the hard heart, and to heal the broken one.
John Newton

To preach means not to make capital out of people's felt frailties (the brainwasher's trick) but to measure their lives by the holy law of God.   *J. I. Packer*

The purpose of preaching is to humble the sinner, exalt the Saviour and promote holiness.   *Charles Simeon*

Flowers are well enough, but hungry souls prefer bread. To allegorize with Origen may make men stare at you, but your work is to fill men's mouths with truth, not to open them with wonder.
C. H. Spurgeon

I wish I could be cut in pieces to preach the gospel, and that every drop of blood might tell it to my perishing fellow-men.
C. H. Spurgeon

It should be our ambition, in the power of the Holy Ghost, to work the entire church into a fine missionary condition.
C. H. Spurgeon

We have done nothing for sinners until, by the power of the Holy Ghost, we bring them to faith; and we only reckon that our preaching is useful to saints as we see them increase in faith. *C. H. Spurgeon*

Exposition is the work of bringing to bear the authority of the Word of God on the totality of a man's being. *Andrew Swanson*

The aim of exposition is to make man understand what God wants him to understand, feel as God wants him to feel and do as God wants him to do.
Andrew Swanson

Teach the tractable, command the obstinate, lay God's charge upon all.
John Trapp

Whenever you preach, be sure that you lift the Saviour high and lay the sinner low.   *John Wilmot*

The ultimate aim of all ministry is to give further cause for glorying in Christ Jesus.   *Geoffrey B. Wilson*

**PREACHING AND PREACHERS —
Christ the Message**

If we can but teach *Christ* to our people, we teach them all.   *Richard Baxter*

There is a wide difference between preaching *doctrine* and preaching *Christ*.
Andrew Bonar

The sermon which is the richest, most profitable, instructive and edifying is the one which is fullest of the Lord Jesus Christ. *John R. de Witt*

Great sermons lead the people to praise the preacher. Good preaching leads the people to praise the Saviour.
Charles G. Finney

Next to Christ I have one joy, to preach Christ my Lord. *Samuel Rutherford*

Preaching is the chariot that carries Christ up and down the world. *Richard Sibbes*

A sermon without Christ as its beginning, middle and end is a mistake in conception and a crime in execution. *C. H. Spurgeon*

Across my pulpit and my tabernacle shall be the mark of the blood; it will disgust the enemy, but it will delight the faithful. Substitution seems to me to be the soul, the life of the gospel, the essence of the gospel; therefore must it be ever in the front. *C. H. Spurgeon*

As for me, I know no other gospel, and let this tongue be dumb rather than it should ever preach any other. Substitution is the very marrow of the whole Bible, the soul of salvation, the essence of the gospel; we ought to saturate all our sermons with it, for it is the life-blood of a gospel ministry. *C. H. Spurgeon*

I do not think a man ought to hear a minister preach three sermons without learning the doctrine of atonement.
C. H. Spurgeon

I wish that our ministry — and mine especially — might be tied and tethered to the cross. *C. H. Spurgeon*

If a man can preach one sermon without mentioning Christ's name in it, it ought to be his last, certainly the last that any Christian ought to go to hear him preach.
C. H. Spurgeon

More and more I am jealous lest any views upon prophecy, church government, politics, or even systematic theology should withdraw one of us from glorying in the cross of Christ.
C. H. Spurgeon

Preach nothing down but the devil, nothing up but the Christ. *C. H. Spurgeon*

We can preach Christ to sinners if we cannot preach sinners to Christ.
C. H. Spurgeon

When we preach Christ crucified, we have no reason to stammer, or stutter, or hesitate, or apologize; there is nothing in the gospel of which we have any cause to be ashamed. *C. H. Spurgeon*

When we preach Jesus Christ, oh! Then we are not putting out the plates, and the knives and the forks, for the feast, but we are handing out the bread itself.
C. H. Spurgeon

No ministry is worthy of anything that is not first and last and all the time a ministry beneath the cross. *James S. Stewart*

PREACHING AND PREACHERS — Dangers

Of all the defects of utterance I have ever known, the most serious is having nothing to utter. *J. W. Alexander*

A pleasing preacher is too often an appeasing preacher. *Anon.*

A preacher should never say 'Finally' — and certainly not more than once. *Anon.*

A sermon's length is not its strength.
Anon.

He who thinks by the inch and talks by the yard deserves to be kicked by the foot.
Anon.

There are three particular temptations that assail Christian leaders: the temptation to shine, the temptation to whine and the temptation to recline. *Anon.*

Herod was eaten by worms because he refused to give God the glory. I am afraid there are a lot of worms being fattened in our churches today. *John Blanchard*

Never put yourself in the position where you have to evacuate the message in order to accommodate the method.
John Blanchard

A man who does not practise what he preaches destroys what he builds.
Bonaventura

The preacher may lose God in his sermon. *E. M. Bounds*

In the work of the ministry, the word *work* forbids loitering and the word *ministry* lording. *John Boys*

There are passages of the Bible that are soiled for ever by the touches of the hands of ministers who delight in the cheap jokes they have left behind them.
Phillips Brooks

One prayerless interpretation of an important text may result in most disastrous consequences ever after to the flippant expounder himself and to all the souls whom he is addressing. *John Burne*

Greed and ambition ... the two sources from which stems the corruption of the whole of the ministry. *John Calvin*

It is too common a fault that men desire to be taught in an ingenious and witty style. *John Calvin*

Teachers ... have no plague more to be dreaded than ambition. *John Calvin*

A ministry that is college-trained but not Spirit-filled works no miracles.
Samuel Chadwick

A self-serving minister is one of the most loathsome sights in all the world.
Walter J. Chantry

We would expect that when men claim to teach the Scriptures, they would imitate the meek and humble Jesus rather than the ostentatious entertainers.
Walter J. Chantry

In pulpit eloquence, the grand difficulty is to give the subject all the dignity it deserves without attaching any importance to ourselves. *C. C. Colton*

It has always been a mark of the false prophets and preachers that they preached what people wanted to hear.
Peter De Jong

Is God so intensely real to us that those who meet us meet him? Or are we little manikins capering professionally through our duties with no true realization of the awesome glory of our Master?
Edward Donnelly

An unconverted ministry and unconverted membership are the devil's chief weapons to oppose the work of God.
Jonathan Edwards

I had rather be fully understood by ten than admired by ten thousand.
Jonathan Edwards

Omitting any truth intentionally in a sermon leads to the denial of it. *John Elias*

The mature man is not threatened by other people's ministries. *Donald English*

A holy office does not make one holy.
Henry C. Fish

If the love of fame be our governing principle, our whole ministry will be tainted by it. *Andrew Fuller*

A lot of preaching misses the mark because it proceeds from the love of preaching, not love of people.
Vance Havner

A lot of what goes for Bible teaching and evangelism is but religious entertainment.
Vance Havner

A preacher who is too big for a little crowd would be too little for a big crowd.
Vance Havner

I trust I am not one who pounds because he can't expound. *Vance Havner*

If you want to be popular, preach happiness; if you want to be unpopular, preach holiness. *Vance Havner*

Popularity has killed more prophets than persecution. *Vance Havner*

Some sermons are all garnish, with not enough meat and potatoes to feed one soul for one day. *Vance Havner*

There is a lot of difference between pouring out one's heart and getting something off one's chest. *Vance Havner*

To become ordained is not necessarily to escape from one's passion for power. It may only serve to canonize it.
Ian Henderson

I don't like those mighty fine preachers who round off their sentences so beautifully that they are sure to roll off the sinner's conscience. *Rowland Hill*

Rash preaching disgusts; timid preaching leaves poor souls fast asleep; bold preaching is the only preaching that is owned by God. *Rowland Hill*

The pastor is called upon to feed the sheep ... He is certainly not to become an entertainer of goats. *William G. Hughes*

I am convinced that the first panic-stricken rush into the arms of the waiting commentators is the death of any originality a man may possess.
George Johnstone Jeffrey

When our zeal is beginning to flag and our ministry becomes formal and professional, we are to go back to the cross.
David N. Jones

Let the preacher beware of any affectation of feeling which he does not possess.
D. P. Kidder

The minister who preaches for his own glory rather than God's glory is guilty of idolatry; but so is the minister who preaches for God's glory and his own.
R. B. Kuiper

I would say that a dull preacher is a contradiction in terms; if he is dull he is not a preacher. *D. Martyn Lloyd-Jones*

If any preacher of the gospel, myself included, gives an impression of cleverness, it is bad preaching. *D. Martyn Lloyd-Jones*

In presenting the Christian gospel we must never, in the first place, make *a direct* approach either to the emotions or to the will. The emotions and the will should always be influenced through the mind.   *D. Martyn Lloyd-Jones*

Sentimentalism is out for the true preacher of the Word.   *R. C. Lucas*

A sermon-subject is like a greased pig. It can slip through the hands with incredibly elusive wriggles.   *Halford Luccock*

When people say, 'What a wonderful messenger', I have problems.
Donald MacLeod

Don't talk down to your congregation. They are not there.   *F. R. Maltby*

Recreation to a minister must be as whetting is with the mower, that is, only to be used so far as is necessary for his work.   *Robert Murray M'Cheyne*

The false preacher is one who has to say something; the true preacher is one who has something to say.
John Henry Newman

A man may preach every day of the week and not have his heart engaged once.
John Owen

No man preaches his sermon well to others if he does not first preach it to his own heart.   *John Owen*

If the truth were known, many sermons are prepared and preached with more regard for the sermon than the souls of the hearers.   *George F. Pentecost*

It is but poor eloquence which only shows that the orator can talk. *Joshua Reynolds*

An unpreaching minister is of little use to the church of Christ. He is a lampless lighthouse, a silent trumpeter, a sleeping watchman, a painted fire.   *J. C. Ryle*

Half the diseases of Christianity have arisen from mistaken notions about the minister's office.   *J. C. Ryle*

None do such injury to the cause of Christianity as unconverted, worldly ministers. They are a support to the infidel, a joy to the devil, and an offence to God.
J. C. Ryle

To be always preaching, teaching, speaking, writing, and working public works is unquestionably a sign of zeal. But it is not a sign of zeal according to knowledge.   *J. C. Ryle*

A crowd is not an achievement, only an opportunity.   *W. E. Sangster*

A man may be a false prophet and yet speak the truth.   *Richard Sibbes*

Every preacher who trims himself to suit everybody will soon whittle himself away.   *J. Harold Smith*

As every sound is not music, so every sermon is not preaching.   *Henry Smith*

An idler has no right in the pulpit.
C. H. Spurgeon

Better abolish pulpits than fill them with men who have no experimental knowledge of what they teach. *C. H. Spurgeon*

Good sermons need not be long, and bad ones ought not to be.   *C. H. Spurgeon*

If I could be an orator, I would not be. The game of eloquence, with the souls of men for the counters, and eternity for the table, is the most wicked sport in the world. *C. H. Spurgeon*

If I thought I could save every soul in this place, or do any other stupendous thing by making the slightest compromise with my conscience, I dare not in the sight of the living God do it. *C. H. Spurgeon*

It is a terribly easy matter to be a minister of the gospel and a vile hypocrite at the same time. *C. H. Spurgeon*

Nonsense does not improve by being bellowed. *C. H. Spurgeon*

The way of salvation is far too important a matter to be the theme of oratorical displays. The cross is far too sacred to be made a pole on which to hoist the flags of our fine language. *C. H. Spurgeon*

I know a minister who is great upon the ten toes of the beast, the four faces of the cherubim, the mystical meaning of the badgers' skins and the typical bearings of the staves of the ark, and the windows of Solomon's temple: but the sins of businessmen, the temptations of the times, and the needs of the age, he scarcely ever touches upon. *C. H. Spurgeon*

The plodding multitudes will never be benefited by preaching which requires them to bring a dictionary to church. *C. H. Spurgeon*

To men of prodigious jaw it may seem a hardship to be confined to time, but a broad charity will judge it better that one man should suffer than that a whole congregation should be tormented. *C. H. Spurgeon*

If it is bad to preach over people's heads, not to preach to their heads at all is worse. *James S. Stewart*

No man ought to be in a Christian pulpit who fears man more than God. *William Still*

It is not too much to say that the preacher who loves to be before the public is hardly prepared spiritually to be before them. *A. W. Tozer*

We who witness and proclaim the gospel must not think of ourselves as public relations agents sent to establish good will between Christ and the world. *A. W. Tozer*

It is unmercifulness to souls to preach so as not to be understood. *Thomas Watson*

Mere promise-mongers are no gospel preachers. *John Wesley*

Observance over the years leads one to say that the appeal to the emotions, while often increasing the results, increases the chaff in greater proportion. *F. C. White*

No ministry can afford to become a museum that embalms the past, but neither can it afford to become a chameleon that spends all its time adjusting to the present. *Warren Wiersbe*

Jealousy is the dominating temptation of the ministry. *Dinsdale T. Young*

PREACHING AND PREACHERS — Divine Calling

There are moments when the minister can derive stimulus and courage for his work only by falling back upon the irrefutable fact of his divine call. *George Barlow*

Christ appoints pastors to his church, not to rule but to serve. *John Calvin*

The sublimest calling which man can attain on earth is that of preaching the Word of God. *J. H. Merle d'Aubigne*

None is a Christian minister who has not been ordained by the laying on of unseen hands. *Richard Glover*

A man cannot really preach until preach he must. If he can do something else, he probably should! *Vance Havner*

God is on the lookout today for a man who will be quiet enough to get a message from him, brave enough to preach it, and honest enough to live it. *Vance Havner*

Ministers can never fill the people's hearts unless Christ first fill their hands. *Matthew Henry*

God never sent a messenger with an empty envelope. *Joel Horne*

A man should only enter the Christian ministry if he cannot stay out of it. *D. Martyn Lloyd-Jones*

A godly preacher is not the organ of a human fraternity but the oracle of a divine gospel. *H. D. McDonald*

Two keys are committed to us by Christ: the one the key of doctrine, by means of which we unlock the treasures of the Bible; the other the key of discipline, by which we open or shut the way to the sealing ordinances of the faith. *Robert Murray M'Cheyne*

The only way in which a man can possibly enter the ministry is when the Holy Spirit of God bestows upon him a gift from the Head of the church. By that gift he is made a minister of Jesus Christ. *G. Campbell Morgan*

A man sent to preach is a man whose mind is constantly turning to this one thing. *Iain H. Murray*

None but he who made the world can make a minister. *John Newton*

Every man who is divinely called to the ministry is divinely equipped. *A. W. Pink*

Do not be a minister if you can help it. *C. H. Spurgeon*

The essence of the minister lies in what God has created him to be rather than in what the church authorized him to do. *John Stacey*

The true minister is not one by his own choice but by the sovereign commission of God. *A. W. Tozer*

I cannot recall, in any of my reading, a single instance of a prophet who applied for the job. *A. W. Tozer*

The ministry is the most honourable employment in the world. Jesus Christ has graced this calling by his entering into it. *Thomas Watson*

An ignorant minister is none of God's making, for God gives gifts where he gives a calling. *Henry Wilkinson*

He who stations the stars has the disposal of his ministers. *Cornelius Winter*

PREACHING AND PREACHERS — Doctrine

Error in the pulpit is like fire in the hayloft. *Anon.*

It is not the man who brings the Word that saves the soul, but the Word which the man brings. *Thomas Arthur*

Preaching should consist in a simple exhibition of the truth. *Albert Barnes*

There is no deceit in the gospel itself; and there should be none in exhibiting it. It should consist of a simple statement of things as they are. *Albert Barnes*

Screw the truth into men's minds. *Richard Baxter*

The power of all genuine ministry is the power of its content, compared with which the most splendid endowments of human ministers are only trivial and irrelevant. *G. W. Bromley*

Preach doctrine, preach all the doctrine that you know, and learn forever more and more; but preach it always not that men may believe it, but that men may be saved by believing it. *Phillips Brooks*

Preaching is not a matter of parts, words or wit; it is Scripture demonstration that works upon the conscience, and that God owns and crowns. *Thomas Brooks*

Preaching is truth through personality. *Phillips Brooks*

Preaching is the communication of truth by man to man. It has in it two essential elements, truth and personality. Neither of those can it spare and still be preaching. *Phillips Brooks*

Starched oratory may tickle the brain, but it is plain doctrine that informs the judgement, that convicts the conscience, that bows the will and that wins the heart. *Thomas Brooks*

All the authority that is possessed by pastors ... is subject to the Word of God. *John Calvin*

The only way you can speak for God with certainty is to speak from the Bible. *Charles Colson*

The doctrine of a minister must credit his life and his life adorn his doctrine. *Jean Daille*

Preach the gospel of the grace of God intelligently, affectionately and without shame — all the contents of the great box, from predestination to glorification. *Christmas Evans*

Authority is inherent in truth. *Henry C. Fish*

Preachers who saturate their sermons with the Word of God never wear out. *Henry C. Fish*

All true Christian preaching must place its emphasis upon something already done by God and offered to the hearers, something which remains true and all-important even if they reject it. *Bryan Green*

We must never teach by persuasion. *William Gurnall*

If a preacher is not doctrinally ready to preach, he is not ready. *Vance Havner*

It has not dawned upon most of us that we do not need some new thing so much as some old things that would be new if anybody tried them!   *Vance Havner*

The very fact that the truth is not popular is all the more reason for preaching it ... It is not our responsibility to make it acceptable; it is our duty to make it available.   *Vance Havner*

What feeds the souls of men is not our trimmings but God's truth. *Vance Havner*

I should rejoice to hear any one of my congregation saying, 'I forget *who* preached, I felt so much the influence of the *truths* he preached.   *Rowland Hill*

Preaching is theology coming through a man who is on fire. *D. Martyn Lloyd-Jones*

Preaching which is nothing but evangelistic is obviously inadequate. Preaching, on the other hand, which is never evangelistic is equally inadequate.
        D. Martyn Lloyd-Jones

What is preaching? Logic on fire! Eloquent reason!   *D. Martyn Lloyd-Jones*

The devil receives his marching orders when the church begins to preach the truth.   *R. C. Lucas*

It is disgraceful for the lawyer to desert his brief; it is even more disgraceful for the preacher to desert his text.
        Martin Luther

Anybody going into the ministry who is not committed to expository preaching is cutting his own throat. *John MacArthur*

Doctrine is only the drawing of the bow; application is hitting the mark.
        Thomas Manton

I like those expositions that take the wings of a dove and fly to the uttermost parts of the text.   *Edward Marbury*

I am just an interpreter of Scripture in my sermons; and when the Bible runs dry then I shall.   *Robert Murray M'Cheyne*

The man who preaches the Word of God has an inexhaustible supply to draw from.
        A. W. Pink

Doctrinal preaching is the only way to get a congregation to know what it believes.   *Klaas Runia*

We have the truth and we need not be afraid to say so.   *J. C. Ryle*

If a minister is not sure about his message, let him keep quiet till he is sure about it.
        C. H. Spurgeon

If people do not like the doctrine of grace, give them all the more of it.
        C. H. Spurgeon

That which cost thought is likely to excite thought.   *C. H. Spurgeon*

We must not stand on the Bible to preach, but we must preach with the Bible above our heads.   *C. H. Spurgeon*

We shall never have great preachers till we have great divines. You cannot build a man-of-war out of a currant-bush.
        C. H. Spurgeon

Preaching is indispensable to Christianity ... For Christianity is, in its essence, a religion of the Word of God.
        John R. W Stott

The Christian preacher is to be neither a speculator who invents new doctrines which please him, nor an editor who excises old doctrines which displease him, but a steward, God's steward, dispensing faithfully to God's household the truths committed to him in the Scriptures, nothing more, nothing less and nothing else.   *John R. W. Stott*

The preacher needs doctrine, to prevent his being a mere barrel-organ, playing over and over again the same tunes.
                    Augustus H. Strong

If we do not possess a positive appetite for the Word, then we are not meant to be preachers. For it is not anything other than the Word that we are called to preach.
                    Arthur Skevington-Wood

PREACHING AND PREACHERS — Earnestness

Cold preachers make bold sinners.
                    Thomas Adams

No man can be a great preacher without great feeling.   *J. W. Alexander*

When people sleep in church, maybe it's the preacher we should wake up. *Anon.*

Deal with sin as sin. And speak of heaven and hell as they are, and not as if you were in jest.   *Richard Baxter*

I preached as never sure to preach again, and as a dying man to dying men.
                    Richard Baxter

I seldom come out of the pulpit but my conscience smiteth me that I have been no more serious and fervent.
                    Richard Baxter

A God who cares cannot be represented by those who don't.   *John Blanchard*

How many souls have been lost for want of earnestness, want of solemnity, want of love in the preacher, even when the words uttered were precious and true!
                    Horatius Bonar

Preaching is a spending, painful work.
                    Thomas Brooks

Something of the quality of enthusiasm must be in every man who preaches. He who lacks it cannot be a preacher.
                    Phillips Brooks

I preached what I did feel, what I smartingly did feel.   *John Bunyan*

If our preaching fails to catch fire it will hardly warm the hearts of our hearers.
                    Frank Colquhoun

There is no rest for a messenger till the message is delivered. *Joseph Conrad*

Preaching is the emission of the soul's energy through speech.   *R. L. Dabney*

I go out to preach with two propositions in mind. First, every person ought to give his life to Christ. Second, whether or not anyone else gives him his life, I will give him mine.   *Jonathan Edwards*

I would have every minister of the gospel address his audience with the zeal of a friend, the generous energy of a father and the exuberant affection of a mother.   *François Fenelon*

Sermons from burning hearts set others on fire.   *Henry C. Fish*

Heart preaching inflames the spirit to worship; head preaching smothers the glowing embers.   *Richard Foster*

The preaching that comes from the soul most works on the soul.   *Thomas Fuller*

The God-sent evangelist … has nothing in common with the political vote-seeker or entertainer. Nothing is more contemptible than a religious clown who cavorts between serious truth and levity.
James R. Graham

A minister without boldness is like a smooth file.   *William Gurnall*

The Word of God is too sacred a thing, and preaching too solemn a work, to be toyed and played with.   *William Gurnall*

A minister should go to every service as though it were the first, as though it could be the best, and as though it might be the last.   *Vance Havner*

Some preachers ought to put more fire into their sermons or more sermons into the fire.   *Vance Havner*

It is not enough that what we say comes from the heart, but it must come from a composed heart, and not from a sudden heat or passion.   *Matthew Henry*

If we are not intensely real we shall be but indifferent preachers.   *J. A. James*

It is not to be doubted that many a well-meant and otherwise good sermon has been wholly inefficient for lack of that energy of purpose which is necessary to impress other minds.   *D. P. Kidder*

I don't like to hear cut-and-dried sermons. When I hear a man preach I like to see him act as if he were fighting bees.
Abraham Lincoln

Preaching is theology coming through a man who is on fire.
D. Martyn Lloyd-Jones

I preach as though Christ was crucified yesterday, rose from the dead today and was coming back tomorrow.
Martin Luther

Speak for eternity.
Robert Murray M'Cheyne

The best way to revive a church is to build a fire in the pulpit.   *D. L. Moody*

The difference between the preaching that does nothing and the preaching that does something is the difference between preaching *before* people and preaching *to* people.   *G. Campbell Morgan*

How much more would a few good and fervent men effect in the ministry than a multitude of lukewarm ones!
Oecolampadius

A sermon is not made with an eye upon the sermon, but with both eyes upon the people and all the heart upon God.
John Owen

It is an easier thing to bring our heads to preach than our hearts to preach.
John Owen

True preaching is the sweating of blood.
Joseph Parker

Genius is not essential to good preaching, but a live man is.   *A. Phelps*

If you want to warm a church, put a stove in the pulpit.   *J. C. Ryle*

A burning heart will soon find for itself a flaming tongue.   *C. H. Spurgeon*

A sermon wept over is more acceptable with God than one gloried over.
C. H. Spurgeon

I dread getting to be a mere preaching machine, without my heart and soul being exercised in this solemn duty.
C. H. Spurgeon

Pray the Lord to save your hearers, then drive at them as though you could save them yourselves. *C. H. Spurgeon*

We shall never get rid of thorns with ploughs that scratch the surface.
C. H. Spurgeon

Each sermon or study should be preached as if it was the first and last. *William Still*

The preacher who talks lightly of sin and punishment does a work strikingly analogous to Satan, when he told Eve, 'Ye shall not surely die.' *Augustus H. Strong*

We are not diplomats but prophets, and our message is not a compromise but an ultimatum. *A. W. Tozer*

That's the best sermon that is digged out of a man's breast. *John Trapp*

Zeal in the ministry is as proper as fire on the altar. *Thomas Watson*

Give me one hundred preachers who fear nothing but sin and desire nothing but God, and I care not a straw whether they be clergymen or laymen, such alone will shake the gates of hell and set up the kingdom of God on earth. *John Wesley*

I love those that thunder out the Word. The Christian world is in a deep sleep. Nothing but a loud voice can awaken them out of it. *George Whitefield*

PREACHING AND PREACHERS — Glory of Preaching

Effective preaching is the dynamic release of a divine word that has gripped the heart and mind of the preacher.
John Blanchard

Every time the gospel is preached it is as if God himself came in person solemnly to summon us. *John Calvin*

Preaching is the public exposition of Scripture by the man sent from God, in which God himself is present in judgement and in grace. *John Calvin*

In the ministry God has committed to a man an office as high as heaven, as deep as hell, as broad as space. *B. H. Carroll*

Every part of your message rests upon the character of God. *Walter Chantry*

Preaching is God in action: it is his chosen method and therefore that which he will honour more than any other.
Brian Edwards

Preaching is the miracle of God communicating himself to a fallen world through the words of a fallen man.
Brian Edwards

With its preaching Christianity stands or falls. *P. T. Forsyth*

God had but one Son in the world and he made him a minister. *Thomas Goodwin*

When the chariot of humanity gets stuck ... nothing will lift it out except great preaching that goes straight to the mind and heart. *David Lloyd-George*

The gift of the ministry is the fruit of Christ's ascension. *Matthew Henry*

God knows, I would much rather preach for nothing than not at all. *Philip Henry*

I would say without hesitation that the most urgent need in the Christian church is true preaching; and as it is the greatest and the most urgent need in the church, it is obviously the greatest need of the world also. *D. Martyn Lloyd-Jones*

Preaching is the most amazing, the most thrilling activity that one can ever be engaged in, because of all that it holds out for all of us in the present, and because of the glorious endless possibilities in an eternal future. *D. Martyn Lloyd-Jones*

To me, the work of preaching is the highest and the greatest and the most glorious calling to which anyone can be called. *D. Martyn Lloyd Jones*

No restoration of biblical standards in worship or evangelism, spirituality or church growth is possible without a restoration of biblical preaching. *Dick Lucas*

The highest worship of God is the preaching of the Word; because thereby are praised and celebrated the name and the benefits of Christ. *Martin Luther*

The pulpit is the throne for the Word of God. *Martin Luther*

No church can rise higher than its pulpit. *Conrad Mbewe*

Preaching is a manifestation of the incarnate Word, from the written Word, by the spoken word. *Bernard Manning*

A holy minister is an awful weapon in the hand of God.
Robert Murray M'Cheyne

The church cannot live above the level of its expository preaching. *Bruce Milne*

Preaching is an ordinance of Christ.
Iain H. Murray

The Christian ministry is the worst of all trades, but the best of all professions.
John Newton

A true sermon is an act of God, and not a mere performance by man. *J. I. Packer*

We have no lack of preachers of prophecy, but we are pitiably short of prophetic preachers. *Leonard Ravenhill*

The issues of life and death are in the pulpit. *John Ruskin*

Draw a circle around my pulpit and you have hit the spot where I am nearest heaven. *C. H. Spurgeon*

If there be a place under heaven more holy than another, it is the pulpit whence the gospel is preached. *C. H. Spurgeon*

What I receive for my ministry is not a tenth of what I could readily earn in an engagement infinitely less laborious and harassing than my present position; although, be it added, I would not leave my ministry for ten thousand worlds.
C. H. Spurgeon

It is one thing to learn the technique and mechanics of preaching; it is quite another to preach a sermon which will draw back the veil and make the barriers fall that hide the face of God.
James E. Stewart

There is more to the ministry than being able to talk. *A. W. Tozer*

If we are God's man for the job we should never make apologies for ourselves or for our preaching.   *Humphrey Vellacott*

A successful preacher wears two crowns: a crown of righteousness in heaven and a crown of rejoicing here upon earth.
Thomas Watson

A minister is a merchant of invaluable jewels.   *Abraham Wright*

PREACHING AND PREACHERS — and the Holy Spirit

Holy eloquence is a gift of the Holy Ghost.   *Thomas Brooks*

No one is a true pastor whom the Lord does not rule by his Spirit.   *John Calvin*

A ministry that is college-trained but not Spirit-filled works no miracles.
Samuel Chadwick

Christian preaching is the preaching of God's grace in Christ, in the power of the Holy Spirit.   *Paul Helm*

The preacher is to be a free man, not bound by study and his script. The curriculum has to be left in the hands of the Holy Spirit.   *Tony Sargent*

All the hope of our ministry lies in the Spirit of God operating on the spirits of men.   *C. H. Spurgeon*

It were better to speak six words in the power of the Holy Ghost than to preach seventy years of sermons without the Spirit.   *C. H. Spurgeon*

Effective sermons are the offspring of study, of discipline, of prayer, and especially of the unction of the Holy Ghost.
J. H. Thornwell

PREACHING AND PREACHERS — Humility

The Christian ministry is not a lordship, but a stewardship.   *George Barlow*

No man who is full of himself can ever truly preach the Christ who emptied himself.   *J. Sidlow Baxter*

It takes more grace for a preacher to listen to preaching than to preach.
John Blanchard

Dispensers of the gospel are the Bridegroom's friends, and they must not speak one word for the Bridegroom and two for themselves.   *Thomas Brooks*

No man can preach Jesus when self fills his vision.   *B. H. Carroll*

No man can give at once the impressions that he himself is clever and that Jesus Christ is mighty to save.   *James Denney*

If ministers know aright what they are, and what they should be, they will be ever throwing themselves on God's mercy.
Patrick Fairbairn

There is not in the universe a more ridiculous nor a more contemptible animal than a proud clergyman. *Henry Fielding*

I can say quite honestly that I would not cross the road to listen to myself preaching.   *D. Martyn Lloyd-Jones*

The pulpit can be a shop-window to display our talents; the closet speaks death to display.   *Leonard Ravenhill*

The gospel minister should be heard, and not seen.   *Maurice Roberts*

A Christian pastor can rule, or he can have the reputation of ruling; but he cannot do both. Real ruling involves a sinking of self, a working through others, a doing of nothing that someone else can be got to do. *Augustus H. Strong*

Make sure it is God's trumpet you are blowing — if it is only yours it won't wake the dead, it will simply disturb the neighbours. *W. Ian Thomas*

Reverence and boasting cannot be found on the same platform. *A. W. Tozer*

Woe be to the church when the pastor comes *up* to the pulpit or comes *into* the pulpit. He must come *down* to the pulpit always. *A. W. Tozer*

We are no less sinners than our audience. *Humphrey Vellacott*

Only once did God choose a completely sinless preacher. *Alexander Whyte*

As ministers commend the mercy of God to others, they must never forget that they need to be partakers of it themselves. *Geoffrey B. Wilson*

PREACHING AND PREACHERS — the Life of the Preacher

A good example is the best sermon. *Anon.*

The minister's life is the life of his ministry. *Anon.*

If it be not your daily business to study your own hearts and to subdue corruption and to walk with God, if you make not this a work to which you constantly attend, all will go wrong and you will starve your hearers. *Richard Baxter*

We must study as hard how to live well as how to preach well. *Richard Baxter*

Accuracy in exegesis is no substitute for reality in experience. *John Blanchard*

An exposition of the truth is no substitute for an exhibition of it. *John Blanchard*

We must not only speak faithfully to our people in our sermons, but live faithfully for them, too. *A. A. Bonar*

Life-giving preaching costs the preacher much — death to self, crucifixion to the world, the travail of his own soul. Crucified preaching only can give life. Crucified preaching can only come from a crucified man. *E. M. Bounds*

Preaching is not the performance of an hour. It is the outflow of a life. *E. M. Bounds*

Study universal holiness of life. Your whole usefulness depends on this. Your sermons last but an hour or two; your life preaches all the week. *E. M. Bounds*

The preacher's sharpest and strongest preaching should be to himself. *E. M. Bounds*

The sermon cannot rise in its life-giving forces above the man. Dead men give out dead sermons, and dead sermons kill. *E. M. Bounds*

If the parsonage does not show the pattern as well as the doctrine, exhortations from thence will only excite the ridicule of the ungodly, and confirm them in their habits of sin. *Charles Bridges*

The minister's life is the people's looking-glass, by which they usually dress themselves. *William Burkitt*

Ministers give occasion of stumbling when by their own faults they hinder the progress of the gospel in those who hear them. *John Calvin*

The man who wishes to make himself useful in Christ's service must devote all his energies to maintaining the honour of his ministry. *John Calvin*

A minister of Christ is often in highest honour with men for the performance of one half of his work, while God is regarding him with displeasure for the neglect of the other half. *Richard Cecil*

Example is more forceful than precept. People look at me six days a week to see what I mean on the seventh day. *Richard Cecil*

The world looks at ministers out of the pulpit to know what they mean when in it. *Richard Cecil*

Let the preacher influence himself; let him reach his own heart if he would reach the hearts of others; if he would have others feel, he must feel himself. *Christmas Evans*

I have never preached a sermon to others that I have not first preached to my own soul. *Henry C. Fish*

How easy is pen-and-paper piety! I will not say it costs nothing; but it is far cheaper to work one's head than one's heart to goodness. I can write a hundred meditations sooner than subdue the least sin in my soul. *Thomas Fuller*

A message prepared in the mind reaches a mind; a message prepared in a life reaches a life. *Bill Gothard*

The ministry will not grace the man; the man may disgrace the ministry. *Joseph Hall*

Many a church thinks it needs a new pastor when it needs the same pastor renewed. *Vance Havner*

The devil will let a preacher prepare a sermon if that will keep him from preparing himself. *Vance Havner*

A man might cast a devil out of others and yet have a devil, may be a devil himself. *Matthew Henry*

Ministers are likely to preach most to the purpose when they can press their hearers to follow their example. *Matthew Henry*

The life of a pious minister is visible rhetoric. *Richard Hooker*

Before God asks evangelists about their faithfulness in preaching the gospel he will ask them about their faithfulness as fathers. *Leo Janz*

The man in whose thought and prayer God ever looms greater knows that in the ministry no man is his competitor. *George Johnstone Jeffrey*

A minister's study should be an upper room and not a lounge. *John Henry Jowett*

Let the preacher beware of any affectation of feeling which he does not possess. Instead let him seek first to experience deeply within his own soul the power of divine grace, and then to make every sermon its organ of communication to the souls of others. *D. P. Kidder*

An office-bearer who wants something other than to obey his King is unfit to bear his office.   *Abraham Kuyper*

Our own spiritual fitness is of first importance.   *Dick Lucas*

The preacher must first and foremost be a spiritual man.   *Donald MacLeod*

There is no heartache to a minister like the heartache of his own heart. *Al Martin*

My people's greatest need is for my own holiness.   *Robert Murray M'Cheyne*

It must be obvious that the most important ingredient of the minister's sermon is his character.   *S. E. McNair*

The man who preaches the cross must be a crucified man.   *G. Campbell Morgan*

A prepared messenger is more important than a prepared message. *Robert Munger*

We do not deal in unfelt truths, but we find ourselves that solid consolation in the gospel which we encourage others to expect from it.   *John Newton*

When you tell me what a man is in the pulpit, you must also tell me what he is out of it, or I shall not know his size.
       John Newton

As a preacher I find it much easier to put the church and the world to rights in a sermon than to hold at bay the dark powers of evil that continually threaten my own soul.   *David Orrock*

If a man teach uprightly and walk crookedly, more will fall down in the night of his life than he built in the day of his doctrine.   *John Owen*

No man preaches that sermon so well to others who does not preach it first to his own heart.   *John Owen*

The most effective preaching comes from those who embody the things they are saying.   *John Poulton*

Laziness and frivolity are bad enough in any profession, but worst of all in that of a watchman for souls.   *J. C. Ryle*

Men may refuse to see the truth of our arguments, but they cannot evade the evidence of a holy life.   *J. C. Ryle*

A man may be a false prophet and yet speak the truth.   *Richard Sibbes*

The life of the preacher should be a magnet to draw men to Christ. *C. H. Spurgeon*

Whatever 'call' a man may pretend to have, if he has not been called to holiness, he certainly has not been called to the ministry.   *C. H. Spurgeon*

The inner man makes the preacher.
       James S. Stewart

Hell is indeed awful unless its preaching is joined to a life laid down by the preacher. How can a man believe in hell unless he throws away his life to rescue others from its torment?   *C. T. Studd*

What a dreadful thing it would be for me if I should be ignorant of the power of the truth which I am preparing to proclaim!   *John Wesley*

Our ministry is as our heart is. No man rises much above the level of his own habitual godliness.   *Thomas Wilson*

It takes a lifetime to prepare a sermon

493

because it takes a lifetime to prepare a man of God.   *Arthur Skevington Wood*

PREACHING AND PREACHERS —
Love

A loveless preacher is a lifeless preacher.
                              John Blanchard

Ministers must so speak to the people as if they lived in the very hearts of the people; as if they had been told all their wants, and all their ways, all their sins and all their doubts.   *Thomas Brooks*

To love to preach is one thing — to love those to whom we preach, quite another.
                              Richard Cecil

The flame of Calvary's love is intense, and should cause a glow in the pulpit.
                              Christmas Evans

The gospel of a broken heart begins with the ministry of bleeding hearts. As soon as we cease to bleed we cease to bless.
                              John Henry Jowett

It is not saying hard things that pierces the consciences of our people; it is the voice of divine love amid the thunder.
                              Robert Murray M'Cheyne

He who preaches to broken hearts always preaches to the times.   *Joseph Parker*

More flies are caught with honey than with vinegar. Preach much on the love of God.   *C. H. Spurgeon*

When love is felt, the message is heard.
                              Jim Vaus

PREACHING AND PREACHERS —
Prayer

One of the gravest perils which besets the ministry is a restless scattering of energies over an amazing multiplicity of interests which leaves no margin of time and of strength for receptive and absorbing communion with God. *Andrew Bonar*

A prayerless ministry is the undertaker for all God's truth and for God's church. He may have the most costly casket and the most beautiful flowers, but it is a funeral, notwithstanding the charmful array.   *E. M. Bounds*

A school to teach preachers how to pray, as God counts praying, would be more beneficial to true piety, true worship and true preaching than all theological schools.   *E. M. Bounds*

As the engine never moves until the fire is kindled, so preaching, with all its machinery, perfection and polish, is at a dead standstill, as far as spiritual results are concerned, till prayer has kindled and created the steam.   *E. M. Bounds*

None but praying leaders can have praying followers ... A praying pulpit will beget praying pews.   *E. M. Bounds*

Prayer puts the preacher's heart into the preacher's sermon; prayer puts the preacher's sermon into the preacher's heart.   *E. M. Bounds*

Preachers who are great thinkers, great students, must be the greatest of prayers, or else they will be the greatest of backsliders, heartless professionals.
                              E. M. Bounds

Let us, even to the wearing of our tongues to the stumps, preach and pray.
                              John Bradford

I never in my life stood up to preach except once — which exception I profoundly regret — without first isolating myself from all human company, even the dearest, and prostrating myself in spirit before the dread and awful God, imploring him, in deepest humility, to bless me that one time.   *B. H. Carroll*

Every minister ought to know that if the prayer meetings are neglected all his labours are in vain.   *Charles Finney*

Prayer . . . is one half of a man's ministry; and it gives to the other half all its power and success.   *Henry C. Fish*

He will make the best divine that studies on his knees.   *John Flavel*

If our lives and ministry are to count for anything today we must solemnly resolve to make time for God.   *Vance Havner*

The preacher who has not learned to curtain off a big corner of his time to stock up on bread from heaven is headed for catastrophe.   *Vance Havner*

Prayer is the principal work of a minister, and it is by this he must carry on the rest.   *Thomas Hooker*

To have prayed well is to have studied well.   *Martin Luther*

I am a leaky vessel, and I need to keep under the tap.   *D. L. Moody*

He that is more frequent in his pulpit to his people than he is in his closet for his people is but a sorry watchman.   *John Owen*

It is in the closet that the battle is lost or won.   *Edward Payson*

Prayer is the first thing, the second thing, the third thing necessary to a minister. Pray, then, my dear brother, pray, pray, pray.   *Edward Payson*

He who does not first hide himself in the secret place to be alone with God is unfit to show himself in the public place to move among men.   *A. T. Pierson*

If we spent twice as much time listening to God as we spend speaking to God, the effectiveness of our sermons would increase a thousand-fold.   *Ivor Powell*

I do not know how a preacher can be much blessed of God who does not feel an agony when he fears that some of his hearers will pass into the next world impenitent and unbelieving.
    C. H. Spurgeon

I frequently find that I cannot pray as a minister; I find that I cannot sometimes pray as an assured Christian, but I bless God I can pray as a sinner. *C. H. Spurgeon*

The pillars on which our ministry rests are, under God, the prayers of our people.   *C. H. Spurgeon*

We should begin to pray before we kneel down and we should not cease when we rise up.   *C. H. Spurgeon*

No man should stand before an audience who has not first stood before God.
    A. W. Tozer

PREACHING AND PREACHERS — Qualifications

Preachers are called to be shepherds, not sheep dogs.   *Anon.*

If I only had three years to serve the Lord,

I would spend two of them studying and preparing. *Donald Grey Barnhouse*

To hold God in awe, to give sound biblical teaching and to live a holy life — these are the fundamental prerequisites for spiritual leadership. *John Benton*

The first qualification for being a spiritual shepherd is to be a good sheep.
John Blanchard

Nearness to Christ, intimacy with him, assimilation to his character — these are the elements of a ministry of power.
Horatius Bonar

The church is looking for better methods; God is looking for better men.
E. M. Bounds

Courage … is the indispensable requisite of any true ministry. *Phillips Brooks*

The three most important ingredients in Christian work are integrity, integrity, integrity. *Charles Colson*

The best sermon is preached by the minister who has a sermon to preach and not by the man who has to preach a sermon. *William Feather*

Every honest minister preaches from a reservoir of guilt and grace.
Gary Gulbranson

The minister is to be a live man, a real man, a true man, a simple man, great in his love, great in his life, great in his work, great in his simplicity, great in his gentleness. *John Hall*

A preacher should have the mind of a scholar, the heart of a child and the hide of a rhinoceros. His biggest problem is how to toughen his hide without hardening his heart. *Vance Havner*

Men who speak for God never merge into the fog around them. *Vance Havner*

The preachers who have moved the world never sold their liberty for a comfortable cage in some ecclesiastical menagerie. Better be a free preacher who can walk into any pulpit responsible only to God, immune to praise or blame, then a ventriloquist's dummy. *Vance Havner*

Ministers must not be afraid of the rich.
Matthew Henry

The man who cannot sincerely rejoice in another man's gifts has no call to the ministry. *George Johnstone Jeffrey*

He is the best preacher that preaches most plainly. *Martin Luther*

Prayer, meditation and temptation make a minister. *Martin Luther*

The fundamental qualification for teaching is learning. *Andrew McNab*

The man who preaches the cross must be a crucified man. *G. Campbell Morgan*

No one has ever been a great preacher or a greatly-used preacher without *living* for preaching. *Iain H. Murray*

The minister who is to preach biblically can only do so as a result of much meditation. *J. I. Packer*

The beginning and end of the pastoral vocation is this: to know Christ Jesus, and in knowing him to then strive with all our being to be like him; and in striving to be like him, to love him; and in loving him to love those whom he has entrusted to our care. *Peter Parkinson*

He who would be a faithful minister of the gospel must deny the pride of his heart, be emptied of ambition, and set himself wholly to seek the glory of God in his calling. *William Perkins*

Trees which stand on top of a cliff need to send their roots deep. *Ivor Powell*

A preacher should know four things — his times, his Bible, his God and himself. *Joseph Sizzoo*

The faithful pastor is an awful weapon in the hands of God. *C. H. Spurgeon*

What manner of men should ministers be? They should thunder in preaching, and lighten in conversation. They should be flaming in prayer, shining in life and burning in spirit. *C. H. Spurgeon*

A ministry of growing power must be one of growing experience. *James Stalker*

Unless a minister has spent the week with God and received divine communications, it would be better not to enter the pulpit or open his mouth on Sunday at all. *James Stalker*

Tearless hearts can never be the heralds of the passion. *James S. Stewart*

The servant of the evangel must be possessed by the message; possessed, heart and mind and soul by the momentous enterprise that has laid its compulsion upon him. *James S. Stewart*

You do not need to be eloquent, or clever, or sensational, or skilled in dialectic: you *must* be real. *James S. Stewart*

Three things make a preacher — reading, prayer and temptation. *John Trapp*

Give me one hundred preachers who fear nothing but sin and desire nothing but God, and I care not a straw whether they be clergymen or laymen; such alone will shake the gates of hell and set up the kingdom of heaven on earth. *John Wesley*

What I believe to be absolutely necessary for a guide of souls is a faith unfeigned, the love of God and our neighbour, a burning zeal for the advancement of Christ's kingdom, with a heart and life wholly devoted to God. *John Wesley*

PREACHING AND PREACHERS — Results

God sometimes blesses a poor exegesis of a bad translation of a doubtful rendering of an obscure verse of a minor prophet! *Anon.*

In a faithful ministry, success is the rule; want of it is the exception. *A. A. Bonar*

Sometimes when I have thought I did no good, then I did the most of all; and at other times when I thought I should catch them I have fished for nothing.
John Bunyan

With me this is a maxim: The sermon that does good is a good sermon. *Adam Clarke*

My test of the worth of a preacher is when his congregations go away saying, not, 'What a beautiful sermon!' but, 'I will do something.' *Francois de Sales*

Preaching is not man's work. Neither is its content or consequence at his disposal. *Peter Y. De Jong*

Every preacher is, or ought to be, a prophet of God who preaches as God bids him without regard to results. *A. C. Dixon*

Application is the life of preaching.
James Durham

God's grace can do anything without ministers' preaching; but ministers' preaching can do nothing without God's grace. *Matthew Henry*

Do not let any conversion astonish you; be astonished rather, that anyone should possibly remain unconverted.
D. Martyn Lloyd-Jones

The hearer's life is the preacher's best commendation. *Thomas Manton*

I would rather beg my bread than preach without success.
Robert Murray M'Cheyne

A faithful ministry will usually be sealed by the conversion of sinners.
Thomas V. Moore

Ministers are seldom honoured with success unless they are continually aiming at the conversion of sinners.
John Owen

He succeeds best who expects conversion every time he preaches.
C. H. Spurgeon

If any minister can be satisfied without conversions, he shall have no conversions. *C. H. Spurgeon*

We must reach the point of preferring to die rather than have a ministry without fruit and without power.
Fernando Vangioni

It is a poor sermon that gives no offence; that neither makes the hearer displeased with himself nor with the preacher.
George Whitefield

If true preaching does not subdue us it is sure to exasperate us. *Alexander Whyte*

PREACHING AND PREACHERS — Trials

In the ministry, to keep on keeping on you will find your chief difficulty. *Anon.*

It would be a parody on the shrewdness of the devil and a libel on his character and reputation if he did not bring his master influences to adulterate the preacher and the preaching. *E. M. Bounds*

Prophets are needed but not wanted.
Vance Havner

True prophets are solitary people; eagles do not fly in flocks. *Vance Havner*

The badge of New Testament ministry is suffering. *R. C. Lucas*

Every wise workman takes his tools away from the work from time to time that they may be ground and sharpened; so does the only-wise Jehovah take his ministers oftentimes away into darkness and loneliness and trouble, that he may sharpen and prepare them for harder work in his service. *Robert Murray M'Cheyne*

The occupational hazard of the Christian ministry and evangelism is discouragement. *John R. W. Stott*

I find it absolutely necessary that gospel ministers should meet with … thorns in the flesh, that both ministers and hearers may know themselves to be but men.
George Whitefield

PREACHING AND PREACHERS — Unction

In the pulpit, as elsewhere, education is no substitute for unction. *John Blanchard*

Preaching ought to be something of an eruption of holy energy and the power of the soul. *John Benton*

Unction in the preacher puts God in the gospel. *E. M. Bounds*

Unction … is heaven's distillation in answer to prayer. *E. M. Bounds*

What is unction? It is the indefinable in preaching which makes it preaching … It is the divine in preaching. *E. M. Bounds*

All the minister's efforts will be vanity or worse than vanity if he have not unction. *Richard Cecil*

Preaching that is without divine power will fall like frost on worship. *Richard Foster*

Preaching has authority only when the message comes as a word from God himself. *J. I. Packer*

Scintillating eloquence may captivate people, but it is the power of God that changes lives. *Ivor Powell*

I would sooner expect a frog to sit down and play Beethoven's *Moonlight Sonata* than expect to see some of the slick preachers of this hour preach with an anointing that would cause godly fear among the people. *Leonard Ravenhill*

Unction is God's knighthood for the soldier-preacher who has wrestled in prayer and gained the victory. *Leonard Ravenhill*

We are tired of men in soft raiment and softer speech who use rivers of words with but a spoonful of unction. *Leonard Ravenhill*

I wonder how long we might beat our brains before we could plainly put into words what is meant by preaching with unction. Yet he who preaches knows its presence, and he who hears soon detects its absence. *C. H. Spurgeon*

Whom God appoints he anoints. *J. H. Thornwell*

PREDESTINATION
(See also: Election — and Conversion)

The reason for the predestination of some, and the reprobation of others, must be sought for in the goodness of God. *Thomas Aquinas*

The Christian's place in heaven was assured before there was a single angel there to help in arranging his accommodation. *John Blanchard*

The obvious answer to those who say that they do not like the idea of predestination is that God does. *John Blanchard*

The predestinating love of God is commended more by those who lead holy and Christ-like lives than by those whose attempts to unravel the mystery partake of the nature of logic-choppers. *F. F. Bruce*

All objections to predestination proceed from the wisdom of the flesh. *Martin Luther*

In the wounds of Christ alone is predestination found and understood. *Martin Luther*

Predestination

Far from relegating the doctrine of predestination to some secondary place, the Bible puts it right at the heart of all its teaching.   *J. Gresham Machen*

The doctrine of predestination is just the doctrine of the divine decrees applied to the special sphere of salvation.
J. Gresham Machen

The doctrine of predestination, so distasteful to human pride, is really the only solid ground of hope for this world and for the next.   *J. Gresham Machen*

When the final result is fore-ordained by God all the steps to it are also fore-ordained.   *J. Gresham Machen*

Instead of shrinking back in horror from the doctrine of predestination, the believer, when he sees this blessed truth as it is unfolded in the Word, discovers a ground for gratitude and thanksgiving such as nothing else affords, save the unspeakable gift of the Redeemer himself.
A. W. Pink

If sinners deserve the punishment inflicted on them, it cannot be unjust in the great Governor of the world to predetermine their condemnation to it.
Thomas Scott

The clamours excited against predestination, if carefully scrutinized, are generally found to be against the thing decreed, and not against the circumstance of its having been decreed from eternity.
Thomas Scott

Predestination is rooted in the character of a personal and righteous God, a God who is the sovereign Lord of history.
R. C. Sproul

I do not believe that there would have ever been a man delivered from this present evil world if it had not been according to the will, the purpose, the predestination of God.   *C. H. Spurgeon*

I question whether we have preached the whole counsel of God unless predestination with all its solemnity and sureness be continually declared. *C. H. Spurgeon*

It is well to fall back every now and then upon the great truth of predestination ... It should be a couch for our refreshment.
C. H. Spurgeon

The difficulties we feel with regard to predestination are not derived from the Word. The Word is full of it, because it is full of God, and when we say God and mean God — God in all that God is — we have said Predestination.
Benjamin B. Warfield

To get rid of predestination we have been willing to degrade our God into a godling.
Benjamin B. Warfield

Let a man go to the grammar school of faith and repentance before he goes to the university of election and predestination.   *George Whitefield*

PREJUDICE

If we were to wake up some morning and find that everyone was the same race, creed and colour, we would find some other causes for prejudice by noon.
George Aiken

Prejudice is a great time saver. It enables you to form an opinion without bothering to get the facts.   *Anon.*

Prejudice is a lazy man's substitute for thinking.   *Anon.*

Prejudice is a loose idea, firmly held.
Anon.

Rare is the person who can weigh the faults of others without putting his thumb on the scales. *Anon.*

Weak-minded characters develop their opinions in the dark-room of prejudice.
Anon.

Man prefers to believe what he prefers to be true. *Francis Bacon*

A prejudice is a vagrant opinion without visible means of support. *Ambrose Bierce*

A little prejudice goes a long way.
John Blanchard

Beware of letting prejudices become principles. *John Blanchard*

Prejudice, which sees what it pleases, cannot see what is plain. *Aubrey de Vere*

Prejudices are rarely overcome by argument; not being founded in reason they cannot be destroyed by logic.
Tryon Edwards

The prejudiced and obstinate man does not so much hold opinions, as his opinions hold him. *Tryon Edwards*

Race prejudice is as thorough a denial of the Christian God as atheism is, and it is a much more common form of apostasy.
Harry Emerson Fosdick

An unprejudiced mind is probably the rarest thing in the world. *Andre Gide*

Beware lest we mistake our prejudices for our convictions. *Harry A. Ironside*

A great many people think they are thinking when they are merely rearranging their prejudices. *William Jones*

The better the brain, the stronger the prejudice. *D. Martyn Lloyd-Jones*

You do not take up a prejudice. It takes you up, and controls you.
D. Martyn Lloyd-Jones

Prejudice is the child of ignorance.
William Hazlitt

There is no prejudice so strong as that which arises from a fancied exemption from all prejudice. *Wiliam Hazlitt*

Prejudice, not being founded on reason, cannot be removed by argument.
Samuel Johnson

All our minds are narrower than we think, and blind spots and obsessions abound in them like bees in clover. *J. I. Packer*

All looks yellow to the jaundiced eye.
Alexander Pope

Water and oil are more compatible than Christianity and prejudice.
William A. Ward

PRIDE — Characteristics

If you want to please the devil, begin to admire yourself. *Anon.*

When a proud man hears another praised, he thinks himself injured. *Anon.*

Most of us have too big an appetite for appreciation. *John Blanchard*

A proud soul is content with nothing.
Thomas Brooks

Pride is the mother of all contempt of God. *John Calvin*

The whole human race is infected with the disease of pride. *John Calvin*

The proud are ever most provoked by pride. *William Cowper*

There is nothing that human pride resents so much as to be rebuked. *G. B. Duncan*

The proud hate pride in others. *Benjamin Franklin*

If the love of fame be our governing principle our whole ministry will be tainted by it. *Andrew Fuller*

You never knew a man full of self-confidence and self-abasement together. *William Gurnall*

Pride is the inmost coat, which we put off last and which we put on first. *Joseph Hall*

Pride is a vice, which cleaves so fast unto the hearts of men, that if we were to strip ourselves of all faults, one by one, we should undoubtedly find it the very last and hardest to put off. *Thomas Hooker*

It is difficult to be high and not to be high-minded. *William Jenkyn*

The devil is content that people should excel in good works, provided he can but make them proud of them. *William Law*

A proud man is always looking down on things and people; and, of course, as long as you are looking down you can't see something that is above you. *C. S. Lewis*

The more pride we have, the more other people's pride irritates us. *C. S. Lewis*

The flesh ever seeks to be glorified before it is crucified. *Martin Luther*

Pride not only withdraws the heart from God, but lifts it up against God. *Thomas Manton*

Every breathing of pride in its first stirrings, if it had its way, would run and tear the crown off God's head. *Al Martin*

The natural man is always play-acting, always looking at himself and admiring himself. *D. Martyn Lloyd-Jones*

No sin is so deeply rooted in our nature as pride. It cleaves to us like our skin. *J. C. Ryle*

We are all naturally self-righteous. It is the family disease of all the children of Adam. *J. C. Ryle*

Pride is intolerable to pride. *Richard Sibbes*

Conceit of our own righteousness clings to us as the skin to the flesh. *C. H. Spurgeon*

Arrogancy is a weed that ever grows in dunghills. *George Swinnock*

The worm of pride breeds soonest in rotten wood. *George Swinnock*

Guard especially against those little tricks by which a vain man tries to bring around the conversation to himself to gain the praise or notice which his thirsty ears drink in so greedily. *Samuel Wilberforce*

PRIDE — Description

Pride is the perverse desire of height. *Augustine*

Pride is the oldest sin in the universe, and shows no signs of growing weaker with age. *John Blanchard*

Pride is the very image of the devil. *Thomas Boston*

As death is the last enemy, so pride the last sin that shall be destroyed in us. *John Boys*

Spiritual pride is a white devil. *Thomas Brooks*

Pride is the master sin of the devil. *E. H. Chapin*

The man who thinks he is too big for a little place is too little for a big place. *Vance Havner*

Pride is the idolatrous worship of ourselves, and that is the national religion of hell. *Alan Redpath*

Pride is over-estimation of oneself by reason of self-love. *Baruch Spinoza*

Pride is the shirt of the soul, put on first and put off last. *George Swinnock*

Pride … that filthy spirit gotten into the midst of men. *John Trapp*

PRIDE — Effects

Pride thrust proud Nebuchadnezzar out of men's society, proud Saul out of his kingdom, proud Adam out of paradise, proud Haman out of the court and proud Lucifer out of heaven. *Thomas Adams*

Pride is such a choking weed that nothing will prosper near it. *Joseph Alleine*

There is no room for God in him who is full of himself. *Anon.*

It was pride that changed angels into devils; it is humility that makes men as angels. *Augustine*

Proud man would perish unless a lowly God found him. *Augustine*

The proud man lives half-way down the slope to hell. *George Barlow*

A proud man is seldom a grateful man, for he never thinks he gets as much as he deserves. *Henry Ward Beecher*

The most effective poison to lead men to ruin is to boast in themselves, in their own wisdom and will power. *John Calvin*

Most of the shadows of this life are caused by standing in one's own sunshine. *Ralph Waldo Emerson*

Pride and grace dwell never in one place. *Thomas Fuller*

A proud heart and a lofty mountain are always barren. *William Gurnall*

Pride of gifts robs us of God's blessing in the use of them. *William Gurnall*

The wind of pride is the life and soul of error; it is the element in which it moves and breathes. *William Jenkyn*

When pride begins, love ceases. *Johann C. Lavater*

Nearly all those evils in the world which people put down to greed or selfishness are really far more the result of pride. *C. S. Lewis*

Pride is the cause of all other sins. *Thomas Manton*

Pride was the sin that changed angels into devils. *Thomas Manton*

As the first step heaven-ward is humility, the first step hell-ward is pride.
John Mason

God has nothing to say to the self-righteous. *D. L. Moody*

All the sin of heathendom, all the sin of Christendom, is but the outgrowth of the one root — God dethroned, self enthroned in the heart of man.
Andrew Murray

The Christ we manifest is too small because in ourselves we have grown too big. *Watchman Nee*

The pride of others offends me, and makes me studious to hide my own.
John Newton

Pride will make hell insufferable.
William S. Plumer

It is easier to save us from our sins than from our righteousness. *C. H. Spurgeon*

Pride destroys all symmetry and grace, and affectation is a more terrible enemy to fine faces than the small-pox.
Richard Steele

God can do little with those who love their lives or reputations. *C. T. Studd*

There is but a step between a proud man's glory and his disgrace. *Publilius Syrus*

Discontent is the daughter of pride.
Augustus M. Toplady

When we take to ourselves the place that is God's, the whole course of our lives is out of joint. *A. W. Tozer*

Pride stops the current of gratitude.
Thomas Watson

The greatest hindrance to revival is pride amongst the Lord's people.
Arthur Skevington Wood

Just as you find it impossible to tear away your shadow so that it may not haunt your body, so you will find it impossible to prevent shame and destruction from dogging the steps of pride. *Spiros Zodhiates*

PRIDE — Essence
(See also: Boasting; Conceit; Egotism; Vanity)

Pride is the mask of one's own faults.
Anon.

It is the devil's masterpiece to make us think well of ourselves. *Anon.*

Pride is a denial of dependence upon God.
John Blanchard

There is no spirit in man more opposed to the Spirit of God than the spirit of pride.
John Blanchard

The root of pride is saying that we can do without God.
James Montgomery Boice

Everyone flatters himself and carries a kingdom in his breast. *John Calvin*

Pride, in the religious sense, is the attitude of autonomy, of self-determination, of independence of God. *J. C. P. Cockerton*

How difficult it is to awaken even Christian people to an understanding of the real nature of pride! *Frank Gabelein*

Pride is to character like the attic to the

house, the highest part and generally the most empty.   *Sydney H. Gay*

Humility is the ornament of angels and pride the deformity of devils.
William Jenkyn

Nothing is as hard to do gracefully as getting down off your high horse.
Franklin P. Jones

You can have no greater sign of a confirmed pride than when you think you are humble enough.   *William Law*

A man is never so proud as when striking an attitude of humility.   *C. S. Lewis*

Other sins are against God's law, but pride is against God's sovereignty.
Thomas Manton

A man needs above all to be saved from what is the root of all sin — his self-will and his pride.   *Andrew Murray*

The essence of sin is arrogance; the essence of salvation is submission.
Alan Redpath

Pride is a sinner's torment, but humility is a saint's ornament.   *William Secker*

To be proud of learning is the greatest ignorance.   *Jeremy Taylor*

There is no pride so insidious and yet so powerful as the pride of orthodoxy.
A. W. Tozer

All pride is idolatry.   *John Wesley*

PRIDE — Folly

He who is proud of his knowledge … has gout in the wrong end.   *Thomas Adams*

A mirror never calls attention to itself unless there are flaws in it.   *Anon.*

If you build upon yourself your edifice will be a mere ruin.   *Augustine*

Man ought to be ashamed of being proud, seeing that God was humbled for his sake.
Augustine

If you think that your best is good enough for God, you have too high an opinion of yourself and too low an opinion of God.
John Blanchard

Proud people breed sad sorrows for themselves.   *Emily Bronte*

None are so near falling as those who are most confident in their own standing.
William Burkitt

A man that extols himself is a fool and an idiot.   *John Calvin*

If we are proud of our talents we betray our lack of gratitude to God. *John Calvin*

Proud men surpass every kind of drunkenness.   *John Calvin*

There is not one of us who can take to himself the least jot of glory without sacrilegious robbing of God. *John Calvin*

There is nothing that tends more to check a foolish eagerness for display than to reflect that we have to deal with God.
John Calvin

This one word 'evil' is a thunderbolt which lays low all human pride.
John Calvin

We ought always to beware of making the smallest claim for ourselves.
John Calvin

Those who think too much of themselves don't think enough.   *Amy Carmichael*

A proud faith is as much a contradiction as a humble devil.   *Stephen Charnock*

I know of no case where a man added to his dignity by standing on it.
Winston Churchill

Of all the marvellous works of God perhaps there is nothing that angels behold with such astonishment as a proud man.
C. C. Colton

The sun should not set upon our anger, neither should it rise upon our confidence.
C. C. Colton

Goodness that preaches undoes itself.
Ralph Waldo Emerson

The one-eyed is easily king among the blind.   *A. R. Fausset*

High places … are slippery places.
Matthew Henry

Pride shuts out grace.
Simon J. Kistemaker

If a man must boast of anything as his own, he must boast of his misery and sin, for there is nothing else but this that is his own property.   *William Law*

Vainglory is the venomous worm of all goodness.   *Robert Leighton*

The Lord would give us great things if only he could trust us not to steal the glory for ourselves.   *David Morgan*

The man who feels he has arrived generally has not.   *Tony Sargent*

No man is weaker than a proud man. For a proud man rests on nothing.
Richard Sibbes

That which is begun in self-confidence will end in shame.   *Richard Sibbes*

Be not proud of race, face, place or grace.
C. H. Spurgeon

Neither God nor man will care to lift up a man who lifts up himself; but both God and good men unite to honour modest worth.   *C. H. Spurgeon*

Pride is the devil's dragnet, in which he takes more fish than in any other, except procrastination.   *C. H. Spurgeon*

The man who clings to his own righteousness is like a man who grasps a millstone to prevent himself from sinking in the flood.   *C. H. Spurgeon*

To glory even in the work of God the Holy Spirit in yourself is to tread dangerously near to self-adulation.
C. H. Spurgeon

If pride and madness go together, so do humility and sanity.   *John R. W. Stott*

The greatest of all disorders is to think we are whole and need no help.
Thomas Wilson

PRIDE — Opposed by God

God assists the humble but resists the proud.   *John Blanchard*

God deliberately sets himself in array against arrogance.   *John Blanchard*

If we insist on our glory, God will withdraw his.   *John Blanchard*

All who exalt themselves wage war with God. *John Calvin*

Pride is God's greatest enemy.
Harry Foster

God sends no one away empty except those who are full of themselves.
D. L. Moody

God is not out to hurt our pride; he is out to kill it. *Donald Pfotenhauer*

God ... though he abominates and resists the proud, yet knows how to bring down the stout heart, not only by the iron rod of his wrath, but by the golden sceptre of his grace. *Thomas Scott*

God abhors them worst who adore themselves most. *William Seeker*

God will not go forth with that man who marches in his own strength.
C. H. Spurgeon

If we think we can do anything of ourselves, all we shall get from God is the opportunity to try. *C. H. Spurgeon*

Nothing that comes from God will minister to my pride or self-congratulation.
A. W. Tozer

Pride is a sin the Lord hates, because it is a sin that sets itself most against God's laws, this is against his being and sovereignty. *Spiros Zodhiates*

PRIDE — Remedy

Swallowing of pride seldom leads to indigestion. *Anon.*

The cure of boasting is to boast in the Lord all the day long. *C. H. Spurgeon*

PRINCIPLES

It is easier to fight for one's principles than to live up to them. *Alfred Adler*

Better be poisoned in one's blood, than to be poisoned in one's principles. *Anon.*

The only standards some people have known are expediency and inclination.
Anon.

Expedients are for the hour; principles for the ages. *Henry Ward Beecher*

All too often we think we are standing on principle when in reality we may only be insisting on our opinion. *Jerry Bridges*

I will stay in prison till the moss grows on my eyebrows rather than make a slaughterhouse of my principles.
John Bunyan

Man's practices are the best indexes of his principles. *Stephen Charnock*

One may be better than his reputation, but never better than his principles.
Nicolas Valentin de Latena

Whenever you put your practice ahead of your principle you run into problems.
Gary Gulbranson

Some people would have higher principles if it wasn't for their interests.
Lucille Harper

Corrupt practices are the genuine end product of corrupt principles.
Matthew Henry

Good principles fixed in the head will produce good resolution in the heart and good practices in the life. *Matthew Henry*

There are no great principles for great duties and little ones for little duties.
Alexander MacLaren

Principles are primers to point to the pathway of power. *F. E. Marsh*

Right is right, even if everyone is against it; and wrong is wrong, even if everyone is for it. *William Penn*

Principles are not like skirts which vary in length and width from one season to another. *Mary S. Wood*

PRIORITIES

The main thing is to make sure that the main remains the main thing. *Anon.*

The last thing one knows is what to put first. *Blaise Pascal*

A man's heart has only enough life in it to pursue one object fully. *C. S. Spurgeon*

PRIVILEGE

Every responsibility is a privilege, and every privilege a responsibility.
John Blanchard

Never did the holy God give a privilege where he did not expect a duty.
Joseph Hall

PROBLEMS — See Difficulties

PROCRASTINATION

Hell is truth seen too late. *H. G. Adams*

Duties delayed are the devil's duties.
Anon.

One of these days is none of these days.
Anon.

One today is worth two tomorrows. *Anon.*

Procrastination is not only the thief of time, it is also the grave of opportunity.
Anon.

The lazier a man is the more he plans to do tomorrow. *Anon.*

Tomorrow is often the busiest day of the week. *Anon.*

Tomorrow must be the longest day of the week — judging by the number of things we are going to do then. *Anon.*

'Too late' is written on the gates of hell.
Anon.

When God says 'Today' the devil says 'Tomorrow'. *Anon.*

For an individual to procrastinate and reject Christ makes his sins more heinous and angers God who was so gracious in giving him an overture of mercy.
Earl Blackburn

God has promised forgiveness to your repentance; but he has not promised tomorrow to your procrastination.
G. B. Cheever

Not to decide is to decide. *Harvey Cox*

Delay is a kind of denial. *Timothy Cruso*

The Bible, which ranges over a period of four thousand years, records but one instance of a death-bed conversion — one that none may despair, and but one that none may presume. *William Guthrie*

The procrastinating man is for ever struggling with ruin. *Hesiod*

Nothing is so fatiguing as the eternal hanging on of an uncompleted task.
William James

He that saith he will be good tomorrow, he saith he will be wicked today.
James Janeway

Some people treat Christian truth like chewing gum. They will chew it over in discussion for hours, but never swallow it.
Kenneth W. Prior

A second lease of life is granted to no man. Then let us resist procrastination as we would resist the devil.
J. C. Ryle

Many think not of living any holier till they can live no longer.
William Secker

A fool lingers on, but time hurries on.
C. H. Spurgeon

Procrastination is the thief of time.
Edward Young

PROFANITY

God has singled out profanity for special treatment on the day of judgement.
John Blanchard

Profanity displays more ignorance than inventiveness.
John Blanchard

Profanity is the use of strong words by weak people.
William A. Ward

PROGRESS — See Growth

PROMISES OF GOD
(See also: Prayer — and the Promises of God)

A little saint may enjoy a great promise.
Anon.

God never promises us an easy time, only a safe arrival.
Anon.

If God gives himself to us in promises, we must give ourselves to him in duties.
Anon.

You cannot starve a man who is feeding on God's promises.
Anon.

God's providence will fulfil all his promises.
John Blanchard

The carrying out of God's promises is as certain as if already in the past tense.
John Blanchard

The possibilities of prayer run parallel with the promises of God.
E. M. Bounds

The resurrection of Christ is the Amen of all his promises.
John Boys

The promises of God are just as good as ready money any day.
Billy Bray

The promises of God are nothing more than God's covenant to be faithful to his people. It is his character that makes these promises valid.
Jerry Bridges

Men many times eat their words, but God will never eat his.
Thomas Brooks

The promises of God will eat their way over all the Alps of opposition.
Thomas Brooks

The whole covenant is a bundle of promises.
Thomas Brooks

We are refugees from the sinking ship of this present world-order, so soon to disappear; our hope is fixed in the eternal order, where the promises of God are made good to his people in perpetuity.
F. F. Bruce

Distrust is cured by meditating upon the promises of God. *John Calvin*

Men ought not to expect more than God promises. *John Calvin*

Our faith should be borne up on wings by the promises of God. *John Calvin*

The promises of God are ... only profitable to us when they are confirmed by the blood of Christ. *John Calvin*

We cannot rely on God's promises without obeying his commandments.
John Calvin

Whatever God can do, he unquestionably will do, if he has promised it. *John Calvin*

The being of God may as well fail as the promise of God. *Timothy Cruso*

God has never promised to solve our problems. He has not promised to answer our questions ... He has promised to go with us. *Elisabeth Elliot*

The greatness of the Promiser enhances the greatness of the promises.
A. R. Fausset

It is better to be as low as hell with a promise than in paradise without one.
John Flavel

God does not parcel himself out by retail, but gives his saints leave to challenge whatever he has as theirs.
William Gurnall

God's promise is never out of his thoughts. *William Gurnall*

Mercy in the promise is as the apple in the seed. *William Gumall*

Oh, it is sad for a poor Christian to stand at the door of the promise in the dark night of affliction afraid to draw the latch!
William Gurnall

The promises are not a common for swine to root in; but Christ's sheep-walk for his flock to feed in. *William Gurnall*

The wise Christian will store himself with promises in health for sickness, and in peace for future perils. *William Gurnall*

We are not taking any risks when we step out on the Word of God. *Vance Havner*

God never promises more than he is able to perform. *Matthew Henry*

God's promises are to be our pleas in prayer. *Matthew Henry*

We must never promise ourselves more than God has promised us.
Matthew Henry

The purposes of God are his concealed promises; the promises — his revealed purposes! *Philip Henry*

My future is as bright as the promises of God. *Adoniram Judson*

God's promises are, virtually, obligations that he imposes upon himself.
F. W. Krummacher

It would be far easier to arrest the sun in its course than to hinder the performance of any promise that God has made to his people. *George Lawson*

God's promise is better than any bond or note on any bank, financial institution, or most stable government, for all these may have to repudiate their bond; God never does so. *R. C. H. Lenski*

What greater rebellion, impiety, or insult to God can there be than not to believe his promises?   *Martin Luther*

We cannot close with Christ without a promise; and we must not close with a promise without Christ.   *Thomas Manton*

Learn to put your hand on all spiritual blessings in Christ and say 'Mine'.
F. B. Meyer

God never made a promise that was too good to be true.   *D. L. Moody*

God's promises are like the stars; the darker the night the brighter they shine.
David Nicholas

It is because God has promised certain things that we can ask for them with the full assurance of faith.   *A. W. Pink*

It is a blessed fact that God's promises are as large as his exhortations, and for each of the latter there is one of the former exactly meeting it.   *A. W. Pink*

Have faith in God, my heart,
Trust and be unafraid;
God will fulfil in every part
Each promise he has made.
Bryn Austin Rees

The promises of God have never borrowed help from moral probabilities.
Thomas Sherlock

God's promises are made conditionally; not that the condition on our part deserves anything at God's hand, but when God hath given the condition he gives the thing promised.   *Richard Sibbes*

Faith always sees the bow of covenant promise whenever sense sees the cloud of affliction.   *C. H. Spurgeon*

God never out-promised himself yet.
C. H. Spurgeon

God promises to keep his people, and he will keep his promise.   *C. H. Spurgeon*

If we would venture more upon the naked promise of God, we should enter a world of wonders to which as yet we are strangers.   *C. H. Spurgeon*

If you appropriate a promise it will not be pilfering: you may take it boldly and say, 'This is mine.'   *C. H. Spurgeon*

My own weakness makes me shrink, but God's promise makes me brave.
C. H. Spurgeon

The Lord does not play at promising.
C. H. Spurgeon

The sight of the promises themselves is good for the eye of faith: the more we study the words of grace, the more grace shall we derive from the words.
C. H. Spurgeon

Faith in the promises works obedience to the precepts.   *George Swinnock*

Upon the two hinges of faith and repentance do all the promises of the Bible hang.
George Swinnock

There is a living God. He has spoken in the Bible. He means what he says and will do all he has promised.
J. Hudson Taylor

Let God's promises shine on your problems.   *Corrie ten Boom*

A great part of a Christian's estate lies in bonds and bills of God's hand.
John Trapp

Faith and the promise meeting make a happy mixture, a precious confection.
John Trapp

The promises are good free-hold.
John Trapp

The Bible is bespangled with promises made to prayer. *Thomas Watson*

The promises are not made to strong faith but to true. *Thomas Watson*

Engraved as in eternal brass,
The mighty promise shines;
Nor can the powers of darkness raise
Those everlasting lines.
Isaac Watts

His every word of grace is strong
As that which built the skies;
The voice that rolls the stars along
Speaks all the promises.
Isaac Watts

I believe the promises of God enough to venture an eternity on them. *Isaac Watts*

God's promises are sealed to us, but not dates. *Susanna Wesley*

You never pray with greater power than when you plead the promises of God.
William J. C. White

Christ is the fulfiller and fulfilment of all the promises of God because he is the sum and substance of them.
Geoffrey B. Wilson

PROPHECY

Nothing is so damaging in the study of New Testament prophecy as to imagine that the eternal God who stands outside and above time is bound by the clocks and calendars of men. *E. M. Blaiklock*

God does not at this day predict hidden events; but he would have us to be satisfied with his gospel. *John Calvin*

Prophecy at the present day is simply the right understanding of Scripture and the particular gift of expounding it.
John Calvin

Prophesying is a dangerous business for those who are not inspired. *R. L. Dabney*

Prophecy takes up approximately one-fourth of all Scripture. And yet we have soft-pedalled what the Bible says about future history ... A tremendously relevant and gripping part of the Christian [hope] has been left out. *Leighton Ford*

I know that some are always studying the meaning of the fourth toe of the right foot of some beast in prophecy and have never used either foot to go and bring men to Christ. *Vance Havner*

No Bible subject holds more practical implications than the matter of prophecy.
Vance Havner

Words of prophecy in the mouth are no infallible evidence of a principle of grace in the heart. *Matthew Henry*

All claims to convey some additional revelation to that which has been given by God in this body of truth are false claims and must be rejected. *George Lawlor*

Since the book of Revelation was completed, no new written or verbal prophecy has ever been universally recognized by Christians as divine truth from God.
John MacArthur

Prophecy is not given to make men prophets, but as a witness to God when it is fulfilled. *Isaac Newton*

An interest in prophecy which is merely speculative and sensational comes perilously close to being sinful.
W. Graham Scroggie

I would not give much for prophetic intelligence if it does not begin, continue and end with the person, work and glory of God.   *H. H. Snell*

It is greatly to be desired that Christians who are so much given to speculate upon the prophecies would turn their thoughts to the perishing myriads by whom we are surrounded and sow in the fields of evangelization rather than in the cloudland of guesswork interpretation.
C. H. Spurgeon

Prophecy is like the German sentence — it can be understood only when we have read its last word.   *Augustus H. Strong*

Much of the Bible is devoted to prediction. Nothing God has yet done for us can compare with all that is written in the sure word of prophecy.   *A. W. Tozer*

PROSPERITY
(See also: Materialism; Money; Possessions; Riches; Wealth)

A full cup must be carried steadily. *Anon.*

Fewer men survive the test of prosperity than the pressure of poverty.   *Anon.*

It takes a strong constitution to withstand repeated attacks of prosperity.   *Anon.*

We do not realize how much we are attached to the good things of this world until they are taken from us. *Augustine*

Watch lest prosperity destroy generosity.
Henry Ward Beecher

We cannot infer from prosperity that God is pleased with us, nor can we infer from adversity that he is displeased with us.
Wilson Benton

Prosperity is not a sign that all is well.
John Blanchard

In the day of prosperity we have many refuges to resort to; in the day of adversity, only one.   *Horatius Bonar*

The snow covers many a dunghill; so doth prosperity many a rotten heart.
Thomas Brooks

The cause of all prosperity is the favour of God.   *John Calvin*

For every one hundred men who can stand adversity there is only one who can withstand prosperity. *Thomas Carlyle*

The comforts of this life are as candles that will end in a snuff. *Stephen Charnock*

If prosperity is regarded as the reward of virtue, it will be regarded as the symptom of virtue.   *G. K. Chesterton*

In prosperity, our friends know us; in adversity we know our friends.
Churton Collins

Prosperity is only an instrument to be used; not a deity to be worshipped.
Calvin Coolidge

To see a man humble under prosperity is one of the greatest rarities in the world.
John Flavel

Abundance, like want, ruins men.
Benjamin Franklin

The saints' spots are most got in peace, plenty and prosperity. *William Gurnall*

Prosperity is a great teacher; adversity is a greater. *William Hazlitt*

Let prosperity be as oil to the wheels of obedience and affliction as wind to the sails of prayer. *Philip Henry*

Material abundance without character is the surest way to destruction.
Thomas Jefferson

Prosperity is good campaigning weather for the devil. *C. S. Lewis*

We can stand affliction better than we can stand prosperity, for in prosperity we forget God. *D. L. Moody*

If a man will make his nest below, God will put a thorn in it; and if that will not do, he will set it on fire. *John Newton*

If we fail to give in prosperity, God will curse what we hold back. *Stephen Olford*

Prosperity is a great mercy, but adversity is a greater one, if it brings us to Christ.
J. C. Ryle

Prosperity teaches men themselves.
Richard Sibbes

I am never afraid for my brethren who have many troubles, but I often tremble for those whose career is prosperous.
C. H. Spurgeon

It is hard to carry a full cup without a spill. *C. H. Spurgeon*

Uninterrupted prosperity is a thing to cause fear and trembling. *C. H. Spurgeon*

If you want to destroy a nation give it too much — make it greedy, miserable and sick. *John Steinback*

Few of us can stand prosperity. Another man's, I mean. *Mark Twain*

Prosperity is a state full of danger. Both the wise and pious have been ensnared by it. *Daniel Wilson*

PROVIDENCE
(See also: Will of God)

God has his hours and his delays.
J. A. Bengel

There are no accidents in the life of a Christian. *Rowland Bingham*

Every blade of grass in the field is measured; the green cups and the coloured crowns of every flower are curiously counted; the stars of the firmament wheel in cunningly calculated orbits; even storms have their laws.
William Blaikie

All the world's thrones are occupied by rulers under God's authority.
John Blanchard

God's providence will fulfil all his promises. *John Blanchard*

The same God who controls the sun cares for the sparrow. *John Blanchard*

I have lived, seen God's hand through a lifetime, and all was for best.
Robert Browning

We cannot be robbed of God's providence. *Jane Welsh Carlyle*

There is nothing of which it is more difficult to convince men than that the providence of God governs this world.
John Calvin

We declare that by God's providence, not only heaven and earth and inanimate creatures, but also the counsels and wills of men, are governed so as to move precisely to that end destined by him. *John Calvin*

That God normally operates the universe consistently makes science possible; that he does not always do so ought to keep science humble. *D. A. Carson*

The mystery of providence defies our attempt to tame it by reason. I do not mean it is illogical; I mean that we do not know enough about it to be able to unpack it.
D. A. Carson

Providence is crowned by the end of it.
Stephen Charnock

God moves in a mysterious way
His wonders to perform;
He plants his footsteps in the sea,
And rides upon the storm.
William Cowper

Happy the man who sees a God employed in all the good and ill that chequers life.
William Cowper

What God *intends,* he decrees; what God *permits,* he has foreseen.
Arthur C. Custance

The longer I live, the more faith I have in providence, and the less faith in my interpretation of providence. *Jeremiah Day*

While providence supports,
Let saints securely dwell;
That hand which bears all nature up
Shall guide his children well.
Philip Doddridge

He that will watch providences will never want providences to watch. *John Flavel*

Providence has ordered that condition for you which is best for your eternal good. If you had more of the world than you have, your heads and hearts might not be able to manage it to your advantage.
John Flavel

Sometimes providences, like Hebrew letters, must be read backwards. *John Flavel*

God's providence is like the Hebrew Bible; we must begin at the end and read backward in order to understand it.
A. J. Gordon

Providence is much more about God's glory than about our happiness.
Geoffrey Grogan

Either directly or indirectly, every providence has a tendency to the spiritual good of those who love God. *Matthew Henry*

God's providence leaves room for the use of our prudence. *Matthew Henry*

God's providences often seem to contradict his purposes, even when they are serving them. *Matthew Henry*

What is corrupt, though of God's permitting, is not of his planting. *Matthew Henry*

Everything that happens to me can help me along in my Christian life.
E. Stanley Jones

God is in the facts of history as truly as he is in the march of the seasons, the revolutions of the planets, or the architecture of the worlds. *John Lanahan*

Nothing is or can be accidental with God.
Henry W. Longfellow

Our Lord God doeth work like a printer,

who setteth the letters backwards; we see and feel well his setting, but we shall see the print yonder — in the life to come.
Martin Luther

Our spirits are most satisfied when we discern God's aim in everything.
Thomas Manton

God not only orders our steps; he orders our stops. *George Muller*

If our circumstances find us in God, we shall find God in our circumstances.
George Muller

If you think you see the ark of God falling you can be sure it is due to a swimming in your head. *John Newton*

All real evil is averted from the people of God, or is so controlled as in the end to do them good. *William S. Plumer*

God is at no loss for means, instruments or agents. Heaven and earth, sea and land, mind and matter are full of them.
William S. Plumer

God rules and overrules.
William S. Plumer

God's government will never fail in any part of the world, in any event of life, or in any tumult of the nations.
William S. Plumer

We need never fear that God will be dethroned, or over-reached or defeated.
William S. Plumer

Nothing was too little for God to create. Nothing is too little for God to preserve.
J. C. Ryle

There's a Divinity that shapes our ends, rough-hew them how we will.
William Shakespeare

Providence is the perpetuity and continuance of creation. *Richard Sibbes*

The keys of providence swing at the girdle of Christ. *C. H. Spurgeon*

God's providence is all exercised through Christ. *Augustus H. Strong*

In the working of God's providence the unseen is prop enough for the seen.
Augustus H. Strong

God's providence and purposes lie behind everything that occurs, but still God himself is not the author of any sinful action. *Geoff Thomas*

God has plans for this world, not problems. There is never a panic in heaven.
W. Ian Thomas

I do not know why God does some things, but I am convinced that nothing is accidental in his universe. *A. W. Tozer*

Not a drop of rain falls in vain.
John Trapp

God is always previous.
Friedrich von Hugel

A firm faith in the universal providence of God is the solution of all earthly problems. It is almost equally true that a clear and full apprehension of the universal providence of God is the solution of most theological problems.
Benjamin B. Warfield

God is to be trusted when his providences seem to run contrary to his promises.
Thomas Watson

God would never permit evil if he could not bring good out of evil.
Thomas Watson

It is a sin as much to quarrel with God's providence as to deny his providence.
Thomas Watson

Providence is a Christian's diary but not his Bible ... We must not think the better of what is sinful because it is successful.
Thomas Watson

If a Christian has to change his plans, it is always because God has something better in store. *Phil Webb*

We turn to God when our foundations are shaking, only to learn that it is God who is shaking them. *Charles C. West*

God is not defeated by human failure.
William J. C. White

PUNISHMENT
(See also: Judgement)

Righteous punishment is a thousand light years away from revenge. *Anon.*

Punishment, that is the justice of the unjust. *Augustine*

If men refuse to be taught by precept they must be taught by punishment.
Thomas V. Moore

PURITY

God requires an inward purity as well as an outward performance. *John Blanchard*

The price of purity is high; but impurity is dirt cheap. *John Blanchard*

Purity lives and derives its life solely from the Spirit of God. *Julius Charles Hare*

Our chastity should be as dear to us as our lives, and we should be as much afraid of that which defiles the body as of that which destroys it. *Matthew Henry*

Those who keep themselves pure in times of common impurity God will keep safe in times of common calamity.
Matthew Henry

The outward modesty which makes itself known in dress is to be accompanied by inward purity and chastity, since the former would otherwise be of no account.
J. E. Hunter

When God purifies the heart by faith, the market is sacred as well as the sanctuary.
Martin Luther

One of the most conclusive evidences that we do possess a pure heart is to be conscious of and burdened with the impurity which still indwells us.
A. W. Pink

Spiritual purity may be defined as undivided affections, sincerity and genuineness, godly simplicity.
A. W. Pink

Genuine purity is internal.
William S. Plummer

The pure in heart shall see God; all others are but blind bats. *C. H. Spurgeon*

God does not demand a beautiful vessel, but he does demand a clean one.
R. A. Torrey

A pure heart breathes after purity.
Thomas Watson

Most men pray more for full purses than for pure hearts. *Thomas Watson*

The pure heart is God's paradise where he delights to walk. It is his lesser heaven.
Thomas Watson

PURPOSE

The two greatest days in a person's life are the day he was born and the day he finds out why he was born.   *Anon.*

All who are ignorant of the purpose for which they live are fools and madmen.
John Calvin

Here is what frightens me: to see the sense of this life dissipated; to see the reason for our existence disappear. That is what is intolerable. Man cannot live without meaning.   *Albert Camus*

The man without purpose is like a ship without a rudder.   *Thomas Carlyle*

What makes life dreary is absence of motive. What makes life complicated is multiplicity of motive. What makes life victorious is singleness of motive.
George Eliot

Those who have a 'why' to live can bear with almost any 'how'. *Victor E. Frankl*

You must have an aim in life if you want to make a hit.   *Nora Grey*

The very idea of purpose could not arise by chance, for purpose and chance are opposites.   *Dave Hunt*

God does nothing in time which he did not design to do from eternity.
William Jay

The least of things with a meaning is worth more in life than the greatest of things without.   *Carl Gustav Jung*

Apart from the bright hope of the gospel everything would be meaningless.
Paul Madsen

One can live on less when he has more to live for.   *S. S. McKenny*

If a man has a why for his life he can bear with almost any how.
Friedrich Nietzsche

Man, made in the image of God, has a purpose — to be in relationship to God, who is there. Man forgets his purpose and thus he forgets who he is and what life means.   *Francis Schaeffer*

Who shoots at the midday sun, though he be sure he shall never hit the mark, yet as sure as he is he shall shoot higher than who aims but at a bush. *Philip Sidney*

Spiritual life depends on the purpose we cherish.   *C. H. Spurgeon*

God made us for himself; that is the first and last thing that can be said about human existence and whatever more we add is but commentary.   *A. W. Tozer*

God made us to be worshippers. That was the purpose of God in bringing us into the world.   *A. W. Tozer*

REASON
(See also: Education; Knowledge; Mind)

A religion small enough for our understanding would not be big enough for our need.   *Anon.*

God does not expect us to submit our faith to him without reason, but the very limits of our reason make faith a necessity.
Augustine

It is no more possible for finite man to comprehend the infinite God than for a child to dip the ocean into a hole he has made in the sand. *Augustine*

No man can understand spiritual mysteries by carnal reason. *Thomas Brooks*

The light of human reason differs little from darkness. *John Calvin*

What madness it is to embrace nothing but what commends itself to human reason! *John Calvin*

God never contradicts reason, he transcends it. *Oswald Chambers*

Water cannot rise higher than its source, neither can human reason.
Samuel Taylor Coleridge

We may as well judge of colours by moonlight as of spiritual things by natural reason. *Elisha Coles*

He that will believe only what he can fully comprehend must have a very long head or a very short creed. *C. C. Colton*

Reason can never show itself more reasonable than in ceasing to reason about things which are above reason.
John Flavel

Before a man can think he must exercise faith in his reason. *John H. Gerstner*

Our use of reason itself is not only wounded and weakened but made wilful and wrong by sin. *Os Guinness*

Without God we cannot trust reason, sense experience, intuition, or any other methods purported to give knowledge.
W. Andrew Hoffecker

Scripture never sets faith and reason over against each other as incompatible. On the contrary, faith can only arise and grow within us by the use of our minds.
Will Metzger

Our belief in the infallibility of Scripture arises not from an ability to prove that Scripture is perfect from start to finish. Rather it rests on Jesus' own witness to Scripture. He believed and taught that it was the Word of God and therefore inherently trustworthy. Our belief in Scripture is dependent on our belief in Jesus. *Peter C. Moore*

The faith that does not come from reason is to be doubted, and the reason that does not lead to faith is to be feared.
G. Campbell Morgan

Reason's last step is the recognition that there are an infinite number of things that are beyond it. *Blaise Pascal*

The supreme achievement of reason is to bring us to see that there is a limit to reason. *Blaise Pascal*

Nothing but faith will ever rectify the mistakes of reason on divine things.
William S. Plumer

Consideration is the high road to conversion. *J. C. Ryle*

To bring our minds under Christ's yoke is not to deny our rationality but to submit to his revelation. *John R. W. Stott*

The devil labours to put out the right eye of faith and to leave us only the left eye of reason. *John Trapp*

Nothing in this world is without reason.
A. W. Tozer

Reason

Where reason cannot wade, there faith
may swim.   *Thomas Watson*

Christians are committed to rationality
because they view the cosmos as the creation of a rational God, and believe
humans are beings made in God's image.
Peter S. Williams

Our reliance upon reason is ultimately an
act of faith.   *Peter S. Williams*

RECONCILLIATION — See Atonement

RECREATION
(See also: Amusements)

When recreation gets ahead of recreation,
then God's house has become a den of
thieves.   *Vance Havner*

We can play, as we can eat, to the glory
of God.   *C. S. Lewis*

Recreation to a minister must be as whetting is with the mower, that is, only to be
used so far as is necessary to his work.
Robert Murray M'Cheyne

Recreation is not the highest kind of
enjoyment, but in its time and place is
quite as proper as prayer.   *S. I. Prime*

REDEMPTION
(See also: Atonement; Salvation)

No one is redeemed except through unmerited mercy, and no one is condemned
except through merited judgement.
Augustine

Life is not worth living apart from
redemption.   *Oswald Chambers*

By Christ's purchasing redemption, two
things are intended: his satisfaction and
his merit; the one pays our debt, and so
satisfies; the other procures our title, and
so merits. The satisfaction of Christ is to
free us from misery; the merit of Christ
is to purchase happiness for us.
Jonathan Edwards

As a race we are not even stray sheep, or
wandering prodigals merely, we are
rebels with weapons in our hands. Our
supreme need from God, therefore, is not
the education of our conscience . . . but
our redemption.   *P. T. Forsyth*

No creature that deserved redemption
would need to be redeemed. *C. S. Lewis*

The believer is not redeemed by
obedience to the law but he is redeemed
unto it.   *John Murray*

Justification and sanctification are two
aspects or the two sides of the one coin
of divine redemption. *W. Stanford Reid*

The heart of the gospel is redemption, and
the essence of redemption is the substitutionary sacrifice of Christ.
C. H. Spurgeon

Jesus came not only to teach but to save,
not only to reveal God to mankind, but
also to redeem mankind for God.
John R. W. Stott

The only thing that a man can contribute
to his own redemption is the sin from
which he needs to be redeemed.
William Temple

The purpose and work of redemption in
Christ Jesus is to raise man as much above
the level of Adam as Christ himself is
above the level of Adam.   *A. W. Tozer*

If I had the wisdom of Solomon, the patience of Job, the meekness of Moses, the strength of Samson, the obedience of Abraham, the compassion of Joseph, the tears of Jeremiah, the poetic skill of David, the prophetic voice of Elijah, the courage of Daniel, the greatness of John the Baptist, the endurance and love of Paul, I would still need redemption through Christ's blood, the forgiveness of sin. *R. L. Wheeler*

There can be no thought of 'cheap' forgiveness when we remember that our redemption cost God the life of his beloved Son. *Geoffrey B. Wilson*

REFORMATION

God brings about reformation when his people return to the Word of God as their sole source of doctrine and practice.
John H. Armstrong

Reformation which springs from any source other than regeneration washes only the outside of the cup. *L. Nelson Bell*

All Christians are called to be reformers.
John Blanchard

The only alternatives to continuing personal reformation are deadness and decay. *John Blanchard*

The foundation of every reformation of the Holy Spirit is the Word of God made plain to the people. *Frank Cooke*

The only true reformation is that which emanates from the Word of God.
J. H. Merle d'Aubigné

Every Christian who thinks of reformation and revival must begin by thinking of how to give glory to God. *Tom Wells*

REGENERATION
(See also: Conversion; Faith — Saving)

Repentance is a change of the mind and regeneration is a change of the man.
Thomas Adams

Regeneration is the fountain; sanctification is the river. *J. Sidlow Baxter*

Seeing we are born God's enemies we must be new-born his sons. *Richard Baxter*

Becoming a Christian is not making a new start in life; it is receiving a new life to start with. *John Blanchard*

Take away the mystery from the new birth and you have taken away its majesty.
John Blanchard

Man's basic need is not a grasp of logic but the gift of life. *John Blanchard*

Regeneration is God's mysterious prerogative. *John Blanchard*

The new birth is infinite in its beginning because its beginning lies in infinity.
John Blanchard

The new birth is not only a mystery that no man can understand, it is a miracle that no man can undertake.
John Blanchard

Faith does not proceed from ourselves, but is the fruit of spiritual regeneration.
John Calvin

When God designs to forgive us he changes our hearts and turns us to obedience by his Spirit. *John Calvin*

Adoption gives us the *privilege* of sons, regeneration the *nature* of sons.
Stephen Charnock

Regeneration is a spiritual change; conversion is a spiritual motion.
Stephen Charnock

Regeneration is a universal change of the whole man … it is as large in renewing as sin was in defacing. *Stephen Charnock*

If the second birth hath no place in you, the second death shall have power over you. *William Dyer*

Regeneration, however it is described, is a divine activity in us, in which we are not the actors but the recipients.
Sinclair Ferguson

Regeneration is the communication of the divine nature to man by the operation of the Holy Spirit through the Word.
A. J. Gordon

Regeneration is a single act, complete in itself, and never repeated; conversion, as the beginning of holy living, is the commencement of a series, constant, endless and progressive. *A. A. Hodge*

Whatever man may do after regeneration, the first quickening of the dead must originate with God. *A. A. Hodge*

Spiritual life is the consequence of spiritual quickening. The baby cries because it is born; it is not born because it cries.
Erroll Hulse

God's work of regeneration is never directly perceived by the soul: it takes place in man within the region of what has now come to be called the subconscious. *Ernest F. Kevan*

To expect Christian conduct from a person who is not born again is rank heresy.
D. Martyn Lloyd-Jones

When God works in us, the will, being changed and sweetly breathed upon by the Spirit of God, desires and acts, not from *compulsion,* but *responsively.*
Martin Luther

We cannot be changed by altering a few of our bad habits. Reformation will not do, for the disease of sin has captured our very life system. We need regeneration, a new heart. *Will Metzer*

The genesis of Christianity as an experience is that of being born again of the Spirit. *G. Campbell Morgan*

Just as in the beginning 'God said, "Let there be light"; and there was light' so, at the moment he appointed for our new birth, he said, 'Let there be life' and there was life. *J. A. Motyer*

We are helpless to co-operate in our regeneration as we are to co-operate in the work of Calvary. *Iain H. Murray*

Regeneration is inseparable from its effects and one of its effects is faith.
John Murray

The embrace of Christ in faith is the first evidence of regeneration and only thus may we know that we have been regenerated. *John Murray*

We are not born again by repentance or faith or conversion: we repent and believe because we have been born again.
John Murray

Let them pretend what they please, the true reason why any despise the *new birth* is because they hate *a new life.*
John Owen

Regeneration has made our hearts a battle field. *J. I. Packer*

Sinners cannot obey the gospel, any more than the law, without renewal of heart. *J. I. Packer*

There is no regeneration without spiritual activities. *J. I. Packer*

Regeneration is the transforming not only of an unlovely object, but of one that *resists* with all its might the gracious designs of the heavenly Potter. *A. W. Pink*

The regenerate have a spiritual nature within that fits them for holy action, otherwise there would be no difference between them and the unregenerate. *A. W. Pink*

The act of God in our regeneration is so momentous that no single category of thought is sufficient to describe the changes it brings about in and for us. *Maurice Roberts*

Grace does not run in families. It needs something more than good examples and good advice to make us children of God. *J. C. Ryle*

If you are never born again, you will wish you had never been born at all. *J. C. Ryle*

There are no still-born children in the family of grace. *William Secker*

Though Christ a thousand times in Bethlehem be born,
If he's not born in thee, thy soul is still forlorn. *Johannes Scheffler*

A dead man cannot assist in his own resurrection. *W. G. T. Shedd*

The very first and indispensable sign of regeneration is self-loathing and abhorrence. *Charles Simeon*

A person is never partially born. He is either regenerate or he is not regenerate. *R. C. Sproul*

Every generation needs regeneration. *C. H. Spurgeon*

Regeneration is a change which is known and felt: known by works of holiness and felt by a gracious experience. *C. H. Spurgeon*

The new creation is as much and entirely the work of God as the old creation. *C. H. Spurgeon*

God regenerates the soul by uniting it to Jesus Christ. *Augustus H. Strong*

Regeneration is a restoration of the original tendencies towards God which were lost by the Fall. *Augustus H. Strong*

Regeneration is essentially a changing of the fundamental taste of the soul. By taste we mean the direction of man's love, the bent of his affections, the trend of his will. *Augustus H. Strong*

Regeneration gives our birth a value and our death a glory. *David Thomas*

Mere outward reformation differs as much from regeneration as white-washing an old rotten house differs from pulling it down and building a new one in its place. *Augustus M. Toplady*

Man's need can only be met by a new creation. *Geoffrey B. Wilson*

RELATIVISM

Even when a person asserts that all morality is relative, he thinks I ought to accept the proposition because it is true.
A. J. Hoover

Although widely assumed in theory, it is widely disregarded in practice ... Few are willing to grant that what they believe and what those who disagree with them believe are both equally right.
Peter C. Moore

The one person a relativist cannot relativize is Jesus Christ. *Peter C. Moore*

The poverty of relativism is demonstrated by its inability to condemn evil on an objective basis. *Robert A. Morey*

If everything is relative including ethics and values then we are in deep weeds: the kind of deep weeds one finds in a jungle. *R.C. Sproul*

If everything is relative to everything else, then there is no ultimate reference point. There is no basis for truth. If everything is relative, then the statement, 'Everything is relative,' is also relative. *R. C. Sproul*

Moral relativism is simply collective moral subjectivism. *Peter S. Williams*

RELIGION

If we make religion our business, God will make it our blessedness.
H. G. J. Adam

A religion without mystery must be a religion without God. *Anon.*

It is religion without love that has been responsible for most of the misery of the world. *Anon.*

Religion is bread for daily use, not cake for special occasions. *Anon.*

Religion is man's search for God, but Christianity is God's search for man.
Anon.

Religion is neither a winter resort nor a last resort. *Anon.*

Religion without Christ is a lamp without oil. *Anon.*

Some people's religion is just like a wooden leg. There is neither warmth nor life in it and although it helps you to hobble along it never becomes part of you, but must be strapped on every morning.
Anon.

Still water and still religion freeze the quickest. *Anon.*

One's religion is what he is most interested in. *J. M. Barrie*

Your daily duties are a part of your religious life just as much as your devotions are. *Henry Ward Beecher*

Although theoretically all religions may be wrong, they cannot all be right, because each has beliefs that claim those of others are false. *John Blanchard*

It as possible to be diligent in our religion yet distant in our relationship.
John Blanchard

Nothing so tends to mask the face of God as religion; it can be a substitute for God himself. *Martin Buber*

Justification by faith is the hinge on which all true religion turns. *John Calvin*

No religion is pleasing to God unless founded on truth.   *John Calvin*

Religion separated from knowledge is nothing but the sport and delusion of Satan.   *John Calvin*

Religion is as requisite as reason to complete a man.   *Stephen Charnock*

Let your religion be less of a theory and more of a love affair.   *G. K. Chesterton*

Men will wrangle for religion, write for it, fight for it, die for it, anything but *live* for it.   *C. C. Colton*

Religion's home is in the conscience.
          T. L. Cuyler

As science is the verification of the ideal in nature, so religion is the verification of the spiritual in human life. *A. J. Dubois*

True religion consists in holy affections.
          Jonathan Edwards

True religion is a powerful thing … a ferment, a vigorous engagedness of the heart.   *Jonathan Edwards*

The religion that is afraid of science dishonours God and commits suicide.
          Ralph Waldo Emerson

Since we cannot suspend judgement about life itself, in the end we cannot be neutral about religious faith.
          C. Stephen Evans

The primary question about any religion is not whether it is useful but whether it is true.   *C. Stephen Evans*

If men are so wicked with religion, what would they be without it?
          Benjamin Franklin

All religions other than Christianity have a kind of points system for obtaining eternal life.   *Stephen Gaukroger*

The story of religious movements is the story of man's search for God.
          Stephen Gaukroger

Religion that does not glow with love is unsatisfactory.   *Richard Glover*

Many Christians have enough religion to make them decent, but not enough to make them dynamic.   *Kenneth Grider*

If religion be worth anything it is worth everything.   *Matthew Henry*

The root of religion is the fear of God reigning in the heart, a reverence of his majesty, a deference to his authority and a dread of his wrath.   *Matthew Henry*

God calls people to worship him with their obedience, and instead they try to fob him off with their religion.
          John Hercus

A man may have as many religious changes in the year as there are changes in the moon, and be unchanged after all.
          Rowland Hill

I would give nothing for that man's religion whose very dog and cat were not the better for it.   *Rowland Hill*

Morality does not make us religious, but religion makes us moral. *Charles Hodge*

Religion is what keeps a nation from chaos — from falling asunder like uncemented sand.   *A. A. Hodge*

Religion's in the heart, not in the knee.
          Douglas Jerrold

Religion

A life that will bear the inspection of men and of God is the only certificate of true religion. *Samuel Johnson*

Formal religion always makes fertile soil for false religion. *Gilbert W. Kirby*

Man is constitutionally religious.
R. B. Kuiper

There are no non-religious activities; only religious and irreligious. *C. S. Lewis*

The core of religion is religious experience. *H. D. Lewis*

Religion is not a matter of fits, starts and stops, but an everyday affair.
David Livingstone

The heart of religion lies in its personal pronouns. *Martin Luther*

Religion is not adorned with ceremonies, but purity and charity. *Thomas Manton*

Most of modern evangelical religion is rotten to the core, because its aim is happiness, not holiness. *Al Martin*

It is sometimes wryly said that all the study of comparative religion does is to make people comparatively religious.
Nigel McCullough

Religion has never been an insurance policy. *Nigel McCullough*

A cheap religion is always a cheat religion. *Thomas V. Moore*

The basic religious question is that of our relation to God. *John Murray*

The heart of true religion is to glorify God by patient endurance and to praise him

for his gracious deliverances. *J. I. Packer*

There is nothing more irreligious than self-absorbed religion. *J. I. Packer*

Men never do evil so completely and cheerfully as when they do it from religious conviction. *Blaise Pascal*

A consciousness of the absence of God is one of the standard incidents of religious life. *Austin Phelps*

A religion which costs nothing is worth nothing. *J. C. Ryle*

Those who fancy that true religion has any tendency to make men unhappy are greatly mistaken. It is the absence of it that does this, and not the presence.
J. C. Ryle

Religion is union between God and the soul. *Paul Sabatier*

The heart of religion is not an opinion about God, but a personal relationship with him. *W. E. Sangster*

People can be inoculated against religion by small injections of it. *W. E. Sangster*

Religion that is merely ritual and ceremonial can never satisfy. Neither can we be satisfied by a religion that is merely humanitarian or serviceable to mankind. Man's craving is for the spiritual.
Samuel Shoemaker

Belief in the immortality of the soul and belief in the accountability of the soul are fundamental beliefs in all religion.
O. J. Smith

No man's religion ever survives his morals. *Robert South*

When people say that all religions are basically the same, they are actually saying that they know little or nothing about world religion.   *R. C. Sproul*

Banish religion and you destroy virtue.
                              C. H. Spurgeon

I would not give much for your religion unless it can be seen. Lamps do not talk, but they do shine.   *C. H. Spurgeon*

If your religion does not make you holy it will damn you. It is simply pageantry to go to hell in.   *C. H. Spurgeon*

Religion is nothing if it is not the foundation of our whole life. *Robert Thornton*

What a mercy to have religion that will do to die by.   *William Tiptaft*

Any untrained, unprepared, unspiritual empty rattletrap of a person can start something religious and find plenty of followers who will listen and pay and promote it.   *A. W. Tozer*

For the true Christian the one supreme test for the present soundness and ultimate worth of everything religious must be the place our Lord occupies in it. *A. W. Tozer*

Frankly, I would much rather have no religion at all than to have just enough to deceive me.   *A. W. Tozer*

No religion has ever been greater than its idea of God.   *A. W. Tozer*

Religion can be a front or a fount.
                              A. W. Tozer

Religion, so far as it is genuine, is in essence the response of created personalities to the creating personality, God.
                              A. W. Tozer

Religion will either make us very tender of heart, considerate and kind, or it will make us very hard.   *A. W. Tozer*

The essence of true religion is spontaneity, the sovereign movings of the Holy Spirit upon and in the free spirit of redeemed man.   *A. W. Tozer*

The whole world has been booby-trapped by the devil, and the deadliest trap of all is the religious one.   *A. W. Tozer*

We have too much religion. *A. W. Tozer*

You can find more carnal, unregenerate, self-centred characters who have religion and are sensitive towards it than you can bury in the Grand Canyon. *A. W. Tozer*

That religion is suspicious which is full of faction and discord. *Thomas Watson*

They who make religion a cloak for their sin shall have a hotter place in hell.
                              Thomas Watson

Religion is the first and the last thing, and until a man has found God, and has been found by God, he begins at no beginning and works to no end.   *H. G. Wells*

Religion is the reaction of human nature to its search for God.
                          Alfred North Whitehead

Unpractical religion is unscriptural religion.   *James Wolfendale*

The only religion ... which is of any use is that which brings us back into harmony with divine law and into the orbit of perfect fellowship with God.
                          Frederick P. Wood

All religions do not point to God. All religions do not say that all religions are the same. *Ravi Zacharias*

Every person who claims that all religions are the same betrays not only an ignorance of all religions but also a caricatured view of even the best known ones. Every religion at its core is exclusive.
Ravi Zacharias

REPENTANCE — Blessings

If sin and thy heart be two, Christ and thy heart are one. *Thomas Brooks*

Nothing will make the faces of God's children more fair than for them to wash themselves every morning in their tears.
Samuel Clark

When we truly comprehend our own nature, repentance is no dry doctrine, no frightening message, no morbid form of self-flagellation. It is, as the early church fathers said, a gift God grants which leads to life. *Charles Colson*

Every man feels more comfort and spiritual joy after true repentance for a sin, than he had in that innocence before he committed the sin. *John Donne*

Real repentance produces confession and forsaking of sin, reconciliation and restitution, separation from the world, submission to the lordship of Christ and filling of the Holy Spirit. *Vance Havner*

Repentance, if it be true, strikes at the root and washes the heart from wickedness.
Matthew Henry

The grief of repentance is never loss in any way; not to experience this grief, that is loss indeed. *R. C. H. Lenski*

Repentance is the next happiest state to that of sinlessness. *Lorinus*

Holy tears are the sponge of sin.
Thomas Manton

The sunshine is always sweeter after we have been in the shade; so you will find Jesus in returning to him.
Robert Murray M'Cheyne

Repentance is the golden key that opens the palace of eternity. *John Milton*

Sorrow for sin is a perpetual rain, a sweet, soft shower which, to a truly gracious man, lasts all his life long. *C. H. Spurgeon*

Upon the two hinges of faith and repentance do all the promises of the Bible hang.
George Swinnock

Those who make their eyes a fountain to wash Christ's feet in shall have his side to wash their souls in. *John Trapp*

It is better to meet God with tears in your eyes than with weapons in your hands.
Thomas Watson

Repentance unravels sin, and makes sin not to be. *Thomas Watson*

REPENTANCE — Essence
(See also: Confession; Contrition; Penitence; Conviction of Sin)

Repentance is a change of the mind and regeneration is a change of the man.
Thomas Adams

According to the greatness of the sin must the repentance be. *Ambrose*

True repentance never exists but in conjunction with faith, while, on the other hand, wherever there is true faith, there is also real repentance.   *Louis Berkhof*

Obedience is the positive side of repentance.   *John Blanchard*

Repentance is an attitude that leads to action.   *John Blanchard*

Repentance is an inner change of heart and mind and an outward change of life.
John Blanchard

True repentance is being broken for sin and from sin.   *John Blanchard*

True repentance is personal, permanent, painful and profitable.   *John Blanchard*

Repentance is ultimate honesty.
Dietrich Bonhoeffer

Repentance is a continual spring, where the waters of godly sorrow are always flowing.   *Thomas Brooks*

No one repents of his own accord.
John Calvin

Repentance is nothing else but a reformation of the whole life according to the Law of God.   *John Calvin*

The beginning of repentance is the confession of guilt.   *John Calvin*

No repentance is true repentance which does not recognize Jesus as Lord over every area of life.   *John C. Chapman*

Repentance is the process by which we see ourselves, day by day, as we really are: sinful, needy, dependent people.
Charles Colson

True repentance arises from the sight by faith of the crucified Saviour.
A. R. Fausset

If we truly believe in Christ it must be penitently; if we repent of sin it must be believingly.   *Sinclair Ferguson*

To forsake sin is to leave it without any thought reserved of returning to it again.
William Gurnall

True repentance does not substitute sacrifice for obedience.   *Vance Havner*

Repentance is the turning of the whole heart from sin and Satan to serve God in newness of life.   *Erroll Hulse*

Repentance is no fun at all. It is something harder than merely eating humble pie. It means unlearning the self-conceit and self-will that we have been training ourselves into for thousands of years.
C. S. Lewis

Repentance is the soul's divorce from sin.
Al Martin

Repentance is the tear in the eye of faith.
D. L. Moody

All true repentance arises from a sight of a dying Saviour, one who has died for us.   *Thomas V. Moore*

It is impossible to disentangle faith and repentance. Saving faith is permeated with repentance and repentance is permeated with faith.   *John Murray*

The broken spirit and the contrite heart are the abiding marks of the believing soul.   *John Murray*

The faith that is unto salvation is a penitent faith and the repentance that is unto life is a believing repentance.
John Murray

Repentance unto life will be repentance in the life. *William Nevins*

Repentance is, fundamentally, a change of direction, a turning from sin to God.
James Philip

Repentance is a thorough change of man's natural heart on the subject of sin.
J. C. Ryle

True repentance begins with knowledge of sin. It goes on to work sorrow for sin. It leads to confession of sin before God. It shows itself before man by a thorough breaking off from sin. It results in producing a habit of deep hatred for all sin.
J. C. Ryle

True repentance has a double aspect; it looks upon things past with a weeping eye, and upon the future with a watchful eye. *Robert South*

Repentance is a plant that never grows on nature's dung-hill. The nature must be changed, and repentance must be implanted by the Holy Spirit, or it will never flourish in our hearts. *C. H. Spurgeon*

There will never be a tear of acceptable repentance in your eye till you have first looked to Jesus Christ. *C. H. Spurgeon*

When the Word of God converts a man, it takes away from him his despair, but it does not take from him his repentance.
C. H. Spurgeon

Man truly repents only when he learns that his sin has made him unable to repent without the renewing grace of God. *Augustus H. Strong*

True repentance takes God's part against ourselves. *Augustus H. Strong*

True repentance hates the sin, and not merely the penalty; and it hates the sin most of all because it has discovered and felt God's love. *W. M. Taylor*

I have discovered that truly repentant men never quite get over it, for repentance is not a state of mind and spirit that takes its leave as soon as God has given forgiveness and as soon as cleansing is realized. *A. W. Tozer*

Repentance is primarily a change of moral purpose, a sudden and often violent reversal of the soul's direction.
A. W. Tozer

Amendment of life is the best repentance.
John Trapp

Repentance, that fair and happy daughter of an ugly and odious mother.
John Trapp

Repentance with man is the changing of his will; repentance with God is the willing of a change. *John Trapp*

Repentance and faith are both humbling graces; by repentance a man abhors himself, by faith he goes out of himself.
Thomas Watson

We must not only abstain from sin but abhor sin. *Thomas Watson*

The true holy water is not that which the pope sprinkles, but is distilled from the penitent eye. *Thomas Watson*

Wouldest thou know when thou hast been humbled enough for sin? When thou art willing to let go thy sins. *Thomas Watson*

O Jesus, full of truth and grace,
More full of grace than I of sin,
Yet once again I seek thy face;
Open thine arms, and take me in,
And freely my backslidings heal,
And love the faithless sinner still.
Charles Wesley

Mourning for sin is anathema to the happy-go-lucky. *Ravi Zacharias*

REPENTANCE — False

Many persons who appear to repent are like sailors who throw their goods overboard in a storm, and wish for them again in a calm. *Anon.*

You can't purify the water by painting the pump. *Anon.*

He who beats his heart, but does not mend his ways, does not remove his sins but hardens them. *Augustine*

Remorse may be a long way from repentance. *John Blanchard*

Repentance without moral change is a contradiction in terms. *John Blanchard*

There is more to repentance than apologizing to God. *John Blanchard*

Unless there is the fruit of repentance in the life, there is no evidence of the root of repentance in the heart.
John Blanchard

If we seek God for our own good and profit, we are not seeking God.
Meister Eckhart

Our pride is disgusted at our faults and we mistake this disgust for true repentance. *François Fenelon*

Esau wept that he lost the blessing, not that he sold it. *William Gurnall*

Repentance is not a change of opinion but of attitude, and there is very little repentance nowadays because of our attitude towards sin. *Vance Havner*

Repentance which is occupied with thoughts of peace is hypocrisy.
Martin Luther

Repentance without faith will lead to sorrow and mere legalistic resolutions.
Will Metzger

Sin may be the occasion of great sorrow, when there is no sorrow for sin.
John Owen

Evangelical repentance is not at the beck and call of the creature. It is the gift of God. *A. W. Pink*

Multitudes desire to be saved from hell (the natural instinct of self-preservation) who are quite unwilling to be saved from sin. *A. W. Pink*

Multitudes seem to think that it is about as easy for a sinner to purify his heart as it is to wash his hands. *A. W. Pink*

Of himself, the fallen sinner can no more repent evangelically, believe in Christ savingly, come to him effectually, than he can create a world. *A. W. Pink*

Let us beware of a repentance without evidence. *J. C. Ryle*

531

This is like weeping with an onion; the eye sheds tears because it smarts.
William Secker

The teaching and the hope of being forgiven while persisting in sin is a great moral impossibility. *A. W. Tozer*

The teaching of forgiveness without any turning from sin is a great error and it has filled the churches with deceived members and helped to fill hell with deceived souls. *A. W. Tozer*

To teach pardon and cleansing where there is no intention to change the life would upset heaven and turn it into a moral insane asylum, and in a hundred years you would not know heaven from hell! *A. W. Tozer*

The eye may be watery and the heart flinty. An apricot may be soft without, but it has a hard stone within. *Thomas Watson*

REPENTANCE — and Holiness

Repentance is the relinquishment of any practice from the conviction that it has offended God. *Joseph Addison*

True repentance is to cease from sin.
Ambrose

Remorse is being sorry. Repentance is being sorry enough to stop. *Anon.*

It is much easier to repent of sins that we have committed than to repent of those we intend to commit. *Josh Billings*

God has nowhere undertaken to forgive a sin that man is not prepared to forsake.
John Blanchard

Repentance is not an idea; it is action.
John Blanchard

He never truly repented of any sin whose heart is not turned against every sin.
Thomas Brooks

You must fall out with sin if ever you fall in love with God. *Thomas Brooks*

A sincere repentance from the heart does not guarantee that we shall not wander from the straight path and sometimes become bewildered. *John Calvin*

Repentance, to be of any avail, must work a change of heart and conduct.
T. L. Cuyler

Repentance without amendment is like continually pumping without mending the leak. *Lewis W. Dillwyn*

Sleep with clean hands, either kept clean all day by integrity or washed clean at night by repentance. *John Donne*

Purity as well as pardon is desired by all true penitents. *Andrew Fausset*

Amendment is repentance.
Thomas Fuller

Those that profess repentance must practise it. *Matthew Henry*

I will take my repentance to the gates of heaven. *Philip Henry*

You should never think of sin without repenting. *Philip Henry*

To do so no more is the truest repentance.
Martin Luther

When our Lord and Master Jesus Christ said 'Repent' he called for the entire life of believers to be one of repentance.
Martin Luther

Repentance begins in the humiliation of the heart and ends in the reformation of the life.   *John Mason*

Real repentance consists in the heart being broken for sin and from sin.
William Nevins

Repentance is an ongoing process ... True repentance affects the whole man and alters the entire lifestyle.
Richard Owen Roberts

I charge you that you do not escape hell if you have no inclination to escape from the things that make it. *David Shepherd*

The faith which receives Christ must be accompanied by the repentance which rejects sin.   *John R. W. Stott*

The idea that God will pardon a rebel who has not given up his rebellion is contrary both to Scripture and to common sense.
A. W. Tozer

There is no danger of repentance where there is no change of heart. *Robert Wilson*

REPENTANCE — Importance
(See also: Conversion; Faith — Saving; Regeneration)

To get the world right, start with yourself.   *Anon.*

Let the quantity of thy sins be the measure of thy repentance. *Isaac Bargrave*

Repentance and faith are graces we have received, not goals we have achieved.
John Blanchard

Repentance and faith are twins.
John Blanchard

The Christian who has stopped repenting has stopped growing.   *John Blanchard*

Whatever the cost of putting a thing right, it can never be more than the cost of leaving it wrong.   *John Blanchard*

When a person becomes a Christian, the repentant sinner becomes a repenting saint.   *John Blanchard*

When man fell into sin he changed his mind – and until he changes it again he can never be right with God.
John Blanchard

I have carried a penitent form around in my heart for half a century or more, and if there is ever any need, instantly I fly there. Jesus waits, loves, pities and never turns away the seeking soul.
Samuel Logan Brengle

Of all acts of man repentance is the most divine. The greatest of all faults is to be conscious of none.   *Thomas Carlyle*

Repentance is an inescapable consequence of regeneration. *Charles Colson*

The saint is a penitent until he reaches heaven.   *R. L. Dabney*

There is no going to the fair haven of glory without sailing through the narrow strait of repentance.   *William Dyer*

All true believers are lifelong repenters.
Jim Elliff

Never will Christ enter into that soul where the herald of repentance hath not been before him.   *Joseph Hall*

The church can do many things after she repents, but she can do nothing else until she repents.   *Vance Havner*

Wherever God designs to give life he gives repentance.   *Matthew Henry*

You should never think of sin without repenting.   *Philip Henry*

Spiritual repentance is the creation of the Spirit.   *Erroll Hulse*

Christianity starts with repentance.
D. Martyn Lloyd-Jones

The first reason for leaving sin is that God commands me to do so.
D. Martyn Lloyd Jones

You cannot drive repentance out of the teaching of Christ without destroying his teaching utterly and entirely.
D. Martyn Lloyd-Jones

Repentance may be old-fashioned, but it is not out-dated as long as there is sin.
J. C. Macaulay

Before God can be received as a friend he must first be worshipped as Lord.
Edward Norman

We make no spiritual progress apart from repentance.   *Maurice Roberts*

Repentance is one of the foundation stones of Christianity.   *J. C. Ryle*

We are all responsible to God for repentance.   *J. C. Ryle*

Repentance is the only gate through which the gospel is received.
Basilea Schlink

Many have the *space of* repentance who have not the *grace of* repentance.
William Secker

Christ and we will never be one until we and our sin are two.   *C. H. Spurgeon*

Repentance and faith are like Siamese twins. If one is sick, the other cannot be well, for they live but one life.
C. H. Spurgeon

Sackcloth and ashes are the court robes of those blessed mourners who shall be comforted.   *C. H. Spurgeon*

You are not living to God as you ought unless you repent daily.
C. H. Spurgeon

An unrepented sin is a continued sin.
Corrie ten Boom

I was born for nothing but repentance.
Tertullian

Exhalation is as necessary to life as inhalation. To accept Christ it is necessary that we reject whatever is contrary to him.
A. W. Tozer

God will take nine steps towards us, but he will not take the tenth. He will incline us to repent, but he cannot do our repenting for us.   *A. W. Tozer*

You can pray till doomsday for revival, but you will never get it without repentance and confession of sin in the Christian life.   *A. W. Tozer*

Our repentance needs to be repented of, and our tears washed in the blood of Christ.   *George Whitefield*

REPENTANCE — Urgency

If we lose our time to repent, we shall repent for ever that we once lost our time.
Thomas Adams

None can be too young to amend that is old enough to die.   *Thomas Adams*

A religion that does not begin with repentance is certain to end there — perhaps too late.   *Anon.*

If we put off repentance another day, we have a day more to repent of, and a day less to repent.   *Anon.*

Though after this life repentance be perpetual, it is in vain.   *Augustine*

The Lord has made a promise *to* late repentance, but where has he made a promise *of* late repentance?
        Thomas Brooks

Death-bed repentance is burning the candle of life in the service of the devil, then blowing the snuff in the face of heaven.   *Lorenzo Dow*

You cannot repent too soon, because you do not know how soon it may be too late.
        Thomas Fuller

Fair-weather repentance might save us many a cloudy day.   *Vance Havner*

Whoever delays his repentance does in effect pawn his soul with the devil.
        Thomas Manton

What insanity is it that persuades multitudes to defer the effort to repent till their death-beds? Do they imagine that when they are so weak that they can no longer turn their bodies they will have strength to turn their souls from sin? Far sooner could they turn themselves back to perfect physical health.   *A. W. Pink*

He that hath promised pardon on our repentance hath not promised to preserve our lives till we repent.   *Francis Quarles*

If God's today be too soon for thy repentance, thy tomorrow may be too late for his acceptance.   *William Secker*

Sin and hell are married unless repentance proclaims the divorce.   *C. H. Spurgeon*

Whatever stress some may lay upon it, a death-bed repentance is but a weak and slender plank to trust our all upon.
        Lawrence Sterne

He who promised forgiveness to them that repent has not promised repentance to them that sin.   *Ralph Venning*

Late repentance is seldom true, but true repentance is never too late.
        Ralph Venning

There's no repentance in the grave.
        Isaac Watts

REPUTATION

A good name keeps its lustre in the dark.
        Anon.

It is better to be despised for the right than praised for the wrong.   *Anon.*

Reputation is often got without merit and lost without fault.   *Anon.*

Reputation is sometimes as wide as the horizon when character is the point of a needle.   *Henry Ward Beecher*

Until we have learned to set very little value upon our own reputation, we will never be inflamed with true zeal in contending for the preservation and advancement of the interest of Divine glory.
        John Calvin

What I do is all that concerns me and not what people think. *Ralph Waldo Emerson*

One may be better than his reputation, but never better than his principles.
Nicolas Valentin de Latena

RESOLUTIONS — See Vows

RESPONSIBILITY
(See also: Duty; Service)

One bird cannot fly to heaven with another bird's wings.   *Thomas Adams*

We are morally responsible to God because we are made in the image of a moral Deity.   *E. H. Andrews*

Some people grow under responsibility, others swell.   *Anon.*

Every responsibility is a privilege, and every privilege a responsibility.
John Blanchard

We must never let our theology rob us of our responsibility.   *John Blanchard*

Man facing God is an encounter in responsibility.   *Martin Buber*

The hours which come fresh to you out of the mercy of your heavenly Father will carry for ever the imprint which your life leaves on them, until all accounts are closed at his Last Assize.
Sinclair Ferguson

It is not what you have that matters. It is what you do with what you have.
Wilfred Grenfell

Initiative is our own personal responsibility. We cannot lay this upon any other person.   *E. F. Hallock*

There are too many people ready to assert their rights who are not ready to assume their responsibilities.
Vance Havner

We are not born for ourselves.
Matthew Henry

Responsibility walks hand in hand with capacity and power.   *John G. Holland*

One cannot be religious by proxy.
William Ralph Inge

If God were less than sovereign, man would be less than responsible. Since God is absolutely sovereign, man is wholly responsible to him.   *R. B. Kuiper*

Good and evil both increase at compound interest. That is why the little decisions you and I make every day are of such infinite importance.   *C. S. Lewis*

Of all the awkward people in your house or job there is only one whom you can improve very much.   *C. S. Lewis*

The sovereignty of God never excuses us from responsibility.   *Will Metzger*

To be a responsible person is to find one's own role and then, funded by the grace of God, to fill this role and to delight in it.   *Cornelius Plantinga*

Responsibility brings accountability.
Ken Robins

The history of America will be written in three phases: the passing of the Indian, the passing of the buffalo and the passing of the buck.   *Will Rogers*

Let it be a settled principle in our religion, that man's salvation, if saved, is wholly of God; and that man's ruin, if lost, is wholly of himself.   *J. C. Ryle*

If God created man then there is someone outside of man to whom he becomes responsible. *Charles Caldwell Ryrie*

To be a man is, precisely, to be responsible. *Saint-Exupery*

My dear friends, you may take it as a rule that the Spirit of God does not usually do for us what we can do for ourselves. *C. H. Spurgeon*

It is easy to dodge our responsibilities, but we cannot dodge the consequences of dodging our responsibilities. *Josiah Stamp*

Men are free to decide their own moral choices, but they are also under the necessity to account to God for those choices. *A. W. Tozer*

The most important thought I ever had was that of my individual responsibility to God. *Daniel Webster*

He who governed the world before I was born shall take care of it likewise when I am dead. My part is to improve the present moment. *John Wesley*

RESURRECTION OF CHRIST

Death died when Christ rose. *Anon.*

The best news the world ever had came from a graveyard. *Anon.*

The angel rolled away the stone from Jesus' tomb, not to let the living Lord out but to let the unconvinced outsiders in. *Donald Grey Barnhouse*

The resurrection of Christ is our receipted bill. *Donald Grey Barnhouse*

The stone at the tomb of Jesus was a pebble to the Rock of Ages inside. *Fred Beck*

The Easter story ends not with a funeral but with a festival. *John Blanchard*

The resurrection of Jesus demands not our applause but our allegiance, not our compliments but our capitulation. *John Blanchard*

The resurrection of Christ is the Amen of all his promises. *John Boys*

The resurrection of Christ is the commencement of his reign. *John Calvin*

The resurrection of Christ is the most important article of our faith. *John Calvin*

If the historical evidence makes it reasonable to believe Jesus rose from the dead, then it is illegitimate to suppress this evidence because all other men have always remained in their graves. *William Lane Craig*

The New Testament preaches a Christ who was dead and is alive, not a Christ who was alive and is dead. *James Denney*

The resurrection is the first and last and dominating element in the Christian consciousness of the New Testament. *James Denney*

At the resurrection, Christ's real self, including his divine nature and his immaterial human nature, were joined to a new, immortal, incorruptible body for ever. *Robert G. Gromacki*

The resurrection of Christ, as the evidence of the sacrifice of his death being accepted, and of the validity of all his claims, is a much more decisive proof of the security of all who trust in him than his death could be. *Charles Hodge*

If Christ be not risen, the dreadful consequence is not that death ends life, but that we are still in our sins.
G. A. Studdert Kennedy

Jesus has forced open a door that had been locked since the death of the first man. He has met, fought and beaten the King of Death. Everything is different because he has done so. *C. S. Lewis*

The man in Christ rose again, not only the God. *C. S. Lewis*

Easter is to our faith what water is to the ocean, what stone is to the mountain, what blood is to the body. *Raymond Linquist*

Our Lord has written the promise of the resurrection, not in books alone, but in every leaf in springtime. *Martin Luther*

I know that my Redeemer lives!
What joy the blest assurance gives!
He lives, he lives, who once was dead;
He lives, my everlasting Head!
Samuel Medley

The same power that brought Christ back from the dead is operative within those who are Christ's. The resurrection is an ongoing thing. *Leon Morris*

Everything antecedent in the incarnate life of our Lord moves towards the resurrection and everything subsequent rests upon it and is conditioned by it.
John Murray

The empty tomb of Christ has been the cradle of the church. *W. Robertson Nicoll*

The victim of Calvary is now … loose and at large. *J. I. Packer*

The Christian church has the resurrection written all over it. *E. G. Robinson*

In an age of abounding unbelief and scepticism, we shall find that the resurrection of Christ will bear any weight that we can lay upon it. *J. C. Ryle*

The resurrection is a fact better attested than any event recorded in any history, whether ancient or modern.
C. H. Spurgeon

Christianity is essentially a religion of resurrection. *James S. Stewart*

This is no appendix to the faith. This is the faith. He is risen! The Lord is risen indeed! *James S. Stewart*

Christianity is in its very essence a resurrection religion. The concept of resurrection lies at its heart. If you remove it, Christianity is destroyed. *John R. W. Stott*

Before Christ's resurrection, it was twilight; it is sunrise now.
Augustus H. Strong

Christ's resurrection is not only the best proof of immortality, but we have no certain evidence of immortality without it.
Augustus H. Strong

The resurrection of Jesus is the Gibraltar of the Christian faith and the Waterloo of infidelity and rationalism. *R. A. Torrey*

The account of the life of Jesus Christ is the only biography known to man that does not end with death and burial — the only record of human life that joyfully hastens on to the next chapter after the last! *A. W. Tozer*

The moral obligation of the resurrection of Christ is the missionary obligation, the responsibility and the privilege of carrying the message and telling the story, of praying and interceding, and of being involved personally and financially in the cause of this great commission.
A. W. Tozer

The resurrection morning was only the beginning of a great, grand and vast outreach that has never ended and will not end until our Lord Jesus Christ comes back again.
A. W. Tozer

The resurrection of Christ and the fact of the empty tomb are not part of the world's complex and continuing mythologies. This is not a Santa Claus tale — it is history and it is reality.
A. W Tozer

Never was there as great an imposture put upon the world as Christianity, if Christ be yet in the grave.
John Trapp

Christ did not rise from the dead as a private person, but as the public Head of the church.
Thomas Watson

The resurrection of Jesus is something to shout about. It is an explosive event whose fall-out affects the whole human race.
Douglas Webster

Our Lord is risen from the dead,
Our Jesus is gone up on high.
The powers of hell are captive led,
Dragged to the portals of the sky.
Charles Wesley

Taking all the evidence together, it is not too much to say that there is no single historic incident better or more variously supported than the resurrection of Christ.
Brooke Foss Westcott

The Gospels cannot explain the resurrection; it is the resurrection which alone explains the Gospels.
John S. Whale

The resurrection is the proof of our reconciliation.
Geoffrey B. Wilson

RESURRECTION OF CHRISTIANS

Our friends bring us to the grace and leave us there, but God will not.
Anon.

Bless God that there is in us resurrection life, and that there awaits us a resurrection.
J. J. Bonar

Christians out-die pagans and the resurrection of Christ is the reason.
T. R. Glover

This world is a great sculptor's shop. We are the statues and there is a rumour going around that some of us are some day going to come to life.
C. S. Lewis

God fits our souls here to possess a glorious body after; and he will fit the body for a glorious soul.
Richard Sibbes

Our bodies shall be *like* Christ's glorious body, not *equal* to it.
Richard Sibbes

At the close of every obituary of his believing children God adds the word 'henceforth!'
A. W. Tozer

The resurrection and the judgement will demonstrate before all worlds who won and who lost. We can wait.
A. W. Tozer

We are more sure to arise out of our graves than out of our beds.
Thomas Watson

REVELATION
(See also: Bible — Divine Authority and Authorship; Knowledge of God)

We must allow God to tell us what he is like. We must seek to discover how he has revealed himself to us. *Simon Austen*

Only God can interpret his own handwriting. *John Blanchard*

To know God without God is impossible; as he is the source of all knowledge, he must be the source of knowledge about himself. *John Blanchard*

Rebellious man is like someone who tries all the buttons on a transistor radio but always gets the same message — he can never entirely turn off God's voice.
John Campbell

Man cannot cover what God would reveal. *Thomas Campbell*

A Christian cannot live by philosophy. Only the light of Christian revelation gives the end as well as the means of life.
John Jay Chapman

God frames his language to our dullness, not to his own state. *Stephen Charnock*

God has not been discovered by reasoning but … has disclosed himself, unexpectedly and dramatically, in the history of a chosen people. *J. C. P. Cockerton*

The message of the gospel is a noise, not a communication, until God tunes the set of man's heart. *Arthur C. Custance*

Revelation never contradicts or sets aside the teachings of natural religion.
J. L. Dagg

Unless God imparts the spiritual ability to hear his voice, one hears nothing but meaningless words. *Ronald Dunn*

No one could ever have found God; he gave himself away. *Meister Eckhart*

Science must always be prepared to alter course when new facts demand such action. Revelation, on the other hand, is final. *Brian H. Edwards*

The need of the world is to listen to God.
Albert Einstein

The one who has come to trust in the salvation of Jesus for his soul will be content to rest in the revelation of Jesus for his mind. *H. Enoch*

It is axiomatic in our understanding of Christian doctrine that it is only in the light of the full revelation of God in Christ that we can perceive the kingdom of darkness clearly enough to understand its powers. *Sinclair Ferguson*

No one less than God can bring us true and reliable information about him: God must give it himself. *Sinclair Ferguson*

If God's speech has an obvious location, that location must be the Holy Scriptures. There simply is no other candidate.
John M. Frame

Nature is a first volume, in itself incomplete, and demanding a second volume, which is Christ. *Charles Gore*

God does not tell us all we want to know about anything, but he will tell us all we need to know. *Vance Havner*

God wants us to reason together with him on the basis of revelation, not on the basis of our poor logic. *Vance Havner*

The natural man can never be educated into apprehension of divine truth.
Vance Havner

By the light of nature we see God as a God above us; by the light of the law we see him as a God against us; but by the light of the gospel we see him as Emmanuel, God with us. *Matthew Henry*

To dust-begotten creatures like ourselves, God is unknowable. The only things we can ever know of him are the things he himself reveals to us. *John Hercus*

God can be described as a heavenly Father, a caring parent who brings human persons into existence and continues to watch over them. Part of that caring is shown in God's desire to communicate with us. *Walter R. Hearn*

Revelation is from the Father, through the Son, by the Spirit. Redemption is to the Father, by the Son, through the Spirit.
A. A. Hodge

Revelation is the act of communicating divine knowledge by the Spirit to the mind. Inspiration is the act of the same Spirit, controlling those who make the truth known. *Charles Hodge*

Whenever anyone knows truth … his knowledge is due to God's illuminating it to his mind. *W. Andrew Hoffecker*

Our need of revelation is like our need of redemption: it is total. *Robert Horn*

There is no Christianity apart from revelation. *D. Martyn Lloyd-Jones*

To the Christian, all knowledge is, in the long run, revelation; and it is almighty God, not us, who ensures that we are able to know what we need to know.
Pete Lowman

Worship is in response to truth about God and the truth about God is revealed in his Word. *John MacArthur*

God does not ordinarily shout to make himself heard. *Gordon MacDonald*

General revelation provides the point of contact for special revelation, this latter alone being [the] saving knowledge of God. *Alister McGrath*

Because God is personal, the only certainty anyone can have about him is the certainty which God gives. In our finitude we are simply not able, by a series of logical arguments, to arrive at certainty about God. *Peter C. Moore*

Our belief in the infallibility of Scripture arises not from an ability to prove that Scripture is perfect from start to finish. Rather it rests on Jesus' own witness to Scripture. He believed and taught that it was the Word of God and therefore inherently trustworthy. Our belief in Scripture is dependent on our belief in Jesus.
Peter C .Moore

We do not believe that God has added, or ever will, anything to his revelation in his Son. *C. B. Moss*

Nothing is to be introduced as doctrine which is not according to revelation.
Henry T. Mahan

Unless thou show us thine own true way, none can find it; Father, thou must lead!
Michaelangelo

Revelation is a disclosure of the divine righteousness. *P. S. Moxom*

Scripture . . . is the only revelation of the mind and will of God available to us. This is what the finality of Scripture means to us; it is the only extant revelatory Word of God. *John Murray*

Apart from special, saving revelation — the revelation that centres upon the Lord Jesus Christ — we do not and cannot know God. *J. I. Packer*

God takes us into his confidence and shares his secrets with us; God finds us ignorant, and gives us knowledge. That is what revelation means. *J. I. Packer*

In revelation, God is the agent as well as the object. It is not just that men speak about God, or for God; God speaks for himself, and talks to us in person. *J. I. Packer*

It is not for us to imagine that we can prove the truth of Christianity by our own arguments; nobody can prove the truth of Christianity save the Holy Spirit. *J. I. Packer*

Revelation is a divine activity: not, therefore, a human achievement. Revelation is not the same thing as discovery or the dawning of insight, or the emerging of a bright idea. Revelation does not mean man fording God, but God finding man, God sharing his secrets with us, God showing us himself. *J. I. Packer*

Since the apostolic age God has said nothing new to men, for he has in fact no more to say to us than he said then. But it is also true that God has not ceased to say to man all that he said then. *J. I. Packer*

Instead of complaining that God had hidden himself, you will give him thanks for having revealed so much of himself. *Blaise Pascal*

There is enough light for those whose only desire is to see, and enough darkness for those of the opposite disposition. *Blaise Pascal*

No man can know the Father any farther than it pleaseth the Son to reveal him. *John Penry*

God's design in all that he has revealed to us is to the purifying of our affections and the transforming of our characters. *A. W. Pink*

God has for various reasons always seen fit to accompany his revelation in all of creation with special revelations of himself. *Richard L. Pratt*

God's revelation in Scripture is given to direct us to true knowledge. *Richard L. Pratt*

The Lord has more truth yet to break forth out of his holy Word. *John Robinson*

The real view of the world is that which revelation presents us. *Hans Rohrbach*

We know nothing from God except by revelation. *Charles Simeon*

Modern man has lost any sense of God's nearness, but Christianity teaches that God reveals himself through every single thing he has ever brought into being, whether a created object or historical event. *R. C. Sproul*

Every genuine revelation of God has this mark upon it, that it makes him appear more glorious. *C. H. Spurgeon*

The nearer we come to God, the more graciously will he reveal himself to us. *C. H. Spurgeon*

Christianity … is the revelation of God, not the research of man. *James A. Stewart*

No man has any right to pick and choose among revealed truths.   *A. W. Tozer*

Unless God give sight as well as light, and enlighten both organ and object, we can see nothing.   *John Trapp*

That which we know about God is not what we have been clever enough to find out, but what divine charity has secretly revealed.   *Evelyn Underhill*

Christianity is the one revealed religion.
Benjamin B. Warfield

Scriptural revelation terminates on the heart.   *Benjamin B. Warfield*

We need every word that God speaks.
David Watson

We should all be incurably agnostic if God had not revealed himself.
David Watson

God is beyond human examination and can be known only by those to whom he chooses to reveal himself.
Geoffrey B. Wilson

In the goodness of God, what could never be discovered by human reason has been revealed to Christians by the Holy Spirit.
Geoffrey B. Wilson

The only revelation from God which Christians still await is the revelation of Jesus Christ at his second coming.
Geoffrey B. Wilson

REVENGE
(See also: Anger; Hatred)

Revenge is a dish that should be eaten cold.   *Anon.*

The smallest revenge will poison the soul.
Anon.

Revenge is the most worthless weapon in the world.   *David Augsburger*

A man who studies revenge keeps his own wounds green.   *Francis Bacon*

Men must not turn into bees and kill themselves in stinging others.
Francis Bacon

Injuries cost more to avenge than to bear.
John Blanchard

Revenge is a passion unbecoming the children of God.   *John Calvin*

The noblest revenge is to forgive.
Thomas Fuller

The only people with whom you should try to get even are those who have helped you.   *John E. Southard*

It is more honour to bury an injury than to revenge it.   *Thomas Watson*

REVERENCE
(See also: Awe; Worship)

Reverence is essential to worship.
Frank Gabelein

We must rejoice in God, but still with a holy trembling.   *Matthew Henry*

The spirit which loses reverence for God turns naturally to sinning.   *John Hercus*

Reverence is the very first element of religion; it cannot but be felt by every-

one who has right views of the divine greatness and holiness, and of his own character in the sight of God.
Charles Simmons

REVIVAL

I believe nothing so distinctly causes the people of God in any generation to 'stand in awe' as when they hear of the great works of God in awakening his people powerfully. *John H. Armstrong*

A revival may produce noise, but it does not consist of it. The real thing is a whole-hearted obedience. *Ernest Baker*

Man can no more organize revival than he can dictate to the wind.
John Blanchard

Revival cannot be planned. It is a divine interruption. *John Blanchard*

It is easier to speak about revival than to set about it. *Horatius Bonar*

Revival is the exchange of the form of godliness for its living power. *John Bonar*

Evangelism is man working for God; revival is God working in a sovereign way on man's behalf. *F. Carlton Booth*

While revivals do not last, the effects of revival always endure. *F. Carlton Booth*

Revival is not the top blowing off but the bottom falling out. *Darrell Bridges*

A revival of religion . . . consists in new spiritual life imparted to the dead and in new spiritual health imparted to the living. *James Buchanan*

In our biblical desire for revival, we must refuse to seek any experience which proposes to eliminate our natural weakness. *Walter Chantry*

No true revival has ever fed the ego of man, or encouraged superficiality.
Bob Cotton

When God is about to do a great work, he pours out a spirit of supplication.
Jonathan Edwards

When God visits his church according to his promises, effects follow that make people shout, 'This is the finger of God!'
John Elias

It is misguided to think that God will revive a people who find no time to commune with him from the heart.
Jim Faucett

All ministers should be revival ministers, and all preaching should be revival preaching. *Charles G. Finney*

Revival is nothing else than a new beginning of obedience to God . . . a deep repentance, a breaking down of heart, a getting down into the dust before God with deep humility, and a forsaking of sin.
Charles G. Finney

There can be no revival when Mr Amen and Mr Wet-Eyes are not found in the audience. *Charles G. Finney*

Every revival that ever came in the history of the world, or in the history of the church, laid great emphasis on the holiness of God. *Billy Graham*

It may seem mysterious that God should permit a work of his own holy and blessed Spirit to be accompanied, marred and

perverted by errors and abuses. But so it has been from the beginning
Ashbel Green

A revival is a work of God's Spirit among his own people. *Vance Havner*

Sunday morning Christianity is the greatest hindrance to true revival.
Vance Havner

There never was a real revival that did not produce heartburn and hallelujahs.
Vance Havner

Revival is God rending the heavens and coming down upon his people.
Vance Havner

Revival is not going down the street with a big drum; it is going back to Calvary with a big sob. *Roy Hession*

In every period when God has awakened his people, the gospel of justification has come to the fore. *Robert M. Horn*

An indispensable sign of true revival is that the Word of God grows mightily and prevails — it spreads widely and grows in power. *Erroll Hulse*

The chief mark of authentic revival is enduring repentance. *Erroll Hulse*

Revival is a sovereign act of God upon the church whereby he intervenes to lift the situation completely out of human hands and works in extraordinary power.
Geoffrey R. King

A revival never needs to be advertised, it always advertises itself.
D. Martyn Lloyd-Jones

You cannot stop a revival any more than you can start it. It is altogether in the hands of God. *D. Martyn Lloyd-Jones*

Revival is a series of new beginnings.
David McKee

Revive thy work, O Lord,
Thy mighty arm make bare;
Speak with the voice that wakes the dead
And make thy people hear.
Albert Midlane

You can have evangelism without revival, but you cannot have revival without evangelism. *Brian Mills*

We ought to be so living that when God begins his great triumphant march we shall fall in with the first battalion, and have part in the first victories.
G. Campbell Morgan

In any biblical revival the norm is heightened; it is not suspended while another type of Christianity is introduced.
Iain H. Murray

The characteristic of a revival is that a profound consciousness of sin is produced in many persons at the same time by an awareness of God. *Iain H. Murray*

Revival is not some emotion or worked-up excitement; it is an invasion from heaven that brings a conscious awareness of God. *Stephen Olford*

Waiting for general revival is no excuse for not enjoying personal revival.
Stephen Olford

The best definition of revival is 'times of refreshing . . . from the presence of the Lord'. *J. Edwin Orr*

Revival

Revival means the work of God restoring to a ... church, in a manner out of the ordinary, those standards which the New Testament sets forth as being entirely ordinary. *J. I. Packer*

The devil keeps step with God, and when revival comes it is always a mixed work, hard to identify just because so much error, fanaticism and disorder are mixed up in it. *J. I. Packer*

Revival is the inrush of God's Spirit into a body which threatens to become a corpse. *D. M. Paton*

True revival has always begun with and resulted in separation. *Vernon Patterson*

Revival is never the end of the church's problems, nor is it intended to be ... but better the problems of life than of death! *Derek Prime*

The most important motive for prayer for revival is the glory of God. *Derek Prime*

There is no revival possible in any fellowship without a price being paid. *Alan Redpath*

A revival out of balance is soon a revival out of power. *Richard Owen Roberts*

Revival is the extraordinary movement of the Holy Spirit producing extraordinary results. *Richard Owen Roberts*

A revival is from God or it is no revival at all. *Wilbur M. Smith*

It is a revival of scriptural knowledge, of vital godliness and of practical obedience. *William B. Sprague*

Christian men should never speak of 'getting up a revival'. Where are you going to get it up from? *C. H. Spurgeon*

Divine omnipotence is the doctrine of a revival. *C. H. Spurgeon*

God is more willing to give revival than we are to receive it. *Erlo Stegan*

You can pray until dooms-day for revival, but you will never get it without repentance and confession of sin in the Christian life. *Erlo Stegan*

The true spirit of revival eludes the grasp of the organizer and the advertiser. It cannot be created by machinery nor promoted by printer's ink. *James A. Stewart*

To prepare our hearts for revival is to prepare for heaven, so that in a true sense we can say that preparation for revival *is* revival. *William Still*

It is useless for large companies of believers to spend long hours begging God to send revival. Unless we intend to reform we may as well not pray. *A. W. Tozer*

They tell me a revival is only temporary; so is a bath, but it does you good. *Billy Sunday*

By definition, revival is not meant to last, though it can pass sooner than intended on account of Christians quenching and grieving the Holy Spirit. *H. N. J. Waite*

There is nothing in the whole scene of religion that is of the order of revival. *H. N. J. Waite*

Revival is divine intervention in the normal course of spiritual things. It is God revealing himself to man in awful holiness and irresistible power. *Arthur Wallis*

In one sense, Pentecost can never happen again. In another sense, it may always be happening, since we live in the age of the Spirit. *Arthur Skevington Wood*

It may be said that revivals thrive on the Word and the Word is exalted in revivals. *Arthur Skevington Wood*

Revival is a sad necessity.
Arthur Skevington Wood

Revival is not an earthly concoction; it is a heavenly creation.
Arthur Skevington Wood

Revival is not something we have and must seek to keep, but something we lack and must plead to receive.
Arthur Skevington Wood

Revival makes the ideal real within the church of God.
Arthur Skevington Wood

The greatest hindrance to revival is pride amongst the Lord's people.
Arthur Skevington Wood

RICHES
(See also: Materialism; Money; Possessions; Prosperity; Wealth)

Riches and content are like two buckets; while one comes up full the other goes down empty. *Thomas Adams*

Gold can no more fill the spirit of man than grace his purse. *Anon.*

If your treasure is on earth, you are going from it; if it is in heaven, you are going to it. *Anon.*

No amount of riches can atone for poverty of character. *Anon.*

Earthly riches are full of poverty. *Augustine*

No man can tell whether he is rich or poor by turning to his ledger. It is the heart that makes a man rich. He is rich or poor according to what he is, not according to what he has. *Henry Ward Beecher*

Of all the riches that we hug ... we can carry no more out of this world than out of a dream. *James Bonnell*

The fullness of the earth can never satisfy the soul. *William Bridge*

As it is not the great cage that makes the bird sing, so it is not the great estate that makes the happy life, nor the great portion that makes the happy soul.
Thomas Brooks

Earthly riches are called thorns, and well they may; for as thorns, they pierce both head and heart; the head with cares in getting them, and the heart with grief in parting with them. *Thomas Brooks*

If the whole world were changed into a globe of gold it could not fill thy heart.
Thomas Brooks

It is the best riches not to desire riches.
Thomas Brooks

You may as well fill a bag with wisdom, a chest with riches, or a circle with a triangle, as the heart of man with anything here below. A man may have enough of the world to sink him, but he can never have enough to satisfy him.
Thomas Brooks

He is rich who has enough to be charitable. *Thomas Browne*

It is not the fact that a man has riches which keeps him from the kingdom of heaven, but the fact that riches have him.
T. Caird

Where there is no want there is usually much wantonness. *John Flavel*

The pride of dying rich raises the loudest laugh in hell. *John Foster*

Not possession, but use, is the only riches.
Thomas Fuller

Riches have made more covetous men than covetousness has made rich men.
Thomas Fuller

Riches may leave us while we live; we must leave them when we die.
Thomas Fuller

Riches rather enlarge than satisfy appetites. *Thomas Fuller*

The truly godly person is not interested in becoming rich. He possesses inner resources which furnish riches far beyond that which earth can offer.
William Hendriksen

Riches, like dust, slip through our fingers even when we hold them fast.
Matthew Henry

Man takes great pains to heap up riches, and they are like heaps of manure in the furrows of the field, good for nothing unless they be spread. *Matthew Henry*

There is a burden of care in getting riches, fear in keeping them, temptation in using them, guilt in abusing them, sorrow in losing them, and a burden of account at last to be given concerning them.
Matthew Henry

It is better being rich in grace than rich in purse. *James Janeway*

No kind of riches is a passport to the kingdom of heaven. *C. S. Lewis*

God commonly gives riches to foolish people to whom he gives nothing else.
Martin Luther

A man may be rich and godly, but it is because now and then God will work some miracles of grace. *Thomas Manton*

God gave us riches as a means to escape wrath, by a liberal and charitable distribution of them to his glory.
Thomas Manton

Riches with a blessing are so far from being a hindrance to grace that they are an ornament to it. *Thomas Manton*

It ill disposes the servant to seek to be rich and great and honoured in this world where his Lord was poor and mean and despised. *George Muller*

Nobody leaves the world richer than when he came in. *Stuart Olyott*

While riches are they are not.
William Secker

Many a millionaire, after choking his soul with gold-dust, has died from melancholia! *E. K. Simpson*

Riches are no curse when they are blessed of the Lord. *C. H. Spurgeon*

I'm glad I did not inherit a fortune. It would have ruined me. *R. A. Torrey*

Riches, as glass, are bright but brittle.
John Trapp

What good is there in having a fine suit with the plague in it?   *John Trapp*

A shoe may have a silver lace on it, yet pinch the foot.   *Thomas Watson*

Riches are but sugared lies, pleasant impostures, like a gilded cover which has not one leaf of true comfort bound up in it.   *Thomas Watson*

The world's golden sands are quicksands.
   Thomas Watson

I fear, wherever riches have increased, the essence of religion has decreased in the same proportion.   *John Wesley*

To lay up treasure on earth is as plainly forbidden by our Master as adultery and murder.   *John Wesley*

Riches are not evil but they are dangerous.   *John White*

RICHES — Spiritual — See Spiritual Riches

RIGHTEOUSNESS — See Christ-likeness; Godliness; Holiness

RITUALISM
(See also: Formalism; Hypocrisy)

Ritualism supplants Christ.
   George Barlow

Christ and ritualism are opposed to each other, as light is to darkness. The cross and crucifix cannot agree. Either ritualism will banish Christ or Christ will banish ritualism.   *Horatius Bonar*

Ritualism has always been the rival of true religion.   *Richard Glover*

The path of piety avoids ritualism and rationalism.   *Richard Glover*

Ritualism, like eczema in the human body, is generally a symptom of a low state of blood.   *A. J. Gordon*

RUMOUR
(See also: Gossip; Slander; Speech)

Trying to squash a rumour is like trying to unring a bell.   *Shana Alexander*

A rumour is about as hard to unspread as butter.   *Anon.*

Rumour is one thing that gets thicker as you spread it.   *Anon.*

There's only one thing as difficult as unscrambling an egg, and that's unspreading a rumour.   *Anon.*

It is said that 'where there's smoke there's fire'; but the smoke may be no more than dust and hot air.   *John Blanchard*

There is no such thing as an 'idle rumour'. Rumours are always busy.   *F. G. Kernan*

I know nothing swifter in life than the voice of rumour.   *Plautus*

Believe not half you hear; repeat not half you believe; when you hear an evil report, halve it, then quarter it, and say nothing about the rest.   *C. H. Spurgeon*

Rumour is a loud liar, like a snowball that gathers as it goes.   *John Trapp*

The first tale is good till the second be heard.   *John Trapp*

The tale-bearer is an incendiary.
   Thomas Watson

SABBATH — See Lord's Day

SACRIFICE

Sacrifice is the ecstasy of giving the best we have to the one we love the most.
Anon.

Sacrifice is the giving up of something we genuinely value in order to express our devotion to God. *John Benton*

He is no fool who gives what he cannot keep to gain what he cannot lose.
Jim Elliot

Too much of our Christianity today is drenched with sentiment, but devoid of sacrifice. *Frank Farley*

Sacrifice without obedience is sacrilege.
William Gurnall

I never made a sacrifice. We ought not to talk of sacrifice when we remember the great sacrifice that he made who left his Father's throne on high to give himself for us. *David Livingstone*

The sign of our professed love for the gospel is the measure of sacrifice we are prepared to make in order to help its progress. *Ralph P. Martin*

God will be our compensation for every sacrifice we have made. *F. B. Meyer*

Self-denial is not so much an impoverishment as a postponement: we make a sacrifice of present good for the sake of a future and greater good. *George Muller*

Nothing less than a living sacrifice is demanded. Not a loan, but a gift; not a compromise, but a sacrifice; not our poorest, but our best; not a dead but a living offering. Each drop of our blood, each ounce of our energy, each throb of our heart, we must offer to God.
Joseph Pearce

A religion which costs nothing is worth nothing. *J. C. Ryle*

God knows all about my health and need of a rest and need of many other things regarded as absolutely necessary ... I gladly laugh at being without them, and rejoice in a living death with a marvellous joy in order to fill the place that others have left unoccupied whatever their reasons for so doing. *C. T. Studd*

If Jesus Christ be God and died for me, then no sacrifice can be too great for me to make for him. *C. T. Studd*

God is looking for some wicks to burn. The oil and the fire are free.
J. Hudson Taylor

The only life that counts is the life that costs. *Frederick P. Wood*

SADNESS — See Sorrow

SALVATION
(See also: Atonement; Redemption)

God's plan and purpose of salvation is like himself, it is eternal. *Eric Alexander*

In creation, God shows us his hand; in salvation, his heart. *Anon.*

The surest token of God's good will towards us is his good work in us. *Anon.*

Perfection demands perfection; that is why salvation must be by grace, and why works are not sufficient.
Donald Grey Barnhouse

Salvation, the salvation of man, is the final purpose of the whole Bible.
J. H. Bernard

There is no such thing as salvation by character; what men need is salvation from character. *John Blanchard*

To save a single soul is beyond the combined legislation of the world's parliaments, the combined power of the world's armies, the combined wealth of the world's banks and the combined skill of the world's orators. *John Blanchard*

We are saved not by merit but by mercy.
John Blanchard

God never saves a spectator.
Robert Brown

They never sought in vain that sought the Lord aright. *Robert Burns*

Our salvation consists in the doctrine of the cross. *John Calvin*

Anyone can devise a plan by which good people may go to heaven. Only God can devise a plan whereby sinners, who are his enemies, can go to heaven.
Lewis Sperry Chafer

The soul was made for God. He who is saved from sin possesses the utmost felicity that the soul can enjoy, in this or the coming world. *Adam Clarke*

The death-struck sinner, like the wan, anaemic, dying invalid, is saved by having poured into his veins the healthier blood of Christ. *Henry Drummond*

If there be ground for you to trust in your own righteousness, then all that Christ did to purchase salvation, and all that God did to prepare the way for it is in vain.
Jonathan Edwards

Souls are not saved in bundles.
Ralph Waldo Emerson

There are as many paths to Christ as there are feet to tread them, but there is only one way to God. *A. Lindsay Glegg*

God did not save us to make us happy but to make us holy. *Vance Havner*

Our salvation includes more than pardon from sin, deliverance from hell and a ticket to heaven. It includes all that we shall need on our journey. *Vance Havner*

Salvation does not come from assent of the head but by the consent of the heart.
Vance Havner

Salvation is not a cafeteria where you take what you want and leave the rest. You cannot take Christ as Saviour and refuse him as Lord and be saved. *Vance Havner*

Salvation is a happy security and a secure happiness. *William Jenkyn*

Salvation is a helmet, not a nightcap!
Vance Havner

A chain is as strong as its weakest link. If but one link of the ten thousand is of the sinner's making, he is hopelessly lost.
R. B. Kuiper

Nowhere does the Bible tell us that salvation is by a faith that does not work.
R. B. Kuiper

Salvation is only by a working faith. In short, good works are the fruit of saving faith. They are also the proof of saving faith. *R. B. Kuiper*

The scriptural doctrine of God and scriptural doctrine of salvation are inseparable and interdependent.   *R. B. Kuiper*

Whatever contribution men make to their salvation they make by the grace of God. And that makes salvation the work of grace a hundred per cent.   *R. B. Kuiper*

Christ is not only the Saviour but the salvation itself.   *Matthew Henry*

Our salvation is so well contrived, so well concerted, that God may have mercy upon poor sinners, and be at peace with them, without any wrong to his truth and righteousness.   *Matthew Henry*

Salvation originates not in man but in God.   *Simon J. Kistemaker*

All our salvation consists in the manifestation of the nature, life and Spirit of Jesus in our inward new man.
William Law

The salvation of a single soul is more important than the production or preservation of all the epics and tragedies in the world.   *C. S. Lewis*

Salvation has nothing what-ever to do with temperament.
D. Martyn Lloyd-Jones

A man cannot be thoroughly humbled until he comes to know that his salvation is utterly beyond his own powers, counsel, endeavours, will and works and is absolutely dependent upon the will, counsel and pleasure of another. *Martin Luther*

If salvation could be attained only by working hard, then surely horses and donkeys would be in heaven.
Martin Luther

No man stands so tall as when he kneels and asks God to set the record straight.
Roy O. McClain

Christ is the final word about salvation. Here, he is not only without a peer, he is without a competitor.
G. Campbell Morgan

God's plan of salvation is not an afterthought; it antedates the work of creation.
J. A. Motyer

Salvation is moving from living death to deathless life.   *Jack Odell*

Feelings of confidence about our salvation need to be tested before they are trusted.   *J. I. Packer*

No sinner was ever saved by giving his heart to God. We are not saved by our giving, we are saved by God's giving.
A. W. Pink

The casting out of demons is ascribed to God's 'finger'; his delivering of Israel from Egypt to his 'hand'; but when the Lord saves a sinner it is his 'holy arm' which gets him the victory.   *A. W. Pink*

The will of the Father is the originating cause of our salvation, the worth of the Son's redemption its meritorious cause and the work of the Spirit its effectual cause.   *A. W. Pink*

Were God only to 'invite', every one of us would be lost.   *A. W. Pink*

Except the names given to God and our Saviour, there is no sweeter word than salvation.   *William S. Plumer*

If there is any greater exercise of power than that which brought all things out of nothing, it is that which brings a clean thing out of an unclean, or makes a saint out of a sinner. *William S. Plumer*

Salvation excels all the miracles ever wrought. *William S. Plumer*

The essence of sin is arrogance; the essence of salvation is submission.
Alan Redpath

All that is necessary for salvation is accomplished in Christ's work, even the guarantee of its application.
Ernest Reisinger

I have no rights to work out my own salvation in the way I choose.
Helen Roseveare

That Christ and a forgiven sinner should be made one, and share heaven between them, is the wonder of salvation; what more could love do? *Samuel Rutherford*

Who could be saved if God were not God, and if he were not such a God as he is?
Samuel Rutherford

Let it be a settled principle in our religion that men's salvation, if saved, is wholly of God; and that man's ruin, if lost, is wholly of himself. *J. C. Ryle*

God gets more out of your salvation than you ever will. *David Shepherd*

Salvation is no precarious half-measure but a foundation laid in heaven.
E. K. Simpson

Christ promises to save his people from their sins, not in their sins. *C. H. Spurgeon*

If any man ascribes anything of salvation, even the very least thing, to the free will of man, he knows nothing of grace, and he has not learned Jesus Christ rightly. *C. H. Spurgeon*

If there is to be in our celestial garment but one stitch of our own making we are all of us lost. *C. H. Spurgeon*

It is not your hold of Christ that saves, but his hold of you! *C. H. Spurgeon*

Many people think that when we preach salvation, we mean salvation from going to hell. We do mean that, but we mean a great deal more: we preach salvation from *sin.* We say that Christ is able to save a man, and we mean by that that he is able to save him from sin and to make him holy, to make him a new man.
C. H. Spurgeon

Salvation *in* sin is not possible; it always must be salvation *from* sin.
C. H. Spurgeon

Salvation is not deliverance from hell alone, it is deliverance from sin.
C. H. Spurgeon

The greatest of all miracles is the salvation of a soul. *C. H. Spurgeon*

There are two hopeless things, salvation without Christ and salvation without holiness. *C. T. Studd*

God does not owe you salvation. You deserve damnation, but he provides salvation. *Billy Sunday*

We need to be delivered from the freedom which is absolute bondage into the bondage which is perfect freedom.
William Temple

It is God alone who saves, and that in every element of the saving process.
Benjamin B. Warfield

Our salvation is a pure gratuity from God.
Benjamin B. Warfield

Not for our duties or deserts,
But of his own abounding grace
He works salvation in our hearts,
And forms a people for his praise.
Isaac Watts

SANCTIFICATION — See Holiness

SATAN — Activity

The devil is not always at one door. *Anon.*

Nothing promotes the activity of the devil more than the Christian's proximity to God. *John Blanchard*

The devil entangles youth with beauty, the miser with gold, the ambitious with power, the learned with false doctrine.
H. G. Bohn

If God were not my friend, Satan would not be so much my enemy.
Thomas Brooks

Satan promises the best, but pays with the worst; he promises honour and pays with disgrace; he promises pleasure and pays with pain; he promises profit and pays with loss; he promises life and pays with death. *Thomas Brooks*

Wherever God has his church, the devil will be sure to set up his chapel; not a chapel of ease for the saints, but a chapel of service for himself. *William Burkitt*

Satan does not work haphazardly but attacks systematically. *Thomas Cosmades*

The devil wrestles with God, and the field of battle is the human heart.
Fyodor Dostoyevski

This world has Satan's graffiti all over it.
Brian Edwards

I think the devil has made it his business to monopolize on three elements: noise, hurry, crowds . . . Satan is quite aware of the power of silence. *Jim Elliot*

Our adversary majors in three things: noise, hurry and crowds.
Richard J. Foster

Satan commonly stops the ear from hearing sound doctrine before he opens it to embrace corrupt. *William Gurnall*

The devil sometimes ... borrows God's bow to shoot his arrows from.
William Gurnall

No sooner is a temple built to God, but the devil builds a chapel hard by.
George Herbert

Satan, the great adversary, directs all his energy to prevent men becoming the subject of that illumination of which the gospel, as the revelation of the glory of Christ, is the source. *Charles Hodge*

The devil makes little of sin, that he may retain the sinner. *Rowland Hill*

The devil is the most diligent of preachers. *Hugh Latimer*

The devil will rather play at small game than no game at all. *Christopher Love*

The devil allows no Christian to reach heaven with clean feet all the way.
Martin Luther

There is no estate to which Satan is so opposed as to marriage. *Martin Luther*

If Satan dared to use Scripture for the temptation of our Lord he will not scruple to use it for the delusion of men.
Donald MacLeod

Satan has no constructive purpose of his own: his tactics are simply to thwart God and destroy men. *J. I. Packer*

The devil's war is better than the devil's peace. Suspect dumb holiness. When the dog is kept out of doors he howls to be let in again. *Samuel Rutherford*

Nowhere perhaps is the devil so active as in a congregation of gospel-hearers.
J. C. Ryle

There is no enemy worse than an enemy who is never seen and never dies, who is near to us wherever we live and goes with us wherever we go. *J. C. Ryle*

Satan is adept in teaching us how to steal our Master's glory. *C. H. Spurgeon*

Satan watches for those vessels that sail without a convoy. *George Swinnock*

The devil, that great peripatetic.
John Trapp

Satan has spite against the new creature.
Thomas Watson

The devil does not care how many sermon pills you take, so long as they do not work upon your conscience.
Thomas Watson

The devil is a busy bishop in his diocese.
Thomas Watson

SATAN — Existence and nature

The devil always leaves a stink behind him. *Anon.*

There is no need for ignorance concerning the devices of the devil, for they are set forth plainly in the Word of God, and they are also visible all around us.
Donald Grey Barnhouse

To deny the fact of Satan is to deny the truth of Scripture. *John Blanchard*

We are opposed by a living, intelligent, resourceful and cunning enemy who can outlive the oldest Christian, outwork the busiest, outfight the strongest and outwit the wisest. *John Blanchard*

To Satan no sight is beautiful but deformity itself, and no smell is sweet but filth and nastiness. *John Calvin*

The devil was educated in the best divinity school in the universe, viz the heaven of heavens. *Jonathan Edwards*

If you don't believe in the devil's existence, just try resisting him for a while.
Charles G. Finney

No player hath so many dresses to come in upon the stage with as the devil hath forms of temptation. *William Gurnall*

The devil is a great student in divinity.
William Gurnall

The devil's *nature* shows his power; it is angelical. *William Gurnall*

God is the Great I AM. Satan is the great 'I am not'; and he is never happier than when he has convinced people that he is non-existent. *Vance Havner*

Satan is not fighting churches; he is joining them. He does more harm by sowing tares than by pulling up wheat. He accomplishes more by imitation than by outright opposition. *Vance Havner*

The devil's image complete is a complication of malice and falsehood.
Matthew Henry

Of all created beings the wickedest is one who originally stood in the immediate presence of God. *C. S. Lewis*

Just as God cannot lie, the devil cannot do anything else. *R. C. Lucas*

I believe Satan to exist for two reasons: first, the Bible says so; and second, I've done business with him. *D. L. Moody*

Satan doesn't care what we worship, as long as we don't worship God.
D. L. Moody

The devil's greatest asset is the doubt people have about his existence.
John Nicola

Satan was the original sinner. *J. I. Packer*

The natural response to denials of Satan's existence is to ask, who then runs his business? *J. I. Packer*

The devil has more knowledge than any of us, and yet is no better for it. *J. C. Ryle*

The devil deserves his name. *Henry Smith*

Certain theologians, nowadays, do not believe in the existence of Satan. It is singular when children do not believe in the existence of their own father.
C. H. Spurgeon

There is something very comforting in the thought that the devil is an adversary. I would sooner have him for an adversary than a friend. *C. H. Spurgeon*

It is the devil's concern to keep his existence, presence, and working, secret. He chooses to work in the dark. *William Still*

SATAN — Limitations

Satan has only a persuading sleight, not an enforcing might. *Thomas Brooks*

Satan ... can do nothing without the command of God, to whose dominion he is subject. *John Calvin*

The whole of Satan's kingdom is subject to the authority of Christ. *John Calvin*

Everything the devil does, God overreaches to serve his own purpose.
Oswald Chambers

God makes the devil a polisher while he intends to be a destroyer.
Stephen Charnock

Satan is God's ape. *Stephen Charnock*

Our arch-enemy is to be cast into hell — and it will take only *one* angel to bind him! *A. Lindsay Glegg*

Did the Christian consider what Satan's power is, and who dams it up, this would always be a song of praise in his mouth.
William Gurnall

God sets the devil to catch himself.
William Gurnall

Satan, as in his first temptation, is still on the losing side. *William Gurnall*

The devil shall never lift his head higher than the saint's heel. *William Gurnall*

Satan cannot give the Christian anything, for he has everything; nor can he take

away anything, because he has nothing.
Vance Havner

Satan can afflict us, tempt us, only with divine permission. *Frank Retief*

Satan, the hinderer, may build a barrier about us, but he can never roof us in, so that we cannot look up. *J. Hudson Taylor*

There are references in the Bible to the devil's wiles and his shrewdness. But when he gambled on his ability to unseat the Almighty he was guilty of an act of judgement so bad as to be imbecilic.
A. W. Tozer

Satan's malice is always frustrated by God and made to minister a blessing to his people. The 'all things' of Romans 8:28 admit of no exceptions.
Geoffrey B. Wilson

The work of Satan is over-ruled so that it assists in bringing to pass the divine purpose, though Satan on his part uses his utmost powers to thwart that purpose.
Geoffrey B. Wilson

SATAN — Power

The devil is old, but not infirm. *Anon.*

The devil has no difficulty in making sin look innocent. *John Blanchard*

Satan is an acute theologian. *John Calvin*

Wherever God erects a house of prayer,
The devil's sure to have a chapel there;
And 'twill be found upon examination,
The latter has the largest congregation.
Daniel Defoe

Adam's fall was the devil's masterpiece.
Elisha Coles

The devil's *nature* shows his power; it is angelical. *William Gurnall*

Satan produces mental and spiritual anaesthetics more potent than any shot from a needle. *Vance Havner*

When Satan fell he may have lost his innocence but he did not lose his intelligence. *Trevor Knight*

Satan's might is such that Almightiness alone exceeds. *Henry Law*

Satan has three titles in the Scriptures, setting forth his malignity against the church of God: a dragon, to note his malice; a serpent, to note his subtlety; and a lion, to note his strength.
Edward Reynolds

Even as great an angel as Michael the archangel did not dare take on Satan alone but called on the Lord to rebuke him. No Christian, then, should ever feel that he is wise enough or powerful enough to engage Satan apart from complete dependence on the Lord.
Charles Caldwell Ryrie

The devil can cite Scripture for his purpose. *William Shakespeare*

He can make men dance upon the brink of hell as though they were on the verge of heaven. *C. H. Spurgeon*

The devil is a better theologian than any of us and is a devil still. *A. W. Tozer*

SATAN — Resisting

It is easy to bid the devil to be your guest, but difficult to get rid of him. *Anon.*

The devil has got to be resisted, not merely deprecated. *Michael Green*

Without a death to self, there is no escape from Satan's power over us.
William Law

'Resisting the devil' does not mean 'rebuking' him by shouting at him. It refers to a godly lifestyle of submission to God, a break with the friendship of the world and a spirit of personal humility.
Frank Retief

Let us learn not to fondle Satan.
Augustus H. Strong

Have the devil for your taskmaster and you will have him also for your paymaster.
John Trapp

SATAN — Subtlety

The devil's boots don't creak.   *Anon.*

Self-righteousness is the devil's masterpiece.   *Thomas Adams*

The devil is usually good-looking.
John Blanchard

The devil is most devilish when respectable.   *Elizabeth Barrett Browning*

Satan paints God with his own colours.
Stephen Charnock

It is one of Satan's deep devices to call off the attention of the church from its own state to the condition of the world without and around her.   *H. G. Fish*

Satan deals in subtleties. Our Lord deals in simplicities.   *Vance Havner*

Satan does far more harm as an angel of light than as a roaring lion. *Vance Havner*

The devil shapes himself to the fashions of all men.   *William Jenkyn*

As an angel of light the devil is utterly self-effacing, so that you would never think to charge him with the sudden trouble that has emerged.   *R. T. Kendall*

Satan's most effective work is done when he deceives people into thinking all is well.   *Will Metzger*

The method of the evil one is to obscure himself behind some other object of worship.   *G. Campbell Morgan*

It is the oldest stratagem of Satan to disfigure the truth by misrepresentation.
Iain H. Murray

Satan is very clever; he knows exactly what bait to use for every place in which he fishes.   *A. W. Pink*

The devil hath power to assume a pleasing shape.   *William Shakespeare*

Sometimes the devil is a gentleman.
Percy Bysshe Shelley

The use of a counterfeit is Satan's most natural method of resisting the purposes of God.   *Stephen Slocum*

If men's trades can be called crafts, the devil's trade may be called craft.
Henry Smith

The fundamental deception of Satan is the lie that obedience can never bring happiness.   *R. C. Sproul*

The devil is by nature a deceiver, and what better occupation than deceiving men about himself!   *William Still*

The devil tries to shake truth by pretending to defend it.   *Tertullian*

The devil hunts more as a fox than as a lion; his snares are worse than his darts.
Thomas Watson

It is only by posing as the champion of truth that the prince of darkness is able to persuade men to swallow his lies.
Geoffrey B. Wilson

SAVING FAITH — See Faith — Saving

SCEPTISM

The sceptic may truly be said to be topsy-turvy; for his feet are dancing upwards in idle ecstasies, while his brain is in the abyss.
G. K. Chesterton

The sceptics' challenge is really presumptuous and arrogant. It is a claim by a finite creature to know how the world should have been created. How could a sceptic know such a thing?
C. Stephen Evans

Scepticism is an intellectual disease which cuts its victim off from everything in the world which is not known by the senses.
John H. Gerstner

Scepticism may be a nice game to play, but there is no way one can live on the basis of it.
Clark H. Pinnock

The city of truth cannot be built upon the swampy ground of scepticism.
Albert Schweitzer

SCIENCE

Science can add years to your life, but only Christ can add life to your years.
Anon.

A God proved by science would not be God. For I can prove only that which is by creation lower than I, that which is at my disposal.
Gerhard Bergmann

Science just does not have knowledge of the beginnings in the genuine sense of the term. It cannot answer the how, much less the why.
R. J. Berry

A miracle is by definition beyond the ability of science to explain and must therefore also be beyond the ability of science to disprove.
John Blanchard

Doing science is going through the process of discovering things that no man has known before, but which God has known all along.
John Blanchard

True science and belief in God have always been in perfect harmony with each other. Trying to drive a wedge between them is ignorance masquerading as intelligence.
John Blanchard

Sometimes people ask if science and religion are opposed to each other. They are, in the sense that the thumb and fingers of my hand are opposed to one another. It is an opposition by which anything can be grasped.
William Henry Bragg

A knowledge of all sciences is mere smoke where the heavenly science of Christ is wanting.
John Calvin

That God normally operates the universe consistently makes science possible; that he does not always do so ought to keep science humble.
D. A. Carson

It is a diabolical science ... which fixes our contemplations on the works of nature and turns them away from God.
John Calvin

Science is but a mere heap of facts, not a golden chain of truths, if we refuse to link it to the throne of God.   *F. B. Cobbe*

We have done wrong to set up any sharp antithesis between science and religion ... There is no other way out of our impasse than to assert that science is one aspect of God's presence. *C. A. Coulson*

The very sciences from which objections have been brought against religion have, by their own progress, removed those objections, and in the end furnished full confirmation of the inspired Word of God.
Tryon Edwards

I only trace the lines that flow from God.
Albert Einstein

Most people say it is the intellect which makes a great scientist. They are wrong; it is the character.   *Albert Einstein*

One thing I have learned in a long life — that all our science, measured against reality, is primitive and childlike.
Albert Einstein

Science can only ascertain what is, but not what should be, and outside its domain value judgements of all kinds remain necessary.   *Albert Einstein*

Science without religion is lame, religion without science is blind. *Albert Einstein*

The religion that is afraid of science dishonours God and commits suicide.
Ralph Waldo Emerson

I have never seen anything incompatible between those things of man which can be known by the spirit of man which is within him and those higher things concerning his future which cannot be known by that spirit. *Michael Faraday*

A true scientist is known by his confession of ignorance.   *A. O. Foster*

Science and religion no more contradict each other than light and electricity.
William Hiram Foulkes

Science cannot explain why the basic laws of nature are as they are. *Rob Frost*

In point of fact, there is no battle between an informed belief in God and the assured results of science.   *Michael Green*

Science knows nothing of rationality and consciousness, of personality and sociability.   *Michael Green*

Sin has got man into more trouble than science can get him out of. *Vance Havner*

Science can give us the 'know-how', but it cannot give us the 'know-why'.
J. N. Hawthorne

Science can in no way establish the claim that nothing supernatural or eternal can be real.   *Walter R. Hearn*

Science is not a process by which we go from no knowledge to some knowledge, or from some knowledge to total knowledge. Rather it is a process by which scientists go from some knowledge to more knowledge. The important feature of science is not that it *always* produces increased knowledge but that *sometimes* it does.   *Walter R. Hearn*

The Bible does not set forth a detailed description of the created world, as scientists seek to do, but repeatedly refers to that world as evidence of God's purposeful activity. The biblical answer to the question, 'Why does anything exist at all?' has not been superseded by scientific discoveries or surpassed by philosophical reasoning. *Walter R. Hearn*

To assume that we could not function as scientists while maintaining our identity and integrity as Christians would be like denying that a football player could also be good at chess. *Walter R. Hearn*

The person who thinks there can be any real conflict between science and religion must be either very young in science or very ignorant in religion. *Philip Henry*

Science helps us to study the cosmos and to increase our knowledge, but its primary function is to prepare us to worship the world's Creator. *W. Andrew Hoffecker*

Science does not of itself provide us with an ethical system, yet it raises many ethical issues. *Rodney D. Holder*

The existence of morality — the concepts of good and evil — are not explicable in mechanistic scientific terms. *Rodney D. Holder*

God pity the man of science who believes in nothing but what he can prove by scientific methods; for if ever a human being needed divine pity he does. *J. G. Holland*

God is not just active in those areas which science cannot explain, as if science were an alternative to God. Instead, our science *is* God's science. He holds the responsibility for the whole scientific story. Our problem is that our thoughts about God are far too small. *John Houghton*

It is impossible to prove scientifically any theory of origins. This is because the very essence of the scientific method is based on observation and experimentation, and it is impossible to make observations or conduct experiments on the origin of the universe. *Scott M. Huse*

Science cannot solve man's moral problems. *Carl Gustav Jung*

Our scientific power has out-run our spiritual power. We have guided missiles and misguided men. *Martin Luther King*

Men became scientific because they expected law in nature, and they expected law in nature because they believed in a Legislator. *C. S. Lewis*

There is nothing in modern science that invalidates the teaching of the Bible regarding God's care for his creatures; nay, there is much that wonderfully confirms it, if only we had eyes to see. Something other than true science has put the mist and darkness over men's eyes. *J. Gresham Machen*

Science is not a barrier to belief. If scientific education must inevitably lead to agnosticism or atheism, why are all great scientists not unbelievers? *Nigel McCullough*

Science that is unconstrained by ethics, or which remakes morality to suit its purposes, is a frightful prospect. *Nigel McCullouch*

The scientific method of observation, experiment and induction does not, and never can, apply to the whole reality of life. *Nigel McCullough*

Every formula which expresses a law of nature is a hymn of praise to God. *Maria Mitchell*

One cannot turn to science to justify science any more than one can pull oneself up by his own bootstraps. *J. P. Moreland*

Questions of meaning and value are outside the limits of science. They are not scientific questions at all. *J. P. Moreland*

There is no ascertained fact of science with which the Bible is out of harmony. There are some hypotheses of scientific investigators which are out of harmony with the biblical revelation. But there is a great difference between hypotheses and established fact. *G. Campbell Morgan*

Science cannot determine origin and so cannot determine destiny. As it presents only a sectional view of creation, it gives only a sectional view of everything in creation. *T. T. Munger*

No sciences are better attested than the religion of the Bible. *Isaac Newton*

Unfortunately for the scientifically minded, God is not discoverable or demonstrable by purely scientific means. But that really proves nothing; it simply means that the wrong instruments are being used for the job. *J. B. Phillips*

The demand for scientific objectivity makes it inevitable that every scientific statement must remain tentative for ever. *Karl Popper*

For every question scientists answer, the more they realize there are new questions to be answered. *Edgar Powell*

Science can never pontificate about origins. *Edgar Powell*

Science is a purposeful activity both because humans have been made lord over creation, and because God reveals his glory through creation. *Edgar Powell*

Scientific theories are simply the best representation of reality we have. Given the present level of knowledge. *Edgar Powell*

Science is a method God has given us to investigate the built-in patterns of physical phenomena. *Alan W. Rice*

'Science', if it contradicts Scripture, is not science but a species of blasphemy. *Maurice Roberts*

Every time a scientist works in his laboratory, he assumes the reality of God though he denies God with his lips. *R. J. Rushdoony*

The true scientist never loses the faculty of amazement. It is the essence of his being. *Hans Seyle*

It is impossible for science to correct the Word of God, but it is possible for science to correct the word of the theologian. *R. C. Sproul*

The very success of science in showing us how deeply ordered the natural world is provides strong grounds for believing that there is an even deeper cause of that order. *Richard Swinburne*

If God said that Jonah was swallowed by a whale, then the whale swallowed Jonah, and we do not need a scientist to measure the gullet of a whale. *A. W. Tozer*

The modern vogue of bringing science to the support of Christianity proves not the truth of the Christian faith but the gnawing uncertainty in the hearts of those who must look to science to give respectability to their faith. *A. W. Tozer*

Whenever I find men running to science to find support for the Bible, I know they are rationalists and not true believers. *A. W. Tozer*

The concept of strict and generally valid laws of nature could hardly have arisen without the Christian concept of creation.
C. F. Vonwezacher

Science has nothing to say to the deepest levels of human experience. What can science say to a heart being chilled by loneliness? What can science say to a heart broken by grief? What relief can science give to a life being turned prematurely grey by unforgiven sin and guilt? *Alan Walker*

Scientific investigation will only succeed if the universe is an intelligible and mathematically comprehensible unity, as theism supposes it to be. *Keith Ward*

Theism does not compete with science, but it does compete with materialism.
Keith Ward

The scientific way of looking at the world is not wrong any more than the glass-manufacturer's way of looking at the window. This way of looking at things has its very important uses. Nevertheless the window was placed there not to be looked at but to be looked through; and the world has failed of its purpose unless it too is looked through and the eye rests not on it but on its God.
Benjamin B. Warfield

True science is never dogmatic. It follows the evidence of eyes and ears wherever it may lead. *Thomas G. West*

Science has proved neither that the material universe is undirected, nor that our material explanations are adequate.
David Wilcox

Even when all possible scientific questions have been answered, the problems of human life remain completely untouched. *Ludwig Wittgenstein*

SCRIPTURE — See Bible

SECOND COMING OF CHRIST

He that rose from the clods we expect from the clouds. *Thomas Adams*

When it comes to belief in the Lord's return there are two kinds of Christians — gazers and goers. *Anon.*

He who loves the coming of the Lord is not he who affirms it is far off, nor is it he who says it is near. It is he who, whether it be far or near, awaits it with sincere faith, stead-fast hope and fervent love.
Augustine

That day lies hid that every day we be on the watch. *Augustine*

It is a bad sign when people start discussing eschatology instead of preparing for the coming of Christ. *John Blanchard*

Many people will be surprised when Jesus comes again — but nobody will be mistaken. *John Blanchard*

The certainty of the Second Coming of Christ should touch and tincture every part of our daily behavior.
John Blanchard

The Christ who rose from the earth and now reigns over earth will one day return to the earth. *John Blanchard*

When Christ returns, the second advent will no longer be a subject for discussion.
John Blanchard

Christ keeps the minds of believers in a state of suspense until the last day.
John Calvin

In the first advent God veiled his divinity to prove the faithful; in the second advent he will manifest his glory to reward their faith. *Chrysostom*

The only remedy for all this mass of misery is the return of our Lord Jesus Christ. Why do we not plead for it every time we hear the clock strike?
Anthony Ashley Cooper

As Christians, we should not be exitists, looking for our going, but adventists, looking for his coming. *William Freel*

The subject of the second coming of Christ has never been popular to any but the true believer. *Billy Graham*

Christ hath told us he will come, but not when, that we might never put off our clothes, or put out the candle.
William Gurnall

Oh, the joy to see thee reigning,
Thee, my own beloved Lord!
Every tongue thy name confessing,
Worship, honour, glory, blessing,
Brought to thee with glad accord —
Thee, my Master and my Friend,
Vindicated and enthroned,
Unto earth's remotest end
Glorified, adored and owned!
Frances Ridley Havergal

Christ will come when he pleases, to show his sovereignty, and will not let us know when, to teach us our duty.
Matthew Henry

When Jesus comes there will be instant job satisfaction for us. *David N. Jones*

If this is not an integral part of the faith once given to the saints, I do not know what is. *C. S. Lewis*

Precisely because we cannot predict the moment, we must be ready at all moments. *C. S. Lewis*

The primitive church thought a great deal more about the coming of Christ than about death, and thought a great deal more about his coming than about heaven. *Alexander MacLaren*

I never preach a sermon without thinking that possibly the Lord may come before I preach another. *D. L. Moody*

Christ is coming to the earth, in such form at least as shall fulfil his purposes of mercy to his friends and justice to his foes.
Thomas V. Moore

I never begin my work in the morning without thinking that perhaps *he* may interrupt my work and begin his own. I am not looking for death, I am looking for *him*. *G. Campbell Morgan*

There is such a danger of our being so occupied with the things that are to come more than with him who is to come.
Andrew Murray

Millions of graves are dug every year, but it is inspiring to think that one generation of Christians will cheat the undertaker. *J. C. Pollock*

Oh, that Christ would make long strides! Oh, that he would fold up the heavens as a cloak, and shovel time and days out of the way! *Samuel Rutherford*

In all our thoughts about Christ, let us never forget his second advent. *J. C. Ryle*

There shall be no time for parting words or a change of mind when the Lord appears. *J. C. Ryle*

Uncertainty about the date of the Lord's return is calculated to keep believers in an attitude of constant expectation and to preserve them from despondency. *J. C. Ryle*

When Christ comes again, the remains of ignorance shall be rolled away. *J. C. Ryle*

If I knew that our Lord would come this evening, I should preach just as I mean to preach; and if I knew he would come during this sermon, I would go on preaching until he did. *C. H. Spurgeon*

Oh, that the Lord would come! He is coming! He is on the road and travelling quickly. The sound of his approach should be as music to our hearts! *C. H. Spurgeon*

The fact that Jesus Christ is to come again is not a reason for star-gazing, but for working in the power of the Holy Ghost. *C. H. Spurgeon*

Since he may come any day, it is well to be ready every day. *J. Hudson Taylor*

He who came in humility and shame will return in spectacular magnificence. *John R. W. Stott*

The imminent return of our Lord is the great Bible argument for a pure, unselfish, devoted, unworldly, active life of service. *R. A. Torrey*

This is pinned as a badge to the sleeve of every true believer — that he looks for and longs for Christ's coming to judgement. *John Trapp*

The Christian hope is not a matter for tickling our minds, but for changing our minds and influencing society. *Stephen Travis*

I am daily waiting for the coming of the Son of God. *George Whitefield*

The brightness of Christ's advent will reveal the true character of those things which were previously hidden by darkness. *Geoffrey B. Wilson*

SECULARISM

Secularism is when the creature declares the Creator redundant. *Dan Beeby*

In attacking the faith which gave it life, secularism has destroyed its own life-blood. *Martin Robinson*

SECURITY

Security is not the absence of danger, but the presence of God, no matter what the danger. *Anon.*

They are well kept whom God keeps. *Anon.*

If the Father has the kingdom ready for us, he will take care of us on the way. *Andrew Bonar*

Should storms of sevenfold thunder roll,
And shake the globe from pole to pole;
No flaming bolt could daunt my face,
For Jesus is my hiding-place. *Jehoiada Brewer*

If God has said, 'I will never leave,' we may well say, 'What shall man do?' *John Brown*

Anyone who has the firm conviction that he will never be forsaken by the Lord will not be unduly anxious, because he will depend on his providence. *John Calvin*

Nothing is more foolish than a security built upon the world and its promises, for they are all vanity and a lie.
Matthew Henry

Everyone who is a man of God has omnipotence as his guardian, and God will sooner empty heaven of angels than leave a saint without defence.
C. H. Spurgeon

This only can my fears control,
And bid my sorrows fly;
What harm can ever reach my soul
Beneath my Father's eye?
Anne Steele

A sovereign Protector I have,
Unseen, yet for ever at hand,
Unchangeably faithful to save,
Almighty to rule and command.
He smiles, and my comforts abound;
His grace as the dew shall descend;
And walls of salvation surround
The soul he delights to defend.
Augustus M. Toplady

Should all the hosts of death,
And powers of hell unknown,
Put their most dreadful forms
Of rage and malice on,
I shall be safe, for Christ displays
Superior power and guardian grace.
Isaac Watts

SELF
(See also: Boasting; Conceit; Egotism; Pride)

A self-made man has no one to blame but himself. *Anon.*

Far too frequently in this life we are interested in only three persons: me, myself and I. *Anon.*

Self is always at home. *Anon.*

Self-will is so ardent and active that it will break a world in pieces to make a stool to sit on. *Anon.*

The hardest victory is victory over self.
Anon.

The man who lives only for himself runs a very small business. *Anon.*

The most common disease in the world is 'I' trouble. *Anon.*

The person who is all wrapped up in himself is overdressed. *Anon.*

The self-made man usually admires his maker. *Anon.*

You never cultivate self into anything but self. *Anon.*

O Lord, deliver me from the lust of always vindicating myself. *Augustine*

The biggest problem with me is 'I'.
Doug Barnett

It is the desiring of one's own way which leads to every other sin in the world.
Donald Grey Barnhouse

The truest self-respect is not to think of self. *Henry Ward Beecher*

No man can really at one and the same time call attention to himself and glorify God. *Louis Benes*

Materialism and self-centredness are forms of idolatry. *John Benton*

Deliver me, O Lord, from that evil man, myself. *Thomas Brooks*

The Christian needs a reminder every hour; some defeat, surprise, adversity, peril; to be agitated, mortified, beaten out of his course, so that all remains of self will be sifted out. *Horace Bushnell*

To live happily the evils of ambition and self-love must be plucked from our hearts by the roots. *John Calvin*

If you open your mouth to vindicate yourself you will lose what you might gain. *Oswald Chambers*

If one devil of self-interest is swept from the soul, seven self-schemes worse than the first will return with it unless the soul is fully employed with living unto him who died and rose again. *Walter J. Chantry*

'Self-centred Christian' is a term of impossible contradiction. *Walter J. Chantry*

Self is the chief end of every natural man. *Stephen Charnock*

Self-interest, of course, is the lowest form of motivation for doing what is morally right. *Mort Crim*

Talk to a man about himself and he will listen for hours. *Benjamin Disraeli*

If you must talk of yourself, let it be behind your own back. *George Eliot*

Self is the poise of the unsanctified heart. *John Flavel*

That household god, a man's own self. *John Flavel*

Beware of no man more than thyself. *Thomas Fuller*

Self is the destruction of safety and sanctity alike. *Richard Glover*

Self is the most abominable principle that ever was. *Thomas Goodwin*

Self is the soul, the spirit of unregeneracy. *Thomas Goodwin*

Self-love is king in unregenerate hearts. *Thomas Goodwin*

The rise of self is the beginning of unfaithfulness. *R. F. Horton*

Self often stands concealed in the shadows of the unconscious. *E. Stanley Jones*

The self-centred are the self-disrupted. *E. Stanley Jones*

Sensitivity about self — is not this one of the greatest curses in life? It is a result of the Fall. We spend the whole of our life watching ourselves. *D. Martyn Lloyd-Jones*

The whole trouble in life is ultimately a concern about self. *D. Martyn Lloyd-Jones*

I am more afraid of my own heart than of the pope and all his cardinals. I have within me the great pope — Self. *Martin Luther*

We never say that self is dead; were we to do so, self would be laughing at us round the corner. *F. B. Meyer*

I have more trouble with D. L. Moody than with any man I ever met. *D. L. Moody*

Nowhere does the self-centred heart of man more quickly take control than when it comes to the machinery of criticism and the promptings of self-interest.
J. A. Motyer

My true knowledge of self comes not from my searching myself but from God searching me. *Watchman Nee*

We have been saved from sin and its consequences in order to be delivered from self and its complexes. *Arthur Neil*

I have read of many wicked popes, but the worst pope I ever met with is Pope *Self.* *John Newton*

No man can free himself from himself.
Herman Olshausen

We can never distrust ourselves too much.
J. I. Packer

The man who lives by himself and for himself is apt to be corrupted by the company he keeps. *Charles H. Parkhurst*

Sin is a man's self. Just as 'I' is the centre letter of sin, so sin is the centre, the moving-power, the very life of self.
A. W. Pink

Most of the small quarrels and conflicts we have in life occur because self is being threatened, challenged or ignored.
Frank Retief

The personal pronoun might well be the coat of arms of some individuals.
Antoine Rivarol

Oh, wretched idol, myself.
Samuel Rutherford

Sinful self is to be destroyed and natural self is to be denied. *William Secker*

The greatest burden we have to carry in life is self. *Hannah Whitall Smith*

Beware of no man more than yourself; we carry our worst enemies within us.
C. H. Spurgeon

I would rather go to heaven doubting all the way than be lost through self-confidence. *C. H. Spurgeon*

How can self drive out self? As well expect Satan to drive out Satan!
John R. W. Stott

Self-derogation is bad for the reason that self must be there to derogate self. Self, whether swaggering or grovelling, can never be anything but hateful to God.
A. W. Tozer

Self-will is a close relative of pride.
A. W. Tozer

So subtle is self that scarcely anyone is aware of its presence. *A. W. Tozer*

Self is the only prison that can bind the soul. *Henry Van Dyke*

SELF-CONTROL
(See also: Discipline)

Never expect to govern others until you have learned to govern yourself. *Anon.*

Conquer yourself and you have conquered the world. *Augustine*

It is impossible to be a follower of Jesus without giving diligent attention in our lives to the grace of self-control.
Jerry Bridges

There is a form of self-control that says 'yes' to what we should do as well as that

which says 'no' to what we shouldn't do.
Jerry Bridges

The beginning of self-mastery is to be mastered by Christ, to yield to his lordship. *D. G. Kehl*

True spiritual self-discipline holds believers in bounds but never in bonds; its effect is to enlarge, expand and liberate.
D. G. Kehl

The man who disciplines himself stands out and has the mark of greatness upon him. *D. Martyn Lloyd-Jones*

No man is free who cannot command himself. *Pythagoras*

SELF-CRUCIFIXION
(See also: Humility; Meekness)

To resist one's cross is to make it heavier.
Henri Amiel

Life offers only two alternatives: crucifixion with Christ or self-destruction without him. *Anon.*

The concept of resurrection is welcomed by all, but the prior concern of self-crucifixion is a higher price than most men are willing to pay. *Anon.*

Self is to be dealt with by crucifixion, not forgiveness. *Donald Grey Barnhouse*

Kill sin before it kills you. *Richard Baxter*

The cross must be borne, carried; we are not at liberty to step over it, or go round to avoid it. *Richard Baxter*

If we truly place ourselves beneath the cross, then we will throw off lives of masquerade, of make-believe, of bluffing, of emptiness and of secret sin.
Gerhard Bergmann

To die to our own comforts, ambitions and plans is of the very essence of Christianity. *John Blanchard*

No man can meditate on the heavenly life unless he be dead to the world and to himself. *John Calvin*

No man is qualified to be a disciple of Christ until he has been divested of self.
John Calvin

The chief praise of Christians is self-renunciation. *John Calvin*

The mortification of the flesh is the quickening of the spirit. *John Calvin*

The only source of our mortification is our participation in the death of Christ.
John Calvin

Put relentless hands down into your hearts, and tear out by the roots everything that will not advance the interests of the Redeemer's kingdom. *B. H. Carroll*

Taking up the cross is the conscious choice of a painful alternative motivated by love for Christ. *Walter J. Chantry*

Without a cross there is no following Christ. *Walter J. Chantry*

All Christians lead a dying life; it is the secret of their strange vitality.
John Cordelier

Crucifixion is something that is done *to us;* it is not something that we do to ourselves. We can only initiate it by picking up the crossbar, that is, by a complete honest determination. *Arthur C. Custance*

God does not want us to think less of ourselves. He wants us not to think of ourselves at all. *Andrew Dhuse*

The believer mortifies because God is pacified towards him; the legalist mortifies that he may pacify God by his mortification . . . that he may have whereof to glory. *Ralph Erskine*

The greatest of all crosses is self — if we die in part every day we shall have but little to do on the last. These little daily deaths will destroy the power of the final dying. *François Fenelon*

There is no other way to live this Christian life than by a continual death to self. *François Fenelon*

You may ask me what is the cure of this love of self. There is no question of a cure; the thing must be killed. *François Fenelon*

No man has a velvet cross. *John Flavel*

We read in Scripture of taking up the cross, but never of laying it down. *J. Ford*

Self is the tumour of the soul, and it grows by what it feeds on. You cannot cure it by a few good resolutions. It requires the most drastic treatment, and Christ prescribes crucifixion as the only way of destroying this root of every kind of bitterness. *R. Moffatt Gantry*

If we do not let go of ourselves we can never reach him who is above us. *Gregory*

We are bid to take, not to make our cross. God in his providence will provide one for us. *William Gurnall*

The only thing we should do with self is consent to its crucifixion and co-operate with God in the process. *Vance Havner*

Let ... corrupt affections ... be mortified and not gratified. *Matthew Henry*

Without a death to self, there is no escape from Satan's power over us. *William Law*

A rejection, or in Scripture's strong language, a crucifixion of the natural self is the passport to everlasting life. Nothing that has not died will be resurrected. *C. S. Lewis*

Die before you die. There is no chance after. *C. S. Lewis*

If you're dead to self you can't hurt any more. *Kay Long*

God creates out of nothing. Therefore until a man is nothing, God can make nothing out of him. *Martin Luther*

You will be dead so long as you refuse to die. *George MacDonald*

Mortified Christians are the glory of Christ. *Thomas Manton*

'Crucified' is the only definitive adjective by which to describe the Christian life. *J. Furman Miller*

The cross is real wood, the nails are real iron, the vinegar truly tastes bitter, and the cry of desolation is live, not recorded. *Malcolm Muggeridge*

There was a day when I died to George Muller; his opinions and preferences, taste and will; died to the world, its approval or censure; died to the approval or blame even of my brethren or friends; and since then I have striven only to show

myself approved unto God.
George Muller

One of the ways of manifesting and maintaining the crucifixion of the flesh is never to use money to gratify it. *Andrew Murray*

What does it mean for me to be 'crucified'? I think the answer is best summed up in the words the crowd used of Jesus: 'Away with him!' *Watchman Nee*

Be killing sin or it will be killing you.
John Owen

He who ceases from mortification lets go all endeavours after holiness. *John Owen*

The choicest believers, who are assuredly freed from the condemning power of sin, ought yet to make it their business all their days to mortify the indwelling power of sin. *John Owen*

The vigour and power and comfort of our spiritual life depends on the mortification of the deeds of the flesh. *John Owen*

Mortification is war. *J. I. Packer*

Do we want 'unction'? Do we want 'power'? Do we want 'revival'? It would be a major step towards all three if we could only learn to crucify our accursed pride more ruthlessly. *Maurice Roberts*

The way of self-mortification is irksome to flesh and blood but it is the only safe way. *Maurice Roberts*

Christ's cross is the sweetest burden that ever I bare; it is such a burden as wings are to a bird or sails to a ship.
Samuel Rutherford

Christianity has a secret unknown to communists or capitalists ... *how to die to self.* This secret makes us invincible.
W. E. Sangster

If you do not die to sin, you shall die for sin. *C. H. Spurgeon*

Prepare yourselves, my younger brethren, to become weaker and weaker; prepare yourselves for sinking lower and lower in self-esteem; prepare yourselves for self-annihilation — and pray God to expedite the process. *C. H. Spurgeon*

We cannot save ourselves and save others; there must be a destruction of self for the salvation of men. *C. H. Spurgeon*

You will never glory in God till first of all God has killed your glorying in yourself. *C. H. Spurgeon*

To be sweet-smelling to God, we must be broken and poured out, not merely containers of a sweet smell. *C. T. Studd*

When you put your life on the altar, when you make ready and accept to die, you are invincible. You have nothing any more to lose. *Josif Ton*

Among the plastic saints of our times Jesus has to do all the dying and all we want to hear is another sermon about his dying. *A. W. Tozer*

The cross is rough, and it is deadly, but it is effective. *A. W. Tozer*

The cross is easier to him who takes it up than to him who drags it along. *J. E. Vaux*

Self-sacrifice brought Christ into the world, and self-sacrifice will lead his followers, not away from sin but into the midst of men. *Benjamin B. Warfield*

SELF-DELUSION

If you feel you have no faults, that makes another one.   *Anon.*

The easiest person to deceive is one's own self.   *Edward Bulwer-Lytton*

The heart of man has so many recesses of vanity, and so many retreats of falsehood, and is so enveloped with fraudulent hypocrisy, that it frequently deceives even himself.   *John Calvin*

The greatest fault is to be conscious of none.   *Thomas Carlyle*

Nothing is easier than self-deceit. For what each man wishes, that he also believes to be true.   *Demosthenes*

Nothing is so easy to deceive as one's self.   *Demosthenes*

Show me a thoroughly satisfied man and I will show you a failure. *Thomas Edison*

Humankind cannot bear very much reality.   *T. S. Eliot*

The fountains of self-deceit are four in number: the rarity of reliable self-knowledge, self's power to deceive self, self letting itself be deceived by others, and self deceived by Satan.
                              Frederick W. Faber

The ultimate tragedy of man's self-understanding is that he believes himself to be free, has all the feelings of a free agent, but does not realize that he is a slave to sin and serves the will of Satan.
                              Sinclair Ferguson

Self-deceivers will prove in the end self-destroyers.   *Matthew Henry*

We lie loudest when we lie to ourselves.
                                    Eric Hoffer

There is much self-delusion in our estimation of ourselves when we are untried, and in the midst of Christian friends, whose warm feelings give a glow to ours which they do not possess themselves.
                       Robert Murray McCheyne

We are so used to disguising ourselves to others that at last we become disguised even to ourselves.
                         Francois Rochefoucauld

Every man is a good man in a bad world —as he himself knows. *William Saroyan*

A sin is two sins when it is defended.
                                   Henry Smith

SELF-DENIAL

When self is not negated, it is necessarily worshipped.   *Anon.*

You deny Christ when you fail to deny yourself for Christ.   *Anon.*

For the proper use of no talent is self-denial more needed than for that of money.   *George Barlow*

Death is half disarmed when the pleasures and interests of the flesh are first denied.   *Richard Baxter*

It is easier to give anything we have than to give ourselves.   *John Blanchard*

All who have not been influenced by the principle of self-denial have followed virtue merely from the love of praise.
                                    John Calvin

Show me a single man who does not

believe in the Lord's law of self-denial, and who yet willingly practises virtue among men. *John Calvin*

The denial of ourselves will leave no room for pride, haughtiness, or vainglory, nor for avarice, licentiousness, love of luxury, wantonness, or any sin born from self-love. *John Calvin*

There is no end and no limit to the obstacles of the man who wants to pursue what is right and at the same time shrinks back from self-denial. *John Calvin*

All of the great spiritual delights we long for come into the world of a Christian's experience attended with the birth-pangs of self-denial. *Walter J. Chantry*

All great virtues bear the imprint of self-denial. *William E. Charming*

As a man goes down in self he goes up in God. *G. B. Cheever*

Surely those who know the great passionate heart of Jehovah must deny their own loves to share in the expression of his! *Jim Elliot*

Whoever will labour to get rid of self, to deny himself according to the instruction of Christ, strikes at once at the root of every evil and finds the germ of every good. *François Fenelon*

To deny self is to become a nonconformist. The Bible tells us not to be conformed to this world either physically or intellectually or spiritually. *Billy Graham*

The first lesson in Christ's school is self-denial. *Matthew Henry*

Self-renunciation is the cardinal ethic of the Christian church. *Charles Inwood*

They that deny themselves for Christ shall enjoy themselves in Christ. *J. M. Mason*

Self-examination is not the same as self-pity, which can be addictive as alcohol, and just as deadly. *Nigel McCullough*

Until we cease to live for self, we have not begun to live at all. *J. R. Miller*

Self-denial is a summons to submit to the authority of God as Father and of Jesus as Lord and to declare lifelong war on one's instinctive egoism. *J. I. Packer*

The severest self-denials and the most lavish gifts are of no value in God's esteem unless they are prompted by love. *A. W. Pink*

There is a great difference between denying yourself things and denying yourself. *Adrian Rogers*

We are as near to heaven as we are from self, and far from the love of a sinful world. *Samuel Rutherford*

Self-emptiness prepares for spiritual fullness. *Richard Stibbes*

We are to rise above our fellow by a superior self-forgetfulness. *C. H. Spurgeon*

Self-denial is indispensable to the enjoyment of religious peace and comfort. *J. H. Thornwell*

There is a sweet theology of the heart that is only learned in the school of renunciation. *A. W. Tozer*

Self-denial is the best touch-stone of sincerity. *Thomas Watson*

Self-denial is the very foundation of spiritual comfort. *Robert Wilson*

SELF-EXAMINATION

An humble knowledge of thyself is a surer way to God than a deep search after learning. *Thomas à Kempis*

Self-inspection is the best cure for self-esteem. *Anon.*

The best eyes look inwards and upwards. *Anon.*

Disciplined self-examination before God, in order to learn what one's weaknesses, blind spots, and deepest needs are, is an ongoing necessity. *John Blanchard*

The more we know of ourselves, the more cause we have to be humble. *John Blanchard*

It is not only the most difficult thing to know oneself, but the most inconvenient one, too. *Josh Billings*

He who knows himself best esteems himself least. *Henry G. Bohn*

No man is worse for knowing the worst of himself. *Henry G. Bohn*

Christ, the Scripture, your own hearts and Satan's devices are the four prime things that should be first and most studied and searched. *Thomas Brooks*

Man never achieves a clear knowledge of himself unless he has first looked upon God's face, and then descends from contemplating him to scrutinize himself. *John Calvin*

Nearly all the wisdom we possess, that is to say, true and sound wisdom, consists of two parts: the knowledge of God and of ourselves. *John Calvin*

Those who know themselves best will fear themselves most. *Donald Cargill*

When I look into my heart, and take a view of my wickedness, it looks like an abyss infinitely deeper than hell. *Jonathan Edwards*

Be soonest angry with thyself. *Thomas Fuller*

Search others for their virtues and thyself for thy vices. *Thomas Fuller*

Self-reflection is the school of wisdom. *Baltasar Gracian*

Whoever has a proper knowledge of himself will be convinced that naturally there is nothing good in him. *Robert Haldane*

Whenever I look inside myself, I am afraid. *C. E. M. Joad*

If you don't do a great deal of preaching to yourself, you are a very poor kind of Christian. *D. Martyn Lloyd-Jones*

If your knowledge of doctrine does not make you a great man of prayer, you had better examine yourself again. *D. Martyn Lloyd-Jones*

No man ever became a Christian without stopping to look at himself. *D. Martyn Lloyd-Jones*

Self-examination is the high road to prayer. *D. Martyn Lloyd-Jones*

The thing we have to watch most of all is our strength, our strong point. We all tend to fail ultimately at our strong point. *D. Martyn Lloyd-Jones*

The way to test yourself, the way to test any man, is to look below the surface.
D. Martyn Lloyd-Jones

No man can produce great things who is not thoroughly sincere in dealing with himself. *James Russell Lowell*

Gracious hearts reflect most upon themselves; they do not seek what to reprove in others, but what to lament in themselves. *Thomas Manton*

Until men know themselves better, they will care very little to know Christ at all.
John Owen

Not only do we know God through Jesus Christ, we only know ourselves through Jesus Christ. *Blaise Pascal*

We cannot too often or too earnestly ask God to make us honest with ourselves.
William S. Plumer

The true cure for self-righteousness is self-knowledge. *J. C. Ryle*

The worst ignorance in the world is not to know ourselves. *J. C. Ryle*

Contemplation is a perspective glass to see our Saviour in; but *examination* is a looking-glass to view ourselves in.
William Secker

Self-examination is the beaten path to perfection. *William Secker*

The reason why there is so little self-condemnation is because there is so little self-examination. *William Secker*

Examination is the eye of the soul.
Henry Smith

An unexamined life is not worth living.
Socrates

The Holy Spirit would lead us to think much upon our own sins. It is a dangerous thing for us to dwell upon the imperfections of others. *Ichabod Spencer*

Secret sins, like secret conspirators, must be hunted out. *C. H. Spurgeon*

The man who does not like self-examination may be pretty certain that things need examining. *C. H. Spurgeon*

A frequent reckoning with ourselves will pluck up sin before it is rooted in the soul.
George Swinnock

Self-knowledge is so critically important to us in our pursuit of God and his righteousness that we lie under heavy obligation to do immediately whatever is necessary to remove the disguise and permit our real selves to be known.
A. W. Tozer

Self-knowledge grows out of man's self-confrontation with God.
Dietrich von Hildebrand

It is good to find out our sins, lest they find us out. *Thomas Watson*

Though not always called upon to condemn ourselves, it is always safe to suspect ourselves. *Richard Whately*

SELFISHNESS

A selfish spirit is unworthy of a Christian. *Joseph Alleine*

People who are self-centred always live in unpleasant surroundings. *Anon.*

Selfishness is a very little world inhabited by one man. *Anon.*

Selfishness tarnishes everything it touches. *Anon.*

Glory built on selfish principles is shame and guilt. *William Cowper*

Somehow, for all the wondrous glimpses of 'goodness' I see in society, there remains the unmistakable stain of selfishness, violence and greed.
John Dickson

Selfishness follows the line of least resistance. *Galen*

Selfishness is the greatest curse of the human race. *W. E. Gladstone*

The self-centred are the self-disrupted.
E. Stanley Jones

Selfishness is not only sin but lies at the root of all sin. *R. B. Kuyper*

Selfishness has never been admired.
C. S. Lewis

No indulgence of passion destroys the spiritual nature so much as respectable selfishness. *George Macdonald*

Where self is the end of our actions, there Satan is the rewarder of them.
William Secker

If I really love God my innate and persistent selfishness will have received its death-blow. *Alexander Smellie*

He who lives only for himself is truly dead to others. *Publilius Syrus*

Selfishness is the enemy of all true affection. *Cornelius Tacitus*

He who lives to benefit himself confers on the world a benefit when he dies.
Tertullian

Selfishness is never so exquisitely selfish as when it is on its knees ... Self turns what would otherwise be a pure and powerful prayer into a weak and ineffective one. *A. W. Tozer*

SELF-PITY

Self-pity is a prison without walls – a sign pointing to nowhere. *Anon.*

Everyone thinks his sack is the heaviest.
Anon.

Self-examination is not the same as self-pity, which can be as addictive as alcohol, and just as deadly. *John Blanchard*

Our tears so blind our eyes that we cannot see our mercies. *John Flavel*

As Christians we should never feel sorry for ourselves. The moment we do so, we lose our energy, we lose the will to fight and the will to live, and are paralysed.
D. Martyn Lloyd-Jones

What poison is to food, self-pity is to life.
Oliver G. Wilson

SELF-RIGHTEOUSNESS

Self-righteousness is the devil's masterpiece. *Thomas Adams*

Never are men's hearts in such a hopeless condition as when they are not sensible of their own sins. *J. C. Ryle*

SEPARATION

For all the world forsake not Christ, but all the world forsake for Christ. *Anon.*

The Christian must live in the world, but he must not let the world live in him.
Anon.

When the world is at its worst, Christians must be at their best. *Anon.*

Is the world against me? … then I am against the world. *Athanasius*

Christians should penetrate the world without ever becoming part of it.
John Blanchard

When a sin is fashionable, Christians should be out of fashion. *John Blanchard*

Before the church can make an impact on the culture it must break with the idolatries and misconceptions that dominate the culture. *Donald Bloesch*

Learn to hold loosely all that is not eternal. *Agnes Maude Boyden*

I have nothing to do with earth, but only to labour in it honestly for God. I do not desire to live one minute for anything which earth can afford. *David Brainerd*

I am sure that you understand that it is not enough to be merely separated from the world. For we can be separated and be quite proud about it. *François Fenelon*

Our lifestyle should not be determined by this age. *Sinclair Ferguson*

We are strangers here. Don't make yourself at home. *Vance Havner*

Beware of separation which leads only to isolation and insulation.
Eric Hutchings

The measure of our discord with the world is the measure of our accord with the Saviour. *Alexander MacLaren*

The glory of the gospel is that when the church is absolutely different from the world she invariably attracts it.
D. Martyn Lloyd-Jones

The world hates Christian people if they can see Christ in them.
G. Campbell Morgan

True revival has always begun with and resulted in separation. *Vernon Patterson*

We must dare to be peculiar. *J. C. Ryle*

If you are in with God you are out with the world. *Rodney (Gipsy) Smith*

A man is known by the company he shuns as well as by the company he keeps.
C. H. Spurgeon

I like to warm my hands; but if I cannot warm them without burning them, I would rather keep them cold. Many things are in a measure desirable, but if you cannot obtain them without exposing yourself to the smut of sin, you had better let them alone. *C. H. Spurgeon*

SERMONS — see Preaching and Preachers

SERVICE — Dignity

God is not greater if you reverence him, but you are greater if you serve him.
Augustine

Christian service has been dignified by Deity. *John Blanchard*

The dignity of serving God is second only to the dignity of belonging to his family.
John Blanchard

Love is the motive for working; joy is the strength for working.   *Andrew Bonar*

Service to God through service to mankind is the only motivation acceptable to God for diligence and hard work in our vocational calling.   *Jerry Bridges*

The highest honour in the church is not government but service.   *John Calvin*

We shall never be fit for the service of God if we look not beyond this fleeting life.   *John Calvin*

There is nothing small in the service of God.   *Francois de Sales*

What dignity the service of God brings to the servants of God.   *Frank Farley*

Man is immortal till his work is done.   *Thomas Fuller*

All Christ's commands are acts of grace; it is a favour to be employed about them.   *William Gurnall*

There are no trivial assignments in the work of the Lord.   *Vance Havner*

If the work be done in Christ's name, the honour is due to his name.   *Matthew Henry*

Service can never become slavery to one who loves.   *J. L. Massee*

Serving God with our little is the way to make it more; and we must never think that wasted with which God is honoured or men are blessed.   *Henrietta Mears*

You do not do God a favour by serving him. He honours you by allowing you to serve him.   *Victor Nyquist*

God wants not slaves but intelligent, grown-up children who show enthusiasm for the family business.   *Cornelius Plantinga*

The world's idea of greatness is to rule, but Christian greatness consists in serving.   *J. C. Ryle*

To serve God is to reign.   *Richard Sibbes*

If you cannot be great, be willing to serve God in that which is small.   *S. F. Smith*

It is better to be God's dog than the devil's darling.   *C. H. Spurgeon*

The meanest work for Jesus is a grander thing than the dignity of an emperor.   *C. H. Spurgeon*

God's work does not need pious lies to support it.   *A. W. Tozer*

SERVICE — God's Part

When God wants a worker he calls a worker.   *Anon.*

We do the works, but God works in us the doing of the works.   *Augustine*

Without God, we cannot. Without us, God will not.   *Augustine*

I was but a pen in God's hand and what praise is due to a pen?   *John Bunyan*

Our service cannot be approved of God except it be founded on his Word.   *John Calvin*

Whatever is laudable in our works proceeds from the grace of God. *John Calvin*

Spirituality is a work of God for his child; service is a work of the child for his God, which can be accomplished only in the power of the indwelling Spirit.

Lewis Sperry Chafer

Spirituality is not gained by service; it is unto service. *Lewis Sperry Chafer*

The Christian worker must be sent; he must not elect to go. *Oswald Chambers*

God does not need your talents, wisdom, holiness and strength. But rather you, in weakness, desperately need the power of his Spirit in your labours.

Walter J. Chantry

It is not what we do that matters, but what a sovereign God chooses to do through us. God doesn't want our success, he wants us. He doesn't demand our achievements; he demands our obedience.

Charles Colson

God will not thank thee for doing that which he did not set thee about.

William Gurnall

Our efficiency without God's sufficiency is only a deficiency. *Vance Havner*

The first thing we need to do in the church these days is to discover that God's work must be done by God's people in God's way. *Vance Havner*

None are allowed to go for God but those who are sent by him. *Matthew Henry*

Those whom God will employ are first struck with a sense of their unworthiness to be employed. *Matthew Henry*

Whatever you do, begin with God.

Matthew Henry

Nothing serves God or worships and adores him but that which wills and works with him. *William Law*

The man who knows the love of Christ in his heart can do more in one hour than the busy type of man can do in a century.

D. Martyn Lloyd-Jones

You never test the resources of God until you attempt the impossible. *F. B. Meyer*

Small numbers make no difference to God. There is nothing small if God is in it. *D. L. Moody*

Divine work must be divinely initiated.

Watchman Nee

You do not do God a favour by serving him. He honours you by allowing you to serve him. *Victor Nyquist*

God hath work to do in this world; and to desert it because of its difficulties and entanglements is to cast off his authority.

John Owen

The most significant gifts in the church's life in every era are ordinarily natural abilities sanctified. *J. I. Packer*

The men that have moved the world for God have done what they have done not because they were strong, but because they were weak, and their weakness was transfigured by grace into an instrument in the hands of God for blessing.

James Philip

Whom God calls he qualifies.

Richard Sibbes

There is nothing in man that God has put there which may not be employed in God's service. *C. H. Spurgeon*

Depend upon it. God's work done in God's way will never lack supplies.
J. Hudson Taylor

All God's giants have been weak men who did great things for God because they reckoned on his being with them.
J. Hudson Taylor

God uses men who are weak and feeble enough to lean on him. *J. Hudson Taylor*

He who serves God has a good Master.
Torriano

God who needs no one has in sovereign condescension stooped to work by and in his obedient children. *A. W. Tozer*

Human sweat can add nothing to the work of the Spirit, especially when it is nerve sweat. *A. W. Tozer*

We should all be willing to work for the Lord, but it is a matter of grace on God's part. *A. W. Tozer*

A master gives his servant work to do, but he cannot give him strength to work; but God, as he cuts us out work, so he gives us strength. *Thomas Watson*

God buries his workmen but carries on his work. *Charles Wesley*

God is more interested in the workman than in the work. *Warren Wiersbe*

To say we have not power to do what God requires of us is blasphemy.
Thomas Wilson

SERVICE — Prayer

Life is fragile — handle it with prayer.
Anon.

You can do more than pray after you have prayed, but you cannot do more than pray until you have prayed. *S. D. Gordon*

To attempt any work for God without prayer is as futile as trying to launch a space probe with a peashooter.
John Blanchard

Do not pray for easy lives. Pray to be stronger men. Do not pray for tasks equal to your powers. Pray for powers equal to your tasks. *Phillips Brooks*

To pray without labouring is to mock God: to labour without prayer is to rob God of his glory. *Robert Haldane*

Never undertake more Christian service than you can cover by believing prayer.
Alan Redpath

SERVICE — Responsibility
(See also: Duty; Responsibility)

God has no larger field for the man who is not faithfully doing his work where he is. *Anon.*

Men who love much will work much.
Anon.

No man's life is for his private use. *Anon.*

Pray for a good harvest, but keep on hoeing. *Anon.*

The world is full of willing workers; some willing to work, and others willing to let them work. *Anon.*

No man has a right to lead such a life of contemplation as to forget in his own ease the service due to his neighbour; nor has any man a right to be so immersed in active life as to neglect the contemplation of God. *Augustine*

God made me for himself, to serve him
here,
With love's pure service and in filial fear;
To show his praise, for him to labour now;
Then see his glory where the angels bow.
Henry William Baker

Christianity is not a sedentary profession
or employment.   *Richard Baxter*

Church greatness consists in being greatly
serviceable.   *Richard Baxter*

Christians should be springs, not sponges.
John Blanchard

Morally, a Christian is called to holiness;
dynamically, he is called to service.
John Blanchard

Go, labour on; spend and be spent —
Thy joy to do the Father's will;
It is the way the Master went;
Should not the servant tread it still?
Horatius Bonar

You can't be reconciled to God without
being recruited.   *Stuart Briscoe*

It is almost as presumptuous to think you
can do nothing as to think you can do
everything.   *Phillips Brooks*

The candle of mercy is set up not to play
by but to work by.   *Thomas Brooks*

The Lord first of all wants sincerity in
his service, simplicity of heart without
guile and falsehood.   *John Calvin*

Whatever ability a faithful Christian may
possess, he ought to possess it for his fellow believers, and he ought to make his
own interest subservient to the well-
being of the church in all sincerity.
John Calvin

We are born into permanent service.
David H. Chilton

A cup can't hold much, but it can overflow a lot.   *Robert Cook*

What is my being but for thee,
Its sure support, its noblest end;
Thy ever-smiling face to see,
And serve the cause of such a Friend?
Philip Doddridge

Your salvation is God's business; his service your business.   *Thomas Fuller*

Make your life a mission — not an inter-
mission.   *Arnold Glasgow*

The vision must be followed by the
venture. It is not enough to stare up the
steps — we must step up the stairs.
Vance Havner

Too many are willing to sit at God's
table, but not work in his field.
Vance Havner

We do not trust God, but tempt him, when
our expectations slacken our exertions.
Matthew Henry

What were candles made for but to burn?
Matthew Henry

Whom God sends he employs, for he
sends none to be idle.   *Matthew Henry*

Christ keeps no servants only to wear a
livery.   *William Jenkyn*

Find out where you can render a service;
then render it. The rest is up to the Lord.
S. S. Kresge

God never gave man a thing to do
concerning which it were irreverent to

ponder how the Son of God would have done it. *George Macdonald*

The measure of a man is not the number of his servants, but in the number of people whom he serves. *Paul D. Moody*

Any man or woman in the church who does not know what it is to share the travail that makes his kingdom come is dishonest and disloyal to Jesus Christ.
G. Campbell Morgan

Faithfulness to God is our *first* obligation in all that we are called to do in the service of the gospel. *Iain H. Murray*

Unless a man's faith saves him out of selfishness into service it will certainly never save him out of hell into heaven.
Mark Guy Pearce

Activity is the mark of the holy spirits and should be the mark of holy men.
C. H. Spurgeon

He is no Christian who does not seek to serve his God. *C. H. Spurgeon*

It is an abomination to let the grass grow up to your knees and do nothing towards making it into hay. God never sent a man into the world to be idle. *C. H. Spurgeon*

Now is the watchword of the wise.
C. H. Spurgeon

We should employ our passions in the service of life, not spend life in the service of our passions. *Richard Steele*

The imminent return of our Lord is the great Bible argument for a pure, unselfish, devoted, unworldly, active life of service. *R. A. Torrey*

It is a truth that stands out with startling distinctness on the pages of the New Testament that God has no sons who are not servants. *H. D. Ward*

The most important place in this church is the back door. *Sandy Williams*

Our humility serves us falsely when it leads us to shrink from any duty. The plea of unfitness or inability is utterly insufficient to excuse us. *Spiros Zodhiates*

SERVICE — Rewards

A candle loses nothing by lighting another candle. *Anon.*

If the love of God sets us to work, the God of love will find us the wages. *Anon.*

Work for the Lord. The pay isn't much, but the retirement benefit is out of this world. *Anon.*

God is not greater if you reverence him, but you are greater if you serve him.
Augustine

The best part of all Christian work is that part which only God sees. *Andrew Bonar*

Christians that would hold on in the service of the Lord must look more upon the crown than upon the cross.
Thomas Brooks

The service of the Lord does not only include implicit obedience, but also a willingness to put aside our sinful desires, and to surrender completely to the leadership of the Holy Spirit. *John Calvin*

The gospel teaches us that while believers are not rewarded on account of their works, they are rewarded according to their works. *R. L. Dabney*

Today, let us rise and go to our work. Tomorrow, we shall rise and go to our reward.   *Richard Fuller*

If you read history you will find that the Christians who did most for the present were just those who did most for the next.
C. S. Lewis

I have had many things in my hands and have lost them all. But whatever I have been able to place in God's hands I still possess.   *Martin Luther*

Oh, how sweet to work all day for God, and then lie down at night beneath his smile!   *Robert Murray M'Cheyne*

Men who expect to be paid in this world for serving God have mistaken God for mammon.   *Thomas V. Moore*

As long as we keep our hopes and dreams alive, as long as we stay involved in life, our spirits will be renewed. There should be no wrinkles on the soul.
Richard E. Morgan

The fruit of Christian service is never the result of allowing the natural energies and inclinations to run riot.   *Leon Morris*

God is a sure paymaster, though he does not always pay at the end of every week.
C. H. Spurgeon

Before the judgement seat of Christ my service will not be judged by how much I have done but by how much of me there is in it.   *A. W. Tozer*

As God will put a veil over his people's sins, so he will in free grace set a crown upon their works.   *Thomas Watson*

The labourer, not the loiterer, is worthy of his hire.   *Henry Wilkinson*

Faithful service is sure to be rewarded, yet this is the reward of grace and not a merited award.   *Geoffrey B. Wilson*

SERVICE — Wholeheartedness
(See also: Zeal)

God does not ask about our ability or our inability, but our availability.   *Anon.*

The man and the whole time is all too little in so great a work.   *Richard Baxter*

What have we time and strength for, but to lay our both for God? What is a candle made for, but to burn?   *Richard Baxter*

God only asks you to do your best.
Robert H. Benson

Christian service is not meant to be a formality burdening the mind, but a fire burning in the heart.   *John Blanchard*

Service is the overflow of super-abounding devotion.   *Oswald Chambers*

Keep us, Lord, so awake in the duties of our callings that we may sleep in thy peace and awake in thy glory.
John Donne

Wherever you are, be all there. Live to the hilt every situation you believe to be the will of God.   *Jim Elliot*

God wants no compulsory service. On the contrary he loves a free, willing heart that serves him with a joyful heart and soul and does what is right joyfully.
Claus Felbinger

Since my heart was touched at seventeen, I believe I have never awakened from sleep, in sickness or in health, by day or by night, without my first waking thought

being how best I might serve my Lord.
Elizabeth Fry

I hate to see a thing done by halves; if it be right, do it boldly; if it be wrong, leave it undone. *Bernard Gilpin*

No duty can be performed without wrestling. The Christian needs his sword as well as his trowel. *William Gurnall*

The service that counts is the service that costs. *Howard Hendricks*

You cannot be too active as regards your own efforts; you cannot be too dependent as regards divine grace. Do everything as if God did nothing; depend upon God as if he did everything. *John Angell James*

Determine never to be idle ... It is wonderful how much may be done if we are always doing. *Thomas Jefferson*

When the heart is right, the feet are swift.
Thomas Jefferson

Ministry that costs nothing accomplishes nothing. *John Henry Jowett*

The danger of mistaking our merely natural, though perhaps legitimate, enthusiasm for holy zeal is always great.
C. S. Lewis

You will certainly carry out God's purpose, however you act, but it makes a difference to you whether you serve like Judas or John. *C. S. Lewis*

The man who tries to do something and fails is infinitely better than the man who tries to do nothing and succeeds.
D. Martyn Lloyd-Jones

The oil of the lamp in the temple burnt

away in giving light; so should we.
Robert Murray M'Cheyne

We never test the resources of God until we attempt the impossible. *F. B. Meyer*

No man ever lost anything by serving God with a whole heart, or gained anything by serving him with half a one.
Thomas V. Moore

No divinely sent opportunity must elude us. *Watchman Nee*

Though you cannot do what you ought; yet you ought to do what you can.
Christopher Nesse

Do little things as if they were great, because of the majesty of the Lord Jesus Christ who dwells in thee; and do great things as if they were little and easy, because of his omnipotence.
Blaise Pascal

Only a burdened heart can lead to fruitful service. *Alan Redpath*

There is no service like his who serves because he loves. *Philip Sidney*

God deserves to be served with all the energy of which we are capable.
C. H. Spurgeon

If the service of God is worth anything, it is worth everything. *C. H. Spurgeon*

When you have kindled your love to Christ at his love to you, then let it burn and spend ... in his service and to his praise. *Robert Traill*

God does sometimes accept of willingness without the work, but never the work without the willingness. *Thomas Watson*

The most willing service to men is rendered by those who are bent on pleasing Christ!   *Geoffrey B. Wilson*

SEX
(See also: Lust)

The first sexual thought in the universe was God's, not man's.   *Doug Barnett*

God thought of sex before man did, and when man leaves God out of his sexual thinking he is in trouble. *John Blanchard*

What would you not give to have the word 'sex' set free from every trace of fear, guilt, shame and impurity?
John Blanchard

All healthy men, ancient and modern, Eastern and Western, know that there is a certain fury in sex that we cannot afford to inflame, and that a certain mystery and awe must ever surround it if we are to remain sane. *G. K. Chesterton*

Sex without love is a dead end.
Fred Catherwood

In nothing did early Christianity so thoroughly revolutionize the ethical standards of the pagan world as in regard to sexual relationships.   *George Duncan*

The powerful sexual drives which are built into man's relationship with woman are not seen in Scripture as the foundation of marriage, but the consummation and physical expression of it.
Sinclair Ferguson

What happens when sex is liberated is not equality but a vast intensification of sexual competition from which there is no sure haven except impotence and defeat.   *George Gilder*

Sexual desire is natural and marriage is provided for its fulfilment.
Norman Hillyer

Homosexual practices are against nature and against revealed truth ... Homosexual indulgence is something which God condemns as the ultimate sign of decadence and degradation in any culture.
O. R. Johnston

The battle of life will probably not rise above the sex battle.   *E. Stanley Jones*

No sinful act desecrates the body like fornication and sexual abuse. In this sense fornication has a deadly eminence.
R. C. H. Lenski

Sexual desire is not love. Desire is quite compatible with personal hatred, or contempt, or indifference. *John MacMurray*

God never intended that man could find the true meaning of his sexuality in any other relationship than that of the total self-giving involved in marriage.
Al Martin

Whereas the charge levelled at the Victorians was 'love without sex', today it is 'sex without love'.   *David Watson*

Sex involves the entire life and personality, and to misuse sex is to abuse oneself as well as one's partner. *Harold P. Wells*

What a man or woman does with his or her sexual energy will decide not only the quality of their own lives, but the kind of world in which they live.
Mary Whitehouse

When sex is deformed, cheapened and exploited then the potentiality of life and the whole social fabric of society deteriorates.   *Mary Whitehouse*

SICKNESS
(See also: Pain; Suffering; Trials)

Sickness shows us what we are.　*Anon.*

Sickness, when sanctified, teaches us four things: the vanity of the world, the vileness of sin, the helplessness of man and the preciousness of Christ.　*Anon.*

All disease is primarily the result of sin, but not always directly so.
John Blanchard

The decay of the outward man in the godless is a melancholy spectacle, for it is the decay of everything; in the Christian it does not touch that life which is hid with Christ in God, and which is in the soul itself a well of water springing up to life eternal.　*James Denny*

Disease is just one of the many results of man's sin, along with death, sorrow, guilt and disasters of nature.
Joni Eareckson Tada

Sometimes sickness serves as God's chastiser to wake us from our sin.
Joni Eareckson Tada

Sometimes Christ sees that we need the *sickness* for the good of our souls more than the *healing* for the ease of our bodies.
Matthew Henry

Sickness is God's messenger to call us to meet with God.　*Thomas Manton*

The chief care of a sick man should be for his soul.　*Thomas Manton*

Medical science recognizes that emotions such as fear, sorrow, envy, resentment and hatred are responsible for the majority of our sicknesses. Estimates vary from 60% to nearly 100%.　*S. I. McMillen*

Be laid aside in bed for a week. You will soon know whether you are a Christian or not!　*D. Martyn Lloyd-Jones*

If cures were to be found for every illness ever known, it would make no essential difference. We should be sick, mad and blind as long as we allowed ourselves to be wholly preoccupied with the hopes and desires of this world.
Malcolm Muggeridge

There is no commentary that opens up the Bible so much as sickness and sorrow.　*James Philip*

Health is a good thing, but sickness is far better if it leads us to God.　*J. C. Ryle*

Sickness is a great leveller.　*J. C. Ryle*

The fact is that many of God's choicest saints are what they are today because God did *not* heal them.　*J. C. Ryle*

The time of sickness is a time of purging from that defilement we gathered in our health ... That is a good sickness which tends to the health of the soul.
Richard Sibbes

I venture to say that the greatest earthly blessing that God can give to any of us is health, with the exception of sickness. Sickness has frequently been of more use to the saints of God than health has.
C. H. Spurgeon

It is impossible that any ill should happen to the man who is beloved of the Lord; the most crushing calamities can only shorten his journey and hasten him to his reward. Ill to him is no ill, but only

good in a mysterious form.
> *C. H. Spurgeon*

Sanctified sickness is far better than unsanctified soundness.
> *George Swinnock*

I am mended by my sickness, enriched by my poverty, and strengthened by my weakness. *Abraham Wright*

SILENCE

A closed mouth gathers no foot. *Anon.*

Better silent than stupid. *Anon.*

Eloquent listening requires as much genius as eloquent talking. *Anon.*

Eloquent silence often is better than eloquent speech. *Anon.*

It often shows a fine command of language to say nothing. *Anon.*

It takes two years to learn to talk and seventy years to learn to keep your mouth shut. *Anon.*

More have repented speech than silence.
> *Anon.*

There are two sciences which every person ought to learn: the science of speech and the more difficult one of silence. *Anon.*

Silence is so rare a virtue where wisdom regulates it, that it is accounted a virtue where folly imposes it. *Thomas Brooks*

Silence is the element in which great things fashion themselves.
> *Thomas Carlyle*

Speech is of time, silence is of eternity.
> *Thomas Carlyle*

Silence is foolish if we are wise, but wise if we are foolish. *C. C. Colton*

God still comes where he can find someone quiet enough to listen and alone enough to heed. *G. B. Duncan*

Blessed is the man who having nothing to say abstains from giving wordy evidence of the fact. *George Eliot*

I think the devil has made it his business to monopolize on three elements: noise, hurry, crowds ... Satan is quite aware of the power of silence. *Jim Elliot*

How rare it is to find a soul quiet enough to hear God speak! *François Fenelon*

Silence is wisdom when speaking is folly.
> *Thomas Fuller*

Silence is one great art of conversation.
> *William Hazlitt*

Better to be silent and be thought a fool than to speak out and remove all doubt.
> *Abraham Lincoln*

To sin by silence when they should protest makes cowards out of men.
> *Abraham Lincoln*

I always feel it a blessed thing when the Saviour takes me aside from the crowd.
> *Robert Murray M'Cheyne*

No human being can establish himself in silence; anyone who thinks he can only shows that he does not know anything about silence. God alone does it... It is God who must immobilize us in silence.
> *Thomas Philippe*

Often silence is the sum of our duties.
William S. Plumer

Speech is … only good when it is better than silence. *Richard Sibbes*

In a still night every voice is heard, and when the body is quiet the mind most commonly is quiet also . . . and when our minds are quiet we are fit to deal with heavenly matters. *Henry Smith*

God can be known in the tumult if his providence has for the first time placed us there, but he is known best in the silence. *A. W. Tozer*

Either keep silence, or speak that which is better than silence. *John Trapp*

Well-timed silence is more eloquent than speech. *Martin Tupper*

A man may wrong another as well by silence as by slander. *Thomas Watson*

SIMPLICITY

Knowledge leads us from the simple to the complex; wisdom leads us from the complex to the simple. *Anon.*

The longer I live, the more I covet simplicity. *Ernest F. Kevan*

The more Christian a person is, the simpler will that person's life be.
D. Martyn Lloyd-Jones

The true hallmark of greatness is simplicity. It is little minds that are complicated and involved.
D. Martyn Lloyd-Jones

Whatever is Christian is always essentially simple. Simplicity is not incompatible with depth.
D. Martyn Lloyd-Jones

A man is rich in proportion to the number of things he can afford to let alone.
Henry Thoreau

SIN — and the Christian

If I grapple with sin in my own strength, the devil knows he may go to sleep.
H. G. J. Adams

Two sorts of peace are more to be dreaded than all the troubles in the world — peace with sin, and peace in sin. *Joseph Alleine*

If hell were on one side I and sin on the other, I would rather leap into hell than willingly sin against my God. *Anselm*

Believers sin less but they are not sinless.
Anon.

It is a great sin to love a small sin. *Anon.*

The Christian has sin in him but not on him. *Anon.*

If sin comes into the life of the believer, he should immediately become concerned about it. It should cause him to rush to the Lord in confession and repentance, and it should cause him to build every bulwark possible against the recurrence of the sin.
Donald Grey Barnhouse

Our sense of sin is in proportion to our nearness to God. *Thomas D. Bernard*

The lost leap into sin and love it; the saved lapse into sin and loathe it.
John Blanchard

It is our duty to feel sin, to fear sin, and to fly sin as far as we can. *John Boys*

A godly man doth mourn for another's sin as well as for his own, because he mourns for sin as sin. *William Bridge*

It is not falling into the water, but lying in the water that drowns. *Thomas Brooks*

Sin may rebel in a saint, but it shall never reign in a saint. *Thomas Brooks*

Whenever a godly man sins, he sins against the general purpose of his soul. *Thomas Brooks*

There is something in man — even regenerate man — which objects to God and seeks to be independent of him. *F. F. Bruce*

The holiest person is ... one who is most conscious of what sin is. *Oswald Chambers*

I preach and think that it is more bitter to sin against Christ than to suffer the torments of hell. *Chrysostom*

Two things in sin chiefly move the godly to mourn for it. One is the dishonour it brings on God. The other is the perdition it brings on the sinner. *David Dickson*

It was sin that made our bodies mortal ... therefore do not yield obedience to such an enemy. *Matthew Henry*

The best of saints may be tempted to the worst of sins. *Matthew Henry*

A sinner falls into sin as a fish, the saint as a child does into the water. *William Jenkyn*

This is one of the sorest trials of a renewed life, that it is built over dark dungeons, where dead things may be buried but not forgotten, and where through open grating rank vapours still ascend. *John Ker*

Even the sinning of the regenerate man differs essentially from that of the unregenerate man. *R. B. Kuiper*

Whatever sin he may commit, the regenerate person always sins against his will. *R. B. Kuiper*

The worst sins of men are spiritual. *C. S. Lewis*

You cannot play with sin and overcome it at the same time. *J. C. MacAulay*

No figure of speech can represent my utter want of power to resist the torrent of sin. *Robert Murray M Cheyne*

The seeds of all sins are in my heart, and perhaps all the more dangerously that I do not see them. *Robert Murray M'Cheyne*

God, in mercy, will never allow children of his to be comfortable in sin. *Will Metzger*

It is one thing for sin to live in us; it is another for us to live in sin. *John Murray*

I do not understand how a man can be a true believer in whom sin is not the greatest burden, sorrow and trouble. *John Owen*

It is not the absence of sin but the grieving over it which distinguishes the child of God from empty professors. *A. W. Pink*

Never was anything more futile than the war against the Lamb. *William S. Plumer*

The grief of a pious soul for sins is not only or chiefly for the misery thus brought on, but chiefly because sin is exceeding sinful and greatly dishonours God.
William S. Plumer

The grace of God which is in a real Christian will not allow him to be at rest in sin. A believer who has sinned is like a man who is required to be his own executioner.
Maurice Roberts

I am convinced that the first step towards attaining a higher standard of holiness is to realize more fully the amazing sinfulness of sin. *J. C. Ryle*

There is no sin so great but a great saint may fall into it. There is no saint so great but he may fall into a great sin. *J. C. Ryle*

The Christian does not have to live in defeat, but he does have to live all his life with the sin nature … and … because God has not made the flesh any better in the believer, because it has not been refined, it is a powerful enemy with which we have to live. *Charles Caldwell Ryrie*

The way we can thank Jesus the most in this life for his act of redemption is no longer to tolerate sin. *Basilea Schlink*

As soon as I learn that a brother states that he has lived for months without sin, I wonder whether his secret vice is lewdness, or theft, or drink, but I feel sure that somewhere or other there is a leak in the ship. *C. H. Spurgeon*

Do believe it, Christian, that your sin is a condemned thing. It may kick and struggle, but it is doomed to die.
C. H. Spurgeon

Of two evils, choose neither.
C. H. Spurgeon

There is a little hell within the heart of every child of God, and only the great God of heaven can master that mischievous indwelling sin.
C. H. Spurgeon

Only the mature believer reaches the place both of self-disgust and self-despair.
John R. W. Stott

For the Christian, to do wrong is to wound his Friend. *William Temple*

Sin in a Christian is like a diver's dress on land — awkward and harassing.
John Trapp

Better starve than go to the devil for provender. *Thomas Watson*

The sins of the godly are worse than others, because they bring a greater reproach upon religion. *Thomas Watson*

Though we [as Christians] are like Christ, having the firstfruits of the Spirit, yet are we unlike him, having the remainders of the flesh. *Thomas Watson*

For the Christian, sin is not the done thing! *Mary S. Wood*

SIN — Deceitfulness

Evil enters like a needle and spreads like an oak tree. *Anon.*

If sin was not such a pleasure it would not be such a problem. *John Blanchard*

No sin is to be regarded as small, because the God who forbids all sin is so great.
John Blanchard

Sin keeps us from knowing the true nature of sin. *John Blanchard*

To understand the deceitfulness of sin, compare its promises and its payments.
John Blanchard

The least sin is infinitely evil.
David Clarkson

If there is anything worse than our sins, it is our infinite capacity to rationalize it away.
Charles Colson

Nothing can deceive unless it bears a plausible resemblance to reality.
C. S. Lewis

No wickedness proceeds on any grounds of reason.
Livy

The most deadly sins do not *leap* upon us; they *creep* upon us.
Stephen Olford

Sin is never less quiet than when it seems to be most quiet.
John Owen

Vice is a monster of such frightful mien
As to be hated needs but to be seen;
Yet seen too oft, familiar with her face,
We first endure, then pity, then embrace.
Alexander Pope

Let's not listen for a minute to the contemptible question, 'What harm is there in it?' There's nothing *but* harm if Christ is not in it.
Scott Richardson

Though Satan's apples may have a fair skin, yet they certainly have a bitter core.
William Secker

A sin is two sins when it is defended.
Henry Smith

All sin is folly; all sinners are fools.
C. H. Spurgeon

Sin may open bright as the morning, but it will end dark as night.
Thomas de Witt Talmage

'Evil' is Hebrew for a fool.   *John Trapp*

Sin may be clasped so close we cannot see its face.   *Richard C. Trench*

A man can no more extract blessedness out of sin than he can suck health out of poison.
Thomas Watson

The most stupendous blunder a man ever made was to think that anything could be made out of sinning.
Frederick P. Wood

SIN — Effects

The real horror of being outside of Christ is that there is no shelter from the wrath of God.   *Eric Alexander*

A little sin will add to your trouble, subtract from your energy and multiply your difficulties.   *Anon.*

As virtue is its own reward, so vice is its own punishment.   *Anon.*

Evil enters like a needle and spreads like an oak tree.   *Anon.*

He who swims in sin will sink in sorrow.
Anon.

Nothing will stop your song quicker than your sin.   *Anon.*

Sin always ruins where it reigns.   *Anon.*

Sin puts hell into the soul and the soul into hell.   *Anon.*

Those who go against the grain of God's laws shouldn't complain when they get splinters.   *Anon.*

Were it not for sin, death would never have had a beginning. Were it not for death, sin would never have an ending.
Anon.

Each man's sin is the instrument of his punishment, and his iniquity is turned into his torment.
Augustine

He that is good is free, though he is a slave; he that is evil is a slave, though he be a king.
Augustine

The punishment of sin is sin. *Augustine*

The sinner sins against himself; the wrongdoer wrongs himself, becoming the worse by his own action. *Marcus Aurelius*

God will give the rebel what he chooses and what he deserves. *Simon Austen*

Vice always renders the mind blind, and the heart hard, and shrouds everything in the moral world in midnight.
Albert Barnes

Our vices have voices; they testify against us.
John Blanchard

Sin denies man the power of God in this life and the presence of God in the next.
John Blanchard

Sin has scarred the ecology of the whole universe.
John Blanchard

There is a high cost in low living.
John Blanchard

Sin has turned the world from a paradise into a thicket; there is no getting through without being scratched. *Thomas Boston*

Sin is the great punishment of sin.
John Boys

Vices are more costly than virtues.
Thomas Brooks

One leak will sink a ship; and one sin will destroy a sinner. *John Bunyan*

The wicked have the seeds of hell in their own hearts. *John Calvin*

This one word 'evil' is a thunderbolt which lays low all human pride.
John Calvin

Sin is the greatest robber that this world will ever know. *Peter Clement*

We cannot do evil to others without doing it to ourselves. *J. F. E. Desmahis*

You cannot do wrong without suffering wrong. *Ralph Waldo Emerson*

Disease is just one of the many results of man's sin, along with death, sorrow, guilt and disasters of nature.
Joni Eareckson Tada

Sin is the most expensive thing in the universe. Nothing else can cost so much.
Charles G. Finney

Sin pays — but it pays in remorse, regret and failure. *Billy Graham*

The pleasure of sin never survives this world. *William Gurnall*

Sin has got people into more trouble than science can get them out of.
Vance Havner

Sin is spiritual cancer, and the man who tries to live with it dies of it. *Vance Havner*

Every wilful sinner ought to be told that he is a dead man. *Matthew Henry*

If we be *ruled* by sin we shall inevitably be *ruined* by it. *Matthew Henry*

No marvel that our sorrows are multiplied when our sins are. *Matthew Henry*

Sin lessens men. *Matthew Henry*

Sinners wilfully lose God for a friend. *Matthew Henry*

That which is won ill will never wear well. *Matthew Henry*

Sins are like circles in the water when a stone is thrown into it; one produces another. *Philip Henry*

The seeds of our punishment are sown at the same time we commit the sin. *Hesiod*

It is the tendency of righteousness to produce blessings, as it is the tendency of evil to produce misery. *Charles Hodge*

If you do Satan's work you must be prepared for his wages. *C. S. Lewis*

The life of sin is always in some sense a life of boredom. *D. Martyn Lloyd-Jones*

The tragedy of sin is that it affects man in his highest faculties. Sin causes us to become fools, and behave in an irrational manner. *D. Martyn Lloyd-Jones*

Sin is an ill guest, for it always sets its lodging on fire. *Thomas Manton*

Sin carrieth two rods about it: shame and fear. *Edward Marbury*

Sin is but hell in embryo; hell is but sin in fulfilment. *Thomas V. Moore*

The most fearful punishment of sinners is simply to leave them to themselves. *Thomas V. Moore*

Sin and shame came in both together. *Christopher Nesse*

Those who are under the rule of sin are also under the wrath of God. *J. I. Packer*

Disobedience has a price. *James Philip*

Sin always comes home to roost. *James Philip*

Sin always leads us much further than we intended to go. *James Philip*

Sin begins with our departure from God; it ends with our departure from God. *James Philip*

The effect sin has on God is to awaken his anger. *James Philip*

We cannot think lightly of sin if we think honestly of its results. *David C. Potter*

Sin would have few takers if its consequences occurred immediately. *W. T. Purkiser*

All wars, disease, sickness, death and even natural disasters can be traced back to that one act of representative disobedience in Eden. *Frank Retief*

Sin has made us all mad as well as bad. *Maurice Roberts*

Of all trades, sin is the most unprofitable. *J. C. Ryle*

God has set it down for an eternal rule that vexation and sin shall be inseparable. *Richard Sibbes*

Sin is fatal in all languages. *Roy L. Smith*

All the sorrows of faith put together do not equal in bitterness one drop of the sorrows of sin. *C. H. Spurgeon*

God must smite sin wherever he sees it. *C. H. Spurgeon*

He cannot smell sweetly who sleeps in a bed of garlic. *C. H. Spurgeon*

It is a glorious truth that God will keep his people, but it is an abominable falsehood that sin will do them no harm. *C. H. Spurgeon*

It is not the nature of sin to remain in a fixed state. Like decaying fruit, it grows more rotten. The man who is bad today will be worse tomorrow. *C. H. Spurgeon*

It were better to die a thousand times than to sin. *C. H. Spurgeon*

Sin drives men mad. Against their reason, against their best interests, they follow after that which they know will destroy them. *C. H. Spurgeon*

Sin is a thief. It will rob your soul of its life. It will rob God of his glory. Sin is a murderer. It stabbed our father Adam. It slew our purity. Sin is a traitor. It rebels against the king of heaven and earth. *C. H. Spurgeon*

Sin is no little thing. It girded the Redeemer's head with thorns, and pierced his heart . . . Look upon all sin as that which crucified the Saviour, and you will see it to be 'exceeding sinful'. *C. H. Spurgeon*

Guilt is related to sin as the burnt spots to the blaze. *Augustus Strong*

All misery calls sin mother. *George Swinnock*

Sin is the weight on the clock which makes the hammer to strike. *George Swinnock*

No sin is small. No grain of sand is small in the mechanism of a watch. *Jeremy Taylor*

The world's turned upside down, from bad to worse, Quite out of frame, the cart before the horse. *John Taylor*

Whatever is wrongfully achieved must lead to ruin. *David Thomas*

One sin liked and loved will make way for every other. *John Trapp*

Pollution is the forerunner of perdition. *John Trapp*

Sin is like the Jerusalem artichoke; plant it where you will, it overruns the ground and chokes the heart. *John Trapp*

All offences against God will either be forgiven or avenged. *A. W. Tozer*

Never underestimate the ability of human beings to get themselves tangled up. *A. W. Tozer*

Sin is the womb of our sorrows and the grave of our comfort. *Thomas Watson*

Sin makes a man worse than a toad or a serpent. *Thomas Watson*

Sin makes sad convulsions in the conscience. *Thomas Watson*

Sin not only makes us unlike God but contrary to God. *Thomas Watson*

Neither the wicked nor the righteous can sin with impunity.   *James Wolfendale*

SIN — Essence

Sin is not only an offence which needs forgiving, it is a pollution which needs cleansing.   *Eric Alexander*

Sin is God's would-be murderer.   *Anon.*

Sin is man's declaration of independence of God.   *Anon.*

Sin is so big that it takes a Christ with a cross to measure it.   *Anon.*

Sin is subservient — the slave of a sovereign God.   *Anon.*

There is no right way to do a wrong thing.   *Anon.*

Any departure by man from what he knows he ought to do, however small his offence may be, slaps the very face of God.   *Saphir R. Athyal*

It is of the heart of sin that men use what they ought to enjoy and enjoy what they ought to use.   *Augustine*

Sin is energy in the wrong channel.   *Augustine*

Sin is the refusal of divine lordship and disobedience to God's will.
    Samuel A. Benetreau

Sin defiles man and defies God.
    John Blanchard

Sin is moral mutiny by man.
    John Blanchard

There is no such thing as a little sin because there is no such person as a little God to sin against.   *John Blanchard*

Sin is a serious business to God, and it becomes serious business to us when we reflect upon the fact that every sin, regardless of how seemingly insignificant it appears to us, is an expression of contempt towards the sovereign authority of God.   *Jerry Bridges*

A will to sin is sin in God's account.
    Thomas Brooks

Every yielding to sin is a welcoming of Satan into our very bosoms.
    Thomas Brooks

No sin against God is little, because it is sin against the great God of heaven and earth.   *John Bunyan*

Sin is the dare of God's justice, the rape of his mercy, the jeer of his patience, the slight of his power and the contempt of his love.   *John Bunyan*

All wickedness flows from a disregard of God.   *John Calvin*

The dimensions of evil are established by the dimensions of God; the ugliness of evil is established by the beauty of God; the filth of evil is established by the purity of God; the selfishness of evil is established by the love of God.
    D. A. Carson

Sin is not wrong doing; it is wrong being; deliberate and emphatic independence of God.   *Oswald Chambers*

The essence of sin is my right to my claim to myself.   *Oswald Chambers*

Every sin is an election of the devil to be our Lord.   *Stephen Charnock*

Sin is essentially rebellion against the rule of God. *Charles Colson*

The sin of the world is not that it does not *do* the will of God but that it does not *choose* the will of God. *Arthur C. Custance*

It is in relation to God that sin assumes its essential significance; sin is not a mere defect or weakness in man, or an unsociable action, but rather an offence against God. *Eryl Davies*

Disease is just one of the many results of man's sin, along with death, sorrow, guilt and disasters of nature. *Joni Eareckson Tada*

Never think to find honey in the pot when God writes poison on its cover. *William Gurnall*

Sin is moral leprosy. *Vance Havner*

Forgetfulness of God is the cause of all the wickedness of the wicked. *Matthew Henry*

Sin is the most unmanly thing in God's world. You never were made for sin and selfishness. You were made for love and obedience. *John G. Holland*

Sinful man does not wish to know God; he wishes himself to be the self-sufficient centre of his universe. *P. E. Hughes*

All sin has its source in apostasy from God. *Erroll Hulse*

Put sin into its best dress, it is but gilded damnation. *William Jenkyn*

What is sin? It is failure to glorify God. *D. Martyn Lloyd-Jones*

Sin is essentially a departure from God. *Martin Luther*

At the heart of everything that the Bible says are two great truths, which belong inseparably together — the majesty of the law of God, and sin as an offence against that law. *J. Gresham Machen*

Sin is not the brute in us; it is, rather, the man in us. *J. Gresham Machen*

In the ways of sin you have a bad master, worse work and the worst wages. *Thomas Manton*

Sin is that abominable thing which God hates. *Thomas V. Moore*

Sin always aims at the utmost ... Every unclean thought or glance would be adultery if it could ... every thought of unbelief would be atheism. *John Owen*

Sin is a kind of allergy in the moral and spiritual system of fallen man. *J. I. Packer*

Sin is not a social concept; it is a theological concept. *J. I. Packer*

We shall never know what sin really is till we learn to think of it in terms of our relationship with God. *J. I. Packer*

Sin is a clenched fist and a blow in the face of God. *Joseph Parker*

All sin is a lie. By it we attempt to cheat God; by it we actually cheat our souls. *William S. Plumer*

If sin had its way it would both dethrone and annihilate God. *William S. Plumer*

No man ever dreaded or hated sin excessively. *William S. Plumer*

The worst thing in every sin is that it is against God. *William S. Plumer*

Sin is the contradiction of God and the antipodes of his nature. *Maurice Roberts*

Sin as a state is unlikeness to God, as a principle is opposition to God, and as an act is transgression of God's law.
E. G. Robinson

Sin is God's one intolerance.
W. E. Sangster

Original sin does not refer to the sin of Adam and Eve. Original sin refers to the *result* of the sin of Adam and Eve. Original sin is the punishment God gives for the first sin. *R. C. Sproul*

The essence of original sin is to hate God.
R. C. Sproul

Sin is an unlimited and unmitigated evil.
C. H. Spurgeon

Sin is Christicide. *C. H. Spurgeon*

Sin is not a splash of mud on a man's exterior; it is filth generated within himself. *C. H. Spurgeon*

Sin is self-coronation. *Vincent Taylor*

Opposition to the divine will is the very essence of all sin. *David Thomas*

We hate sin not merely because its consequences are disastrous, or its forms repugnant to our tastes and sensibilities, but because it is a reflection upon God.
J. H. Thornwell

Sin is basically an act of moral folly, and the greater the folly, the greater the fool.
A. W. Tozer

The essence of sin is rebellion against divine authority. *A. W. Tozer*

A sinner is a devil in man's shape.
Thomas Watson

Sin has the devil for its father, shame for its companion and death for its wages.
Thomas Watson

Sin is a little word with only three letters, but the biggest is I.
Arthur Skevington Wood

SIN — Fact

Sin is like seed — to cover it is to cultivate it. *Anon.*

Every sin is reprehensible, because the sinner is responsible. *John Blanchard*

People used to argue as to whether the world was square or round — but the Bible says it is crooked! *John Blanchard*

The two greatest facts in life are sin and death. *John Blanchard*

We are born in sin and spend our lives coping with the consequences.
John Blanchard

Man cannot cover what God would reveal. *Thomas Campbell*

The only dreadful thing is sin.
Elisha Coles

There is in truth only one religious problem in the world — the existence of sin. Similarly there is only one religious solution to it — the atonement.
James Denney

Sin is a matter of what we are, not what we learn. *Brian Edwards*

The doctrine of sin is the foundation of the doctrine of grace. *David Jussely*

Christianity begins with the doctrine of sin. *Soren Kierkegaard*

Mere time does nothing either to the fact or the guilt of sin. *C. S. Lewis*

How could a holy God, if he is all-powerful, have permitted the existence of sin? What shall we do with the problem? I am afraid we shall have to do with it something that is not very pleasing to our pride; I am afraid we shall just have to say that it is insoluble. *J. Gresham Machen*

Many have puzzled themselves about the origin of evil; I observe that there is evil, and that there is a way to escape it, and with this I begin and end. *John Newton*

Good and evil are not the same to the living God: whichever side you are on, and for whatever reason you do it, evil is evil, and the nature of the cause you support makes no difference to the evils you perform. *James Philip*

The right measure of sin's sinfulness is the dignity of him who came into the world to save sinners. If Christ is so great, then sin must indeed be sinful! *J. C. Ryle*

The alienation of man from God is a fact. It is our business not to deny it but to end it. *William Temple*

If the best man's faults were written in his forehead, it would make him pull his hat over his eyes. *John Trapp*

Men's sins feast the devil. *Thomas Watson*

Sin is an irrational thing. *Thomas Watson*

Sin is worse than hell; for the pains of hell are a burden to the creature only, but sin is a burden to God. *Thomas Watson*

The evil of sin is not so much seen in that one thousand are damned for it, as that Christ died for it. *Thomas Watson*

SIN OF OMISSION
(See also: Negligence)

Sinful omissions lead to sinful commissions. *Thomas Brooks*

Our minds should not dwell upon the good we do, but upon that which we neglect to do. *Gregory the Great*

Sins of omission are aggravated by knowledge. *Thomas Manton*

I do not know any subject that so much distresses me, humbles me and lays me in the dust, as the thought of my omissions. It is not what I have done about which I think so much as of what I have not done. *C. H. Spurgeon*

Not doing good fits the heart for doing evil. *George Swinnock*

Some sins of omission are like great men, that never go without great followers. *George Swinnock*

Every man is guilty of all the good he didn't do. *Voltaire*

SIN — Power

Sin is the strength of death and the death of strength. *Thomas Adams*

A swarm of locusts can do more damage to a field than a full-grown cow.   *Anon.*

Sin's misery and God's mercy are beyond measure.   *Anon.*

There is no sin so little as not to kindle an eternal fire.   *Anon.*

Sin has two great powers; it reigns and it ruins.   *John Blanchard*

Sin is not a toy, it is a tyrant.
John Blanchard

Those sins that seem most sweet in life will prove most bitter in death.
Thomas Brooks

What a thing is sin, what a devil and master of devils is it, that it should, where it takes hold, so hang that nothing can unclinch its hold but the mercy of God and the heart-blood of his dear Son!
John Bunyan

When the will is enchained as the slave of sin, it cannot make a movement towards goodness, far less steadily pursue it.   *John Calvin*

A man may die as well by a fly choking him as by a lion devouring him . . . so likewise, little sins will sink a man to hell as soon as great sins.   *Daniel Cawdray*

Our sin is a step to another more heinous.
David Dickson

Sin cannot be reduced to manageable proportions.   *Sinclair Ferguson*

How deep is the pollution of sin that nothing but the blood of Christ can cleanse it!
John Flavel

Our use of reason itself is not only wounded and weakened but made wilful and wrong by sin.   *Os Guinness*

God's wounds cure; sin's kisses kill.
William Gurnall

We must deal with the seeds of sin in our hearts. If neglected the seeds soon become weeds.   *Vance Havner*

A slight sore, neglected, may prove of fatal consequence, and so may a slight sin slighted and left unrepented of.
Matthew Henry

Sin has turned the world upside down; the earth has become quite a different thing to man from what it was when God made it to be his habitation.
Matthew Henry

The way of sin is downhill; a man cannot stop himself when he will.
Matthew Henry

Duty is the greatest liberty, and sin the greatest bondage.   *Thomas Manton*

We have been created for eternal life — and that has been frustrated by sin, which diverts us from God and creates a sense of emptiness by so doing.
Alister McGrath

He that hath slight thoughts of sin never had great thoughts of God.   *John Owen*

There is no death of sin without the death of Christ.   *John Owen*

We are ourselves so infected and affected by sin that we are altogether incapable of estimating its due merits.   *A. W. Pink*

All sin hardens the heart, stupefies the conscience and shuts out the light of truth.
William S. Plumer

Sin has digged every grave.
William S. Plumer

Sin is worse than all other evils. It makes earth like hell, and it makes hell what it is. *William S. Plumer*

Sin is arguably the greatest power in existence but for the power of God himself. It is not only an evil but an infinite evil. It is not merely against God but absolutely and entirely against God.
Maurice Roberts

Sin is never satisfied. *Maurice Roberts*

Sins begin like cobwebs, but become iron clamps. *J. C. Ryle*

Men hate their sins but cannot leave them.
Seneca

Sin and death are an adamantine chain and link that none can sever. Who shall separate that which God in his justice hath put together? *Richard Sibbes*

Part of the sinfulness of sin is seen when people begin to call the truth a lie, or call a lie the truth. *R. C. Sproul*

Sin is sovereign until sovereign grace dethrones it. *C. H. Spurgeon*

Sin will reign if it can: it cannot be satisfied with any place below the throne of the heart. *C. H. Spurgeon*

The more men suppress the truth of God which they know, the more futile, even senseless, they become in their thinking.
John R. W. Stott

The least sin is damnable ... A pistol will kill as dead as a cannon.
George Swinnock

No sin is small. It is against an infinite God and may have consequences immeasurable. No grain of sand is small in the mechanism of a watch.
Jeremy Taylor

No place can be so pleasant but sin will lay it waste. *John Trapp*

Pollution is the forerunner of perdition.
John Trapp

Little sins unrepented of will damn thee as well as greater. Not only great rivers fall into the sea, but little brooks; not only greater sins carry men to hell, but lesser; therefore do not think pardon easy because sin is small. *Thomas Watson*

There is in sin a commanding and a condemning power. *Thomas Watson*

As a very little dust will disorder a clock, and the least grain of sand will obscure our sight, so the least grain of sin which is upon the heart will hinder its right motion toward God. *John Wesley*

SIN — and Satan

Sin is an odious thing, the devil's drivel or vomit. *John Trapp*

Sin stamps the devil's image on a man.
Thomas Watson

The sinner's heart is the devil's mansion house. *Thomas Watson*

SINCERITY
(See also: Honesty; Integrity)

We are not saved by sincerity, but we may certainly be lost through insincerity.
Robert Black

It is better to be ingenuous than ingenious.
John Blanchard

Be what you seem! Live your creed!
Horatius Bonar

Sincerity is the very queen of virtues.
Thomas Brooks

The Lord first of all wants sincerity in his service, simplicity of heart without guile and falsehood.
John Calvin

Sincerity is the salt which seasons every sacrifice.
Stephen Charnock

We may truly be said to worship God though we lack perfection, but we cannot be said to worship God if we lack sincerity.
Stephen Charnock

Sincerity is the face of the soul.
S. Dubay

Sincerity is the highest compliment you can pay.
Ralph Waldo Emerson

Be as you would seem to be.
Thomas Fuller

Sincerity doesn't make wrong facts right.
Stephen Gaukroger

Sincerity! It is the life of all our graces and puts life into all our duties.
William Gurnall

Sincerity ... keeps the soul pure in the face of temptation.
William Gurnall

Sincerity makes the soul willing.
William Gurnall

I know no religion but sincerity.
Matthew Henry

Nothing is more pleasing to God than sincerity and plain-dealing.
Matthew Henry

No one can produce great things who is not thoroughly sincere in dealing with himself.
James Russell Lowell

Never has there been one possessed of complete sincerity who did not move others.
Mencius

Sincerity is of the essence of the life of godliness.
Iain Murray

We are to receive our reward not according to our success, but according to our sincerity.
John Oldfield

To be true to convictions is the life of sincerity.
John Owen

The primary condition for sincerity is the same as for being humble: not to boast of it, and probably not even to be aware of it.
Henri Peyre

The strength of every grace lies in the sincerity of it.
A. W. Pink

There is no substitute for godly sincerity.
William S. Plumer

Whatever we are in our religion, let us resolve never to wear a cloak. Let us by all means be honest and real.
J. C. Ryle

Sincerity is the truth of all grace.
William Secker

He that is sincere is sincere in all places and at all times.
Richard Sibbes

Sincerity is the prime requisite in every approach to the God who requires 'truth in the inward parts' and who hates all hypocrisy, falsehood and deceit.
Geoffrey B. Wilson

The conduct of our lives is the only proof of the sincerity of our hearts.
Robert Wilson

SINFUL NATURE
(See also: Depravity; Guilt; Man — a Sinner; Sin)

We all carry about with us material that Satan can work upon.   *Anon.*

The greatest struggles that life can know are not within the unsaved, but within the saved.   *Donald Grey Barnhouse*

Ourselves are the greatest snares to ourselves.   *Richard Baxter*

Not only the worst of my sins, but the best of my duties speak me a child of Adam.   *William Beveridge*

Our sinful natures are neither removed at our regeneration nor refined by our sanctification.   *John Blanchard*

Sin in a wicked man is like poison in a serpent; it is in its natural place.
Thomas Brooks

The man without a navel still lives in me.
Thomas Browne

In the conversion of man, the properties of our original nature remain entire.
John Calvin

The procuring cause of our misery is in ourselves.   *John Calvin*

Man without God is a beast, and never more beastly than when he is most intelligent about his beastliness.
Whittaker Chambers

Nothing leads to self-repudiation so much as spiritual meditation on the corruption and wickedness of your heart.
Walter J. Chantry

The ground of the soul is dark.
Meister Eckhart

Evil is the real problem in the hearts and minds of men.   *Albert Einstein*

The real problem is in the hearts and minds of men. It is not a problem of physics but of ethics. It is easier to denature plutonium than to denature the evil spirit of man.   *Albert Einstein*

Embellished nature is nature still.
John Flavel

Original sin is the malice that is ever flickering within us.   *Eric Hoffer*

The flesh is the womb where all sin is conceived and formed, the anvil upon which all is wrought, the Judas that betrays us, the secret enemy within that is ready on all occasions to open the gates to the besiegers.   *Thomas Jacomb*

All the old primitive sins are not dead but are crouching in the dark corners of our modern hearts — still there, and still as ghastly as ever.   *Carl Gustav Jung*

In youth, mid-age, and now after many battles, I find nothing in me but vanity and corruption.   *John Knox*

The true Christian's nostril is to be continually attentive to the inner cesspool.   *C. S. Lewis*

Man today is as rotten as he was the moment he fell in the Garden of Eden.
D. Martyn Lloyd-Jones

Human nature is like a drunk peasant. Lift him into the saddle on one side, over he topples on the other side. *Martin Luther*

I more fear what is within me than what comes from without. *Martin Luther*

Original sin is in us, like the beard. We are shaved today and look clean, and have a smooth chin; tomorrow our beard has grown again, nor does it cease growing while we remain on earth. *Martin Luther*

No figure of speech can represent my utter want of power to resist the torrent of sin. *Robert Murray M'Cheyne*

None but God knows what an abyss of corruption is in my heart.
Robert Murray M'Cheyne

The seeds of all sin are in my heart, and perhaps all the more dangerously that I do not see them.
Robert Murray M'Cheyne

It is one thing for sin to live in us; it is another for us to live in sin. *John Murray*

Flesh is an affection which focuses on the enjoyment of the creature, without primary reverence for and worship of the Creator. *Tom J. Nettles*

I find not one corruption of my vile heart is dead, though some seem now and then asleep. *John Newton*

I have a vile heart, capable of every evil; and I, in myself, am as prone to change as a weathercock. *John Newton*

Whosoever contends against indwelling sin shall know and find that it is present with them, that it is powerful in them.
John Owen

The flesh is radically and wholly evil.
A. W. Pink

No prayer is complete which does not contain a petition to be kept from the devil. *J. C. Ryle*

The evil that is in us is all our own.
J. C. Ryle

There is far more wickedness in all our hearts than we know. *J. C. Ryle*

The seeds of every wickedness lie hidden in our hearts. They only need the convenient season to spring forth into a mischievous vitality. *J. C. Ryle*

The Christian does not have to live in defeat, but he does have to live all his life with the sin nature … and … because God has not made flesh any better in the believer, because it has not been refined, it is a powerful enemy with which we have to live. *Charles Caldwell Ryrie*

Impress the young convert from the very beginning with the conviction that God has called him into his kingdom to struggle with the corruptions of his heart.
William B. Sprague

All the devils in hell and tempters on earth could do us no injury if there were no corruption in our own natures.
C. H. Spurgeon

Beware of no man more than of yourself; we carry our worst enemies within us.
C. H. Spurgeon

During my first week the new life that was in me had been compelled to fight for its existence, and a conflict with the old nature had been vigorously carried on. This I knew to be a special token of the indwelling of grace in my soul.
C. H. Spurgeon

Our old man is crucified, but he is long at dying. *C. H. Spurgeon*

The saints are sinners still. *C. H. Spurgeon*

There is no doctrine more true to experience than this, that corruption remains even in the hearts of the regenerate, and that when we would do good evil is present with us. *C. H. Spurgeon*

There may be persons who can always glide along like a tramcar on rails without a solitary jerk, but I find that I have a vile nature to contend with, and spiritual life is a struggle with me. I have to fight from day to day with inbred corruption, coldness, deadness, barrenness, and if it were not for my Lord Jesus Christ my heart would be as dry as the heart of the damned. *C. H. Spurgeon*

Our old nature is no more extinct than the devil; but God's will is that the dominion of both should be broken.
John R. W. Stott

Human nature … is not a green apple to be perfected by mere growth, but an apple with a worm at the core, which left to itself will surely rot and perish.
Augustus H. Strong

The human personality has … been invaded by an alien army which is always campaigning within it. *R. V. G. Tasker*

Sins are because sin is. *A. W. Tozer*

I have never heard of a sin being committed without knowing full well that I had the seed of it within myself.
Johann Wolfgang von Goethe

I see no fault that I might not have committed myself.
Johann Wolfgang von Goethe

Though we (as Christians) are like Christ, having the firstfruits of the Spirit, yet we are unlike him, having the remainders of the flesh. *Thomas Watson*

Original sin is a sea that will not, in this life, be dried up. *Thomas Watson*

Believers are no more able now *of themselves* to think one good thought, to form one good desire, to speak one good word, or to do one good work, than before they were justified. *John Wesley*

Worst of all my foes, I fear the enemy within. *John Wesley*

The biblical view is that all events are God's events. *David Wilkinson*

SLANDER
(See also: Gossip; Rumour; Speech)

Slander, like coal, will either dirty your hand or burn it. *Anon.*

Slanders are the devil's bellows to blow up contention. *Anon.*

Slander is almost invariably verbal cowardice. *John Blanchard*

The surest method against slander is to live it down by perseverance in well-doing. *Hermann Boerhaave*

No one should say behind a man's back what he dare not, or would not, say to his face. *William Booth*

No greater injury can be inflicted upon men than to wound their reputation. *John Calvin*

If you are slandered, never mind; it will all come off when it is dry. *Charles G. Finney*

Slander is best answered with silence. *Ben Johnson*

Slander has a marvellous way of driving us into the arms of our heavenly Father. *Stuart Olyott*

Lies and false reports are among Satan's choicest weapons. *J. C. Ryle*

Slander is a vice that strikes a double blow, wounding both him that commits and him against whom it is committed. *Jacques Sauin*

Whispered insinuations are the rhetoric of the devil. *Johann Wolfgang von Goethe*

SLEEP

For what else is sleep but a daily death which does not completely remove man hence nor detain him too long? And what else is death, but a very long and very deep sleep from which God arouses man? *Augustine*

Sleep is, in fine, so like death I dare not trust it without my prayers. *Thomas Fuller*

SLOTH — See Indolence

SOCIAL RESPONSIBILITY

A man ought to carry himself in the world as an orange-tree would if it could walk up and down in the garden — swinging perfume from every little censer it holds up to the air. *Chrysostom*

Social service need not be the 'social gospel' . . . It means doing something about ... pain and suffering, for the sake of Christian love, and not insinuating at every turn that what we do is in order to get people into our churches and to take up our form of creed. *Jose D. Fajardo*

If God is God and man is made in his image, then *each* man is significant. *Os Guinness*

The Christian with social concern must champion all those who need champions, not just those whose championing is currently popular. *Os Guinness*

The church cannot be concerned with the redemption of men in such a way that their becoming Christians means that they must withdraw from God's creation. *Paul Helm*

To live as contemporary Christians means at least this — to take account of the fact that our neighbours are made in the image of God. *Paul Helm*

Church members who deny in fact their responsibility for the needy in any part of the world are just as much guilty of heresy as those who deny this or that article of the faith. *W. A. Visser 't Hooft*

However we do it, the Christian faith requires us to have sensitivity to social need and oppression. This is not a social gospel. This is not the gospel. It is a fruit of the gospel. *Alan Kreider*

A born-again Christian without a social conscience is irrelevant, and a social activist without a regenerate heart is irresponsible. *Gordon Moyes*

Christianity was never meant to interfere with a man's obedience to the civil power. *J. C. Ryle*

We have no liberty to say that our sole responsibility as Christians is to preach the gospel of salvation, since moral and social righteousness will then follow normally. *John R. W. Stott*

It's a mistake to assume that God is only interested in religion. *William Temple*

The New Testament churches did not have specific programmes of social reform in their community action, but they did have Christ and the gospel so that social reform in the community inevitably came, and with awful and positive power. *Foy Valentine*

Whatever makes men good Christians makes them good citizens. *Daniel Webster*

The gospel of Christ knows of no religion but social, no holiness but social holiness. *John Wesley*

SOLITUDE

It is far better to be alone than to be in bad company. *Anon.*

Solitude is often the best society. *Anon.*

Observe what directions your thoughts and feelings most readily take when you are alone, and you will form a tolerably correct opinion of your real state. *J. A. Bengel*

Solitude is the soul's best friend. *Charles Cotton*

You are only what you are when no one is looking. *Robert C. Edwards*

Conversation enriches the understanding, but solitude is the school of genius. *Edward Gibbon*

People who cannot bear to be alone are the worst company. *Albert Guinon*

It is what we do with our solitude that makes us fit for company. *C. S. Lewis*

Have we not all known what it is to find that, somehow, we have less to say to God when we are alone than when we are in the presence of others? *D. Martyn Lloyd-Jones*

What I am in secret, that I am in reality. *Arthur Neil*

Not till we have lost the world do we begin to find ourselves. *Henry Thoreau*

In the poverty of solitude all riches are present. *Paul Tillich*

SORROW

Sorrow commonly comes on horseback but goes away on foot. *Thomas Adams*

How amazing it is that we have so few tears these days when there is so much to weep about! *Issac H. A. Ababio*

Every lock of sorrow has a key of promise to fit it. *Anon.*

Godly sorrow is better than worldly joy. *Anon.*

Joys are our wings; sorrows are our spurs.
Anon.

He who does not sigh as a pilgrim will never rejoice as a citizen. *Augustine*

Night brings out stars as sorrow shows us truths. *Gamaliel Bailey*

How fast we learn in a day of sorrow!
Horatius Bonar

There is nothing that so makes us acquainted with Christ himself as sorrow.
Horatius Bonar

The heaviest thing in the world is a heavy heart. *John Burroughs*

The soul would have no rainbow had the eyes no tears. *John Vance Cheney*

If one man should suffer all the sorrows of all the saints in the world, yet they are not worth one hour's glory in heaven.
Chrysostom

Sorrow is given us on purpose to cure us of sin. *Chrysostom*

The finest flowers are often found growing in the soil of sorrow. *G. B. Duncan*

No matter how great a sorrow may be, God has already suffered it.
Meister Eckhart

Christ takes no more delight to dwell in a sad heart than we do to live in a dark house. *William Gurnall*

No marvel that our sorrows are multiplied when our sins are. *Matthew Henry*

Weeping must never hinder worship.
Matthew Henry

Sorrows and joys alike are temporary. In a moment all may be changed. Therefore to one who judges rightly, earthly grief is not over grievous and earthly joy not over joyous. *J. B. Lightfoot*

You learn your theology most where your sorrows take you. *Martin Luther*

Earth has no sorrow that heaven cannot heal. *Thomas Moore*

I wonder, many times, that ever a child of God should have a sad heart, considering what his Lord is preparing for him.
Samuel Rutherford

There is no commentary that opens up the Bible so much as sickness and sorrow. *J. C. Ryle*

Better to have a Christian's days of sorrows than a worldling's joys.
C. H. Spurgeon

Sorrows are visitors that come without invitation. *C. H. Spurgeon*

There is a sweet joy that comes to us through sorrow. *C. H. Spurgeon*

This only can my fears control,
And bid my sorrows fly;
What harm can ever reach my soul
Beneath my Father's eye?
Anne Steele

All misery calls sin mother.
George Swinnock

There are such things as consecrated griefs, sorrows that may be common to everyone but which take on a special character when accepted intelligently and offered to God in loving submission.
A. W. Tozer

Sorrow

One Son God hath without sin, but none without sorrow. *John Trapp*

Melancholy gives the devil great advantages; it pulls off the chariot wheels.
Thomas Watson

SOUL
(See also: Heart)

Man does not have a soul, he is a soul.
James Barr

As God's eternal decrees have an end without a beginning, so the souls of men have a beginning without an end.
John Boys

Soul is that by which we live naturally; spirit is that by which we live through grace supernaturally. *John Boys*

The soul is the breath of God, the beauty of man, the wonder of angels and the envy of devils. *Thomas Brooks*

As the man is more noble than the house he dwells in, so is the soul more noble than the body. *John Bunyan*

The soul is such a thing, so rich and valuable in its nature, that scarce one in twenty thousand counts of it as they should. *John Bunyan*

The body is the prison of the soul.
John Calvin

The soul, being a spirit, conveys more to the body than the body can to it.
Stephen Charnock

If the soul be lost, the man is lost.
John Flavel

The soul pays a dear rent for the tenement it now lives in. *John Flavel*

The fundamental error of sinners is undervaluing their own souls.
Matthew Henry

The soul is the man. *Matthew Henry*

The real value of an object is that which one who knows its worth will give for it. He who made the soul knew its worth, and gave his life for it. *Arthur Jackson*

Your own soul is your first and greatest care. *Robert Murray M'Cheyne*

The soul is the place where man's supreme and final battles are fought.
Abraham Neuman

Where the eternal interests of the soul are concerned, only a fool will give himself the benefit of the doubt. *A. W. Pink*

The whole world cannot make up to a man for the loss of his soul. *J. C. Ryle*

Our souls are like the mill that grinds what is put into it. *Richard Sibbes*

The meaning of earthly existence lies, not as we have grown used to thinking, in prospering, but in the development of the soul. *Alexandr Solzhenitsyn*

None but God can satisfy the longings of the immortal soul; as the heart was made for him, he only can fill it.
Richard C. Tench

The moral character of the soul depends upon its central object. *David Thomas*

SOUL-WINNING
(See also: Evangelism; Witnessing)

A good fisherman keeps himself out of sight.   *Anon.*

If we would win some we must be winsome.   *Anon.*

I remember no one sin that my conscience doth so accuse me and judge me as for doing so little for the saving of men's souls and for dealing no more fervently and earnestly for their conversion.
Richard Baxter

The greatest thing in life is to bring others to Jesus Christ.
Henry Ward Beecher

You do not choose to be in the business of bringing men to Christ; you choose Christ and you are at once in the business.
Joe Blinco

Go for souls — and go for the worst!
William Booth

Some like to live within the sound of church or chapel bell; I'd rather run a rescue shop within a yard of hell.
William Booth

Some men's passion is for gold. Some men's passion is for art. Some men's passion is for fame. My passion is for souls.
William Booth

I cared not where or how I lived, or what hardships I went through, so that I could but gain souls to Christ. *David Brainerd*

There was nothing of any importance to me but holiness of heart and life, and the conversion of the Indians to God.
David Brainerd

The longing of my heart would be to go all round the world before I die, and preach one gospel invitation in the ear of every creature.   *William Burns*

Nothing is more useless than a Christian who does not try to save others . . . I cannot believe in the salvation of anyone who does not work for his neighbour's salvation.   *Chrysostom*

The solemn one thing of my life shall be to save souls.   *Thomas Collins*

I long for the conversion of souls more sensibly than anything else besides.
Philip Doddridge

The level of our concern for the salvation of others reflects the condition of our own souls.   *Owen French*

No man can be a Christian who is unconcerned for the salvation of others.
Richard Haldane

Lord, speak to me, that I may speak
In living echoes of thy tone;
As thou hast sought, so let me seek
Thy erring children lost and lone.
Frances Ridley Havergal

The best publicity the gospel will ever have is a new Christian out to win others.   *Vance Havner*

I would think it a greater happiness to gain one soul for Christ than mountains of silver and gold for myself.
Matthew Henry

If we do not catch men we are in danger of losing even the desire to catch them.
John Henry Jowett

The joy of catching a soul is unspeakable. When we have got one soul we become possessed by the passion for souls. Get one and you will want a crowd.
John Henry Jowett

The glory of God, and, as our only means to glorifying him, the salvation of souls, is the real business of life. *C. S. Lewis*

The salvation of a single soul is more important than the production or preservation of all the epics and tragedies in the world. *C. S. Lewis*

The salvation of souls is a means to the glorifying of God because only saved souls can duly glorify him. *C. S. Lewis*

I feel there are two things it is impossible to desire with sufficient ardour — personal holiness and the honour of Christ in the salvation of souls.
Robert Murray M'Cheyne

What would I not give for the power to make sinners love *him! Edward Payson*

The best soul-winners are those who go when it is convenient, and then go when it is not convenient. *John Rice*

A man's religion may well be suspected when he is content to go to heaven alone.
J. C. Ryle

One single soul saved shall outlive and outweigh all the kingdoms of the world.
J. C. Ryle

Better indeed for us to die than to live if souls be not saved. *C. H. Spurgeon*

Ere the sun goes down think of some one action which may tend to the conversion of some one person, and do it with all your might. *C. H. Spurgeon*

Have you no wish for others to be saved? Then you are not saved yourself. Be sure of that. *C. H. Spurgeon*

I would sooner bring one sinner to Jesus Christ than unpick all the mysteries of the divine Word. *C. H. Spurgeon*

If anybody had told me, 'Somebody has left you £20,000,' I should not have given a snap of my fingers for it, compared with the joy which I felt when I was told that God had saved a soul through my ministry. *C. H. Spurgeon*

The soul-winner must first be a soul-lover. *C. H. Spurgeon*

To be a soul-winner is the happiest thing in this world. And with every soul you bring to Jesus Christ you seem to get a new heaven here upon earth.
C. H. Spurgeon

What are all your kings, all your nobles, all your diadems, when you put them together, compared with the dignity of winning souls to Christ? *C. H. Spurgeon*

Winners of souls must first be weepers for souls. *C. H. Spurgeon*

You do not love the Lord at all unless you love the souls of others.
C. H. Spurgeon

It is a great work to make people fit for the cemetery. *William Tiptaft*

I would rather win souls than be the greatest king or emperor on earth; I would rather win souls than be the greatest general that ever commanded an army ... My one ambition in life is to win as many as possible. Oh, it is the only thing worth doing, to save souls; and, men and women, we can all do it. *R. A. Torrey*

Our joy until we die is to win men for the Lord.   *Nicolaus Ludwig Von Zinzendorf*

No Christian has any right ever to feel comfortable as long as there are any anywhere who do not know Christ.
Max Warren

We have one business on earth — to save souls.   *John Wesley*

Give me souls or take away my soul!
George Whitefield

To bring souls to Christ should be our master passion.   *Frederick P. Wood*

SPEECH
(See also: Eloquence; Gossip; Rumour; Slander)

It is easier to look wise than to talk wisely.
Ambrose

A bird is known by his note, a man by his talk.   *Anon.*

A sharp tongue is no evidence of a keen mind.   *Anon.*

Actions don't always speak louder than words — your tongue can undo everything you do.   *Anon.*

His heart cannot be pure whose tongue is not clean.   *Anon.*

In company, guard your tongue — in solitude, your thoughts.   *Anon.*

Lord, make my words gracious and tender, for tomorrow I may have to eat them!
Anon.

No physician can heal the wounds inflicted by the tongue.   *Anon.*

Nothing is so opened more by mistake than the mouth.   *Anon*

One thing you can give and still keep is your word.   *Anon.*

The Christian should learn two things about his tongue: how to hold it and how to use it.   *Anon.*

The tongue is but three inches long, yet it can kill a man six feet high.   *Anon.*

There are two sciences which every person ought to learn: the science of speech and the more difficult one of silence.   *Anon.*

What is in the well of your heart will show up in the bucket of your speech.   *Anon.*

When you speak, remember God is one of your listeners.   *Anon.*

Words are leaves — deeds are fruit. *Anon.*

The tongue is the hinge on which everything in the personality turns.   *T. C. Baird*

It is a sad fact that the tongues of professing Christians are often all too busy doing the devil's work.
Donald Grey Barnhouse

One of the first things that happens when a man is really filled with the Spirit is not that he speaks with tongues, but that he learns to hold the one tongue he already has.   *J. Sidlow Baxter*

Gentle words fall lightly, but they have great weight.   *Derick Bingham*

A sanctified heart is better than a silver tongue.   *Thomas Brooks*

Of all the members in the body, there is none so serviceable to Satan as the tongue.   *Thomas Brooks*

We know metals by their tinkling and men by their talking.   *Thomas Brooks*

A word spoken is physically transient but morally permanent.   *Francis Burkitt*

The vice of the tongue spreads and prevails over every part of life. It is as active and potent for evil in old age as ever it was in the days of our youth. *John Calvin*

There is nothing more slippery or loose than the tongue.   *John Calvin*

During a long life I have had to eat my own words many times and I have found it a very nourishing diet. *Winston Churchill*

When you have nothing to say, say nothing.   *C. C. Colton*

Think all you speak but speak not all you think.   *Patrick Delaney*

The worst of speaking without thinking is that you say what you think.
                        James Denney

Let thy speech be better than silence, or be silent.   *Dionysius the Elder*

Nothing is often a good thing to say.
                        Will Durant

Kind words are the music of the world.
                    Frederick W. Faber

The heart of a fool is in his mouth, but the mouth of a wise man is in his heart.
                    Benjamin Franklin

If I speak what is false, I must answer for it; if truth, it will answer for me.
                        Thomas Fuller

The jawbone of an ass was a killer in Samson's time. It still is. *Morris Gilber*

A sanctified heart is better than a silver tongue.   *Thomas Goodwin*

If the mouth be bad, the mind is not good.
                        Matthew Henry

It is bad to think ill, but it is worse to speak it.   *Matthew Henry*

If nobody said anything unless he knew what he was talking about, what a ghastly hush would descend upon the earth!
                        A. P. Herbert

There will come a time when three words, uttered with charity and meekness, shall receive a far more blessed reward than three thousand volumes written with disdainful sharpness of wit.
                        Richard Hooker

Many people would be more truthful were it not for their uncontrollable desire to talk.   *Edgar Watson Howe*

There is a time for saying nothing; there is occasionally a time for saying something; there is never a time for saying everything.   *Hugh of St Victor*

A sharp tongue is the only edged tool that grows keener with constant use.
                    Washington Irving

A fool is hardly discerned when silent; his picture is best taken when he is speaking.   *William Jenkyn*

An evil speaker is his own scourge.
                        William Jenkyn

If you can hold your tongue you can hold anything.   *E. Stanley Jones*

Sharp tongues have a way of sharpening other tongues.   *E. Stanley Jones*

Better to remain silent and be thought a fool than to speak out and remove all doubt.   *Abraham Lincoln*

Blessed are they who have nothing to say and who cannot be persuaded to say it.
James Russell Lowell

The tongue is the ambassador of the heart.
John Lyly

When the hands are idle, the tongue is usually very active.   *Henry T. Mahan*

A tongue that is set on fire from hell shall be set on fire in hell.   *Thomas Manton*

Evil words show a wicked heart, and idle words a vain mind.   *Thomas Manton*

Most of a man's sins are in his words.
Thomas Manton

If you think twice before you talk once, you will speak twice the better for it.
William Penn

Man's speech is like his life.   *Plato*

A word spoken is physically transient but morally permanent.   *J. C. Ryle*

Our words are the evidence of the state of our hearts as surely as the taste of the water is an evidence of the state of the spring.   *J. C. Ryle*

By the striking of the clapper we guess at the metal of the bell.   *William Secker*

Speech is the index of the mind. *Seneca*

When I think over what I have said, I envy dumb people.   *Seneca*

Speech is ... only good when it is better than silence.   *Richard Sibbes*

If we cannot be believed on our word, we are surely not to be trusted on our oath.
C. H. Spurgeon

The word of a man is as powerful as himself.   *Richard Sibbes*

Some men's tongues bite more than their teeth.   *C. H. Spurgeon*

Tongues are more terrible instruments than can be made with hammers and anvils, and the evil which they inflict cuts deeper and spreads wider. *C. H. Spurgeon*

Whatever moves the heart wags the tongue.   *C. T. Studd*

The heart is the metal of the bell, the tongue but the clapper. *George Swinnock*

Speech is the mirror of the soul; as a man speaks, so he is.   *Publilius Syrus*

A man is hid under his tongue.
Ali Ibn-Ali-Talib

Evil tongues are the devil's bellows.
John Trapp

A ready tongue without an informed mind, a devout character and a holy life will hinder rather than advance the cause of Christ.   *Curtis Vaughan*

How can Christ be in the heart when the devil has taken possession of the tongue?
Thomas Watson

Words are the looking-glass of the mind.
Thomas Watson

SPIRITUAL DARKNESS

It is no advantage to be near the light if the eyes are closed. *Augustine*

The blindness of unbelievers in no way detracts from the clarity of the gospel; the sun is no less bright because blind men do not perceive its light. *John Calvin*

There is no greater darkness than the ignorance of God. *John Clavin*

A blind man will not thank you for a looking-glass. *Thomas Fuller*

Man lives in the dark and even his nuclear flashlight cannot pierce it. *Vance Havner*

Spiritual darkness is spiritual bondage. *Matthew Henry*

Those that love darkness rather than light shall have their doom accordingly. *Matthew Henry*

The penalty of living in the darkness is not merely that one does not see, but that one goes blind. *David Smith*

Blindness is the cause of unbelief, whoever the unbeliever may be. *John R. W. Stott*

The human intellect, even in its fallen state, is an awesome work of God, but it lies in darkness until it has been illuminated by the Holy Spirit. *A. W. Tozer*

A blind eye is worse than a lame foot. *Thomas Watson*

SPIRITUAL GIFTS

The things that count most cannot be counted. *Anon.*

All Christ's gifts are like himself, spiritual and heavenly. *Thomas Brooks*

All know that the gift of healing was not perpetual ... The anointers of this day are no more ministers of the grace of which James speaks than the player who acted Agamemnon on the stage was a king. *John Calvin*

All the gifts and power which men seem to possess are in the hands of God, so that he can, at any instant ... deprive them of the wisdom which he has given them. *John Calvin*

If we are proud of our talents we betray our lack of gratitude to God. *John Calvin*

If we listen to the instruction of Scripture we must remember that our talents are not of our own making, but free gifts of God. *John Calvin*

There is none so poor in the church of Christ who may not impart to us something of value. *John Calvin*

Whatever ability a faithful Christian may possess, he ought to possess it for his fellow believers, and he ought to make his own interest subservient to the well-being of the church in all sincerity. *John Calvin*

Spiritual gifts are not toys with which to play; they are tools of the Spirit with which to do the Lord's work effectively. *G. Raymond Carlson*

To claim credit for the Lord's gifts to us or to undervalue our particular charisma is in either case to lose sight of the essential nature of any gift. *Herbert M. Carson*

Spiritual gifts are no proof of spirituality. *Samuel Chadwick*

It is dangerously easy to fix our hearts on the blessing rather than the Blesser.
Ronald Dunn

Salvation is promised to those who have the graces of the Spirit, but not to those who have merely the extraordinary gifts. Many have these last, and yet go to hell.
Jonathan Edwards

There is a great deal of unmapped country within us.
George Eliot

You cannot have the *gifts* of Christ apart from the *government* of Christ.
A. Lindsay Glegg

Grace is too much neglected where gifts are too highly prized.
William Gurnall

Pride of gifts robs us of God's blessing in the use of them.
William Gurnall

A drop of grace is worth a sea of gifts.
William Jenkyn

The best gifts are those which benefit the whole body. You don't find many people asking for the gift of liberality.
Harry Kilbride

To consider the charismata as intended merely to adorn and benefit the person endowed would be just as absurd as to say, 'I light the fire to warm not the *room* but the *stove*.'
Abraham Kuyper

We cannot get Christ's gifts without himself.
Alexander Maclaren

Gifts are but dead graces, but graces are living gifts.
Christopher Nesse

All through the New Testament, when God's work in human lives is spoken of, the ethical takes priority over the charismatic.
J. I. Packer

The most significant gifts in the church's life in every era are ordinarily natural abilities sanctified.
J. I. Packer

To place ourselves in range of God's choicest gifts, we have to walk with God, work with God, lean on God, cling to God, come to have the sense and feel of God, refer all things to God.
Corneluis Plantinga

It is very hard to behold our own gifts without pride, and the gifts of others without envy.
Vavasor Powell

Men forget that gifts without grace save no one's soul, and are the characteristics of Satan himself.
J. C. Ryle

We are all talented people. Anything whereby we may glorify God is a talent.
J. C. Ryle

SPIRITUAL HUNGER

God promises to fill those who hunger and thirst after righteousness, yet the sign that he is doing so is that they go on hungering and thirsting.
John Blanchard

It is easy to mistake intellectual curiosity for spiritual hunger.
François Fenelon

A deep and sober daily concern to please God is the rarest of rarities.
Vance Havner

If there is a man anywhere who is hungering after God and is not filled, then the Word of God is broken. We are as full as we want to be.
A. W. Tozer

If there is anything in your life more demanding than your longing after God, then you will never be a Spirit-filled Christian.
A. W. Tozer

Taking in its widest latitude, to 'hunger and thirst after righteousness' means to yearn after God's favour, image and felicity. *A. W. Pink*

Desires for more grace, and groanings which cannot be uttered, are growing pains, and we should wish to feel them more and more. *C. H. Spurgeon*

They who do not thirst for righteousness shall be in perpetual hunger and thirst. *Thomas Watson*

O for a heart to praise my God,
A heart from sin set free;
A heart that always feels thy blood
So freely shed for me.
Charles Wesley

SPIRITUAL RICHES

Treasures in heaven are laid up only as treasures on earth are laid down. *Anon.*

It's wiser to have your bank in heaven than to have your heaven in a bank. *Anon.*

The saint's enduring riches are in the future, locked up in the heavenly casket. *George Barlow*

God, and God alone, is man's highest good. *Herman Bavinck*

God's purposes always have God's provision. *John Blanchard*

Union with Christ entitles to all that is his. *Elisha Coles*

If we are spiritually impoverished, it is not because the hand of grace is tight-fisted; it is because the hand of faith is too weak. *Ronald Dunn*

A man is just as rich as his investment in the bank of heaven. *Vance Havner*

God wants no man to be more prosperous than his soul. *Vance Havner*

It takes a radical break to turn from earth's trash to heaven's treasure. *Vance Havner*

The trees of the age to come extend their branches over the wall on this side and we may enjoy some of their fruits here and now. *Vance Havner*

A man with God on his side is always in the majority. *John Knox*

Shame on us for being paupers when we were meant to be princes. *D. Martyn Lloyd-Jones*

My Father, help me to learn that I am heir to possessions which exceed my present holding! *George Matheson*

Learn to put your hand on all spiritual blessings in Christ and say, 'Mine'. *F. B. Meyer*

If ever you are tempted to say, 'I wish someone were to die and leave me something in his will,' allow me to tell you, 'Someone has!' *David Shepherd*

There's a huge inheritance to be claimed by repenting sinners. *David Shepherd*

God is the portion of his people, and the chosen people are the portion of their God. *C. H. Spurgeon*

The *All-Sufficient* is sufficient for my largest want. He who is sufficient for earth and heaven is certainly able to meet the case of one poor worm like me. *C. H. Spurgeon*

The way of uprightness is the way of heavenly wealth. *C. H. Spurgeon*

With the goodness of God to desire our highest welfare, the wisdom of God to plan it, and the power of God to achieve it, what do we lack? *A. W. Tozer*

It is unlikely that God will entrust us with spiritual riches until he sees that we are genuinely serving him, not mammon. *David Watson*

All Christ's subjects are kings. *Thomas Watson*

How vast the treasures we possess!
How rich thy bounty, King of grace!
This world is ours, and worlds to come;
Earth is our lodge, and heaven our home. *Isaac Watts*

SPIRITUAL WARFARE

The hardest victory is victory over self. *Anon.*

The call to Christian commitment is not basically a call to enjoy happiness but to endure hardness. *John Blanchard*

For the Christian, this world is an arena, not an armchair. *John Blanchard*

Spiritual depression cannot be resisted by flight, but must be struggled with and resisted. *John Cassian*

All whom the Lord has chosen and received into the society of his saints ought to prepare themselves for a life that is hard, difficult, laborious and full of countless griefs. *John Calvin*

God has appointed this whole life to be all as a race or a battle; the state of rest, wherein we shall be so out of danger as to have no need of watching and fighting, is for another world. *Jonathan Edwards*

Jesus invited us not to a picnic but to a pilgrimage; not to a frolic but to a fight. *Billy Graham*

No duty can be performed without wrestling. The Christian needs his sword as well as his trowel. *William Gurnall*

The constant challenge in this life we call Christian is the translation of all we believe to be true into our day-to-day lifestyle. *Tim Hansel*

We are not here to commune with darkness but to conquer it. *Vance Havner*

We do not become saints in our sleep. *Vance Havner*

Scars are the price which every believer pays for his loyalty to Christ. *William Hendriksen*

Our journey is uphill, with a dead body upon our backs, the devil doing what he can to pull us down. *Philip Henry*

It is impossible to be a true soldier of Jesus Christ and not fight. *J. Gresham Machen*

Sometimes we are praying when we should be resisting Satan. *D. Martyn Lloyd-Jones*

There can never be peace in the bosom of a believer. There is peace with God, but constant war with sin. *Robert Murray M'Cheyne*

Keeping our heads despite the pull of pleasure is as hard a task as any for the affluent believer. *J. I. Packer*

Regeneration has made our hearts a battlefield. *J. I. Packer*

Christianity is a battle — not a dream.
Wendell Phillips

There is no winning without warfare; there is no opportunity without opposition; there is no victory without vigilance. *Alan Redpath*

There is only one attitude possible for us if we mean to get to heaven. We must wage a ceaseless warfare against sin within us all the days of our life.
Maurice Roberts

You will not get leave to steal quietly to heaven in Christ's company without a conflict and a cross. *Samuel Rutherford*

The believer may be known by his inward warfare as well as by his inward peace. *J. C. Ryle*

There is no holiness without a warfare.
J. C. Ryle

Where there is grace there will be a conflict. *J. C. Ryle*

What greater encouragement can a man have to fight against his enemy than when he is sure of the victory before he fights — of final victory? *Richard Sibbes*

I have never won an inch of the way to heaven without fighting for it.
C. H. Spurgeon

I thank God with all my heart that I have never known what it is to be out of the seventh of Romans, nor out of the eighth of Romans either: the whole passage has been solid truth to my experience.
C. H. Spurgeon

It strikes me that conflict is the principal feature of the Christian life this side of heaven. *C. H. Spurgeon*

Dead fish go with the stream, living ones against it. *William Tiptaft*

The Christian life is not a playground; it is a battle-ground. *Warren Wiersbe*

SPIRITUALITY

You are only as spiritual as you are scriptural. *Myron Augsburger*

Attitudes to God, especially as we come to him in worship, are the true monitor of spirituality. *John Benton*

It is very rare for the spirituality of a group of Christians to exceed that of its leaders. *John Benton*

A man's true spiritual quality is to be judged by his graces, not his gifts.
John Blanchard

Spirituality is a work of God for his child; service is a work of the child for his God, which can only be accomplished in the power of the indwelling Spirit.
Lewis Sperry Chafer

Spirituality is not gained by service; it is *unto* service. *Lewis Sperry Chafer*

The best measure of a spiritual life is not its ecstasies but its obedience.
Oswald Chambers

Spirituality is the genius of the gospel.
Stephen Charnock

No man is living at his best who is not living at his best spiritually.
W. Marshall Craig

Sentiment is the main opponent of spirituality. *Art Glasser*

The carnal mind sees God in nothing, not even in spiritual things. The spiritual mind sees him in everything, even in natural things. *Robert Leighton*

Every Christian would agree that a man's spiritual health is exactly proportional to his love for God. *C. S. Lewis*

The measure of our spirituality is the amount of praise and thanksgiving in our prayer. *D. Martyn Lloyd-Jones*

The more spiritual we are, the more we shall think about heaven.
D. Martyn Lloyd-Jones

The ultimate test of our spirituality is the measure of our amazement at the grace of God. *D. Martyn Lloyd-Jones*

In the biblical sense, the spiritual man is the man who has been begotten again, and has not had part of his nature but all of his nature transformed by the supernatural act of the Spirit of God.
J. Gresham Machen

Prayer is conditioned by one thing alone and that is spirituality. *Leonard Ravenhill*

Learn to hold loosely all that is not eternal. *Agnes Maude Royden*

Spirituality begins to have real meaning in our lives as we begin to exhibit simultaneously the holiness of God and the love of God. *Francis Schaeffer*

In spiritual things there is no envy.
Richard Sibbes

Spiritual things are against the stream; heaven is up the hill. *Richard Sibbes*

Real spirituality always has an outcome.
Oswald J. Smith

Our estimate of Christ is the best gauge of our spiritual condition. *C. H. Spurgeon*

SPORT — See Amusements; Recreation

STEWARDSHIP
(See also: Giving; Tithing)

Our temporary stewardship will determine our permanent ownership.
John Blanchard

We are to get, not just in order to have, but in order to give. *Anon.*

The fundamental truth in the matter of stewardship is that everything we touch belongs to God. *John Blanchard*

It was not an accident that seventeen of the thirty-six parables of our Lord had to do with property and stewardship.
William James Dawson

Poor stewardship amounts to nothing less than with-holding from the Lord that which is his. *Frank Gabelein*

Stewardship is what a man does after he says, 'I believe'. *W. H. Greaves*

Stewardship is the acceptance from God of personal responsibility for all of life and life's affairs. *Roswell C. Long*

Stewardship is not the leaving of a tip on God's tablecloth; it is the confession of an unpayable debt at God's Calvary.
Paul S. Rees

The use of our possessions shows us up for what we actually are.
Charles Caldwell Ryrie

STUBBOBNESS

A stiff neck usually supports an empty head. *Anon.*

Nothing is more like real conviction than simple obstinacy. *Anon.*

Man's impotency lies in his obstinacy. *Thomas Brooks*

Ignorance is closely followed by obstinacy. *John Calvin*

Hardness of heart makes a man's condition worse than all his other sins besides. *Thomas Watson*

Hell is full of hard hearts; there is not one soft heart there. *Thomas Watson*

SUBMISSION
(See also: Abandonment; Consecration; Zeal)

He who abandons himself *to* God will never be abandoned *by* God. *Anon.*

We should give God the same place in our hearts that he holds in the universe. *Anon.*

I dare not choose my lot; I would not if I might. Choose thou for me, my God, So shall I walk aright. *Horatius Bonar*

Nothing on earth do I desire,
But thy pure love within my breast;
This, only this, will I require,
And freely give up all the rest.
Antoinette Bourignon

If you lay yourself at Christ's feet he will take you into his arms. *William Bridge*

All life should be subject to the kingly rule of God. *Martin Buber*

Shall I, I pray Thee, change thy will my Father
Until it be according unto mine?
But no Lord, no, that never shall be, rather
I pray thee blend my human will with thine.
Amy Carmichael

The path of submission is the way to peace. *Herbert Carson*

Jesus will not be a Saviour to any man who refuses to bow to him as Lord. *Walter J. Chantry*

The Lord is King! Who then shall dare
Resist his will, distrust his care,
Or murmur at his wise decrees,
Or doubt his royal promises?
Josiah Conder

One of the miracles of the grace of God is what he is able to do with the torn nets of lives surrendered to him. *G. B. Duncan*

Submission to God is the only true balm that can heal the wounds he gives. *Nathaniel Emmons*

There are no disappointments to those whose wills are buried in the will of God. *Frederick W. Faber*

Make this simple rule the guide of your life: to have no will but God's. *François Fenelon*

Refuse nothing to God. *François Fenelon*

Promotion, publicity, personality, politics, popularity and even prosperity we have in abundance. But there is a dearth of God-empowered men and women with a deep love for the Saviour, unconditional commitment to him and complete indifference to their own wellbeing. *James R. Graham*

There is nothing got by scuffling with God. *William Gurnall*

Let him rule man who said, 'Let us make man.' *Matthew Henry*

Terms with God must always be *his* terms, not yours. *John Hercus*

If you don't surrender to Christ you surrender to chaos. *E. Stanley Jones*

We get no deeper into Christ than we allow him to get into us. *J. H. Jowett*

My times are in thy hand;
My God, I wish them there;
My life, my friends, my soul I leave
Entirely to thy care.
William Freeman Lloyd

It has always been my ambition to have no plans as regards myself.
Robert Murray M'Cheyne

Let God have your life; he can do more with it than you can. *D. L. Moody*

What I have to do, as his child, is to be satisfied with what my Father does, that I may glorify him. *George Muller*

I want nothing for myself; I want everything for the Lord. *Watchman Nee*

Men must choose to be governed by God or they condemn themselves to be ruled by tyrants. *William Penn*

Man is most truly himself, not when he struts about in pride of ability and possession, but when he sees himself as a creature of God and submits to the will of his Creator which is his true happiness. *Warren A. Quanbeek*

There are times when God asks nothing of his children except silence, patience and tears. *Charles Seymour Robinson*

The awesome purchase price of the very life of the Son of God should be more than ample motivation to make every child of God eagerly want to yield back to the Lord the very freedom which his death bought. *Charles Caldwell Ryrie*

The capital of heaven is the heart in which Jesus Christ is enthroned as King.
Sadhu Sundar Singh

To bring our minds under Christ's yoke is not to deny our rationality but to submit to his revelation. *John R. W. Stott*

We are not truly converted if we are not intellectually and morally converted, and we are not intellectually and morally converted if we have not subjected our minds and wills to the yoke of Jesus Christ.
John R. W. Stott

When all that you are is available to all that God is, then all that God is is available to all that you are. *Ian Thomas*

Father, I wait thy daily will;
Thou shalt divide my portion still;
Grant me on earth what seems thee best,
Till death and heaven reveal the rest.
Isaac Watts

May the mind of Christ my Saviour
Live in me from day to day,
By his love and power controlling
All I do and say.
Katie Barclay Wilkinson

SUCCESS

No one ever climbed the ladder of success with his hands in his pockets. *Anon.*

The dictionary is the only place where you can find success before work. *Anon.*

The highest branch is not the safest roost.
Anon.

Always expect to succeed, and never think you have succeeded.
Thomas Arnold

If the devil cannot use failure to drag you down, he will use success.
John Blanchard

To find his place and fill it is success for a man. *Phillips Brooks*

Men of great honour and worldly glory stand but in slippery places.
Thomas Brooks

It's a dangerous and misguided policy to measure God's blessing by standards of visible, tangible, material 'success'.
Charles Colson

The dangers to our spiritual welfare from success are far greater than the dangers from failure. *Arthur C. Custance*

The secret of success is constancy of purpose. *Benjamin Disraeli*

Try not to become a man of success but rather try to become a man of value.
Albert Einstein

There is a glare about worldly success which is very apt to dazzle men's eyes.
A. W. Hare

Success can feather our nest so comfortably that we forget how to fly.
Vance Havner

Visible success has never been the proof of Jesus or his followers. *Vance Havner*

Pray that success will not come any faster than you are able to endure it.
Elbert Hubbard

It is difficult to be high and not to be high-minded. *William Jenkyn*

Many who are climbing the ladder of success have their ladders leaning against the wrong walls. *Erwin W. Lutzer*

Even success in the Lord's work is a broken reed if we lean on it for security.
John W. Sanderson

The mania to succeed is a good thing perverted. *A. W. Tozer*

The man who is elated by success and cast down by failure is still a carnal man. At best his fruit will have a worm in it.
A. W. Tozer

The resurrection and the judgement will demonstrate before all worlds who won and who lost. We can wait! *A. W. Tozer*

Nothing recedes like success.
Walter Winchell

Success without God only makes temporary friends and admirers.
Spiros Zodhiates

SUFFERING
(See also: Pain; Sickness; Trials)

God sometimes has to put us on our backs in order to make us look up. *Anon.*

The face of Jesus must be very near our own when the thorns from his crown of suffering are pressing our brow and hurting us. *Anon.*

We can sometimes see more through a tear than through a telescope. *Anon.*

There is as much difference between the sufferings of the saints and those of the ungodly as there is between the cords with which an executioner pinions a condemned malefactor and the bandages wherewith a tender surgeon binds his patient.   *John Arrowsmith*

Suffering so unbolts the door of the heart that the Word hath easier entrance.
Richard Baxter

Weakness and pain helped me to study how to die; that set me on studying how to live.   *Richard Baxter*

Tears are often the telescope by which men see far into heaven.
Henry Ward Beecher

God would sooner we had holy pain than unholy pleasure.   *John Blanchard*

Pain and suffering are not necessarily signs of God's anger; they may be exactly the opposite.   *John Blanchard*

Strictly speaking, the atheist has no questions to ask about suffering; neither does he have any answers.   *John Blanchard*

Those who sing loudest in the kingdom will be those who on earth had the greatest bodily suffering. We pity them now, but then we shall almost envy them.
Andrew Bonar

Suffering ... is the badge of the true Christian.   *Dietrich Bonhoeffer*

In suffering one learns to pray best of all.
Harold A. Bosley

Suffering times are teaching times.
William Bridge

God understands our suffering because he has experienced it.   *Francis Bridger*

To ask God to step in constantly to prevent human or natural causes of suffering would be to ask for a puppet-master, nothing less.   *Francis Bridger*

Suffering times are a Christian's harvest times.   *Thomas Brooks*

We must suffer patiently, because impatience is rebellion against the justice of God.   *John Calvin*

The sovereign and utterly good God created a good universe. We human beings rebelled; rebellion is now so much a part of our make-up that we are all enmeshed in it. Every scrap of suffering we face turns on this fact.   *D. A. Carson*

The staying power of our faith is neither demonstrated nor developed until it is tested by suffering.   *D. A. Carson*

There is a certain kind of maturity that can be attained only through the discipline of suffering.   *D. A. Carson*

Because Jesus drank so deeply of bitter suffering, he is able to steady our hand as we drink what for us is a bitter draught but is, by comparison with his, a diluted cup.   *Herbert Carson*

Suffering is God's furnace in which he tests the quality of our faith.
Herbert Carson

To be human is to face the issue of suffering.   *Herbert Carson*

We must not assume that because someone is suffering deeply it is a sign of God's judgement on him individually.
Herbert Carson

Suffering

Out of suffering have emerged the strongest souls; the most massive characters are seared with scars.   *E. H. Chapin*

The soul would have no rainbow had the eye no tears.   *John Vance Cheney*

Sufferings are but as little chips of the cross.   *Joseph Church*

God sometimes washes the eyes of his children with tears in order that they may read aright his providence and his commandments.   *T. L. Cuyler*

Tears are part of existence on this earth. They have flowed from Eden right down through history to the present day.
          Wayne Detzler

I am convinced that the Christian answer to the question of suffering is positive and hopeful.   *Brian Edwards*

There is no authentic Christian service that does not have suffering written into it.   *Donald English*

Without a doubt, what helps us most in accepting and dealing with suffering is an adequate view of God — learning who he is and knowing he is in control.
          Joni Eareckson Tada

Scripture teaches that not all suffering builds character. Unbelievers suffer and often learn no lessons from it.
          John M. Frame

To a lesser or greater degree, we all contribute to the suffering in the world.
          Stephen Gaukroger

A Christian never moves so swiftly to heaven as when he is under a sanctified cross.   *Andrew Gray*

Suffering often awakens a consciousness of sin in the sufferer. *D. Edmond Hiebert*

Many parts of religion relate entirely to suffering, and every part receives a lustre from it.   *William Jay*

There is a sanctity in suffering when meekly borne.   *D. Jerrold*

Although the world is full of suffering, it is full also of the overcoming of it.
          Helen Keller

Suffering prepares us for glory.
          David Kingdon

God whispers to us in health and prosperity, but, being hard of hearing, we fail to hear God's voice in both. Whereupon God turns up the amplifier by means of suffering. Then his voice booms.
          C. S. Lewis

The real problem is not why some pious, humble, believing people suffer, but why some do not.   *C. S. Lewis*

Suffering is a choice instrument for shaping character, and without its touch the most delicate chasing on the vessel would be impossible.   *Ian Maclaren*

There is a great want about all Christians who have not suffered. Some flowers must be broken or bruised before they emit any fragrance.
          Robert Murray M'Cheyne

There is nothing the body suffers that the soul may not profit by. *George Meredith*

Good men are often great sufferers.
          William S. Plumer

It is and should be the care of a Christian not to suffer for sin, nor sin in suffering.
Vavasor Powell

Saints should fear every sin, but no sufferings. *Vavasor Powell*

Our sufferings are not always reasonable.
Frank Retief

Probably one of the hardest aspects of suffering to endure is the fact that our suffering is not explained. It would be much easier if we knew why. *Frank Retief*

We must do away once and for all with the great myth that suffering is never part of God's will. *Frank Retief*

There are no gains without pains.
J. C. Ryle

Outward weaknesses are oft a means to restrain men from inward evils. God usually sanctifies the pains and griefs of his servants to make them better.
Richard Sibbes

We must shed tears if we would hereafter have them wiped away.
Richard Sibbes

All the suffering I could possibly endure could not earn me a place in heaven.
R. C. Sproul

God does not witness to the world by taking his people out of suffering, but rather by demonstrating his grace through them in the midst of pain.
C. Samuel Storms

I would . . . suggest that some form of suffering is virtually indispensable to holiness. *John R. W. Stott*

A man is not known by his effervescence but by the amount of real suffering he can stand. *C. T. Studd*

If God made a world without suffering, it would be a world in which humans had little responsibility for each other and for other creatures. *Richard Swinburne*

The best of saints have borne the worst of sufferings. *George Swinnock*

The Bible has a great deal to say about suffering and most of it is encouraging.
A. W. Tozer

It is worth noting that suffering only becomes a problem when we accept the existence of a good God. *David Watson*

Suffering can often produce great depths of character, mature understanding, warm compassion and rich spirituality.
David Watson

Calvary is God's great proof that suffering in the will of God always leads to glory.
Warren Wiersbe

SUICIDE

No man must let the tenant out of the tenement till God the landlord call for it.
Thomas Adams

Suicide is a grave sin and scandal in a Christian, such as even throws doubt on the sincerity of his Christian profession. But there is no reason to think that the old man, still dwelling in the flesh of the regenerate, is quite incapable of such an act. *Roger Beckwith*

We must cast the world out of our hearts, not cast ourselves out of the world.
N. Bifield

We may not ourselves loose our souls, but let God let them out of prison.
John Boys

Man was not born for his own pleasure, neither must he die at his own lust.
Henry Smith

He that would not die when he must, and he that would die when he must not, are both of them cowards alike.
George Swinnock

No creature but man willingly kills itself.
Thomas Watson

SUNDAY — See Lord's Day

SUPERSTITION

Superstition is godless religion, devout impiety. *Joseph Hall*

The devil divides the world between atheism and superstition. *George Herbert*

Superstition is not, as has been defined, an excess of religious feeling, but a misdirection of it, an exhausting of it on vanities of man's devising.
Richard Whately

SURRENDER — See Abandonment; Consecration; Submission; Zeal

SWEARING — See Profanity

SYMPATHY

Sympathy is two hearts tugging at the same load. *Anon.*

Next to love, sympathy is the divinest passion of the human heart.
William Burke

Sympathy is a supporting atmosphere.
Ralph Waldo Emerson

God does not comfort us to make us comfortable but to make us comforters.
J. H. Jowett

Sympathy is no substitute for action.
David Livingstone

Empathy is your pain in my heart.
Halford E. Luccock

It is good manners to be an unbidden guest at a house of mourning.
George Swinnock

TELEVISION

All television is educational television. The only question is, what is it teaching?
Nicholas Johnson

Television is called a medium because so little of it is rare or well done. *Fred Allen*

Television is chewing gum for the eyes.
Fred Allen

The easiest way to find more time to do all the things you want to do is to turn off the television. *O. A. Battista*

If a man's leisure-time exercise consists only of changing channels, it is not only his legs that will become atrophied.
John Blanchard

The primary danger of the television screen lies not so much in the behaviour it *produces* as the behaviour it *prevents* — the talks, the games, the family activities, and the arguments through which much of the child's learning takes place and his character is formed.
Urie Bronfenbrenner

If you have half a mind to turn on the television, it is all you will need for many of the programmes.   *M. R. De Haan*

Television is an invention that permits you to be entertained in your living room by people you wouldn't have in your home.   *David Frost*

Television is the literature of the illiterate.   *Lee Loevinger*

I find television very educating. Every time somebody turns on the set I go into the other room and read a book.
Groucho Marx

Television is the main sustainer of our addiction to superficiality and triviality.
John Piper

TEMPER

A man who can't control his temper is like a city without defences.   *Anon.*

The most important time to hold your temper is when the other person has lost his.   *Harold Smith*

TEMPTATION — Avoiding and Resisting

We have many leaders into temptation, but it is our fault if we follow them.
Thomas Adams

Following the lines of least resistance makes men and rivers crooked.   *Anon.*

He who avoids the temptation avoids the sin.   *Anon.*

It takes two to make a successful temptation, and you are one of the two.   *Anon.*

Most people who fly from temptation usually leave a forwarding address. *Anon.*

Never invite trouble — it always accepts.
Anon.

No one can be caught in a place he does not visit.   *Anon.*

There is no merit in abstaining from what one is not tempted to do.   *Anon.*

We are never strong enough to risk walking into temptation.   *Anon.*

If you don't want the devil to tempt you with forbidden fruit, you had better keep out of his orchard.   *Doug Barnett*

Better shun the bait than struggle in the snare.   *John Dryden*

To realize God's presence is the one sovereign remedy against temptation.
François Fenelon

Unless there is within us that which is above us, we shall soon yield to that which is about us.   *P. T. Forsyth*

If you don't want to trade with the devil, stay out of his shops.   *Vance Havner*

Those that would avoid sin must not parley with temptation. *Matthew Henry*

Those that would be kept from harm must keep out of harm's way. *Matthew Henry*

What makes resisting temptation difficult for many people is that they don't want to discourage it completely.
Franklin Jones

In the line of duty adult Christians are bound to face many temptations, but to expose oneself needlessly to temptation is to tempt God. *R. B. Kuiper*

Each temptation leaves us better or worse; neutrality is impossible. *Erwin W. Lutzer*

Our response to temptation is an accurate barometer of our love for God.
Erwin W. Lutzer

The more of the divine nature in you, the more you are able to stand against temptations. We are easily carried aside, because we have more of man than God in us. *Thomas Manton*

There is a time for holy running. *Al Martin*

Christ will not keep us if we carelessly and wantonly put ourselves into the way of temptation. *F. B. Meyer*

Temptations are never so dangerous as when they come to us in a religious garb.
D. L. Moody

Temptation is like a knife, that may either cut the meat or the throat of a man; it may be his food or poison. *John Owen*

Temptations ... put nothing into a man, but only draw out what was in him before. *John Owen*

God is better served in resisting a temptation to evil than in many formal prayers.
William Penn

The best defence against the temptation to stray from God is the possession by experience of his rich gifts that meet all desires. *James Philip*

Weak doctrines will not be a match for powerful temptations. *William S. Plumer*

It is much easier to suppress a first desire than to satisfy those that follow.
Francois Rochefoucauld

To pray against temptation, and yet to rush into occasion, is to thrust your fingers into the fire, and then pray they might not be burnt. *Thomas Secker*

If you hold the stirrup, no wonder if Satan gets into the saddle. *William Secker*

He cannot smell sweetly who sleeps in a bed of garlic. *C. H. Spurgeon*

Learn to say 'NO'; it will be of more use to you than to be able to read Latin.
C. H. Spurgeon

Of two evils, choose neither.
C. H. Spurgeon

One reason that sin flourishes is that it is treated like a cream-puff instead of a rattle-snake. *Billy Sunday*

Things forbidden have a secret charm.
Tacitus

Temptation rarely comes in working hours. It is in their leisure time that men are made or marred. *W. T. Taylor*

Temptation can cause us to succumb, sink, sin or stand. *William A. Ward*

It is not laying the bait that hurts the fish if the fish do not bite. *Thomas Watson*

Temptation is a trial of our sincerity.
Thomas Watson

TEMPTATION — Blessing

Every temptation is an opportunity of our getting nearer to God.
John Quincy Adams

Temptations discover what we are.
Thomas à Kempis

It is good to be without vices, but it is not good to be without temptations.
Walter Bagehot

Find out what your temptations are and you will find out largely what you are yourself.   *Henry Ward Beecher*

Tempting times are teaching times.
William Bridges

The more you are tempted by Satan, the more you are pitied by God.
William Bridges

Temptation provokes me to look upward to God.   *John Bunyan*

Temptations are a file which rub off much of the rust of our self-confidence.
François Fenelon

If it takes temptation and sin to show God in his true colours and Satan in his, something has been saved from the wreck.
Michael Green

Temptation has its uses. As we grapple we grow.   *E. Stanley Jones*

My temptations have been my masters in divinity.   *Martin Luther*

One Christian who has been tempted is worth a thousand who haven't.
Martin Luther

Temptation and adversity are the two best books in my library.   *Martin Luther*

Nothing is so conducive to real humility as temptation. It teaches us how weak we are.   *Donald MacDonald*

TEMPTATION — Certainty

There is no order so holy, no place so secret, where there will be no temptation.
Thomas à Kempis

God promises a safe landing but not a calm passage.   *Anon.*

Temptations are everywhere, *and so is the grace of God.*   *Anon.*

Temptations, like foul weather, come before we send for them.   *Anon.*

Temptation is something we must never excite, but always expect.
John Blanchard

How daily, hourly, is the struggle with sin and fear and temptation — it is never over!   *J. J. Bonar*

Jesus was tempted, not because he was bad, but because he was important.
G. B. Duncan

There is no devil so bad as no devil.
Ralph Erskine

The best of saints may be tempted to the worst of sins.   *Matthew Henry*

The greatest temptation out of hell is to live without temptation.
Samuel Rutherford

You are not tempted because you are evil; you are tempted because you are human.
Fulton J. Sheen

The man who has never been tempted doesn't know how dishonest he is.
Josh Billings

The greatest temptations sometimes follow the highest manifestation of God's love.   *William Bridge*

Christ is no sooner out of the waters of baptism than he is in the fires of temptation; whence we learn that great manifestations of the love of God are usually followed with great temptations from Satan.   *Francis Burkitt*

There are as many forms of temptation as there are Christians. *Edward Donnelly*

If you have not been through the devil's sifter, you are probably not worth sifting!   *Vance Havner*

Sin is seldom, if ever, original.
       Maurice Roberts

Some temptations come to the industrious, but all temptations attack the idle.
       C. H. Spurgeon

There is no ripe fruit unpecked by the birds.   *C. H. Spurgeon*

We shall always be in danger as long as we are here.   *C. H. Spurgeon*

TEMPTATION — and Satan
(See also: Satan)

Satan, like a fisher, baits his hook according to the appetite of the fish.
       Thomas Adams

Even on the brink of Jordan I find Satan nibbling at my heels.   *Anon.*

As Satan can tell how to suit temptations for you in the day of your want, so he has those that can entangle you in the day of your fullness.   *John Bunyan*

We cannot stand against the wiles of the devil by our wits.   *Oswald Chambers*

Temptation is the tempter looking through the key-hole into the room where you are living; sin is your drawing back the bolt and making it possible for him to enter.   *J. Wibur Chapman*

O Lord, help us to hear the serpent's rattle before we feel its fangs.
       Thomas De Witt Talmage

God never tempts any man. That is Satan's business.   *Billy Graham*

No player hath so many dresses to come in upon the stage (with) as the devil hath forms of temptation.   *William Gurnall*

There is a spark of hell in every temptation.   *William Gurnall*

We must not so much as taste of the devil's broth, lest at last he brings us to eat of his beef.   *Thomas Hall*

An empty heart is an invitation to the devil.   *Vance Havner*

The devil can go no farther than God permits.   *Vance Havner*

Sometimes we are praying when we should be resisting Satan.
       D. Martyn Lloyd-Jones

All Satan's temptations … are so many 'welcome' notices along the broad road that leads to destruction.   *J. I. Packer*

We must not blame the devil for our choices.   *Frank Retief*

The devil's temptations have no need to be original because the old, well-tried

snares of the past are usually successful enough in each succeeding generation.
Maurice Roberts

He who will fight the devil with his own weapons must not wonder if he finds him an overmatch. *Robert South*

Idle Christians are not tempted of the devil so much as they tempt the devil to tempt them. *C. H. Spurgeon*

Temptation is the devil looking through the keyhole; yielding is opening the door and inviting him in. *Billy Sunday*

Satan never sets a dish before men that they do not love. *Thomas Watson*

It must not be expected that the devil will let those rest who are labouring to destroy his kingdom. *Thomas Wilson*

TEMTATION — and Sin

Temptation always promises more than it produces. *John Blanchard*

Temptation is the fire that brings up the sum of the heart. *Thomas Boston*

Temptation has its source not in the outer lure but in the inner lust.
D. Edmond Hiebert

Let us beware of making light of temptations because they seem little and insignificant. There is nothing little that concerns our souls. *J. C. Ryle*

No degree of temptation justifies any degree of sin. *Nathaniel Parker Willis*

Temptation is not sin; it is the call to battle. *Frederick P. Wood*

TESTING — See Trials

THANKSGIVING
(See also: Gratitude)

No duty is more urgent than that of returning thanks. *Ambrose*

God's giving deserves our thanksgiving.
Anon.

Thanksgiving is the vibration of the soul's heart-strings under the soft touch of God's benevolence. *Anon.*

To give thanks sincerely, one must give more than thanks. *Anon.*

I give it as my testimony that there is a marvellous therapy in thanksgiving.
John Blanchard

Thanksgiving is not a natural virtue; it is a fruit of the Spirit, given by him.
Jerry Bridges

As the Lord loves a cheerful giver, so likewise a cheerful thanksgiver. *John Boys*

A thankful man is worth his weight in gold. *Thomas Brooks*

A thankful heart has a continual feast.
W. J. Cameron

How worthy it is to remember former benefits when we come to beg for new.
Stephen Charnock

We should spend as much time in thanking God for his benefits as we do in asking him for them. *Vincent de Paul*

Thankfulness grows best in the seed-bed of conviction, just as some plants must be placed in the soil in the winter if they

are to flower in the summer.
Sinclair Ferguson

The thankfulness of the receiver ought to answer to the benefit of the bestower as the echo answers to the voice.
Thomas Fuller

Those blessings are sweetest that are won with prayers and worn with thanks.
Thomas Goodwin

Thanksgiving is an act of self-denial.
William Gurnall

Joy untouched by thankfulness is always suspect. *Theodor Haecker*

Prayer without thanks-giving is like a bird without wings. *William Hendriksen*

Every stream should lead us to the fountain. *Matthew Henry*

In thanking God, we fasten upon his favours to us; in praising and adoring God, we fasten upon his perfections in himself. *Matthew Henry*

Thanksgiving is good but thanks-living is better. *Matthew Henry*

Every virtue divorced from thankfulness is maimed and limps along the spiritual road. *John Henry Jowett*

Thankfulness is a flower which will never bloom well excepting upon a root of deep humility. *J. C. Ryle*

He enjoys much who is thankful for little. *William Secker*

Our thanks should be as fervent for mercies received, as our petitions sought.
Charles Simmons

It is sad when there is nothing for which we feel grateful to God, but it is serious when there is something and we fail to show gratitude. *William Still*

Every furrow in the book of Psalms is sown with the seeds of thanksgiving.
Jeremy Taylor

Hearty thanks must be given to God: such as cometh not from the roof of the mouth but the root of the heart. *John Trapp*

Thanks must be given and held as still due. *John Trapp*

The Christian is suspended between blessings received and blessings hoped for, so he should always give thanks.
M. R. Vincent

Thanking God for whatever he gives us is one sure way of resisting the devil.
Spiros Zodhiates

THEOLOGY
(See also: Bible; Doctrine)

All my theology is reduced to this narrow compass — Christ Jesus came into the world to save sinners.
Archibald Alexander

Beware of a theology produced by spontaneous generation. *Anon.*

Every question is ultimately a theological question. *Hilaire Belloc*

Every Christian should be a theologian.
John Blanchard

We must never let our theology rob us of our responsibility. *John Blanchard*

Theology can never be a science, on account of the infirmities of language.
Horace Bushnell

All theology, when separated from Christ, is not only vain and confused, but is also mad, deceitful and spurious. *John Calvin*

None but a theology that came out of eternity can carry you and me safely to and through eternity. *T. L. Cuyler*

I have not the slightest interest in a theology which doesn't evangelize.
James Denney

Deep theology is the best fuel of devotion; it readily catches fire and, once kindled, it burns long. *Frederick W. Faber*

The price of theological integrity, like that of liberty, is eternal vigilance.
Timothy George

Our theology must become biography.
Tim Hansel

The truth of God is a boundless expanse. Definitions were made for man, not man for definitions. *A. A. Hodge*

Whereas God's existence is the last or highest proof of philosophy, it is the *first* truth of theology. *W. Andrew Hoffecker*

The basic questions of all theology are 'Who is God?' and 'Who is man?'
R. B. Kuiper

Theology should be empress, and philosophy and the other arts merely her servants. *Martin Luther*

The more we know of God, the more unreservedly we will trust him; the greater our progress in theology, the simpler and more child-like will be our faith.
J. Gresham Machen

Your theology is what you are when the talking stops and the action starts.
Colin Morris

All true theology has an evangelistic thrust, and all true evangelism is theology in action. *J. I. Packer*

If we pursue theological knowledge for its own sake, it is bound to go bad on us. It will make us proud and conceited.
J. I. Packer

Theology's proper goal is to equip the disciples of Jesus Christ for obedience.
J. I. Packer

Think of theologians as the church's sewage specialists. Their role is to detect and eliminate intellectual pollution, and to ensure, so far as man can, that God's life-giving truth flows pure and unpoisoned into Christian hearts. *J. I. Packer*

Never study theology in cold blood.
E. G. Robinson

Let us come to Jesus — the person of Christ is the centre of theology.
H. B. Smith

A sound theology must be a theology where grace is central to it. *R. C. Sproul*

No Christian can avoid theology.
R. C. Sproul

Our errors in theology are rooted in our pride and our slothfulness. *R. C. Sproul*

To commit theological error is to commit sin. *R. C. Sproul*

Believe that all theology is rotten rubbish which is not the Word of the Lord.
C. H. Spurgeon

If your theology doesn't change your behaviour it will never change your destiny.   *C. H. Spurgeon*

My entire theology can be condensed into four words: 'Jesus died for me'.
C. H. Spurgeon

Rest assured that there is nothing new in my theology except that which is false.
C. H. Spurgeon

Theology is a rational necessity.
Augustus H. Strong

To be either true or useful, theology must be a passion.   *Augustus H. Strong*

Theological beliefs may get one into a church, but not into the kingdom of God.
Stanley I. Stuber

Loose theology leads to loose morality.
R. A. Torrey

Theological truth is useless until it is obeyed.   *A. W. Tozer*

The secret of life is theological and the key to heaven as well.   *A. W. Tozer*

We being what we are and all things else being what they are, the most important and profitable study any one of us can engage in is without question the study of theology.   *A. W. Tozer*

The plague of Christendom has been the passion of theology to define what God has not defined and to discover what he has kept secret.   *Henry Van Dyke*

THOUGHTS
(See also: Imagination; Mind)

A man is not what he thinks he is, but what he thinks, he is.   *Anon.*

Give burning thoughts time before they become flaming words.   *Anon.*

In company, guard your tongue — in solitude, your thoughts.   *Anon.*

The probable reason some people get lost in thought is because it is unfamiliar territory to them.   *Anon.*

Thinking evil is the same as doing it.
Anon.

Pure thoughts cannot produce evil deeds.
Augustine

Thought is a kind of sight of the mind.
Augustine

A man's thoughts dye his soul.
Marcus Aurelius

One must live the way one thinks or end up thinking the way one has lived.
Paul Bourget

Our minds are mental greenhouses where unlawful thoughts, once planted, are nurtured and watered before being transplanted into the real world of unlawful actions.   *Jerry Bridges*

We allow in our minds what we would not allow in our actions, because other people cannot see our thoughts.
Jerry Bridges

To think is an effort; to think rightly is a great effort; and to think as a Christian ought to think is the greatest effort of a human soul.   *Oswald Chambers*

As the image on the seal is stamped upon the wax, so the thoughts of the heart are printed upon the actions.
Stephen Charnock

Thoughts are the immediate spawn of the original corruption. *Stephen Charnock*

If you would voyage Godward, you must see to it that the rudder of thought is right.
W. J. Dawson

Think all you speak but speak not all you think. *Patrick Delaney*

A man is what he thinks about all day long. *Ralph Waldo Emerson*

What is the hardest task in the world? To think. *Ralph Waldo Emerson*

How we think is one of the great determining factors in how we live.
Sinclair Ferguson

Thy thoughts are vocal to God.
John Flavel

It is bad to think ill, but it is worse to speak it. *Matthew Henry*

The actions of men are the best interpreters of their thoughts. *John Locke*

Thoughts are the spies and messengers of the soul. *Thomas Manton*

We grow like the things we think about.
Daniel L. Marsh

It is right for us to take thought, but not for thought to take us!
D. Martyn Lloyd-Jones

More souls are lost through want of consideration than in any other way.
Robert Murray M'Cheyne

At every point right living begins with right thinking. *Bruce J. Milne*

We cannot afford the luxury of careless thinking. *Irwin Moon*

Controlling and directing one's thoughts is a habit, and the more one practises it the better one becomes at it. *J. I. Packer*

Thoughts, even more than overt acts, reveal character. *William S. Plumer*

The spiritual battle, the loss of victory, is always in the thought-world.
Francis Schaeffer

Vain thoughts defile the heart as well as vile thoughts. *William Secker*

Ill thoughts are little thieves.
Richard Sibbes

Thoughts are the seeds of actions.
Richard Sibbes

God will not live in the parlour of our hearts if we entertain the devil in the cellar of our thoughts. *C. H. Spurgeon*

The secret of clean living is clear thinking. *John R. W. Stott*

Thoughts have a moral character.
David Thomas

Every normal person can determine what he will think about. *A. W. Tozer*

If we would think God's thoughts, we must learn to think continually of God.
A. W. Tozer

Whatever engages my attention when I should be meditating on God and things eternal does injury to my soul. *A. W. Tozer*

Thoughts

What we think about when we are free to think about what we will — that is what we are or will soon become. *A. W. Tozer*

Jesus is no stranger to your thoughts.
Geoff Treasure

Guard well your thoughts; our thoughts are heard in heaven. *Owen D. Young*

TIME — and Eternity

The world began with time and time with it. *Thomas Adams*

Time is a file that wears and makes no noise. *Anon.*

Time is but the fringe of eternity. *Anon.*

Time writes no wrinkle on the brow of the Eternal. *Anon.*

What we weave in time we wear in eternity. *Anon.*

The great weight of eternity hangs upon the small wire of time. *Thomas Brooks*

If we look around us, a moment can seem a long time, but when we lift up our hearts heavenwards, a thousand years begin to be like a moment. *John Calvin*

Time is nothing to God.
Oswald Chambers

Time cannot be infinite. *Stephen Charnock*

It is difficult for me to understand how an intelligent person can spend all of time building for this world and have no time for the future world. *Billy Graham*

God doesn't rush men; he owns time.
John Hercus

All that is not eternal is eternally out of date. *C. S. Lewis*

God created time when he created finite things. *J. Gresham Machen*

All space of time should be small to them that know the greatness of eternity.
Thomas Manton

Eternity depends upon this moment.
Thomas Manton

Time is the chrysalis of eternity.
Jean Paul Richter

There is a time appointed by the Father when the whole machinery of creation shall stop, and the present dispensation shall be changed for another. *J. C. Ryle*

God is not subject to time.
Dorothy L. Sayers

Right now counts for ever. *R. C. Sproul*

Time is not God's master, but his servant. *William Still*

God hath given man a short time here upon earth, and yet upon this short time eternity depends. *Jeremy Taylor*

You cannot kill time without injuring eternity. *Henry David Thoreau*

God dwells in eternity, but time dwells in God. He has already lived all our tomorrows as he has lived all our yesterdays. *A. W. Tozer*

I am not careful for what may be a hundred years hence. He who governed the world before I was born shall take care of it likewise when I am dead. My part is to improve the present moment.
John Wesley

We give so little thought to the fact that God made time as a preparation for eternity, and this earth the place where we acquire our entry either to heaven or hell.
Spiros Zodhiates

TIME — Misuse

Kill time and you murder opportunity.
Anon.

Lost time is never found. *Anon.*

Time can be wasted, but it can never be re-cycled. *Anon.*

Wasting time is a kind of unarmed robbery. *Anon.*

I would I could stand on a busy corner, hat in hand, and beg people to throw me all their wasted hours. *Bernard Berenson*

To waste time is to squander a gift from God. *John Blanchard*

Do not squander time, for it is the stuff of which life is made. *Benjamin Franklin*

As good have no time as make no good use of it. *Thomas Fuller*

Those who dare lose a day are dangerously prodigal; those who dare misspend it, desperate. *Joseph Hall*

Time and money are the heaviest burdens of life, and the unhappiest of all mortals are those who have more of either than they know how to use. *Samuel Johnson*

Too often a man handles life as he does bad weather. He whiles away the time as he waits for it to stop. *Polger*

All that time is lost which might be better employed. *Jean Jacques Rousseau*

Misspending a man's time is a sort of self-homicide. *George Savile*

We are always complaining that our days are few and at the same time acting as if they would never end. *Seneca*

You cannot kill time without injury to eternity. *Henry Thoreau*

A man has no time for which he is not accountable to God. If his very diversions are not governed by reason and religion he will one day suffer for the time he has spent in them. *Thomas Watson*

TIME — Urgency

Today is the tomorrow you worried about yesterday. *Anon.*

Tomorrow is a post-dated cheque. Today is cash. *Anon.*

Time never takes time off. *Augustine*

What is past cannot be recalled; what is future cannot be insured.
Stephen Charnock

It is better to lose anything than to lose time; we can recover lost money, but time is irrecoverable. *Chrysostom*

Time goes, you say? Ah, no! Alas, time stays, *we go!* *Henry A. Dobson*

Time is not a commodity that can be stored for future use. It must be invested hour by hour, or else it is gone for ever.
Thomas Edison

One today is worth two tomorrows.
Benjamin Franklin

The morning hour has gold in its hand.
Benjamin Franklin

There is not a single moment in life that we can afford to lose.

Edward M. Goulburn

We live by demands when we should live by priorities. *J. A. Motyer*

Time is urgency. *Paul S. Rees*

Time is the deposit each one has in the bank of God and no one knows the balance. *Ralph W. Sockman*

We have much to do and little time in which to get it done! *A. W. Tozer*

He who neglects the present moment throws away all he has.

Johann von Schiller

TIME — Use

Give me a Christian that counts his time more precious than gold. *Joseph Alleine*

Life is too short for us to do everything *we* want to do; but it is long enough for us to do everything *God* wants us to do.

Anon.

I have these forty years been sensible of the sin of losing time; I could not spare an hour. *Richard Baxter*

Spend your time in nothing which you know must be repented of; in nothing on which you might not pray for the blessing of God; in nothing which you could not review with a quiet conscience on your dying bed; in nothing which you might not safely and properly be found doing if death should surprise you in the act. *Richard Baxter*

The whole man and the whole time is all too little in so great a work. *Richard Baxter*

Time should not be spent, it should be invested in the kingdom of God.

John Blanchard

We speak of spending time, the Bible speaks of buying it. *John Blanchard*

Time is not yours to dispose of as you please; it is a glorious talent that men must be accountable for as well as any other talent. *Thomas Brooks*

I count that hour lost in which I have done no good by my pen or tongue.

John Bradford

There is nothing puts a more serious frame into a man's spirit than to know the worth of his time. *Thomas Brooks*

We are to redeem the time because we ourselves are redeemed. *Richard Chester*

God never places any real emphasis on the present — except as preparation for the future. *Joni Eareckson Tada*

The surest method of arriving at a knowledge of God's eternal purposes about us is to be found in the right use of the present moment. Each hour comes with some little faggot of God's will fastened upon its back.

Frederick W. Faber

Those to whom God has taught the value of time feel that it has little need to be 'killed'; it goes away from us all too quickly without that. *Robert Johnstone*

The year is made up of minutes. Let these be watched as having been dedicated to God. It is in the sanctification of the small that the hallowing of the large is secure.

G. Campbell Morgan

Time is not a utility, it is an opportunity.
Edward Norman

Have you time enough to eat, to drink, to sleep, to talk unprofitably, it may be corruptly, in all sorts of unnecessary societies, but have not time to live unto God? *John Owen*

Half our life is spent trying to find something to do with the time we have rushed through life to save. *Will Rogers*

Great men never complain about the lack of time. Alexander the Great and John Wesley accomplished everything they did in twenty-four hour days. *Fred Smith*

I do not have time to be in a hurry.
John Welsey

TITHING
(See also: Giving; Stewardship)

If God gave you ten times as much as you give him could you live on it? *Anon.*

The tithe is not meant to be a ceiling at which we stop giving, but a floor from which we start. *John Blanchard*

Giving a tenth is nothing to brag about.
Samuel Chadwick

Shall we grudge the expenses of our religion, or starve so good a cause?
Matthew Henry

We are all congenitally allergic to tithing. *R. T. Kendall*

God demands the tithe, deserves the offerings, defends the savings and directs the expenses. *Stephen Olford*

If you are not a tither you are a robber.
Stephen Olford

It could be argued that in the Old Testament tithes were *paid,* and therefore do not, strictly speaking, come under the heading of giving at all. Christian giving only begins when we give more than a tenth. *Kenneth F. W. Prior*

TOLERANCE

Tolerance is seeing certain things with your heart instead of your eyes. *Anon.*

In the great things of religion, be of a mind: but when there is not a unity of sentiment, let there be a union of affections. *Matthew Henry*

We ought not to make any conditions of our brother's acceptance with us but such as God has made the conditions of their acceptance with him. *Matthew Henry*

TONGUE — See Speech

TRIALS — Blessings
(See also: Pain; Sickness; Suffering)

Times of affliction are usually gaining times to God's people. *Joseph Alleine*

Adversity introduces a man to himself.
Anon.

Affliction is God's shepherd dog to drive us back to the fold. *Anon.*

Affliction is the school of faith. *Anon.*

Affliction, like the iron-smith, shapes as it smites. *Anon.*

Afflictions are often God's best blessings sent in disguise. *Anon.*

Crosses are ladders that lead to heaven.
Anon.

Fire is the test of gold, adversity of strong men. *Anon.*

Our great Teacher writes many a bright lesson on the blackboard of affliction. *Anon.*

Some hearts, like evening primroses, open more beautifully in the shadows of life. *Anon.*

The Christian justifies tribulation. Ten thousand times ten thousand saints . . . are ready to witness that their most manifest and rapid spiritual growth is traceable to their periods of trial. *Anon.*

The darker the night, the brighter the stars; the hotter the fire, the purer the gold. *Anon.*

The gem cannot be polished without friction, nor man perfected without trials. *Anon.*

The hammer shatters glass, but forges steel. *Anon.*

The more a tree of righteousness is shaken by the wind, the more it is rooted in Christ. *Anon.*

The water that dashes against the wheel keeps the mill going; so trial keeps grace in use and motion. *Anon.*

Trial is the school of trust. *Anon.*

Where there are no trials in life, there are no triumphs. *Anon.*

The purpose of the tests of life are to make, not break us. *Maltbie Babcock*

Prosperity is the blessing of the Old Testament; adversity is the blessing of the new. *Francis Bacon*

Night brings out stars as sorrow shows us truths. *Gamaliel Bailey*

Suffering so unbolts the door of the heart that the Word hath easier entrance. *Richard Baxter*

Weakness and pain helped me to study how to die; that set me on studying how to live. *Richard Baxter*

The brook would lose its song if you removed the rocks. *Fred Beck*

Troubles are often the tools by which God fashions us for better things. *Henry Ward Beecher*

For the Christian, trials and temptations are not only means for proving his faith but for improving his life. *John Blanchard*

I have learned more from life's trials than from its triumphs. *John Blanchard*

The Christian's midnight is brighter than the sinner's noon. *John Blanchard*

The trials of life are meant to make us better, not bitter. *John Blanchard*

Affliction is the shaking of the torch that it may blaze the brighter. *Horatius Bonar*

We have got more from Paul's prison-house than from his visit to the third heaven. *Andrew Bonar*

It is the usual way of providence with me that blessings come through several iron gates. *Thomas Boston*

Afflictions are blessings. *Thomas Brooks*

Afflictions are but as a dark entry into our Father's house. *Thomas Brooks*

Afflictions are the mother of virtue.
Thomas Brooks

Affliction is an excellent comment upon the Scriptures. *Thomas Brooks*

Afflictions ripen the saint's graces.
Thomas Brooks

Afflictions, they are but our Father's goldsmiths who are working to add pearls to our crowns. *Thomas Brooks*

God's house of correction is his school of instruction. *Thomas Brooks*

Stars shine brightest in the darkest night. Torches are the better for beating. Grapes come not to the proof till they come to the press. Spices smell sweetest when pounded. Young trees root the faster for shaking. Vines are the better for bleeding. Gold looks the brighter for scouring; and juniper smells sweeter in the fire.
Thomas Brooks

The grand design of God in all the afflictions that befall his people is to bring them nearer and closer to himself.
Thomas Brooks

The vinegar of adversity quickens our graces. *Thomas Brooks*

As threshing separates the wheat from the chaff, so does affliction purify virtue.
Richard E. Burton

The Lord uses his flail of tribulation to separate the chaff from the wheat.
John Bunyan

Thou art beaten that thou mayest be better. *John Bunyan*

Afflictions ought ever to be estimated by their *end*. *John Calvin*

In the darkness of our miseries the grace of God shines more brightly. *John Calvin*

Our afflictions prepare us for receiving the grace of God. *John Calvin*

Our faith is really and truly tested only when we are brought into very severe conflicts, and when even hell itself seems opened to swallow us up. *John Calvin*

The more we are afflicted by adversities, the more surely our fellowship with Christ is confirmed! *John Calvin*

Whatever poison Satan produces, God turns it into medicine for his elect.
John Calvin

The staying power of our faith is neither demonstrated nor developed until it is tested by suffering. *D. A. Carson*

There is a certain kind of maturity that can be attained only through the discipline of suffering. *D. A. Carson*

The saint knows not why he suffers as he does, yet he comprehends with a knowledge that passes knowledge that all is well. *Oswald Chambers*

The brightest crowns that are worn in heaven have been tried, and smelted, and polished, and glorified through the furnace of tribulation. *E. H. Chapin*

We often learn more under the rod that strikes us, than under the staff that comforts us. *Stephen Charnock*

Affliction makes saints eminent.
Chrysostom

In prosperity, our friends know us; in adversity we know our friends.
Churton Collins

It is not until we have passed through the furnace that we are made to know how much dross there is in our composition.
C. C. Colton

Calamity is the perfect glass wherein we truly see and know ourselves.
William Davenant

There is no education like adversity.
Benjamin Disraeli

Fiery trials make golden Christians.
William Dyer

Eminent virtue always shows brightest in the fire. Pure gold shows its purity chiefly in the furnace.   *Jonathan Edwards*

Great men are made greater by their misfortunes.   *Minucius Felix*

Afflictions … are as necessary for our waftage to heaven as water is to carry the ship to her port.   *William Gurnall*

God's wounds cure; sin's kisses kill.
William Gurnall

God sometimes snuffs out our brightest candle that we may look up to his eternal stars.   *Vance Havner*

It takes the grindstone to sharpen the axe.
Vance Havner

It is better to drink of deep griefs than to taste shallow pleasures.   *William Hazlitt*

The Lord doesn't take us into deep water to drown us but to develop us.
Iry Hedstrom

Afflictions are continued no longer than till they have done their work.
Matthew Henry

Afflictions are sent for this end, to bring us to the throne of grace, to teach us to *pray* and to make the word of God's grace precious to us.   *Matthew Henry*

Extraordinary afflictions are not always the punishment of extraordinary sins, but sometimes the trial of extraordinary graces.   *Matthew Henry*

If we cry to God for the removal of the oppression and affliction we are under, and it is not removed, the reason is not because the Lord's hand is shortened or his ear heavy, but because the affliction has not done its work.   *Matthew Henry*

It has been the advantage of God's people to be afflicted.   *Matthew Henry*

Many are taught with the briars and thorns of affliction that would not learn otherwise.   *Matthew Henry*

Of the many that are afflicted and oppressed, few get the good they might get by their affliction. It should drive them to God, but how seldom is this the case!
Matthew Henry

Outward losses drive good people to their prayers, but bad people to their curses.
Matthew Henry

Sanctified afflictions are spiritual promotions.   *Matthew Henry*

Sometimes God teaches us effectually to know the worth of mercies by the want of them and whets our appetite for the means of grace by cutting us short in those means.   *Matthew Henry*

The injuries men do us should drive us to God, for to him we may commit our cause.   *Matthew Henry*

Let prosperity be as oil to the wheels of obedience and affliction as wind to the sails of prayer.   *Philip Henry*

Affliction is the medicine of the mind.
                    John P. K. Henshaw

The great blows of God are designed to make a man stand up.   *John Hercus*

Afflictions are the cause of eternal glory. Not the meritorious cause, but still the procuring cause.   *Charles Hodge*

Afflictions are unavoidable; they occupy a large proportion of life, and of godliness.   *William Jay*

The Christian is more formed from his trials than from his enjoyments.
                    William Jay

As the wicked are hurt by the best things, so the godly are bettered by the worst.
                    William Jenkyn

Trouble is only opportunity in work clothes.   *Henry J. Kaiser*

Only in the hot furnace of affliction do we as Christians let go of the dross to which, in our foolishness, we ardently cling.   *David Kingdon*

This school of trial best discloses the hidden vileness of the heart and the vast riches of a Saviour's grace. *Henry Law*

Christian people are generally at their best when they are in the furnace of affliction and being persecuted and tried.
                    D. Martyn Lloyd-Jones

Trials and tribulations are very good for us in that they help us to know ourselves better than we knew ourselves before.
                    D. Martyn Lloyd-Jones

Affliction is the Christian's theologian.
                    Martin Luther

I never knew the meaning of God's Word until I came into affliction. *Martin Luther*

No man, without trials and temptations, can attain a true understanding of the Holy Scriptures.   *Martin Luther*

We should never see the stars if God did not sometimes take away the day.
                    Kenneth Macrae

God's children never gain so much honour as in their troubles. *Thomas Manton*

Trial is not only to approve, but to improve.   *Thomas Manton*

Affliction is the whetstone of prayer and obedience.   *Edward Marbury*

Trouble is the structural steel that goes into character-building. *Douglas Meador*

A dark hour makes Jesus bright.
                    Robert Murray M'Cheyne

Affliction is the school in which great virtues are acquired, in which great characters are formed.   *Hannah More*

No pain, no palm; no thorns, no throne; no gall, no glory; no cross, no crown.
                    William Penn

One breath of paradise will extinguish all the adverse winds of earth.   *A. W. Pink*

Afflictions often possess remarkable power to remind us of our sins.
                    William S. Plumer

It is a blessed thing when our trials cure our earnest love for things that perish.
                    William S. Plumer

By afflictions God is spoiling us of what otherwise might have spoiled us — when he makes the world too hot for us to hold, we let it go. *John Powell*

The hiding places of men are discovered by affliction. *S. I. Prime*

I have never met with a single instance of adversity which I have not in the end seen was for my good — I have never heard of a Christian on his deathbed complaining of his affliction.
Alexander M. Proudfit

Afflictions clarify the soul.
Francis Quarles

Afflictions are a fan in God's hand to separate between good and evil men.
Maurice Roberts

No enemy of Christ's cause ... has it in his competence to inflict so much as one naked blow on the Christian or on the church. Every blow is parried for our good. Every curse aimed at us is sweetened into a blessing. Every poisonous dart is deflected. Every wound is healed. Every accusation is silenced.
Maurice Roberts

Grace grows best in the winter.
Samuel Rutherford

Affliction is a searching wind which strips the leaves off the trees and brings to light the bird's nests. *J. C. Ryle*

In the resurrection morning ... we shall thank God for every storm. *J. C. Ryle*

Let us settle it firmly in our minds that there is a meaning, a needs-be and a message from God in every sorrow that falls upon us. *J. C. Ryle*

Prosperity is a great mercy, but adversity is a greater one, if it brings us to Christ.
J. C. Ryle

There are no lessons so useful as those learned in the school of affliction.
J. C. Ryle

The tools that the great Architect intends to use much are often kept long in the fire, to temper them and fit them for work.
J. C. Ryle

Trials are intended to make us think, to wean us from the world, to send us to the Bible, to drive us to our knees. *J. C. Ryle*

Trials are the resistances God gives us to strengthen our spiritual muscles.
George Seevers

Misfortune is an occasion to demonstrate character. *Seneca*

No one appears to me more pitiable than the man who has never known misfortune. *Seneca*

We become wiser by adversity. *Seneca*

Afflictions should be the spiritual wings of the soul. *Richard Sibbes*

After conversion we need bruising, to see that we live by mercy. *Richard Sibbes*

Poverty and affliction take away the fuel that feeds pride. *Richard Sibbes*

When the afflictions of Christians are doubled, then they are commonly most humbled. *Richard Sibbes*

As Jacob was blessed and halted both at one time, so a man may be blessed and afflicted both together. *Henry Smith*

A true Christian's losses are gains in another shape. *C. H. Spurgeon*

I am afraid that all the grace that I have got out of my comfortable and easy times and happy hours might almost lie on a penny. But the good that I have received from my sorrows, and pains, and griefs, is altogether incalculable. What do I not owe to the crucible and the furnace, the bellows that have blown up the coals, and the hand which has thrust me into the heat? *C. H. Spurgeon*

I am sure I have derived more real benefit and permanent strength and growth in grace, and every precious thing, from the furnace of affliction, than I have ever derived from prosperity. *C. H. Spurgeon*

I bear my witness that the worst days I have ever had have turned out to be my best days. *C. H. Spurgeon*

I can bear my personal testimony that the best piece of furniture that I ever had in the house was a cross. I do not mean a material cross; I mean the cross of affliction and trouble. *C. H. Spurgeon*

I owe more than I can tell to the graver's tool, and I feel the lines of its cutting even now. *C. H. Spurgeon*

In shunning a trial we are seeking to avoid a blessing. *C. H. Spurgeon*

None of us can come to the highest maturity without enduring the summer heat of trials. *C. H. Spurgeon*

On some few occasions I have had troubles which I could not tell to any but my God, and I thank God I have, for I learned more of my Lord then that at any other time. *C. H. Spurgeon*

Our troubles have always brought us blessings, and they always will. They are the dark chariots of bright grace. *C. H. Spurgeon*

Stars may be seen from the bottom of a deep well, when they cannot be discerned from the top of a mountain. So are many things learned in adversity which the prosperous man dreams not of. *C. H. Spurgeon*

The anvil, the fire and the hammer are the making of us. *C. H. Spurgeon*

The Christian gains by his losses. He acquires health by his sickness. He wins friends through his bereavements, and he becomes a conqueror through his defeats. *C. H. Spurgeon*

The tears of affliction are often needed to keep the eye of faith bright. *C. H. Spurgeon*

There are some of your graces which would never be discovered if it were not for your trials. *C. H. Spurgeon*

There is nothing that makes a man have a big heart like a great trial. *C. H. Spurgeon*

We find no sword-blades so true in metal as those which have been forged in the furnace of soul-trouble. *C. H. Spurgeon*

Jesus was transfigured on the hilltop, but he transforms us in the valley. *J. Charles Stern*

It takes a world with trouble in it to train men for their high calling as sons of God and to carve upon the soul the lineaments of the face of Christ. *J. S. Steward*

A sanctified person, like a silver bell, the harder he is smitten, the better he sounds.
George Swinnock

Cold blasts make a fire to flame the higher and burn the better.   *George Swinnock*

God's rod, like Jonathan's, is dipped in honey.   *George Swinnock*

We are safer in the storm God sends us than in a calm when we are befriended by the world.   *Jeremy Taylor*

For a Christian, even the valleys are on higher ground.   *D. Reginald Thomas*

Despise not the desert. There is where God polishes his brightest gems.
R. A. Torrey

As the hotter the day the greater the dew at night; so the hotter the time of trouble the greater the dews of refreshing from God.   *John Trapp*

Better be preserved in brine than rot in honey.   *John Trapp*

Better be pruned to grow than cut up to burn.   *John Trapp*

Troubles are free school-masters.
John Trapp

Affliction is God's flail to thresh off our husks.   *Thomas Watson*

Christians are commonly best in affliction.   *Thomas Watson*

Is it any injustice in God to put his gold into the furnace to purify it?
Thomas Watson

Jonah was sent into the whale's belly to make his sermon for Nineveh.
Thomas Watson

The eyes that sin shuts affliction opens.
Thomas Watson

The whale that swallowed Jonah was the means of bringing him safe to land.
Thomas Watson

There is more evil in a drop of sin than in a sea of affliction.   *Thomas Watson*

When God lays men on their backs, then they look up to heaven.   *Thomas Watson*

Whilst I continue on this side of eternity, I never expect to be free from trials, only to change them. For it is necessary to heal the pride of my heart that such should come.   *George Whitefield.*

We know not what we lose when we pray to be delivered out of afflictions, because God always increases his consolation and grace as afflictions abound.
Thomas Wilson

I am mended by my sickness, enriched by my poverty, and strengthened by my weakness.   *Abraham Wright*

What fools we are, then, to frown upon our afflictions! These, how crabbed so ever, are our best friends. They are not intended for our pleasure, they are for our profit.   *Abraham Wright*

Among my list of blessings infinite stands this the foremost that my heart has bled.
Edward Young

TRIALS — Certainty

A saint is often under a cross, never under a curse.   *Anon.*

God's people are not without trial — nor without God in time of trial.   *Anon.*

There never yet was an unscarred saint.
                                                  Anon.

The Christian life is a bed of roses — thorns and all.   *Doug Barnett*

God promises the Christian heaven after death, not before it.   *John Blanchard*

Sin has turned the world from a paradise into a thicket; there is no getting through without being scratched. *Thomas Boston*

Saints have their winter seasons.
                                        Thomas Brooks

As we are adopted in Christ we are appointed to the slaughter.   *John Calvin*

The disciples of Christ must walk among thorns, and march to the cross amidst uninterrupted afflictions.   *John Calvin*

Spiritual believers are honoured with warfare in the front line trenches.
                                Lewis Sperry Chafer

The Scriptures show conclusively that tribulation is a natural by-product of genuine Christianity.   *William E. Cox*

Perpetual sunshine is not usual in this world, even to God's true saints.
                                Jonathan Edwards

No man has a velvet cross.   *John Flavel*

None are crowned till they have striven.
                                Thomas Goodwin

There is far more agony than ecstasy in this world of things as they are.
                                Vance Havner

Afflictions are in the covenant, and therefore they are not meant for our hurt but are intended for our good.
                                Matthew Henry

Christ went by the cross to the crown, and we must not think of going any other way.   *Matthew Henry*

The corn of God's floor must expect to be threshed by afflictions and persecutions.   *Matthew Henry*

Testing is important, inevitable ... because we must be revealed to ourselves.
                                J. Russell Howden

Every Christian is a cross-bearer.
                                Martin Luther

Every true saint is heir to the cross.
                                Martin Luther

As the way to Canaan lay through a howling wilderness and desert, so the path to heaven lies through much affliction.
                                Thomas Manton

Crosses seldom come single.
                                Thomas Manton

A believer is to be known not only by his peace and joy, but by his warfare and distress.   *Robert Murray M'Cheyne*

There is no guarantee that men faithful to God will be recognizable by their numbers, their talents or their success.
                                Iain H. Murray

To hold on to the plough while wiping our tears, that is Christianity.
                                Watchman Nee

Why should I complain
Of want or distress,

Temptation or pain?
He told me no less;
The heirs of salvation,
I know from his Word,
Through much tribulation
Must follow their Lord.
John Newton

God promises no immunity from crosses.
Richard Sibbes

There are no crown-wearers in heaven
that were not cross-bearers here below.
C. H. Spurgeon

Trouble-free living is not the lot of the
children of Adam, even when they
become the children of God. *Frank Retief*

It is winter with the saints sometimes,
when the tree has no leaves, yet the life
is in it. *Daniel Rowland*

God hath called you to Christ's side and
the wind is now in Christ's face in this
land; and seeing ye are with him, ye
cannot expect the lee-side or the sunny
side of the brae. *Samuel Rutherford*

You will not get leave to steal quietly to
heaven without a conflict and a cross.
Samuel Rutherford

The grace of God exempts no one from
trouble. *J. C. Ryle*

How can I look to be at home in the
enemy's country, joyful while in exile, or
comfortable in a wilderness? This is not
my rest. This is the place of the furnace
and the forge and the hammer.
C. H. Spurgeon

Christianity promises us no escape from
the opposition of wicked men; indeed it
teaches us to expect it. *David Thomas*

You must not always expect the wind to
be at your back all the way to heaven.
William Tiptaft

He that escapes affliction may well
suspect his adoption. *John Trapp*

Afflictions fit for heaven. *Thomas Watson*

Life and trouble are married together.
Thomas Watson

Though Christ died to take away the curse
from us, yet not to take away the cross
from us. *Thomas Watson*

While there is a devil and a wicked man
in the world never expect a charter of
exemption from trouble. *Thomas Watson*

TRIALS — God the Sender

God breaks the cistern to bring us to the
fountain. *Anon.*

God loves his people when he strikes
them as well as when he strokes them.
Anon.

God promises a safe landing but not a
calm passage. *Anon.*

God sends nothing but what can be borne.
Anon.

God sometimes puts his children to bed
in the dark. *Anon.*

The pressures of life are the hands of the
Potter. *Anon.*

Those whom God loves he takes to
pieces; and then puts them together again.
Anon.

Paradoxical as it may seem, God means not only to make us good, but to make us also happy, by sickness, disaster and disappointment.   *C. A. Bartol*

Men think that God is destroying them when he is tuning them.
Henry Ward Beecher

We are always in the forge or on the anvil; by trials God is shaping us for higher things.   *Henry Ward Beecher*

God may call you to endure difficulties, but he will never cause you to experience defeat.   *John Blanchard*

God sometimes puts us in the dark to show us he is the light. *John Blanchard*

Nothing that happens to the Christian is accidental or incidental. *John Blanchard*

The storms of life no more indicate the absence of God than clouds indicate the absence of the sun.   *John Blanchard*

Affliction is the expression of paternal love.   *Horatius Bonar*

The Lord has given me both vinegar and honey, but he has given me the vinegar with a teaspoon and the honey with a ladle.   *Billy Bray*

Wherever souls are being tried and ripened, in whatever commonplace and homely way, there God is hewing out the pillars of his temple.   *Phillips Brooks*

Many crosses spring forth to us from the root of God's favour.   *John Calvin*

Our Father does not afflict to destroy or ruin us, but rather to deliver us from the condemnation of the world. *John Calvin*

We are not afflicted by chance, but through the infallible providence of God.
John Calvin

When visited with affliction, it is of great importance that we should consider it as coming from God, and as expressly intended for our good.   *John Calvin*

Slum clearance is not an end in itself simply to satisfy the town planners, its ultimate aim is to move people to better homes. So in all God's dealings, which may at times appear harsh, he is gently and graciously preparing us for removal.
Herbert Carson

Suffering is God's furnace in which he tests the quality of our faith.
Herbert Carson

By suffering God's will, we learn to do God's will.   *Thomas Case*

God's way of answering the Christian's prayer for more patience, experience, hope and love often is to put him into the furnace of affliction.   *Richard Cecil*

God does not do what false Christianity makes out—keep a man immune from trouble.   *Oswald Chambers*

If God has made your cup sweet, drink it with grace. If he has made it bitter, drink it in communion with him.
Oswald Chambers

It is a great thing, when the cup of bitterness is pressed to our lips, to feel that it is not fate or necessity, but divine love working on us for our good ends.
E. H. Chapin

God measures out affliction to our need.
Chrysostom

649

Count each affliction, whether light or grave, God's messenger sent down to thee. *Aubrey T. De Vere*

I had rather have God's vinegar than man's oil, God's wormwood than man's manna. *John Donne*

God's pruning is purposeful.
Sinclair Ferguson

Trials ... are not threats to God's purposes, but further indications of how meticulously faithful he is to that purpose.
Sinclair Ferguson

God does not always spare us trouble, but he does succour us in trouble.
Vance Havner

The grace, the groans and the glory are all part of the eternal purpose. Where there is no groaning there is no growing now, nor glory to come. *Vance Havner*

God ne'er afflicts us more than our desert,
Though he may seem to over-act his part.
Sometimes he strikes us more than flesh
   can bear,
But yet still less than grace can suffer
   here.
Robert Herrick

God retains his kindness for his people even when he afflicts them.
Matthew Henry

God sometimes brings his people into a wilderness that there he might speak comfortably to them. *Matthew Henry*

God's design in afflicting his people is their probation, not their destruction; their advantage, not their ruin. *Matthew Henry*

There may be love in Christ's heart while

there are frowns in his face.
Matthew Henry

Winds and clouds are in God's hands, are designed to try us, and our Christianity obliges us to endure hardness.
Matthew Henry

Good when he gives, supremely good,
Nor less when he denies.
E'en crosses from his sovereign hand
Are blessings in disguise.
James Hervey

It is a great consolation to know that dissensions ... are not fortuitous, but are ordered by the providence of God, and are designed, as storms, for the purpose of purification. *Charles Hodge*

God will not look you over for medals, degrees or diplomas, but for scars.
Elbert Hubbard

Troubles appear to be in God's catalogue of mercies, and we cannot do without them. *Thomas Jones*

Adversity is the diamond dust heaven polishes its jewels with. *Robert Leighton*

God, who foresaw your tribulation, has specially armed you to go through it, not without pain but without stain. *C. S. Lewis*

The great thing, if one can, is to stop regarding all the unpleasant things as interruptions of one's own or real life. The truth is of course that what one calls the interruptions are precisely one's real life — the life God is sending one day by day.
C. S. Lewis

God often puts us in situations that are too much for us so that we will learn that no situation is too much for him.
Erwin W. Lutzer

Let God lay on a burden, he will be sure to strengthen the back.   *Thomas Lye*

Afflictions are but the shadow of God's wings.   *George Macdonald*

If God sends us on stony paths he will provide us with strong shoes.
Alexander MacLaren

Affliction by itself does not sanctify; it exhausts and embitters, it depresses and entices. It is the presence of God and the use made of it by him, as he relates it to our lives as a whole . . . that makes adversity salutary.   *Donald MacLeod*

God sends us miseries, not to make us worse but to make us better.
Thomas Manton

God will never permit any troubles to come upon us unless he has a specific plan by which great blessing can come out of the difficulty.   *Peter Marshall*

I always feel much need of God's afflicting hand.   *Robert Murray M'Cheyne*

If nothing else will do to sever me from my sins, Lord send me such sore and trying calamities as shall awake me from earthly slumbers.
Robert Murray M'Cheyne

If we only saw the whole, we should see that the Father is doing little else in the world but training his vines.
Robert Murray M'Cheyne

Our heavenly Father never takes anything from his children unless he means to give them something better.   *George Muller*

Trials are medicines which our gracious and wise physician prescribes, because we need them; and he proportions the frequency and weight of them to what the case requires.   *John Newton*

Affliction is a talent, entrusted to us by God, which he expects us to improve to his glory and to our own everlasting good.
Brownlow North

It is true that *God tempts none,* as temptation formally leads into sin; but he *orders temptations.*   *John Owen*

God has lessons for us to learn in our times of trouble, and he is strong enough to resist our piteous cries for relief until the discipline of pain does its gracious work in our souls.   *James Philip*

Having called believers into his grand designs, which means into fellowship with his sufferings, God is not slow to share with them the fruits of his travail, in terms of blessing and glory, here and hereafter.   *James Philip*

An affliction at God's hands is better than a joy of our own creation.
William S. Plumer

God loves his own children too well to exempt them from affliction.
William S. Plumer

The whole of life is a test, a trial of what is in us, so arranged by God himself.
William S. Plumer

By afflictions God is spoiling us of what otherwise might have spoiled us. When he makes the world too hot for us to hold, we let go.   *Thomas Powell*

No matter how long our trial may be, it will never be too long for God's intention.
P. B. Power

Trials — God the Sender

God permits no suffering or trials without a purpose, even though that purpose may be hidden from us. *Frank Retief*

I bless the Lord that all our troubles come through Christ's fingers, and that he casts sugar among them. *Samuel Rutherford*

I would wish each cross were looked in the face seven times, and were read over and over again. It is the messenger of the Lord and speaks something.
Samuel Rutherford

There is no cross or misery that befalls the church of God or any of his children, but it is related to God.
Samuel Rutherford

Every cross is a message from God and intended to do us good in the end.
J. C. Ryle

Let no man think himself the better because he is free from troubles. It is because God sees him not fit to bear greater.
Richard Sibbes

Affliction is not sent in vain from the good God who chastens those he loves.
Robert Southey

It is the Lord's way to tear before he heals. This is the honest love of his heart and the sure surgery of his hand.
C. H. Spurgeon

Our Lord's letters often come to us in black-edged envelopes. *C. H. Spurgeon*

The Lord gets his best soldiers out of the highlands of affliction. *C. H. Spurgeon*

The refiner is never very far from the mouth of the furnace when his gold is in the fire. *C. H. Spurgeon*

Trials are no evidence of being without God, since trials come from God!
C. H. Spurgeon

We never have such close dealings with God as when we are in tribulation.
C. H. Spurgeon

Mountains are God's methods.
J. Charles Stern

While the storm gathers let us by faith rejoice in our place behind the shut door — in Christ. *J. Charles Stern*

God tempers the wind to the shorn lamb.
Laurence Sterne

God and adversity will be good company.
George Swinnock

A sculptor does not use a manicure set to reduce the rude, unshapely marble to a thing of beauty. *A. W. Tozer*

God is ingenious in making us crosses.
A. W. Tozer

If God has singled you out to be a special object of his grace you may expect him to honour you with stricter discipline and greater suffering than less favoured ones are called upon to endure. *A. W. Tozer*

God's wounds are better than Satan's salves. *John Trapp*

Affliction is a badge of adoption.
Thomas Watson

God afflicts with the same love as he adopts. *Thomas Watson*

God never promises to save us from adversity, only to be with us in the midst of it. *David Watson*

Usually, when the Lord intends us some signal mercy, he fits us for it by some eminent trial.   *Thomas Watson*

Whoever brings an affliction, it is God who sends it.   *Thomas Watson*

God doesn't save people from punishment or pain. He saves them by giving them the strength and the spirit to bear it.
          Leonard Wilson

We may feel God's hand as a Father upon us when he strikes us as well as when he strokes us.   *Abraham Wright*

The God of circumstances will not place one upon us that is heavier than we can bear.   *Spiros Zodhiates*

TRIALS — Response

Reckon any matter of trial to thee among thy gains.   *Thomas Adams*

Adversity does not make us frail; it only shows us how frail we are.   *Anon.*

Come then, affliction, if my Father wills, and be my frowning friend. A friend that frowns is better than a smiling enemy.
          Anon.

It is better to get to heaven battered, bruised and bleeding than to go happily to hell.   *Anon.*

The longer we dwell on our misfortunes, the greater is their power to harm us.
          Anon.

If you are swept off your feet, it's time to get on your knees.   *Fred Beck*

We cannot infer from prosperity that God is pleased with us, nor can we infer from adversity that he is displeased with us.
          Wilson Benton

God has done a mighty work in our hearts when we can praise him in every pain, bless him for every burden, sing in every sorrow and delight in every discipline.
          John Blanchard

We are called upon to reflect the love of God as much in trial as in tranquility.
          John Blanchard

If you meet with misfortunes, consider that you merit greater ones.
          Petrus Blesensis

In the day of prosperity we have many refuges to resort to; in the day of adversity, only one.   *Horatius Bonar*

It is more commendable to bear affliction patiently than to be busy in good works.   *Bonaventura*

Had we a clearer view of the other world, we should make so much of either the smiles or frowns of this. *Thomas Boston*

The person who is patient under mistreatment by others is the person who has developed such a confidence in the wisdom, power and faithfulness of God that he willingly entrusts his circumstances into his hands.   *Jerry Bridges*

Trials always change our relationship with God. Either they drive us to him, or they drive us away from him.
          Jerry Bridges

I do not pray for a lighter load but for a stronger back.   *Phillips Brooks*

A gracious soul may look through the darkest cloud and see God smiling on him.   *Thomas Brooks*

If you would not have affliction visit you twice, listen at once to what it teaches.
James Burgh

Lord, how happy it is when strong afflictions from thee raise in us strong affections for thee!   *Francis Burkitt*

Every chastisement is a call to repentance.
John Calvin

In every affliction, we ought immediately to review our past life. When we do so, we shall certainly find that we have deserved such chastisement. *John Calvin*

It is a genuine evidence of true godliness when, although plunged into the deepest afflictions, we yet cease not to submit ourselves to God.   *John Calvin*

Worship God in the difficult circumstances and, when he chooses, he will alter them in two seconds. *Oswald Chambers*

Afflictions are blessings to us when we can bless God for afflictions.
William Dyer

It lightens the stroke to draw near to him who handles the rod.   *Tryon Edwards*

A cross which comes from God ought to be welcomed without any concern for self.   *François Fenelon*

Learn how to suffer, for that is the most important of all lessons.
François Fenelon

Shall light troubles make you forget weighty mercies?   *John Flavel*

If the sun of God's countenance shine upon me, I may well be content with the rain of affliction.   *Joseph Hall*

We should be more anxious that our afflictions should benefit us than that they should be speedily removed from us.
Robert Hall

God has not departed because the day is dark.   *Vance Havner*

We should glory in our infirmities, but not glorify them.   *Vance Havner*

Days of trouble must be days of prayer.
Matthew Henry

Perils and frights should drive us *to* God, not *from* him.   *Matthew Henry*

Such is the nature of our trials that while they last we cannot see the end.
Martin Luther

When I consider my crosses, tribulations and temptations, I shame myself almost to death thinking of what they are in comparison to the sufferings of my blessed Saviour, Jesus Christ.
Martin Luther

The cup which the Saviour giveth me, can it be anything but a cup of salvation?
Alexander Maclaren

A Christian is a bird that can sing in winter as well as in spring. *Thomas Manton*

To lie down in the time of grief, to be quiet under the stroke of adverse fortune, implies a great strength. *George Matheson*

While the fire is hot, keep conversing with the Refiner.   *F. B. Meyer*

No affliction would trouble a child of God if he knew God's reasons for sending it.
G. Campbell Morgan

The man who measures things by the circumstances of the hour is filled with fear; the man who sees Jehovah enthroned and governing has no panic.
G. Campbell Morgan

Bearing wrong is a glorious part of the fellowship with Christ's sufferings.
Andrew Murray

A Christian should never let adversity get him down except on his knees.
Mae Nicholson

Our present sufferings are like an ugly porch which leads us to the threshold of an unspeakably glorious mansion.
Stuart Olyott

Seek holiness rather than consolation.
John Owen

We ought as much to pray for a blessing upon our daily rod as upon our daily bread.
John Owen

As mature or maturing Christians we should realize that God may not always want us to have an easy time — which is in effect what we ask for when we ask for affliction to be removed. *James Philip*

There is a strange perversity in men concerning their trials in life, and only grace can cure it.
William S. Plumer

Many a man has thought himself broken up, when he has merely been made ready for the sowing.
Hugh Redwood

Praise God for the hammer, the file and the furnace!
Samuel Rutherford

Saints must be best in worst times.
Samuel Rutherford

When I am in the cellar of affliction I look for the Lord's choicest wines.
Samuel Rutherford

Why should I start at the plough of my Lord, that maketh the deep furrows on my soul? I know he is no idle husbandman; he purposeth a harvest.
Samuel Rutherford

It is never legitimate to be angry with God. To do so is an affront to God's holiness. It is an unspoken declaration that God has done an injustice.
R. C. Sproul

Be it ours, when we cannot see the face of God, to trust under the shadow of his wings.
C. H. Spurgeon

Cast your troubles where you have cast your sins.
C. H. Spurgeon

Cry for grace from God to see God's purpose in every trial, and then for grace to submit to it, at once; to accept it, to rejoice in it. This is usually the end of trouble.
C. H. Spurgeon

Faith always sees the bow of covenant promise whenever sense sees the cloud of affliction.
C. H. Spurgeon

Let no excess of suffering drive us away from the throne of grace, but rather let it drive us closer to it.
C. H. Spurgeon

Let us be sure to praise God when things go ill with us!
C. H. Spurgeon

Let us love a chiding God. *C. H. Spurgeon*

When a train goes through a tunnel and it gets dark, you don't throw away your ticket and jump off. You sit still and trust the engineer.
Corrie ten Boom

Nothing influences the quality of our life more than how we respond to trouble.
Erwin G. Tieman

We are all good until we are tired.
William Tiptaft

Never in history has the Lord left his people clueless in a time of calamity.
David Wilkerson

TRIALS — Temporary Nature

When God's hand is on thy back, let thy hand be on thy mouth, for though the affliction be sharp it shall be but short.
Thomas Brooks

The punishments inflicted by God on his servants are only temporary, and intended as medicine.
John Calvin

You can't get to tomorrow morning without going through tonight.
Elisabeth Elliot

The skirmish may be sharp, but it cannot last long. The cloud, while it drops, is passing over thy head; then comes fair weather and an eternal sunshine of glory.
William Gurnall

Though your life be evil with troubles, yet it is short — a few steps and we are out of the rain.
William Gurnall

All the tribulations of this life are but incidents on the road from groans to glory.
Vance Havner

How soon you will find that everything in your history, except sin, has been *for you*. Every wave of trouble has been wafting you to the sunny shores of a sinless eternity.
Robert Murray M'Cheyne

What matter in eternity the slight awkwardnesses of time?
Robert Murray M'Cheyne

It was well worth standing a while in the fire, for such an opportunity of experiencing and exhibiting the power and faithfulness of God's promises.
John Newton

No pain, no palm; no thorns, no throne; no gall, no glory; no cross, no crown.
William Penn

The ills of this present life ... cannot harm us. For they are simply introductory, a kind of preface to the main theme; they are not what the real story is about.
James Philip

He who has fixed the bounds of our habitation has also fixed the bounds of our tribulation.
C. H. Spurgeon

The punishment of sin is everlasting, but the fatherly chastisement of it in a child of God is but for a season. *C. H. Spurgeon*

The rod may make us smart, but the sword shall not make us die.
C. H. Spurgeon

God does not mock his children with a night that has no ending; and to every man who stands resolute while the darkness lasts there comes at length the vindication of faith and the breaking of the day.
James S. Stewart

He that rides to be crowned will not think much of a rainy day.
John Trapp

Affliction has a sting, but withal a wing; sorrow shall fly away.
Thomas Watson

Affliction may be lasting, but it is not everlasting.
Thomas Watson

Correction may befall the saint, but not destruction. *Thomas Watson*

Lights are the pains that nature brings;
How short our sorrows are,
When with eternal future things
The present we compare!
Isaac Watts

TRINITY — See Godhead

TRUST — See Faith

TRUTH
(See also: Honesty; Integrity)

He who sets one great truth afloat in the world serves his generation.
James W. Alexander

Add one small bit to the truth and you inevitably subtract from it. *Anon.*

The man who speaks the truth is always at ease. *Anon.*

The trouble with stretching the truth is that people are apt to see through it. *Anon.*

God forbid that we should ever be satisfied either with heated ignorance or frozen truth. *John Blanchard*

The claim 'There is no such thing as absolute truth' self-destructs, because if there is no such thing as absolute truth, the statement itself cannot be absolute truth. *John Blanchard*

To say that something can be 'true for you, but not for me' is virtually to reduce truth to a matter of personal opinion.
John Blanchard

Truth is objective, not subjective, so sincerity or passion is no guarantee of a claim's validity. *John Blanchard*

Whatever you add to the truth subtracts from it. *John Blanchard*

Truth needs no defence; it is beyond attack. *James Bolen*

Truth is not the feeble thing which men often think they can afford to disparage. Truth is power; let it be treated and trusted as such. *Horatius Bonar*

Truth exists; only falsehood has to be invented. *George Braque*

Keep the truth and the truth will keep you.
William Bridge

If a thousand old beliefs were ruined in our march to truth we must still march on. *Stopford A. Brooke*

Truth is always strong, no matter how weak it looks, and falsehood is always weak, no matter how strong it looks.
Phillips Brooks

Every parcel of truth is precious as the filings of gold; we must either live with it, or die for it. *Thomas Brooks*

I thirst for truth, but shall not reach it till I reach the source. *Robert Browning*

Naked truth is too hard for armed error.
Francis Burkitt

Nothing is deemed more precious by God than truth. *John Calvin*

When truth is silent, false views seem plausible. *Walter J. Chantry*

Truth is incontrovertible. Panic may resent it; ignorance may deride it; malice may distort it; but there it is.
Winston Churchill

If all heretical doctrines and ways and the memory of them were rooted out of the world, the heart is bad enough in one day to set them all on foot again; therefore guard the truth.   *John Collins*

Always tell the truth. Then you don't have to worry about what you said last.
   Robert Cook

Truth is the foundation of all knowledge and the cement of all societies.
   John Dryden

If God were able to backslide from truth, I would fain cling to truth and let God go.   *Meister Eckhart*

The truth does not vary because men forget or ignore or traduce it.
   Irwin Edman

The grandest homage we can pay to truth is to use it.   *Ralph Waldo Emerson*

Do not merely speak the truth, but live truthfully, openly and honestly with one another.   *Sinclair Ferguson*

It cannot be overemphasized that men and women who have accomplished anything in God's strength have always done so on the basis of their grasp of truth.
   Sinclair Ferguson

Speak boldly and speak truly. Shame the devil!   *John Fletcher*

A lie stands on one leg, truth on two.
   Benjamin Franklin

Truth fears no trial.   *Thomas Fuller*

Truth is not finally a matter of philosophy but of theology.   *Os Guinness*

All truth is God's truth and is true everywhere, for everyone, under all conditions. Truth is true in the sense that it is objective and independent of the mind of any human knower. Being true, it cannot contradict itself.   *Os Guinness*

Truth is true even if nobody believes it and falsehood is false even if everybody believes it.   *Os Guinness*

We must not just debate the truth, we must know the truth. If we would live free, we must not just know the truth, we must live in truth and we must become people of truth.   *Os Guinness*

Godliness is the child of truth, and it must be nursed ... with no other milk than that of its own mother.   *William Gurnall*

News may come that truth is sick, but never that it is dead.   *William Gurnall*

The farther a soul stands from the light of truth, the farther he must needs be from the heat of comfort.   *William Gurnall*

The temple of truth will not be damaged half so much by woodpeckers on the outside as by termites on the inside.
   Vance Havner

Whenever unbelief thinks it has buried the truth, the 'corpse' always comes to life in the midst of the funeral to outlive all the pallbearers.   *Vance Havner*

With the loss of truth we forfeit profundity; we are deprived of depth.
   Seamus Heaney

Truth is never diminished by asking questions.   *Walter R. Hearn*

Some people live their whole lives just around the corner from the world of truth.
Carl F. H. Henry

Truth is always as honest in its recognition of darkness as it is exultant in its understanding of light. *John Hercus*

Whenever anyone knows truth, his knowledge is due to God's illuminating it to his mind. *W. Andrew Hoffecker*

O faithful Christian, search the truth, hear truth, learn truth, love truth, speak the truth, hold the truth till death. *John Hus*

Every truth, like a lease, brings in revenue the next year as well as this.
William Jenkyn

Truth reforms as well as informs.
William Jenkyn

Write nothing, say nothing, think nothing that you cannot believe to be true before God. *Joseph Joubert*

According to Christianity, the acid test of truth and goodness is scripturalness.
R. B. Kuiper

Absolute truth belongs to God alone.
Gotthold Lessing

Truth is always about something, but reality is that about which truth is.
C. S. Lewis

The business of the truth is to set us free from sin. *D. Martyn Lloyd-Jones*

It is better that the heavens fall than that one crumb of truth perish. *Martin Luther*

Peace if possible, but truth at any rate.
Martin Luther

Seek not greatness, but seek truth and you will find both. *Horace Mann*

Truths are concocted and ripened by meditation. *Thomas Manton*

God and his truth cannot be changed; the gospel is not negotiable. *John Marshall*

Nothing sets the heart on fire like truth.
Will Metzger

Belief or unbelief has no bearing on the validity of an argument. *Robert A. Morey*

Truth must not be suppressed because men are wicked and blind.
Wolfgang Musculus

The claims of truth are paramount.
John Murray

Truth lives in the cellar, error on the doorstep. *Austin O'Malley*

It is truth alone that capacitates any soul to give glory to God. *John Owen*

Right is right, even if everyone is against it; and wrong is wrong, even if everyone is for it. *William Penn*

Truth often suffers more by the heat of its defenders than by the arguments of its opposers. *William Penn*

There are none so bitter against the truth as those who have departed from it.
James Philip

There are no victories like those of truth.
William S. Plumer

Truth needs no flowers of speech.
Alexander Pope

If truth is a fantasy then life has no meaning. *Vaughan Roberts*

Truth and morality are inextricably connected. *Martin Robinson*

There is no power on earth more formidable than the truth. *Margaret Lee Runbeck*

Truth has no responsibility to make us comfortable. *David L. Russell*

We have the truth and we need not be afraid to say so. *J. C. Ryle*

Let us rejoice in the truth, wherever we find its lamp burning. *Albert Schweitzer*

Truth without godliness is a human knowledge of divine things.
Richard Sibbes

Truth is always the strongest argument.
Sophocles

If our foundation for truth is true, all other truth can only support and enhance it.
R. C. Sproul

What is true or not true can never be determined by an analysis of what men desire or do not desire to be the truth.
R. C. Sproul

A thousand errors may live in peace with one another, but truth is a hammer that breaks them all in pieces. *C. H. Spurgeon*

It is in the way of truth that real peace is found. *C. H. Spurgeon*

It is more to God's glory that the world should be conquered by the force of truth than by the blaze of miracles.
C. H. Spurgeon

Long ago I ceased to count heads. Truth is usually in the minority in this evil world. *C. H. Spurgeon*

Men to be truly won must be won by truth. *C. H. Spurgeon*

Opinions alter, but truth certified by God can no more change than the God who uttered it. *C. H. Spurgeon*

The practice of truth is the most profitable reading of it. *C. H. Spurgeon*

Truth wears well. *C. H. Spurgeon*

Nothing sets the heart on fire like truth.
John R. W. Stott

Our Lord Jesus Christ called himself the Truth not the Custom. *Tertullian*

The devil tries to shake the truth by pretending to defend it. *Tertullian*

Truth does not blush. *Tertullian*

Truth in propositions is powerful; truth in example is more powerful.
David Thomas

The shining of truth, like the shining of the sun, wakens insects into life, which otherwise would have no sensitive existence. Yet, better for a few insects to quicken than for the sun not to shine!
Augustus M. Toplady

Truth engages the citadel of the human heart and is not satisfied until it has conquered everything there. *A. W. Tozer*

We should never retreat before truth simply because we cannot explain it.
A. W. Tozer

Truth is like our first parents — most beautiful when naked.   *John Trapp*

Truth must be spoken, however it be taken.   *John Trapp*

Truth seldom goes without a scratched face.   *John Trapp*

God is the source of all truth, and every discovery is a means of glorifying him.
Gene Veith

Truth is not ashamed of its name of nakedness; it can walk openly and boldly.
Ralph Venning

The truth is always daunting but always worth knowing.   *Thomas Winning*

All truth is God's truth, and all must ultimately be one.   *J. Stafford Wright*

UNBELIEF
(See also: Agnosticism; Atheism; Impiety)

If you are an unbeliever when you die, Christ did not die for you.   *Ambrose*

Living without faith is like driving in a fog.   *Anon.*

Unbelief in the face of evidence is either stupidity or sin.   *Anon.*

All unbelief is the belief of a lie.
Horatius Bonar

In all unbelief there are these two things: a good opinion of one's self and a bad opinion of God.   *Horatius Bonar*

Can any man perish more justly than they who refuse to be saved?   *John Calvin*

Infidelity is always blind.   *John Calvin*

Our own unbelief is the only impediment which prevents God from satisfying us largely and bountifully with all good things.   *John Calvin*

The blindness of unbelievers in no way detracts from the clarity of the gospel; the sun is no less bright because blind men do not perceive its light.   *John Calvin*

Unbelief ... is always proud. *John Calvin*

Unbelief makes us rebels and deserters.
John Calvin

Unbelieving and irreligious men have no ears.   *John Calvin*

As faith is the greatest grace, so that which is opposite to it must be the greatest sin.   *Stephen Charnock*

Is not he as much guilty of his own death that rejects a medicine as he that cuts his own throat?   *Stephen Charnock*

Unbelief was the first sin, and pride was the first-born of it.   *Stephen Charnock*

When God is not believed we must needs give credit to the devil.
Stephen Charnock

Christ distinguished between doubt and unbelief. Doubt says, 'I can't believe.' Unbelief says, 'I won't believe.' Doubt is honest. Unbelief is obstinate.
Henry Drummond

Disobedience and unbelief are two sides of the same coin.   *Ronald Dunn*

What loneliness is more lonely than distrust?   *George Eliot*

Alongside getting faith out of a heart that is utterly hostile and unbelieving, making a silk purse out of a sow's ear or getting blood from a turnip is child's play.
John H. Gerstner

Unbelief is always conceited.
Richard Glover

Unbelief in the biblical view is not passive, an innocent but inaccurate view of the world that has unfortunately 'got it wrong' at a few points. Rather, unbelief is active, driven by a dark dynamism.
Os Guinness

God excludes none if they do not exclude themselves.
William Guthrie

Gospel light is justly taken away from those that endeavour to extinguish it.
Matthew Henry

Nothing is more offensive to God than disbelief of his promise and despair of the performance of it because of some difficulties that seem to lie in the way.
Matthew Henry

There are those who will trust Christ no further than they can see him . . . ; as if he were tied to our methods, and could not draw water without our buckets.
Matthew Henry

Unbelief is apt to mistake recruits for enemies, and to draw dismal conclusions even from comfortable premises.
Matthew Henry

Unbelief is at the bottom of all our staggerings at God's promises.
Matthew Henry

Unbelief is at the bottom of what sinners do ignorantly.
Matthew Henry

Unbelief is the great obstruction to Christ's favours.
Matthew Henry

Unbelief may truly be called the great damning sin, because it leaves us under the guilt of all our other sins; it is a sin against the remedy.
Matthew Henry

Unbelief, or distrust of God, is a sin that is its own punishment.
Matthew Henry

Unbelief is the shield of every sin.
William Jenkyn

Unbelief ... makes the world a moral desert, where no divine footsteps are heard, where no angels ascend and descend, where no living hand adorns the fields, feeds the birds of heaven, or regulates events.
F. W. Krummacher

Unbelief is a matter not only of the head but of the heart. The unbeliever's trouble is that his heart is not right with God.
R. B. Kuiper

Unbelief is radically all other disobedience.
Robert Leighton

The Bible itself gives us one short prayer which is suitable for all who are struggling with the beliefs and doctrines. It is: Lord I believe, help Thou my unbelief.
C. S. Lewis

When you are arguing against God you are arguing against the very Power that makes you able to argue at all. *C. S. Lewis*

No difficulty in believing the gospel is intellectual, it is always moral.
D. Martyn Lloyd-Jones

As no one can give himself faith, neither can he take away his unbelief.
Martin Luther

Birds lack faith. They fly away when I enter the orchard, though I mean them no ill. Even so do we lack faith in God.
Martin Luthe

Unbelief is the mother of sin, and misbelief the nurse of it. *Thomas Manton*

Ultimately, the acceptance of the gospel is a moral problem not an intellectual problem. *Will Metzger*

Unbelief is not failure in intellectual apprehension. It is disobedience in the presence of the clear commands of God.
G. Campbell Morgan

The natural man does not want to believe that God has spoken. *Tom Nettles*

For the most part we live upon successes, not promises. Unless we see and feel the print of victories we will not believe.
John Owen

Unbelief makes God a liar and, worse still, a perjurer, for it accounts him as not only false to his word, but to his oath.
A. T. Pierson

Unbelief is far, far more than entertaining an erroneous conception of God's way of salvation: it is a species of hatred against him. *A. W. Pink*

Unbelief is not simply an infirmity of fallen human nature, it is a heinous crime.
A. W. Pink

No maniac ever reasoned more illogically than the unbeliever. *William S. Plumer*

The errors of faith are better than the best thoughts of unbelief. *Thomas Russell*

If men do not have eternal life it is never

because God did not love them, or because Christ was not given for them, but because they did not believe on Christ. *J. C. Ryle*

No sin makes less noise, but none so surely damns the soul, as unbelief.
J. C. Ryle

The difficulties of Christianity no doubt are great; but depend on it, they are nothing compared to the difficulties of infidelity. *J. C. Ryle*

Unbelief about the existence and personality of Satan has often proved the first step to unbelief about God. *J. C. Ryle*

We can never be too much on our guard against unbelief. It is the oldest sin in the world. *J. C. Ryle*

Those who deny God are bound to bestow all his attributes on flesh and blood. *Isaac Bashevis Singer*

The revelation of the gospel is to a world that is already under indictment for its universal rejection of God the Father.
R. C. Sproul

Those who spurn the gospel challenge not the power of the church but the sovereignty of God. *R. C. Sproul*

There are no infidels anywhere but on earth. There are none in heaven and there are none in hell. *C. H. Spurgeon*

Unbelief calls itself 'honest doubt', and not without cause, for we should not have known it to be honest if it had not labelled itself so. *C. H. Spurgeon*

Unbelief will destroy the best of us. Faith will save the worst of us. *C. H. Spurgeon*

Unbelief is so deeply rooted in the human heart that when God performs miracles on earth, unbelief doubts whether he can perform them in heaven, and when he does them in heaven, whether he can do them on earth. *Friedrich Tholuck*

If the way to heaven is so narrow, and so few seek it, what will become of those who never seek it? *William Tiptaft*

Every man will have to decide for himself whether or not he cannot afford the terrible luxury of unbelief. *A. W. Tozer*

Human unbelief cannot alter the character of God. *A. W. Tozer*

I do not believe there is anybody who ever rejects Jesus Christ on philosophical grounds. The man who continues in his rejection of Christ has a pet sin somewhere — he's in love with iniquity.
A. W. Tozer

It is unbelief that prevents our minds from soaring into the celestial city, and walking by faith with God across the golden streets. *A. W. Tozer*

A great many believers walk upon the promises at God's call in the way to heaven even as a child upon weak ice, which they are afraid will crack under them and leave them in the depth.
Robert Traill

Infidelity is the mother of apostasy.
John Trapp

Faith unlocks the divine store-house, but unbelief bars its doors. *Curtis Vaughan*

Unbelief is the foul medley of all sins, the root and receptacle of sin.
Thomas Watson

Unbelief is the root of apostasy.
Thomas Watson

The root of all apostasy is the primal sin of unbelief. *Geoffrey B. Wilson*

UNCERTAINITY
(See also: Doubt)

The fact that a Christian is uncertain does not mean that he is insecure.
John Blanchard

Nothing in the world causes so much misery as uncertainty. *Martin Luther*

The only thing people are certain about is their uncertainty. *George Bernard Shaw*

UNITY — Church — See Church unity

UNIVERSALISM

Universalism is the curse of the universe.
John Blanchard

Universalism abstracts from the radical condition of man as a sinner before God.
Jakob Jocz

Universalism is the evangelist's 'By-Path Meadow'. We shall do well to stick to the road. *J. I. Packer*

URGENCY

Live your best, and act your best, and think your best each day, for there may be no tomorrows. *Anon.*

Making the most of today is the best way to be ready for tomorrow. *Anon.*

Paul's calendar had only two days — 'today' and 'that day'. *Anon.*

We must take the opportunity of a life-time in the lifetime of an opportunity.
Anon.

God says 'today'; the devil says 'tomorrow'.
Basil

Now if ever, now for ever, now or never, up and be doing, lest you be for ever undone.
William Dyer

Harvest time is always the ever-present *now!*
Billy Graham

It is later than it has ever been before, and the smartest thing any man can do is to set his watch by God's clock.
Vance Havner

The big word with God is *now.*
Vance Havner

Today is God's time. Tonight your soul may be required. Set your watch with heaven and not the faulty timepieces of earth.
Vance Havner

We shall have all eternity in which to celebrate our victories, but we have only one short hour before the sunset in which to *win* them.
Robert Moffatt

Opportunity is headlong bald behind, having never a lock to catch hold of.
Christopher Nesse

Opportunities are for eternity, but not to eternity.
William Secker

Now is the watchword of the wise.
C. H. Spurgeon

There is only one time that is important — *now.*
Leo Tolstoy

VANITY
(See also: Boasting; Conceit; Egotism; Pride)

Some people are so sensitive that when you pat them on the back their head swells.
Anon.

We know nothing vainer than the minds of men.
John Calvin

Guard against that vanity which courts a compliment, or is fed by it.
Thomas Chalmers

We are all imbued with the love of praise.
Cicero

Of all our infirmities, vanity is the dearest to us; a man will starve his other vices to keep that alive.
Benjamin Franklin

A vain mind is as bad, and as odious to God, as a vicious life.
Thomas Manton

It is hard to carry a full cup without spilling, and not to lift up ourselves when we are raised up by God.
Thomas Manton

Vanity is the fruit of ignorance.
Alexander Ross

VICTORY

Be careful that victories do not carry the seeds of future defeats.
Anon.

We will be controlled either by Satan, by self or by God. Control by Satan is slavery; control by self is futility; control by God is victory.
Anon.

A victory inside of us is ten thousand times more glorious than any victory can be outside of us.
Henry Ward Beecher

Victory

Let us be as watchful after the victory as before the battle. *Andrew Bonar*

The more anyone excels in grace, the more he ought to be afraid of falling. *John Calvin*

There is only one answer to defeat and that is victory. *Winston Churchill*

A victorious Christian life is not a superior brand of Christianity reserved for the elite of the elect. It is the normal Christian life for every Christian. *Ronald Dunn*

God's victories are won only on the battlefield of the human heart. *H. H. Farmer*

God has not called us to fumble through life. *Stephen Olford*

There is no more dangerous moment in our lives than that which follows a great victory. *Stephen Olford*

There can be no victory where there is no combat. *Richard Sibbes*

The first step on the way to victory is to recognize the enemy. *Corrie ten Boom*

God wants us to be victors, not victims; to grow, not grovel; to soar, not sink; to overcome, not to be overwhelmed. *William A. Ward*

VIGILANCE

The permanent presence of the old nature guarantees that in the Christian life there is no victory without vigilance. *John Blanchard*

Let us be as watchful after the victory as before the battle. *Andrew Bonar*

True grace always produces vigilance rather than complacency; it always produces perseverance rather than indolence. *Jerry Bridges*

The more anyone excels in grace, the more ought he to be afraid of falling. *John Calvin*

Keep us, Lord, so awake in our callings that we may sleep in thy peace and awake in thy glory. *John Donne*

Christian, seek not yet repose;
Cast thy dreams of ease away;
Thou art in the midst of foes:
Watch and pray. *Charlotte Elliott*

Many a saint, for want of keeping a tight rein, and that constantly, over some corruption which they have thought they had got the mastery of, has been thrown out of the saddle. *William Gurnall*

Our enemies are on every side, so must our armour be. *William Gurnall*

Set a strong guard about thy outward senses. These are Satan's landing-place, especially the eye and ear. *William Gurnall*

The humble Christian is the wary Christian. *William Gurnall*

Those whom God has promised to save he has promised to render watchful. *Charles Hodge*

Eternal vigilance is the price of liberty. *Thomas Jefferson*

The best way never to fall is ever to fear. *William Jenkyn*

All sins are rooted in love of pleasure. Therefore be watchful. *Thomas Manton*

When we partake of the divine nature, we do not put off the human; we ought to walk with care, but yet with comfort. *Thomas Manton*

No stage of experience takes away the need for vigilance. *J. A. Motyer*

Unless we keep a strict watch, we shall be betrayed into the hands of our spiritual enemies. *John Owen*

If we know anything of true, saving religion, let us ever beware of the beginnings of backsliding. *J. C. Ryle*

True conversion gives a man security, but it does not allow him to leave off being watchful. *C. H. Spurgeon*

A wandering heart needs a watchful eye. *Thomas Watson*

VIOLENCE
(See also: War)

Where violence reigns, reason is weak. *Sebastein Chamfort*

Somehow, for all the wondrous glimpses of 'goodness' I see in society, there remains the unmistakable stain of selfishness, violence and greed. *John Dickson*

Any man who knows the nature of his own heart realizes that violence is not another man's problem. *Os Guinness*

Violence is normal in a fallen world. *Os Guinness*

Violence is an involuntary quest for identity. *Marshall McLuhan*

VIRGIN BIRTH
(See also: Incarnation —Jesus Christ)

Those who deny that Jesus was without a human father must explain how he was without a human failure. *John Blanchard*

The God who took a motherless woman out of the side of a man took a fatherless man out of the body of a woman. *Matthew Henry*

The New Testament presentation of Jesus is not an agglomeration, but an organism, and of that organism the virgin birth is an integral part. Remove the part and the whole becomes harder and not easier to accept. *J. Gresham Machen*

For history the really strong argument in favour of the virgin birth is the difficulty of accounting for the story otherwise than on the assumption of its truth. *H. R. Mackintosh*

It seems far more difficult to believe that the God of eternity would become a man by natural human procreative processes than to believe that he would be miraculously conceived and virgin-born! *Henry M. Morris*

As bread is made of wheat, and wine is made of the grapes, so Christ is made of a woman. His body was part of the flesh and substance of the virgin. *Thomas Watson*

The virgin birth at the very least points to a world unbounded by sheer naturalism. *Ravi Zacharias*

VIRTUE
(See also: Ethics; Goodness; Morality)

Virtue consists in doing our duty in the various relations we sustain to ourselves, to our fellowmen and to God, as it is made known by reason, revelation and providence. *Archibald Alexander*

Virtue

Virtue flourishes in misfortune.   *Anon.*

Virtue is the only true nobility.   *Anon.*

Virtue never needs the help of vice; she is self-sufficient.   *Aristotle*

Negative virtue is not enough; we must do good.   *William S. Plumer*

Virtue is a state of war, and to live in it we have always to combat with ourselves.
Jean-Jacques Rousseau

VOWS

Many resolutions are like impressions made on the sand: the first wave washes them away.   *Anon.*

Christians are not to make vows to God. Sometimes the devil tempts us along this line, but it is only a shrewd attempt to get us back on the ground of law, where we can be dealt a heavy blow.
Donald Grey Barnhouse

Good resolutions are like cheques drawn on a bank where you have no account.
Oscar Wilde

WAR
(See also: Violence)

A great war leaves the country with three armies — an army of cripples, an army of mourners and an army of thieves.
Anon.

If there is anything in which earth, more than any other, resembles hell, it is its wars.   *Albert Barnes*

In war all humanity and equity is buried.
John Calvin

War is one of God's judgements.
John Calvin

War is pleasant to those who never tried it.   *John Calvin*

Jesus treats wars and natural disasters not as agenda items in a discussion of the mysterious ways of God, but as incentives to repentance.   *D. A. Carson*

The tragedy of war is that it uses man's best to do man's worst.
Harry Emerson Fosdick

Woes may come from peace but they must come from war.   *Thomas Fuller*

During war we imprison the rights of man.   *Jean Giraudoux*

War is a tragedy which commonly destroys the stage it is acted on.
Matthew Henry

War is not an act of God but a crime of man.   *Cordell Hull*

What a fine-looking thing is war! Yet ... what is it but murder in uniform?
Douglas Jerrold

Mankind must put an end to war, or war will put an end to mankind.
John F. Kennedy

The most persistent sound that reverberates through men's history is the beating of war drums.   *Arthur Koestler*

If active service does not persuade a man to prepare for death, what conceivable concatenation of circumstances would?
C. S. Lewis

War is a specific product of civilization.
Louis Mumford

Let men who delight in the cruelties of war remember that their day is coming.
William S. Plumer

Truth is the first casualty in any war.
John Nevin Sayre

O war! Thou son of hell!
William Shakespeare

No calamities have ever befallen nations that are so much to be deplored as the atrocities of war. *C. H. Spurgeon*

In war there is no such thing as victor and vanquished ... There is only a loser, and that loser is mankind. *U. Thant*

The noise of war drowns the voice of laws. *John Trapp*

War is the slaughter-house of mankind, and the hell of this present world.
John Trapp

WEALTH
(See also: Luxury; Materialism; Money; Possessions; Prosperity; Riches)

Wealth can do us no good unless it help us toward heaven. *Thomas Adams*

A golden bit does not make a better horse.
Anon.

Chains of gold are stronger than chains of iron. *Anon.*

Gold is the heaviest of all metals, but is made more heavy by covetousness. *Anon.*

The two great tests of character are wealth and poverty. *Anon.*

Wealth is no harm, but the inability to give it up is deadly. *Anon.*

Wealth is not only what we have, but what we are. *Anon.*

The greater our wealth, the greater our dangers. *Aristotle*

Whenever wealth keeps a man from thinking about God it is not a blessing but a curse. *John Blanchard*

All the wealth of this world is nothing else but a heap of clay. *John Calvin*

It is only when the rich are sick that they fully feel the impotence of wealth.
C. C. Colton

Our wealth is often a snare to ourselves and always a temptation to others.
C. C. Colton

Without the rich heart, wealth is an ugly beggar. *Ralph Waldo Emerson*

Wealth consists not in having great possessions but in having few wants.
Epicurus

Disquieting care is the common fruit of an abundance of this world, and the common fault of those that have abundance.
Matthew Henry

Poor people are as much in danger from an inordinate desire towards the wealth of the world as rich from an inordinate delight in it. *Matthew Henry*

Worldlings make gold their god; saints make God their gold. *Matthew Henry*

Gold will be slave or master. *Horace*

The real measure of our wealth is how much we'd be worth if we lost all our money. *John Henry Jowett*

Few people have the spiritual resources to be both wealthy and godly. *Erwin W. Lutzer*

God gave us wealth, not that we should be hoarders but dispensers. *Thomas Manton*

Wealth often ends in pride. *Thomas Manton*

Glory and glitter are not synonymous terms. *J. McIlmoyle*

Keeping our heads despite the pull of pleasure is as hard a task as any for the affluent believer. *J. I. Packer*

Wealth is no mark of God's favour. Poverty is no mark of God's displeasure. *J. C. Ryle*

Wealth ruins far more souls than poverty. *J. C. Ryle*

The wealthiest man is he who is contented with least. *Socrates*

Wisdom outweighs any wealth. *Sophocles*

Many a man's gold has lost him his God. *George Swinnock*

The streets of gold do not have too great an appeal for those who pile up gold here on earth. *A. W. Tozer*

Wealth must be processed through a philosophy of life that is greater than wealth itself. If not, it shapes the mind for bitter disappointments. *Ravi Zacharias*

WIFE — See Family Life

WILL
(See also: Free Will)

When the will is won, all is won. *Thomas Brooks*

The Holy Spirit teaches us in Scripture that our mind is smitten with so much blindness, that the affections of our heart are so depraved and perverted, that our whole nature is vitiated, that we can do nothing but sin until he forms a new will within us. *John Calvin*

To will is human, to will the bad is of fallen nature, but to will the good is of grace. *John Calvin*

Man's will always acts in accordance with its disposition. *Jonathan Edwards*

The essence of the virtue and vice of dispositions of the heart and acts of the will lies not in their cause but in their nature. *Jonathan Edwards*

Such biblical emphasis on man's will as there is tends to emphasize its bondage rather than its freedom. *Sinclair Ferguson*

What the foot is to the body, the will is to the soul. *William Gurnall*

All the wickedness of the wicked world is owing to the wilfulness of the wicked will. *Matthew Henry*

The will is the basal, fundamental force in personality. *John Henry Jowett*

What we call the will is just the whole person making choices. *J. Gresham Machen*

Will is character in action.
William McDougall

If there were no will there would be no hell. *Christopher Nesse*

The will itself is not weak or strong; it is our motivation that is weak or strong.
John Powell

God looks more at our wills than at our works. *William Secker*

The sinner in his sinful nature could never have a will according to God.
J. Denham Smith

The root of all evil in human nature is the corruption of the will. *A. W. Tozer*

The will is the deciding factor in everything that we do. In every sphere of life it settles alternatives. *Frederick P. Wood*

WILL OF GOD
(See also: Guidance; Providence)

The will of God is the measure of things.
Ambrose

The study of God's Word for the purpose of discovering God's will is the greatest discipline which has formed the greatest character. *Anon.*

A man's heart is right when he wills what God wills. *Thomas Aquinas*

The moral will is the only will of God of which we may be certain in our experience. *Jack Arnold*

All heaven is waiting to help those who will discover the will of God and do it.
J. Robert Ashcroft

Nothing, therefore, happens unless the Omnipotent wills it to happen: he either permits it to happen, or he brings it about himself. *Augustine*

A man in the centre of God's will is never just anything. *John Blanchard*

Nothing is right for a Christian if it is not God's will for him. *John Blanchard*

Our duty is found in the revealed will of God in the Scriptures. Our trust must be in the sovereign will of God, as he works in the ordinary circumstances of our daily lives for our good and for his glory.
Jerry Bridges

God cannot approve of anything that is not supported by his Word. *John Calvin*

If we would avoid a senseless natural philosophy we must always start with this principle: that everything in nature depends upon the will of God, and that the whole course of nature is only the prompt carrying into effect of his orders.
John Calvin

By suffering God's will, we learn to do God's will. *Thomas Case*

God's will is the rule of righteousness, and his righteousness is the rule of his will. *Elisha Coles*

Jesus taught us that we are to be obsessed with living according to the will of God.
Herbert W. Cragg

Nothing lies beyond the power of man if it is within the will of God.
James E. Crowther

The sin of the world is not that it does not *do* the will of God but that it does not

choose the will of God.
Arthur C. Custance

Perfect conformity to the will of God is the sole sovereign and complete liberty.
J. H. Merle D'Aubigne

God's will is not an itinerary but an attitude.
Andrew Dhuse

The will of God is not something we are just to understand; it is something we are to undertake.
G. B. Duncan

Inside the will of God there is no failure. Outside the will of God there is no success.
Bernard Edinger

If you think that you know the will of God for your life . . . you are probably in for a very rude awakening, because nobody knows the will of God for his entire life.
Elisabeth Elliot

There are no disappointments to those whose wills are buried in the will of God.
Frederick W. Faber

Make this simple rule the guide of your life: to have no will but God's.
François Fenelon

It should be the aim of every Christian to have his will directed by the will of God revealed in Scripture.
Sinclair Ferguson

Only in obedience can we discover the great joy of the will of God.
Sinclair Ferguson

There is no avoiding, and no substitute for, the sometimes long, arduous experience of discovering the will of God in our own lives.
Sinclair Ferguson

The will of God is shaped in the image of his Son's cross.
Sinclair Ferguson

The will of God means death to our own will, and resurrection only when we have died to all our own plans.
Sinclair Ferguson

Wisdom and the will of God are intimately related ... Nothing is more vital for practical knowledge of the purposes of God than wisdom.
Sinclair Ferguson

The revealed will of God is either manifested to us in his Word or in his works.
John Flavel

Seek neither more nor less than God's will for you.
Vance Harmer

Once the will of God to me was a sigh; now it is a song.
Frances Ridley Havergal

All moral obligation resolves itself into the obligation of conformity to the will of God.
Charles Hodge

God will always reveal his will to one who is willing to do it.
Hilys Jasper

To walk out of God's will is to walk into nowhere.
C. S. Lewis

Doing the will of God leaves me no time for disputing about his plans.
George Macdonald

The choices of God's will are always — not sometimes, but always — determined by the ends which his infinite knowledge and his infinite wisdom place before him.
J. Gresham Machen

'Not as I will, but as thou wilt.' To be able to say these words and truly mean them is the highest point we can ever hope to attain.
Malcolm Muggeridge

Most people don't want to know the will of God in order to do it; they want to know it in order to consider it. *William Pettingill*

God's will is the law of universal nature.
William S. Plumer

To understand the will of God is my problem; to undertake the will of God is my privilege; to undercut the will of God is my peril. *Paul S. Rees*

We must do away once and for all with the great myth that suffering is never part of God's will. *Frank Retief*

That soul shall have his will of God who desires nothing but what God will.
William Secker

Whether you shall live to reach home today or not depends absolutely upon God's will. *C. H. Spurgeon*

There is no other will but the Master's will, for all other wills subserve his, whether they will or no. *William Still*

God's heavenly plan doesn't always make earthly sense. *Charles R. Swindoll*

Contentment with the divine will is the best remedy we can apply to misfortune.
William Temple

The power of God is identified with his will; what he cannot do is what he will not do. *Tertullian*

Opposition to the divine will is the very essence of all sin. *David Thomas*

The greatest folly in the universe is to oppose the will of God. *David Thomas*

The will of God is the place of blessed, painful, fruitful trouble! *A. W. Tozer*

WISDOM

Knowledge leads us from the simple to the complex; wisdom leads us from the complex to the simple. *Anon.*

True wisdom is a divine revelation.
George Barlow

Wisdom has never made a bigot, but learning has. *Josh Billings*

Wisdom gives a balance to character.
John Blanchard

Nearly all the wisdom we possess, that is to say, true and sound wisdom, consists of two parts: the knowledge of God and of ourselves. *John Calvin*

This is our wisdom, to be learners to the end. *John Calvin*

To search for wisdom apart from Christ means not simply foolhardiness but utter insanity. *John Calvin*

True wisdom consists in being wise according to the law of God. *John Calvin*

Wisdom is not the growth of human genius. It must be sought from above.
John Calvin

The only way to know is to will to do God's will. *Oswald Chambers*

Knowledge is the fountain of wisdom.
Stephen Charnock

Wisdom must be from God, because it can be found only in relation to him.
Edmund P. Clowney

Humility is the hallmark of wisdom.
Jeremy Collier

There is no solid wisdom but in true piety. *John Evelyn*

Wisdom and the will of God are intimately related ... Nothing is more vital for practical knowledge of the purpose of God than wisdom. *Sinclair Ferguson*

True wisdom is always humble. *Richard Fuller*

No man is really wise unless he lives in the will and for the glory of God. *Geoffrey Grogan*

If you lack knowledge, go to school. If you lack wisdom, get on your knees! Knowledge is not wisdom. Wisdom is the proper use of knowledge. *Vance Havner*

Heavenly wisdom is better than worldly wealth, and to be preferred before it. *Matthew Henry*

It is better to get wisdom than gold. Gold is another's, wisdom is our own; gold is for the body and time, wisdom for the soul and eternity. *Matthew Henry*

Modesty is the badge of wisdom. *Matthew Henry*

Such is the degeneracy of human nature that there is no true wisdom to be found with any but those who are born again and who, through grace, partake of the divine nature. *Matthew Henry*

He who has a constant longing for wisdom will persistently pray for it. *D. Edmond Hiebert*

Unaided wisdom, with its strongest wing, can only flutter in the vale of vanity. No earth-born eye can catch a glimpse of God. *Henry Law*

The next best thing to being wise is to live in a circle of those who are. *C. S. Lewis*

Surely the essence of wisdom is that before we begin to act at all, or attempt to please God, we should discover what it is that God has to say about the matter. *D. Martyn Lloyd Jones*

Wisdom opens the eyes both to the glories of heaven and to the hollowness of earth. *J. A. Motyer*

Not until we have become humble and teachable, standing in awe of God's holiness and sovereignty ... acknowledging our own littleness, distrusting our own thoughts, and willing to have our minds turned upside down, can divine wisdom become ours. *J. I. Packer*

The kind of wisdom that God waits to give to those who ask him is a wisdom that will bind us to himself. *J. I. Packer*

Wisdom is God-centred. *Michael Parsons*

Wisdom is always an overmatch for strength. *Phaedrus*

The greatest wisdom on this earth is holiness. *William S. Plumer*

Wisdom is the knowledge which sees into the heart of things, which knows them as they really are. *J. Armitage Robinson*

The desire of appearing to be wise often prevents our becoming so. *Francois Rochefoucauld*

Wisdom is to the mind what health is to the body. *Francois Rochefoucauld*

The wisest mind has something yet to learn. *George Santanaya*

If ... our wisdom has been acquired without any of that eagerness and painful diligence with which the covetous man desires and seeks for his riches, it is a shrewd conjecture that it is not of the genuine sort. *Thomas Scott*

Wisdom in ruling is justice; wisdom in speech is discretion; wisdom in conduct is prudence; wisdom in evaluation is discernment. *George Seevers*

Wisdom is easy to him that will understand. *Richard Sibbes*

To know God, and Jesus Christ whom he has sent, is the highest principle and perfection of man. This attainment, infinitely above all others, constitutes true wisdom. *Charles Simeon*

Wisdom outweighs any wealth.*Sophocles*

We can be certain that God wants us to be wise, just as we are sure that he wants us not to sin. *R. C. Sproul*

Conviction of ignorance is the doorstep to the temple of wisdom. *C. H. Spurgeon*

The sublimity of wisdom is to do those things living which are to be desired when dying. *Jeremy Taylor*

The wisest person in the world is the person who knows the most about God. *A. W. Tozer*

The true test of wisdom is works, not words. *Curtis Vaughan*

It is a fact that those whose lives are daily being conformed to the Word and purposes of God will be given the ability to see issues more plainly. *Malcolm Watts*

If the Lord Jesus Christ is a stranger to you, the best you can hope for is to become a philosopher, like Socrates of old. But apart from Christ there is no wisdom. *Spiros Zodhiates*

The one who has wisdom in his head and heart does not need to shout at others. *Spiros Zodhiates*

Wisdom, the wisdom of God, is not something that is acquired by man, but something that is bestowed by God upon his elect. It is a divine endowment and not a human acquisition. *Spiros Zodhiates*

WITNESSING
(See also: Evangelism; Soul-Winning)

Anyone who is not doing personal work has sin in his life. *C. M. Alexander*

Every Christian occupies some kind of pulpit and preaches some kind of gospel. *Anon.*

The real mark of a saint is that he makes it easier for others to believe in God. *Anon.*

We are not Christ's lawyers; we are his witnesses. *Anon.*

Witnessing is not something we do; it is something we are. *Anon.*

What I live by, I impart. *Augustine*

A Christian is called to be a witness, not counsel for the prosecution. *Doug Barnett*

Men may not read the gospel in seal-skin, or the gospel in morocco, or the gospel in cloth covers; but they can't get away from the gospel in shoe leather. *Donald Grey Barnhouse*

675

Witnessing

Every believer is a witness whether he wants to be or not.
Donald Grey Barnhouse

If you want your neighbour to know what Christ will do for him, let your neighbour see what Christ has done for you.
Henry Ward Beecher

If you can't shine, at least twinkle!
Alistair Begg

Christians should penetrate the world without ever becoming part of it.
John Blanchard

The object of witnessing is not to win an argument but disciples. *John Blanchard*

The secret of reaching men is to know the secret of reaching God.
John Blanchard

We are called not merely to be advocates of Christianity but witnesses to Christ.
John Blanchard

A Christian's life should be nothing but a visible representation of Christ.
Thomas Brooks

The Bible calls the good man's life a light; and it is the nature of light to flow out spontaneously in all directions, and fill the world unconsciously with its beams.
Horace Bushnell

Witnessing is not an effort, it is an over-spill. *Robert Cook*

The Christian is the visual aid which God brings on to the stage when he begins to speak to an unconverted person.
H. W. Cragg

Cry the gospel with your whole life.
Charles de Foucauld

If you were arrested for being a Christian would there be enough evidence to convict you? *David Otis Fuller*

Jesus, and shall it ever be,
A mortal man ashamed of thee,
Ashamed of thee, whom angels praise,
Whose glories shine through endless days?
Joseph Grigg

Witnessing is not just something a Christian says, but what a Christian is.
Richard C. Halverson

Too many Christians live their Christian lives inside their heads; it never gets out through hands and feet and lips.
Vance Havner

We are the salt of the earth, not the sugar, and our ministry is truly to cleanse and not just to change the taste. *Vance Havner*

Wherever we go, let us not fail to take our religion along with us.
Matthew Henry

The Christian's task is to make the Lord Jesus visible, intelligible and desirable.
Len Jones

A witness in a court of law has to *give* evidence; a Christian witness has to *be* evidence. It is the difference between law and grace! *Geoffrey R. King*

In the New Testament we find the prophethood as well as the priesthood of all believers. *Geoffrey R. King*

You can never speak to the wrong man about Christ. *Peter McFarlane*

A Christian is the world's Bible — and some of them need revising. *D. L. Moody*

Nothing locks the lips like the life.
D. L. Moody

Our secrets are for sharing. *J. A. Motyer*

Faith is not created by reasoning, but neither is it created without it. There is more involved in witness than throwing pre-arranged clumps of texts at unbelieving heads. *J. I. Packer*

I was never fit to say a word to a sinner, except when I had a broken heart myself. *Edward Payson*

We are not responsible for conversion, but we are responsible for contact.
A. T. Pierson

Witnessing is the whole work of the whole church for the whole age.
A. T. Pierson

Faithful witness is truth telling, not head counting. *Don Posterski*

If it is possible for your closest contacts to be neutral about Christ then there is something wrong with your Christianity.
Alan Redpath

God has no dumb children. *J. C. Ryle*

Love — and the unity it attests to — is the mark Christ gave Christians to wear before the world. Only with this mark may the world know that Christians are indeed Christians and that Jesus was sent by the Father. *Francis Schaeffer*

Christians are in the world to be witnesses, and they must concentrate on their calling. *Paul B. Smith*

The sermons most needed today are sermons in shoes. *C. H. Spurgeon*

The real problem of Christianity is not atheism or scepticism, but the non-witnessing Christian trying to smuggle his own soul into heaven. *James S. Stewart*

Nothing shuts the mouth, seals the lips, ties the tongue, like the poverty of our own spiritual experience. We do not bear witness for the simple reason that we have no witness to bear. *John R. W. Stott*

Testimony is not a synonym for autobiography! When we are truly witnessing, we are not talking about ourselves but about Christ. *John R. W. Stott*

To be a witness does not consist of engaging in propaganda or in stirring people up. It means to live in such a way that one's life would not make sense if God did not exist. *Emmanuel Suhard*

The light of religion ought not to be carried in a dark lantern. *George Swinnock*

My heart is full of Christ, and longs
Its glorious matter to declare!
Of him I make my loftier songs,
I cannot from his praise forbear;
My ready tongue makes haste to sing
The glories of my heavenly King.
Charles Wesley

Only the sheer rapture of being lost in the worship of God is as exhilarating and intoxicating as telling someone about Jesus Christ. *Donald S. Whitney*

The most powerful ongoing Christian witness has always been the speaking of God's Word by one who is living in God's Word. *Donald S. Whitney*

WONDER — See: Awe; Worship

WORK

A dictionary is the only place where you will find success before work. *Anon.*

Too many Christians worship their work, work at their play and play at their worship. *Anon.*

A lot can be achieved by an ounce of talent and a ton of hard work.
John Blanchard

Every Christian should pursue excellence of workmanship and service in whatever vocational calling he finds himself.
Jerry Bridges

Service to God through service to mankind is the only motivation acceptable to God for diligence and hard work in our vocational calling. *Jerry Bridges*

He who disregards his calling will never keep the straight path in the duties of his work. *John Calvin*

Men were created to employ themselves in some work, and not to lie down in inactivity and idleness. *John Calvin*

I never did anything worth doing by accident, nor did any of my inventions come by accident; they came by work.
Thomas Edison

Man was made to work, because the God who made him was a 'working God'.
Sinclair Ferguson

God gives every bird its food, but he does not throw it into the nest.
Josiah G. Holland

Do your work with your whole heart and you will succeed — there is so little competition! *Elbert Hubbard*

The best preparation for good work tomorrow is to do good work today.
Elbert Hubbard

If a man is called to be a street sweeper, he should sweep streets even as Michelangelo painted, or Beethoven composed music, or Shakespeare poetry.
Martin Luther King

Throw your soul into the work as if your one employer were the Lord!
R. C. H. Lenski

There can be intemperance in work just as in drink. *C. S. Lewis*

A dairymaid can milk cows to the glory of God. *Martin Luther*

Instead of letting a mob of hoodlum tasks surround and trample me to death, I force them into a single file and handle them one at a time. *Don Mallough*

Work for the world is done best when work for God is done first. *John C. Ryland*

One of the greatest blessings of humanity is that divine law which requires men to work for their livelihood. *David Thomas*

No race can prosper until it learns that there is as much dignity in tilling a field as in writing a poem.
Booker T. Washington

No labour is servile when the Lord's approval is the paramount consideration.
Geoffrey B. Wilson

WORKS — Good — See Good Deeds

WORLD
(See also: Worldliness)

The world counterfeits every Christian grace, but never is able to produce a coin with the right ring.
Donald Grey Barnhouse

Worldly glory is but a breath, a vapour, a froth, a phantom, a shadow, a reflection, an apparition, a very nothing.
Thomas Brooks

The created world is but a small parenthesis in eternity.   *Thomas Browne*

What a charming place this world would be if it was not for the inhabitants.
Esther Burr

The world is all appearances, like our clothes: the truth lies underneath.
Thomas Carlyle

As long as there are spots in the moon it is vain to expect anything spotless under it.   *Thomas Fuller*

The world's smiles are more dangerous than its frowns.   *Matthew Henry*

This world is our passage and not our portion.   *Matthew Henry*

Enemy-occupied territory — that is what the world is.   *C. S. Lewis*

There is no neutral ground in the universe: every square inch, every split second, is claimed by God and counter-claimed by Satan.   *C. S. Lewis*

It is a hard matter to enjoy the world without being entangled with the cares and pleasures of it.   *Thomas Manton*

The world belongs to God and he wants it back.   *David Pawson*

The money, the pleasures, the daily business of the world are so many traps to catch souls.   *J. C. Ryle*

The earth is big in our hopes, but little in our hands.   *William Seeker*

Thorns will not prick of themselves, but when they are grasped in a man's hand they prick deep. So this world and the things thereof are all good, and were all made of God for the benefit of his creatures, did not our immoderate affection make them hurtful.   *Richard Sibbes*

Nothing in the world can be properly understood unless it is understood in terms of God's design and plan.
R. C. Sproul

The world would not hate angels for being angelic, but it does hate men for being Christians. It grudges them their new character; it is tormented by their peace; it is infuriated by their joy.
William Temple

Without God the world would be a maze without a clue.   *Woodrow Wilson*

WORLDLINESS
(See also: World)

There is no surer evidence of an unconverted state than to have the things of the world uppermost in our aim, love and estimation.   *Joseph Alleine*

If we loved the world the way God loves it, we wouldn't love it the way we shouldn't love it.   *Anon.*

If you have a distorted view of the Christian life you have let the world develop the negative. *Anon.*

The Christian must live in the world, but he must not let the world live in him. *Anon.*

If you are wise, let the world pass, lest you pass away with the world. *Augustine*

A man caught up with this world is not ready for the next one. *John Blanchard*

Jesus did not pray that his Father would take Christians out of the world, but that he would take the world out of Christians. *John Blanchard*

I looked for the church and I found it in the world; I looked for the world and I found it in the church. *Horatius Bonar*

The stars which have least circuit are nearest the pole; and men whose earths are least entangled with the world are always nearest to God and to the assurance of his favour. *Thomas Brooks*

The two poles could sooner meet, than the love of Christ and the love of the world. *Thomas Brooks*

It is infinitely better to have the whole world for our enemies and God for our friend, than to have the whole world for our friends and God for our enemy. *John Brown*

The mind of a Christian ought not to be filled with thoughts of earthly things, or find satisfaction in them, for we ought to be living as if we might have to leave this world at any moment. *John Calvin*

We are of the world, and until Christ rescues us from it, the world reigns in us and we live unto it. *John Calvin*

There are Christians living on spiritual stale bread and mouldy cheese when they might be enjoying roast turkey from heaven! *A. Lindsay Glegg*

Nothing is more contrary to a heavenly hope than an earthly heart. *William Gurnall*

The bee will not sit on a flower where no honey can be sucked, neither should the Christian. *William Gurnall*

If you find yourself loving any pleasure better than your prayers, any book better than the Bible, any house better than the house of God, any table better than the Lord's table, any person better than Christ, any indulgence better than the hope of heaven — take alarm! *Thomas Guthrie*

If you stand on the Word you do not stand in with the world. *Vance Havner*

Many Christians are still in the wilderness, longing for garlic instead of grace, melons instead of manna! *Vance Havner*

The path of the Word and the path of the world do not run parallel. *Vance Harmer*

We cannot have a heavenly fellowship if we allow a hindering fellowship. *Vance Havner*

We must deal with the carnalities if we desire the spiritualities. *Vance Havner*

When the night-club invades the sanctuary it ought not to be difficult for any Bible Christian to discern the time of day. *Vance Havner*

Worldliness is rampant in the church. The devil is not fighting churches, he is joining them! He isn't persecuting Christianity, he is professing it.   *Vance Havner*

Worldlings make gold their god; saints make God their gold.   *Matthew Henry*

Whoever marries the spirit of this age will find himself a widower in the next.
                    William Ralph Inge

To forsake Christ for the world is to leave a treasure for a trifle ... eternity for a moment, reality for a shadow.
                        William Jenkyn

Worldliness is a spirit, a temperament, an attitude of soul. It is life without high callings, life devoid of lofty ideals. It is a gaze horizontal, never vertical. Its motto is 'Forward', never 'Upward'.
                    John Henry Jowett

It is better to trust in the Lord than in men or princes; whereas who-ever will live on worldly principles must carry the same strain and care as does the man of the world.   *G. H. Lang*

God lays down one programme of life for his children; the world proposes another and totally incompatible programme for its servants. So love for the one excludes love for the other.
                        Robert Law

The health of our bodies, the passions of our minds, the noise and hurry and pleasures and business of the world, lead us on with eyes that see not and ears that hear not.   *William Law*

The carnal mind sees God in nothing, not even in spiritual things. The spiritual mind sees him in everything, even in natural things.   *Robert Leighton*

The legitimate courtesies of life become positively sinful when they take priority over the interests of the Lord Jesus.
                    William MacDonald

A carnal Christian is the carcass of a true Christian.   *Thomas Manton*

The world and grace are incompatible.
                        Thomas Manton

The world is a dirty, defiling thing. A man can hardly walk here but he shall defile his garments. The men of the world are dirty, sooty creatures. We cannot converse with them but they leave their filthiness upon us.   *Thomas Manton*

Depend upon it, as long as the church is living so much like the world, we cannot expect our children to be brought into the fold.   *D. L. Moody*

If I walk with the world, I can't walk with God.   *D. L. Moody*

The only ultimate disaster that can befall us is to feel ourselves at home on this earth.   *Malcolm Muggeridge*

Conformity to the world can be overcome by nothing but conformity to Jesus.
                        Andrew Murray

The spirit of this world is devotion to the visible.   *Andrew Murray*

There is nothing the Christian life suffers more from than the subtle and indescribable worldliness that comes from the cares or the possessions of this life.   *Andrew Murray*

Being of the world means being control-led by what preoccupies the world, the quest for pleasure, profit and position.
                        J. I. Packer

Those who love the world serve and worship themselves every moment: it is their full-time job. *J. I. Packer*

Worldliness means yielding to the spirit that animates fallen mankind, the spirit of self-seeking and self-indulgence without regard for God. *J. I. Packer*

Worldliness and Christianity are two such ends as never meet. *Nehemiah Rogers*

It is dangerous dressing for another world by the looking-glass of this world. *William Secker*

To accommodate to the world spirit about us in our age is nothing less than the most gross form of worldliness in the proper definition of that word. *Francis Schaeffer*

It strikes me that some people want only as much of God's salvation as will keep them out of hell, and they measure out with unconscious precision how much worldliness and sin they can still hang on to without jeopardizing their chances. *David Shepherd*

He that loves the world is a worldling. *Richard Sibbes*

All earthly things are as salt water, that increases the appetite, but satisfies not. *Richard Sibbes*

The world's fashion is the worst fashion of all. *Richard Sibbes*

You might as well talk about a heavenly devil as talk about a worldly Christian. *Billy Sunday*

A worldly Christian is spiritually diseased. *C. H. Spurgeon*

He who has the smile of the ungodly must look for the frown of God. *C. H. Spurgeon*

Take care if the world does hate you that it hates you without cause. *C. H. Spurgeon*

Worldly policy is a poor short-sighted thing, and when men choose it as their road it leads them over dark mountains. *C. H. Spurgeon*

Worldliness is a spirit, an atmosphere, an influence permeating the whole of life and human society, and it needs to be guarded against constantly and strenuously. *W. H. Griffith Thomas*

If I find anyone who is settled down too snugly into this world, I am made to doubt whether he's ever truly been born again. *A. W. Tozer*

It is scarcely possible in most places to get anyone to attend a meeting where the only attraction is God. *A. W. Tozer*

Of all the calamities that have been visited upon the world, the surrender of the human spirit to this present world and its ways is the worst, without any doubt. *A. W. Tozer*

Pleasure, profit, preferment are the worldling's trinity. *John Trapp*

There is not a minute to waste in getting the world out of the church and the church into the world. *Foy Valentine*

If men do not put the love of the world to death, the love of the world will put them to death. *Ralph Venning*

He that is in love with the world will be out of love with the cross. *Thomas Watson*

Make no mistake about it, the world with its unbelief is a spiritual ice-house, and too much contact with it will quickly cool the spirit.   *Malcolm Watts*

Identification with the world and its needs is one thing; imitation of the world and its foolishness is quite another.
                              Warren Wiersbe

WORRY
(See also: Anxiety; Fear)

The devil would have us continually crossing streams that do not exist. *Anon.*

Worry gives a small thing a big shadow.
                                     Anon.

Worry is like a rocking chair; it will give you something to do, but it won't get you anywhere.   *Anon.*

Worry is the interest we pay on tomorrow's troubles.   *Anon.*

Worry over tomorrow pulls shadows over today's sunshine.   *Anon.*

You can't change the past, but you can ruin a perfectly good present by worrying about the future.   *Anon.*

Worry is to life and progress what sand is to the bearings of perfect engines.
                               Roger Babson

Fretting is the caressing of the old nature.   *Donald Grey Barnhouse*

Worry and worship are mutually exclusive.   *John Blanchard*

Worry is an indication that we think God cannot look after us. *Oswald Chambers*

Worry is an intrusion into God's providence.   *John Edmund Haggai*

Never attempt to bear more than one kind of trouble at once. Some people bear three kinds — all they have had, all they have now and all they expect to have.
                           Edward Everett Hale

It is not work but worry that kills, and it is amazing how much wear the human mind and body can stand if it is free from friction and well oiled by the Spirit.
                               Vance Havner

Disquieting care is the common fruit of an abundance of this world, and the common fault of those that have abundance.
                              Matthew Henry

Worry is sin against the loving care of the Father.   *E. Stanley Jones*

Worry is the traitor in our camp that dampens our powder and weakens our aim.   *William Jordan*

The essence of worry ... is the absence of thought, a failure to think.
                         D. Martyn Lloyd-Jones

Worry has an active imagination.
                          D. Martyn. Lloyd Jones

A day of worry is more exhausting than a week of work.   *John Lubbock*

Not work, but worry makes us weary.
                              S. I. McMillen

Be careful for nothing, prayerful for everything, thankful for anything.
                                 D. L. Moody

Worry over poverty is as fatal to spiritual fruitfulness as is gloating over wealth.
                                  A. W. Pink

Worry

Worry is a thin stream of fear trickling through the mind. If encouraged, it cuts a channel into which all other thoughts are drained. *A. S. Roche*

Half our miseries are caused by things that we think are coming upon us.
J. C. Ryle

If a case is too small to be turned into a prayer it is too small to be made into a burden. *Corrie ten Boom*

Worry is faith in the negative, trust in the unpleasant, assurance of disaster and belief in defeat. *William A. Ward*

I dare not fret any more than I dare curse and swear. *John Wesley*

WORSHIP — Blessings

Worship is to Christian living what the mainspring is to the watch.
Lawrence R. Axelson

Worship renews the spirit as sleep renews the body. *Richard C. Cabot*

This is, indeed, the proper business of the whole life, in which men should daily exercise themselves, to consider the infinite goodness, justice, power and wisdom of God, in this magnificent theatre of God.
John Calvin

It is only when men begin to worship that they begin to grow. *Calvin Coolidge*

In our worship there should be the power of the supernatural which brings home a sense of God. *Bryan Green*

An attitude of worship can cut down an avalanche of words. *Vance Havner*

By doing obeisance we are learning obedience. *Matthew Henry*

If worship does not change us it has not been worship. *John MacArthur*

If we want to know God and to be blessed of God, we must start by worshipping him. *D. Martyn Lloyd-Jones*

Worship liberates the personality by giving a new perspective to life, by integrating life with the multitude of lifeforms, by bringing into the life the virtues of humility, loyalty, devotion and rightness of attitude, thus refreshing and reviving the spirit. *Roswell C. Long*

In the most lofty devotion we become unconscious of self. *Austin Phelps*

God is most glorified in us when we are most satisfied in him, and we are most satisfied in him in worship. *John Piper*

Worship alone of all the activities of the believer will continue in heaven and will occupy the redeemed host for ever.
Robert G. Rayburn

There is more healing joy in five minutes of worship than there is in five nights of revelry. *A. W. Tozer*

I know of no pleasure so rich, none so pure, none so hallowing in their influences and constant in their supply as those which result from the true and spiritual worship of God. *Richard Watson*

WORSHIP — Essence

True worship exalts God to his rightful place in our lives. *Anon.*

Worship does not have to be dull to be deep. *John Blanchard*

Devotion is not an activity; it is an attitude towards God. *Jerry Bridges*

Christian worship is at once the Word of God and the obedient response thereto. *W. H. Cadman*

The beginning and perfection of lawful worship is readiness to obey. *John Calvin*

To adore God is to be lifted outside ourselves. To bow in wonder before this transcendent majesty whose glory fills the heavens and whose mighty power spans the wide compass of history and reaches with unerring accuracy into every crevice of time and space, this is to mount up from a grovelling obsession with our own needs to an awe-inspiring glimpse of the glory of the eternal God. *Herbert Carson.*

To worship God is to realize the purpose for which God created us. *Herbert M. Carson*

Worship is the declaration by a creature of the greatness of his Creator. *Herbert M. Carson*

Worship is transcendent wonder. *Thomas Carlyle*

Without the heart it is no worship. It is a stage play. It is an acting a part without being that person, really. It is playing the hypocrite. *Stephen Charnock*

The dearest idol I have known,
Whate'er that idol be,
Help me to tear it from thy throne,
And worship only thee.
William Cowper

It is impossible to use God and worship him at the same time. *Larry Crabb*

True worship is seen not in the ingredients of the service but in the inclination of the heart. *Brian H. Edwards*

Reverence is essential to worship. *Frank Gabelein*

Our Lord approved neither idol worship nor idle worship, but ideal worship, in spirit and truth. *Vance Havner*

True worship is a blend of godly fear and trembling together with joy that we are accepted in the Beloved. *Erroll Hulse*

Worship is the sum total of all our response to God as his children. *Robert M. Horn*

God is more real to me than any thought or thing or person. *William James*

Worship is Christian living. *Dick Lucas*

Worship begins in holy ecstasy; it ends in holy obedience — or it isn't worship. *John MacArthur*

You cannot worship God in a vacuum. You cannot worship God apart from his revelation. *John MacArthur*

Worship is that to which we give our interest, our enthusiasm and our devotion. *Clarence E. MacCartney*

Worship is giving to the Lord the glory that is due in response to what he has revealed to us and done to us in Jesus Christ his Son. *Oswald B. Milligan*

Worship that costs us nothing is worth precisely what it costs. *Leon Morris*

Worship is the adoration of a redeemed people, occupied with God himself.
A. W. Pink

Worship is the activity of the new life of a believer in which, recognizing the fulness of the Godhead as it is revealed in the person of Jesus Christ and his mighty redemptive acts, he seeks by the power of the Holy Spirit to render to the living God the glory, honour and submission which are his due.
Robert G. Rayburn

Worship is the adoring contemplation of God as he has revealed himself in Christ and in his Word.   *J. Oswald Sanders*

To worship God in truth is to worship him as he commands.   *R. C. Sproul*

Worship is the submission of all our nature to God. It is the quickening of conscience by his holiness, the nourishment of the mind with his truth, the purifying of the imagination by his beauty, the opening of the heart to his love, the surrender of the will to his purpose.
William Temple

In true worship men . . . have little thought of the means of worship; their thoughts are upon God. True worship is characterized by self-effacement and is lacking in any self-consciousness. *Geoffrey Thomas*

No worship is wholly pleasing to God until there is nothing in me displeasing to God.   *A. W. Tozer*

True worship is to be so personally and hopelessly in love with God that the idea of a transfer of affection never even remotely exists.   *A. W. Tozer*

True worship seeks union with its beloved, and an active effort to close the gap between the heart and the God it adores is worship at its best! *A. W. Tozer*

Worship in all its grades and kinds is the response of the creature to the Eternal.
Evelyn Underhill

In every part of our worship we must present Christ to God in the arms of faith.
Thomas Watson

Worship is a response to greatness.
Tom Wells

To worship God in spirit is to worship from the inside out.   *Donald S. Whitney*

WORSHIP — Importance
(See also: Awe; Fear of God)

What we worship determines what we become.   *Harvey F. Ammerman*

The best eyes look inwards and upwards.
Anon.

Attitudes to God, especially as we come to him in worship, are the true monitor of spirituality.   *John Benton*

If we worshipped as we should, we wouldn't worry as we shouldn't.
John Blanchard

Life ought not merely to contain acts of worship; it should be an act of worship.
John Blanchard

Worship comes before service, and the King before the King's business.
John Blanchard

The first foundation of righteousness undoubtedly is the worship of God.
John Calvin

Does not every true man feel that he is himself made higher by doing reverence to what is really above him?
Thomas Carlyle

The man who does not habitually worship is but a pair of spectacles behind which there is no eye. *Thomas Carlyle*

None reverence the Lord more than they who know him best. *William Cowper*

What greater calamity can fall upon a nation than the loss of worship? Then all things go to decay . . . literature becomes frivolous and society lives on trifles.
Ralph Waldo Emerson

Carnal men are content with the 'act'of worship; they have no desire for communion with God. *John W. Everett*

Nothing prepares the heart more for worship of the Lord than to contemplate his beauty and perfection. *Frank Gabelein*

Worship ought to describe everything the people of God do when they come together, and above all in the preaching of the Word of God. *Graham Harrison*

As secret worship is better the more secret it is, so public worship is better the more public it is. *Matthew Henry*

Public worship will not excuse us from secret worship. *Matthew Henry*

Those cannot worship God aright who do not worship him alone.
Matthew Henry

Where we have a tent God must have an altar; where we have a house he must have a church in it. *Matthew Henry*

Worship is the highest function of the human soul. *Geoffrey R. King*

We need to worship and adore as well as to analyse and explain. *Isobel Kuhn*

Devotion signifies a life given or devoted to God. *William Law*

A man can no more diminish God's glory by refusing to worship him than a lunatic can put out the sun by scribbling the word 'darkness'on the walls of his cell.
C. S. Lewis

We — or at least I — shall not be able to adore God on the highest occasions if we have learned no habit of doing so on the lowest. *C. S. Lewis*

Every man becomes the image of the man he adores. He whose worship is directed to a dead thing becomes a dead thing. He who loves corruption rots. He who loves a shadow becomes, himself, a shadow.
Thomas Merton

Honest dealing becomes us when we kneel in God's pure presence.
David McIntyre

Our whole life . . . should be so angled towards God that whatever strikes upon us, whether sorrow or joy, should be deflected upwards at once into his presence.
J. A. Motyer

What or whom we worship determines our behaviour. *John Murray*

Our minds are so constituted that they cannot at one and the same time be stayed upon the Lord and fixed upon next winter's new coat or hat. *A. W. Pink*

Where God is truly known, he is necessarily adored.   *A. W. Pink*

Worship is as much God's due as anything can be.   *William S. Plumer*

Worship requires us to be as adult, as responsible, as serious, as concentrated in our thoughts as we are capable of being.
Alwyn Pritchard

A man's worship is governed by what he believes, for worship is man's means of ascribing to God that adoration, reverence, praise, love, and obedience of which he sincerely believes God to be worthy.   *Robert G. Rayburn*

We must take our whole heart to the house of God, and worship and hear like those who listen to the reading of a will.
J. C. Ryle

He who knows God reverences him.
Seneca

I am called to worship a God I cannot see, but not to submit to a God I cannot know and prove.   *David Shepherd*

All places are places of worship to a Christian. Wherever he is, he ought to be in a worshipping frame of mind.
C. H. Spurgeon

He whose soul does not worship shall never live in holiness.   *C. H. Spurgeon*

I like, sometimes, to leave off praying, and to sit still, and just gaze upwards till my inmost soul has seen my Lord.
C. H. Spurgeon

Soul worship is the soul of worship, and if you take away the soul from worship you have killed the worship.
C. H. Spurgeon

Nowhere in Scripture is true worship portrayed in other than serious terms.
Geoff Thomas

Because we were created to worship, worship is the normal employment of moral beings.   *A. W. Tozer*

God made us to be worshippers. That was the purpose of God in bringing us into the world.   *A. W. Tozer*

God wants worshippers before workers; indeed, the only acceptable workers are those who have learned the art of worship.   *A. W. Tozer*

I can safely say, on the authority of all that is revealed in the Word of God, that any man or woman on this earth who is bored and turned off by worship is not ready for heaven.   *A. W. Tozer*

I mean it when I say that I would rather worship God than do anything else.
A. W. Tozer

I say that the greatest tragedy in the world today is that God has made man in his image and made him to worship him, made him to play the harp of worship before the face of God day and night, but he has failed God and dropped the harp. It lies voiceless at his feet.   *A. W. Tozer*

If there is any honesty left in us, it persuades us in our quieter moments that true spiritual worship is at a discouragingly low ebb among professing Christians.
A. W. Tozer

If you will not worship God seven days a week, you do not worship him on one day a week.   *A. W. Tozer*

Man is a worshipper and only in the spirit of worship does he find release for all the powers of his amazing intellect.
A. W. Tozer

The whole course of the life is upset by failure to put God where he belongs.
A. W. Tozer

We are called to an ever-lasting preoccupation with God. *A. W. Tozer*

What comes into our mind when we think about God is the most important thing about us. *A. W. Tozer*

Where there is not worship there is discord from the broken strings. *A. W. Tozer*

Worship is a moral imperative.
A. W. Tozer

Worship, then, is not part of the Christian life; it is the Christian life.
Gerald Vann

To pray is less than to adore.
Clarence Walworth

Posture in worship is too often imposture. *Thomas Watson*

Worship is the only fitting response to God's bounty. *Geoffrey B. Wilson*

Man is not made to question, but adore.
Edward Young

YOUTH

Every adult Christian generation owes its young people a divine demonstration of the reality of what it believes and preaches. *Anon.*

Tell me what are the prevailing sentiments that occupy the minds of your young men and I will tell you what is to be the character of the next generation.
Edmund Burke

I believe young people are indifferent to the church today, not because the church has required too much of them, but because it has demanded so little. *Mort Crim*

A young sinner will be an old devil.
William Gurnall

Demoralize the youth of a nation and the revolution is already won. *Nikolai Lenin*

When we are out of sympathy with the young, then I think our work in this world is over. *George Macdonald*

Many teenage troubles are a revolt against an unfriendly world. *Alan Redpath*

My character, tastes and ideals were, in the main, fixed by the time I reached the age of sixteen . . . the seed had been sown, and could only produce a growth of a certain species. *Bertrand Russell*

The passions of the young are vices in the old. *Joseph Joubert*

We cannot always build the future for our youth, but we can build our youth for the future. *Franklin D. Roosevelt*

Youth is a time of life wherein we have too much pride to be governed by others, and too little wisdom to govern ourselves.
Henry Scougal

ZEAL

(See also: Abandonment; Consecration; Passion; Service — Wholeheartedness; Submission)

Not all Christians have great mental powers, or are extrovert personalities, but all should be zealous.
Timothy G. Alford

It's easier to cool down a fanatic than warm up a corpse.   *Brother Andrew*

Unless I go about my business of saving the souls of men with an energy and a zeal almost amounting to madness, nobody will take any notice of me, much less believe what I say and make everlasting profit out of it.   *William Booth*

I cared not when or how I lived, or what hardships I went through, so that I could gain souls for Christ.   *David Brainerd*

Zeal is like fire; in the chimney it is one of the best servants, but out of the chimney it is one of the worst masters.
Thomas Brooks

Zeal without doctrine is like a sword in the hand of a lunatic.   *John Calvin*

Attempt great things for God; expect great things from God.   *William Carey*

Give me the love that leads the way,
The faith that nothing can dismay,
The hope no disappointments tire,
The passion that will burn like fire.
Let me not sink to be a clod;
Make me thy fuel, Flame of God.
Amy Carmichael

Men ablaze are invincible. Hell trembles when men kindle.   *Samuel Chadwick*

It is better to wear out than to rust out.
Richard Cumberland

Unless a man undertakes more than he can possibly do, he will never do all that he can.   *Henry Drummond*

Am I ignitable? God deliver me from the dread asbestos of 'other things'. Saturate me with the oil of the Spirit that I may be a flame.   *Jim Elliot*

Zeal without knowledge is fire without light.   *Thomas Fuller*

Those who in time past have wrought great things for God have possessed a sanctified energy totally devoid of sloth.
James R. Graham

Earnestness commands the respect of mankind. A wavering, vacillating, dead-and-alive Christian does not get the respect of the church or of the world.
John Hall

We cannot grow a harvest for God with one eye on the weather.   *Vance Havner*

We need an outbreak of holy heartburn, when hearers shall be doers, when congregations shall go out from meetings to do things for God.   *Vance Havner*

In those things in which all the people of God are agreed, I will spend my zeal; and as for other things about which they differ, I will walk according to the light God hath given me, and charitably believe that others do so too. *Philip Henry*

True zeal makes nothing of hardships in the way of duty.   *Matthew Henry*

Oh, that I was all heart and soul and spirit to tell the glorious gospel of Christ to perishing multitudes!   *Rowland Hill*

Without Christ, not one step; with him, anywhere! *David Livingstone*

A disciple can be forgiven if he does not have great mental ability. He can be forgiven also if he does not display outstanding physical prowess. But no disciple can be excused if he does not have zeal. If his heart is not aflame with a red-hot passion for the Saviour, he stands condemned. *William Macdonald*

The disgrace of the church in the twentieth century is that more zeal is evident among Communists and cultists than among Christians. *William MacDonald*

I feel there are two things it is impossible to desire with sufficient ardour — personal holiness and the honour of Christ in the salvation of souls.
Robert Murray M'Cheyne

Oh, how I wished that I had a tongue like thunder, that I might make all hear; or that I had a frame like iron, that I might visit everyone, and say, 'Escape for thy life!' *Robert Murray M'Cheyne*

No divinely sent opportunity must elude us. *Watchman Nee*

Misplaced zeal is zeal *for* God rather than the zeal *of* God. *William L. Pettingill*

He who has no zeal has no love to God.
William S. Plumer

Mix a conviction with a man and something happens! *Adam Clayton Powell*

A zealous man in religion is a man of one thing. He only sees one thing, he cares for one thing, he is swallowed up in one thing; and that one thing is to please God. *J. C. Ryle*

A zealous Saviour ought to have zealous disciples. *J. C. Ryle*

As well a chariot without its steeds, a sun without its beams, a heaven without its joy, as a man of God without zeal.
C. H. Spurgeon

I'd rather be a lean bird in the woods than a fat bird in a cage. *C. H. Spurgeon*

If by excessive zeal we die before reaching the average age of man, worn out in the Master's service, then glory to God, we shall have so much less of earth and so much more of heaven. *C. H. Spurgeon*

The supreme need of the church is the same in the twentieth century as in the first: it is men on fire for Christ.
James S. Stewart

Nothing sets the heart on fire like truth.
John R. W. Stott

Be extravagant for God or the devil, but for God's sake don't be tepid. *C. T. Studd*

No craze so great as that of the gambler, and no gambler for Jesus was ever cured, thank God. *C. T. Studd*

One live coal may set a whole stack on fire. *John Trapp*

Zeal without knowledge is like wild fire in a fool's hand. *John Trapp*

A fanatic is a person who loves Jesus more than you do. *George Verwer*

I have one passion only: It is he! It is he!
Nicolas von Zinzendorf

Zeal is as needful for a Christian as salt for the sacrifice or fire on the altar.
Thomas Watson

Zeal

My talents, gifts and graces, Lord,
Into thy blessed hands receive;
And let me live to preach thy Word,
And let me to thy glory live;
My every sacred moment spend
In publishing the sinners' Friend.
Charles Wesley

Get on fire for God and men will come
and see you burn. *John Wesley*

Lord, let me not live to be useless!
John Wesley

The world is my parish. *John Wesley*

I am never better than when I am on the
full stretch for God. *George Whitefield*

O Lord, make me an extraordinary Christian.
George Whitefield

Does our fire for God warm others, or
does it burn them? If it burns them, it will
burn us too. *Spiros Zodhiates*

———————————————

Subject Index

Abandonment — see also: Consecration; Submission; Zeal

Abortion

Actions — see also: Duty, Good deeds, Service

Activism — see also: Service

Addiction — see Habit

Adoption

Adoration — see Awe; Worship

Adversity — see Pain; Sickness; Suffering; Trials

Advice

Affections

Affliction — see Pain; Sickness; Suffering; Trials

Age — see Old Age

Agnosticism — see also: Atheism; Unbelief

Aim — see Purpose

Alcohol — see also: Drunkenness

Ambition

Amusements — see also: Recreation

Angels — see also: Demons

Angels — Fallen — see Demons

Anger — see also: Hatred; Revenge; Passion

Anger — Righteous

Annihilation — see also: Death; Eternity; Judgement

Antichrist — see also: Satan — Existence and Nature

Antinomianism

Anxiety — see also: Fear; Worry

Apathy — see also: Complacency; Indifference

Apostasy

Appreciation

Arrogance — see Boasting; Conceit; Egotism; Pride; Vanity

Art

Ascension — see Jesus Christ — Ascension

Assurance

Atheism — see also: Agnosticism; Unbelief

Atonement — see also: Cross; Forgiveness by God; Jesus Christ — Death; Redemption

Authority

Avarice — see Greed

Awe — see also: Adoration; Fear of God; Worship

Backsliding

Beauty

Behaviour — see Actions

Belief — see Faith

Bible — Authority — see also: Divine Authority and Authorship

Bible and Christ

Bible —
  Divine Authority and Authorship
  Fulness
  and the Holy Spirit
  Inerrancy and Infallibility
  Influence and Power
  Preservation
  Purpose
  Relevance
  Submission to
  Supremacy
  Unity

Bible Study

Bigotry

Blasphemy

Blessings — see Spiritual Gifts

Boasting — see also: Conceit; Egotism; Pride; Vanity

Bravery — see Courage

Brokenness — see Humility; Repentance; Self-Crucifixion; Submission

Chance
Character
Charity — see also: Generosity; Giving;
   Kindness
Chastening — see also; Trials
Children — see Family Life
Christ — see Jesus Christ
Christian — see also: Christianity
Christianity —
   Characteristics
   Definition
   Uniqueness
Christlikeness — see also: Godliness;
   Holiness
Church —
   Attendance and Membership
   Blemishes
   and Christ
   Divisions
   Duties
   Fellowship
   Glory
   Oneness
   Power
   Security in God's purposes
Church Unity
Circumstances
Cleansing — see Forgiveness by God;
Clothing
Commitment — see Abandonment;
   Consecration; Submission; Zeal
Common Grace — see Grace —
   Common Grace
Communion with Christ — see also:
   Communion with God; Love for
   Christ; Meditation; Prayer
Communion with God — see also:
   Comminion with Christ; Love for
   God; Meditation; Prayer
Communism
Companionship — see Fellowship;
   Friendship
Compassion — see also: Kindness;
   Love for Others; Mercy to Others
Complacency — see also: Apathy
Complaining — see Murmuring

Compromise
Conceit — see also: Boasting; Egotism;
   Pride; Vanity
Confession — see also: Contrition;
   Conviction of Sin; Penitence; Repen-
   tance
Confidence — see Assurance
Conflict — see Spiritual Warfare
Conformity — see Compromise
Conscience —
   and the Bible
   and God
   Importance
   Power
   and Sin
Consecration — see also: Abandon-
   ment; Submission; Zeal
Consistency — see Faithfulness
Contempt
Contentment
Contrition — see also: Confession;
   Conviction of Sin; Penitence;
   Repentance
Controversy
Conversion — see also: Faith —
   Saving; Regeneration; Repentance
Conviction — see Assurance
Conviction of Sin
Conviction of Sin — see also:
   Confession; Contrition; Penitence;
   Repentance
Convictions
Courage
Courtesy
Covenant
Covetousness — see also: Gluttony;
   Greed
Cowardice
Creation — see also: Evolution; Nature
Criticism by Others — see also:
   Criticism of Others
Criticism of Others — see also:
   Criticism by Others
Cross — see also: Atonement; Jesus
   Christ — Death
Curiosity
Cynicism

Blessings
Characteristics
Essence
False
Importance
Humour — see Happiness; Joy
Hunger — Spiritual — see Spiritual Hunger
Hurry
Husband — see Family Life
Hypocrisy see also: Formalism; Ritualism

Idleness — see Indolence
Idolatry
Ignorance
Imagination — see also: Mind; Thought
Immorality — see Sex
Immortality — see also: Destiny; Eternity; Eternal Life; Heaven
Impatience
Impenitence
Impiety — see also: Atheism; Unbelief
Incarnation — Jesus Christ — see also: Virgin Birth
Inconsistency
Indifference — see also: Apathy; Complacency
Indolence
Infidelity — see Unbelief
Influence — see also: Example
Ingratitude
Injustice
Insecurity
Inspiration — see Bible
Integrity — see also: Honesty; Truth
Intolerance

Jealousy — see also: Envy
Jesus Christ —
    Ascension
    Birth — see Incarnation
    Death — see also: Atonement; Cross; Forgiveness by God
    Deity and Humanity
    Glory

Holiness
Humility
Intercession
Life and Influence
Lordship
Love
Perfection
Power
Resurrection
    — see Resurrection of Christ
Second Coming — see Second Coming of Christ
Sympathy
Teaching
Uniqueness
Joy — see also: Happiness; Humour
Judgement — see also: Destiny; Eternity; Eternal Life; Heaven; Hell; Punishment
Justice
Justification — see also: Faith — and Deeds; Holiness — and Justification

Kindness — see also: Compassion; Love for Others; Mercy to Others
Kingdom of God
Knowledge — see also: Education; Mind; Reason
Knowledge of God — see also: Revelation

Law of God
Laziness — see Indolence
Leadership
Legalism
Leisure
Liberalism
Liberality — see Generosity; Giving
Liberty
Life
Literature
Loneliness
Longsuffering — see Patience
Lord's Day
Love for Christ — see also: Communion with Christ; Meditation; Prayer

of Omission — see also: Negligence
Power
and Satan
Sincerity — see also: Honesty; Integrity
Sinful Nature — see also: Depravity;
Man — a Sinner; Sin
Slander — see also: Gossip; Rumour;
Speech
Sleep
Sloth — see Indolence
Social Responsibility
Solitude
Sorrow
Soul — see also: Heart
Soul-Winning — see also: Evangelism;
Witnessing
Speech — see also: Eloquence; Gossip;
Rumour; Slander
Spiritual —
Darkness
Gifts
Hunger
Riches
Warefare
Spirituality
Sport — see Amusements; Recreation
Stewardship — see also: Giving;
Tithing
Stubbonness
Submission — see also: Abondonment;
Consecration; Zeal
Success
Suffering — see also: Pain; Sickness;
Trials
Suicide
Sunday — see Lord's Day
Superstition
Surrender — see Abandonment; Consecration; Submission;
Swearing — see Profanity
Sympathy

Television
Temper
Temptation —

Avoiding and Resisting
Blessing
Certainty
and Satan — see also: Satan
and Sin
Testing — see Trials
Thanksgiving — see also: Gratitude
Theology — see also: Bible; Doctrine
Thoughts — see also: Imagination;
Mind
Time —
and Eternity
Misuse
Urgency
Use
Tithing — see also: Giving; Stewardship
Tolerance
Tongue — see Speech
Trials —
Blessings — see also: Pain;
Sickness; Suffering
Certainty
God the Sender
Response
Temporary Nature
Trinity — see Godhead
Trust — see Faith
Truth — see also: Honesty; Integrity

Unbelief — see also: Agnosticism;
Atheism; Impiety
Uncertainity — see also: Doubt
Unity — Church — see Church Unity
Universalism
Urgency

Vanity — see also: Boasting; Conceit;
Egotism; Pride
Victory
Vigilance
Violence — see also: War
Virgin Birth — see also: Incarnation —
Jesus Christ
Virtue — see also: Ethics; Goodness;
Morality
Vows

A wide range of Christian books is available from Evangelical Press. If you would like a free catalogue please write to us or contact us by e-mail. Alternatively, you can view the whole catalogue online at our website:

www.evangelicalpress.org.

Evangelical Press
Faverdale North, Darlington, Co. Durham, DL3 0PH, England

e-mail: sales@evangelicalpress.org

Evangelical Press USA
P. O. Box 825, Webster, New York 14580, USA

e-mail: usa.sales@evangelicalpress.org